His Excellency Dr. Ghoulem Berrah

A Dream for Peace

A Memoir

To Nabila –
May Allah bless you always.

PUBLISHED BY DR. GHOULEM BERRAH FOUNDATION

Copyright © 2017 by Dr. Ghoulem Berrah

First Published French edition *Un Rêve Pour la Paix* 2018
by les Éditions de l'Archipel in Paris, France

Algerian edition published December 2018
by les Éditions Dalimen in Algiers, Algeria

A Dream for Peace, American edition 2019
published by Dr. Ghoulem Berrah Foundation
www.berrahfoundation.org

All rights reserved, including the rights of reproduction
in whole or in part in any form.

Dr. Ghoulem Berrah Foundation
18851 NE 29th Avenue Suite 700
Aventura, FL 33180 (USA)

P.O. Box 800037
Aventura, Florida 33280
(USA)

ISBN 978-0-578-46076-5
ISBN 978-0-578-42043-1 (ebook)

Edited by Nana Yalley

Proceeds from *A Dream for Peace* will be donated
to develop the Dr. Ghoulem Berrah Interfaith Center
and to other charitable causes.

Printed and bound in the United States of America

To my beloved mother. You molded me with your love, wrapped me with your prayers, and shaped the man I became.

Contents

Prologue	1
Editor's Toast	11
CHAPTER ONE: Birth to University	15
CHAPTER TWO: Hardship and Prison	49
CHAPTER THREE: Initiation to the Struggle in Morocco	65
CHAPTER FOUR: Struggle in Morocco—Organization	93
CHAPTER FIVE: My American Experience—Becoming a Scientist	123
CHAPTER SIX: The Call of Africa	171
CHAPTER SEVEN: Bonding with President Houphouët	217
CHAPTER EIGHT: Murky Waters of Love	241
CHAPTER NINE: The Abidjan-Algiers Axis	285
CHAPTER TEN: Israel and Palestine—Our Plea for Peace	309
CHAPTER ELEVEN: Our Common Faith	373
CHAPTER TWELVE: Memos from the Cold War	441
CHAPTER THIRTEEN: Concord in Africa	465
CHAPTER FOURTEEN: Diplomacy of Smiles	505
CHAPTER FIFTEEN: Côte d'Ivoire's Political Radar	521
CHAPTER SIXTEEN: Algeria—Cry of the Crestfallen Heart	563
CHAPTER SEVENTEEN: Dialogue for Humanity's Sake	601
Epilogue	613
Acknowledgments	627
Photo Credits	631

Prologue

Memories of a Muslim Brother
By H. E. Monsignor Justo Mullor Garcia

In spite of the many invitations, as a principle, I am against writing my diplomatic memoirs. In his autobiography, titled *Mémoires d'Outre-Tombe*, French writer François-René de Chateaubriand set a standard for memoirs that is hard to emulate; however, the endeavor of reminiscing the exceptional brotherly bond with a friend—he, a Muslim, and myself an Apostolic nuncio—having both served as diplomats, I am writing in the twenty-first century about bits of a common life in a still emerging Africa that presents itself as a great continent to both her children and admirers.

Both Dr. Ghoulem Berrah and I came from different backgrounds. He was born in an Algeria that was still looking to reclaim its original identity and which was, as I often called it, the "anti-geographic" part of France. I was born in a Spanish-German family, with a touch of Jewish blood from my father's side. We had nothing in common before meeting each other in the exceptional country of Côte d'Ivoire led by President Houphouët-Boigny in the 1980s. Dr. Berrah arrived in Côte d'Ivoire through complex and unusual paths; one such notable journey was to China's Forbidden City, where he stood next to Mao Zedong. Listening to him talk about it was like reliving a dream grounded in such an effective reality and an experience easily framed in an era beyond any historical realm. Compared to his biography, mine seems completely ordinary and remains too typical. We were nonetheless both believers in God, he, in accordance with the Qur'an and I, in accordance with the Gospels. This did not prevent either the profound meaning of our religiosity or the sincere friendship that compelled us to call each other brother.

Everybody in Abidjan knew that he was the diplomatic advisor to the president of the Republic and that I was accredited as the Apostolic nuncio to Côte d'Ivoire. The president, and also Father of the Nation, had served as a minister in several of Charles de Gaulle's administrations, and just like De Gaulle, he also embodied a profound sense of secularism. Secularism does not imply ignorance of religious faith, much less the persecution of those who have a sensitive conscience to what the existence of divine laws dictates in the process of offering a moral compass to the personal or social actions of each individual. The *laïcité ouverte* (open secularism) proposed by extremely intelligent philosophers, as well as first-class politicians, was a natural setting in President Houphouët-Boigny's Côte d'Ivoire. The chapter "Notre Foi Commune" ("Our Common Faith") in this memoir is proof of such reality. In addition to serving as the Apostolic nuncio, I also had the privilege of being the Dean of the Diplomatic Corps. A few days after my arrival in Abidjan, I was surprised by the number of people who greeted me in the city and introduced themselves as belonging to a different religion. It was clear that Pope John Paul II had many Ivorian admirers, and the general climate in the city was one of deep respect for everything pertaining to religion.

It was not unusual to encounter Ivorians of different religions at any faith-based ceremony. This was a way of showing respect for the faith of others, as well as displaying certain openness toward the realities of different faiths. Such was the case for some Animists, Muslims, and Protestants, who loved listening to the Catholic sermons.

The vicinity of the president's private residence to the

Prologue

nunciature, as well as my special relationship with him, created particular circumstances that allowed me to celebrate the Eucharist at his place on the eve of Sunday, which was attended by family and some of his aides. For President Houphouët-Boigny, I was, first and foremost, his closest neighbor and most importantly, a Catholic priest, whose friendship and insight he had come to appreciate.

Thus, Dr. Berrah and his wife, a devout Catholic, very well known within the circle of the faithful, were always present at my open celebrations. The atmosphere was similar to that of missionary organizations where followers of other religions, who sincerely respect the Catholic faith, never failed to attend; this belongs to what I call *Africanité vécue* (Living Africanity).

For Dr. Berrah and myself, the most significant example of this "Living Africanity" happened without a doubt throughout the construction of Abidjan's new Catholic cathedral, an edifice sought after by the entire Ivorian population, backed by President Houphouët-Boigny, and inaugurated by Pope John Paul II. The day of consecration has been marked in Côte d'Ivoire's history. I could never forget the comment made by a Jewish technician when I once paid a visit to the construction site: *"In this cathedral, we all work with the same enthusiasm: Catholics, Muslims, Jewish, and Animists."* It was an obvious "ecumenical reality."

In his memoirs, my friend and brother Dr. Berrah talks about that *Living Africanity* within the religious sphere, especially in the chapter "Our Common Faith." The obvious meaning is rooted in the respect that everyone has for another's religion. Making mention of his friend, our mutual friend Essy Amara, ambassador to the United Nations and also married to a Catholic, Dr. Berrah cites a very real and noteworthy example: *"Essy and I decided to join forces with the local villagers and set up a fund to build a Catholic church and a mosque. We were the first ones to make a financial contribution to the fund. I informed the president about our plans, and not surprisingly, he liked the vision behind the idea. He pledged his support by making a significant contribution. As a Muslim, the project brought much joy to my heart, because we planned to erect the two buildings close to each other and shine a light on our common faith... At the project's completion, we inaugurated the mosque and the church on the same day and organized a major celebration for the entire village... I was full of pride for the hard workers and praised the Almighty for allowing me to witness an exemplary harmonious characteristic in the atmosphere."*

That same "harmonious and exemplary" perfume, stemming from my brother Ghoulem's sensitivity, is expressed in his memoirs when he notes his recollection of a visit to the Holy Sepulchre of Jerusalem, next to his wife, who I also consider my sister. The quote is telling: *"As we entered the basilica, I was concerned about my wife's reaction. According to the Christian faith, it is the revered place known as Calvary. This is where Christ was crucified, and it is here his tomb resides. The Holy Sepulchre, the most revered shrine in Christendom, is the most visited place of pilgrimage by the faithful. When we finally entered the basilica, my Love experienced strong emotions and was overwhelmed by tears. I held her hand strong in mine and said a few soothing words to cheer her up. We stood at the heart of Christianity, and the magnitude of the moment illuminated the deep beams of her faith."*

There is another significant example that shows the respect this great Muslim friend had for the Catholic faith. On the eve of the inauguration of Our Lady of Peace Basilica in Yamoussoukro, I had arrived from Geneva, where I was assigned as the Vatican's Permanent Observer to the United Nations, to take part in the event. The construction of the basilica was heavily contested by a segment of the international public opinion, especially the Europeans. Because the ultimate goal of the project was unknown to me, I learned about the different architectural features of the new basilica in the company of Dr. Berrah. As we surveyed the site, the editor of a French television channel who had recognized me came

Prologue

up and asked my personal opinion regarding the significance of the new place of worship. Beside me was Dr. Berrah. My response was instantaneous: *"I'm here with a dear Muslim friend; please do ask for his opinion."* Dr. Berrah's answer was very clear: *"I wonder why the Europeans, who are so proud of their Middle Age–era cathedrals, are so surprised to see a cathedral built from the ground up by Africans as a gift to themselves today."* That same evening, many of our French friends of various religious and political beliefs, who knew about the interview and our answers, did not fail to give us a call.

I will not dwell on all the other facets Dr. Berrah mentioned in his memoirs, for they belong to other times within his history; besides, I must also add the history of Côte d'Ivoire and of Africa where I lived for some unforgettable years that were filled with intense personal and professional experiences. One example is adequate to illustrate the value of this experience; I am reminded of a phrase from Pope John Paul II, which will always remain vivid in my memory as a priest and as a diplomat of the Holy See: *"It would suffice one more head of state such as the one I met in Côte d'Ivoire to change Africa and perhaps the world."*

Naturally, in regard to and especially out of respect and love for Africa and Africans, I feel compelled to refrain from judging the events that have characterized Côte d'Ivoire in recent years. I belong to a generation of Europeans and papal diplomats who love and respect history. For me, Côte d'Ivoire with its greatness and its limitations is the place I resided alongside numerous missionaries, ambassadors, Ivorian families that I met and loved, as well as others, foreigners that had settled there to help with its development. For me, it was a delight to witness this development over the span of seven years, witness it as a concrete reality that could be enjoyed to varying degrees by all social classes. As a representative of the pope, I did not just travel throughout the Catholic diocese; I also traveled down Côte d'Ivoire's innermost roads, and more than once, I did so accompanied by some of my colleagues and their families, to whom I wanted to introduce the religious and social work of the missionaries.

All continents are still suffering from the consequences of the two world wars but also from the political and economic ideologies that caused them. Even though the ideal of European unity sprung to answer the "demons" that were the source behind these disasters, there still awaits a better and more accurate definition. Countries such as Côte d'Ivoire that once experienced colonization know that their history is exposed to all the temptations that these "demons" have sown in their lands. The solution to the various problems that arose during the growth of their true and definitive identity must be found in the totality of a comprehensive and effective education. It is the seal that the wise Creator Father of the new Côte d'Ivoire stamped in many of his achievements.

As a conclusion in these considerations, while introducing Dr. Ghoulem Berrah's memoir, I welcome the fact that on the occasion of the end of Ramadan, the first message to Muslims from the new pope, elected just four months ago (I write in August 2013) and who chose the significant name of "Francis," had a very revealing title for both my friend and brother and myself: *promoting mutual respect between Christians and Muslims through education*. In reading the text, I imagined the joy of my friend while in Paradise, where every sincere and profound religious life such as his will eventually end. Thus was our conviction in respecting the faith of one another and of our respective religious families, as well as that of the Jews; as such, allowing the Almighty God to enlighten this mystery to all monotheist mystics and believers.

I will refrain from any citation in this important text by the current pope and will limit myself to a single one, which would have filled my friend and brother with joy, but also the wise imams of Abidjan, to whom I have each year extended a similar message on behalf of John Paul II. My quote is very short and reminds me of

Prologue

my Ivorian memories: *It is not possible to establish true links with God, while ignoring other people. Hence it is important to intensify dialogue among the various religions, and I am thinking particularly of dialogue between Islam and Christian.* I sense a deep joy when thinking about the many Ivorian Catholics, Muslims, as well as animists who have lived this advice before the aforementioned letter during the years of my memorable stay in Abidjan.

+ *Justo Mullor*
Rome, 6 aout 2013

H. E. Monsignor Justo Mullor García
A Brief Biography

His Excellency Monsignor Justo Mullor García was born on May 8, 1932, in Los Villares (Jaén), Spain, where his family, originating from Enix (Almería), had been transferred due to his father's work at the Ministry of Development. He was just a child when his father was shot by dictator General Francisco Franco's troops, prompting his family to return to Enix. As the only child in an Almerían family, he had it all, but he decided to embrace the vocation to priesthood and went to study at the Almería Seminary. He was ordained a priest in 1954 at the tender age of twenty-two, and because of his leadership qualities, he was dispatched by the Bishop of Almería for further studies at the Gregorian University in Rome, where he obtained a Doctorate in Canon Law. In 1957, he entered the Pontifical Ecclesiastical Academy to lay the foundation for a diplomatic career in the Holy See.

He began his service as the Nunciature of Belgium in 1967 and transferred to Portugal after three years. Five years later, he was named the Permanent Observer of the Holy See to the Council of Europe, and in

A Dream for Peace

1979, he was ordained Archbishop Titular of Emerita Augusta by Pope John Paul II before moving on to serve as nuncio in Côte d'Ivoire and pro-nuncio in Burkina-Faso and Niger until 1985. He was transferred once again to serve in Geneva as the Holy See's Permanent Observer to the United Nations.

After the collapse of the Iron Curtain in 1991, Pope John Paul II appointed him the first Apostolic Nuncio to the Baltic States of Estonia, Latvia, and Lithuania. He was the entrusted Apostolic Administrator of Estonia. In 1994, he was named Titular Archbishop of Bolsena (Volsinium), and in 1997, he was appointed nuncio to Mexico. It was there he uncovered and denounced the double life of a priest, who was the founder of the Legion of Christ in Mexico. That was Monsignor Mullor's last function in the Holy See as a nuncio. Wherever he represented the Holy See, Monsignor Mullor always managed to organize visits by Pope John Paul II, who appointed him in 2000 as president of the Pontifical Ecclesiastical Academy in Rome, to oversee the development of all future diplomats of the Holy See.

He presented his resignation to Pope Benedict XVI at the age of seventy-five. His Holiness made him a member of the Congregation for the Causes of Saints in 2009. Though he spent his last years in Rome, living in the Via de l'Erba building for retired nuncios, the city of Almería named a plaza in his honor. Furthermore, the town of Los Villares, his birthplace, paid homage a few years ago by dedicating a street to him. The municipality of Enix did the same and named him their favorite son. After two years of weakening health, Monsignor Mullor passed away peacefully in Rome, on Friday, December 30, at the age of eighty-four. His mortal remains were laid to rest in the Cathedral of Almería on Wednesday, January 4, 2017.

A Dream for Peace

Dr. Ghoulem Berrah

Homage to the Author
by Nana Yalley

To do justice to the life and accomplishments of His Excellency Dr. Ghoulem Berrah would take more than a few paragraphs of recollections from my memory. Certainly, this single-volume autobiography will do its part to manage the task and deliver to the reader a competent portrait of a great man.

One anecdote that is worth mentioning was his persistence in reminding me of how much he loved his wife. It was a repetitive pattern that never ceased to amaze me. Each time we were together, he would interrupt our conversation as soon as his wife left his side, just to say how much he adored her. *"You know, I wouldn't be who I am, were it not for her,"* he would say. His opening statement was always the same as the accolades that followed, peppered with many praiseworthy tributes to his beloved wife. He would go on and on until she returned, and then he would immediately switch back to the conversation, as if to shield her from his affectionate poesy. He was always that way, and I came to cherish those moments. I looked forward to hearing his reaffirmation of genuine love—something so sacred. There was an elevated level of candid conviction that illuminated the persona of my dear friend and brother.

Never have I known an individual with so much compassion for his fellow brethren, always chasing a selfless drive to do what was best to achieve peace. When we met several years ago, it was at the boardwalk, on the water's edge, in South Florida. Our encounter, brief as it may have been, was borne out of Celestine Prophesy. Standing tall, with broad shoulders, exhibiting a fashionable and classy swag in a striped fitted navy-blue suit, he smiled at me from afar as I approached, drenched in sweat, on my usual power-walk path. *"Hello, my friend, how are you today?"* he greeted with his signature smile. I stopped to take his outstretched hand. *"I am doing well. Thank you for asking. How are you?"* That was how it began. A friendship at first sight, which would by God's design motivate him to finally decide to write his life's story. We were neighbors, but for the chance happenstance, our paths might never have crossed.

As time went by, we seemed to gel on many levels. I discovered a lot about the man and his boundless accomplishments. Our conversations were always deep and farsighted, at times spirited, yet very funny. I was hard-pressed not to pose the question, *"When will you write your story?"* His accounts of diplomatic rapprochement saw many gains in global political corridors, but there were also some painful losses that hit close to home. He spearheaded innovations that produced impactful outcomes in the world of biological science, and he recorded many selfless pilgrimages in strict harmony with his deep religious faith. I found him fascinating. He had chronicled a life that transcended the typical norm for high achievers, gone further than most humans in professional achievements and spiritual adeptness, yet those characteristics did not define his humble nature.

Throughout his life, he held firm to his honor in situations where it was severely tested. From him, I learned that the longer one struggles with something, the more we come to cherish it in the long run. His penchant to love deeply, and his disciplined engagement with his maker, were carved into his soul. Dr. Berrah faced the turmoil of political discourse head-on and challenged the status quo to embrace next practices. In the upper echelons of power, where he sat with diverse and cultured political leaders, he did his best work as a steward for peace, and from the grassroots, he empowered laymen to strive to reach their greatest potential.

When Dr. Berrah left the shores of his native Algeria as a young man to embark on studies in France, his heart was heavy, but his mind was set to return soon to help liberate his country from French colonial rule—by any means necessary. He had seen enough and lived a painful reality of subjugation, but he never accepted the policy of second-class citizenry. He refused to bow to any man or genuflect to any system of oppression. His story, *A Dream for Peace*, is intricately woven in a delicately balanced oratorical sampling of episodes that chronicle a life's journey, seemingly hapless at times, yet with successful outcomes that serve as proof that his mission here on earth was ordained by a higher power. I continue to believe that greatness in a man or a nation is not by fluke. It is therefore necessary to harness the tenets of profound faith and constant prayer. Dr. Berrah had in him an endless fountain of living waters from which he drew an undaunted source of inner faith. Henceforth, his heartfelt involvement in the welfare of the average person did not distract him from the complex problems of the world at large. It is fair to say that all those who have met him have surrendered unconditionally to his sincerity, nobility, and witty personality.

With these few words, I salute my friend and brother, the traditional realist who did his very best work for Mideast peace, sewed the seeds of concord among people of different faiths, and served with distinction in his pursuit of Afro-Arab harmony. In so doing, he promoted the essence of dialogue for the ideals that are at their core, sustained by a sense of purpose. He was a true class act, an indisputable gentleman, who, out of his precepts of duty and honor, answered a greater call to serve in Africa and transmit to the world a diplomatic message for the greater good.

A Dream for Peace

I was born into a humble but strong and very proud family. A mausoleum of my ancestors is set high in the Aurès Mountains in the town of Chechar, above the village of Ariss, where the Benboulaid brothers fired the first shots of the Algerian Revolution.

Chapter One

Birth to University

I was born in Aïn Beïda, a small town in the province of Constantine, at the foot of the Aurès Mountains, in northeastern Algeria. In those days, the government of France had annexed my country as a part of the French mainland. Algeria was divided into three departments—Algiers was in the central, Oran in the west, and Constantine in the eastern department. Growing up, I constantly saw French settlers enjoying casual walks in the beautiful flower garden situated at the town's center. Life was always serene and pleasant. We experienced severe winters at times, but the summer evenings were rather lovely. Most southerners loved to spend their summer vacations in my hometown. The settlers played their music and danced beside a kiosk in the heart of the garden during the holidays, but native Algerians were never allowed in the area. My people were not bothered by such pernickety rules. We were content with minding our own business in our fatherland.

The region was notorious for its recurrent lapses in security. Exacerbated by complex tribal bonds spanning centuries, central government forces that were charged with enforcement of the law were frequently scoffed at by the locals. My father's tribe, the Saighi, had its origins in the hotbed of rebellious Arabized Berbers who marched to the beat of their own drum. They are part of a powerful dominant clan, the Chaouis, a cluster of diverse tribal elements from the Aurès Mountain region. Famous for their tenacious determination and battle prowess, the Chaouis spearheaded the destruction of many Arab dynasties over the centuries, and carved for themselves an indomitable reputation that continues to live on through the sound bites of folklore. Because of their bravery and strength, there is a popular saying in Algeria: *"Stubborn like a Chaoui."* A proud Saighi tribesman, my father, Hamadi Berrah, loved to hunt, and like most of the men in the region, he was often seen carrying a rifle around town.

My father.

Occasionally, members of the colonial police force came to our community with about ten, sometimes more than a dozen officers, just to issue a single arrest warrant. The city and the region remained outside the control of the government long after President Houari Boumédiène ascended to power (June 1965 to December 1978) about three years after our independence. Football games were very popular across the country, providing an enjoyable pastime for many passionate supporters. When our home team lost the match to a visiting team during a crucial playoff game in

Birth to University

Aïn Beïda, many angry supporters blamed the referee for the loss. The ensuing protests quickly turned to mass riots, and the police force, plagued by limited resources, lost control of the crowds. Things rapidly got out of hand and spread through parts of the town, where several vehicles were burned and the local police station was ransacked.

In the immediate aftermath of the incident, an irate President Boumédiène condemned the entire town. His strong reaction backfired, as angry inhabitants deemed the blanket condemnation an overreach and vowed revenge. Months later, residents set up an inconvenient roadblock shortly before Boumédiène's presidential motorcade passed through en route to his hometown in the nearby Sedrata township. In retaliation, the full-fledged municipality of Aïn Beïda, a town with a city council and a city hall, was denied the title of Wilaya (province) by the government. Instead, the honor was bestowed upon Canrobert, a small military hamlet with a handful of residents. Until today, the administrative structure remains the same—the town which was once the epicenter of robust activities remains a Daïra (district zone) surrounded by Wilayas: Khenchela, Oumbouagui, and Tebessa.

I was born into a humble but strong and very proud family. A mausoleum of my ancestors is set high in the Aurès Mountains in the town of Chechar, above the village of Ariss, where the Benboulaid brothers fired the first shots of the Algerian Revolution. My father was a jeweler. Most of his finest works were forged by Jewish silversmiths.

My mother was from La Meskiana, in the easternmost part of Algeria, along the Tunisian border. The region was just as uncontrollable as my father's. Her family, the Mechakras, were a humble and proud clan. When she lost her parents as a young girl, she was taken in by her oldest sister, Lalla Aïcha, who was married to a wealthy landowner at the time. Barely a teenager, my mom, Lalla Zebida, was married off to my father in a colorful ceremony marking his fourth nuptial. Dad's first two marriages ended with the death of both spouses, and the third was terminated in divorce court. Back then, marriages between young women and older men were a common occurrence. Typically, couples were culled from the same bloodline, and cousins were joined in matrimony. Interfamily marriages were mostly sealed before a child's birth. Rarely were there any exceptions to the rule, but in my parents' case, the long traditional customs were circumvented. Mom was wise beyond her years. She was also very devout, and the elders soon began to take note. Though it was against convention to invite anyone her age to participate in family councils, they decided to forgo principles of folklore and pull her into the huddle. Very often, the elders came to seek her counsel on private matters.

In those days, life was shaped by weddings. I attended many beautiful ceremonies where women from either side of the aisle wore long, loose dresses popularly known in the region as *gandouras*. What stood out was the embroidered stitching and matching golden belts that were studded with genuine gold coins. Celebrations were larger than life, and colorful meals were masterfully laid out for the outstanding feast. Classic traditional music reverberated in sync with the finest choreographed dancers, handpicked from among the region's best, who stomped and entertained with memorable dance routines. It wasn't unusual for most parties to go on for a few days. Some wealthy families ensured that the festivities lasted an entire week. My favorite event was the traditional fantasia exhibition. The age-old display of unmatched gallantry by professional equestrians who rode proudly on beautiful Algerian Barb horses attracted people from far and near. Crowds immersed themselves in dazzling colors and braced for jaw-dropping stunts. The riders galloped along on the dirt fields in their traditional garb, with either a brown or blue burnoose, complimented by a prominent golden threaded turban, adorned with detailed motifs. Their polished handmade leather boots were fitted with shiny golden spurs, and they sat on cultured designer saddles held in place by colorful bejeweled girths.

The cavalier horsemen were always ready to put on a spectacular show with their shiny rifles. Some in the crowd screamed in amazement when the daredevils heaved themselves across the underbelly of fast-moving horses and flipped back onto their saddles with exceptional agility. They choreographed the firing of bullets into the air as they galloped along the rope line with effusive spectators looking on. Wind bursts stroked the horses' manes and caressed the glistening curls that sparkled through the powder of exploding dust. It was an instant motion blur that teased the mind into capturing the moment as if it were projected onto a still frame that forced the eyes to focus on the hooves of the galloping horses in full suspense above the ground. Every rider tried to outdo the other with genius creativity and bravado. At one memorable event, I stared wide-eyed at a man who galloped just inches past my feet, standing upright on his saddle like a statue. The reins lay gently in his outstretched palm. I marveled at his display of elegance and grace, and dreamed of becoming Aïn Beïda's most famous acrobatic rider someday.

Issues of dignity stood above all else, and marriages were looked upon as transactions to establish alliances among families. The bride and the groom were not consulted and would not meet until the night of the wedding. It was customary in Muslim tradition, and similarly in the old Jewish tradition, for the girl to practice abstinence. Her abstinence would be affirmed on the night of the wedding, and she would be the pride of her parents, cementing their honor and consecrating the union of both families. *"If one wants to draw water from the ground, one would have to ensure that there are enough troops for the task."* This was an old saying passed on by generations of old, because water was a rare commodity in the region. Marriages, therefore, were merely strategic alliances in search of strength in numbers.

Agriculture and the breeding of livestock was an extensive vocational undertaking. The lack of silos during harvest season ensured that grains of wheat and barley were piled mountain high on the grounds of the storage facilities. Mass production of grains was always the case, generating enough quantities to cater to domestic consumption as well as exports to France and Japan. There were sheep, lined up by the thousands and grouped in flocks of a hundred each. A single shepherd was assigned to his own flock. The vast majority of landowners owned hundreds of flocks.

Livestock markets were open on a weekly basis for each village. In Aïn Beïda, the market was open on Mondays. Sheep were queued up and taken to the market by their shepherds for haggling with prospective buyers. The bargaining process begins with the first bidder offering a thousand francs to buy one sheep from a shepherd. Without taking the money, the shepherd accepts the offer and the bidder moves along to continue shopping for other wares elsewhere at the market. When a second customer approaches the shepherd and inquires about pricing for the same sheep, he is told that an offer has been made and accepted. The fervent customer raises the bid to eleven hundred francs and disappears into the crowd. *"You have been offered eleven hundred francs for your sheep,"* the shepherd informs the first bidder when he returns to the scene. There was a sense of dignity and honor among the folks. Even though the initial transaction for the sheep may not have been finalized, there was regardless a customary commitment by both sides, and it was always worth the hassle.

The market was closed whenever there was a tribal dispute. Some disputes led to violence, people were injured, and on occasion, someone was killed. Peace was always restored after prolonged negotiations, with either side accepting some form of compensation to settle the dispute.

Neither my father nor my mother had a memorialized birth date. My parents were born around a certain date, with supplementary judgments from the colonial era authenticating their existence. Mom never had an identification card, and she never traveled outside the village.

There was great harmony among the families; husbands were very respectful of their wives and vice versa. Divorces were rare. Spouses were never called by their names in public; they would refer to each other as "she" or "he." When they addressed their children, he would say, "Your Mommy," and she'd say, "Your Daddy."

In a perfect world, there would have been six of us children from my mother's side of the family—three girls, Fifi, Missa, Yasmina; the twin boys, Hassan, Hussein; and I. Sadly, the first of the twins died at birth, and the second passed away at the age of seven, when I was three years old. When my father passed away, Fodil, his son from a previous marriage, stepped into the role as the family head. I was only five at the time. He worked at the local pharmacy and had earned himself quite a reputation because of the nature of his profession. There was a great deal of respect in the community for civic servants, doctors, pharmacists, and teachers. With an ever-absent boss at the pharmacy where he worked, Fodil therefore became the accidental beneficiary of all the accolades and gained a very high profile around town. He was quite the personality.

I had twelve uncles and we lived on Charles Stora Street, aptly named by the French colonialists. The exclusive strip of roadway was ours in a literal sense, and the natives dubbed it "Saighi Street" in honor of my father's tribe. Trade was not allowed anywhere near the street, and among the locals, it was clear that only those who knew my family would venture beyond the infamous street. Within the five families in the estate of my ancestors, there were never any problems—no issues among my uncles. Problems among the women and children were rare. We all lived in harmony as one big, happy family.

Ensuring that I had an excellent education was an honorable endeavor and a matter of high priority for my mom. Her concern for my well-being was also extended to her nephews and nieces—the children and grandchildren of her older sister. After the death of my father, Mom watched over my schooling with rigor. Although, I was told that there were many who asked for her hand in marriage, she refused all marriage proposals, fearing that a new man in her life may not raise us in accordance with her standards. She tried her best to be a gentle disciplinarian. But as a five-year-old boy, I believed that my routine was difficult. She would ease me out of a deep sleep at five o'clock in the morning—the exact time when the elders awoke for their morning prayers—and walk me through my morning ritual until I was ready for the Qur'anic school about two blocks away. I'd return home at about seven o'clock, eat my breakfast, and head to kindergarten.

School for native Algerian children.

When I reached the appropriate age for school, I was sent to a newly built facility for indigenous citizens. Under colonial law this was a requirement, but Mom did not seem to mind that aspect of the law. As a matter of fact, she thought it was an important step, since her family comprised of intellectuals with educational credentials from colonial and traditional Qur'anic institutions. The

Saighis symbolized a proud tradition in high education and intellect. My cousin, Tahar Zemouchi, was the first teacher in the village, and my other cousin, Fatima Cid, was the first pharmacist in Algeria. Education was a serious matter for our mother.

Throughout my final years of primary school, she kept me up late into the night to teach me how to memorize and recite my French comprehension, alongside my history and geography lessons. If I stumbled or hesitated a little bit during my exercises, she sent me off to reread the material, more than ten times, and return to recite everything from scratch, as many times as she deemed necessary. Much later in life, I pondered the question of how she managed to coach me through the process. She did not comprehend the French language, let alone speak it.

Qur'anic school.

My mother showered me with deep love, and I expressed my deepest love and sentiments for her in return. I loved her; she was tender, gentle, attentive, kind, and very intelligent. Each and every

A Dream for Peace

night, she'd tuck me into bed and place a piece of chocolate in my mouth. When I felt her tender fingers touch my lips, I submerged myself in her sweet and gentle good-night kiss on my face. She always worried that she might lose me, just as she lost my twin brothers before me. There were nights when I woke up and saw her standing by my bedside, staring adoringly at me.

In our tribal tradition, it was customary for women to pierce the ear of a surviving son after losing multiple boys at a young age. When I turned three, almost immediately after we lost my older brother, my right ear was pierced. I thought nothing of it. When I turned six, I grew increasingly weary of the persistent banter by schoolmates, who called me a girl, despite my very strong boyish appearance. On a hot sunny afternoon, I broke from lunch and stormed into the house to express my frustration to Mom: "Look, Mom, you have but one choice. Either you remove the earring, or I will rip off my ear to get rid of it." She sensed the rage and seemed horrified. "My dearest Aziz," she empathized with a most soothing tone, addressing me using the endearing Arabic term for "sweetheart," "it's all right, son. Don't say such horrible things. Come and sit with Mom. I will remove the earring." Relief at last. I was finally free.

Like a united clan, my uncles often ate their meals together. They held each other in such reverence that when a decision was made to give away a niece in marriage by an uncle, the father of the girl would merely accept the decision without any hesitation. The siblings never stood in each other's way. We could eat our meals and spend the night at the respective homes of our cousins without letting our parents know ahead of time.

The town of Aïn Beïda was more like an Israeli kibbutz; everybody knew their neighbor, and we all helped each other. When the head of a family was out of town, a child of any relative could be called upon to run errands or fetch water for the family. My mother would usually ask that I go to the house of her two Jewish friends every Sabbath to turn on the lights for them. The precepts of their religion forbade them from engaging in certain mechanized activities. Our local friendly teachers from the indigenous school, comprised of Frenchmen and some Kabyle tribesmen, were respected and seen as extended family members. They taught us the French language, history, mathematics, geography, and other essential curricular subjects, with the exception of the history and geography of Algeria.

Our teachers had been indoctrinated to instill in us that France was our motherland. As a kid, I wasn't too sure that their attempt to inculcate us with a "respect for France" always resonated. During a lesson in civics, one of my classmates demonstrated such lackluster knowledge when the teacher posed a question, using a form of matriarchal reference to the French nation, "Who is France?" He looked sternly at the little timid boy. Quite innocently, yet in his own solemn way, he answered, "France is Bouziane's mother." Bouziane was his neighbor. Our class erupted in laughter.

We knew the history of France from its origins and were acutely familiar with French culture—the succession of the kings of France, their geography with all the rivers, railway lines, railway stations, and train intersections. All these facts we were expected to know by heart, but we knew absolutely nothing about our Algerian heritage. At times, the system seemed tactfully designed to make us forget our Algerian heritage.

As a norm, we were expected to tackle the syllabus on Algeria at the end of the school year and "study the details" on our own. We rarely received questions regarding our Algerian homeland. This was either a political calculation or, perhaps, sheer coincidence.

Notwithstanding, we did indeed receive a solid education. For six days each week, we attended the indigenous schools; five of those days were for academic education and the sixth day was dedicated to vocational tutelage, mainly carpentry and steel workshops. As a matter of fact, we demonstrated a higher proficiency level of the French language than our young French counterparts. We were so well versed in the language that we bypassed the usual colloquial revisions because we did not speak French at home. Nonetheless, to our parents, French remained the "language of the foreigners."

There were approximately sixty students at the indigenous primary school. Upon completion of our primary school program, we received the Certificat d'Études, tantamount to our first graduate degree. It was an honor to receive one, and we aspired to reach that milestone. Our parents viewed it as an instrument but not as a major educational challenge. For them, the ultimate test was to ensure our thorough comprehension of the Qur'an and Islam.

After earning the Certificat d'Études, five or six of the best students from the indigenous school were cleared to enroll in the Cours Complémentaire, a four-year syllabus attended exclusively by a majority of French students, which concluded at the middle school level with a certificate of completion. The educational process was very intense, but unlike the indigenous school, where we interacted with our native Algerians, the environment was imperiled by blatant racism.

The milieu was worsened by the fomentation of anti-colonial sentiments among the natives. My feelings and instincts became visibly anti-colonialist, and the effects were on full display during a mathematics class taught by Mr. Millet, the principal. The school's heating system was a wood-burning cast-iron furnace. Due to the overwhelming levels of smoke that flowed into the classroom whenever fresh firewood was placed in the unit, no student was permitted to put logs in it during recess. Whenever we were cold, we huddled around the furnace to keep ourselves warm. One day, the stationmaster's daughter, a girl by the name of Spiteri, tossed a log in the stove, right before the end of recess. We had barely returned to our respective seats when Mr. Millet arrived on the premises and saw the gradual release of black smoke coming out of the furnace. Without hesitating, he turned to me and yelled, "This is an *Arab* deed." "No, sir," I replied, "this is a *French* deed." Obviously irritated, he stared me in the eye and posed the question directly, "So, who is responsible for the faux pas?" "I do not know," I replied with a child's insolence. "Let the culprit come forward," he said. I shrugged. Spiteri stayed quiet, and so did everyone.

He had singled me out because I was the only Algerian in math class. As far as he was concerned, my audacity was an act of disobedience, meriting a three-day suspension. My first revulsion against racism and colonialism did not merit the severe punishment. At the time, I believed in my heart that his reaction amounted to an unjustifiable form of hazing. My mother was not particularly happy with my behavior, but the incident was soon forgotten. At least I impressed upon Mr. Millet my tight-lipped disposition, and he learned that I would not tattle on my peers.

Upon completion of the Cours Complémentaire program, Fodil asked me to pursue teaching as my major. He explained that the salary was good and that free housing was also provided to every teacher. Elaborating further, he even suggested that I would be able to buy a car, because all the French teachers had one. Not to mention the fact that they were also entitled to taking three months off from work each year and if I chose that path, I would be able to help him support the family. But I was not interested in becoming a teacher. I could not see myself working for the French colonial administration for the rest of my life, nor could I begin to bear the thought of me going down that road. I wanted to continue my studies and finish high school. Mom supported my plans, but Fodil was determined to stop me at all cost. He intentionally dragged his feet on submitting my school application until the registration deadline had passed, effectively limiting my chances of getting into the Lycée d'Aumale (Reda Houhou), the best school in the province of Constantine. I was left with the only available option—to enroll at the Collège de Batna, an all-boys high school for average students, where I spent a year waiting for the next registration opportunity.

Sometime that year, Loucif, a classmate at school, introduced

A Dream for Peace

me to the Benboulaid brothers, Mustapha and Omar, owners of a bus line servicing the Batna–Ariss route in the Aurès Mountain range. We used to meet on most weekends. A majority of my classmates joined the "Maquis" underground guerrilla fighters when the Algerian Revolution began a few years later. My close friends Benbaatouche, Gouaref, and many others died as martyrs. The Benboulaid brothers were the ones who started the revolution in Ariss, when they ordered the hijacking of their own bus and took the passengers hostage. Consequently, the head of regional administration for North Africa, known locally as a *caïd*, was killed along with a French teacher, whose wife survived with severe injuries.

    I worked very hard to achieve high academic scores during the school year. At the graduation ceremony, I received almost every award, including one for excellence, and the prestigious City of Batna Award, a top prize normally reserved for the best student from among the collective secondary schools in the city. A separate City Award was given to the top girl in her class. All the girls in the elite schools were French. Mr. Malpel, the pompous and racist colonial mayor of Batna, presided over the award ceremonies. We stood in line for several minutes, waiting to go on the podium. As a rule, those who were up for the most prestigious awards were expected to be at the head of the queue. I was second in line behind a French girl. When she walked up to receive her prize, Mr. Malpel planted a kiss on her cheek, congratulated her, and handed over the prize. She walked off, beaming with pride. I moved into position and reached for a handshake, but instead, he shoved the award in my hand to avoid making skin contact and quickly turned to look at the students behind me. I was stunned and hurt, almost frozen in place for a few seconds. Without hesitation, I staged an immediate anti-colonial protest on the spot and dropped the large, beautifully engraved hardcover book. It crash-landed with a thud on the ornate table, and the audience gasped. I stared into the eyes of my bewildered classmates and ambled off to my seat.

Birth to University

The year I spent at the Collège de Batna had all but secured my admission to the Lycée d'Aumale with flying colors. I received a scholarship upon admission and was assigned supervisory duties to oversee the junior high students. I was given the keys to the high school, with full access to the buildings at all times. I even ate my meals in a separate area with the other school prefects.

There was a direct bus line between Aïn Beïda and Constantine. Occasionally, Mom would send my sister Missa to the station with freshly baked *baklava*, a favorite dessert, made with filo dough, nuts, butter, and honey. Each time, the driver received his own special package and brought my parcel to school. I enjoyed many assortments of pastries from my mother on a regular basis and shared some with my closest friends. The motherly routine carried over from my days at Batna.

Like most teenage boys, I always dreamed about owning a motorbike. But the thought of me on the back of a bike scared my mother more than anything. She warned against the "dangerous" machine and made me promise not to ever get on a motorbike. At school, a few of my French buddies teased with their superb maneuvers on their bikes, imploring me to take a spin, but I never took the bait. Needless to say, I just couldn't resist when a friend talked me into testing out his noisy little Vespa scooter. I sat on the bike and accelerated, totally oblivious to the nature of the engine's mechanics or how to regulate the speed. As I quickly began to lose control, I cried out "Mommy..." and took a nasty fall onto the road. Luckily, the wounds on my knees were superficial, but the emotional distress was more profound. I never telegraphed the incident to anyone. I just returned the bike to my friend and went to receive first aid from the school nurse at the infirmary.

School closed for the summer vacation, not long after my minor accident. Mom was always happy to welcome me home. She embraced me as soon as I walked through the door, looked deeply into my eyes, ruffled my hair, and kissed my forehead. Walking behind me as I sauntered along, towing my belongings, I could almost feel her breathing down my neck. "Aziz," she said. "Yes, Mom," I replied, turning to look at her. "You know, I had a strange feeling that something had happened to you at school." She forced a smile. "Son, please roll up your pants and show me your knees." I stood there and wondered quietly about her psychic abilities. "But Mom, I am not a little boy anymore. Why would I show you my knees?" In an instant, she seemed irritated. "Because you were on a motorbike, and I heard you cry out *'Mommy!'* as you fell off the bike. I even saw your bleeding knees." I was speechless, but more convinced than ever that she was a natural clairvoyant. I thought of what to say as I rolled up my pants to the knees. "Don't worry, Mom, there's no more pain. As you can see, the scars are healing well." She stared right into my soul, and I felt horrible. Her sustained silence was more punishing than any words she could have uttered. From that day forward, I was more than certain about her deep maternal intuition. We shared an effervescent bond that grew more powerful, long after the umbilical chord had been cut from her womb. Our souls were truly connected.

The curriculum at Lycée d'Aumale was an excellent one. Our syllabus was up to par with the elite schools in Paris. There were very few Algerians enrolled at the school. We excelled in all subjects, including the dead languages: Ancient Greek and Latin. It was common practice for our teachers to give us some homework at the end of each school week. The best and most proficient student in the Latin program was my cousin, Mohamed Zemmouchi. He was known to spend his weekend sabbatical completing assignments on Latin themes and versions. When we returned to school on Sunday evenings, some classmates would approach and ask for copies of his Latin assignments. Zemmouchi would impose an "embargo" until those who were interested in receiving a copy paid a fee.

My grades in physics, chemistry, and mathematics were always high. Occasionally, a classmate, the son of the Commandant de Cercle (Regional Commander) would invite me to spend the weekends and help him polish up on the subjects. We stayed in a nice suite at the Hotel de France, the largest hotel in Constantine, and exchanged privileges: every meal we ate was served to us on fine silverware, and I gladly taught him the formulas.

When I earned my baccalaureate upon graduation, my stepbrother resurfaced again, insisting that I become a teacher. Having received a scholarship to continue my studies wherever I wanted, I remained unhinged and hard to persuade. Mother was still very supportive of me. But he persistently suggested that I enroll at the University of Algiers—an institution filled with racists and practitioners of nepotism. We haggled back and forth for a couple of weeks before reaching a compromise. He agreed to let me go on to France to continue my university studies with a caveat: "Absolutely not in Paris," he said. "Well, okay. You have my word," I promised. Soon after the conversation, I packed my few belongings into a military duffel bag and went to say goodbye to my mother.

Graduating class at Lycée d'Aumale.

A Dream for Peace

I had parted ways with my mom before. The first time was for a local departure to my boarding school in Batna, and then a year later, when I said goodbye prior to departing for my high school in Constantine. But this time was much different, because I was going overseas to a far-away place to pursue a higher education, and I knew it would be a while before I saw her again. We were both very emotional. I tried hard not to look into her teary eyes, so as not to trigger my own tears from streaming down my cheeks. She hugged and blessed me, promising to keep me in her prayers. Again and again, she recited prayers imploring Allah to ensure that I would forever be blessed and surrounded by greener pastures on my journeys.

The plan was for me to travel by sea aboard a cattle transport ship setting sail from the city of Bône, present-day Annaba. On the eve of my departure, I stayed with the Audiberts—parents of a friend from France, who I used to help with homework assignments in Aïn Beïda. They owned the largest hardware store in town and had moved to Bône after acquiring a hotel by the harbor, near the very famous Cours Bertagna, a town square where Arabs had no access. I was given free accommodation and escorted to the boat in the morning. Aboard, I sat on a folding chair in the ship's hold with a flock of sheep. For the very first time in my life, I left the shores of my fatherland, no passport required. The French had annexed my country; therefore, I was a French subject. I slept very little on the journey because of the constant bleating by the flock. But at my age, being in the company of the flock was the least of my worries.

The boat docked at Marseille harbor in the morning. I disembarked and went to the University of Aix-Marseille. After taking some time to explore the city for a few hours, I decided it didn't meet my expectations. I rushed to the station to catch the next train to Lyon. The University of Lyon wasn't what I'd envisioned either. I turned around and went back to the station to catch a train to Paris. My cousin, Abdelhak Berrah, welcomed me to his home at 14

Rue des Arcades. The building was a former brothel with beautifully furnished rooms that had been remodeled to accommodate area students. After a few days with him, the city life grew on me, but I'd been warned: this was the "forbidden city" I'd promised Fodil I would avoid at all cost.

I went to Poitiers, only to discover that the city was absolutely lifeless and devoid of the robust metropolitan energy I'd experienced in Paris. I thought the local university was too small. I spent a few days wrestling with my decision. Finally, I decided to head south, to Bordeaux. It was there that I realized I had come to the end of my journey.

I arrived by train on a Saturday afternoon and headed straight to the offices of the National Students' Union of France (UNEF) in search of accommodation. Normal working hours were over, and there were a few people on the grounds. I was still holding my backpack, staring at the notes on a bulletin board, when a student walked up to me. "The offices are closed until Monday." He extended his hand and said, "Hi, my name is Lamine Ben Ahmed. I am from Tunisia." I was certain he could detect the desperation on my face, because he understood immediately that I was desperately in need of accommodation. "You are more than welcome to stay at my place until you find a room." I took him up on the offer without any hesitation. I could not afford to stay at a hotel, but I still had a few days to find a permanent place to stay. I was thankful for his kind gesture.

He jumped on his Lambretta scooter, and I sat behind him for the short ride to his place. As soon as we entered the room, I looked around and found a place for my belongings. He offered his bathroom to me to freshen up. I was in urgent need of a good shower. It was a Saturday night, and he suggested we go to a nightclub. "What kind of place is that?" The word "nightclub" did not ring a bell. "It is a place where one goes to listen to music and meet girls with whom one can dance," he explained, a bit surprised at my naiveté. I wondered what we would be wearing to this so-called nightclub. I had no suit and no tie, only the bare necessities in my luggage—two pairs of shoes, two pairs of pants, several shirts, and a pullover. He offered me a suit that fit somewhat perfectly. I was soon dressed and ready to discover the unknown.

Though we were total strangers, my Tunisian brother was quite courageous. He was willing to trust me enough to share his small living space. "I am a medical student," he said. "Oh, how convenient. I am also seeking enrollment into the medical program here. I guess I can pick your brains over the coming days." He seemed flattered. "I'd be more than happy to help." He was a very interesting young man, totally carefree and generous in every way. I was quite impressed by his intuitive abilities too. He guessed accurately that I did not have enough money at my disposal, and he knew right away that I had no place to stay.

My first experience at a nightclub did not impress me. The music was too loud for my liking, and I felt a bit awkward. I sat and observed the action on the dance floor over a cold soft drink. Lamine seemed to enjoy himself very much. We returned to his place after a few hours. Over the next few days, we became more acquainted and soon after I registered at the university, I found a room in another part of town. We remained very good friends throughout my stay in Bordeaux. Over time, I interacted with several students from Morocco, Algeria, Tunisia, Vietnam, Madagascar, and the sub-Saharan French colonies. There was strong synergy among us, since we happened to be in the same boat, having to deal with constant discrimination and racism. We met at the same coffee place, Le Régent, and discussed all the problems we encountered. Eventually, we came together for a common purpose under the banner of the Association of North African Muslim Students (AEMNA), and then we constituted the UGET[1] for the Tunisians and the UNEM[2] for the Moroccans. At this juncture, I had been in med school for a little over two years, and my studies were proceeding fairly well. During a field study at a local hospital in Bordeaux, our medical professor demonstrated a unique technique by which a handkerchief could substitute for a stethoscope, just in case we ever found ourselves without one. We were truly amazed by the creativity involved in the borderline medical experiment. I never could have imagined that a piece of cloth could serve as a device for listening to the lungs. A retiring medical professor taught us about all the typical medical mistakes that could prove costly in our practice and emphasized the discipline of ensuring quality outcomes through the use of self-regulatory methods. The medical program at school was very advanced.

I continued to juggle my student union activities along with my medical studies in a seamless undertaking that brought immense satisfaction, because my continued commitment and dedication had a sense of purpose. We had organized the North African workers in the community. Law students met with illiterate workers to type up administrative letters and help defend their rights. Literature majors wrote letters on behalf of the workers to their families. I led a team of medical students to provide basic medical assistance for some workers. Those with more severe cases were accompanied to the hospital, and since a significant majority did not speak French, we helped secure the necessary aid for them. We also visited some inpatients to provide moral support and ensure that they were well cared for. The situation paved the way for us to hold political meetings and solidify our base. We began establishing similar movements at universities in Paris and other major university towns around France.

---

[1] General Union of Tunisian Students
[2] General Union of Moroccan Students

A Dream for Peace

A good friend, Jamil Ben Bouzid, often accompanied me to the Gare Saint-Jean train station in Bordeaux. He was the son of a former captain of the French army, who happened to be a prominent Aïn Beïda citizen. On an urgent trip to Paris in midwinter, I wore a short-sleeved shirt to the train station. He took off his sweater and placed it on my shoulders, putting himself at risk for catching the flu. He was down to a short-sleeved shirt when he left the station.

After attending several meetings with our brothers in Paris, I returned to Bordeaux to begin organizing local factory workers and Algerian brothers at the university. Manifestations of racism were visible everywhere we went, and it helped us build solidarity among Algerians and comrades from other colonized countries. We couldn't even rent a room without going through the UNEF. On a daily basis, we held meetings to evaluate our options in light of the oppressive climate, discuss our objectives, and make decisions on various actionable items. The meetings were usually in the basement of a locale in the center of town—Le Café Français. We were often victims of physical violence. Mohammed Khemisti, who later became the first foreign minister of President Ahmed Ben Bella,[3] was beaten up in Montpellier by the ultra-rightist Mousseron Ballan group.[4]

In retaliation, I recruited some guys from the Algerian underground, led by Chouki, an Algerian bouncer, who was a hired gun for the Corsican Mafia. Members of the Bordeaux underground had initially confided in me, promising to convert to moral citizens of society. It was the occasion to honor their word and embrace our cause. They ransacked the university restaurant belonging to the French rightists (BEC).[5] I was later arrested, interrogated by the French anti-terrorist squad throughout the night, and charged with procurement. My comrades from the UNEF intervened and secured my release. I was the vice president for the Bordeaux

---

[3] Algeria's first president.
[4] Leader of ultra-rightist movement.
[5] Bordeaux Students Club.

branch at the time. From then on, I was closely monitored by the police, hence, I spent the night at different locations with the help of my most trusted colleagues, who always went out of their way to see to my comfort. Typically, rooms were very small—just enough to fit a junior-size bed and a tiny desk. That was the standard accommodation for most students. But above all else, the generosity of my friends was beyond imagination. Everywhere I spent the night, my host gave me the mattress off their bed, and they went to sleep on the squeaky box springs with nothing but a blanket. I always tried to argue my way out of it, because I'd rather have been the one on the box springs, but it didn't matter to them how much I protested. My dear brothers were always prepared to endure the discomfort. They were more than willing to do anything to accord me the courtesy of a peaceful night's sleep. Our brotherly spirit was branded in everyone's nature, and no one gave a second thought to such noble actions. Though the colonialists had imposed undue hardship on all of us, circumstances had united everyone under the banner of an exemplary solidarity. To such extent, even when we ran out of meal coupons at the end of the month, we knew that all we had to do was to show up at the cafeteria on campus, where any of our colleagues would offer up a coupon, even if it was their last remaining one. Once in a while, if there were no coupons left, someone would go back for seconds (usually served without any meat) and share the meal with his mate. We took care of each other with brotherly affection and called on the phone regularly to ensure that none of us had been arrested.

I was studying in France in 1954 when I received word that my mother had fallen seriously ill. The news came as a surprise because she had kept me in the dark about her condition, knowing fully well that I would have dropped everything to be with her. But Mom was not one to interfere with my studies. She held on until the end was near before summoning me to her side.

My flight to Algiers, although short, felt like several hours long. I made my way to Aïn Beïda by bus, where a few relatives were on hand to welcome me. But as luck would have it, so were the two Frenchmen, agents from the General Intelligence Unit, waiting in the shadows to escort me to the police station. "Are you on your way to Cairo?" the interrogator pressed, ogling down at me as I sat on a stool in the confines of a small windowless room. "I came to see my dying mother. If I planned to go to Cairo, I would have flown there directly from France." I was plain mad and made no secret of my disdain for the inconvenience.

The Algerian Revolution had just begun a few weeks earlier on November 1. It was initiated by nine members of a revolutionary group, the Comité Révolutionnaire d'Unité et d'Action (CRUA), who adopted the name Front de Libération Nationale (FLN). They formed an external delegation in Cairo, charged with garnering diplomatic support for Algeria's liberation while overseeing the supply of arms and ammunition for the revolution. This was all done with the blessing of the Egyptian president, Gamal Abdel Nasser. Meanwhile, members in Algeria were primed to spread the guerrilla warfare around the country in a synchronized action on the same day. Due to the ferocious nature of activities in the Aurès Mountains by hardened combatants, our region became the epicenter of the revolution. The French authorities grew extremely paranoid and started to crack down at transit points across the region. As a result of the call to arms by the FLN from the Cairo headquarters, security forces proceeded to arrest suspected sympathizers, mostly young men from my hometown, in a desperate attempt to stem the flow of potential recruits into Egypt.

I spent a few hours at the station before being released from custody, after my uncles came to demand a legal reason and justification for holding me. Once I got to Mom's side, my composure was shaken to the core. She was a picture of vibrant health when I saw her last, just her old self, full of laughter, life, and energy. I had a hard time accepting the fact that the unexpected was unfolding right in front of me. At my young and tender age, I was ill prepared to be listening to the dying wish of my mom. But I sat quietly by her bedside, clutching her hand so close to me and trying very hard to keep from crying. She asked that I promise to take very good care of my sisters, especially Yasmina, the youngest. I just nodded and gave her my word, hoping to soothe her emotional agony. As she whispered, her words, so soft, yet profoundly pointed, echoed gently past my earlobes like a cool stream of heavenly wind gusts and cloaked me with goose bumps. I kept saying repeatedly that Allah was watching over her. She passed away three days later. Words cannot describe the pain and anguish of losing my dearly beloved mom. She had been a pillar of support throughout my challenges, and the void was intensely immense. I consoled myself by acknowledging that I had been fortunate enough to spend the last few days with her. I thanked Allah for according me the privilege of being there for the funeral.

Following the burial ceremonies, I mourned with my sisters for a few days. We comforted ourselves, believing that our mother would continue to watch over us. Each night, I purposely retired early to bed, just to be alone. I reflected on every memory that came to me, like my teenage years when I used to hug Mom, a short and frail woman, and braced her head close to my chest, teasingly asserting my dominance. "*Aziz, you may be tall, but I'm still your mom,*" she would say. Her infectious giggle reverberated like a soothing melody through my body, and I would release my hold on her. She was not a fan of pictures, but that was because she wanted to preserve traditions of old. All she left me was an everlasting memorable portrait that lived safely in the depths of my heart.

It was because of her I wanted to succeed in my medical studies, just to make her happy and prove to her that her consistent support had not been in vain. She was very proud of me, and it showed in every way. "Ghoulem, I am waiting for you to become a *toubib* ["doctor" in Arabic] so that you can remove my heart, cleanse

A Dream for Peace

it, and put it right back," my lovely aunt once quipped in front of the family, and I watched Mom beam with pride. Suddenly, it dawned on me that she would not be coming to my graduation.

It wasn't long before I understood that she never left my side. I knew that I would continue to feel her presence in my entire life. I often reflected on her words in prayer—those same words she uttered when she prayed that I would always be surrounded by greener pastures.

Days later, it was time to go back to Bordeaux. Among the family members who accompanied me were some elders who could not resist giving me an earful because of the incident at the bus station. From the onset, there had been murmurs among some uncles about my "political activism in France," but they bit their tongue and said nothing. They assumed the cops may have been tracking my every move and decided to arrest me upon arrival. Alas, when it was time to send me off, they thought it very appropriate to set me straight. *"You young people are ostentatious. You think you can beat France and take down NATO with it? Use your head, Ghoulem, and keep a low profile. Stay out of trouble and go make us proud, son."* My very opinionated uncle, a hard-edged rebel, respected among his siblings for his fearlessness, was especially blunt. I shrugged him off with all due respect to the other elders and acknowledged with a subtle nod. I hugged everyone firmly and said an emotional goodbye.

In France, my political activities were ramped up more than usual. I managed to balance politics and medical studies with ease. I met with Vietnamese students on occasion to gain some insight on the events of Dien Bien Phu and acquired some knowledge about the remarkable victory over the French army by Viet Minh forces. My interactions with them became quite interesting over the coming days as I became increasingly curious. The very notion that such a small nation had stood their ground against Algeria's colonial power was confounding. My Vietnamese comrades shared every bit of information with me. Within days, I was up to speed on the geographical layout of the forestry terrains in the heart of the region.

Birth to University

The opulent fragrances of jungle flowers in the misty dusk air was known to be responsible for Dien Bien Phu's memorable atmospheric essences that filtered throughout the contours of endless mountain ranges, full of wild baboons that played peak-a-boo in the giant bamboo groves. Fields of rice plantations meandering freely into each other in a checkered layout graced the green valleys along winding natural river basins. It sounded like a beautiful part of the world, much too serene for war and bloodshed. I planned on visiting someday.

The heroic story of General Võ Nguyên Giáp, commander of the Viet Minh forces, was told in tales that shifted from version to version every single day. As the story goes, he craftily drew the French army into a deadly battle in the Dien Bien Phu valley and isolated them from vital supplies. The French capitulated after a few months and called for a cease-fire, ending a bitter eight-year struggle against the Viet Minh. This historic event was a powerful take-home lesson for the Algerian liberation war, which began some six months later.

More than three decades after General Giáp's magnificent victory, I was pleasantly surprised when my dear friend, Dr. Trần, a Swiss gentleman of Vietnamese origin, offered to organize a trip to Vietnam. "Well, you can definitely count me in," I told him. "Dien Bien Phu is on my bucket list." His cousin in Hanoi, Dr. Truong Xuân Dàn, was a medical professor and retired general who had served as a doctor in the army. When we met at his home in a quiet neighborhood on the city outskirts, I was really thrilled. A mild-mannered and soft-spoken war veteran, he shared a most harrowing account of the combat and gave me a firsthand glimpse into the mind of one of the best military strategists of our time. We toured the famed battleground in Dien Bien Phu, where he recounted some heroic activities by the hardened infantrymen who scaled mountainous terrains on bicycles, pulling along artillery and other weapons.

A Dream for Peace

Standing at the summit and looking across the valley, I asked him, "How did you do it, my friend?" He cast a long gaze at the distant mist and spoke proudly, "We were energized by the love for our motherland. We were ready to sacrifice our lives to gain our independence. That was all that mattered to us." I knew exactly what he was saying, because we shared the same belief in our own quest for independence.

My life on campus in Bordeaux was quite hectic. I had a full schedule after class and progressively began to shape a permanent routine of going from meeting with Vietnamese students, to joining Malagasy student groups for discussions regarding the struggle in Madagascar, and on occasion I met with members of the Federation of Black Franco-African students (FEANF). Meetings with citizens of French West African colonies were highly spirited. Everyone was full of iconoclastic ideas. I was particularly motivated by calls to promote a more patrician vision of Africa's future after colonialism. Although we were very passionate and forceful during some of our discussions, we remained tempered in our expectations and resolute in our commitment. It was, after all, our ancestral heritage that was under attack by a colonial power whose sole aim was to vanquish any trace of our cultural existence. We pledged to defend our people at all cost and endeavor to device ways to implement achievable objectives. Each topic at every meeting revolved around similar virtues, regardless of the nature and makeup of the organization. Independence and national sovereignty were held in the highest order of importance, and we were ever mindful of the magnitude of the fight ahead. The Guinean students repeatedly highlighted the importance of steering away from the French educational system in order to foster our own African identity and culture, which was being undermined by the colonists.

I became the president of the Comité de Liaison des Étudiants d'Outre Mer (overseas students), and with the help of fellow overseas students, as we were called then, I drafted a program for the Anti-Colonial Commemoration Day demonstration, which was held on February 21, 1955. The event was grand. Students from different countries set up their various booths for traditional exhibition of cultural goods and artifacts, and there were activities of all kinds.

I sent out a personal invitation to the guest of honor and keynote speaker for the evening—Professor André Mandouze, a French academic and journalist. He was a Catholic, an anti-fascist, anti-colonialist activist, and an avid supporter of Algeria's struggle for independence. He was later awarded the position of Director of Higher Education at the University of Algiers, after Algeria gained independence. His love for Algeria was linked to the fact that it was the birthplace of Saint Augustine, to whom he dedicated his thesis at the Sorbonne in Paris. Saint Augustine symbolized the connection between Africanism and Universalism.

It was a snowy winter day. There was so much snow on the ground that it made it impossible to travel by car. I went to his place, and we walked back together to the festivities. When we arrived at the exhibition, we learned that the mayor of Bordeaux, Jacques Chaban Delmas, had cut off the electricity. We did not despair. We simply waited for the power to be restored, and the event proceeded without any further interruptions.

Professor Mandouze was very spirited on the podium. He made an eloquent presentation in a powerful speech that called for a cessation in colonial dominance of Africa and Asia. Students were really fired up, and the solidarity among those of us from the colonized countries was greatly strengthened.

In the days following the events, we took to the streets and demonstrated in support of the citizens of Vietnam and in favor of Malagasy independence. Vietnamese students were the most discreet, yet the most active. Beyond taking on the responsibility of distributing leaflets, which they printed at the Communist Party offices, the Guinean students were always ready for demonstrations.

A Dream for Peace

They were highly effective at revolutionary journalism, always headlining the African peoples quest to gain their freedom. The many bright activists among the various movements were inspired by the belief that independence and traditional culture were one and the same. The Algerian union preceded the formation of the General Union of Algerian Muslim Students (UGEMA), an offspring of the FLN, which later became the most important and the most revolutionary organization. Always mindful of our nationalist struggle for independence, I participated in strategic meetings with FLN organizers in France to help formulate our rhetoric on how to engage the colonial powers for the liberation of our people.

We were ahead of our political elders. We had laid the foundations for the unity of North Africa through the AEMNA, and our grassroots organizations lived on until Algeria's independence. But within the student community of Algeria, the unity proved to be more difficult. There were two divisions initially: on one side, the National Union of Algerian Students, led by Mohammed Harbi, who later became a famous historian, and on the other, there was the nationalist UGEMA led by Belaid Abdesselam, Ahmed Taleb Ibrahimi, and Abdelmalek Benhabiles, also known as Socrates. The second group would prevail after the first group left the door open to non-Muslims and welcomed the children of French colonialists. The French Communist Party helped the UGEMA gain an advantage over the National Union of Algerian Students.

We founded the UGEMA and convened our initial congress in July 1955 to elect our first committee directors, comprising of nineteen others and myself. Thereafter, the duly elected committee directors voted to nominate executive committee members, comprising of students from the Paris sector. We established the various sectors in the different university towns by order of importance. Ahmed Taleb was elected president of UGEMA, Mohammed Khemisti was elected president of the Montpellier sector, and I was picked to be the president of the Bordeaux sector.

When we held our first convention, there were some among the Algerian students who were anti–Messali Hadj. Even the chef at the North African university restaurant was a strong Messalist.[6] Some students decided to take down the portrait of Messali Hadj, the famed Algerian patriot, claiming that the picture had been hanging on a rusty nail on the wall and risked falling off. We knew this was a lame excuse at best, but it was their main reason for removing the awesome portrait, which had dominated the great hall of the North African university restaurant.

We continued to coexist under difficult conditions until one fateful day in May of 1956, when the Organization of the Secret Army (OAS), an underground movement at the time, organized the massacre of students at the University of Algiers. Although they were officially rolled out in 1961, the dissident French paramilitary organization had been very active since the beginning of the Algerian struggle in 1954. Following the senseless attack, the UGEMA sector for Algiers, which was headed by Mohamed Benyahia, Allaoua Benbaatouche, and my dear friend and brother Lamine Khane, decided to retaliate by embarking on an immediate general strike. Our members abstained from studies and work in Algeria. The irony for us and all other member students in France was the fact that our finals were fast approaching. Hence, we were caught off guard by the grave situation.

The members convened the UGEMA committee in Paris and decided to send Belaid Abdesselam to Algiers for a briefing. He was chosen because of his experience in the Parti du Peuple Algérien (PPA)[7] and its various branches. We expected him to return with a detailed report. During his twenty-four-hour trip, he met with Lamine Khane, who had already elected to join the health services wing of the ALN—the military arm in the suburbs of Algiers. As soon

---

[6] Members of the Algerian patriot Messali Hadj's political party.
[7] Algerian political party founded by Messali Hadj.

as he returned, we convened a board meeting to hear his report and elected to vote either for or against the decision of the Algiers sector.

The meeting was held at the Paris headquarters of the AEMNA, located at 115 Boulevard Saint Michel, cradle of the Tunisian, Moroccan, and Algerian revolutions. When the discussions became highly spirited and animated, I suggested that only the elected members of the board, who had the power and authority to make decisions, remain in the boardroom. I was out-voted by the members. My second proposition was for us to find a solution to re-settle the striking students in countries that were willing to receive them: If we were to go on a general strike, our decision could have some dire consequences on the future of an independent Algeria. When the matter was put to a vote, I was outvoted on that as well. The issue of going on a general strike was then put to a vote. By a show of hands, the majority voted to go on strike. We made a blind decision that only a few of us were convinced was the right thing to do, but we were all outraged by the situation and sensed the urgent call to action.

A Dream for Peace

I spent all my time praying and reading the Bible in Spanish—a language I barely understood—but I kept reading to improve my comprehension. I used a spoon to mark the wall, whenever I imagined that a full day had passed. I prayed that God would someday set me free so that at the very least, I could live one single day in an independent Algeria.

Chapter Two

Hardship And and Prison

The meeting that induced a solemn and unanimous vote in favor of a general strike was a difficult one: the consequences of our action could have dire repercussions for Algeria's future, potentially depriving the country of all of its intellectuals. Many students were in the process of taking their final exams—some had begun taking their oral tests. I tried my hardest to convince the members to allow those who were taking their oral exams to complete the process before we went on strike, but I wasn't successful.

Emotions were further intensified by the killing of our brothers at the University of Algiers by OAS assassins. At the end of our deliberations, the final decision was taken by a show of hands, and I had to submit to the weight of the unanimous decision by a majority of our members. The closing statement was drafted, signed, and published immediately. Redha Malek, who was supposed to sign the declaration after I was done signing it, sat on my left side. He simply advised me to execute the document with a *tkhenticha*-style signature—a cabalistic sign to render my signature illegible to the Special Services at a later time. However, like everyone else, I put my official signature on the document, which may have since disappeared into the annals of history.

After arriving at the decision to go on strike, we were invited by Layachi Yaker to meet with Ferhat Abbas[8] at La Rue Blanche, behind the Saint Lazare train station in Paris. He was a member

---

[8] Algerian political Leader and nationalist.

A Dream for Peace

of the JUDMA[9] and years later, he joined President Boumédiène's cabinet as his Minister of Commerce. The meeting was held at the home of Ahmed Boumendjel,[10] with attendees Ferhat Abbas, Ahmed Francis[11], and Boumendjel. Abbas, a great speaker, explained his vision in succinct detail, outlining a path forward for the Algerian struggle that was in stark contrast to the rhetoric of the extremists. After politely indulging him, we were unanimous in telling him that his explanations were not sufficient, given the current state of events. We believed strongly that the only way to achieve our goal was to join forces and unite. We learned a few days later that he had decided to go to Cairo to participate in the armed revolution.

We decided to spread the news about the decision to go on strike—to all our friends and brothers. We visited the various precincts to get the word out. I was responsible for the southwest region of France. I called on the students at the universities and went to ensure that the workers with whom I had become very acquainted due to my work with FLN's Federation of France were given the message.

I visited Poitiers, a city I knew all too well. I had been there on a previous occasion, hoping to register at the local university's Faculty of Medicine, but I reversed course and decided to enroll at the university in Bordeaux. My job on the campus was easy. I gave a long speech and engaged my comrades in heated debates until we arrived at a near unanimous decision. Although I'd planned to make Bordeaux my last stop, I decided to continue on to Toulouse, the "Pink City," nicknamed for its pink flamingos. The situation in the local sector was more complicated: Belkhouja, a future Minister of Planning in President Boumédiène's administration, was at the time the head of the Toulouse sector. He refused to participate in the strike. He was in the midst of completing his oral exams and

---

[9] Youth of the Democratic Union of the Algerian Manifesto.
[10] Algerian politician and nationalist.
[11] Algerian politician and nationalist (member of JUDMA).

thought the timing was just terrible; however, the vast majority of students in Toulouse agreed to support our decision.

After the tumultuous meeting, I returned to Bordeaux, where the discussions seemed much easier. I had been in contact with my headquarters, and they had the situation under control. But the biggest question for all the students was, "What shall we do, and where do we begin?" This was the key question that I had also raised during our board meeting. I had presented my question clearly: "How were we going to move all the students, or at least the vast majority, and allow them to continue their education outside of France—and how were we planning to support them?"

While waiting for frantic emotions to subside, I found myself a job at the annual Bordeaux fair in Quai des Chartrons. I was hired by the daughter of the owner of Vidal and Manega Tarpaulin Company and was immediately promoted to the position of foreman. Without hesitation, I hired about thirty of my comrades to help ease their financial burdens. The vast majority of students did not have regular contacts with their families who lived in remote villages across Algeria and were isolated from the rest of the world. We had all made a decision to embark on a general strike, without consulting our parents, and as expected, everyone grew increasingly apprehensive.

My political activities became more intense. When I returned to Toulouse to meet with the Algerian working class brothers again, I found that many of them were working in the quarries in the southwest. I went into more details about the reasons for our decision. Though they did not fully understand why, they still accepted our decision. I returned to Bordeaux, reassured of their commitment.

As soon as I got off the train at the Saint Jean station, I was approached by two undercover police officers in trench coats from the Internal Security Police. They seemed to have come out of nowhere. I was ordered to join them for a quick stroll and warned about making any sudden movements. My interrogation began in a small room at the Rue du Cerf Volant division, where I was grilled on all my activities before and after the meeting in Paris. They were well versed on the minute details of my movements. It was clear they'd been following me around like a shadow for sometime. Right then, I felt the noose beginning to tighten around my neck. My most urgent desire was to be released from custody. Luckily, they had nothing on me, and I was released after several hours.

Back on campus, I received word that the dean wished to see me the next day. When I knocked on the door, I was greeted by the sight of an impatient man sitting behind a large desk, wearing a stoic look on his pale face. He gestured for me to take a seat, looking right at me with piercing eyes. "Your actions are having a negative effect on your cohorts," he opened in a firm voice, before launching into a barrage of accusations. "You are motivating them to go on strike and asking them to drop out of school. Need I remind you that the reason their families sent them to France in the first place was to ensure that they earned their degrees for a professional career in Algeria?" I sat quietly and listened.

He raged on and threw accusations and threats at me; then he paused and took a deep breath. I watched him gather his thoughts, and then he became quite animated. "Listen, I know that you do not have any money." He slipped a signed check across the table to me. "Wow," I thought. It was a blatant and shameless attempt at bribery. I had to stop myself from laughing. The entire scene had an aroma of comedic exhibition. "I have got a job, sir." I was audacious. We stared each other down for a few seconds. "I received a scholarship from the French government to study in your country. It is tantamount to a contract, which I have clearly breached, hence, I have no right to claim the scholarship." "Your so-called strike only began on the twenty-sixth," he fired back. I replied: "*I was planning for the twenty-sixth before the twenty-sixth. This is exactly why I am refusing to accept the scholarship. We have nothing against the French, or against the education system in France, but the events from last week, when OAS members, mostly students, shot and killed dozens of our brothers with impunity at the University of Algiers, is cause for concern. Had we been in Algiers, we would have suffered the same fate. This is why we are marching in solidarity."*

There was a sudden whiff of cold tension in the room. I got up and closed the door behind me. In an interesting twist, I realized that I had inadvertently uncovered a plot: the police were spying on us and relaying information to the university. I was the "white wolf" in the student community—the president of the Bordeaux section of the UGEMA, chairman of the Liaison Committee for the Overseas Students, and vice president of the Student Union of France. I knew then that I was an obvious target and concluded it was time for me to leave the country.

Shortly after midnight, I walked briskly toward the Public Garden of Bordeaux, where I was renting a room in a small house behind the park. Moving stealthily like a cat in the night, I was on full alert, when I realized that the house was surrounded by both plainclothed and other police officers. I stood in the shadows for a minute and snuck away quietly without being noticed. I was perturbed, not because they had caused me some inconvenience, but by the fact that I had exposed my landlords to the bedlam. I thought about the warmhearted wife and mother of a ten-year-old boy who had opened her home to me and pledged to do everything to help and protect me. She even told me that if she passed away someday, she prayed her son would encounter some semblance of hospitality on his journey through life.

I faded into the dark of night, needing no further convincing that the big foot of the law was planted steadfast on my neck. Jamil Ben Bouzid, an old friend from Aïn Beïda, was home when I knocked. He was not under surveillance, but he knew that I was being watched. Like me, he was an only son. While international and domestic phone calls were a rare means of communication due to infrastructure limitations, almost everyone communicated

A Dream for Peace

by writing letters. In our small community, whenever our mothers received a letter from either of us, they shared every intimate detail with each other. They were always thrilled to receive our letters. Jamil was committed to our cause. Even if he did his part in his own timid way, he was still a lovely boy. I spent the night at his place.

His room had always been a safe haven, but I had chosen not to use it on a frequent basis for the sake of protecting him. In the immediate days ahead, I kept a very low profile, and we maintained a strict routine. I began working with the FLN's Federation of France to coordinate and strategize over escape plans. I stayed with different comrades and moved around under the radar until a friend of Algeria, a young French student whose instincts were on high alert, came to warn me that the police had put together ample evidence to serve an arrest warrant. He was the nephew of the chief of the central police station. He boldly suggested that I go and stay in the gardener's cottage on his uncle's property. That was astonishingly brilliant and clever. We were both convinced that the last place the police would contemplate searching for a fugitive would be in the backyard of their boss. He was smart, and I trusted him enough. I took him up on his offer, knowing fully well that we risked incriminating both of us. It was in the gardener's cottage I spent my final days and fine-tuned my escape plans to prepare for D-day.

From the moment I began my activities with the various student organizations, I had been steadfast in my commitment to doing everything to help my beloved Algeria gain its freedom, no matter the cost. I was acutely aware that my passionate activism in and out of campus would subject me to intense abuse and harassment by a very determined police force. Regardless, I was full of life with limitless positive energy like most young student activists. Months earlier, on February 21, 1955, during the Anti-Colonial Commemoration Day events, my comrades and I joined other students from countries under French control to manifest a call for change. Many French students showed up in force to

Hardship And and Prison

lend their support. That day, I met and befriended Antoinette, a beautiful young woman from Côte d'Ivoire. I quickly discovered from talking to her that she was just like me—a militant and vocal political activist. From the moment she learned about my activities, she made it clear that she would cooperate with us regarding the Algerian cause. More and more, she took a keen interest in our activities and volunteered to help with our outreach objectives.

She and I soon took a liking to each other, and our relationship quickly blossomed into a romantic one. I admired her for her many qualities and found her depth and command of political facts to be quite impressive. Within a matter of weeks, she became an integral part of our ground organization. She was assigned a permanent role to meet, greet, and welcome my fellow Algerian brothers at the train station. She was also given the role of receiving and distributing all of our mail.

The practice of cash-for-vouchers was not unusual among the various political parties. They were used as a way to enroll individuals when they affirmed their accreditation to a political party. The monies went to pay for essential activities and to sustain the party's agenda. In her capacity as mail recipient, Antoinette intercepted a suitcase full of stamped vouchers belonging to a rival political organization, Parti du Peuple Algérien (PPA). The vouchers, an important source of funds for the PPA, were valued at several thousand francs. When she brought the suitcase to me, I took the decision to engage in an act of sabotage by dumping the suitcase in the Gironde River. I did so to ensure that the FLN would stand out as the sole political voice for the Algerian people.

On the eve of my departure, a comrade from the FLN Federation of France told me that Antoinette was under surveillance. I went to warn her to take extreme caution and brought her up to speed on my escape plans. When I told her that I would be enlisting in the Maquis guerrillas, she surprised me by asking to come along. "After all," she said, "the Maquis could always use a nurse." Even after I expressed concerns about the high-risk nature of the mission, she remained resolute in her decision and pressed me hard to honor her wishes.

I snuck out of the gardener's cottage in the dark of night and met up with her at the secret location where our trusted comrades were directed to pick us up. They pulled up in a black Citroen Traction Avant, which had been customized to hide us. I found out on the way to our drop-off point that she had not bothered to say goodbye to her sister who was her roommate and, like her, a nursing student.

There were five of us in the car, including Chouki, the Algerian pimp, who had played an instrumental part in avenging the beating of Khemisti. We headed south and arrived in the town of Saint Jean Pied de Port at the Franco-Spanish border, around ten or eleven o'clock at night, and met up with some smugglers. They asked for and received payment in advance. Chouki and the driver wished us luck. We followed the smugglers and vanished into the foggy night.

The border crossing was more like boot camp endurance training on an obstacle course. We trekked across the Pyrénées mountain range—a tough terrain with ancient trees, massive rocks, and gravels. To avoid detection, we crawled on our knees and elbows for several exhaustive hours until we arrived in Pamplona, Spain, in the early morning.

Tired beyond belief, we went to search for a place to eat breakfast. We had a quick meal at a small café somewhere in town and went to surrender to the Spanish Civil Guard. We came clean and told them we lacked the necessary identification papers. Nonetheless, they were assured that we were French citizens. When news of our escape was published in the French newspapers the next day, the Spaniards thought they had arrested a "big fish"—an important leader of the FLN. I had never thought of myself as an important figurehead. We spent the entire day at the station in an empty office, with nothing to do. We just stared at the walls and engaged in small talk for several hours. The civil guardsmen were very respectful and communication was easy, because everyone at the station was bilingual. It was clear that their leaders had been debating what to do with us and by the late evening, we were informed that they were not equipped to accommodate our stay. They pointed to a nearby hotel and asked me to go and rent some bedsheets and blankets. We were told to order our meals at the adjacent restaurant in case we were hungry. When we returned after dinner, they found a place at the station for us to sleep. Sometime in the day, we were given a tour of the city of Pamplona and its surrounding areas in a police car. They left us alone for the most part, and we spent the night at the station again. Shortly after returning from our breakfast, we were driven to the largest prison in the country. This was where dictator General Francisco Franco's political opponents, the Rojos, were incarcerated during his rule. We were happy to hear that they were not considering locking us up in there.

Our summary detention lasted until we received a visit from an important administration official in a neatly ironed uniform adorned with golden insignias. He informed Antoinette that the French government demanded her extradition. She was the daughter of Dr. Salmon, a physician to a French government minister by the name of Félix Houphouët-Boigny. She refused extradition. He left us at the station, promising to return after reviewing the matter. When he came back the next day, he informed us that our place was no longer at the Civil Guard station. For security reasons, he had been ordered to oversee our transfer to the dreaded prison of the Rojos. They shipped us off that same evening. We arrived at the processing center, and Antoinette began to cry as we were being separated. I assumed she was fearful of going to prison and tried my best to console her, explaining that it was still time to accept extradition. But she thought it was peculiar that I would think that. The idea hadn't even crossed her mind. She was only crying because the prison guards were about to shave her head. Either way, the guards were nice enough to let us say goodbye to each other. She was transferred to the women's prison, and I did not hear from her again. I was escorted to a building reserved for male prisoners and given prison garments. The clerk listed my belongings on a sheet of paper and had me look it over and sign off on the items before they were confiscated.

Hardship of prison life was just beginning. I was led down a hallway to a holding cell in a dark and musky basement. The heavy metal door squeaked on its rusty hinges and swung open. I walked in and looked around, and wondered how I could cope with my new surroundings. The two guards kept a watchful eye from the doorway before slamming the door shut. One of them peeked through the spyhole for a quick second, and then I heard their footsteps echoing to a gradual fade down the hall. I'd been told that they placed me in solitary confinement for "my own protection." I sat down on the cold concrete slab that would be my bed for the foreseeable future.

The cell measured three by two meters. A constantly flickering light bulb hanging from a short string on the ceiling provided some dim luminance. The aged Turk toilet in the corner was covered in dust, and a maze of spiderwebs stretched across to a small sink on the corroded wall. I immediately tried to tighten the faucet handle to stop the intermittent dripping of water, but it was much too loose to shut off completely. The unit was screwed floppily against the tainted metallic backsplash a few feet above the tank. I knew right then that I had to figure out a way to block the reverberating sound of water drops from driving me insane. When I bowed my head to Allah and recited some verses from the Qur'an to end my prayers for the day, I gave thanks for the privilege of having some water to purify my physical self and cleanse my spirit.

Since the ambiance was not favorable to a tranquil sleep, I stayed awake the entire night, praying and reciting more verses from the Qur'an.

In the coming days, coping with the persistent drops became an unnerving psychological exercise. Though it was a source of constant torture, I was more bothered by the overwhelming stench from the toilet, which I did my very best to remedy by flushing as much as I could. I also ran water down the sink to mask the scent. After a while, I had no concept of day or night.

I had no idea how long I would be in my predicament. The constant reminder that I was in fact a prisoner in limbo, with no official charges filed against me, worsened my plight. I had been incarcerated for a while and never been in front of a judge. I wondered if the punishment fit the crime of crossing a border without documentation.

When the prison chaplain came to visit, my circadian rhythm was totally off. I didn't know if it was day or night. He offered some cigarettes and gave me a Bible, speaking in fluent French. I refused to take the cigarettes because I had never smoked before, but I listened to his lecture about religion. We spent several minutes together before he left, after promising to bring some candies on his next visit. I was very happy to receive the Bible; it would not only serve as good reading material, but it became my only companion in the lonesome cell. I was equally pleased to receive the chaplain whenever he made time to visit. He was the only human that served as a reminder that there were considerate people around me.

Occasionally, the sound of large keys dangled around the security locks, and the door swung open once, and again, shortly thereafter. The guards barely set foot in my "home" and I never saw their faces, just the gloved hand that heaved the bowl of soup across the floor. The concoction was always prepared in a hot, salty water base, complimented with some floating chickpeas, or French beans. Within a couple of minutes after slamming the door, his colleague unlocked it again and tossed a piece of bread at me. The routine was the norm, but every so often my reflexes got the best of me, and a guard would nail me on the face with a piece of dry bread.

From our interactions, I began to sense that the chaplain was nurturing the thought of converting me to Christianity. I addressed

A Dream for Peace

the matter during one of his visits. "Father, I do not believe that you can succeed in converting me. If you'd like to continue trying, I can assure you that you'd have as much chance of converting me to Christianity as I would trying to convert you to Islam." He stopped coming. I missed him, and I yearned for our conversations. He had been the only one I could socialize with.

I spent all my time praying and reading the Bible in Spanish—a language I barely understood—but I kept reading to improve my comprehension. I used a spoon to mark the wall, whenever I imagined that a full day had passed. I prayed that God would someday set me free so that at the very least, I could live one single day in an independent Algeria.

Soon, I could not count the days anymore. I no longer had reference points. I was fetched by two burly prison guards one early morning and escorted to the prison's rooftop; it was nice to breathe some fresh air and see the light of day. I observed ten prisoners doing some construction work on the grounds. Two men struggled to push a wheelbarrow with a pile of red bricks across the yard. There were four men waiting to receive them by the prison's main wall. They picked up the bricks, one at a time, and passed them off to four prisoners on wooden ladders. For a moment, I watched them stack the bricks on the wet cement at the wall's summit, and I turned around to face the guards, as if to ask if they expected me to participate in the hard labor. A menacing-looking bully pointed at the men and ordered me to join them. I shook my head and roared in French, "I have nothing to do with General Franco. You have absolutely no reason to subject me to forced labor." Before he had a chance to react, an older prisoner stepped between us and placed his hand on my shoulder: "How many years have you been sentenced for?" He spoke in a perfect French accent. "I don't have the slightest idea." I shrugged him off. "This is serious; yours is a very serious situation." He was genuine. "The prisoners here have already been sentenced—some to life, others to fifty, a hundred years or more. You, *mon garçon*, must have been condemned to more years than everyone around here. You are better off picking up the bricks." I hesitated momentarily, but the concerned look in his eyes spoke volumes. I rolled up my sleeves and got to work, serving a hard labor sentence. In the coming days I actually looked forward to coming out and joining my fellow convicts in the yard. It was a way out of my dark cell, and besides, I could breathe some clean air. Our backbreaking toil left its mark on history. Pamplona's most notorious prison walls were extended and reinforced with impenetrable concrete.

With the exception of my Bible, each passing day in prison was identical—darkness and solitude.

One fateful day, some plain-clothed police officers came and took me out of isolation. I did not know why. They took me to the office of the director of the prison, and I was pleasantly surprised to see that Antoinette was waiting for me. She was wearing the same outfit she wore when I last saw her. The director handed my confiscated clothes and belongings back to me: these included a green pullover, a pair of pants, my favorite moccasin shoes, and some money. I signed a release form, and we were set free. Mute like a fish, we were ushered to the back of a waiting car. The officers sat in front and drove off at high speed in silence. They led us in an unknown direction, and I began to fear the worst. We did not say anything, but Antoinette and I shared inquisitive glances from time to time. I did not know Spain, and I could not even imagine where they drove us. In fact I did not think we were released; I really thought the worst. When the car drove through a forest, I thought we were about to meet an imminent end. We were sure the police were certainly ready to kill us. We drove through villages and hamlets. When we finally approached a populated area, we became less anxious and even more elated when we saw the welcome sign as we entered the city of Madrid.

After an endless and exhaustive journey, we crisscrossed

the city to reach the central police station. We were pulled out of the car and taken inside a huge building to the office of the police commissioner, who sat across a desk in a neatly ironed uniform that was adorned with many golden insignias. Sitting next to him was a handsome man in civilian clothes who spoke fluent Arabic and French. "I am Abdel Kebir El Fassi, leader of Morocco's Istiqlal[12] Party in Spain. You are free." We could not believe our ears. "God is great! Thank you very much, Mr. El Fassi." He promised to accompany us to Morocco and oversee our handover. I knew of their long, drawn-out struggle to liberate their country from Spain. Although the FLN and Istiqlal parties had been involved in their own unique liberation struggles, they had established an alliance to enable military cooperation between the two organizations.

The Moroccan Liberation Army was the military arm for the Moroccans in their political struggle, and the Armée de Libération Nationale (ALN) represented Algeria's military wing in our fight against French occupation. Because of the cooperative alliance, the FLN asked the Istiqlal to help secure my release. I was still in a daze when we cosigned the release documents with Mr. El Fassi. Our short trip to the magnificent Spanish Colonial hotel was like a vivid dream in real time. Just the mere thought of checking into a clean space with modern amenities brought a smile to our faces. I listened attentively to the details regarding our release. We were part of a prisoner swap involving six prisoners of war from Spain who had been held by the Moroccan Liberation Army in northern Morocco, a region that was still under Spanish occupation. Once we were checked in, we expressed immense gratitude to our liberator.

We met with him in the early morning for a hasty breakfast and thanked him again. The car took us to the port of Almeria in southern Spain, just in time to catch the ferry to the northern coastal city of Tangier. We sailed across the Mediterranean and

---

[12] Arabic word for "independence."

drove to the town of Tétouan, nested on the northeastern coast of Morocco. Seized by an overwhelming feeling of relief, I expressed my sentiments to Antoinette—*"Oh, how beautiful it is to be free."*

A Dream for Peace

At times, we washed little or not at all, and we ate boiled chickpeas, lentils, and some canned sardines with a spoon coiled from container lids. We slept on the floor and woke up early to begin our boot camp drills on obstacle courses. I taught the newcomers how to dismantle and rebuild a machine gun.

Chapter Three

Initiation to the Struggle in Morocco

At the time, I did not realize that the affable, mild-mannered gentleman who welcomed us with open arms in Tétouan was of very high repute. Dr. Abdelkrim El Khatib exuded infectious confidence and a palpable ethical acumen that made me feel right at home. In 1951, he became Morocco's first surgeon, and when I met him, he was the head of the Moroccan Liberation Army.

Dr. Abdelkrim El Khatib.

In the midst of the liberation struggle, he occasionally took a break from his duties with the Maquis to practice medicine in Casablanca. After the welcome ceremony, he pulled me aside and told me that Antoinette's place was not in Tétouan. He explained that he had studied her case and knew of her bravery in fighting the extradition request while we were in Pamplona. He suggested that she should stay with his older brother Mahfoud El Khatib, a father of several girls, who lived in Rabat. I gave my consent without knowing how much time would pass before I saw her again. In the coming weeks, I was introduced to Dr. El Khatib's family, and they practically adopted me as family. I remained in Tétouan, and like a fish in water, I enjoyed my newfound freedom.

Although the Algerian war was within the borders of Algeria, the battle was also fought along the eastern and western border regions of Tunisia and Morocco. Most covert operations involved cross-border incursions into and out of Algeria. I took up arms with the resistance in Morocco to help liberate my country.

Our benefactor in Tétouan, Hadj Barakat, was a man of large stature who showed us great hospitality. He received the entire Moroccan Liberation Army on his huge property, before they retreated to El Mantaka in the Spanish zone. There were over a hundred of us, packed in a shed with several beds, and he ensured that we were fed appropriately. Among us were fighters from a special unit known as La Main Noire, who went on covert missions within the French zone in the southern region. By signing up for the unit, the men had submitted themselves to a form of suicidal pact in the process. Upon completing their missions, they were to escape to the northern zone. However, if they were captured during a mission, they kept a strychnine pill in their pocket to take their own lives. Such was the case of Zerktouni, who died a martyr rather than risk being taken into custody and succumbing to torture and placing his network at risk. The men of La Main Noire were responsible for capturing the six Spanish soldiers for whom we were exchanged.

I lived among the Moroccan Liberation Army under the direction of Dr. El Khatib. I was constantly away on missions, traveling with my companions from Tangier to western Algeria. The border in this part of the region of Ahfir and Ajdir was highly porous, and the French made matters worse by placing barbed wire and land mines on the ground. As a precaution, we used mules and donkeys for transportation. We also crossed the border to deliver weapons and ammunition to the area known as Maroc Oriental ou Remo,[13] before it became an established Wilaya. We penetrated deeply into Algeria a few times to store arms caches in areas that we identified carefully with military maps, in anticipation of an occupation by the French army. I was given the code name Mahjoub Ben Abdallah and a passport from Tangier, an international city-state at the time. It was a light blue colored booklet with a five-pointed black star imprint on its cover. I traveled on covert missions to Spain without fear of being arrested. We occupied a significant area of the region until the French colonial army took up their positions in the zone. That was when our casualty count began to increase.

We repatriated a fighter who had been dismembered in hand-to-hand combat when he attempted to wrestle a weapon away from a French soldier. In order to disengage from the Moroccan, the soldier unpinned a grenade on his belt and set it off between the two of them. Although our martyr lost both hands, he managed to throw the recovered weapon with his dismembered limbs while crying out victoriously: "The gun fell on our side, the gun . . ." We rushed to pick up our shell-shocked brother and sent him off to a hospital in Tétouan.

There was also the case of another brother who had been engaged in a brutal combat which scarred him badly enough that whenever he heard the sound of a broken exhaust or a weapon, he would throw himself facedown on the street. The cases of psychiatric trauma in the Moroccan Liberation Army were heart wrenching.

One day, Dr. El Khatib notified me that a highly ranked Algerian who was passing through town had asked to see me. The official, a tall man of thin stature, whom I later learned suffered from lung

---

[13] Oriental Morocco

problems, was Mohammed Boudiaf.[14] We sat across from each other and spoke for a while, mainly about the FLN and its organizational structure in Morocco. He impressed me as a brave and generous personality for having dedicated his life to the struggle. However, he was somewhat vague when I pressed him on his thoughts about Algeria's future and his world vision. At the end of our conversation, I had become rather doubtful about the future of the revolution for which I had enlisted.

Although the Moroccan war had come to an end, sporadic fighting continued in the Rif zone where I was situated and in pockets of French and Spanish territorial regions. By the autumn of 1956, Sultan Sidi Mohammed Ben Youssef was still overseeing the gradual restoration of independent Morocco after successful negotiations with both France and Spain. The reform that transformed Morocco into a constitutional monarchy with a democratic form of government was still in its infancy, and Dr. El Khatib remained committed to a strategic plan to accommodate the incoming Algerian fighters who were involved in a fierce battle for our country's independence.

A year before the sultan assumed the title of king and was crowned Mohammed V, Morocco's Royal Armed Forces were created. Fourteen thousand Moroccan personnel from the French army and ten thousand from the Spanish armed forces transferred into a newly formed Armed Brigade, but notably absent were members of the Moroccan Liberation Army, whose plight would soon become a cause célèbre for Dr. El Khatib.

At this juncture, Dr. El Khatib had embraced me as his brother in arms, and we worked side by side to ensure the efficient integration of fighters into the Algerian struggle. I accompanied him to oversee the handover of a Moroccan Liberation Army training camp to the ALN of Algeria, in the French zone. The plan was for me to stay at the

---

[14] Algerian political leader.

Initiation to the Struggle in Morocco

camp on an abandoned farm in Khemisset,[15] near the city of Meknes, until the ALN fighters arrived. When we got there, I was introduced to about thirty Moroccan Chleuhs[16]—noble volunteer fighters who were awaiting orders to transfer into Algeria to help their brothers in the liberation struggle. They wore *djellaba*[17] clothing, strategically chosen to hide their weapons and ammunition.

The camp was fully fortified with a communication center and sophisticated equipment. Dr. El Khatib left to go on a mission to a different region, and I remained behind with the fighters until he came back two weeks later with a large utility vehicle. We had already taken the time to break down and box up the communication equipment while he was away. The fighters and I loaded all the gear into the truck, and they took off into Algerian territory to open a new front for the Maroc Oriental ou Remo, an idea stemming from Dr. El Khatib's long-held vision.

A few days later, a team of twenty Algerian fighters arrived at the camp. I received them and made it clear there was hardly any food to eat. Water was scarce because the drinking well was practically empty. Two of the fighters, code-named Omar I and Omar II, took immediate possession of the camp. Mabed, their superior commander who wasn't there, was the head of the ALN in Rabat. I later discovered that the real name of Omar I was Dr. Gueniche, from the northwestern coastal city of Oran.

We recorded new recruits on a regular basis, mainly Algerians. High school students in Morocco of Algerian origin were also forced to enlist. Due to my experience with the Moroccan Liberation Army, I was considered a seasoned fighter and given the privilege to help turn the new recruits into soldiers. Uniforms, *pataugas*, and handguns were distributed to all, and everyone received a code name; I kept mine—Mahjoub Ben Abdallah. Since we had no running water, we

---

[15] Town in Zemmour Province of Morocco.
[16] Berber ethnic group in southwest Morocco.
[17] North African traditional outfit.

rationed the well water for drinking and washing ourselves. At times, we washed little or not at all, and we ate boiled chickpeas, lentils, and some canned sardines with a spoon coiled from container lids. We slept on the floor and woke up early to begin our boot camp drills on obstacle courses. I taught the newcomers how to dismantle and rebuild machine guns. I also catered to the needs of those who became ill.

The girlfriend of Omar I, a left-leaning French journalist, came to tour the training camp one sunny afternoon. In anticipation of the arrival, he had made preparations for a barbeque luncheon in honor of his guest. I found the idea to be somewhat insensitive to our state of affairs, because our young fighters only ate chickpeas and boiled lentils on the premises. I went to remind him that it had been a while since our soldiers had the opportunity to get a whiff of the sweet aroma of grilled meat. Around the camp, I was known for my straight talk and resolve in ensuring that everyone always respected our protocol. He didn't take kindly to my meddling in his affairs and reacted by ordering my immediate arrest. I was hustled off by two soldiers and thrown in a small room guarded by one of his heavily armed bodyguards.

The barbeque proceeded as scheduled, but by nightfall, there was a major uprising on my behalf. Some of the fighters decided to revolt for my sake, because I was still locked up and they considered it unjustified. Indeed, I was the only just and courageous soldier who was capable of defending them against Omar I's antics. The Mabed wing of the ALN was more or less a mafia organization that was behind the spread of terror in the Algerian expat community. Omar I and Omar II were assassins who executed those who opposed them by hauling them off to camp with their heads covered in a bag, placing them beside two or three cars, and running the engines to muzzle the sound of the guns. This was the typical form of execution for many valiant fighters. They were the group that had tried unsuccessfully to eliminate Omar Benboulaid, the fighter who shot the first bullet of the revolution in Arris, in the Algerian Aurès region—further proving that the revolution often fed on the blood of their own martyrs.

Motivated by my comrades' show of force, Omar I succumbed to the pressure and ordered my release in the morning. There was no clear resolution in the matter, and the incident left me wondering if this was just a premonition of things to come in Algeria's future.

Not long afterward, an epidemic of dysentery broke out in the camp, and I wasn't immune to the outbreak. We were totally overwhelmed because the anti-diarrheal drugs provided by a pharmacy in Meknes did not produce the desired results. I helped transport the severely ill to a special department reserved for the Moroccan Liberation Army at the Moulay Youssef hospital in Rabat. The department was without a doctor, and it only had one Algerian nurse. It was, however, well stocked with medication. I took upon myself the responsibility of providing medical aid to help the Moroccan Liberation Army fighters and the ALN patients at the hospital. The director of the transfusion center came to assist me with the process at a later time. The Algerians were transported to the Khemisset camp as soon as they recovered, but I remained at the hospital and continued to assist the many sick Moroccans. That was when I was introduced to Mr. Benhima, chief of staff for the Ministry of Health. Not long after we met, he came to see me to discuss an issue regarding a particular health care facility in Taounate, a Moroccan town in the Rif region that had been abandoned by its resident French physician. He was hoping that perhaps if I relocated to the area, my presence would have an impact. Although at the time Dr. El Khatib and I were working on a very important case regarding the Maquis veterans, I knew that it was an urgent matter that needed my commitment. I took him up on his offer to allocate my services as soon as the Maquis issue was settled.

Among the Moroccan fighters present at the hospital were some homeless veterans, casualties of the liberation war. Most of

A Dream for Peace

them had lost their homes to fire or war-related destruction and were using the hospital as a shelter. Despite many unsuccessful attempts, Dr. El Khatib continued to work with the administration, hoping that they would enact legislation for some funding to be made available to help substitute their living conditions and rebuild their homes. He grew increasingly exasperated by the ever-stagnating process. But after a long period of frustrations, tireless efforts hampered by intransigence and bureaucratic policies, the authorities paved the way for a seamless integration of the fighters into the Royal Armed Forces (RAF).

We still had to overcome an insurmountable obstacle in the form of a rigid RAF physician, Lieutenant Benkemoun, who had been given the power to decide the fate of every eligible soldier's suitability for integration. Dr. El Khatib and I were surprised by the strenuous prerequisite for integration which required us to put the men thorough a rigorous medical and aptness protocol to ensure their fitness to serve. Our fighters were mainly peasants and mostly illiterate men from the Maquis who obviously could not meet the criteria. I grew increasingly perturbed by the many rejections. The military hierarchy that was writing the rules were veterans from the upper echelon of the French army who had no business subjecting the Maquis vets to such humiliation. The men were valiant fighters of the Moroccan Liberation Army who had nothing else to offer but their sheer determination and courage. I took it upon myself to go and confront the lieutenant at a military clinic in Rabat's Suissie forest. "Lieutenant, when these men signed up for the Maquis to liberate their country, they were neither asked for a medical certificate nor a record of their physical. You need to make an exception and allow them to be integrated for a year or two, until they reach the age of retirement. This is all they are asking the government to do for them at this juncture."

My passionate plea fell on deaf ears, but I wasn't discouraged. I persisted in pushing for a change, and my tireless efforts finally paid off after several attempts. He finally sought the authorization of his superiors and the royal palace, and we received the green light to move ahead with our proposal.

As soon as we completed the integration of the combatants, I gathered a few belongings and left to serve as a physician in Taounate. I arrived in the town sometime in the midafternoon. The doctor's quarters were just above the infirmary. I met with the staff, made preparations for the next day, and went to bed. At about five o'clock in the early morning, I was startled by a series of knocks in rapid succession on my door, followed by a yell:

"The fish mongers have arrived!" I rushed to open the door, slightly bewildered. It was the male nurse. "What's going on?" I asked.

"The fish mongers have arrived with their fish." I was still puzzled.

"What have I got to do with fish?"

"The fish cannot be sold until they have been inspected and examined by a doctor and a certificate of sale has been issued to the merchants. Without this certificate, the sale is prohibited."

I was bemused. "But I am not a veterinarian."

"I understand. But sir, this is not fish of a superior quality, and the examination does not require special training. You look at the eyes of the fish—if they are open and bright, you are off to a good start. Next, you open the gills—if they are pink, the fish is good to be sold. Otherwise, the certificate cannot be issued, and the fish must be thrown away."

Oh well, I thought to myself. This is a unique moment, and I guess I would have to rise to the challenge. We went to examine the crates of fish, mostly sardines. He was more of an expert than I. We authorized the fish that could be sold and rejected those that were not fresh enough for consumption. I learned something new that day.

A few days later, I discovered that I was not acting exclusively as a fish veterinarian. A cow was brought to me in the early morning

A Dream for Peace

by a local peasant. "Sir, I am begging you to do something for us," the very concerned owner pleaded. "My entire family lives off this cow's milk. If you do not save our maternal mother, we are all lost: my wife, our four children, and myself." I thought long and hard about the unusual options before me. In order to save the cow, I'd have to take some valuable time away from the human patients who were desperately in need of care. When I solicited the opinion of my nurse on the matter, we decided to ask the peasant to describe the cow's symptoms. "For several days, the ear of the animal has been runny, and the secretion is smelly," he told us. Fortunately, we had enough streptomycin in stock. When the nurse returned with the meds, we dropped five bottles in the animal's infected ear. I asked the peasant to come back again the following three days to receive the same treatment. Eventually, the cow was cured of its ailment, and the owner was divinely grateful. Likewise, the nurse and I were very pleased with the outcome.

I had barely been in Taounate for a little more than a few weeks when the Ministry of Health summoned me to the office of Mr. Benhima in Rabat. On behalf of the ministry, he thanked me for my services and spoke about a new assignment: "There is an older hospital in the southeast, in the charming hamlet of Missour. Recently, the French completed a new health care facility in the area but left without furnishing the building. They also built a new hospital in the roadside township of Boulemane which is well equipped and functional." He used a map to illustrate his point. "As you can see, the area extends five hundred kilometers to the border fringes of Algeria. The effects of war have decimated the entire region, and the five resident French doctors have abruptly left the country without any warning. Under the French protectorate, the province comprised of five medical districts headed by each of the five doctors. They also practiced mobile health care and brought their services to patients in remote villages. This is an area that needs you more than Taounate." I was aware that the region had been very active during the liberation war. He made it clear to me that many doctors had declined to take on the assignment, claiming security lapses in the area.

I reassured him that I would consider the opportunity. I later went to see Dr. El Khatib to gain some insight. Without any hesitation, he gave a strong endorsement to the idea, after describing passionately what amounted to senseless acts of sabotage by the French on their way out of the region. With reckless abandonment, they exacted revenge on fragile tents made from camel hair strands and destroyed the few standing brick houses in the various habitats. His words cut to the core of my beliefs, and I assured him there was no need to convince me to go to the poverty-stricken area. I was ready to take on the task without delay.

Upon hearing from me again, the Health Ministry gave me the assignment and issued an official Land Rover Jeep to be used at my disposal. I drove the vehicle back to Taounate and stopped at the infirmary to bid farewell to the nurse. Although I was tired from the long drive, the sense of urgency I was feeling at the moment gave me an extra bit of energy. I went to pack my belongings and took a nap. I woke up at dawn to say my morning prayers, and I embarked on the long journey shortly after. By sunrise, I was navigating the terrain of a mountain pass known for its severe snowfalls to get to the village of Boulemane. I drove through the small hamlet of Immouzer des Marmouchas—a mountain camp with steep slopes, made famous during the revolution—and finally arrived in Missour, the capital of the province, a town that owes its life to the Moulouya River. During the days of colonial rule, the French built a residence worthy of the great cities of Morocco, with a tennis court and a miniature golf course. This was all done to appease and retain the district commander.

Missour was completely isolated from the rest of the world. It was centrally located, connected by a single bus station: the Fes-to-Taza route. I soon discovered that the blue bus was our only form of transportation for everything, including courier services, mail deliveries, and salary disbursements to civil servants. At times, we even used the bus to evacuate critically ill patients to the town of Fes. I was greeted by Si Ahmed, a mild-mannered Algerian sporting a worn silk *tabani* turban. He was joined by Abderrhamane, a Moroccan helper, and two male nurses in white community hospital uniforms. The local school had no principal, and the town had no *caïd*.

Recognizing the sacrifices of the province, Dr. El Khatib had assigned a native of Marmouchas, Mohammed Ou-El-Hadj El Marmouchi, as a *caïd*. This was his reward for bravery during the revolution. He was a valiant fighter who had driven the French out of the village of Immouzer des Marmouchas. As the story goes, he and his comrades made their way to the top of the mountain with barrels of gasoline on the backs of dozens of donkeys. They poured the gasoline into gutters, ignited the fuel, and set the village ablaze. The French army, mainly Foreign Legionnaires, and the hamlet's settlers immediately fled for their lives. From then on, he earned the moniker Mohammed Ou-El-Hadj El Marmouchi. He had become a man of the people, revered for being astute, analytical, and resolute in tough situations.

The region lacked so much of everything in all the various sectors. I was willing to do whatever was within my power to help as much as I could. I knew I would be stretched thin if I availed myself to conduct duties apart from my hectic schedule at the hospital, but I also knew that if I managed my time and delegated responsibilities to my staff, I would be able to take on some temporary assignments outside the hospital. Once I had established a more efficient routine, I began to take on some extra duties: I became the advisor to the *caïd* and volunteered to be the local school's interim principal until they found a replacement. The Mouloya riverbed was always dry in the summer, but in the rainy season, the river overflowed and washed away camels, cows, makeshift houses, bridges, and everything in its path. When I was told about a dispute among the resident landowners along the Mouloya River, I volunteered my time to educate them on water conservation, and I offered solutions to help them implement rules for sharing water with adjoining lands. They had faced the complex seasonal occurrence without ever figuring out a remedy due to a lack of resources. The key all along was for them to find a way to salvage and conserve some water for use in the dry season.

The Health Ministry had budgeted for the renovation of the hospital in Missour to begin shortly after my arrival, and on my watch, the place underwent a series of renovations. During the first few weeks, I received a selection of medical equipment, including some new beds. I oversaw the construction of a fully equipped operating room and a new kitchen, and I reserved a special area in the ward for wounded Algerian combatants. With the help of friends from the Moroccan Liberation Army, I loaded the old equipment onto several trucks and sent them off to the ALN.

For security reasons, I always wore a holster with a pistol underneath my white doctor's overall, everywhere I went. Ahmed, whom I respectfully addressed as *Si*, Arabic for "Mister," accompanied me on weekly visits to surrounding villages to treat patients infected with tuberculosis, an epidemic in the region at the time. Young children and infants were the hardest hit. Whenever we came to a village, we usually set ourselves up at a market in the town's center to ensure easy access to our services. As the people lined up to get treated for their ailments, Si Ahmed would boil our needles and syringes in a bowl of water on a Primus kerosene stove. He usually sat on a wooden chair and made enough room on his seat for each patient to place their foot next to him. This was the more expedient way to administer the injection. In a single morning, he managed to deliver about two hundred injections of streptomycin. He even attended to those patients with dental issues that same morning and removed more than twenty teeth and molars with great professionalism. Our basic equipment was more than adequate for the process.

    I was full of admiration whenever I watched him work. He performed dental surgeries with impeccable dexterity without using anesthesia on his patients, and a majority barely reacted to the pain. The folks in Missour, where he had lived for about twenty years, were fond of him. He was respected by everyone. He also loved to hunt and was quite skillful at it. On our trips across the region he brought his hunting rifle, and we crisscrossed many rough terrains in the vast forestlands, hoping to spot some wild game along the way. Occasionally, we returned to Missour with a gazelle or some other type of game animal.

    I traveled several miles to respond to emergency calls in remote villages. At times, I was summoned by the chief of a village to deliver a baby. Years after my services, I ran into one of my cousins and his Algerian wife in Geneva. He introduced her and told me that she lived in Morocco around the same time I was stationed in Missour. She was impressed to learn that I had served in the region during the liberation war. "As a matter of fact, I do recall that there was a young Algerian doctor in Missour, by the name of Dr. Mahjoub. He helped deliver my youngest sister, Rachida, but he soon disappeared from the face of the earth. We always wondered what happened to him." I was abruptly surprised. "Mahjoub was my code name," I said to her, almost rattled by the unexpected revelation. In an instant, her calm demeanor gave way to extreme excitement. What were the odds of having delivered my cousin's sister-in-law decades earlier? She became quite animated, understandably, because they had assumed for years that I was a casualty of war. Not only was I heartened by the sheer magnitude of the moment, but also the probability of such a fateful occurrence was beyond anything I could ever have imagined.

    In my monthly reports to the health department in Fes, Morocco's second largest city, I usually wrote about the difficult conditions faced by the population in Immouzer township and its surrounding villages. I also made it a point to stress the fact that there was an urgent need to rebuild the shattered lives of the people as promised by the government and continued to do my part to help the local communities as much as I could. Dr. El Khatib tried very hard to secure assistance for the peasants. He kept pushing the local authorities even after many unsuccessful attempts.

In the mountain region of Immouzer, Jews and Moroccan Chleuhs lived in harmony. The Jewish community had been established there since the days of the Spanish Inquisition, and they even learned to speak the local language. I was well known in the area and highly respected by everyone. The local rabbi called upon me one morning to ask if I could issue certificates of abstinence to young Jewish girls on the eve of their weddings. I found his request quite unusual and sought to clarify that my general medicine assignment did not include such unique services. He did not seem concerned at all. He came back to see me several times, and each time, I would dismiss him politely with the same explanation. Like clockwork he returned again to plead with me and insist that I take on the task. He was an exceptionally nice person. I finally threw in the towel and told him that I would take on the task as long as the examination was conducted in the presence of an elderly woman from the community. He smiled and said, "That shouldn't be a problem." Within days, I began to conduct my services in strict accordance with their tradition. I eventually got to know the entire community, mostly very nice and very humble folks. There were so many feasts, and I was always invited. At times, they snuck a little surprise delivery of some traditional Jewish cakes to my office at the hospital.

At the far end of Missour village, there was a Foreign Legion barracks midway to Fes. The barren road out of Boulemane village stretched far across the sandy terrain, straight through the desert, into the village of Injil. I was returning from a mission in Fes when my green Opel broke down in the middle of the desert a few miles before I got to Injil. After waiting for several hours on the desolate road, I hailed down the first car I saw. Fortunately, the driver pulled up to me and stopped. He was European in civilian clothing. I had a feeling he was a Foreign Legionnaire on his day off. He looked at me and thought I looked familiar. He recognized me from the hospital, but I did not recall seeing him before. Other than physicians and high-ranking officers, most Legionnaires usually wore civilian attire outside the barracks. I greeted him: "As you can see, my car broke down. I believe it's the engine, but what do I know; I lack any knowledge in automobile mechanics. I only know how to drive these things." He was kind enough to get out of his car and look under my hood. Within minutes of poking around, he concluded that the issue was a faulty ignition system and went to grab a toolbox from his trunk to begin fixing the car. I helped as much as I could, handing him tools and putting some away like a good apprentice. When he asked me to try restarting the engine, the vehicle started after the first crank. I kept it idling and got out to shake his soiled hand. "Thank you very much. This means a lot to me," I said. "My pleasure. Glad I could help. Drive safely." He started his car and disappeared down the road.

    Soon after that incident, I learned about a covert organization within the FLN that smuggled escaped Legionnaires into East Germany. In return, the FLN received substantial kickbacks from the East German government. I was approached by some Legionnaires at the local market one morning. They wanted to know if I would be interested in getting involved with the scheme. I gladly consented, and we arranged to meet sometime that evening. I showed up to the location as scheduled and met a fine gentleman who went by the code name Mostefa. He was an East German embed in the FLN, fluent in French, and a former Legionnaire himself. I became a part of a team that had managed to infiltrate the Legionnaire camp. Those interested in escaping knew how to get in touch with us. Code language was used to filter communications through the proper channels until it got to me. My personal residence served as a safe house and a point of transit for escapees. We planned with precision and executed our missions flawlessly. On occasion, I embarked on a road trip from Missour to Fes to deliver fugitive soldiers to Mostefa. His job was to receive and ensure the safe passage of the Legionnaires into East Germany.

We saw the operation as a way to undermine and weaken the Foreign Legion, but the escapees were mostly burned out from the futile and unjust war. When my comrades at the FLN headquarters in Fes recommended that we expand the process to include weapons, escapees began to smuggle guns and ammunition on their way out of the barracks. It was a high-stakes game, and we were highly successful despite the odds.

Among the Legionnaires that I helped escape was a young soldier who happened to be a longtime liaison and an invaluable asset in the operation. When I went to pick him up at nightfall to deliver him to the network, I learned that he had stolen the gun of the unit commander before his escape. It is considered an affront to a supreme military leader who loses his weapon of command. His reckless action placed the entire operation in danger. The colonel had discovered the theft within minutes, and we pulled away just in time, but not before we were spotted heading toward the village. As I hustled him past the backyards of some houses in the moonlit night, we were seen by Bahlouli, the village teacher. He waved at us and I waved back. We had barely entered my house when I heard the rumbling sounds of military tanks in the distance. Soon, the entire village was surrounded. The fuming unit commander visited the residence of the *caïd* and ordered him to do everything in his power to get his weapon back.

The *caïd* was not aware of the Legionnaire's escape and did not suspect that I was involved. He knew that in the past, I had authorized the resident physician for the Legionnaires to use the new local civilian hospital for emergencies. I had continued to cooperate with them, knowing that their barracks was isolated from the rest of the world, just as we were. After ensuring that the escapee was safely hidden inside my house, I snuck out. Just as I was about to turn the corner, I saw Bahlouli approaching. He motioned for me to follow him into the Moulouya River valley. "Rid yourself of your white uniform to avoid exposure," he hissed. My white medical uniform was glowing beautifully in the moonlit night. I quickly took off my shirt and pants, and we lay quietly for a few seconds on our bellies to study our surroundings. When we saw that the coast was clear, we began to crawl on our elbows and knees until we made it to the other side of the riverbank. Thankfully, it was the dry season and the riverbed was not entirely muddy. We hid in some grass on high ground and observed the village below for several minutes, until the tanks began to break away from their positions.

I thanked Bahlouli for risking his life to help me evade detection and threw my clothes back on before we crossed the riverbed to get into the village. Safely back in my room, I quickly immersed myself in the shower and disinfected the minor lesions on my body. The Legionnaire was safe, and no one had been in the house. But then, I heard a knock on the door as I was getting dressed and went to see who it was. The trusted servant of the *caïd* had come to inform me that his boss wanted to meet with me. I quickly put my shoes on and went to the house. He was very calm when I walked in and greeted him. I sat next to him on a traditional sofa in the living room, curious but patient, expecting to learn some valuable details. He began by telling me that the furious colonel had threatened to burn down the village if his gun was not immediately released. He had responded to the threat through an interpreter, with a few powerful words that summed up his resolve: "I am Mohammed Ou-El-Hadj El Marmouchi. Where were you when I made the move in Immouzer?" The French colonel stood in stunned silence and pondered the statement. He weighed his options for several minutes and smartly followed his instincts. He could sense that the stubborn and steadfast *caïd* was not about to succumb to his threats. He paced the compound before ordering his forces to retreat to their barracks.

I waited for two days until the situation had calmed before informing the *caïd* that I would be going on a mission to Fes. "Oh my, how convenient. I would like to come with you, if you don't mind. I have some business to attend to in Fes." That was quite a coincidence. We agreed to leave at about four o'clock in the morning. He was ready when I pulled up at his residence. The Legionnaire was sitting in the back seat of my Opel, disguised as a village woman in a *djellaba* with a white veil. After getting in the car, the *caïd* asked me about the passenger. "She's just the cleaning lady hitching a ride to see some friends in Fes." I quickly changed the subject and began chatting endlessly about whatever came to my mind.

Midway through the drive, we experienced engine problems and came to a sudden stop in Boulemane heights. Both the *caïd* and I got out to give the car a push, but the coupé was so heavy that the two of us managed to gain a few feet. I knew then and there we needed the extra manpower. I called the escapee to lend a helping hand. "Please no. Don't bother the woman," the *caïd* pled. As he exited the car, his hairy muscular legs were revealed beneath the dress, right in front of the observant *caïd*. He did not immediately comment about what he had just witnessed. We managed to push the car and get it started again. When we arrived in Fes, I dropped him off at his destination and took the Legionnaire to Mostefa's. He showed off the colonel's gun, triggering a very interesting and animated conversation, before I left to go on my errands.

I picked up the *caïd* on the way back to Fes. "Si Mahjoub." His voice had a slight pitch shift. I looked over at him. "It is quite obvious that you have been hiding something." I remained relaxed, a forced sardonic smile expressed on my face. "Who was the 'woman' in the car with us?" I laughed it off and gave him the details along the way. We even revisited the issue of the colonel and imagined what could

A Dream for Peace

have happened if he had followed through with his threat to burn down the village. The jokes were plenty, and we laughed hard until it hurt. "Congratulations, Si Mahjoub, for overseeing an exceptional covert operation. See you soon." He wandered onto his compound and called it a night.

On occasion, he summoned me to monitor his health and advise him on medical matters. During one such visit, he had a migraine and I concluded it was related to his high blood pressure. I prescribed some meds for him and recommended that he give a blood sample in the morning. Being a heavyset man, I guessed accurately that he had high cholesterol and suggested a lean diet with mostly vegetables. In the coming days, his migraines gradually disappeared. As a token of gratitude, he invited me for dinner at his home one evening, and I watched him indulge in a succession of high-caloric meals. It seemed he didn't heed my recommendations, or just couldn't help himself. After eating our fill, he clapped to summon the butler. "Please bring the special diet to the table. Let's make the doctor happy." Soon, I was staring down at more food, although this time, the pots and pans were full of veggies and some lean white meat stew. I realized then that he thought I'd asked him to eat his usual meal regimen and cap it off with the lean diet. I made light of the situation and wished him well.

During the internal struggle among the leaders of the FLN, it was in fact an escaped Legionnaire who delivered the booby-trapped radio that exploded and killed the valiant Mustapha Benboulaid. His brother Omar, who took refuge for some time in Casablanca, was also the victim of an attack by the FLN in Morocco. Luckily for him, all three handguns of his chosen killers jammed when they attempted to kill him on a busy street, and he managed to escape.

Throughout the duration of the Algerian liberation war, the inhabitants of the Marmouchas region demonstrated a high level of bravery and generosity. Despite being of Moroccan origin, they volunteered to join their Algerian brothers in the struggle. Although they were poor, family members pulled their resources together and donated a donkey to the cause. This became a widespread practice across the region, and it yielded hundreds of animals to my care. I had all the donkeys herded to Taza by some seasoned tribesmen and delivered to the head of the FLN in the region. The people from the village of Boulemane were a courageous and extremely generous clan of brave mountaineers. I often received Algerian fighters from the frontlines of battle, who came to the village for some well-deserved rest.

There were several occasions when the *caïd* of Boulemane, El Lahcen Youssi, asked me to come to the rescue of passengers trapped in the mountain pass, and I always obliged with pleasure. His cousin was a member of a group that laid the groundwork for the return of the sultan, who had been exiled in Madagascar for some time. Among the group was Mbarek Bekkai, a war veteran who had lost a leg in the Vietnam war fighting for the French and was willing to sacrifice the other leg for Morocco.

The rise of the Istiqlal in Morocco was not entirely celebrated by the first governor of Tafilalet Province, Addi Ou Bihi. When the party set about influencing the local politics in the country, he saw their imposition of a new constitution as an infringement on the rights of the people. Reasoning that he should protect King Mohammed V's interests from the political maneuverings of the Istiqlal, he decided to shut down the party's offices in his province and imprison their representatives. Coincidentally, he did so while the king was on a Mediterranean cruise. Crown Prince Hassan, commander of the Royal Armed Forces at the time, ordered the military to put down the insurrection. On their way, the Royal Army was trapped in the Boulemane mountain pass due to heavy snowfall and low visibility. Overheated engines in tanks and heavy utility vehicles rendered the battalion immobile. I happened to be stranded in the mountain pass at the same time, having pulled over minutes earlier. As I sat in my idling Jeep, doing my very best to keep warm until the storm

A Dream for Peace

passed, a couple of high-ranking officers approached and asked if I knew where they could find some water. "There is snow and there is your helmet," I said to them, a bit surprised. Watching as they sauntered off into the fog, I wondered how they hadn't made the connection between snow and water. They looked pitiful. The storm subsided after several minutes, and I began the slow journey down the treacherous terrain. I finally made it into the village of Boulemane and sought refuge at the home of Caïd Lahcen El Youssi. He served some mint tea with traditional pastries and clarified why the mountaineers were against the invading powers of the Istiqlal and the Fassis.

    The Boulemane mountain pass was often closed during harsh winter storms. But I was always authorized to go across and tend to medical emergencies. Such was the case when I braved hazardous conditions on the slopes to go and assist some stranded travelers. Occasionally, I approved the use of the hospital as shelter for travelers based on availability. Caïd El Youssi invited some stranded travelers to dine with him in the evening and called on me to attend. Per protocol, I sat at his right-hand side, and on his left, he placed the wife of a high-ranking technical assistant from Europe. We were served a sumptuous meal. Per tradition, toward the end of the dinner, *méchoui*, a whole animal, barbecued to perfection, was served. We all enjoyed the very tasty roast. "What kind of *méchoui* is this?" the lady asked shortly after finishing her third serving. "A gazelle," he responded proudly. He was an avid hunter. Seemingly rattled, she stopped eating and began repeating again and again, "The poor beast," as she cried. But it was too late to be remorseful, since she had already eaten her fill.

    My situation was undermined several months into my tenure in the region after Bahlouli, the village teacher, went to reveal my real identity to the authorities at the headquarters of the Ministry of Health in Fes. As a result, I received an impromptu visit from a Legionnaire commander serving as the regional surgeon general.

Initiation to the Struggle in Morocco

Without further warning, he decided to conduct a thorough inspection of both hospitals in operation to see if everything was up to code. He quickly discovered that the sanctity of both facilities were intact, but he decided to hold a meeting with the chief accountant, the nurses, and I to focus on other matters. "Please explain to me why the inpatient food expenses account for more patients than are in the ward registry." It was obvious that he was looking for a problem. I was the source of his suspicion, targeted because of my position as head of the service department. He was acutely familiar with regional culture but chose to play dumb. It was not unusual for family members to accompany the patient to the hospital and stay with them. "I conduct my services conscientiously and compassionately," I spoke calmly and sincerely. "You do realize that parents of the children are extremely poor, and some of them travel from remote villages to come here. They have no relatives locally, hence nowhere else they can go. They only consent to their child's hospitalization as long as they are allowed to stay with them in the ward." He listened intently but seemed unmoved. I emphasized one last point: "Those patients with a severe bout of tuberculosis had to be quarantined. I am sure you are aware that there is an epidemic in the region." He remained compassionless and unimpressed with my explanation. "Your decisions are still against the rules." I stayed calm: "Sir, it is impossible to open such a beautiful hospital and keep it closed to the people who need it the most." Everyone chimed in to lend a voice of support for my position. He remained unmoved. He suggested accompanying us on our morning rounds across parts of the region first thing in the morning. We agreed to meet at the hospital at 5:00 a.m. As soon as he left, we all breathed a sigh of relief and went to Si Ahmed's house for dinner.

    His wife prepared a delectable royal meal for us and made sure we ate our fill. We thanked them for a perfect evening. It was a welcome escape from the stressful episode at the hospital. We kicked back and blew off some steam for a while before dispersing

A Dream for Peace

into the late night.

Everyone was on time, bright and early at 5:00 a.m. Fridays were market days in the town of Outat El Hadj, about a two-hour drive from the hospital. We looked forward to attending to the medical needs of the throngs of patients that lined up to receive treatment at the crowded market.

I drove the service Jeep—a solid Land Rover with a bikini top and two benches in the back. The surgeon general was wearing khaki uniform and a Stetson hat to shield from the harsh sunlight. He sat in the passenger seat next to me, clutching a worn leather briefcase on his lap. Si Ahmed bounced back and forth on the bench behind me and held on to the rear-mounted spare tire for dear life. We accelerated across the shifty and bumpy terrain until we got to the Taza–Fes road and pushed toward the Mouloya River. The bridge had succumbed to raging currents on multiple occasions, leaving the public works engineers with no other alternative but to build a concrete sedimentation pathway at the foundation. I drove into the deep end of the basin and did my best to maneuver the four-wheel-drive vehicle along the slippery surface. At times, it seemed as though the Jeep might tilt over, but I kept using the gears to prevent the tires from skidding. "So, Mr. Mahjoub, I was told that you are Algerian?" I looked over at him for a brief second and felt the vehicle tip sideways onto two tires. I quickly turned the steering wheel counterclockwise and then back to regain traction. There was a hint of suspicion in his tone, I thought, and I knew immediately that Bahlouli had blown my cover. Perhaps, he had even revealed sensitive details about our covert operations, and the man had known all along that I was more than just a doctor. It quickly dawned on me that he might pull out a gun from his briefcase. I abruptly hit the brakes. "Get out of the car, or I'll make you." I placed my right hand on the butt of my revolver. He jumped out without delay. Si Ahmed begged for forgiveness on his behalf, but I ignored him.

Initiation to the Struggle in Morocco

I looked back in my rearview mirror to see if he would pull out a gun to shoot at us. He just stood there and watched us disappear into the distance. I breathed a sigh of relief and set my thoughts on the many patients in Outat El Hadj who awaited my weekly visit. Not relenting, Si Ahmed climbed over into the front seat and continued to plead with me, even kissing my hand. "Dr. Mahjoub, please have mercy on the man. The road is empty, and we are the only ones on this path. If he remains at the bottom of the riverbed, he will drown in the flash floods." Although I was convinced that he wasn't armed, I drove for a few minutes and composed myself before turning around. As I approached, I saw him marching in our direction. Relieved, yet still panicky, he stayed quiet in his seat and stared at the road for the remainder of the trip. When we got to Outat El Hadj, he went to complete his task with Si Ahmed while I was examining my patients. He gave us the silent treatment on the return trip to Missour. Like a freed caged bird, he climbed out of the Jeep and got in his car, and then I saw him raise his hand to wave before thundering along the free road to Fes, accelerating into the vistas that opened up ahead.

When I was summoned by Governor Fatmi Benslimane only days after the incident, I wasn't very surprised. He was married to Dr. El Khatib's aunt, but we had also crossed paths months earlier, soon after I had taken up arms with a group of Moroccan Liberation Army fighters to evict his predecessor, an entrenched colonial-era colonel who had served as the regional commander. We went to liberate El Batha palace after the Frenchman and his bodyguards hunkered down and refused orders to vacate the premises. The rebellion was brought to an end after a very intense confrontation, and when it was all over, we went to hand the keys to Mr. Benslimane.

He recognized me when I walked into his office to deal with the incident regarding the surgeon general. "You wanted to assassinate the French surgeon general for the region of Fes?" He was still in disbelief and needed to hear my side of the story from the moment he received the report. "The man uncovered my clandestine identity. The question had not been asked when I was sent to the region to fill the void left by five French doctors who had left their assignment without notice. At the time, every physician in the Fes region refused to take on those responsibilities. The chief of staff for the Ministry of Health warned of the insecurities in the region, and this was also the case with my first assignment in Taounate." He nodded in agreement, but said nothing. I still had a lot to get off my chest. "A month later, I was asked if I would go to Missour, Boulemane, and Outat El Hadj . . ." He gestured with a hand wave to interrupt. "Please, please, calm yourself down. You know, you are like family to me. Let me figure out a way to appease the surgeon general. Please return to your duties, Dr. Mahjoub. I will find an appropriate solution."

I thanked him for treating me like family and gave him a hug before leaving his office. Less than a month later, I was summoned to see him again. He had spoken to the Minister of Health, and they agreed that I should be given a new assignment in Salé. It was an excellent position in a region that would place me closer to my friends on the outskirts of Rabat. He gave me the necessary documents for my accommodations.

I returned to Missour and informed everyone that I'd been transferred. They were distressed to hear the news. The *caïd* voiced his dismay at losing "a doctor and a friend." I was really sad. I wrapped up my workday at evening's end and went home to begin packing my belongings. It took a week for the moving van to arrive. Many villagers, including some of my friends from the Jewish community, came to help me load my belongings onto the van. My heart was very heavy that day. We bid an emotional farewell to each other, and I promised to return someday soon. Those who knew me well could not stomach the thought of seeing me leave for perhaps the last time. As the van peeled off slowly, I waved goodbye, and no one could stop from crying.

A Dream for Peace

As a result of my activities, I was invited to the People's Republic of China to represent the FLN and the youth of the Third World. We did not have an FLN branch in China for lack of diplomatic relations with the Chinese government, and unlike the Eastern European countries, we had no students in the country. I was the de facto ambassador.

I had the opportunity to meet face-to-face with Mao Zedong.

Chapter Four

Struggle in Morocco—Organization

I embarked on the long journey to the town of Salé, a Rabat suburb, and located my new residence, a colonial-style property that used to belong to the director of the local sanatorium. It was a beautiful house adorned with a lovely garden on the other side of the Bou Regreg River. I reunited with Antoinette, and we settled down together. Although my lifestyle kept me busy twenty-four hours of the day, we lived a very quiet and peaceful life for a while. At some point, Dr. El Khatib asked me to commit to marrying her. Islamic principles forbade us to co-habituate out of wedlock. After several months in the country, I had grown very close to the family. His mother, Lalla Meryem, was a native of Morocco, but she was deeply Algerian. She was born into the Guebbas family. Her father graduated magna cum laude from Oxford University and was one of the first prime ministers in the government of King Mohammed V's father. Fondly known by the citizenry as "Fkeh"—the Arabic word for "the Great Erudite"—he was an esteemed and dignified family man. She married an Algerian, and her kids grew up entirely devoted to the liberation struggle. Despite her old age, she stood upright like a reed. She was not only physically fit; she was also sharp and conscientious in her reasoning. She was very fond of her son and affectionately referred to me also as "my son."

I neither said much, nor did I express my innermost thoughts, fears, and concerns during my conversation with Dr. El Khatib. Marriage had been the furthest thing from my mind, but I agreed with him that I should respect Islamic principles. We were definitely on the same page about living in strict accordance with my faith.

A Dream for Peace

I did, however, overestimate my level of emotional readiness to become a good husband to anyone. Antoinette had been heroic and courageous when she followed me to Morocco, and we'd grown very close because of everything we had been through. When we discussed the matter, it became clear to me that she was more than ready to get married. We agreed to take the plunge.

My first wife, Antoinette.

There was an upcoming wedding for Yaya Benslimane, the son of the governor of Fes, at El Batha palace. Dr. El Khatib proposed that we initiate our nuptials at the same time. We tied the knot in

Struggle in Morocco—Organization

the magnificent historic chamber where the Treaty of Fes[18] was signed. My wife had been working as a pediatric nurse and earning a decent salary. She was not very fluent in Arabic, but with the help of an interpreter, she managed to get around. I began working at the main hospital in Salé.

Once in Rabat, I was poised to work with the FLN leadership to find ways to strengthen their influence within the expat community of Algerians. I had been led to believe that the organization was securely intact, but I was disappointed to discover the dysfunctional state of affairs for both the FLN and the Liberation Army. The patriarch at the head of the FLN was Cheikh Kheireddine, a highly regarded theologian and a former member of the Association of the Oulemas, a group of theologians who aimed to promote the cultural and religious identity of Algerians. He had settled in Morocco for several years and run the FLN, assisted by his Algerian Chief of Protocol. I went to meet up with him on occasion to seek his counsel on very important matters, but I quickly determined that he lacked the power to do anything. Each time I visited, I found him sitting cross-legged on a chair, smoking tobacco. I noticed that our Moroccan collaborators did all the work for him and soon learned that the corrupt head of the ALN in Rabat, Mabed, had marginalized him. After enduring months of terror at the hands of the group, he pulled back gradually and let them continue with their shenanigans.

The mere mention of the name Mabed sent shivers down the spine of some in the Algerian community. Under his leadership, military officials were known to seek out attractive married women, kidnap them, and force their husbands to the front lines of battle. Nonetheless, I continued to ponder my options and solicit ideas on what I could do to help my country as well as my brothers who had migrated to Morocco with the noble intention of serving their country, yet were subjected to acts of injustice and humiliation by

---

[18] Signed on March 30, 1912, the treaty made Morocco a French protectorate.

the Mabed organization. I figured out that an independent UGEMA in Rabat was long overdue. I had enough time on my hands to put it all together. Due to my work at the hospital, I opened some doors and won over the hearts of some highly influential personalities in politics and certain social circles. I met the Jaedi, the Aouad, and the Hassar families, all of whom were highly influential in the Istiqlal Party. I visited their homes to provide medical care and got to know them very well. Eventually, I became very close to Fatima Hassar, niece of Dr. El Khatib, and her husband. She was a very dynamic person, full of humor and always ready to serve others. Her husband, Si Larbi, and her were both high-ranking members in the Istiqlal Party. He owned a pharmacy in Salé, and she served as the president for the Association of Moroccan Women.

I was completely absorbed into their family, always present at many delectable traditional Moroccan lunches at their home in Salé. I ate together from the same bowl with everyone, including her brother Hosni, his mom, dad, and mother-in-law. The mild-mannered and organized Si Larbi was also a teacher at the Istiqlal private school in Salé, which made him a recurrent latecomer to our lunches.

It was widely known within the Algerian community in Rabat that I was very well connected. An elderly Algerian man came to see me once, seeking help to get back his only son who had been forced to enlist at the training camp right after he got married. His daughter-in-law had also been kidnapped, and he had no idea where she was. This had become a typical occurrence in the community, pointing directly to the ugly fingerprints of the Mabed group. Unfortunately, under the circumstances, I was powerless and couldn't do much to help him. Even with my extensive resources, no one dared to interfere in the ALN's internal affairs.

Struggle in Morocco—Organization

Mr. and Mrs. Hassar.

The Hassar family gave me their unwavering and unlimited support. Before moving into their new house in Souissi, an affluent suburb of Rabat, their vast property in Salé was wide open to all Algerians who came to serve or take refuge in Morocco. They even took in a young woman by the name of Chafikha, who claimed to have escaped from Algeria with the help of the Jeanson network, a little-known underground organization that collaborated with the FLN. Shortly after she became acclimated, they gave her away in marriage to a young man by the name of Ahmed, who had only recently arrived from France. He was recruited into the police force by the director of Sûreté Nationale (National Security), Mr. Mohammed Hassar, Si Larbi's cousin. Although some Algerians remained at the mansion in Salé for several days while seeking employment, they usually returned to the front if they were unsuccessful. Years later, Ahmed went back to Algeria to take on the position of chief of staff for Belaid Abdesselam, a minister in the government of President Boumédiène.

A Dream for Peace

In order to gain legal authorization to organize the Algerian students in Morocco, I enrolled in law school, because there was no medical school. Prince Abdallah, with whom I became friends, was in the same program at the university, where there was neither a student nor other youth organization for Algerians. I immediately began to implement my plans to organize and build a very active section of the UGEMA.

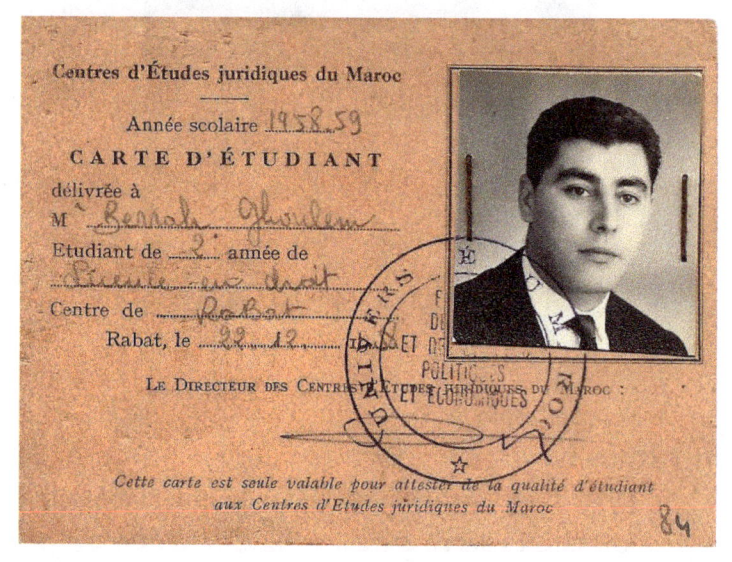

My law school ID.

Mahjoub Ben Seddick, president of the Moroccan Labor Union, was introduced to me by Mrs. Hassar. He donated a villa at 1 Rue de Savoie in the L'agdal neighborhood to be used as our headquarters. I was elected by the new members to become the president of the Rabat branch, and for our secretary-general, we elected Miss Rahal, a descendant of a family of Algerian interpreters who had served as indirect administrators for Morocco under the French colonists. Young people came from Europe to join the organization, and we grew into a formidable force. Mehdi Ben Barka, leader of the Moroccan Students Union and the brain trust of the Moroccan youth, proposed to absorb UGEMA into the Moroccan students movement. I spoke to him and clarified why it wouldn't be a good idea. He understood our position and committed to helping us whenever necessary. We remained very active and maintained contacts with other student organizations around the world.

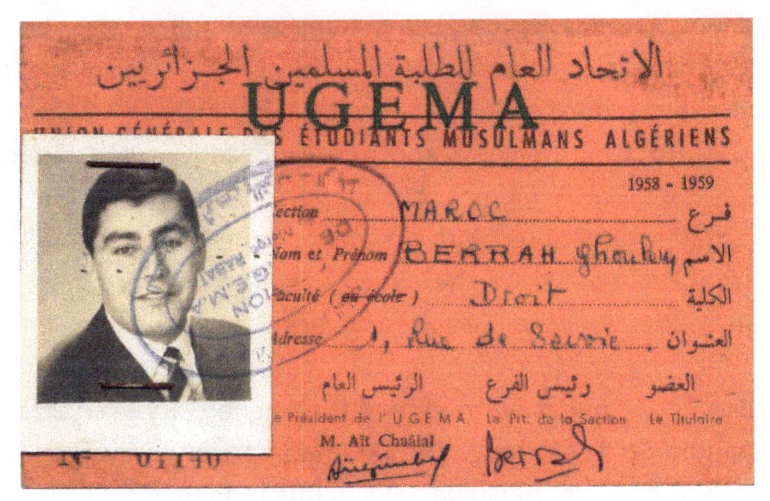

My official UGEMA membership ID.

The Hassar couple introduced me to Abu Bakr El Kadiri, a member of Istiqlal's Executive Committee. From a very young age, he had been a militant nationalist and taken up the cause to fight against the occupation until his country was liberated from colonial rule. When I met him, he was quite the intellectual—an academic writer and an influential politician who was revered as one of the signatories of the Manifesto of Independence. He related to me in more ways than one and understood my objectives. As one of the forerunners of modern education in Morocco, having founded several free educational institutions in the 1930s and 1940s (against colonial opposition), he assured me of his support and remained steadfast in that regard.

Believing that it was my responsibility to create opportunities and broaden the horizons for my fellow Algerian students, I continuously sought the help and support of the Hassar family. They saw to it that I was invited to major events at most of the accredited embassies in Rabat. I met several ambassadors and managed to secure some scholarships for my fellow Algerian students. The director of Sûreté Nationale—a sanctioned body for foreign document issuance, among other things—supplied passports to the Algerian scholarship recipients so they could travel abroad and pursue their studies.

Moroccan families and other organizations continued to support the UGEMA. Many of our supporters dropped by our local office to give donations. With assistance from the Maroc Oriental organization, we moved the aid to the Algerian border to help the army and refugees. Despite the lackluster behavior of some ALN officers, our Moroccan backers were not deterred by their conduct. They continued to extend their generosity even after an Algerian officer took things too far and imprisoned the governor of the Moroccan city of Oujda. Cheikh Kheireddine quickly went to apologize to the Moroccan authorities for the unfortunate heresy.

Messaoud Ait Chaalal, head of the Lausanne branch of the organization, continued to visit every country that expressed friendship with Algeria, in search of academic scholarships and other forms of assistance for UGEMA member students who had escaped from France. He persisted in the tradition of the organization and visited us in Morocco for meetings on several occasions. One such visit coincided with the bombardment of the village of Sakiet Sidi Yousef in Tunisia. The French, who had long claimed the right to pursue Algerian fighters across the border into Tunisia in an attempt to stop FLN and ALN incursions, authorized their air force to attack the village. The bombardment left scores of Tunisian civilian casualties. In solidarity with our brethren, Ait Chaalal helped me organize a demonstration to the French Embassy in Rabat. We marched on a rainy day with the national union of Moroccan students. Their president, Seghrouchni, myself, and Ait Chaalal led the march. The Moroccan police had set up a barricade a few blocks from the French

Struggle in Morocco—Organization

Embassy. As soon as we encountered them, we were arrested and transported to the offices of the Sûreté Nationale and locked away in the basement. At day's end, Mr. Mohammed Hassar ordered our release and offered his apologies for the inconvenience.

I was invited to tour Eastern Europe by the International Union of Students (IUS), a communist-leaning organization that was established in Prague in 1946 as the antithesis to the United States National Student Association (USNSA). I went on the journey, accompanied by Mohammed Aberkane, to examine the lifestyle and conditions under which our fellow Algerian students were living. Our first trip was to the Czech Republic to meet our World Youth Federation counterparts in the UIE. While visiting some of the Algerian students in the region, I observed and recorded a few minor lapses in their accommodations. Per my request, the leaders of the UIE agreed to make improvements in their living conditions wherever feasible. Our trip concluded after a visit to Hungary and the Republic of Yugoslavia.

At the time, the world was divided into two parts—communists on one side, and the capitalists on the other. We took advantage of both political movements and prepared for the future of an independent Algeria by training our students to be experts in all fields, and in all languages, while maintaining our neutrality. For all our efforts, most of us in the Algerian student community were not called upon to be a part of the Conseil National de la Revolution (CNR) or given the recognition we deserved from our political leaders. Mohammed Benyahia, Lamine Khane, and Redha Malek were the only student representatives to serve on the board of the Gouvernement Provisoire de la République Algérienne (GPRA).

As a result of my activities, I was invited to the People's Republic of China to represent the FLN and the youth of the Third World. We did not have an FLN branch in China for lack of diplomatic relations with the Chinese government, and unlike the Eastern European countries, we had no students in the country. I was the de facto ambassador. Like the accredited ambassadors in Beijing, I was invited to every event that required the invitation of the diplomatic corps in the same capacity. For example, on the occasion of the Dalai Lama's escape, I was invited to a high-level meeting by the Chinese government that included Liu Shaoqi, the president of the Republic, and Prime Minister Zhou Enlai with the entire members of the diplomatic corps.

The two officials gave the first speech to inform us of the situation. They complained about India's Prime Minister Jawaharlal Nehru and the state of affairs with a brotherly country that had chosen to give asylum to the Dalai Lama. About half an hour later, Chairman Mao came and took center stage on the podium. Directly contradicting the previous speakers, he stated:

"If my brother Nehru needs ten million more than those who followed the Dalai Lama, and if he can feed them, I would be more than happy to send them immediately."

As the de facto FLN representatives, we were invited to listen to a clarification of the "great leap forward" and the Cultural Revolution. I realized during our trip that I was witnessing a historic national transformation in a unique moment in time. We visited all the universities in Beijing, made friends with many students, and gave lectures on the Algerian war. At a conference hosted in the village of a Chinese martyr, my companion, Mohammed Aberkane, gave a speech and thanked Marshal Josip Broz Tito for lending a helping hand to the liberation struggle. Our perpetual interpreter on the trip was a strong patriot and a very opinionated gentleman. He enjoyed drinking hot mint tea like a connoisseur, slurping the steaming liquid through his front teeth to avoid burning his tongue.

It seemed a customary habit from a tea tradition dating back a thousand years, but it was reminiscent of the exact tea drinking etiquette practiced by most Arabs. During an early morning visit to my room on the day after the conference, he seemed intent on addressing a statement in Aberkane's speech. "Comrade, your partner spoke about Tito the deviationist?" I hadn't given it much thought, but I gave my best diplomatic response: "I apologize if this has offended our Chinese comrades, but you are the interpreter—it was your call to censor the statement, if you thought it was inappropriate." "I am sworn in my task," he replied. "We are also sworn to accurately report the history of the Algerian Revolution." He shrugged it off, as if to say it wasn't really a big deal.

With Mohammed Aberkane and Chinese hosts.

Under the policy of "letting a hundred flowers bloom and a hundred schools of thought contend," Mao Zedong encouraged citizens to openly express their views and opinions of the communist regime. We arrived in China at a time when the government had grown weary of the brief period of cultural liberalization and instituted a massive crackdown of dissenting voices across the country. We witnessed the disappearance of some students barely a day after they had made an innocent statement. Initially, I wasn't aware of what was going on. I had gotten to know some of those students and when I couldn't find them, I asked our interpreter if he had any idea where they were. "Comrade, you must not seek after them. They are guilty of deviationism." The dreary response did not give me a sense of discomfort, but I felt a tad bit uneasy.

Chairman Mao enjoyed talking with young people. For the youth orientation phase of our trip, he received us along with other student representatives from many African countries, most of whom I had met in France when I served as the chairman of the Liaison Committee for the Overseas Students. I stood next to him in at least one picture, surrounded by the other students. The picture in question was displayed for years at the front entrance of the Beijing airport and was only removed after Chairman Mao's passing. It was also reproduced in a large souvenir book that the Chinese authorities in the capital offered to dignitaries whenever they visited the country.

I had the opportunity to meet face-to-face with Mao Zedong. On the occasion of one such meeting, an official car preceded by police escort picked me up at the hotel, a few blocks from Tiananmen Square. Sitting next to the driver was a presidential representative, and sitting beside me was my interpreter. We circled the same buildings several times before I finally realized what was going on. When I asked my interpreter why we were going around the same block, he responded firmly, expressing the importance of an early arrival rather than later, and driving around in circles in order to be on time—"We do not make the Great Leader wait."

When we arrived at our destination, I was left waiting in an office that seemed modest for the big chief—the great leader of what was at the time the largest country in the world, based on population. He soon arrived with his interpreter. There were three of us at the meeting. Over traditional Chinese tea, Chairman Mao bombarded me with questions about Africa, colonization, the Algerian Revolution, global issues, and challenges facing my fellow Third World students. He talked about many issues that China was facing, and the need for the people of the Third World to unite.

"I dream of the day when I can give a bowl of rice to each

Struggle in Morocco—Organization

citizen of China before they go to sleep."

His words had a profound resonance, and the reverberations are even stronger today as I witness the development of China as a major world power.

Perhaps, it was his innate ability to express himself so passionately and modestly that has forever left an imprint on my psyche. I came away with an ineffaceable impression of a great leader at the head of eight hundred million people, who felt as though he was being harassed domestically and internationally. Unwavering and resolute, he was intent on instilling an unmatched discipline upon a diverse people on a vast continent—a large populace that remained united because of a shared purpose.

On more than one occasion, I was invited to attend debates at the People's Assembly. The speeches were interminable, because they were translated into six different Chinese languages. Chairman Mao was not only respected, he was also revered as a great politician and a poet. I traveled across many regions and witnessed a hardworking people in every sector of the society. They seemed energized and unstoppable. I was scheduled to give lectures at some local factories and universities in the southernmost part of the country. Walking to the train station with my interpreter in the early morning, I observed several workers replacing the pavement by Tiananmen Square in preparation for the National Day events of October 1. I did not see any construction machinery. They passed buckets of sand and crates of pavestones along a human chain link. Next to a huge pile of sand, a laborer had fallen asleep with a shovel in his hand. I stopped and pointed at him. My interpreter smiled and brushed it off like a normal occurrence. "He is tired, but as soon as he wakes up, he will resume work." I stood for about a minute and watched the men at work, marveling at the hectic scene, but I was not convinced that the work could be completed by the deadline. "They are very close to the target date. We are a month away from the events." As far as my interpreter was concerned, missing the deadline was unthinkable—"They will complete the job on time."

We moved on to the station and hopped on a train to Shanghai. I visited the local university to conduct my first lecture on the Algerian Revolution for some political science students. Speaking in Arabic at a large lecture hall, I paused after each sentence for the interpreter to translate my words into Mandarin. I received some positive feedback from the students who came up and wished good luck to the Algerian people. Everyone was very supportive, and from what I could understand, their words were uplifting. Their gestures and encouraging words were very heartwarming.

Helping workers at Tiananmen Square.

We spent the remainder of the afternoon at a steel plant, where a select group of workers gathered to hear me speak about the Algerian struggle. I highlighted the perils of oppression and gave a moving narrative on the colonial transgressions that had triggered the Algerian war. They released some confetti at the end of my speech amid overwhelming applause, and I offered the mike for an interactive session with some of the workers. We embarked

Struggle in Morocco—Organization

on similar tours across the Shanghai region for a few days, using the same format of lecture in open forums.

On the way to Guangzhou, we arrived at the banks of the vast Yangtze River at nightfall. There were no bridges at the time. The train's carriages were transported by barges in pairs and reconstructed on the other side of the river. As we floated downstream, my interpreter was quick to point out that Chairman Mao swam in the river in 1956. Each of the carriages had a large container with hot water, next to a box of tea and several teacups. Drinkers would make tea by adding two or three buds of tea leaves to some hot water. The sanitary conditions on the train were not optimal. Water had to be boiled, and most people wore white surgical masks to protect themselves from airborne diseases. We stayed in Guangzhou for a few days until my assignments were complete. Back in Beijing, I observed that the workers had done a spectacular job. The pavement at Tiananmen Square was ready for the festivities.

Overall, life in China was pleasant, but those in the remote country regions had it more difficult. Men and women dressed alike in Mao-style uniforms designed in China blue colors. Women's physiques were hidden in their clothing to avoid giving an obvious appearance of their femininity. There was a great push for gender equality in every sector of society. I was even invited to tea by the president of the All-China Women's Federation. With 250 million members, the organization was a formidable force in Chairman Mao's China. I expected to be paying a courtesy visit to their offices, but the reception was surprisingly bigger than I anticipated. I sat at a long conference table in a magnificent hall at their headquarters, with a group of district leaders and students from various universities. The president of the association and I engaged in a question and answer session, with occasional follow-ups from some of the women. For over four hours, the topic was focused on cultural issues, matters concerning women in China, Africa, and specifically Algeria. When

A Dream for Peace

I told them that most women in Africa were housewives, our discussions became slightly heated and animated. She responded with a passionate narrative about the disadvantages of reducing a woman's role in society. She thought that by not empowering women, a country would be deprived of half its potential. I disagreed with her position, of course, because I believed that women should focus on educating the children at home. It was only natural that their intellectual abilities should be utilized to instill sound principles that couldn't be learned at school.

"*A country suffers when women are too busy working to fulfill their obligations to society, because in so doing, very little emphasis is placed on raising and empowering children to strengthen the foundation of humanity. I also believe that a child who is truly showered with love will give love back to society.*"

I spoke in Arabic, she spoke in Mandarin, and my interpreter translated our words back and forth. She said something, and they all laughed. He laughed and transmitted back to me, "She said you are a dirty bourgeois." I laughed as much and said, "Perhaps you are right. I may be a bourgeois, but I'm not dirty."

At a childcare facility.

I enjoyed a visit to a nursery and childcare facility with a group of my fellow students, where all the children were almost the same age and very beautiful. Each time we entered a classroom, the toddlers ran up and hugged us. They all wore the same uniforms, and it was impossible to distinguish the boys from the girls. The Chinese government had instituted a law banning couples from having more than one child. Hence, those who did not use contraceptives found themselves aborting baby girls until a boy was born.

We also visited a variety of farms, historic monuments, and places where the army of the Long March fought their battles. I was picked up one evening before dinner and transported to a venue where an event was being held for some veterans of Chairman Mao's People's Liberation Army. At the end of the event, I took to the podium to give a speech about the Algerian struggle and our fight against the French army and NATO. I focused heavily on the atrocities committed by France, against women, children, and the elderly. At the end of my speech, the vets bombarded me with one question after another and heaped praises on the efforts by the FLN. Some were impressed by the fact that at my young age, I had already accomplished a lot and continued to give so much to our cause.

I received a call from the hotel reception about an ALN delegation in the lobby. They had come to visit with me unannounced, in the early morning. I rushed downstairs to greet them. We stood in the reception area for a few minutes and shared stories about the Algerian Revolution. A member of the delegation introduced himself as Commandant Azzedine and asked to speak to me in private. We moved away from the group to a corner in the reception area. He seemed eager to unload some information and set the record straight about something. Perhaps, I thought, a painful matter had been eating away at him for sometime. Before opening up to me, we spoke at length about my trip and got along very well. I had long heard the rumors about him being a traitor to our struggle, but I was surprised to learn that he wanted to speak to me about the topic.

A Dream for Peace

He clearly hated being viewed in a manner unbefitting his character, and as a matter of fact, he said it caused him a lot of pain. He had been wounded in combat and captured by the French. As a prisoner of war, the French had sought to strike a deal for his release by attempting to coerce him to infiltrate the Maquis. He accepted the deal, only as a way to get out of jail, but had no intention to fulfill his part of the bargain. To escape their wrath, he snuck into Tunisia and went underground in Tunis. I told him that I was impressed by his version of events and that I always knew there were two sides to every story. I made no further comments. We took some pictures before he left. He autographed a card for me and wrote these words: "Come what may, the revolution must learn to trust me."

I longed to return to familiar surroundings to join my fellow combatants in serving the revolution. I sent word to our hosts, informing them that we were ready to depart the country. They made the necessary arrangements and organized a big farewell dinner for us on the eve of our departure.

Shortly after setting foot in Rabat, I was summoned to see Mabed at the ALN offices on Rue Temara. He needed seven young Algerian men with blond hair to go on a secret mission. I told him that other than the students on the UGEMA membership list, I had no idea where to find any such recruits. At the time, I did not know that he was planning to send the men on a mission to blow up a fuel depot in Mourepiane, near Marseille. Without knowing his intentions, I volunteered myself, Miss Rahal, the secretary-general of the UGEMA, and other leaders, in that order. "Are you kidding me?" he asked angrily. "Are you making fun of the Algerian Revolution?" I calmed him down, explaining that I could not hide in the background and send young people to volunteer for missions without first seeking their opinions. I knew, however, about the convictions of Miss Rahal and myself. It took some more persuasion for him to finally understand that I was being sincere. He adjourned the meeting abruptly after I apologized for not being able to help.

Struggle in Morocco—Organization

Despite all his bluster and chest pumping, Mabed turned out to be more of a disappointment to all who had sacrificed for the struggle. Shortly before the war came to an end, he escaped to the city of Toulouse and purchased a large stud farm with stolen money from the revolution.

I continued to have access to the royal palace, the Istiqlal Party, the Moroccan Liberation Army, and the Communist Party. The leadership of the Communist Party included, among others, Dr. Messouak, a well-known ENT, Abdelaziz Belal, an economics professor, and Bachir Aouad, a bookstore owner. Bachir moonlighted as a translator for the Russian Embassy from time to time. Due to their flirtations with communism, the Istiqlal authorities were constantly monitoring these gentlemen. Whenever they received word about an imminent dragnet, they sent me to clean out their offices and hide all printing equipment before the authorities swooped in. I kept all the evidence in the trunk of my car until the coast was clear.

In 1957, Dr. El Khatib and Mahjoubi Aherdan formed their own political party, El Haraka Echabia—"the Popular Movement." Months later, I participated in drafting their statutes and watched the number of militants grow exponentially in what became a very dynamic party over a short period. One day, I accompanied them to bury the remains of Si Abbas, the martyr, in a manner worthy of his rank. Si Abbas was the resistance leader in the Rif Mountains. He was assassinated and buried in Fes. Leaders for the Liberation Army contemplated transferring his body to the Rif Mountains, because they concluded he had been buried in a manner that was disrespectful to his honor. There was a big celebration at the cemetery in Fes when his body was exhumed and returned to his hometown. The burial ceremony ruffled the feathers of the Istiqlal leadership. I had just returned to Rabat from the event, when I found out that M'hamed Boucetta, a powerful Istiqlal Party affiliate and a member of Dr. El Khatib's family, had signed an arrest warrant for the leaders of El Haraka Echabia.

I received a distressful call in the morning from Lalla Hiba, Fatima Hassar's mother, informing of the sudden arrest of her brother, Dr. El Khatib. I quickly jumped in my car and drove to her house in Rabat. Within minutes, she and I were on our way to his Casablanca home to inquire about his whereabouts. He had been transported to the Fes prison in the mainland, about a couple of hours by car from where he lived. As I drove at very high speeds to get to her brother, she remained very calm and kept me engaged in little conversations along the way. I had known her as a very bighearted individual, but she demonstrated an impressive level of courage and maintained her composure throughout the entire ordeal. When we arrived at the prison sometime in the midafternoon, the entire compound was surrounded by the police. The guards let us in, and we found Dr. El Khatib and Aherdan in a large room, sitting cross-legged on mats, encircled by some curious prisoners. They were revered because they had gained some notoriety as political prisoners, and everyone seemed to know who they were. Before long, they gave us their version of the events that led to their arrest, but they reassured us of their innocence and Lalla Hiba instantly felt relieved. We spent the rest of the day with them, discussing our thoughts and soliciting some strategic information on ways to help expedite their release. The ideas were abundant, but at the time, I underestimated the complexity of the situation. Before leaving, I promised to do my best to get the word out. We got back to Rabat in the evening.

The next day, the city was under total political turmoil. I reported the situation to the head of the FLN in Morocco, Cheikh Kheireddine, focusing on the Algerian origins of Dr. El Khatib and especially the invaluable assistance he brought to the war in Algeria. I also reminded him that he was responsible for organizing the East Moroccan front. He broke his silence—"This is between the Moroccans. If you commit yourself to anything, it will be at your

Struggle in Morocco—Organization

own risk."

I felt alone and isolated. Despite being a friend of the Istiqlal Party and the Communist Party, I did not know which way to turn. The political situation in Morocco was deteriorating. Having seized control of the central government, the Istiqlal Party had grown more powerful and pervasive. King Mohammed V's influence had waned, and there were more political gridlocks within the corridors of government than ever before. The perilous state of affairs and massive bureaucratic red tape made it extremely difficult for the former fighters of the Moroccan Liberation Army to get their dues as veterans. But nonetheless, the party was not really unified. There were internal struggles among the left wing and those on the right. I knew that if the Hassar family had any leverage left, they would have done whatever it took to secure the release of the political prisoners.

I visited them at the Fes prison the next day. With the Popular Movement still in its infancy, most of the activists did not know each other, except for the former Liberation Army fighters and the Chleuhs. The prisoners were neither allowed by the authorities to consult with their lawyers, nor were they permitted to see a judge. In that regard, we saw no other alternative but to resort to a popular revolt. We decided that I had to go to the Marmouchas region to inform the leadership of the fate of their dear friend, Dr. El Khatib. His nephew, Abdelkrim Benslimane, who had committed his body and soul to the struggle for his uncle's liberation, drove with me to Missour and Immouzer des Marmouchas. We attended one strategic meeting after another, followed by one gathering after another, and received unconstrained passionate support. At each gathering, everyone answered in a unified voice, "You just have to lift the finger, Si Mahjoub, and by any means necessary, we will light a fire with the little we have left." Our task was made easy because most of the folks in the region had a beef to pick with the government over its failed promises to rebuild their homes, which had been destroyed by the French colonists during the war. By the time we left the region, I was satisfied that we were poised to revolt.

The groundswell had already begun when I reported back to the prisoners in Fes a few days later. On my way out of their cell, Aherdan asked me to pick up his machine gun from his house and deliver it to Captain Ben Miloudi in the town of Oulmes. The captain was admired for his courage and respect for the given word.

I drove directly to Aherdan's home in the early morning and announced my arrival to some family members on the compound. Faced with a difficult situation, Meriem, his wife, a classy French woman, held it together very well. She kept the conversation brief and went to pick up the gun, which I strapped onto my shoulder to conceal beneath my *djellaba*. We left in my car and headed to the El Khatib residence to pick up his wife, Meftaha, for the four-hour trip back to Fes. I always held Meftaha in great esteem because of her deferential strength and caring nature. Seeing her, it was hard to tell that she was going through a very tough situation. She appeared dignified and her demeanor was composed. Meriem sat in the passenger's seat to my right, and Meftaha made herself comfortable in the back of the car. I had printed some flyers in support of the political prisoners and hidden them beneath her seat. We were only ten kilometers from Fes when we came to a stop at a military checkpoint. There were about twenty cars ahead of us. I paused to think for a moment and made a quick decision to lean on the horn and drive around the cars in the opposite lane. Luckily, my car was still registered in Missour with a physician's sticker on the windshield. A high-ranking military officer waved us down and stormed angrily toward the car. I apologized for my impulsive action and explained that I was on an emergency call to help deliver a baby. That was good enough for him. He pulled back and moved some vehicles around for me to proceed. I breathed a sigh of relief, knowing in my heart that we had only gotten away with my actions because of God's intervention. I went to drop off the ladies at the prison and headed back on the road to Missour. The *caïd*, Mohammed Ou El Hadj El Marmouchi, was expecting my arrival. After updating him on the situation, I spent a few hours in the region distributing the flyers. It was almost dusk when I returned to Fes to pick up the ladies for the long drive back to Rabat.

I went to hand over Aherdan's machine gun to Ben Miloudi the following day. Not long after receiving the weapon, Ben Miloudi was injured in combat while toting that same gun. On my very next visit to the prison, Aherdan angrily blamed me for giving away his weapon. I found it quite odd, but he was clearly shaken up. I could tell that he felt guilty about the unfortunate incident, but even so, I was still baffled by his convenient memory loss. He totally ignored me when I reminded him that the decision to give the weapon to Ben Miloudi was his. When he made comments about the risks of pulling off a successful rebellion, I responded philosophically, "While in the water, one no longer fears the rain." He was in prison, I wondered, what was the worse thing that could happen to him? He smiled at me, nodding approvingly at my confidence, and then proceeded to discuss strategy.

I returned to law school and kept up a normal appearance. I met with Prince Hassan's younger brother, Moulay Abdallah, and gave him the details of the plan. He wasn't a fan of the Istiqlal Party. Therefore, he was more than happy to help. He promised to get me some weapons. I was invited to his residence a few days later to pick up a large designer suitcase containing three submachine guns, four machine guns, and some ammunition. I took the weapons to the home of Dr. El Khatib's elder brother, Si Mahfoud El Khatib, for safekeeping, and waited a few days to ensure that no one was onto us before delivering the suitcase to our Marmouchas comrades.

The rebellion began right then and grew stronger by the day. Slowly but surely, the government's grip on power started to weaken. Dr. El Khatib and Mahjoubi Aherdan were suddenly released from prison after two months of incarceration. Due to their unpopular policies, the Istiqlal administration was greatly damaged. We saw King Mohammed V consolidate control and become more powerful. It was yet another reaffirmation and a vivid reminder that prison remains the antechamber of power in underdeveloped countries.

Dr. El Khatib went on to become the Minister of Employment and Social Affairs under King Mohammed V and held other ministerial positions under King Hassan II. Most notably, he was the first president of the Moroccan Congress. Mahjoubi Aherdan served as the Minister of Defense for several years in Morocco.

I was summoned by Dr. Francis Hammond, the Director of Cultural Affairs for the US Embassy, with whom I had been in contact for some time. We had come to know and respect each other. He was an African-American with dual Doctor of Letters degrees from an American university and the University of Louvain in Belgium. As an avid supporter of the Algerian Revolution, he did his best to distance himself from diplomats at the French Embassy. Mohammed V's daughter, Princess Lalla Aicha, adored Dr. Hammond's little girls and often invited them to a play day at the palace. He was highly regarded by the royal family and local political leaders. When we met, he informed me about a situation concerning ten scholarships that the US government had offered to Moroccan students. He had gone through several difficult processes to secure the scholarships for the students, but the Moroccan government had declined to take up the grants for no apparent reason. He felt personally embarrassed by their decision.

He was hoping I'd be able to help him figure out a way to redirect the awards to Algerian students. "Not a bad idea," I told him. But of course, I knew that it would be easier said than done, because the students would have to travel on Moroccan passports. He had thought long and hard before contacting me, and the only practical suggestion he could offer, were I to accept the scholarships, was for me to figure out a way to ask Princess Lalla Aicha for her assistance. The final decision rested on the Moroccan government's willingness to award the scholarships to members of the UGEMA. The other hurdle to overcome would be to figure out a way for the US government to recognize the interim government of Algeria. Thoughts raced through my head in many directions. I asked him for some time to reflect on the matter. On my way home, I reflected on the timing of such a once-in-a-lifetime opportunity. At stake was a dazzling potential for upward mobility and a chance to embark on higher education in America.

As usual, the Hassars and I dined together that evening, and I shared the details with Fatima, a good friend of Dr. Hammond's. She volunteered without hesitation to lend a helping hand. I heard from her a week later. She had spoken with Princess Lalla Aicha, and she was more than delighted to assist. When I called the number she gave me to make an appointment to see the princess, the secretary told me that they were expecting to hear from me.

Princess Lalla Aicha received me at the residence in Rabat's Suissie neighborhood in a royal setting with stately courtesy. We spoke at length for about an hour on the war in Algeria. She was very knowledgeable in world affairs and North Africa politics. Over traditional tea, we brainstormed the situation and discussed our approach. When we were done talking, she promised to get in touch with Dr. Hammond and assured me she would spare no effort in obtaining the scholarships for us.

Meanwhile, I stayed in touch with Dr. Hammond and got the word out to my UGEMA compatriots. They were split on whether we were morally obligated to turn down the offer. How could one accept a scholarship from the US, France's NATO ally, whose weapons had been used against the martyrs of the Algerian liberation? It was a tough one to swallow. At our offices, the debate got even more heated among the members. I tried my best to convince everyone that it was a fleeting situation and that we faced a once-in-a-lifetime opportunity that could bring recognition to our struggle by a great power like America. I also reminded them that we had no formal commitment from the US government. It was premature to be all up in arms about something that wasn't a sure bet. No one knew at that moment if the proposal would be accepted.

In the coming days, however, Dr. Hammond was able to achieve a major milestone with the help of Princess Lalla Aicha. The Moroccan government offered the scholarships to the UGEMA. Though it was a crucial first step, he cautioned that since the US government had no intention of dealing with the GPRA, he was still pondering his next move. I continued to meet with him at his home, or sometimes at the home of Mrs. Fatima Hassar. We chose to meet discreetly in private residences in order to avoid any diplomatic fallout, because the US government did not want an incident with their ally, France. I was impressed by his great courage and tenacious dedication. During one of our meetings at a neutral location, he informed me that he had spoken on record to the ambassador and told him that if the US government rejected the process, he would tender his resignation. He knew that he would always be welcome at the University of Louvain, where he'd obtained his PhD.

At that juncture in the waiting game, I felt overwhelmed and conflicted. It wasn't because I was juggling many responsibilities in Morocco, but the defective nature of the political environment within the FLN had played a part in the decline of my morale. The movement was rife with injustices and abuses by those who sought to get rich at any cost. I had a nagging suspicion that matters would be worse in Algeria after independence. I grew anxious by the day, and I looked forward to a change in environment.

The good news came as a surprise at a lunch meeting with Dr. Hammond. As soon as I entered his house, he gave me a bear hug and said the US had consented. Smiling broadly, I slapped his palm and held on to a firm handshake.

"Oh, my goodness. That is such great news. I am very relieved to hear that the decision came down in our favor. Thank you very much, Dr. Hammond." He kept smiling and nodding his head. "Thanks for finding your way around the bureaucrats."

"You are very welcome." But then, the brief smile faded from his face. "Just a word of caution, Ghoulem. The French Embassy has heard about the situation, and they are pressuring my government to reverse our decision. As far as they are concerned, the UGEMA is a terrorist group."

He had been in intense negotiations with them for several days and said he was doing all he could to change their views and, perhaps, their policy. At the time, Algerians were considered French citizens. They saw our student organization as a fringe movement against their colonial dominance. In that regard, their ally, the US, could not interfere in their domestic affairs. The diplomatic standoff went on for weeks. At times, it felt as though the French government had the upper hand. But through skillful diplomacy and some good luck, they eventually relented.

Finding the best and most qualified students within the UGEMA organization was not the easiest task. There were more heated debates at our headquarters in the coming days, until finally, cooler heads prevailed. We decided to vote on the matter, and the majority consensus was for the committee members to interview some of the students and sort out their qualifications. I included myself on the list, despite only having a year left to complete my bachelor's degree in law studies at the Faculty of Law and Political Sciences. We had to go through an arduous selection process to find the nine most qualified students to meet the requisite criteria necessary to gain acceptance into the scholarship program. After narrowing down the candidates, we worked with the US Embassy to apply for admission into a select group of universities. Within a couple of weeks, we received admission letters from most of the schools on our list. I gained admission to Columbia University.

As we approached the departure date, we held a strategic meeting to figure out a way to get Moroccan passports. I went to see Mr. Mohammed Hassar at his office to seek his counsel on the matter. True to form, he was like a family member who couldn't wait for the opportunity to help me get ahead in life. The passport issue was solved on the spot. I waited until we received our travel documents before reserving our airline tickets. When I went to pick up the tickets from Dr. Hammond, I spotted a sinister plot by the French in our transit routing. It seemed the French secret service had influenced the local travel agency to ensure a stopover in Paris, where authorities would be waiting to take us off the plane. Our entire fate would have fallen in the hands of the French justice system. The arrest of ten Algerian "terrorists" would have been great propaganda material for the colonial government. He was glad we exposed the scheme before it was too late. I asked him to reroute our flight through Brussels and thanked him for his vigilance.

Sadly, Antoinette and I were about to be separated again for sometime. Because of the manner in which the opportunity had presented itself, I wasn't able to include her in the process. We pondered a different plan for us to reunite again in the United States and talked extensively about what I could do to procure a scholarship for her. I truly believed there was a possibility for her to come and join me sooner than later and promised to leave no stone unturned until we were reunited again. When I went to break the news to Dr. El Khatib on the eve of my departure, I found him in a melancholic state. He needed me more than ever, he said, but realized the situation represented a once-in-a-lifetime opportunity.

He took me to the Casablanca airport the next morning. *Before parting ways, he gave me a miniature Qur'an adorned with mother-of-pearl from Jordan—a gift I have cherished to this day. I returned the gesture by giving him my permanent companion, a revolver.* Saying goodbye was really tough for the two of us. Having fought side by side in many battles, we had finally arrived at a different chapter.

We gave a bear hug as the tears rolled down our cheeks and

wished each other good luck.

Looking back at the difficult journey on the path to securing the highest level of education for my fellow Algerian brothers and myself, I can't help but appreciate the onerous task involved in eliciting the support of my fellow UGEMA members when the opportunity came my way. Those that came along went on to help shape the backbone of Algeria's future. Nouredine Ait El Hocine became the president of SONATRAC.[19] Chakib Khelil was appointed Minister of Energy and Mines and doubled as the director of the Trans-Mediterranean Pipeline. Bachir Ould Driss was Algeria's representative to the United Nations.

---

[19] Algeria's state oil company.

A Dream for Peace

I was the first scientist to ever give a hypothesis on what was later identified by Professor Howard Temin as the "Reverse Transcriptase Enzyme"—which is a factor in enabling specific RNA viruses to induce certain forms of cancer. As a result of my initial discovery in 1961, and my hypothesis at the Houston Conference in 1962, Temin managed to isolate the enzyme's immunologic structures later in the 1970s while conducting further research at the University of Wisconsin in Madison.

Chapter Five

My American Experience—Becoming a Scientist

Upon landing in New York, we were separated and sent off to begin our English workshops at different universities. I arrived at Bennington College, an all women's liberal arts school in Vermont, offering "Intensive English Studies" to scholarship recipients from the Third World. The program was designed to last for three months. I lived on campus throughout the entire period and enjoyed a relaxed and pampered lifestyle—a stark contrast to the undue privation in the Maquis. We were treated like royalty and placed in groups of ten per tutor. Some of us were frequent guests at the School of Music, known for its weekly concerts by a variety of invited artists. I attended a gigantic event at an outdoor concert by the great Arthur Rubinstein and a choir of three hundred. It was quite a spectacle. Throughout the entire performance, I sat transfixed and followed his every riff on the grand piano. I had long been an admirer of the great classical music maestros, dating back to my days at Lycée d'Aumale. But this was my very first major live concert—a captivating experience that sent me on an unforgettable musical journey. The genius of Rubinstein—a prolific classical pianist, bolstered by the angelic voices of the choir on a big stage—was for me, a profound reminder of the larger-than-life nature of the United States. It dawned on me, right then and there—I had arrived in a new world to begin a brand new chapter in my life.

From the moment we arrived on US soil, volunteers from the Institute of International Education (IIE), working with the US State Department, saw to our safety, security, and comforts. They also accompanied us everywhere. The first three months went by quickly. At the end of the course, I received an invitation by the US Senate Committee on Foreign Relations to give a presentation in Washington, DC. Perhaps the fact that I was the UGEMA point person had something to do with the invite. But also at the time, the Senate body was very interested in colonial affairs across the globe. I did not know then that in July 1957, about two years before I came to the States, Senator John Kennedy had proposed on the Senate floor that the US *"must support Algeria's efforts to gain independence from France."*

    I arrived at the Capitol in the early morning and toured the great halls of Congress. When I walked into the chamber, I approached each of the senators on the bench and gave a firm handshake. The atmosphere was very cordial, but I still didn't know what to expect. I sat behind a polished mahogany table, flanked by two IIE handlers who were there to help with necessary translation. From behind a circular bench on a platform across from us, the senators smiled—at times looking down at their notes. When the committee chairman called the meeting to order, I quickly understood that they had very relevant information about my background and travels behind the Iron Curtain, yet they had limited knowledge of the oppression that the citizens of Algeria continued to endure on a daily basis. Given the opportunity to speak, I seized the moment and with only a few words, I painted a portrait of life as an Algerian in my homeland:

    "Honorable Senators, please allow me to illustrate for you one of many despicable actions by the French colonialists in Algeria. First and foremost, there are several segregated zones all over my country with posted signs explicitly forbidding access to Arabs and dogs."

    My voice cracked. I felt emotional. They sat in silence, with stoic expressions. I continued to elaborate on the systemic destruction of our culture, the degradation of our traditional values, the painful war for our liberation, and the fact that the FLN was not a communist organization. Furthermore, I emphasized that my

My American Experience—Becoming a Scientist

trips behind the Iron Curtain were motivated by the needs of the revolution.

"We were given weapons by those who had become our friends. They had become our friends because they either delivered or sold weapons to help us defend ourselves against the French colonists. It is the love of liberty that makes us admire the US for the example she gave the world in the fight that led to her liberation from England. We have nothing against your French allies, except that they use NATO's weapons to exterminate our people. In the same manner as Americans have become friends with the British, your former colonial masters, we do not reject the possibility of becoming friends with the people of France."

Prompted by a senator on the panel with a question about my thoughts on the war in Vietnam, I paused briefly to reflect. As an Algerian, I knew that my people had a long history of solidarity with the people of Vietnam because of our common struggle against the French. During my stay in France, I had been passionately involved in the overseas student movement as a political activist and kept abreast of the political debates in all the French colonies across the globe. I composed myself before delivering my blunt yet detailed opinion: "France attempted to win the war in Dien Bien Phu; they were unsuccessful in their quest. I don't believe any other country will ever succeed in defeating the Vietnamese, because the French did all they could to infiltrate their society and still came up short. They learned to speak the language, married Vietnamese women, set up factories, and established rubber plantations, but ultimately, their plans were in vain. They only realized that all was lost after the war came to an end. *No country in the world, regardless of their power, can fight a war, let alone win it, when its main bases are tens of thousands of kilometers away.*" One of the senators nodded and said something, but his words were muzzled because he was looking away from the microphone, over at the chairman. Nonetheless, they laughed and I heard someone mention something about a "brilliant young man." The chairman muttered, "Yes, yes, well done, young fella. We will now adjourn for lunch."

In the cafeteria, I sat at a table with a couple of committee members. One senator sought to explain the virtues of having a Fulbright scholarship and gaining admission to an American university as prestigious as Columbia School of Law in New York. His colleague emphasized that New Yorkers were in general exposed to the influence of the United Nations. He was sure that most New Yorkers were well informed about world events and certainly the war in Algeria. Needless to say, he planted a seed in my head and suggested that if I wanted to help the Senate and the US government, I could also choose to pursue my studies in the Midwest and bring attention to the Algerian cause. By staying engaged in the community, I could perhaps enlighten those who believed that Algerians flirted with communism and were allied with the USSR and China. The other senator was quick to interject and add that states in the Midwest were politically conservative. I listened intently and imagined how my life would be impacted by my decisions in the coming days. Before leaving, I thanked them for everything and promised to ponder my choices.

On the flight to New York, I thought long and hard about the conversation and spoke at length with my IIE minder. I had not given much thought to the demographics and political layout of the US until my Senate encounter. The opportunities in the country seemed endless. I recalled our heated conversations at the last UGEMA meetings, where I won over my comrades with the idea that coming to America would help us raise awareness for the Algerian cause. My brief journey down memory lane was interrupted by the mechanized sound of the plane's landing gear. I stared out of the window at the amazing Manhattan skyline. We landed in New York City, about an hour after taking off from DC, and took a cab to a hotel across the street from the IIE headquarters, a few blocks away from the United Nations building. After checking me in, he went over our

My American Experience—Becoming a Scientist

schedule and left for the day.

When we met at the front desk in the morning, he directed me to the office of the FLN representative to the United Nations, on 46th Street. I walked a few blocks down the street, marveling at the awesome architecture and the crowds, walking briskly in all directions. It seemed as though everyone was on a mission and they had to get there on time. After several minutes, I arrived at the building and asked to meet with the head of the Diplomatic Mission. In a cramped yet active office space, Mr. Abdelkader Chanderli, a bright and cultured fellow, welcomed me with a traditional Algerian brotherly affection. He was a former journalist at the New York bureau of *Il Tempo*, an Italian newspaper. We were immediately joined by his assistant, Raouf Boudjakdji, a man as charming as his boss. In those days, coming across a fellow Algerian in America was not an everyday occurrence. Neither of the two gentlemen pretended not to be surprised at my impromptu visit. I gave them a more detailed orientation about the great efforts of our brothers in the Moroccan border regions. After getting to know my story, Mr. Chanderli spoke of a number of Algerian students who had come to the States on scholarships from the US National Student Association, in cooperation with the UGEMA office in Lausanne, Switzerland. Raouf was warm, personable, and supportive. He had a big heart and an eloquent manner of voicing his discontent at the French for their war crimes. He seemed very touched by the sacrifices of our brothers on the front lines and prayed that our struggle would soon come to an end. I was impressed by the work they were doing, offering their very best to remind the world about our cause, with very little resources at their disposal. Mr. Chanderli invited me to join them for lunch the next day.

We sat at a restaurant a few yards away from the UN and talked about my Senate encounter. Chanderli thought that embarking on scientific studies in the Midwest was an idea worth exploring. I wasn't quite sure of what to make of my broadening horizons. The new school year was fast approaching. I felt the need to make a decision. When I visited the IIE office the next day, they seemed more accommodating than usual. As soon as I saw my minder, he asked if I had made a decision. I flashed a quick smile and shook my head. He was prepared to help me. After all, he said, the choice was mine to make, and either way, my decision would be respected. We walked into an office with one of his coworkers and studied a large map on the wall, featuring every major university in the States. Pointing at the University of Indiana, he gave a brief overview about the statewide conservative culture, the people's political leanings, and the excellent curriculum at the College of Arts and Sciences. I was impressed. The fog in my head had cleared up in an instant. I began to ask some very detailed questions about the school's academic orientation, and the final destination became apparent. There was a collective sigh of relief in the room. I gave a thumbs-up and asked them to begin processing my paperwork for admission to the University of Indiana. I went to inform Mr. Chanderli first thing in the morning. The ever-accommodating IIE had booked my flight to Indianapolis in no time. They even provided a bus ticket to Bloomington.

It was the first time I had been alone since my arrival in the US When my flight landed in Indianapolis, I was met by two staff members from the IIE at the airport. On the way to the bus station, I was assured that an official from the university awaited my arrival in Bloomington. I felt very much at ease, because every necessary preparation had been made for me. I just sat back and allowed myself to immerse into the system. In Bloomington, I was received by a fine gentleman. He understood that my English was limited and so he did his very best to keep the conversation at a basic level. We drove to the "Commons"—a university hotel with a large restaurant—and registered my name at the front desk. He gave me a check for general expenses before I rushed off to drop my bags in the room. We had an appointment with Mr. Dayi'nin, the Dean of

My American Experience—Becoming a Scientist

Foreign Students. "Welcome to our university." The handshake was firm, and his eyes pierced into mine. I smiled back and mustered a quick "Thank you. I am very happy to be here." He sat back down at his desk. "Please take a seat. Have you checked in at the Commons?" he asked. "Yes. I have. Very nice hotel." He said, "Of course this is only temporary. You will be moving into a newly furnished mobile home tomorrow." I was really impressed by the flawless process. "Well, make yourself at home. I am sure you are in good hands." "Thank you, sir," I answered. I left his office and thought about my appointment with the faculty of the School of Biology.

I was accompanied by an IIE minder to a meeting the next morning. We walked into a conference room and greeted a group of professors at a round table. I was still dealing with limitations in my English language comprehension and my minder understood very little French, hence I sat through the entire orientation without fully grasping everything. Either way, the interaction was stress-free, and I was amazed by the ease at which they walked me through the process. One of the professors agreed to tutor and ensure my maximum preparedness for the upcoming assessment test. Internally, I was quietly wrestling with thoughts of my linguistic limitations; I barely spoke English—I was beginning to feel like an incapable swimmer being cast off into a vast ocean. Following the meeting, I was taken to my brand-new mobile home at 134 Walnut Grove. I was stunned by the magnificent living space. Not so long ago, I had been sleeping on a bunk bed at the Khemisset camp with fellow freedom fighters. Looking around the space, it was as if I was about to move into a little mansion. It was a two-bedroom apartment with a living room, a dining room, a kitchen, and a nice-sized bathroom. All the furnishings were brand new. I even had access to hot and cold water, a heater, and an air-conditioning unit.

Having successfully completed my assessment test, I enrolled in the department of microbiology. I was offered a place in the laboratory of my academic advisor and tutor, Professor Walter

Konetzka. The US government took care of everything: my studies, housing, and books. All I had to do was roll up my sleeves and get to work. I was really off to a great start. I felt like Alice in Wonderland—except I was dealing with overwhelming responsibilities. The brand-new biology building was conveniently located within walking distance from my mobile home. I enrolled in a workshop to brush up on biology, biochemistry, and genetics, and I sat in the front row of my first bacteriology class for beginners, taught by Professor Konetzka. Later that day, I attended a biochemistry class given by the world-renowned eminent professor, Felix Haurowitz, an American from the Czech Republic, who also spoke French. He was the author behind the metaphoric key-in-the-lock theory—the simplified explanation for the more complex antigen-antibody interaction.

I was the only foreign student in my classes, and English was not my strongest subject. But I quickly grew accustomed to a nurturing milieu, always surrounded by professors and students who helped me out whenever necessary. By the time the second week came along, I had fostered a warm relationship with Dr. Konetzka. He was kind enough to invite me to meet his family. The house was close to campus, not very far from my mobile home. His wife, Lillian, an astute and witty personality, welcomed me to their charming home. They were Polish-Americans with three young boys and a girl. I marveled at the calm disposition of their kids. They were very friendly and curious. My heavy French accent didn't seem to bother them at all. He was the ideal family man, patient and self-assured. Within minutes, I fell in love with their adorable children. Walter Jr., Kevin, Michael, Elizabeth, and I played little games for a while, before their mother invited us to sit at the dinner table. The food and conversation were a combined treat. It had been such a long time since I felt a true sense of nurturing in a family setting. The hours passed quickly, and I had to leave. I felt rejuvenated after it was all over, and happily, this was the beginning of many visits to come. I ended up spending my very first Thanksgiving holiday with them.

Our relationship blossomed into a stronger bond in the following days and weeks. They took on the responsibility of ensuring my well-being and adopting me into their family as if I were one of their very own. Their support was invaluable. At every opportunity, he introduced me on campus as a serious personality, "someone who is passionately dedicated to the independence of his country." He was always there when I needed him. Especially, when I informed him about my plans to reunite with my wife. He immediately sought the involvement of the university. Within a few months, he managed to help me secure a scholarship from the American Red Cross for her. Antoinette finally came to the US to pursue her studies and be by my side again.

Dr. Walter Konetzka.

At the university, I began earning high marks for my studious habits, prompting more scrutiny among some of my jealous classmates. Because the English language had been harder for me to speak than to read or write, a few of my classmates were puzzled by my consistency in outshining everyone. Oddly enough, this had been the experience of my fellow Algerian students who were dispersed across the country and were facing similar challenges. Every so often, we spoke on the telephone to keep ourselves apprised of the trials and tribunals of acclimation.

As the leader of the group, I was also the emergency contact for everyone. We looked to each other for support, especially, when we struggled with homesickness, which was a prevalent emotional issue among us. It had gotten so bad for one of the guys who was enrolled at Seattle University that he suffered a nervous breakdown and was admitted to the intensive care unit of a local hospital. I received a call from the patient relations department and drove nonstop across the country to see him. His situation was quite severe. He embraced me very hard and cried about his desire to return to familiar surroundings, to be closer to the traditions of his people. Because of the state he was in, I knew that I could not leave his side until I was assured that he wouldn't succumb to major depression. For three days, we walked the grounds of the hospital after our morning prayers, shielding ourselves from the constant Seattle rains, and talked about the things we missed the most. It was therapeutic for both of us. The day after my arrival, he felt much stronger and began to eat again. I kept on reminding him that Algeria needed us to make such sacrifices. I told him again and again that in order for us to play an essential role in our country's future, and to be there for our people after independence, our selfish needs must be secondary to the stability of a new Algeria. When he was ready to return to campus, I oversaw his discharge and went back to Bloomington.

There was always a particular group of students in my class who had a habit of rushing to my desk every time we received our test results. Their behavior was borne out of curiosity, because they could not fathom my innate ability to score such high grade points in light of the language limitations. I knew that my comprehensive techniques could be traced back to the Qur'anic School days. "*As a*

My American Experience—Becoming a Scientist

young boy attending the Qur'anic School back in my country, I learned that memorizing was an art form. I was taught how to memorize the verses of the Holy Book. It was like a magic box. By and by, everything became clear in my mind and spirit," I explained proudly to some classmates who demanded to know the "secret" behind my exceptional prowess. However, it was not always that easy. During a biochemistry exam, I stumbled on the English word "buffers," but luckily, Professor Haurowitz had been standing next to my desk. Looking down, he saw that I was hesitant and indecisive, and pointed to the word. *"Tampons,"* he said. I immediately responded, *"Aaahh, merci,* page 256 of the biochemistry book." In a flash, I raced to finish my test.

Indiana University

This certificate is presented to

GHOULEM BERRAH

in recognition of high scholastic achievement at Indiana University during the year preceding

Founders' Day
May 2, 1962

I had been speaking about Algeria and the liberation war before I could even express myself in the English language. But by the end of the 1950s, Third World affairs had not gained much prominence in American news media. Among the student population, the Algerian war was not a familiar subject matter, because studies in history and geography were largely focused on the American continent. I finally came to grips with what I learned from my meetings with US senators and my fellow Algerian, Chanderli. I began targeting churches, temples, colleges, and universities across the Hoosier State. As the word got around, I received invitations to speak in other forums, and at every opportunity, I did my very best to shine some light on the dark trenches of colonial tyranny. To further attract national attention to the Algerian cause, I joined the NAACP and the Congress of Racial Equality. I was cognizant of the fact that both organizations were focused on racial inequality issues in America, but I aimed to bridge the geographical gap by highlighting historical ties with the African continent, and in so doing, I brought more attention to the issue of colonial subjugation in Africa. The topic rapidly evolved with my vigorous activism, and Algeria's independence became a part of the discourse. Slowly but surely, various liberation movements began to sprout out of the grassroots in support of the Algerian cause. Congressional representatives received petitions from constituents imploring them to push for a cessation in the war against my people. I soon realized that my tireless efforts had awakened the consciousness of many who until then had not been familiar with our struggle. The call for freedom and liberty is in the DNA of every American, hence it wasn't long before the message resonated and snowballed beyond my wildest imagination.

I befriended Sharon Ann Wilson, a leader of the local NAACP chapter and a social movement activist, who had never ceased to vigorously advocate on behalf of African-Americans. She became an integral part of my ambitious plans and helped garner support for the Algerian liberation struggle. Her unyielding activism attracted members of the black elite who had been marginalized, despite their wealth and status. Together, we stood shoulder to shoulder in the fight for social equality for all people. By the time Algeria gained independence in 1962, most African-American activists who

My American Experience—Becoming a Scientist

had been following our political progress were keen to visit the country. Several members of the Black Panther group, who were under persecution in America, took refuge in Algiers after Eldridge Cleaver, a popular leader of the organization, was granted asylum by President Boumédiène's administration.

My Algerian upbringing exposed me to racial discrimination and repression, mostly at the hands of the French colonial settlers who were doing to my people what a majority of white America was doing to the "colored" people in that era. I struggled to come to grips with the stubborn institutional racism that existed, especially, in the state of Indiana, where groups like the Ku Klux Klan flourished. Prior to my admission to IU, the Klan attempted to kidnap the daughter of a prominent Indianapolis physician from her dorm at a local university campus, all because she had joined a "whites-only" sorority. The beautiful girl was mixed, but the nature of her complexion made it difficult to detect that she wasn't Caucasian. Ultimately, her secret was revealed, and it wasn't long before the Klan trespassed on the lawn of the sorority in the dark of night and set a cross ablaze. Thanks to the timely intervention of campus security, she barely escaped with her life. I wondered where all the widespread animosity from the privileged class stemmed from. Why the insecurity? I used to ask myself. America was the world's beacon of light, and the one country I believed could transcend all forms of injustices. If change could happen, it would be the good people of this great nation that would carry the torch of freedom, liberty, and justice for all.

Armed with more knowledge and scientific acuity, I came into my second year prepared to pursue excellence in microbiology. Dr. Konetzka had among his subjects a topic that had been causing some major anguish in the scientific community since the later months of the 1950s, through the early 1960s, dealing with the inhibition of DNA synthesis. Scientists had been searching for a chemical compound which could inhibit Gram-negative bacteria without inhibiting the Gram-positive. For those in the field, the subject matter seemed foolish, because Gram-negative bacteria are more resistant than Gram-positive. We focused on experimenting with phenethyl alcohol, which was used to isolate Gram-positive bacteria in a petri dish. My experiment was conducted in a "liquid media" at different concentrations. At 0.25 percent concentration, the organic compound inhibited the proliferation of the *Escherichia coli* bacillus while the individual bacteria stretched like spaghetti. I cleansed the transformed bacteria and soaked them in a fresh "liquid media" without using phenethyl alcohol. The action prompted the bacteria to divide rapidly. I repeated the experiment several times, until I was convinced beyond a semblance of a doubt, and then, with a sudden boost of courage, I rushed over to see Dr. Konetzka. In my beginner's English, I informed him that the chemical compound had selectively inhibited DNA synthesis without interfering with RNA and proteins. He laughed in my face and said: "In the largest laboratories in the world, researchers are desperately seeking a way to selectively block the synthesis of DNA. Nobody has succeeded to this date. But lo and behold, here you come, straight from the bush, to calmly break the news to me." I was not discouraged by his reaction. I rushed back to the lab to review my experimentation results again, just to be absolutely sure of my conclusion. When I repeated the experiment several times and came up with the same results, I reached out to him again, but he was still dismissive.

The following week, he asked that I conduct the same experiment. This time, I was supposed to be focusing on a bacteriophage T2, which consisted only of DNA and an envelope of proteins. When the virus was treated with phenethyl alcohol, it multiplied and emptied the envelopes, thereby eliminating DNA. I followed up with the electronic microscope, and it confirmed that the envelopes were empty. However, when I cleansed the T2 virus-producing cells to rid them of the phenethyl alcohol action before the multiplication process began, normal viruses were produced.

My American Experience—Becoming a Scientist

Dr. Konetzka remained unconvinced. He was preoccupied with lectures and had been providing research assistance to students during the day. Meanwhile, I was also working very hard on my experiments under his tutelage, direction, and supervision. At times, he collaborated with me in his lab to ensure that my formularies were adjusted properly and calibrated to produce the expected results. When he got a break in his hectic schedule, he set aside some time to have me redo the experiment in his presence one evening. Professor Eugene Weinberg, a specialist on the physiology of iron, was lecturing students in the nearby laboratory. I began by charting my entire methodology under Dr. Konetzka's close observation. He helped me inoculate one of the preparations with phenethyl alcohol, but there was no inoculation of phenethyl alcohol in the second preparation, which served as base reference. After the experiment, I placed the two preparations into the incubator at 37 degrees centigrade, and with his permission, I left for the night. He stayed at the lab and spent the entire night in the incubator, monitoring the results closely. The next morning, I came to the laboratory very early, and found the word "WOW" written with white chalk in extra bold letters across the blackboard.

When he arrived at the laboratory at his usual time, he was ecstatic. He exclaimed, "Wow!" and gave me a bear hug. "Ghoulem, this is a miraculous breakthrough. Oh my God. This is a big deal! Big, big, big deal! This will set the scientific community on fire." He broke into a rapturous laughter. At last, I felt a great sense of relief. We gave each other multiple high-fives and decided to publish our findings. "We've got to move very quickly and publish our findings, before someone else beats us to the punch. We will put your name before mine this time, and in the next publication, we will put my name first, followed by yours." Humility was a natural trait of his, and I saw no inconvenience in the suggestion. We quickly wrote the article on our discovery and sent it out for publication. It was immediately picked up by the *Journal of Bacteriology* in 1961 and the *Biochemical and Biophysical Research Communication* in 1962. As a result, our laboratory took on an international reputation, and requests for our procedural formulas came in from all over the world. The University of Indiana had a great reputation even prior to our discovery. Salvador Luria[20] and James D. Watson,[21] both Nobel Prize winners, were among my predecessors in the department of microbiology. James Watson codiscovered the structure of DNA in 1953 with Francis Crick, when they proposed the double helix, or spiral staircase structure of the DNA molecule, using X-ray diffraction data collected by Rosalind Franklin. I was fortunate enough to have studied genetics under the tutorship of Professor Herman J. Muller,[22] a Nobel Prize winner in genetics.

Much to my surprise, I was elected an associate member of the Sigma Xi society in 1962. I became a part of an international multidisciplinary research society and a fraternity for eminent scientists, whose programs and activities, while honoring scientific achievement, continue the tradition of promoting the health of scientific enterprise. I was also listed in *The American Men of Science*, a biographical reference on leading scientists in the United States.

Prior to our discovery, many scientists had halted their research on the subject matter for lack of concrete evidence, because there were many hypotheses about the integration of DNA from donor cells to recipient cells floating around. Scientists were asking if this was a physical phenomenon—a thesis defended by the French scientists Jacob, Monod, and Lwoff—or if this was a biological phenomenon that did not require the synthesis of DNA. By using our compound, some in the community confirmed that it was a biological phenomenon because when the DNA synthesis was blocked, the genome part that had penetrated the recipient cell did not integrate.

---

[20] Italian microbiologist, 1969 Nobel Prize winner.
[21] American geneticist, 1962 Nobel Prize winner.
[22] American geneticist, 1946 Nobel Prize winner.

My American Experience—Becoming a Scientist

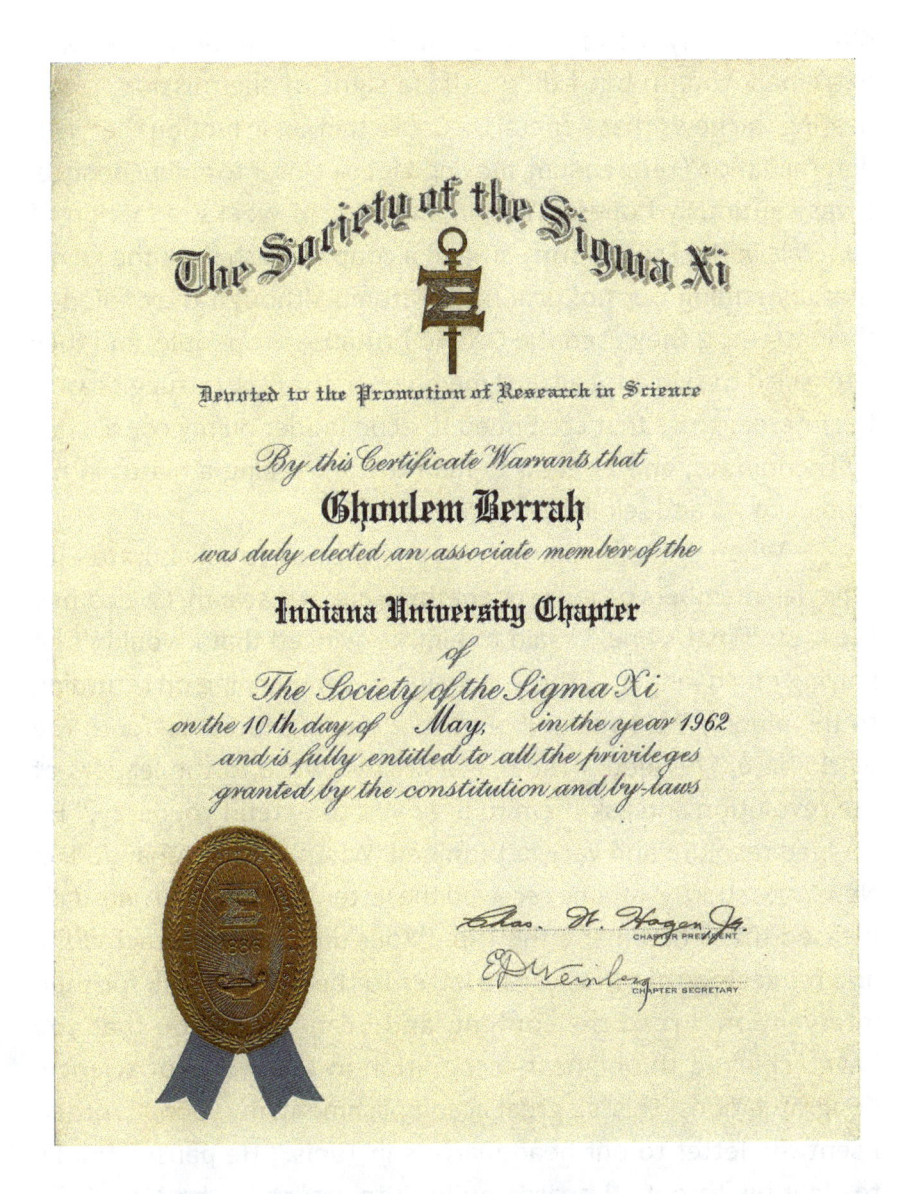

Despite my success in research, being absent from the frontlines of the Algerian liberation war began to cause me some distress. Even though I found myself at the vanguard of scientific innovations, all of my accomplishments seemed meaningless as long as my countrymen continued to die in the quest for independence.

A Dream for Peace

Maintaining my steadfastness and focus at the university was extremely tough, but I did not lose sight of the mission. Upon hearing the news that General De Gaulle had set in motion the "self-determination" referendum, moving Algeria closer to independence, I was cautiously hopeful. Within a matter of weeks, a faction of generals in the French army staged a coup to push back the gains, thereby stifling our political momentum. Although they failed in their attempt, they used the OAS to brutalize my people, and they intensified the violence against members of the FLN. I struggled with the internal strife that continued to echo louder on my conscience by the minute, and I began to lean toward taking a hiatus in my studies to go and rejoin the fight.

When Dr. Konetzka asked my permission to collaborate with other lab members on more phenethyl alcohol research, I welcomed the idea. "That's fine," I said to him, convinced that I wouldn't be staying much longer at the university. "I am planning on returning to the Maquis." He seemed puzzled. "You are more useful to the world here," he pled. "The university will write to the leaders of the revolution and ask them to urge you to extend your stay." He seemed resolute and very determined. When I visited Chanderli in New York, shortly after he received the letter, he appeared unusually pleased that I had made the trip. "Your university contacted me and requested that I forward a letter to the GPRA to ask for their intervention. I read the content, and I can assure you that you have achieved the highest recognition in the world of science. Congratulations! This is a great accomplishment, my young brother. I sent the letter to our headquarters in Tunis." He paused briefly to clear his throat. "I heard you long to return to the Maquis." I nodded in agreement and attempted to speak. "Hear me out for a second," he said. "The fight for our independence is almost over. I can assure you that things are slowly moving our way. Despite all the massacres of our people and the suffering, we are headed in the right direction. At least for now, the French are secretly talking

My American Experience—Becoming a Scientist

with the GPRA."

It was always helpful to hear from those who were close to the situation. I listened and parsed his words in my head. We were both very passionate about our nation's struggle for independence. "Ghoulem, my young brother, in a future independent Algeria, we will need our highly educated brethren to serve and help rebuild our nation. I must strongly urge you to reconsider your decision." My concerns were eased quite a bit. I felt a slight sense of relief, knowing his dedication and personal commitment to our struggle. Thanks to his assurances, I began to feel some respite from the weight.

Weeks later, the chief of staff for the GPRA's Minister of Education, Belaïd Abdesselam, sent a congratulatory letter containing a special scholarship offer. Because I was a benefactor of a Fulbright scholarship and a National Institutes of Health research grant at the time, I declined the offer. The congratulatory letter was published in the US edition of the Algerian students newspaper.

At every opportunity, Mr. Chanderli introduced me to his peers as *"Algeria's scientific assistant to the US."* One such notable introduction was made to the French ambassador to the United Nations.

I attended classes during the day and continued to conduct research in the laboratory at night. This was my lifestyle at the university as I endeavored to complete my PhD. I had already achieved my Master of Science degree within two years and hoped to work very hard to earn my PhD in the following two years. I even took up painting as a hobby to help alleviate stress and stimulate my creative juices. In between long and arduous hours of studies in the library, juxtaposed with laboratory experimentations, I traversed the surface of a canvas with my paintbrush to produce many colorful portraits, mostly of natural elements and contemporary abstracts.

I only realized the magnitude of what I had accomplished years later in the 1970s, during a visit to the university. When I knocked on the door of Dr. Konetzka's office and walked in with my wife, he stood up from his chair to receive us with open arms. "Ghoulem, we were just talking about you earlier this week at the University Council, during a student assessment meeting," he said. "We warned them that if they did not double their efforts, they would run the risk of being expelled. I told them that only once in the history of the university have we convened a meeting with an international student to warn him of health risks associated with habitual studying. Guess who I was talking about." We joined him in laughter. It is true that as a post-graduate student, I had the keys to the library, and after everyone had left for the day, I would often continue studying until the wee hours and leave around eight o'clock in the morning, when the librarian arrived.

Despite all the efforts, there were skeptics in the scientific community who were not convinced by the findings in our publication. Many of our colleagues around the world kept asking for reprints and samples of our experimentation compound. The skepticism continued until the day we were invited to the Annual Symposium on Fundamental Cancer Research in Houston, Texas, in 1962.

There was an intense level of curiosity in the atmosphere. My cohorts could not wait to see me on the podium. A friendly gentleman in the reception area, who introduced himself as Howard Temin from the University of Wisconsin–Madison, approached me. He wanted my opinion and further elaboration on the inhibitive process of DNA and RNA synthesis. We engaged in a brief conversation, and I informed him that I would be sharing some more details from the podium. On this day, Dr. Konetzka was in heaven. He was beaming from ear to ear as if he was the happiest person in the world.

When I finally stood up to begin my presentation, I was immediately bombarded with questions from many of the attendees. One of the most virulent voices was Professor Norton Zinder, a friend of Dr. Konetzka's. His voice echoed through the conference room as he engaged me in a brief discussion on a premise that phenethyl

My American Experience—Becoming a Scientist

alcohol did not just inhibit the synthesis of DNA, but that the process had a similar effect on RNA. Although, he'd requested and received a reprint with a sample of the compound that I originally used in the experiments, he claimed to have conducted more experiments on a type of RNA virus known as the F2 virus, and thus arrived at a different conclusion. I immediately begged to differ: "What you are saying is patently false. Phenethyl alcohol selectively inhibits DNA and not RNA. The RNA is the slave; it cannot substitute itself for DNA, which is the master. The information it carries goes to the DNA, and then returns to the RNA, which in turn transmits the information to proteins."

I was the first scientist to ever give a hypothesis declaring that the discovery of an enzyme was necessary to effectuate the process of transmission. The enzyme was later identified by Professor Howard Temin as the "reverse transcriptase enzyme," which is a factor in enabling specific RNA viruses to induce certain forms of cancer.

As a result of my initial discovery in 1961, and my hypothesis at the Houston symposium in 1962, Temin managed to isolate the enzyme's immunologic structures later in the 1970s while conducting further research at the University of Wisconsin in Madison. I was elected an active member of the New York Academy of Sciences in 1966, and I became a permanent member in 1983. Professor Temin, along with David Baltimore and Renato Dulbecco, shared the 1975 Nobel Prize for Physiology or Medicine. In the same year that I became a permanent member of the Academy of Sciences, Dr. Montagnier and his team discovered the HIV1 and HIV2 strains. Their research went beyond the development of measures to prevent the transmission of AIDS, a retrovirus, which reverses the normal pattern of replication in RNA. They discovered that retroviruses depend on the reverse transcriptase enzyme to use the genetic material in the white blood cells that they infect, in order for the virus to have the proteins they need to survive.

A Dream for Peace

This is to certify that

Ghoulem Berrah

has been elected an Active Member

of

The New York Academy of Sciences

President

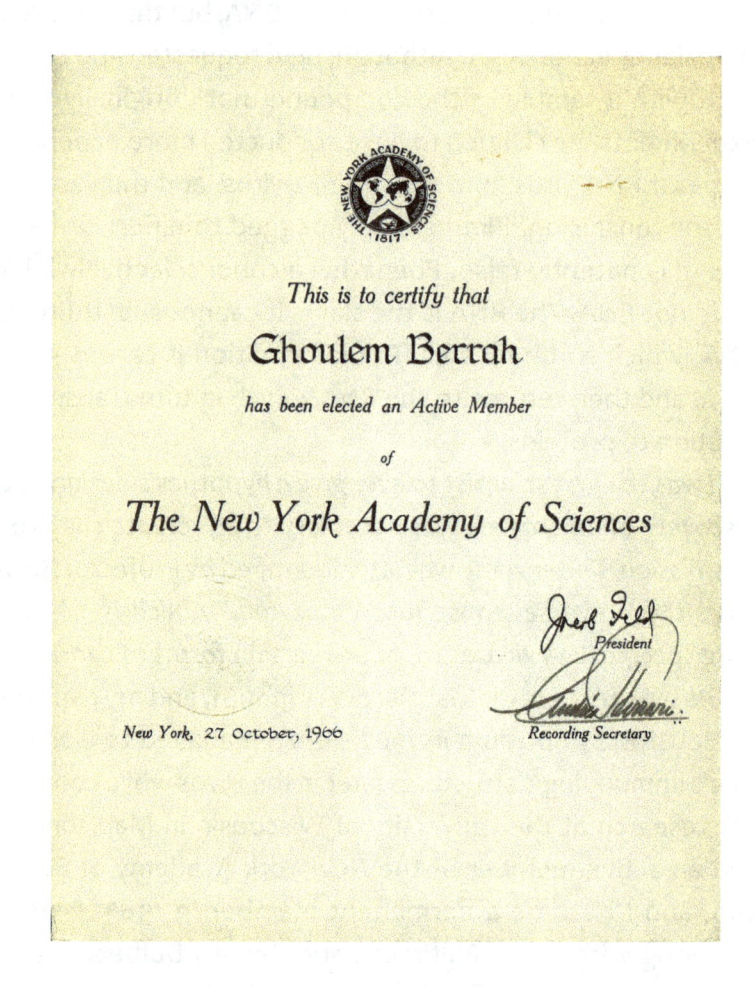

New York, 27 October, 1966

Recording Secretary

We remained in Houston for four days. I began receiving teaching offers from many prestigious universities that were interested in my work, i.e., Yale, Johns Hopkins, Columbia, University of California in Los Angeles, and also the US National Institutes of Health. Each of them offered a faculty position and asked that I join the research team even before I completed my thesis and doctorate program. Dr. Konetzka felt strongly that Yale was a better choice for me. I returned to UI to complete my thesis and earn my doctorate.

Whenever I visited the UN, I was often the guest of

My American Experience—Becoming a Scientist

Ambassador Usher Assouan, a longtime friend from my days in Bordeaux, who served as Côte d'Ivoire's Permanent Representative. I used to sit next to him on the Ivorian bench and listen in on some interesting debates. Back then, the debates were mostly about the newly independent African countries and overall developmental concerns regarding the continent. I was also a regular visitor to his house at the end of the final session. That was my last stop for lunch before hitting the road. I earned the nickname "Côte d'Ivoire's Algerian" from some Algerian diplomats who'd been keenly observing my frequent visits to the Ivorian annex.

Presidents Kennedy and Houphouët-Boigny, with First Ladies.

I was pleasantly surprised when Usher called sometime in May of 1962 to inform me that President Houphouët-Boigny, the Ivorian president, had asked to meet me in New York. He was on a historic visit in the US for talks with President John F. Kennedy.[23] I let Usher know that I could not wait to have an audience with the

---

[23] Video of the event: The American Journey: President and Madame Houphouët-Boigny May 1962, https://www.jfklibrary.org/asset-viewer/archives/USG/USG-01-K/USG-01-K

president—a leader with whom I shared a lot in common. I was a long-time admirer and a fan of his notable accomplishments in France. Usher made the necessary arrangements for a two-day stay at the Waldorf Astoria hotel, where the president was staying.

Antoinette and I left Bloomington at night and drove across three state lines to get to New York in my Plymouth. We arrived in the morning and checked in at the front desk. My father-in-law, the president's personal physician, came to greet us at the lobby. He was there as part of a large presidential entourage.

At the presidential suite, the president approached in a polka-dot robe with his arms wide open. He received me like a family member with a bear hug and motioned to a nearby seat. I instantly felt relaxed. He started the conversation with questions about my studies and research at the university. The interaction was easy and courteous. As a former freedom fighter himself, he'd chosen the path of dialogue rather than combat, yet he was quite inquisitive about my involvement in the Algerian Revolution. He believed that his choice of dialogue embodied his political vision for a more balanced world order. When we spoke about my future plans, I elaborated on my dream to return to Algeria after independence to help develop my beloved country. He liked what he heard. He said:

"More so than the United States, Africa is in much need of you. We are in the process of development. Come and help us. You will be free to leave and go wherever you want to go, when you tire. We have many things to do together."

My initial impression was of a visionary leader who came across as profoundly evocative, and I sensed a level of wisdom that hinted at a larger call to service. I did not know what to make of his statement at that particular moment, but I paused to digest his words. The brief silence was quickly interrupted by the butler asking to pour some coffee. "Côte d'Ivoire is the third largest coffee producer in the world," the president said, "but the Ivorians do not drink coffee—they sell it." He smiled broadly. I was surprised to hear him say that. As I pondered the irony of his statement, he asked about how I met my wife. When I began narrating our story, he listened and nudged the tall tale along with occasional quips and wordplays that made me laugh. He laughed at his own jokes. I liked his sense of humor. Antoinette came in to greet him and stayed for a few minutes. As soon as she left us, he declared he had been waiting to hear about our escape from France and the much-publicized arrest in Spain. Reliving the ordeal was a painful experience for me, because it had been a while since I took a mental trip down that road. I re-created each and every moment as I spoke, and he sat silently, nodding a few times as if he felt my pain. I was completely comfortable in his presence, and the time just flew by. I thanked him for the meeting and returned to my room to join my wife and father-in-law.

We were the president's guests for two days. Each time we came around, I sensed a higher level of curiosity among some in his entourage. It seemed they had been awaiting our arrival with much interest. I found out that rumors of our adventurous escape from France to Spain had spread like wildfire. When I saw Usher at dinner that evening, he told me that the president had also been curious for a while and he looked forward to a meeting with the "Algerian revolutionary." On the third day of our stay, my father-in-law joined my wife and I in thanking the president again for his hospitality. I returned to Bloomington to focus on completing my thesis.

Barely two months after seeing the president, Algeria, my beloved country, gained her independence. She was finally free from the vestiges of colonial bondage and oppression. I was overjoyed when I heard the news. But I was more curious to know about the details of the transition of power. I immediately got in my car and headed for the highway—destination, New York. I quickly searched the radio and tuned in to the Voice of America station. They were broadcasting directly from Algiers. Pundits spoke about the hysterical enthusiasm that greeted GPRA President Ben Khedda when he landed in Algiers. I thought I was dreaming. The countryside,

My American Experience—Becoming a Scientist

they said, seemed to be awash in green and white Algerian flags, confetti was being tossed from the top balconies of apartments, and everyone from small children to elderly veiled women and bent men were waving frenziedly. All the frenzy was captured in the background as the journalist spoke. It was unbelievable. The emotions weighed heavily on my heart, and I became extremely homesick. When I pulled up at the mission after several hours of driving, the celebrations were in full effect. Chanderli, Boudjakdji, and a few others were all ecstatic. Everyone was speaking loudly and hugging each other. Some of the brothers waved our flag at the corner of the street, and many passing drivers honked their horns in support. It was a very proud day for all of us.

Not long after the euphoria had died down, I dropped everything and boarded a flight to Algiers. Some old comrades from the war arranged a meeting with Mr. Ben Bella, Algeria's first president. My initial impression of the man wasn't very good. He lacked the necessary requisites for our newly independent country. Nothing about our encounter seemed to persuade me to think otherwise. He had neither a coherent vision, nor a pack of sound ideas to start the country moving in the right direction. When we sat down

A Dream for Peace

to speak in a dimly lit office at a secret location, he was quick to get down to business. "What would you like to do in my administration?" he inquired impatiently—a bit too abrupt for my liking. "*Actually, I want nothing. I am here to serve my newly independent country. An office with a camping bed and some hardworking personnel will be a good start. I am sure you can appreciate that there are more difficult challenges ahead than we encountered during our armed struggle,*" I said. My heart was in the right place, but his views on education were contradictory to my principles. It was a disappointing encounter. He went on and on about his philosophy, sounding off with self-aggrandizing belligerence that became predictably destructive to our discussion. I thanked him for his time and left him sitting in the shadow.

At the time, there was a mass exodus of French immigrants, including Algerian Jews who held French nationality. The "*pieds noirs*," as they were called, were given a stark choice between "the suitcase or the coffin." They chose the suitcase. I was vehemently opposed to the policy. Either way, the government distributed vacated properties to our war veterans. But there were many ordinary citizens who took advantage of the opportunity and commandeered some homes for their families. Had the *pieds noirs* chosen to stay, they were promised a date with a coffin. I just could not understand why Ben Bella failed to take any action to stop the practice amid the rampant chaos in Algiers. I personally witnessed many fleeing French families, some of whom managed to make it to the port of call to join the masses that were already gathered there, waiting to board a ship. The situation was much worse at the ports of Annaba and Oran. In the midst of the unpredictable conditions on the ground, I became extremely frustrated and disappointed. Upon discovering that Ben Bella had opted for an orientation toward a bold form of socialism, surrounding himself with Trotskyists, I decided to return to the United States after only ten days. The warning signs had been there during the struggle. But I hoped our

My American Experience—Becoming a Scientist

leaders would seize the opportunity and take the high road—for an immediate peace and justice for all who chose to stay and help our new nation rebuild itself and become a strong democracy. On the long journey back to the States, I felt my heart grow heavier with each mile of separation from my dearest motherland. Despite my overwhelming sadness, I rested assured in the dream of returning someday to my ideal utopia.

President Ben Bella's first trip outside of Algeria was to New York to raise the flag for the admission of a newly independent country into the United Nations. From there, he flew directly to Havana to meet with Fidel Castro, despite objections by President Kennedy. His visit definitely placed Algeria in a unique category. It seemed he was eager to let the world know that he was planning on pushing the country into communism.

Toward the end of my doctorate, Ambassador Usher offered to have Antoinette join the Ivorian mission at the UN as his secretary. I gave my approval, despite knowing fully well that in so doing, we would end up living far apart. For her own sake, I knew that she would enjoy working around fellow Ivorians. Still, he convinced me that the move would also help boost her credentials and strengthen her résumé. At least in the interim, I thought I could commute between New Haven and Manhattan with ease, whenever I had a break from my teaching obligations. But even if the constant back and forth took its toll, we planned to put up with the situation until she gained the experience and could use the job as a reference in the future. She moved into a corporate apartment on 33rd Street in East Manhattan. In hindsight, I recognize that all the signs were there—the gesture of goodwill toward my wife was intended to draw me closer to Côte d'Ivoire. I continued to maintain contacts with President Houphouët-Boigny through Ambassador Usher.

In August of 1963, Sharon Ann Wilson and I enlisted to help organize the historic march on Washington, DC, which was led by the Reverend Martin Luther King Jr. It was a demonstration unlike no other. Police in the capital estimated that the participants had come from all over the US, amounting to over two hundred and fifty thousand, but that figure was challenged by objective minds to be around half a million. The organization of the event was impeccable—a fact that astonished many white Americans: it was a meticulously cultivated grassroots operation, organized for large numbers of people across state lines, and it was all done in an orderly fashion. The march lasted the entire day and culminated with the famous "I Have a Dream" speech by the charismatic civil rights leader.

Back in Bloomington, I successfully completed my doctorate and accepted the job at the Yale School of Medicine in 1963. I was deeply distraught when I went to part ways with the Konetzkas. The feeling was mutual. I bid farewell for the last time and promised I'd return to see them again. Although I had completed my educational commitments, there was still a part of me that felt the need to tackle the widespread racism around the very conservative state. I had managed to win the hearts and minds of the people, but sadly, there wasn't much I could do to help resolve their historic problems. Still, I was comforted by the fact that I had done my part to bring about a deeper understanding for the Algerian struggle. Such was the mood at the time of my departure.

I spent a week in New York with Antoinette and left to begin my professorial duties at Yale. The university's administration had reserved a stunning contemporary apartment in an exclusive East Haven complex for me. To my surprise, I was not allowed to continue with my research program at the university. I collaborated with Professor J. F. McCrea on cancerous tumors induced by the action of viruses and alumina on the belly of young rabbits. He had long been working on an idea supported by his late professor—the hypothesis that the abrasion of alumina mixed with the vaccinia virus promoted the formation of a melanoma. I made some significant strides in my own research on the topic and attained the prestigious Brown Coxe

My American Experience—Becoming a Scientist

Postdoctoral Fellowship in two consecutive years (1964 and 1965) at the School of Medicine.

I was the youngest professor at the School of Medicine, teaching students, some around my age or older. Those who took my virology class respected my style of teaching, and the syllabus quickly became very popular. The mostly sociable classes spurred innovative discussions, and at times, I engaged some of the brightest minds to see how far I could push them. I was strict when I needed to be, constantly urging everyone to work very hard, while still remaining approachable. I even befriended a few of my students. On my way to class during an early morning downpour in the spring, I ran into a student who didn't seem to be herself. When she walked up to me, I couldn't quite make out what she was saying. Her words slipped out softly through her quivering lips, and the tears welled up in her deep blue eyes. At first, I thought I overheard her mumble something about her grades. "Professor Berrah," she said, "I have decided to commit suicide." The tears rolled down her cheeks, and I couldn't believe my ears. "I beg your pardon? That is a very bad decision. Life is supposed to be a journey, not an end in itself." I stood silent for a second and asked her to follow me to my office. When she sat across from my desk, I gave her a cup of water and placed a call to her counselor, who wasn't at her office. While waiting for a call back, I found out that the poor girl was totally distraught and despondent over a breakup with her boyfriend. "Listen, I understand that you are in so much pain, but I won't sit here and pretend to know exactly what you must be feeling inside." She sobbed and clenched her jaws, and I offered some tissues.

I finally managed to get her to open up to me, and I listened until she poured her heart out. I noticed she was feeling better as we continued to speak. It seemed she just needed an outlet to vent and express her regrets. "I hope you will reconsider your decision. There is a lot more to live for. And you know, you will have many occasions to kill yourself, but now is not the right time, my dear." She smiled, and I knew the unintended humor had struck a positive chord. "I want you to remember that the university provides counseling and support to help you get through the tough times." I wrote down her counselor's number and handed it to her. "Thank you. Thanks for talking to me," she said. "Anytime," I replied. We walked out of my office. I didn't see her in class that day, but she seemed fine when I saw her a few days later.

The recent assassination of President Kennedy had taken a toll on the American psyche. Like most Americans, I was still in disbelief. In the immediate days after his funeral, I replayed in my mind tidbits of information from an editorial in a Moroccan newspaper about his speech on the Senate floor, imploring President Eisenhower to work with France, a staunch ally of the US, to bring the war to an end. I remember saying to some friends that I hoped he would become president someday. He was a senator in 1957, when he put forth a resolution proposing that the US should use its full powers to ensure Algeria's independence from France. Every Algerian applauded his position, and I vowed to follow his political career. At the time, I did not know what the future had in store for me. I was at Indiana University when he became president, and America was at its very best during the few years of his presidency. But the shock waves in the aftermath of the Dallas incident had brought an entire nation to its knees—a nation that wrestled with its conscience, while students on campuses everywhere struggled to cope.

He was assassinated about sixteen months after Algeria gained independence, at a time when I believed that his influence would have helped the US craft policies that were aimed at cultivating stability across Africa and most of the world. I visited the UN as often as I could and paid particular attention to how the US saw its role in Africa. I watched and listened to the debates and analyzed the words of Ambassador Adlai Stevenson so that I could dissect the details with my comrades at the Algerian mission. But ever since our independence, my visits to the mission seemed to attract a few criticisms from newly appointed diplomats, who assumed that they had reason to question my patriotism. Some never failed to bombard me with innuendos, utter rubbish, and nonsensical questions about my plans to return home: "Our country is independent now, brother Ghoulem. When will you go back to Algeria?" Oddly enough, I always shrugged them off and never once volunteered to let anyone know about my recent visit to our homeland. Without a doubt, nationalistic fervor was sustained at a fever pitch, after an almost eight-year battle for liberation that brought so much bloodshed to our people. Finally, we were all beaming with pride and euphoria, but I wasn't mad at those who observed me closely and seemed to question my lifestyle without any basis. I brushed off the gossip as just wildly exaggerated assumptions run amok and took their postulations with a grain of salt. I laughed at those who asked if I was a pragmatic capitalist who "switched cars every year," and when I overheard someone mentioning to an associate that the "love of luxury" was what kept me in the United States, I thought that the silliness would soon dissipate with the tide. Unbeknownst to them, I had quietly begun to grow more apprehensive about the bleak future that I foresaw in the cards for our beloved country under Ben Bella's Trotskyist policies. A major part of me felt that we were on an ill-conceived trajectory that could alter the soul of our nation. However, in those days, only a handful of Algerians understood what was at stake: we were going adrift with Ben Bella. It was only a matter of time.

    For several months, I kept a close eye on political developments in Algeria and continued to teach at Yale. I grew accustomed to commuting to New York on the weekends and perhaps became much too comfortable on the open highway. On the way back to New Haven, I was adrift in deep thoughts as I planned for the week ahead. Without the sound of sirens and flashing lights behind me, I wouldn't have realized how fast I was driving. The cop who pulled me over on the shoulder of the Hartford Highway

A Dream for Peace

in Connecticut on a late Sunday night said he'd clocked my speed at several miles above the limit. He ordered me to exit the car and hauled me off to the police station, where I was hit with a $300 fine. Since I wasn't carrying that much money in my wallet, I was allowed to place a call to a good friend of mine. He came to bail me out at around eight in the morning. I arrived on campus just in time to deliver my lecture. "Class, for your information, I prepared these notes in my cell at the Hartford police station, where I spent the night." There was a sudden burst of laughter, and some inquiring voices wanted to know if I was serious. "Yup. I was held up for speeding." I began the lecture. As soon as the class ended, a student handed me the key to his Porsche and asked if I would like to take it for a spin. "As long as you promise to sit next to me with your driver's license," I remarked. We had a good laugh. I headed straight to the lab to revisit an ongoing research project.

Although I was content with my life, I secretly nursed a chronic void in my beating heart. I had an overwhelming feeling that something was always amiss and my life's purpose was not being fulfilled. There was no doubt in my mind that my life's mission was somewhere out there, waiting patiently for me to rise to the occasion. Like many, I also wrestled with the Vietnam War and struggled to understand the disturbing US policies that seemed increasingly inconclusive and misguided. Past experience had taught me all I needed to know about the interference of major powers in the affairs of smaller sovereign nations. The situation seemed eerily familiar to me, very reminiscent of Algeria's liberation struggle.

Slowly but surely, my dreams morphed into voices that echoed louder on my conscience. I began to feel a burning desire to engage—to work for a better world—to help achieve peace and harmony among all humans. I was convinced that an equal level of development was the only way to accomplish such an objective. As I pondered the idea, I wrestled with a Gordian knot: continuing with my research on virus and cancer and making advances on curing the sick, or committing

My American Experience—Becoming a Scientist

to the pursuit of a long-standing dream to participate in Africa's development—to go and serve healthy people who often lacked the bare minimum.

I was full of mixed emotions when I finally arrived at the decision to cease all further research and teaching at Yale. I tendered my resignation letter at the chancellor's office and called Usher to notify him. He was absolutely delighted. He contacted the president immediately to relay the message and called back to inform me that the Ivorian leader looked forward to my arrival.

I addressed my peers at the end of the faculty's last meeting in December and announced my decision to leave. Upon learning that I was placing my scientific career on hold to move to Côte d'Ivoire, they were beyond shocked. A couple of professors in the room chimed in to ask that I reconsider. "It is the dream of many young people in America to come to Yale," said one associate. "And you, a professor, are quitting your position to pursue an adventure in the African bush?" I wasn't surprised at the question, but I ignored him with a subtle laugh. Perhaps, they took me for a madman or an enlightened zealot. Still, I remained undeterred. I thanked them graciously for their measured support and left.

A Dream for Peace

Dr. Walter A. Konetzka
September 8, 1923 – August 23, 1992

This chapter is dedicated to the memory of my dear friend and exceptional tutor, Dr. Walter A. Konetzka, Professor Emeritus, University of Indiana. I had the greatest honor and painful duty to deliver the eulogy at his memorial service.

My American Experience—Becoming a Scientist

Reprinted from JOURNAL OF BACTERIOLOGY
Vol. 83, No. 4, pp. 738-744   April, 1962
Copyright © 1962 by The Williams & Wilkins Co.
Printed in U.S.A.

SELECTIVE AND REVERSIBLE INHIBITION OF THE SYNTHESIS OF BACTERIAL DEOXYRIBONUCLEIC ACID BY PHENETHYL ALCOHOL

GHOULEM BERRAH AND WALTER A. KONETZKA

Department of Bacteriology, Indiana University, Bloomington, Indiana

Received for publication October 11, 1961

ABSTRACT

BERRAH, GHOULEM (Indiana University, Bloomington) AND WALTER A. KONETZKA. Selective and reversible inhibition of the synthesis of bacterial deoxyribonucleic acid by phenethyl alcohol. J. Bacteriol. 83:738-744. 1962.—The selective inhibitory effects of phenethyl alcohol on gram-negative bacteria were confirmed with a variety of species. At a concentration of 0.25%, phenethyl alcohol was bacteriostatic for gram-negative bacteria; gram-positive cells were unaffected. *Pseudomonas fluorescens* required higher concentrations of the compound for inhibition than did the other gram-negative bacteria, and the gram-positive, acid-fast mycobacteria resembled the majority of gram-negative bacteria in sensitivity.

In the presence of phenethyl alcohol, gram-negative cells formed long filaments. There was no net synthesis of deoxyribonucleic acid (DNA) in such cells, whereas protein and ribonucleic acid (RNA) syntheses were unaffected. Upon removal of phenethyl alcohol, multiplication of the cells immediately ensued, with concomitant DNA synthesis. Yeast extract stimulated both RNA and protein synthesis in phenethyl alcohol-treated *Escherichia coli*, but no detectable stimulation of DNA synthesis occurred under these conditions.

In 1953, Lilley and Brewer suggested the incorporation of phenethyl alcohol in nutrient media as a means of selecting for gram-positive bacteria from mixed flora. Phenethyl alcohol at a concentration of 0.25% in Trypticase soy agar completely inhibited the growth of seven gram-negative enteric organisms; under the same conditions, *Staphylococcus aureus*, *Streptococcus faecalis*, and *Diplococcus pneumoniae* formed colonies.

Because phenethyl alcohol is one of the few compounds which is more inhibitory to gram-negative than to gram-positive bacteria, this investigation was undertaken to determine the mechanism of the selective inhibitory action of phenethyl alcohol on gram-negative bacteria.

MATERIALS AND METHODS

Bacteria. The bacteria employed were obtained from the departmental stock culture collection and are listed in Table 1. Stock cultures on Trypticase soy agar slants were maintained at 5 C and transferred biweekly.

Preparation of inocula. Erlenmeyer flasks (50-ml), each containing 10 ml of Trypticase soy broth, were inoculated from the stock culture and incubated on a shaker for 18 hr at 37 or 30 C (depending on the optimal temperature of the bacteria). From these cultures appropriate dilutions were made in Trypticase soy broth, to obtain the desired initial cell concentration for a particular experiment.

Growth determinations. Viable counts were made by dilution of the cultures in sterile distilled water at room temperature and by spreading 0.1-ml samples on the surface of Trypticase soy agar plates. The colonies which developed were counted after 48 hr of incubation. Total counts were determined with a Petroff Hausser counting chamber. When turbidimetric measurements were desired, the cultures were grown in side-arm flasks consisting of a 250-ml Erlenmeyer flask to which an optically calibrated 18-mm test tube had been attached. The optical density of the cultures was determined in a Coleman Universal spectrophotometer at a wave length of 660 mμ.

Chemical assays. Samples (40-ml) of cultures of *Escherichia coli* H treated with 0.25% phenethyl alcohol were chilled and washed twice with cold distilled water. The washed cells were extracted with 10 ml of 0.25 N perchloric acid at 0 C for 30 min. After centrifugation, the pellet was extracted twice with 4 ml of 0.5 N perchloric acid at 70 C for 15 min. The combined extracts were used to assay for ribonucleic acid (RNA) by the orcinol reaction (Mejbaum, 1939) and for deoxyribonucleic acid (DNA) by the diphenyl-

738

amine reaction (Burton, 1956). The pellet from the hot perchloric acid extract was dissolved in 1 N NaOH at 90 C for 30 min, and protein was determined by the method of Lowry et al. (1951). Purified salmon-sperm DNA, purified yeast RNA, and bovine albumin were used as standards for DNA, RNA, and protein, respectively.

Phenethyl alcohol. The phenethyl alcohol was obtained from Matheson Coleman and Bell (lot no. 343248). After passage through a sterile sintered-glass filter, the compound was added to sterile medium to give the desired concentration. Any solution added to a culture containing phenethyl alcohol was prepared to contain the same concentration of phenethyl alcohol, to avoid dilution of the compound.

TABLE 1. *Effect of concentration of phenethyl alcohol on bacteria grown on Trypticase soy agar*

Bacteria	Control	0.1%	0.25%	0.35%	0.5%
Gram negative					
Acetobacter gluconicum 9.4*	+†	+	−	−	−
A. peroxydans 10.2*	+	+	−	−	−
A. xylinum X*	+	+	−	−	−
Aerobacter aerogenes 45	+	+	−	−	−
A. aerogenes 68	+	+	−	−	−
Chromobacterium violaceum X	+	+	−	−	−
Escherichia coli B	+	+	−	−	−
E. coli H	+	+	−	−	−
E. coli K12	+	+	−	−	−
Erwinia amylovora S	+	+	−	−	−
Klebsiella pneumoniae 56	+	+	−	−	−
Neisseria perflava 12	+	+	−	−	−
Proteus mirabilis H1	+	+	−	−	−
P. morganii A	+	+	−	−	−
P. vulgaris 1	+	+	−	−	−
Pseudomonas fluorescens X	+	+	+	+	−
Rhizobium japonicum UW	+	+	−	−	−
R. trifolii CB	+	+	−	−	−
Salmonella enteritidis X47	+	+	−	−	−
Serratia marcescens NIM	+	+	−	−	−
Shigella dysenteriae I	+	+	−	−	−
S. sonnei SBH	+	+	−	−	−
Gram positive					

TABLE 1.—*Continued*

Bacteria	Control	0.1%	0.25%	0.35%	0.5%
Bacillus cereus var. *mycoides* EM	+	+	+	−	−
B. megaterium EU	+	+	+	+	−
B. subtilis M	+	+	+	+	−
Corynebacterium hoagii X	+	+	+	+	−
Lactobacillus plantarum 17-5	+	+	+	+	−
Leuconostoc mesenteroides P60	+	+	+	+	−
Mycobacterium phlei X39	+	+	−	−	−
M. smegmatis 601	+	+	−	−	−
Staphylococcus aureus 209P	+	+	+	+	−
Streptococcus faecalis 10C1	+	+	+	+	+
S. lactis Tol	+	+	+	+	+

* These organisms were grown on glucose yeast infusion agar.

† Symbols: +, growth; −, complete absence of growth in 5 days.

RESULTS

Inhibition of bacterial growth. Bacteria were streaked on Trypticase soy agar containing different concentrations of phenethyl alcohol. The presence or absence of growth on the plates was determined after 5 days of incubation at the optimal temperature of each organism. The results (Table 1) confirm and extend those obtained by Lilley and Brewer (1953). The gram-negative bacteria were inhibited at a concentration of 0.25%; the gram-positive bacteria grew at this concentration and, in most cases, at a concentration of 0.35%. However, a few exceptions were noted. The gram-negative bacterium *Pseudomonas fluorescens* was not inhibited at 0.35%; on the other hand, the gram-positive, acid-fast *Mycobacterium phlei* and *M. smegmatis* were inhibited at a concentration of 0.25%. At a concentration of 0.5%, all organisms tested were inhibited except the streptococci.

Action of phenethyl alcohol in liquid media. Although the gram-positive bacteria formed colonies on solid media, such colonies required more time to become visible than they did on media without phenethyl alcohol. This observa-

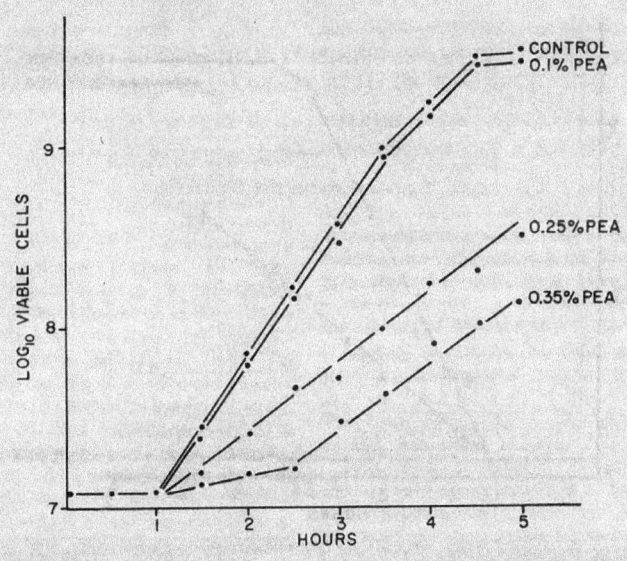

FIG. 1. *Effect of concentration of phenethyl alcohol (PEA) on growth of Staphylococcus aureus 209P in Trypticase soy broth.*

tion suggested that there was some inhibition of the gram-positive species. Consequently, phenethyl alcohol at different concentrations was added to Trypticase soy broth at the time of inoculation, and viable counts were made at 30-min intervals.

In Trypticase soy broth, phenethyl alcohol at a concentration of 0.1% had no effect on *S. aureus* 209P, but at 0.25 and 0.35%, the compound was progressively more inhibitory, as reflected by the decreased rate of growth (Fig. 1); however, the maximal crop of cells was eventually obtained. Similar results were obtained with *Bacillus subtilis* M. Although 0.1% phenethyl alcohol inhibited the growth rate of *E. coli* H, 0.25% completely inhibited multiplication of this bacterium (Fig. 2). These data also indicate that the phenethyl alcohol was not bactericidal, since the viable count of *E. coli* remained constant for 9 hr in the presence of 0.25% phenethyl alcohol. Essentially identical results were obtained with *Aerobacter aerogenes* 68.

Bacteriostatic action of *phenethyl alcohol. E. coli* H was inoculated into Trypticase soy broth and incubated until a concentration of 5×10^7 cells/ml was reached. The culture was divided into three equal portions, two of which received phenethyl alcohol at a final concentration of 0.25%. After 3 hr of incubation, one of the cultures which contained phenethyl alcohol was centrifuged, washed twice, and resuspended in Trypticase soy broth and incubation continued. Viable counts were made at 30-min intervals on all three cultures (Fig. 3). It is apparent (Fig. 2 and 3) that phenethyl alcohol is truly bacteriostatic, since upon removal of the compound the cells began dividing and at a rate higher than in the absence of phenethyl alcohol. This observation suggested that the cells were filamenting in the presence of phenethyl alcohol. Microscopic examination and measurements of the treated cells revealed that they had increased in length; within a few hours the cells were seven to ten times as long as the untreated cells.

Effect of penicillin on phenethyl alcohol-treated cells. Since *E. coli* H continued to increase in length in the presence of phenethyl alcohol, an experiment was performed to determine whether cell-wall synthesis continued under such conditions. Trypticase soy broth was inoculated with *E. coli* H and incubated at 37 C until the cell concentration reached 2.3×10^8 cells/ml. Phen-

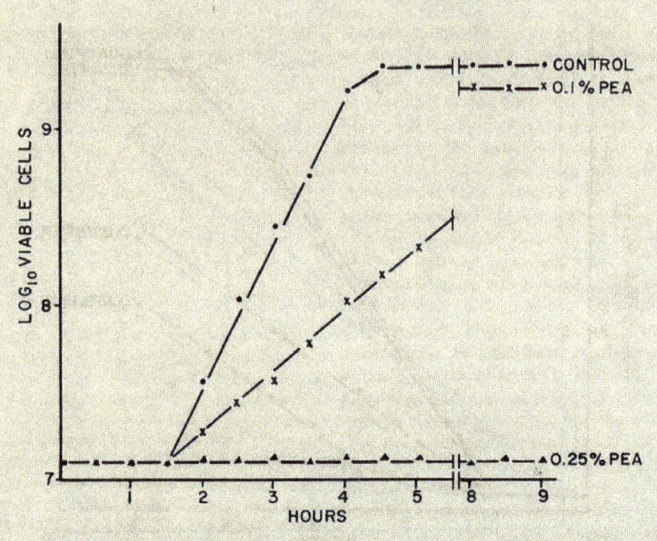

FIG. 2. *Effect of concentration of phenethyl alcohol (PEA) on growth of Escherichia coli H in Trypticase soy broth.*

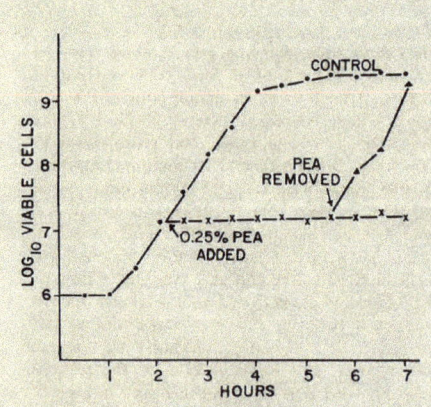

FIG. 3. *Bacteriostatic effect of phenethyl alcohol (PEA) on Escherichia coli H in Trypticase soy broth.*

TABLE 2. *Action of penicillin on phenethyl alcohol-treated Escherichia coli H*

Additions	Viable count Before addition	Viable count After addition (2.5 hr)	Kill
			%
None	2.3×10^6	7.2×10^8	—
PEA* (0.25%)	2.3×10^6	2.5×10^6	0
PEA (0.25%) + 10 units penicillin/ml	2.3×10^6	2.6×10^6	0
PEA (0.25%) + 25 units penicillin/ml	2.3×10^6	1.6×10^4	99.3
Penicillin (10 units/ml)	2.3×10^6	7.4×10^8	—
Penicillin (25 units/ml)	2.3×10^6	1.0×10^3	99.9

* PEA = phenethyl alcohol.

ethyl alcohol (0.25%) was added to five of the flasks; one flask received no phenethyl alcohol and served as the control. After the cultures had incubated at 37 C for 2.5 hr, viable counts were made and penicillin was added to four of the five flasks at the desired concentration. The cultures were incubated for an additional 2 hr, and the viable count of each culture was determined. The cells were killed to the same extent as they were in the presence of penicillin alone (Table 2). These results indicate that cell-wall

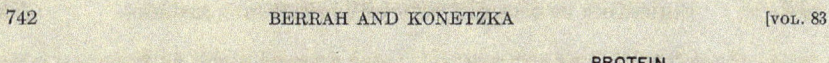

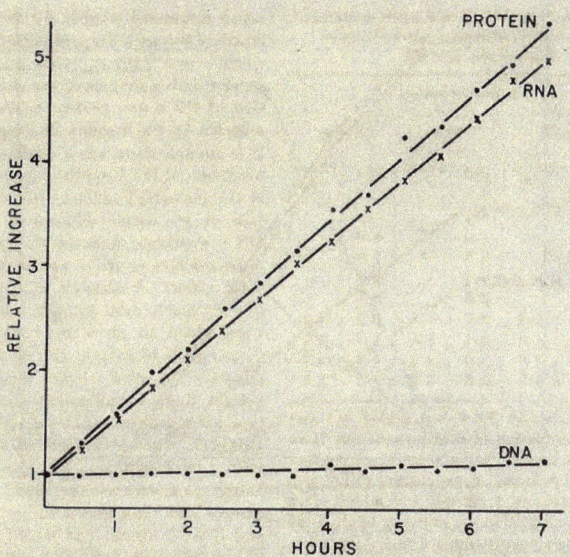

FIG. 4. *Effect of 0.25% phenethyl alcohol on the synthesis of proteins, RNA, and DNA in Escherichia coli H. The viable count remained at 5×10^7 cells/ml throughout the experiment. DNA: $1 = 3$ µg/5×10^7 cells. RNA: $1 = 13$ µg/5×10^7 cells. Protein: $1 = 50$ µg/5×10^7 cells.*

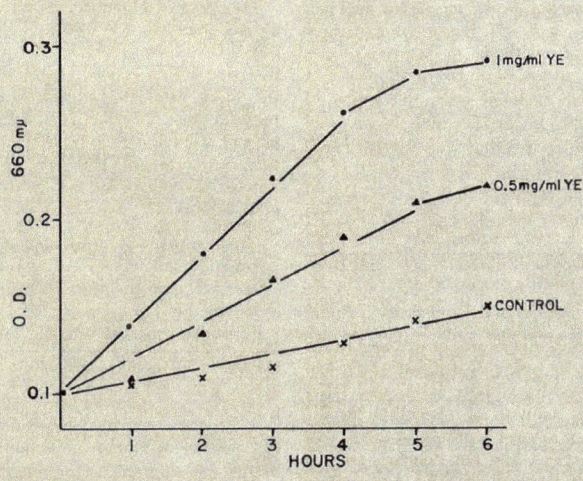

FIG. 5. *Effect of yeast extract (YE) on the turbidity of a culture of Escherichia coli H in Trypticase soy broth containing 0.25% phenethyl alcohol.*

TABLE 3. *Stimulation of RNA and protein synthesis by yeast extract in phenethyl alcohol-treated Escherichia coli H**

Time	Relative increase					
	DNA		RNA		Protein	
	PEA	PEA + YE	PEA	PEA + YE	PEA	PEA + YE
hr						
0	1.0		1.0		1.0	
1	1.0		1.5		1.6	
2	1.0		2.2		2.3	
2.5	1.0		2.5		2.7	
3	1.0	1.0	2.7	3.1	2.9	3.3
4	1.0	1.0	3.4	4.1	3.5	4.6
5	1.3	1.0	4.0	5.4	4.2	5.9
7	1.3	1.2	5.0	7.2	5.2	8.0

* Phenethyl alcohol (PEA) was added (0 time) at a final concentration of 0.25% to *E. coli* H in Trypticase soy broth when the total count had reached 5×10^7 cells/ml. Yeast extract (YE), at a final concentration of 1 mg/ml, was added after the cells had incubated in the presence of PEA for 2.5 hr. The initial concentrations of DNA, RNA, and protein per 5×10^7 cells were the same as those reported for Fig. 4.

synthesis continued during the inhibition of multiplication by phenethyl alcohol.

Action of phenethyl alcohol on nucleic acid and protein synthesis in E. coli. Because disturbances in the rates of synthesis of macromolecules result, in many instances, in the development of long filamentous bacterial cells, the action of phenethyl alcohol on protein and nucleic acid synthesis was investigated. Trypticase soy broth was inoculated with an overnight culture of *E. coli* H at a concentration of 5×10^6 cells per ml and incubated at 37 C until the culture had reached 5×10^7 cells per ml. Phenethyl alcohol was added at a concentration of 0.25% and the incubation continued; 40-ml samples were removed every 30 min for 7 hr and immediately chilled. After plating an appropriate dilution for viable counts, each sample was centrifuged in the cold, washed twice with cold distilled water, and the cells analyzed for protein, RNA, and DNA (Fig. 4). Upon addition of phenethyl alcohol there was little if any net synthesis of DNA, and after 7 hr the DNA had not doubled. On the other hand, net synthesis of RNA and protein had increased approximately fivefold in 7 hr, which accounted roughly for the increase in the length of the cells. The concentration of phenethyl alcohol was critical, since at concentrations greater than 0.25% there was considerable inhibition of RNA and protein synthesis, which was reflected by the inability of the cells to elongate. It is obvious there was a selective and reversible inhibition of DNA synthesis, since upon removal of the phenethyl alcohol, either by washing the cells or by simple dilution of the compound, DNA synthesis immediately proceeded.

Stimulation of RNA and protein synthesis by yeast extract. A number of complex materials (liver extract, meat extract, and yeast extract) were added to phenethyl alcohol-treated cells in an effort to reverse the inhibitory action of phenethyl alcohol. Upon addition of yeast extract, there was an apparent reversal of inhibition when determined turbidimetrically (Fig. 5). However, when examined microscopically, the cells were found to have simply increased in length. Analyses of the cells to which yeast extract had been added indicated that protein and RNA synthesis was stimulated, while there was no effect on net DNA synthesis (Table 3). The substance or substances responsible for the stimulation are under investigation.

DISCUSSION

The selective inhibitory properties of phenethyl alcohol originally described by Lilley and Brewer (1953) have been substantiated by this investigation, and with a greater variety of bacteria. For the most part, the growth of gram-negative bacteria was inhibited by 0.25% phenethyl alcohol, while the gram-positive bacteria grew at this concentration. However, there were two notable exceptions to this generalization. The gram-negative *P. fluorescens* was not inhibited until the concentration of phenethyl alcohol reached approximately 0.5%. The other exception was the gram-positive, acid-fast mycobacteria, which resemble the gram-negative cells in their sensitivity to phenethyl alcohol. This observation may imply that the solubility of phenethyl alcohol in lipids may play a role in its selective action, since the gram-negative bacteria contain a greater content of lipid material in their cell walls than do the gram-positive bacteria (Salton, 1960).

Although the mechanism for the selective inhibitory activity of phenethyl alcohol on gram-negative bacteria was not resolved by these studies, the compound was shown to be bacteriostatic at the concentrations usually employed. More significantly, however, the bacteriostatic action of the compound can be explained by its ability to inhibit selectively and reversibly DNA synthesis. The stimulation by yeast extract of RNA and protein synthesis in phenethyl alcohol-treated cells offers additional evidence for this selective inhibition of net DNA synthesis, for the addition of yeast extract resulted in an almost twofold increase in protein and RNA without any increase in DNA. This stimulation by yeast extract was unexpected, because the phenethyl alcohol-treated cells were in a complex medium, Trypticase soy broth. Yeast extract must be supplying some substance(s) which is limiting in Trypticase soy broth, since the turbidity increase appears to be a function of the yeast-extract concentration, without concomitant increase in cell numbers.

The formation of filamentous forms in the presence of phenethyl alcohol is similar to the observations of Barner and Cohen (1954) on a thymine-requiring strain of $E. coli$ and by Shiba et al. (1959) with mitomycin C. In each instance, the inhibition of DNA synthesis led to filament formation. However, inhibition with phenethyl alcohol differs in a number of important aspects. In the absence of thymine, the thymine-requiring strain rapidly loses the ability to form colonies (Barner and Cohen, 1954), while cells inhibited with phenethyl alcohol remain viable for at least 9 hr. Inhibition of DNA synthesis with mitomycin C is not reversible, but removal of phenethyl alcohol results in immediate initiation of cell division and DNA synthesis. Phage synthesis was not inhibited in the absence of thymine in the $E. coli$ mutant (Barner and Cohen, 1954) nor in the presence of mitomycin C with normal cultures of $E. coli$ (Sekiguchi and Tagaki, 1960). However, we have found a striking inhibition of T2 synthesis in the presence of phenethyl alcohol. The results of these experiments will be reported elsewhere.

The data obtained thus far do not allow for speculation of the mechanism by which phenethyl alcohol inhibits DNA synthesis. It is significant, however, that, in addition to being a reversible inhibitor of DNA synthesis, phenethyl alcohol is effective against a variety of bacteria, and therefore should prove a valuable asset in the study of the relationships between the synthesis of nucleic acids and the synthesis of proteins.

ACKNOWLEDGMENT

This investigation was supported by a grant (E-2570-C2) from the U. S. Public Health Service.

LITERATURE CITED

BARNER, H. D., AND S. S. COHEN. 1954. The induction of thymine synthesis by T2 infection of a thymine requiring mutant of *Escherichia coli*. J. Bacteriol. **68**:80–88.

BURTON, K. 1956. A study of the conditions and mechanism of the diphenylamine reaction for the colorimetric estimation of deoxyribonucleic acid. Biochem. J. **62**:315–323.

LILLEY, B. O., AND J. H. BREWER. 1953. The selective antibacterial action of phenylethyl alcohol. J. Am. Pharm. Assoc., Sci. Ed. **42**:6–8.

LOWRY, O. H., N. J. ROSEBROUGH, A. L. FARR, AND R. J. RANDALL. 1951. Protein measurement with the Folin phenol reagent. J. Biol. Chem. **193**:265–275.

MEJBAUM, W. 1939. Über die Bestimmung kleiner Pentosemenger, insbesondere in Derivaten der Adenylsaüre. Z. physiol. Chem., Hoppe-Seyler's **258**:117–120.

SALTON, M. R. J. 1960. Microbial cell walls. John Wiley and Sons, New York.

SEKIGUCHI, M., AND Y. TAGAKI. 1960. Effect of mitomycin C on the synthesis of bacterial and viral deoxyribonucleic acid. Biochim. et Biophys. Acta **41**:434–443.

SHIBA, S., A. TERAWAKI, T. TAGUCHI, AND J. KAWAMATA. 1959. Selective inhibition of formation of deoxyribonucleic acid in *Escherichia coli* by mitomycin C. Nature **183**:1056–1057.

INHIBITION OF REPLICATION OF BACTERIOPHAGE T2 BY PHENETHYL ALCOHOL*

Walter A. Konetzka and Ghoulem Berrah

Department of Bacteriology, Indiana University, Bloomington, Ind.

Received July 2, 1962

Berrah and Konetzka (1962) reported that the bacteriostatic action of phenethyl alcohol can be attributed to the selective and reversible inhibition of DNA synthesis in susceptible bacteria. This communication deals with the effect of phenethyl alcohol on the replication of the bacteriophage T2 in *Escherichia coli* H.

METHODS

Phenethyl alcohol, at a concentration of 0.34%, was added to an exponentially growing TSB culture of E. coli H at 5×10^7 cell/ml. The culture was incubated for 2 hrs, during which time there was no significant increase in cell numbers nor any net synthesis of DNA. However, RNA and protein increased approximately 3-fold. The methods employed for these determinations have been described previously (Berrah and Konetzka, 1962). After the 2-hr incubation period, 20 ml of the culture were filtered through a Millipore HA filter (47 mm), and the collected cells were resuspended in 5 ml of TSB + 0.34% PEA. One-tenth ml of a suspension of T2 at 5×10^{10} PFU/ml was added and the mixture aerated for 5 min. Two and one-half ml samples of the suspension were then filtered through a Millipore HA filter. One sample was washed on the filter with 3 separate

---

* This investigation was supported, in part, by a grant (E-2570-C2) from the U. S. Public Health Service.

Abbreviations: DNA - deoxyribonucleic acid; RNA - ribonucleic acid; PEA - phenethyl alcohol; TSF - Trypticase soy broth; PFU - plaque forming units; dCMP - deoxycytidine-5'-phosphate.

40 ml volumes of TSB + 0.34% PEA, and the cells were finally resuspended in 10 ml of the same medium; another sample was treated in an identical manner, except that the last 40 ml volume of TSB did not contain PEA, and the cells were resuspended in 10 ml of TSB without PEA. This procedure removed over 99.9% of the unadsorbed phage. The infected cells were appropriately diluted into TSB + 0.34% and TSB without PEA, respectively, incubated at 37 C, and samples were withdrawn at intervals and plated in the usual manner for the determination of a single step growth cruve (Adams, 1959). Samples were also treated with chloroform before plating to determine the intracellular phage (Séchaud and Kellenberger, 1956).

The methods for the single cell bursts were identical to those employed for the single step growth curve except that the infected cells were diluted immediately after the 5 min adsorption period to contain 0.7 infected cells/ml of broth with and without 0.34% PEA. The diluted samples were incubated at 37 C for 1 1/2 hrs before being plated. The addition of 2.5 ml of the seeded top agar to the PEA-containing samples diluted the compound sufficiently so that it was not inhibitory to the plating cells.

Bacterial cell counts were determined by means of a Petroff Hausser counting chamber.

RESULTS

A normal burst of approximately 200 PFU was observed in the control cells (Table 1), although these cells were in the presence of PEA for 2 hrs prior to infection and for the 5 min interval during the adsorption period. Despite the fact that DNA synthesis in the cells had been prevented for 2 hrs, removal of the PEA allowed normal replication of T2. However, in the presence of PEA there was a marked inhibition of T2 replication, as determined by the single step growth curve experiment. The burst size of the cells in the presence of PEA was approximately 4. The infected bacteria in the presence of PEA lysed to the same extent as the control cells, but there was no substantial increase in PFU. The number of morphologically identi-

Table 1

Effect of PEA on T2 Replication in E. coli H

Minutes after Adsorption	PEA Removed after Infection		PEA Present after Infection	
	PFU x 10^7/ml	Bacterial Cell Count x 10^7/ml	PFU x 10^7/ml	Bacterial Cell Count x 10^7/ml
10	4.8 (<0.01)*	5.6	5.1 (<0.01)	4.7
15	4.5		4.9	
20	5.1 (<0.01)		4.8 (<0.01)	
25	5.1		5.0	
30	4.6 (0.16)		4.9 (0.16)	
35	4.7		12.1	
40	1070.0 (1030.0)		19.3 (17.6)	
45	1070.0		16.2	
50	942.0 (976.0)		18.8 (15.9)	
55	960.0		22.6	
60	978.0 (954.0)	<0.5	18.8 (19.4)	<0.5

* The figures in parentheses represent PFU in the equivalent chloroformed samples.

fiable bacteria decreased over 90% in each case. The inhibition of T2 replication was further substantiated by the results of the single cell burst experiment (Table 2). The control cells released a normal number of PFU, but the PEA-treated cells released only 1-9 PFU/cell.

DISCUSSION

The selective and reversible inhibition of DNA synthesis by PEA is strikingly demonstrated by the effect of this compound on T2 replication. According to the data obtained from the single step growth curve experiment, synthesis of T2 is inhibited approximately 98%. However, this inhibition may indeed be 100%. With the high multiplicity of infection employed and the percent infection attained, the cells are probably multiply infected and, consequently, the infective units released from the PEA-treated cells may simply represent the "protein coating" of the input T2 DNA. The results also imply that phage proteins are being synthesized

Table 2

Effect of PEA on Single Cell Bursts of T2

Control Cells (PEA removed after infection):
  Number of Plates with plaques: 6
    Plaque counts: 124, 182, 251, 315, 352, 366
  Number of Plates without plaques: 42

PEA-inhibited Cells:
  Number of plates with plaques: 8
    Plaque counts: 1, 1, 2, 5, 6, 7, 7, 9
  Number of Plates without plaques: 40

---

in the PEA-treated T2-infected cells, for not only do the infected bacteria lyse (Table 1), but they also form phage-induced dCMP deaminase at about the same rate as untreated infected cells (Keck et al., 1960). An increase in phage proteins can also be detected by complement-fixation procedures. A detailed report of these findings is in preparation.

REFERENCES

Adams, M.H. 1956. Bacteriophages Interscience Publishers, Inc., N.Y.
Berrah, G. and Konetzka, W.A. 1962. J. Bacteriol., 83, 738.
Keck, K., Mahler, H.R. and Fraser, D. 1960. Arch. Biochem, Biophy., 86, 85.
Sechaud, J. and Kellenberger, E. 1956. Ann. inst. Pasteur, 90, 102.

A Dream for Peace

I understood exactly why he embodied such a strong desire to cater to the needs of the poor. We shared a common disposition—a strong belief to serve those in need. The synergy between us was quite natural. There were no absolute barriers in our beliefs, and our communal principles were integral to our core.

Chapter Six

The Call of Africa

On a bright and beautiful morning in 1965, I responded to the call of Côte d'Ivoire—the Call of Africa.

The words of the president had lingered in my thoughts ever since our fateful meeting at the Waldorf Astoria hotel: "More so than the United States, Africa is in much need of you. We are in the process of development. Come and help us. You will be free to leave and go wherever you want to go, when you tire. We have many things to do together." Those were the words that helped convince me that an equal level of development was the only path to peace and understanding among all people. I purchased my plane ticket for the maiden journey to the city of Abidjan—on a mission to serve Africa.

The moisture-laden subtropical breeze caressed my face and stroked my hair with a gentle touch as I moved swiftly across the tarmac with a group of passengers in the humid Ivorian climate. A welcoming party was waiting at the airport to usher me through immigration and customs. We sped off into the night as soon as my luggage was loaded into the trunk. Despite the long flight, I wasn't the least bit jet-lagged when I met the president at his official residence. We were like old friends who hadn't seen each other in quite sometime. He laid out a flawless welcome decorum in an intimate setting and immersed me in his signature hospitality. I learned right then that it was his nature to make one feel as though they were all that mattered in the moment. The evening's dinner reception was attended by family members who did their very best to make me feel at home.

Bright and early the next morning, I stepped out of the apartment to explore my new neighborhood and found myself immersed in beautiful greenery right outside my door. Perfectly trimmed cascading bougainvillea hedges with purple and white flowers lined the long walkway, stopping only to hug the large trunk of an ancient mango tree. I got in my car and drove on the shady street, awestruck by the unique formation of centuries-old baobab and silk cotton trees with extended overhead branches that crisscrossed each other to form a tunnel of leafy stems. I recalled a time when I marveled at something of the kind during a previous trip to Hawaii. Farther along the way, I approached the Ébrié Lagoon and was met by a spectacular array of bright orange poinciana trees in full bloom along the shore. It seemed the city had been built around the lagoon. I envisioned a future that was full of potential for further development.

My first day on the job, the president's chief of staff was assigned the responsibility of acquainting me with the cabinet and shepherding me into the system. In the beginning, I spent most of my time at the presidential palace among the curia of French advisors who had entrenched themselves like despots. They made no secret of the fact that they saw me as a competitor. The environment had an unwelcoming feel to it. In only a matter of days, the president sensed that I was not feeling comfortable around the members of his cabinet. When he appointed Ambassador Usher to the position of Minister of Foreign Affairs, he asked me to join him at the Foreign Ministry, although I continued to work directly with the president on an "as needed" basis. I became an advisor to the Foreign Ministry, mostly collaborating with Usher on missions. Due to the president's fear of flying, Usher represented him at every summit of the Organization of African Unity (OAU) and the General Assembly meetings at the UN.

The people of Côte d'Ivoire were always cheerful and

The Call of Africa

welcoming. When I first arrived, I noticed the many roadside vendors in the heart of the city. Sellers of souvenirs, artifacts, and produce quickly surrounded every vehicle that came to a brief stop in traffic. Most vendors sat at small tables by the roadside and sold tropical fruits or prepared meals in big pots and pans, set on large, colorful steel trays. After completing each transaction, they placed the cash beneath the tray and moved on to the next customer. Some women balanced their baked goods atop their heads and went after cars to haggle with passengers. I once found myself pulling over and calling out to a vendor to ask for directions. The unassuming woman left her stall of oranges and mangos and approached my vehicle, mindful of the money beneath her tray, but she did not seem to care. She stood beside my car and peeled an orange with the skill of an artisan, broke down the directions, and presented the fruit to me. I paid her and drove off. The culture was unique in that way. People seemed to trust each other.

Occasionally, I'd break away from the office and head out to Treichville market, the heartbeat of the city, to mingle with regular folks. This was my favorite place to go for leisurely walks in Abidjan. The ambiance was always lively in the picturesque market, swamped with tons of people, walking and bumping into each other. Most beggars I encountered seemed to share a common pattern. I'd give some money to one and they'd search for some change to split the money with their friends.

There were hoards of vibrant items for sale. I always walked casually through the many throngs of people, until I arrived at the fabrics section—one of the most intriguing and spectacular parts of the market. The highly popular clothing fabric *pagne*, an intricately woven cloth with multicolored patterns, was sold en masse. Each time I passed by, the boisterous vendors called out or tugged on my shirt to draw my attention to their merchandise. Stall after stall, I'd sift through artfully arranged fabric neatly laid out in rows across tables and mats.

A Dream for Peace

Creative vendors personalized their fabrics by naming them. Names such as *"my foot, your foot,"* referencing a pattern depicting the feet of an inseparable couple, or *"the capable husband,"* for a husband who takes good care of his wife, were very popular. The *pagne* fabric was common among women from the central and southern part of the country, but those from the north mostly wore a *boubou*, an embroidered traditional flowing wide-sleeved robe.

I was drawn like a magnet to their unique style of fashion and quickly learned the characteristics of customary attire. Some women's clothing were sewn as a long skirt, and married women distinguished themselves by draping an additional piece of cloth around their hips. Usually, the *camisole*, a blouse, is worn to complement the dress. A distinct *camisole* characterized the elegance of the Ivorian woman.

Through my friend Usher, I found out that the *pagne* played a major role in the country's customs. He expressed with such passion and pride a tradition that had filtered down through many generations—the young bachelor bringing the fabric to ask for the hand of the love of his heart. The number of *pagnes* brought to her home served as a measure of the dowry's value. Such was the nature of the ancestral practices of the ethnic Akan group. During funerals, *pagnes* were selectively chosen to accompany the deceased to his or her final resting place. Along with condolences, the fabric was also offered to members of the grieving family as a genuine gesture of sympathy.

I became a recurrent customer, patronizing a particular vendor who sold a unique fabric known as *kente*. The Ashanti tribe of the Gold Coast, modern-day Ghana, invented the traditional cloth, which is typically woven from silk, although I saw other varieties woven from threads such as rayon. When I first touched the cloth and learned about a tradition that had been passed down many generations since its inception when *kente* was produced exclusively for royalty, I was impressed. What makes it unique is the weaving technique used, coupled with the types of chosen colors and patterns, but more importantly, the skill of the designer. Like *pagne*, *kente* is also widely worn by both men and women. I just couldn't get enough of the traditional artists who designed the cloth with their own distinctive touch. I got to a point where I'd trace my fingers across the textile, and I knew I had to have it. I became a staunch collector before long.

In the arts and crafts section of the market, I shopped for wooden artifacts and beautiful ivory sculptures carved by exceptionally talented artists. Masks with wily expressions endowed with special ancestral meaning, carved wooden relics known as Ashanti dolls, and some copies of ancient masks, artificially aged to give an antiquated characteristic, were always on display. I looked forward to exploring the culture and traditions by mingling with the people, especially, on the weekends. My first exposure to a mini carnival of sorts came during a Sunday afternoon visit, when I heard the beating sounds of African drums in the Ébrié quarter of Treichville. As I inched closer, I could see from the distance two colorful stilt walkers in masks, towering above the crowds and gyrating to music. They were mounted several feet high, enough to touch the roofs of some local houses. I peered through the tight space and hovered above the shoulders of some onlookers to catch a glimpse of the troupe. The two stilt dancers wore white pants and straw skirts with striped indigo tops. "Ahhh! The *Dan Yacouba* dancers," I heard a shopkeeper say. The ethnic group was known for the historic tradition. Their performers marveled with acrobatic maneuvers and pulsating dance routines to the beats of *djembe* and *gangan* drums, among other traditional instruments. I was totally transfixed. It felt like the heartbeat of Africa in full regalia. I indulged for several minutes and applauded with everyone when a young girl, about four years old, was catapulted toward a knife-wielding daredevil who caught her without incident. I placed some money in a large calabash as soon as a masquerading dancer held it up to my face.

The humming rhythms remained in my mind for sometime, and I promised myself that I would someday learn about the roots of local traditional dances. Within months, I became acquainted with the different folklores and performances, and connected their origins to specific tribes. Dancers and customary festivities were integral to welcoming ceremonies for visiting dignitaries and during state jamborees. Names of dances such as the Goly and the Kotou stemmed from the Baoulé tribe; the Zaouli was a Gouro tribal dance. Every dance had ancestral significance and ritualistic connotation. Whenever I returned to the market on the weekends, I frequently bartered with merchants selling gold and silver filigree jewelry, mostly from Senegal and Guinea. The market was a melting pot of tribes from all over West Africa. Several languages, dialects, and variations of the French language were spoken loudly everywhere. It seemed everyone felt at home in the country. There was much fraternity and harmony among the citizens and immigrants. Things looked promising, and the country was poised for growth under its visionary leader.

In my first official meeting with President Houphouët-Boigny, I informed him that I was committed to serve with a purpose—to help improve the conditions of life for all people, and to achieve peace, justice, and harmony among all humans. "Côte d'Ivoire has chosen the path of capitalism," I said. "This in my opinion is a policy that typically imposes a degree of hardship on some citizens in society." He smiled and said, "My son, what matters is not the label but the contents in the bottle. Slogans do not matter, as long as we keep moving in the path of progress." From that moment, I felt very close to him—both spiritually and politically.

The president unveiled an ambitious agenda to build a modern Côte d'Ivoire, and he adjusted his policies accordingly. He had long nurtured these plans since his entry into politics. Each and every time we sat down together, he recounted his struggles to me, as he reflected on his journey and life's purpose. *"When I was a child, I had an affliction for mangoes. I never missed an opportunity to climb up a mango tree just to pluck some ripe fruit. But one day, I almost lost an eye to a swinging tree branch that grazed my cornea as I reached for a mango. I promised to never eat the fruit again."* "Mr. President," I said, "you have a peculiar way of looking at things." We laughed. I was pleasantly surprised to also learn that he had a passion for dancing, and he'd become a very good dancer over the years. *"I gave up the habit at the age of twenty, when I graduated from medical school. I decided not to be a slave to my passions."*

After graduating at the top of his class from the School of Medicine in Dakar, he returned to Côte d'Ivoire. *"I took on the fight against colonial injustices. While working at the main hospital in Abidjan, I organized my fellow African doctors to protest against substandard conditions in the African patients' wing of the hospital."* He paused briefly to reflect. *"The Europeans, of course, were housed in a separate wing, very high-quality facilities, and given the utmost care."* In retaliation, the ruling colonial government transferred him to a medical center with extremely poor facilities in Guiglo, a region in western Côte d'Ivoire. *"I took on the challenges under extreme circumstances and remained undeterred. I had committed to serving for the good of the people. In fact, I invested my personal funds and began providing limitless assistance, not just to the local population but also to the medical center."*

The excellent evaluation given by different French health inspectors that visited the medical center impelled the colonial administration to send him on a new assignment to Abengourou, a region in the eastern part of the country. Due to the sizeable French immigrant population in the area, the local medical center was exclusive to European doctors. There were large numbers of cocoa and coffee plantations in the region, and the labor force was subjected to all sorts of injustices. Confronted with the deplorable situation, he sought to remedy certain abusive trade practices by

A Dream for Peace

intermediary buyers who purchased cocoa from local farmers at ridiculously low prices. As a result of exaggerated fluctuations in the base wholesale values, prices fell dramatically on occasion without a logical explanation. Realizing the nature of the scheme, he pushed the farmers to refuse the sale of their products. He could relate to the situation, because he had been raised in a family of farmers that owned the most extensive lands and plantations in the region of Yamoussoukro. He organized the farmers of Abengourou, formed an association to defend their interests, and pushed the government to include a fair index pricing structure for their products.

President Houphouët-Boigny promoting rural farming.

Abuses were widespread and not limited to farmers alone. Landowners were also victims of some malpractices. Although they had the responsibility of cultivating crops on their own land, farmers were required to spend a specific number of hours working on farms belonging to colonial settlers. The president referred to the colonial law as disguised slavery. "I was not about to sit idly by and watch such deplorable acts of malfeasance continue without a fight. I started to organize the workers and petition for the abolition of forced labor, but the tension between the colonialists and the farmers began to rise when they refused to perform their duties under the forced labor act."

"You see, my son, in the midst of dealing with the social unrest, I fell in love with a young woman of exceptional beauty." The president had a habit of making light of a serious affair. I laughed at the unexpected segue. "But seriously, she was from the Agni[24] traditional royal family of Abengourou—a Muslim. Her name was Khadija.[25] I'm sure you know the name's origin—a prestigious name in Islam?" I agreed. "Her father thought I was unfit to marry her because I was not a Muslim." Nonetheless, after overcoming many obstacles, her family finally accepted him, and their union was sealed. She remained a devout Muslim, he remained a practicing Catholic, and they were blessed with five children.

Having arrived at a stalemate, amid continuing rising tensions between the colonial administration and farmers, he wrote an article, titled "We are besieged by grand theft." Published under a fictitious name in *Le Trait d'Union*, a French socialist newspaper, he condemned and denounced oppressive colonial practices. With the worsening situation, the administration soon deemed him a troublemaker, and he was transferred to Dimbokro township in the center part of the country. Barely a few weeks on the job, he was again reassigned to the town of Toumodi, near his hometown of Yamoussoukro. Due to the untimely passing of his brother, he decided to stop practicing medicine and moved to take on the duties of a tribal chief in Yamoussoukro.

He had been born into chiefdom and stood in line to inherit the responsibility of becoming the traditional king of the Baoulé tribe of Akoués. He was only five years old at the time the throne

---

[24] An ethnic group in southeast Côte d'Ivoire and Ghana.
[25] Wife of Prophet Muhammad (peace and blessings be upon him).

was vacated. I told him, "At five years old, Mr. President, I was in kindergarten, learning to read and recite the Qur'anic verses." He smiled. "You were lucky, because my sadness began at the age of five." I could not begin to imagine the emotional impact on him. "That was an awesome responsibility for a boy. You had not even lost your first tooth." He laughed. The elders knew that he was too young to ascend to power; hence, his stepfather was assigned the responsibilities of a regent. By the time his stepfather passed away, Félix Houphouët was pursuing a career in medicine. He asked his younger brother to take the reins. "I wanted to travel the country to help the indigents who were desperately in need of care."

I understood exactly why he embodied such a strong desire to cater to the needs of the poor. We shared a common disposition, a strong belief to serve those in need. The synergy between us was quite natural. There were no absolute barriers in our beliefs, and our communal principles were integral to our core. "In my case, Mr. President, I traversed the remotest regions and braved many treacherous terrains in Morocco to care for several patients. That was my calling, and it beckoned loudly. I know exactly what you must have felt in your heart." We connected so deeply on many levels. Looking right at me, at times seemingly expressing a subtle impassiveness, he appeared to gather his thoughts. "When my younger brother passed away, I was left with no other choice. I settled into my role in Yamoussoukro and assumed responsibility for the vast family plantations." As a farmer, he began to cultivate a plan to use the chieftaincy as a platform for positive change. "My unwavering support for farmers' rights became an integral part of my life," he told me. "That was an amazing transition, Mr. President," I said. "You went from one side of the spectrum to the other, but the mission remained the same—to improve the lives of the downtrodden by using God's gifts as a force for good." He nodded in agreement. "So, I quickly came up with a strategy to organize the nation's farmers."

The Call of Africa

He cofounded the Syndicat Agricole Africain[26] (SAA) in Abidjan in 1944, doing so with the help of some rich farmers, including Joseph Anoma, a very charming and sophisticated gentleman, whom I had the highest regard for. The national organization united the majority of Ivorian farmers and helped promote Nana[27] Houphouët's ideas. His objective was to impose a better remuneration for agricultural products, improve the wages for farm workers, and abolish forced labor. He recounted the entire ordeal to me. "In those days," he said, "the average daily wage of a farm worker was fixed at 3.50 *francs*. When I was called to head the union of African farmers by the landowners, I immediately increased their wages to 20 *francs*, and despite the increase, my calculations revealed that the agricultural process was still profitable." As expected, the colonial powers dragged him to court. "This was an attempt to intimidate you, Mr. President."

A sardonic smile appeared on his face. "But of course. Little did they know that I was steadfast. I wasn't about to bow to their wishes. They lodged a complaint against me in Paris, at Rue Oudinot—the Colonial Ministry." "Ahhh. I'm not surprised, Mr. President," I said. He continued: "Lucas, then Director of Political Affairs, was sent to Abidjan to investigate the allegations, and I was dragged all the way to Dakar, to the office of then Governor General Digo, to face charges." I agreed: "They were relentless. I know the colonialists. They are always insistent on having their way." He nodded and took a glass of water from the butler. I grabbed a glass of orange juice from the tray. "A jurist by the name of Joste was the spokesman for the colonialists. I began to illustrate with chalk on a blackboard to prove the point that even by paying a 20 *francs* daily wage to workers, operations would continue to remain profitable. As a consequence of my ingenious argument, Digo presumptively

---

[26] The African agricultural union.
[27] Tribal king (chief) in the Akan culture.

A Dream for Peace

concluded that the colonialists could continue paying their farm workers 3.50 *francs*, but they could not impose their decision on African landowners who chose to pay higher wages to their farm workers." I was impressed. "Congratulations, Mr. President. Their heartless behavior pushes us to fight for justice." "Indeed, my son," he responded. "I also managed to convince them that one could not force everyone to work for 3.50 *francs* per day. As well, those who owned over two hectares of land could no longer be forced to leave their plantation to work on the farms of the colonial masters."

Despite the favorable verdict, he knew there was still more work to do. He believed that the decision should also apply to all landowners and workers, not just the privileged few. This had to be done by legislation, and he understood that he would have to embark on a political struggle in order to dismantle the entrenched powers of colonial exploitation. "So that was the reason why you ran for office and became a congressman?" I asked. "Absolutely. I needed them to put the verdict into law. And at the right moment, the legislative order allowing for the candidacy of Africans from francophone colonies into the French National Assembly paved the way for me to do just that. I ran for office and won the election." "Congratulations, Mr. President," I said. A boyish smile appeared on his face. One of his aides walked in and mentioned an important phone call. "Pardon me, but I have to take that call. Let's continue our conversation in Yamoussoukro. Please make the necessary preparations to come with me for the weekend." "Certainly," I said. "Much obliged. I look forward to spending the weekend with you."

He took me to see his sisters on a Saturday morning, shortly after breakfast at his residence, and introduced me as a "new family member." They were very curious and expressive. Though I couldn't quite make out what they were saying in their native Baoulé language, it seemed they were more than happy to welcome me into their home. We spent about half an hour with them and left to tour the president's ancestral museum. He personally delighted in

The Call of Africa

giving me an orientation into the past, ensuring that I understood and appreciated the minutest details of ancestral craftsmanship. It was as if his mere presence in the museum had thrust him back into his traditional role as a chief. His energy was transformed into a purveyor of unparalleled cultural decency. The pride was unabashedly genuine and authentic. I learned a whole lot about my new family.

Back at his office, we continued our conversation about his ascension into political relevance. "It seems to me that the independence of your country was not an immediate objective once you arrived in Paris." The question had been on my mind since our last conversation. "Of course, my son. But timing is everything. An independent Côte d'Ivoire was always the main objective, but when I arrived in Paris as a congressman in the Assemblée Nationale, my first act was to introduce a bill to abolish forced labor in the francophone African territories. The so-called Houphouët-Boigny Act was adopted in 1947. You know, I was pragmatic enough to realize that things should happen progressively. I believed that the people needed to become academically astute in order to manage their political affairs at the national level." In fact, his goal was to spread the vision beyond the borders of Côte d'Ivoire, into the entire community of francophone African territories. "In the year 1946, I joined Modibo Keïta [Mali's future president] and a few friends from other francophone colonies to launch the Rassemblement Démocratique Africain[28] [RDA] in Bamako. Our initial aim was to push for the emancipation of the people of Africa, but we also organized ourselves into major political parties across the francophone territories. Keep in mind that I had already forged ahead with the formation of the Parti Démocratique de Côte d'Ivoire[29] [PDCI] months earlier, and that became the Ivorian branch of the RDA."

---

[28] African Democratic Rally.
[29] Democratic Party of Côte d'Ivoire.

A Dream for Peace

In the next elections, he campaigned for the Second Constituent Assembly. Promising during his travels throughout the regions of Haute and Basse Côte d'Ivoire that, if elected, he would not go to Paris alone, he planned to take along with him many young Ivorian students on a mission to advance their education. They would return to help develop their country. "This was an unprecedented visualization of the future, Mr. President, and a very wise move. How did you get it off the ground?" He placed both hands on the table and smiled. I observed the sparkle in his eyes. "After I won, I kept my promise and immediately set things in motion. Through a highly competitive process, we selected three hundred of the best students from every *école primaire secondaire* [EPS] in the country and propositioned the administration to help enroll them in secondary schools around France. There were no high schools in Côte d'Ivoire at the time." The central colonial administration systematically dismissed the initiative. In the end, the number of children able to depart from Abidjan was reduced to 148, including 13 girls, although there were still several obstacles to overcome. The students who had come to Abidjan from all over the country, had to endure a long wait—from the beginning of August to the end of October. Assemblyman Houphouët-Boigny applied for a scholarship for the candidates, but the central colonial administration opposed it, arguing that the colony did not have sufficient resources to meet such expenses. Thankfully, he was the president of the SAA at the time. He appealed to the organization and convinced its members to take on the responsibility of paying for the scholarships for the sake of the country's future.

Not to be outdone, the colonial administration put up some more roadblocks. He persevered and sent his representative, Dr. Auguste Denise, to the Ministry of Colonies in Paris to present the union's account statement and show proof of funds. Upon submitting the statement, the Minister of Colonies finally gave his approval. When he thought they had overcome the final hurdles,

The Call of Africa

little did he know that incoming passenger vessels would not be allowed to dock at the port of Abidjan. No one seemed to know the reason why. When he was told about the blockade, he contacted the governor of Côte d'Ivoire, André Latrille, and asked him to intervene. The governor had been a supporter of the initiative, but unfortunately, he lacked the authority to make decisions. He received his orders from the central administration in Paris. This time was different, however, and without waiting to hear from Paris, Latrille took the courageous initiative to requisition a French battleship at the port of call in Abidjan. The children were able to board the Frigate, *L'Aventure*, and set sail for France. The entire episode was later dubbed "Aventure 46."

The poor children were confined to the main deck of the battleship, under very difficult conditions, until they docked at the port of call in Dakar. There, they switched ships and boarded an ocean liner to Marseille. As fourth-class passengers, they were kept in the lowest decks. The president recounted how he held his breath while awaiting the news of their arrival. "I was in Paris at the time, praying daily and imploring the Almighty to oversee the success of the expedition." He heard about their arrival in Marseille through a friend and fellow assemblyman from Côte d'Ivoire, Daniel Ouezzin Coulibaly, who received and housed them in the comforts of a large villa.

They arrived in the month of November, in the chill of winter, wearing clothes that were well suited for the tropics. "I saw to it that the Red Cross took on the responsibility of clothing them before they boarded the train to Paris," he said. "I am sure you were relieved at last, Mr. President." He smiled broadly. "I was beyond relieved, my son. I can't begin to describe the joy I felt in my heart when I finally welcomed them in Paris." I smiled, watching him get a little animated as he relived the historic event. "My friend Léon Robert was counselor of the French Union at the time. He organized their enrollment into various schools across France and toured the establishments occasionally to ensure their well-being. I received them regularly at my own residence in a suburb of Paris, and I made sure they went to Côte d'Ivoire for the holidays every two years." I was impressed. "That was quite an undertaking, Mr. President. The nation owes a debt of gratitude to Léon Robert."

His gaze traced the dusky horizon, and he seemed to drift into space. "Mr. President, as a matter of fact, we share something in common." He turned his gaze back to me and smiled. I began to narrate the events of 1956: "After the massacre of students by the OAS at the University of Algiers, the UGEMA leadership held an emergency meeting to look into the merits of embarking on a general strike. I was extremely concerned about the future repercussions that a decision of such magnitude would impose on Algeria once we achieved independence. I pointed out that we stood to lose our young intellectuals unless we organized a resettlement for those students who might abandon their studies in France. Either way, I was outvoted. When I arrived in Rabat, I mobilized the union and met with diplomats from different embassies. In the end, I procured scholarships for our students and had them admitted into universities in Eastern Europe." He beamed from ear to ear—"*Ah bon, ah bon.*" We had been seated in his office for a couple of hours. I looked over at the presidential desk and thought of the day's tasks, which entailed more of the same—transcribing his policy dictations and reviewing the Foreign Ministry's mission strategy. But we were in a reflective mood that day. He marveled about my audacious involvement in the Algerian Revolution and recalled his own actions at the French National Assembly in 1947, when he led a major effort to prevent an armed conflict between France and his "Algerian brothers." Breaking from the assembly members, he spoke out against the introduction of a bill that institutionalized an unjust establishment of a dual electoral college system by the French leadership in colonial Algeria's assembly. It was a despicable attempt at voter suppression. The decree established unfair practices of vote tabulation and declared that a single vote by a French citizen from the first college was equivalent to eight votes of Algerian Muslims in the second college. "I denounced the proposal, but sadly I was outvoted and the legislative body moved to adopt the measure." I was fascinated by the fact that he had been a force for good and had done his part to help bring some fairness to the process in Algeria. "President Houphouët was an early proponent of a peaceful resolution in the Algerian conflict?" I asked just to be sure. "This is quite amazing." He was impassive. "I was opposed to any escalation in the Algerian war. I was also concerned about the mounting casualties and the toll on the Algerian people. But once he became president, my dear friend and confidant, General De Gaulle, informed me of his intention to liberate Algeria. It was clear that he knew what was at stake, and he was mindful of the military that had been key to his ascension, hence he planned to take incremental steps to avoid upsetting them, even if it was his wish to move swiftly."

I really appreciated being led behind the scenes to learn about the inner workings of the political apparatus that was at play during our liberation war. The more I absorbed the president up close, the more smitten I became by his compassion and dexterity. Like a traditional Akan chief, wise beyond his years, he embodied very likeable characteristics that were mostly rooted in his love of the Almighty and peace among men. He was never one to speak too much about his accomplishments, hence our conversations always left me mesmerized. "You know, a very good Algerian friend of mine, Ferhat Abbas, once a congressman and colleague at the National Assembly, was quite the eloquent speaker," he recalled. "I always beamed with pride whenever he stood at the podium to plead the Algerian case. During a debate about introducing Social Security in Algeria, speaker after speaker stood at the dais and spoke against the proposal. Most of our colleagues pointed out that since Muslim men could take on several wives, Social Security would be very difficult to implement. The vast majority seemed to agree with that line of reasoning. When Ferhat Abbas took to the podium, he said, "*My fellow assemblymen, I beg to differ with you on this point. Stop the hypocrisy. At least, unlike you, we don't have concubines. We marry our women and make it official.*" According to the president, there were murmurs and subtle laughter in the hall.

Despite the fact that the RDA was a large movement comprising of sixteen francophone African colonies, there were two representatives from each colony at the National Assembly. At the time, the French Communist Party, a much larger organization, was the only group that shared some of the RDA party's positions. The two parties merged for strategic reasons and gained more seats in the assembly as a result. But the staunch opposition to France's stranglehold on its colonies created the perception that the partnership was a threat to the government's colonial interests. Not to mention, because of the Cold War, the Communist Party's positions became increasingly favorable toward Moscow. Soon enough, the floor of the assembly was rife with derogatory slogans and name-calling, interlaced with caricatures of communists and RDA members. "A few of my fellow assemblymen gave me the nickname 'Houphouët the Stalinist.' I decided to pull the RDA away from the Communist Party and join forces with l'Union Démocratique et Socialiste de la Résistance[30] [UDSR], when party members in Côte d'Ivoire began to face unwarranted persecutions by the French, who were adamant on stopping the spread of communism."

He worked in the administration of Guy Mollet and cowrote the Loi-cadre (Reform Act) with Gaston Defferre, a law that granted domestic autonomy to the overseas territories. In his new position, he managed to help francophone Africa reach an unprecedented milestone. "I was a Minister of State and a member of the Constitutional Committee. Upon my recommendation, De Gaulle

---

[30] The Democratic Socialist Union of the Resistance.

inserted an article in the constitution of 1958, allowing for each of the members of the community to seek independence at any time. Without that, no African state would have managed to get out of the community of francophone nations." Under the framework, Côte d'Ivoire chose to become an independent nation in 1960. It was around the same time that the "*Aventure 46*" students graduated from universities across France. There were several doctors, pharmacists, engineers, teachers, attorneys, dentists, civil servants, and diplomats who returned to help build a modern Côte d'Ivoire. Some of them were assigned ministerial posts in his administration. President Houphouët honored Governor André Latrille's actions by dedicating one of the largest boulevards in Abidjan to his memory.

With cabinet members in 1956—Houphouët-Boigny, seated.

I was not only impressed by the success of his visionary prowess, but above all, his patience and tenacious acumen were highly transmittable attributes. Mulling over his words, I was overcome by an overwhelming sense of purpose. While I pondered the magnitude of the challenges that lay ahead, I digressed briefly to refocus my thoughts on a detailed orientation of his chosen method of governing—through a one-party system, the PDCI. "There is much synergy between the government and the PDCI itself. We cooperate on everything and discuss ideas in think tanks to try and find common ground between party directives and governmental actions. In other words, the government ultimately implements the party's policies and ideas." I found it to be an interesting approach to the science of politics. At first glance, one would be tempted to think that the format leaned toward a complex experiment—a form of totalitarianism in public policy, but then again, that would be a reductive vision. I listened intently. "Normally, the various political ideas that evolve within the party are expressed freely through an ongoing dialogue. We hold a party convention every five years to outline party policies and elect a president who determines our charter. The party appoints a secretary-general to oversee the management and coordination of the organization." Under the secretary-general's leadership, there are national secretaries and departmental delegates who take on responsibilities akin to pulleys equipped with upward and downward transmission belts. They were charged with communicating the party's ideas and decisions to the many sectors and subsectors of the general public. It was also their responsibility to share the concerns expressed by the party's base and report their findings to the leadership. To ensure that the commoner on the street would have a voice, the party's base was encouraged to present ideas and suggestions on their shared concerns. Members of the Bureau Politique, the central advisory body of the party, as well as those of the Committee of Wise Men and those of the Grand Conseil, were also appointed at the convention.

    Back in 1963, the president was told about a conspiracy to overthrow his government on two occasions. The country's security apparatus was placed on high alert, and a number of individuals were arrested, tried, and imprisoned for crimes against national security. He later discovered that he had been misled by the secret service. The facts had been uncovered only a few weeks prior to my conversation with him, and he had taken the necessary steps to rectify the rather unfortunate miscarriage of justice. He remained saddened by the episode, and the thought of incarcerating the innocent victims caused him great agony. "What happened was a total miscarriage of justice, and I have since taken measures to ensure better oversight. Although, it is a bit too late for those who were falsely accused." He was sure that such incidents would not be repeated.

In August 1967, President Houphouët-Boigny and his wife were invited to the White House by President Lyndon B. Johnson. After the state dinner, the president returned to New York and stayed at the Waldorf Astoria for a couple of days. Around midday, he called and asked me to greet Senator Robert Kennedy in the lobby. I brought the small delegation to his suite. The two men originally met when the senator represented the US at Côte d'Ivoire's independence celebrations in 1960. They met again in DC during an official state visit and continued to stay in touch after President John Kennedy's assassination.

I remained with the guests at the request of President Houphouët. After disappearing for a brief moment, he soon reappeared with a souvenir and handed it to the senator's interpreter, indicating that his services wouldn't be needed. "Who will be the translator, Mr. President?" I whispered in his ear. "You." I was absolutely taken aback. "But I am not an interpreter," I muttered. "Success comes only after you put out the effort. Try your hardest. I am sure you will succeed." I escorted the interpreter to the elevator and returned to take up my new assignment. It felt like a daunting challenge. Though I stumbled multiple times, the president and the senator were very patient and gracious. After that experience, I studied very hard in the ensuing days until I was confident that I had acquired the swiftness to switch with ease from one language to the other.

A Dream for Peace

Côte d'Ivoire's official interpreter was a young woman at the Foreign Ministry. But at times, the president called on me to translate his statements for visiting English-speaking dignitaries. Hence, I was the interpreter at a welcoming ceremony for President Julius Nyerere of Tanzania. Upon arrival at the airport in Abidjan, he first spoke in English and then he switched to say a few words in Swahili, a language infused with about 25 percent Arabic. I caught some of the nuances but lost track of the gist. When I stopped with the translation, he paused to smile at me, as if to signal that he understood why I could not go further, prompting his interpreter to take over the process. "I hope that this visit will bring about a more beneficial meaning for both countries and for the African continent. I am bringing brotherly greetings from Tanzanians to the people of Côte d'Ivoire, and I wish to pay tribute to President Houphouët-Boigny for ensuring the independence of this great nation." The president thanked him and delivered his statement: "Nothing in our view symbolizes more profoundly the will of the countries of our great African continent and the desire of its people to understand each other and cooperate with a view to unite. Nothing underlines better their will to reduce instances and particularities to a scale that corresponds to reality than your visit to our country at this moment in time."

After the welcoming ceremonies, Dr. Nyerere handed me an envelope containing a speech he had prepared for the gala dinner. "Would you mind looking this over and translating the speech for this evening's event?" "But of course. I will be delighted," I replied. There was very little time to translate both presidential speeches. I scurried off to the home office and began working feverishly to beat the deadline. The persistent ringing of the phone went ignored until I finally rushed to answer the doorbell to save my eardrums from the extra knocking. To my surprise, Ambassador Essienne, the chief of staff at the Ministry of Foreign Affairs, along with the president's security team breathed a collective sigh of relief. "Sorry to disturb you. We have a problem," he said. "The president has just suspended the afternoon meeting and he is requesting your presence." I acted *avion par terre*, as they say in Côte d'Ivoire, and scurried off with them to the palace. The afternoon meeting was for the Ivorian and Tanzanian committees, and both presidents were expected to attend. The young woman was the official translator for the event. When I arrived at the presidential palace and walked into the president's office, he expressed disbelief at my not being by his side while he was receiving an English-speaking head of state. I explained the reason for my absence and wondered if something had gone amiss. He voiced his disappointment at what had transpired while he was making his speech. "The audience listened attentively as I spoke with the interpreter translating. But suddenly, everyone seemed astounded. They were all staring at me bewildered. *It was as if yours truly was speaking utter nonsense.*"

With President Houphouët and Dr. Julius Nyerere.

In his speeches, the president had a habit of intellectualizing his views in such a way that an inattentive interpreter could be caught off guard. I accompanied him to the venue and took over the translation. At the end of the meeting, I rushed home to complete the impossible task of transcribing one speech into French and the other into English. With only a limited amount of time, I kept my eye on the clock and went to complete my assignment successfully at the gala dinner.

President Tubman inspects honor guard at Abidjan port.

President William Tubman of Liberia arrived at the port of Abidjan in his yacht, shortly after I had been admitted to the Treicheville hospital cardiology center and strapped to an IV pole for medication administration. I was laying in my bed, stricken with malaria, doing my best to breathe away the agonizing headache, when the phone rang at around ten or eleven o'clock in the morning. It was the president. "How are you, Mr. President," I asked. "Oh, tired, but you know I feel obliged to go and welcome our guest at the port. And you—how are you?" he asked. I was the only aide whom he addressed in a formal manner. "I am doing well, Mr. President." After a brief moment, he asked, "Will you be coming to the welcoming ceremony for our guest?" I answered in the affirmative and removed the IV from my arm. When I began to put on my clothes, I glanced over at the hospital monitor. My blood pressure was low—90/60. I could barely stand up; I had to keep leaning against the wall or sit down. Finally, after much exertion, I managed to saunter out of the room and head for the official event. I arrived in time to conduct my duties as expected and continued working for the entirety of the Tubmans' visit.

On the red carpet with Presidents Houphouët and Tubman.

With Presidents Houphouët and Tubman at the gala dinner.

A Dream for Peace

With hypotension and battling feverish symptoms, I wasn't the ideal image of an interpreter, but I put forth my best effort and met the expectations of the man who had placed his trust in me. Minutes after crawling into bed at the ward, my irate doctor walked in to check my vitals and give me a strong reprimand.

President Houphouët awards Tubman a medal.

I was feeling much better by the time Zambia's President Kenneth Kaunda visited the country. It was the first of two consecutive visits to Abidjan within a span of eight months.

When we arrived at the airport with a large presidential entourage that included the Chief of Protocol, we kept a hectic pace because we had been informed that his visit was going to last about six hours. Only two days earlier, he had met with President De Gaulle at the Élysée, a critical meeting that was encouraged in large part by President Houphouët-Boigny. When we arrived at the presidential palace, the two leaders shared the same couch, and I stood between them, hovering closely behind the couch. I interpreted his positions and points of views, which were positive and uplifting. The main focus of discussions was about their mutually adopted positions against an OAU resolution that refused to support a Biafra state in Nigeria's civil war. At the time, both Zambia and Côte d'Ivoire had recognized the sovereignty of the breakaway eastern region of Nigeria. After lengthy talks, President Houphouët invited him to return, and he vowed to do so for more substantive discussions on how best to incorporate some of Côte d'Ivoire's internal advancements into his own domestic agenda.

With President Kaunda and President Houphouët.

As promised, he came back to the country after eight months and began a four-day visit. He received a customary but lavish reception at the airport. President Houphouët praised him as someone who was *"not a stranger, but a friend and a brother."* He delivered a speech which I'd prepared days earlier in French, and I translated: *"A reputation has preceded you, which gives your visit great value in our eyes—that of an intransigent fighter for whom the responsibilities of power have naturally transformed into a realistic head of state, that of a man of action who draws from his religious humanism, the possibility of contributing human and African solutions to the problems of the moment."*

President Kaunda and President Houphouët.

President Kaunda smiled the entire time I was translating. His face exuded a humble composure inside an unassuming personality. He seemed at ease and at home. I looked over at him just as President Houphouët paused momentarily to get his reaction. He nodded: *"Finally,"* President Houphouët continued, *"the reputation of the representative of a country that refuses to interfere in other people's affairs, a country that means to strengthen its young and difficult independence, a country that cherishes the difficult ambition of serving by using as an example the cause of dialogue, tolerance, and peace. Moreover, Côte d'Ivoire sees in the action of your government, an inspiration—a turn of mind, and even attitudes, that are very often close to their own. I am pleased to see in this the presage of a very pleasant stage and fruitful conversations."*

He paused again for some applause before President Kaunda began his introductory remarks: "We have come here to learn and draw upon your wisdom, your profound knowledge, not only in the field of African politics, but also in that of world politics..." I wrote down his statements in shorthand while he was speaking in English, and I verbalized every word in French for President Houphouët on the fly. We had not been given an advance copy of his speech.

There were several events organized for the four-day visit. Dr. Kaunda met the diplomatic corps, and then we went to the Abidjan town hall where he received the "key to the city." We boarded a helicopter the next morning for a tour of some very innovative agricultural projects in the farming communities outside the city. This particular visit was something he had been looking forward to because he was very interested in moving Zambia away from its dependence on mineral production, which was the country's most vital natural resource. He saw a brighter future in the diversification of resources and a pathway into more lucrative agricultural production. I liked his vision and agreed with most of what he said about a self-reliant domestic policy.

On a two-day tour of the interior, we stopped in Bouaké and wound up in Yamoussoukro for the day. It was there I really warmed up to him in a more casual setting that seemed to bring out his most personable side. When we returned to Abidjan, both leaders got together again for a more formal exchange of ideas. This time, the advisors were an integral part of the discussions, and everyone engaged each other in a working session. One thing was abundantly clear at the meeting: the Zambians were impressed by the Ivorian miracle, and Dr. Kaunda was eager to emulate our accomplishments in his homeland. He expressed his gratitude to President Houphouët

A Dream for Peace

for the opportunity to learn so much in a short time.

Foreign dignitaries continued to flock to Côte d'Ivoire on a frequent basis. Many curious African leaders, motivated by rumors of the Ivorian miracle, came on diplomatic missions and insisted on touring some of the country's innovative industries. The mayor of Abidjan had his hands full on occasion when certain leaders were invited to the city hall. One such dignitary was Ghana's newly elected leader, Dr. Kofi Abrefa Busia, who arrived for talks with the president in May of 1970. The mayor proclaimed him a friend of the city. We went to city hall for the "key to the city" ceremonies. After receiving the award, I stood with him on stage and translated his speech to the audience:

With Ghana Prime Minister Dr. K. A. Busia.

"Mr. Mayor, your excellencies, ladies and gentlemen . . . you are right Mr. Mayor, the tumultuous welcome my colleagues and I have received from the people of Abidjan has borne undoubted testimony to the genuine warmth and cordiality of their feelings. I wish to express to you all the citizens of Abidjan our very sincere thanks. My colleagues

and I are happy to be among you today. Our presence here as members of a government elected to power by the people of Ghana in free and fair elections itself gives evidence of a unique achievement of which we are proud. We in Ghana set out and led the way to independence full of great hopes and good intentions. As you have recalled, Mr. Mayor, our hopes were disappointed, and we exchanged colonial rule for oppression, from which our gallant armed forces and police rescued us on the twenty-fourth of February 1966."

His last sentence was in reference to the armed coup d'état that led to the overthrow of Ghana's first president, Dr. Kwame Nkrumah. I delivered his wording verbatim to the attendees, and everyone applauded with so much zeal. We shook hands, and he expressed to me his pleasure with my astute performance. He was in a very jovial mood during his visit, and we connected on several fronts. Our friendship endured long after he was forced out of office by the military. While in exile in London, where he spent his last days as a sociology professor at Oxford University, his hopes for restoration of democracy in Ghana never faded.

Visits by world leaders and others from the private sector, such as industrial and financial leaders, yielded very positive outcomes. President Houphouët was well known for his supportive and inspiring nature, but more profoundly, he was highly revered by many for his prudence. Domestic and international politics and economics went hand in hand, and we took pride in the fact that Côte d'Ivoire's trajectory toward modernizing its industrial sector was on sound footing. The country's needs were always front and center in our daily briefings. Most importantly, the president believed that constant investment infusion was essential to laying the foundation for many projects in the pipeline. At every meeting, especially those with the ministerial council, he reinforced the need for broader and diversified cooperation in order to ensure unhampered dynamic economic development.

A Dream for Peace

With President Houphouët and Robert McNamara.

    Not long after the Finance Ministry began to conduct studies to determine if there were synergies with the World Bank's lending program for nations that were poised for rapid growth, we received word that Mr. Robert McNamara had taken on the mantle of leadership at the institution. He arrived in Abidjan from Dakar during a West African tour and held two days of very constructive talks with the president and other ministers. I sat in on the meetings to ensure accuracy in communications. We drilled down on the country's financial needs and negotiated the terms of an agreement under which the World Bank would invest in palm oil and coconut plantations. In the end, Mr. McNamara committed to a $17.1 million loan. It was at the time three times the amount of all the money the bank had lent to the country. To gain some clarity on the minute details of the agreement, I caught up to him at the waiting Mercedes and solicited some pertinent answers for the record. He assured me that the bank's efforts were geared toward achieving economic progress in African countries and that his team would be ready to come to the aid of developing nations in the years to come.

The Call of Africa

While keeping up with the demands of my hectic diplomatic schedule, I was enduring some difficult challenges in my private life. Back when I decided that it was time to leave the promise of America behind and respond to a higher call, I anticipated starting my life anew in a country that was native to my wife but foreign to me. I really looked forward to immersing myself in the customs and adapting to my new surroundings with Antoinette by my side. We'd had our difficulties in the past, but ultimately, recurring problems overwhelmed our best judgment and interfered with our plans to sustain a happy marriage. Despite many attempts to mend our differences, we failed miserably and had to call it quits. Predictably, the annulment of our marriage left me without a family in my new homeland, but thankfully, the president kept his promise to treat me like a son from the moment I set foot on Ivorian soil. His family members stepped up in a big way and welcomed me into their immediate nucleus without hesitation. Like a sibling, I grew closer to them each day and continued to focus on the future.

It was in my nature to do everything in my power to stay away from the limelight if I could help it. But nonetheless, my frequent appearances on television, standing next to or behind the president, caused immense jealousy among certain individuals of affluence, especially those who had tried to unseat me from my position. I found it quite remarkable. I had made enormous sacrifices to come to Côte d'Ivoire. I left the US where I lived an extraordinarily comfortable life to come and live with no air-conditioning in a tropical climate where I was constantly defenseless against malaria-transmitting mosquitoes. I felt reassured in my commitment to the continent and knew that despite the drivel, I needed to be patient. *I had but one ambition: to serve Africa.* In return, I received the unparalleled confidence and esteem of the president, who continued to behave increasingly like a father figure and a friend. Frequently during our conversations, he would reiterate the words, *"We have many things to do together..."*

With each passing day, I felt closer to him. "The president has requested that I ask if you would be willing to become an Ivorian citizen." Minister Usher posed the question while we were on a diplomatic mission. I was taken by surprise. The thought had never crossed my mind. "Prior to asking me to convey the message to you, he gave a great deal of consideration to the idea. You are, after all, well versed on all state secrets, but he did not wish to ask you directly." I gave an affirmative answer to the proposition.

I was on a mission to Paris when the president called to thank me for agreeing to naturalize. "Mr. President," I said in my earnest response. "*I was born without a nationality. I had the nationality of the French colonialists, which I always rejected. And then, I vanquished my Algerian nationality by way of fighting a war. But sharing your nationality, even on an isolated island like Robinson Crusoe, is something I would do with pleasure.*"

Article 2 of the naturalization decree stipulates: "*His naturalization being of the particular interest of Côte d'Ivoire, he is relieved from the limitations under paragraphs 2 and 3 of Article 43 of the aforementioned Act.*" He felt a sense of relief and delight. "You could become the president of the Ivorian republic tomorrow, you know . . ." He was kidding. He knew fully well that I would never entertain the thought.

His domestic agenda was bolstered by powerful strategic alliances with countries on the international stage, whose leaders hoped to develop stronger ties with Côte d'Ivoire. On occasion, Minister Usher and I encountered foreign diplomats at the UN who expressed their openness to engaging our nation on specific matters of mutual benefit. However, some Arab countries were hesitant and a bit reserved because of Minister Usher's unwavering position on issues in the Middle East. I was approached by a few diplomats who were frustrated by his biasness toward the Israeli nation. I was fully aware of the fact that he harbored an undeniable friendship with the country, and he was not very subtle about playing favoritism.

The Call of Africa

With Minister Usher and US Secretary of State Dean Rusk.

Usher and I often went over to meet with Israeli foreign ministers at their headquarters in New York's Carlyle Hotel at the end of the UN General Assembly sessions. The press published a story of one such meeting with Mrs. Golda Meir in a newspaper, and I was widely criticized by my Arab brethren for crossing a red line. In those days, both the Israelis and Arabs were intent on demonizing each other. But I was determined to draw attention to the humanitarian crisis in the Palestinian camps. I had waited patiently for an opportunity to speak with then Foreign Minister Meir to engage her maternal sensibilities and express my sentiments on the dire nature of the refugee issue. I said, *"What unites Arabs, Israelis, and all others is our common humanity. If the situation were reversed, and Israeli women and children were being committed to live and suffer in refugee camps, I would be by your side, seeking justice on behalf of the Jews."* Perhaps my words found a way to her heart, but she seemed tongue-tied. I left without saying another word. As far

A Dream for Peace

as I was concerned, something needed to be done very quickly, and I was intent on cultivating patience for the long haul. I challenged myself to dedicate all my energy and diplomatic resources to help solve the Israeli-Palestinian crisis, no matter what the cost may be. I knew there was a taboo associated with being seen as cozying up to an Israeli, and in the high-stakes political drama, I was risking my life every single day. Yet, in the ensuing months, I continued to accompany Usher on consultations with Golda Meir's successor, Abba Eban. Despite the heated rhetoric that followed my every move, I was neither concerned nor deterred by the lack of popular appreciation and understanding among my Arab brethren.

    I gained a reputation for demonstrating an impeccable conviction for straight and impartial diplomacy. Around diplomatic circles, it was widely known that I always showed professional courtesy and kindness to every diplomat, including those in the Israeli delegations that visited Côte d'Ivoire. Because of that, I earned the wrath of my Algerian brothers. When an Israeli colonel in charge of civic services came to the Ivorian city of Bouaké to conduct studies on the construction of a large kibbutz-like training center, the visiting press corps took a picture of me posing in the middle of the accompanying delegation. Algeria's ambassador to Côte d'Ivoire sent a copy of the picture with a negative caption to his Minister of Foreign Affairs. At the time, my cousin, Abdel Hamid Adjali, Director of Political Affairs at the Foreign Ministry, contacted me to share his thoughts. I shrugged it off and asked him not to worry. But the rumors and innuendos continued to cast false aspersions on me without any substantiated facts. By contrast, the Israeli government advised a newly appointed ambassador to Côte d'Ivoire to ask that I look over his speech before he presented his credentials to President Houphouët. It was an unheard of diplomatic gesture to me at a time when there was a great deal of mistrust between Jews and Arabs. Nonetheless, I took the initiative and returned the gesture by reading his speech and wishing him success on his mission.

The Call of Africa

Minister Usher and I were constantly targeted by progressives at the OAU and the UN. Regardless, he remained resolute against the many attacks directed at Côte d'Ivoire for our firm and unwavering position on critical issues. As his second in command, I always stood by him, staunchly committed to our policies, irrespective of the repercussions. The Algerian delegate who often sat in front of us was a cousin of mine. In the midst of the bombastic statements, he would come up to our section and ask that I use my influence to have Usher temper the rhetoric. I usually ignored him. Remaining true to my solemn commitment to the Ivorian republic, I stood steadfast by our policies. It was assuring to have the unwavering confidence of President Houphouët, who was a great source of support in the midst of all the pandemonium.

I was constantly subjected to all kinds of tribulations. In one episode, when Minister Usher presented a list of nominations for an ambassadorship position, he had strategically placed my name at the top of the list, although he was mainly considering awarding the opportunity to an individual with an academic background who had helped him reform the university. After the cabinet meeting, the chief of staff did not hesitate to inform me that a majority of the ministers had opposed my nomination. It made no difference to me whatsoever, but notwithstanding, I felt like they misunderstood who I really was. I was neither an opportunist, nor was I looking for any particular position. I was there to serve the nation and the president. He expressed confidence in my professional acumen when we spoke a few days later: "To me, you are more than an ambassador." I was soon promoted to the position of Special Advisor to the President.

My first adventure with Algeria began on the occasion of the OAU summit in Algiers in September 1968. I was making my way through the concourse of the Club des Pins,[31] our meeting location, when I walked past Algeria's new president, Boumédiène. He was

---

[31] Name of a resort located in the province of Algiers.

A Dream for Peace

smoking a cigar in the company of a group of cabinet members, including his Minister of Education, Ahmed Taleb Ibrahimi, and Kasdi Merbah, the head of military security. I overheard him ask Ahmed Taleb if that was "Berrah" who just walked by. He must have said yes, because he asked him to call out to me. I went over to see them. After we exchanged courtesies, he made a heartfelt appeal: "You must come home; I need you by my side." "I am more useful where I am, in sub-Saharan Africa, than here," I responded in all modesty, but my remark fell on deaf ears. "No, I want you here," he insisted. I walked away. Of course, like a flash, Kasdi Merbah caught up to me and told me that we would "discuss" my return home that same evening. He was known for "fixing" state problems expeditiously. I informed Usher as soon as I joined the Ivorian delegation, and he kindly advised that I share his room just to be on the safe side. I thought it would be better if I left immediately. I had in my possession a pre-booked Air France ticket from Algiers to Paris, in the name of Siméon Aké, the Ivorian ambassador to the UN. I hastily prepared a report of my activities and handed it over to the Ivorian ambassador to Algiers and left for the airport with Ambassador Aké's passport in my possession. Upon arrival, I presented his passport to the protocol services. They went through the routine security check and issued a stamped boarding pass. Before handing his passport over to my Ivorian diplomatic escort, I removed the boarding pass, slipped it into my passport, and went to board the plane. In those days, VIP passengers were not subjected to as much scrutiny. Later that night, when Kasdi Merbah and his agents came searching, they discovered to their astonishment that I was nowhere to be found. From then on, my relationship with my fatherland became increasingly difficult.

On the occasion of a medical conference in Abidjan, the dean of the School of Medicine at the University of Algiers came to present a paper on trachoma, an eye disease that affected many people in the Algerian Sahara. Stating that he was presenting it on behalf of Algeria at the Congress on Trachoma in Mexico, he asked me to read it and give my opinion. I took the paper and studied it that evening and came back the following day with two observations. I asked him if he wanted a review of convenience or a fair comment; he preferred the latter. I proceeded to tell him that the experiments that led to the drafting of the communication were not scientific. He requested that I advise him further, and I explained my point of view, which led to him soliciting my help. I realized that Algeria's honor was at stake, and so I told him I would do it with pleasure. My only caveat was for him to place my name above that of all the foreign scientists. Other than that, being cited after the Algerians was not a problem. This fateful occurrence was the antecedent that imposed my name in the archives of the University of Algiers without having ever attended the institution. When he began soliciting my help on scientific matters on a more regular basis after that, I insisted he go through the official channels since my position as special advisor to President Houphouët-Boigny could potentially be a conflict of interest. I asked that the Algerian government submit an official request to my boss. He presented the proposal to the cabinet at the meeting of ministers, through the Minister of Education, Ahmed Taleb. President Boumédiène was exasperated—"How can I ask a foreign president for the right to use an Algerian brain?"

That was the complex nature of the relationship between Algeria and Côte d'Ivoire. It was a delicate situation. I decided to do everything in my power to improve relations between my two countries for the sake of peace and reconciliation. In 1969, while I was focused on working to improve relations between the two leaders, President Houphouët called to tell me about a diplomatic standoff with Algiers: the ambassadors of Algeria and the USSR had fomented an uprising with the dockers' union at the port of Abidjan, and they proceeded to submit official reports to their respective governments.

The French secret service, not their Ivorian counterparts, intercepted the diplomatic briefcases and secretly photocopied the incriminating reports. They sealed the briefcases and shipped them off as if nothing had happened. President Houphouët broke off diplomatic relations with the USSR in the midst of the fracas and asked me to contact Algeria's ambassador, Mr. Ali Abdellaoui, to inform him of his discontent and outrage, among other things. I went to deliver the impromptu missive to him at a meeting in the official ambassadorial residence instead of his office. He was clearly surprised to see me. I had never been to the residence before. Over a cup of coffee, I gave further details on the reason why I had come to see him. He reacted swiftly: "This is a serious violation of the Vienna Convention. How can my diplomatic briefcase be opened?" He jumped off his seat and paced the room in stunned amazement. I sat quietly and waited for him to calm down before interjecting my opinion. "If you do not want your secrets to be violated, all you have to do is follow the example of the superpowers and have your diplomatic briefcase handcuffed to the wrist of one of your diplomats." He knew I wasn't kidding. "As a matter of fact, the briefcase containing the highly classified content could have been handcuffed to the wrists of two of your most trusted diplomats with instructions to place it between their knees on the flight." He sat speechless. I thanked him for his time and left.

President Houphouët dispatched Foreign Minister Usher and I on a three-nation secret mission to see Morocco's King Hassan II, President Boumédiène, and Tunisia's President Habib Bourguiba. We went to inform them in the most discreet manner of the incident with Algeria. We met and briefed King Hassan II in Skhirat.[32] The ambassador of Algeria to Morocco informed us that President Boumédiène was traveling in western Algeria, and he was ready to meet with us near the border town of Oujda. I asked Usher to go on that meeting by himself, because I thought my presence could aggravate the situation. I waited for him at the border. When he

---

[32] A city in Morocco.

returned, he disclosed that President Boumédiène had protested angrily and said he would recall his ambassador. "It was unacceptable to him that his diplomatic courier had been violated," said Usher. I had done well not to go with him on the volatile mission. We flew to Tunis to meet with President Bourguiba before heading back to Abidjan.

The precarious situation caused me a lot of anguish and distress. I knew that I'd have to double down on my diplomatic efforts to bring the two heads of state closer, regardless of their dissimilar characteristics, background, and orientation. President Boumédiène, a colonel and former chief of staff of the ALN, was less prone toward diplomacy and more militant. He had an unflinching commitment to the total liberation of the African continent and made no secret about his support for most liberation fighters who received training at a safe haven in Algeria. He even sent some troops to support his Arab brethren in the Six-Day War with Israel. By contrast, President Houphouët-Boigny never fought in an armed conflict to liberate his country. He had a different style about him; he preferred a method of dialogue and diplomacy. His international positions were mostly in line with France and the US, and progressives labeled him "the Valet of Imperialism." Nonetheless, they were both nationalists who loved Africa with undaunted passion, and they also shared a common vision for the development and honor of the continent. However, the stalemate continued until the tenth summit of the OAU in Addis Ababa. For the African leaders, the summit was a must-attend because it commemorated the tenth anniversary of the organization. Relations were extremely tense even before the summit. The two countries had each recalled their ambassadors months earlier.

I began to prepare President Houphouët sometime before we arrived in Addis Ababa by warming him up to the idea of a meeting with President Boumédiène. When I arrived at the meeting for the Ministers of Foreign Affairs ahead of the presidents, the interaction between the delegations of Côte d'Ivoire and Algeria were somewhat strained. My cousin Abdelhamid Adjali, Algeria's Director of Political Affairs, led the delegates. These types of meetings usually lasted for a couple of days before the commencement of the presidential meeting of the summit.

But on their scheduled day of arrival, I took it upon myself to go and welcome the Algerian presidential delegation at the airport. I greeted President Boumédiène and informed him that President Houphouët-Boigny wished to meet with him. Algeria's Director of Protocol, Abdelmajid Allahoum, called the very next morning to confirm that his president was ready to meet with my president at 8:00 a.m. the next day. I was ecstatic. I even forgot the rules of protocol: the president of Côte d'Ivoire was older than the Algerian president, and he ascended to his presidency before him. In that regard, the Ethiopian government honored him by deference and housed him on the fourteenth floor of a high-rise apartment building. President Boumédiène was placed on the eleventh floor. The appropriate procedure would have been to arrange for President Boumédiène to come up and see President Houphouët. But the thought did not cross my mind at the time. All I wanted was the enemy brothers to reconcile and begin breaking bread.

When I went into President Houphouët's suite early in the morning, I was met with a chorus of dissenting voices from my cabal of Ivorian brothers—"Berrah wants to humiliate President Houphouët. He wants him to go down to the level of the Algerian president." They sounded like a broken record. It was a rambunctious reminder of my having accidentally neglected the use of proper protocol in presidential affairs. I ignored them and went to catch the elevator. I didn't have to say very much, because President Boumédiène understood what was at stake. "Everything is ready here; it's not a matter of protocol. President Houphouët is my big brother, and I respect him a lot. Please let him come, and tomorrow, I will reciprocate and pay him a courtesy visit," he said. I went back up to see President Houphouët and report on the minor oversight. He assured me that it did not matter.

We took the elevator down to President Boumédiène's suite at exactly five minutes to eight o'clock. President Houphouët held my right hand firmly in his left hand: *"What do you wish that I say to him?"* he asked calmly. *"Everything. Especially the role you played in preventing the partition of Algeria while you were Minister of State and confidant of General De Gaulle. And the role you played in advising the French president not to make the mistake of tracing a new border between Morocco and Algeria, at the expense of Algeria."* He smiled.

President Houphouët advised De Gaulle that he shared the same views as King Mohammed V in regards to the issue of the border demarcation with Algeria. King Mohammed V had taken the position that he preferred to solve the problem with his Algerian brothers once they achieved independence.

We expected the meeting to have lasted about fifteen minutes, but it went on for forty-five minutes. The two leaders spoke like old friends who had a lot of catching up to do. President Boumédiène was impressed by President Houphouët's political track record. He admitted that he was absolutely oblivious to the president's achievements in subtle behind-the-scenes diplomacy. Throughout their discussion, his forthrightness and emotional demeanor spoke of a man who was truly delighted. At the end of the meeting, the valedictions were very friendly. As promised, Boumédiène reciprocated and came to see President Houphouët. They met again and again at every opportunity during the summit. I breathed a big sigh of relief and swam freely like a fish in water. I accompanied my president to each and every meeting throughout the historic summit.

From then on, there was nothing less than mutual respect between the two leaders. The OAU summit marked the beginning of very meaningful relations between President Houphouët-Boigny and President Boumédiène. As I took it all in, I reminisced about

A Dream for Peace

Kasdi Merbah's veiled threat to "discuss" my return home with me at the previous OAU summit in Algiers in 1968. In the final analysis, the ultimate outcome was that peace was achieved. The harmonious relationship established between the two leaders resonated across the African continent and beyond, with profoundly constructive consequences. My sacrifices had not been in vain.

Their friendship solidified over the coming months. A year after their encounter, they had bonded and become like family, knitted from the same thread. President Boumédiène once said to President Houphouët-Boigny, "*I think it is useless to speak in depth about the personal relationship and fraternal friendship that we have so far woven slowly but surely. I wish I had known you sooner. There is an Algerian proverb that goes, 'Whomever you ignore is somehow, someone lost to you, by virtue of the friendship and support he can bring to you.' These personal relationships have growing fraternal and friendly effects on the relationship between Algeria and Côte d'Ivoire. He who has not known you has lost you to time. I did not know you, and I regret it even more in each of our contacts, even if they are indirect.*

"*Since I met and have gotten to know you, I have constantly expressed sincere feelings of friendship and respect toward you. I have a great admiration and esteem for your frankness, your sincerity, your political acumen and wisdom. You are the only one able to nicely combine all these qualities with discretion and a sense of humanity.*"

A Dream for Peace

Besides having me serve as his special advisor, the president associated me with everything, including his personal and family affairs. When I tried to keep away out of respect to give him his space during some very private discussions, he'd say, "It's okay. You can stay. I have nothing to hide from you."

Chapter Seven

Bonding with President Houphouët

The portrait of our affectionate relationship expressed the depths of our unfettered love for peace and dialogue among all humankind. As I reflect through the following recollections from our shared experience, I am reminded of the purity of my bond with President Houphouët-Boigny, which was truly filled with trust and intimacy.

His displays of affection touched me to the depths of my heart and made me blush. On Fridays, when I was held back at the mosque for prayer, he often delayed his lunch until I was done. Whenever I was sent on a mission, he kept an empty seat next to his chair at the dining table as he awaited my return. He always referred to the chair as "Berrah's chair" and went to extents to ensure no one sat in it. When he called me by my last name, he did so with much fondness in his heart, because in his Baoulé mother tongue, "Berrah" was the name of a very rare exotic bird that was cherished by his ancestors. He knew that I had no extraneous designs beyond the scope of my position. I had no ethnic or tribal interests to defend, and I never hesitated to speak my mind or share my opinion if I disagreed with him.

I acted with the utmost discretion at all times and adjusted to my assigned role in whatever field he chose, conducting my duties to the best of my abilities. He knew that there were no limits to my availability. I kept the old habits of the combatant, ready to serve

A Dream for Peace

at any time. On the many occasions that he called in the middle of the night (about three or four o'clock), he always asked, "Are you asleep?" I'd answer in a sound and clear voice, "No, Mr. President, I am ready to serve." And immediately, I would engage him in a conversation.

He was a man of extreme thoughtfulness. I accompanied him to Algiers for the Non-Aligned Movement summit in September 1973

and went to see him at his hotel in the early morning. The summit had just ended, and he was getting ready to depart for Abidjan. He surprised me by suggesting that we go and see my family. I was thrilled. I called my oldest sister, Fifi, the mother figure in my life, and instructed some other family members to arrange a meeting. We planned to gather at the house of my cousin, Abdelhak Berrah, a Professor of Internal Medicine and the family patriarch. From the moment we decided to go on the unplanned private visit, I knew we would impose some extra security measures on the host country. The summit had brought together a hundred heads of state, and our last-minute changes were enough to cause major disruptions in the security detail that was charged with overseeing the departure of the large number of presidential delegations. When I contacted the Office of Protocol for the Algerian government, I immediately apologized for the inconvenience. Still, they were not very amused at the pending logistical nightmare. Nonetheless, our impromptu itinerary was formally instituted into an actionable plan, and our presidential convoy was rerouted to my cousin's home. When we reached downtown Algiers, we caused a major traffic gridlock that lasted for over an hour. The entourage was speechless and totally stumped when the convoy suddenly came to a stop in front of the house.

Members of my family were deeply moved and impressed by the president's humility, and he was heartened by the ubiquitous loving atmosphere. Abdelhak's wife, Hacina, served some tea, coffee, and freshly squeezed orange juice with traditional pastries, including my favorites: *baklava*, *makrout*, and *brajs*. We engaged in small talk and mostly lighthearted conversation for the short duration of the visit, and at the end, we headed back to the airport and boarded the presidential plane. When the aircraft reached cruising altitude, President Houphouët-Boigny, despite having a fear of flying, made his way to my seat to thank me for sacrificing so much love and affection in order to come and help him in Côte d'Ivoire. I thanked him in return and told him that the pleasure and joy was indeed a privilege of mine.

While in Beirut on a mission to see Chairman Yasser Arafat in October 1973, I received word that the president wished to see me in Washington, DC. He was on an official visit to the US at the behest of President Richard Nixon. My flight to DC connected in Paris after a quick layover. I arrived in a little over twelve hours and jumped in the waiting limousine to Blair House, the official residence for visiting presidential guests.

A wide grin awaited my entrance into his suite. "*Bonjour, ça va?* How was your trip?" Amid the warmhearted reception, a bear hug in classic President Houphouët style, it was clear that he seemed more eager than usual to discuss other topics. "*Bien, merci,*" I replied. "Are you sure you're not tired?" he asked. "No, no, I am doing very well. And you, how are you doing?" "I have no choice. I am well," he said. I chuckled at his humor. "How was your encounter with Pokou Koffi in Paris?" he asked. "Did he hand you the documents?" He was referring to his trusted personal assistant. "Sorry, Mr. President, Pokou and I did not cross paths on this trip, but I will return to the airport and board a flight to Paris. Kindly have him meet me there." The president got ahold of him on the phone and spoke briefly. "He experienced some minor delays. I asked him to board a flight from Abidjan tonight. He will link up with you in Paris." "*Trés bien,*" I responded. I left my suitcase in the presidential suite and headed to the airport. Finding a flight was not that difficult. Within hours, I was flying across the Atlantic. The Ivorian ambassador picked me up and drove to the Vaneau hotel in the 7th Arrondissement. The old boutique hotel had been a popular lodge for President Houphouët-Boigny and fellow African assemblymen in colonial times. I quickly checked into a room and went to sleep in my shirt, because my personal belongings were back in DC. Pokou knocked on the door first thing in the morning and handed over a small briefcase.

Bonding with President Houphouët

On my return flight, an air hostess observed what seemed like a briefcase that was permanently glued to my chest and offered to take it off my hands. I declined and thanked her. But she returned to ask again if she could give me a break. My response was still the same. Her caring companions were not very far behind. They came at me, one after the other, and asked to place the briefcase in the overhead compartment. Finally, I sought to clarify the situation to one of them: *"Miss, it is not the briefcase that accompanies me; it is I who is accompanying the briefcase."*

I jumped into the waiting limousine on the tarmac in DC and went to meet the president, who was relieved to see me again. He took quite some time to convey his sentiments and share his gratitude and appreciation for what I had done. "I looked after your suitcase. I kept it safe and secure while you were away," he teased, and asked the butler to fetch my suitcase. I thanked him and went to my hotel to catch up on some much-needed rest.

We arrived for the welcoming ceremony at the South Lawn of the White House on the morning of October 9. President Nixon delivered a heartwarming welcoming speech, and President Houphouët took to the microphone to return the favor. Although relations between the United States and Côte d'Ivoire were at their best, the Israeli-Palestinian conflict was a hot-button issue at the time. The topic took center stage as soon as we commenced the official talks. Initially, discussions between the two leaders focused on the economic cooperation between our countries, but by day's end, discussions shifted to the war in the Middle East. President Nixon asked President Houphouët to share his thoughts on how to bring the nations together for a common purpose—to not only bring an end to the fighting but to also find a way to build a new structure of peace in the Mideast. The president responded by delivering a constructive narrative about the root causes of the political unrest in the Mideast and factored in an overview of international quandaries by linking the problems in Africa to a viable solution for

A Dream for Peace

achieving global harmony among all nations. He was like a shortwave radio, transmitting far and wide, yet often he was best captured by outsiders than by his own countrymen.

At the end of the visit, the entire delegation traveled to New York. When we met with the president at the Waldorf Astoria hotel, he informed everyone that he would leave the US aboard the famous *Paquebot France*[33] with his wife, a few bodyguards, and myself. The rest of the entourage was instructed to return by air. We set sail the next day and arrived at the port of Le Havre in France after five nights and four days. Along the way, the president and I really bonded. We spoke for several hours each day and enjoyed many delicious meals with his wife. At times, we punctuated our contrasting views on capitalism and socialism with passionate debates, but world affairs and the Palestinian issue dominated our daily conversations. Our talks usually began with him addressing me as *"my son,"* but that changed to *"my young brother"* the moment we started digging deeper into the issues. I grew accustomed to the habit over time. He had a way of expressing the value of the free market. "The venture capitalists will not decide to dismantle their industrial plants and ship them off after having already constructed the real estate," he said several times during our talks. "Similarly, those who have already invested in our roads and infrastructure will not roll up the roads like a red carpet and take off with them. Capitalism and socialism are only words," he emphasized. "It is not the label that matters, but the content in the bottle." This was a favorite line and a typical segue for him. "But I practice a strong social policy to prevent capital flight. We will do many things together," he repeated, as he always did, whenever we had our deep talks.

---

[33] SS France, a famous French ocean liner.

Back in Côte d'Ivoire, I continued to help him in whatever capacity he wished and rose to the occasion each time he requested that I work with him to help resolve various conflicts around the world. But oddly enough, my non-Ivorian friends nagged about my continued commitment to President Houphouët-Boigny. They highlighted my personal credentials in an attempt to point out that I could do much better. To those dissenting voices, I'd always say these words: "A candle can only light another candle to create a candlelight; President Houphouët-Boigny is a lighthouse."

Besides having me serve as his special advisor, the president associated me with everything, including his personal and family affairs. When I tried to keep away out of respect to give him his space during some very private discussions, he'd say, "It's okay. You can stay. I have nothing to hide from you." When official duties made it impossible for him to leave the country, he called upon me to accompany his wife on a private visit to the United States. During the trip, she reaffirmed that the president had nothing but confidence in me. He was a leader, a virtuoso, who, when given the first note in the score, would play it better than everyone else.

"Be careful about the corruption that you will be exposed to from the immigrant communities as well as your secretaries," the president warned me from the very beginning. "All your documents must be written by hand, and their confidentiality must be absolute. Their secrets must remain between you and me." Such was the nature of my assignments—I had to maintain a very delicate balance at all times.

During one of my missions to see President Anwar Sadat, the ambassador of Côte d'Ivoire who was accredited to Egypt wanted to accompany me to the meeting. I tried to make him understand that I could not grant his request because of the confidential nature of the discussions. He continued to insist on accompanying me because he had "never met with President Sadat before." I inquired as to why that was the case, since he was the ambassador to the country and must have presented his official credentials to the president. "Unfortunately, for unknown reasons, I presented my credentials to Vice President Hosni Mubarak because the president was not available at the time," he said. I thought fast and figured something out. At least he could be a part of the official pictures. I cleared the plan with Egyptian protocol, and he was happy with the compromise. When the ambassador and I arrived at the palace the next day, we exchanged formal greetings and proceeded with the photo op with President Sadat and Vice President Mubarak. Both he and the vice president recused themselves before the meeting began in earnest. The particulars of the content made it one of my most difficult missions, but our discussions were very cordial. When I was done with the assignment, the ambassador expressed his gratitude at having finally met the Egyptian head of state.

Over the years, all the successive foreign ministers who followed in each other's shoes understood the nature of my clandestine position. Therefore, there was no friction among us. At an annual meeting for our foreign diplomatic corps, some ambassadors complained that they were unaware of the content of my missions to their designated host countries. The president moved expediently to address their concerns and put them at ease.

At the behest of the president, I attended the foreign affairs ministers' meeting with Ambassador Siméon Aké on the eve of the 1977 OAU summit in Libreville. Even though he knew how close I was to Usher, the president trusted me enough to reveal his intention to appoint Ambassador Aké as the Minister of Foreign Affairs. It was understood between he and I that our discussions would always remain strictly confidential. Nonetheless, the situation did not absolve me from criticisms by Usher's closest friends, who accused me of "abandoning him" even though I was not involved in that particular executive decision. But despite the false innuendos, Usher and I continued to be very close.

Upon leaving the government, Usher remained very active. He became a partner in a law firm in Abidjan. In his capacity as an accredited attorney, he was retained by the African Development Bank (ADB) to help promote the brand and raise some capital from non-African sources, such as Japan and West Germany. He informed me that he had attempted to reach President Houphouët to update him about a prospective deal but had been unsuccessful. The president did not take immediate action on the matter after I conveyed the message. On his way to his weekend retreat in Yamoussoukro, I walked up and tapped on the window of the presidential limousine to remind him to call Usher. They discussed the merits of circumventing our Arab allies to solicit capital into the ADB from other nonregional investment sources, but the president knew that the heads of Arab countries that were heavily vested in the success and relevance of the ADB were viscerally opposed to any such deal. He asked me to take preemptive measures to soothe their concerns.

I thought it was best to focus on the fact that the African

A Dream for Peace

Development Fund (ADF), which had been set up in 1973 to supplement the activities of the ADB, would be the beneficiary of the investment infusion. Therefore, I was motivated to target a couple of the nineteen state participants in the ADF at the time. I discussed the case for the ADB's intended objective, which was to broaden its funding activities and widen its membership base by reaching out to nonregional prospects. Both the president and I were convinced that the move would bolster the promotion of development projects for the economic and social advancement of member states and provide for a more active policy to invest in the growth of agriculture and rural development. When I embarked on my diplomatic quest to secure some relevant feedback from my selected sources, I encountered a higher level of intense opposition from some finance ministers, who were hesitant to open the door to nonregional institutions. As such, I met with the president to brainstorm on imposing a realistic approach to address the reservations of our Arab brothers before I advised Usher on the best line of recommendations for a draft study. Ultimately, the formal ADF replenishment talks were taken up by the Board of Governors in Libreville in May 1978.

I sometimes got myself involved in situations that got out of hand. In one episode, I told the president about a young ambassador whom I had met and taken a liking to. He was intelligent and very active, and I appreciated his performance on some of our many missions. The president soon promoted him to a ministerial position in his administration. After a few months in his highly confidential position, the minister became involved in some shady commercial dealings with a friendly country. The president was not very happy when the activities came to his attention, and he pondered firing him. He sent me to see him to express his revulsion and disappointment. The minister denied the entire affair, despite overwhelming evidence. I was already disenchanted with him because I was the one who made the recommendation to the president. Appalled, I shared my dismay and left. A few days later, the president ended the young man's ministerial career. I was totally embarrassed by the ordeal and emphasized my lapse in judgment when I apologized to the president.

Within the president's cabinet, the manifestations of jealousy were obvious, and to my surprise, even the highly respected chief of staff, Guy Nairay, revered by the ministers and every member of the cabinet, was no exception. For the most part, I thought the behavior was very childish. He had an issue with me being the president's designated special advisor in charge of the Middle East, the Arab

A Dream for Peace

world, and all of the socialist African countries. During a presidential trip to Paris, we were informed about a disparaging article in a journal from a Middle Eastern country. The editorial regarding President Houphouët's positions on some political matters was devoid of facts. When the president expressed his displeasure to me, I immediately contacted the country's ambassador in France to discuss the situation and correct the many distortions in the publication. He promised to look into the matter. The next edition included a formal apology to the president and a factual clarification of his positions. Soon after Guy Nairay found out about the incident, he decided to take up the matter with me at the VIP lounge in the Charles de Gaulle Airport while we were waiting for our flight to Geneva. "I am the chief of staff!" he blurted out from where he sat a few feet away from me. "And nothing should escape me concerning the cabinet's affairs." When I looked up and realized that I was the target of his misdirected frustrations, I walked over to respond, "I'm not a part of your cabinet. Need I remind you that I do not have an office in the cabinet? You, on the other hand, have two offices." He composed himself and said nothing more. Months after the episode, we found a way to bridge our differences. His son was pursuing his studies at Yale University. "The Yale Man," he would usually call out to me whenever we ran into each other. Weeks later, he introduced me to his son during one of his visits to Côte d'Ivoire.

All presidential appointments had to go through the secretary-general of the government. It had been a while since the president issued a decree for my official appointment as special advisor and given instructions to the secretary-general. However, he sat on the presidential directive for eight years. I only stumbled upon the fact that it had never been published when I was conducting a search for some documents. Upon being notified, the president had it published retroactively to the date of his original directive. When we discussed the matter, he responded with his very personal philosophy, *"One does not envy mediocre people. The day nobody*

Bonding with President Houphouët

envies you is the day I will start to worry, because it will mean that you have become mediocre." From then on, peace and harmony prevailed. The chief of staff and the secretary-general became more cooperative and consulted me on various matters of state.

There were occasional communication lapses within the ranks of the president's Security Services and Office of Protocol. I had a feeling some of the incidents were purposely designed to derail my efforts and hamper our progress toward achieving certain objectives. But I wasn't sure if there were anti-Arab agents at play or an infiltration by pro-Israeli influences within our security system. In the midst of the Mideast crisis, a Palestinian delegation came to Côte d'Ivoire to deliver a message from Chairman Arafat to the president. I was given the green light by the president to prearrange the meeting a couple of days earlier, after receiving a telex from Chairman Arafat's advisor, Dr. Isam Sartawi.

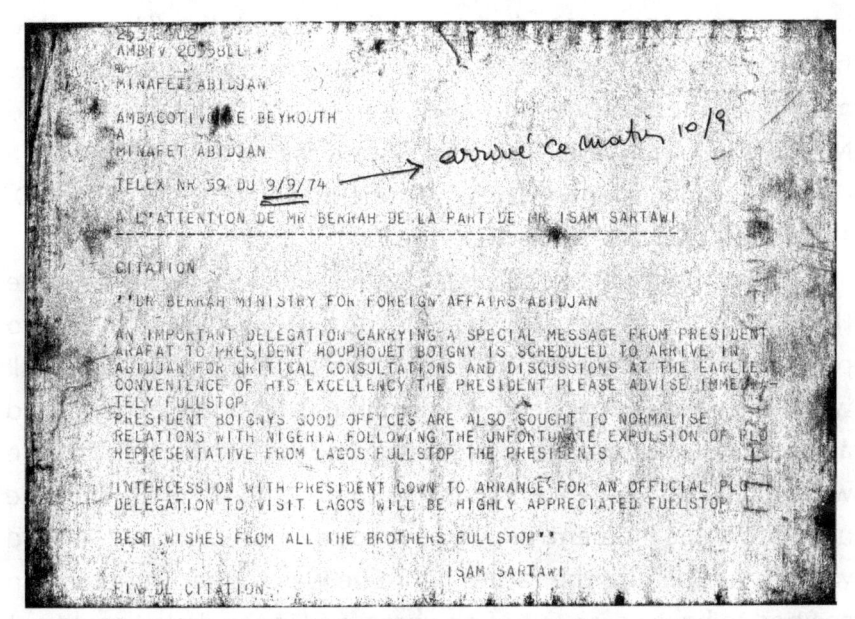

Dr. Sartawi's original telex.

When the delegation arrived in the country, the head of protocol ignored them, and an appointment to see the president was never officially entered into the books. The Palestinians waited patiently at their hotel for a lengthy period without hearing from anyone. They finally reached out and asked for my intervention. I was not only embarrassed by the rampant display of substandard comportment, but the shoddy conduct was more than I could bear, because impartiality had long been deeply enshrined in our golden rule. I immediately rushed to the residence. "Mr. President, there is a delegation of six who are here to see you. I'm sorry to say that if you do not receive them, there will be seven of us leaving the country." He was slightly surprised, not quite clear on why I was so livid. I had to backtrack and explain the situation to him. "There is a Palestinian delegation here to see you. They have not come to compel you to do anything out of the ordinary; they are here to ask for your intervention in a matter concerning the president of Nigeria, who has threatened to close the PLO offices in Lagos. This is in response to the misconduct of a PLO representative." He reacted favorably and compassionately. "I will receive the delegation in the morning." The meeting went well. As soon as they left, he called Nigeria's head of state, General Yakubu Gowon, and pressed for a renewed commitment on the government's relations with the PLO. The matter was resolved during the call.

  On an official trip to Lagos, we stayed at the Federal Palace Hotel. Shortly after we arrived at his suite, the president made two phone calls to his family. He had just begun dialing the third call when the phone went dead. A few minutes later, we experienced a sudden power outage. The entire floor went dark and there was an unsettling silence, but I tried to breathe some life into the uncomfortable moment. *"Papa, have you ever been happy?"* I asked warmly, addressing the father figure he was to me. The question seemed to have come out of nowhere, and in the dark, I could not tell if he looked puzzled. "Berrah, what is going on? Are you in a philosophical mood?" I smiled gently. "No, not quite. Just curious, that's all." He pondered my question for a brief second. *"As a matter*

Bonding with President Houphouët

of fact, I have. Each time it happened, it lasted with lightning speed. If my happy moment lasted longer than lightning speed, I would always turn to the Almighty and pray, 'Lord, you have deprived me of your divine grace.'" I mused over his words. "Papa, that is quite profound. I am sorry to say this, but what you are describing is a masochistic philosophy." He burst out laughing. As the lights came on, I noted the change in his mood. He was relaxed and laid back.

The president valued my opinions regarding his vision for the country's direction. I always gave my very best in the interest of the republic. Over the years, I was given more responsibilities, including overseeing the transparency in some affairs of the state. An Algerian gentleman, Abderraouf Benbrahim, had been placed in charge of the World Bank for greater West Africa. Ever since he came onto the international stage, he continually made decisions that were detrimental to the financial health of Côte d'Ivoire. I briefed the president, and he immediately acted by recommending that I send an official letter to his boss seeking Benbrahim's removal. This was a vital decision necessary to preserve the relationship between the World Bank and Côte d'Ivoire.

Abidjan, September 24, 1987

To Mr. Serageldin
Director of Africa Department World Bank
Washington, D.C.

Mr. Director:
    Further to instructions from the President of the Republic and in order to preserve the excellent relationship between Côte d'Ivoire and the World Bank, we would greatly appreciate the replacement of Mr. Benbrahim from his position.
    Please accept, Mr. Director, the expression of my distinguished consideration.

  On behalf of the President
  Dr. Ghoulem Berrah
  Special Advisor

A Dream for Peace

P.R.C.S/BM.001

A

MONSIEUR SERAGELDIN

DIRECTEUR DU DEPARTEMENT
GEOGRAPHIQUE N° 1 DE LA
REGION AFRIQUE
BANQUE MONDIALE

<u>W A S H I N G T O N</u>

MONSIEUR LE DIRECTEUR,

SUR INSTRUCTION EXPRESSE DU CHEF DE L'ETAT ET DE MANIERE A PRESERVER L'EXCELLENCE DES RELATIONS ENTRE LA BANQUE MONDIALE ET LA REPUBLIQUE DE COTE D'IVOIRE, JE VOUS SAURAIS GRE DE PROCEDER AU REMPLACEMENT DE MONSIEUR BENBRAHIM.

JE VOUS PRIE D'AGREER, MONSIEUR LE DIRECTEUR, L'EXPRESSION DE MA CONSIDERATION DISTINGUEE.

P. LE PRESIDENT DE LA REPUBLIQUE

LE DOCTEUR G. BERRAH
CONSEILLER SPECIAL.

The year 1987 was a period when the World Bank exerted pressure on developing countries by calling for an increase in the price of goods. There were massive demonstrations across Africa. Tunisia, for example, had to face down a revolt due to the rising price of bread. Côte d'Ivoire, which stood as the world's number one producer of cocoa, saw a sudden drop in the price of the commodity four months after the country had signed the cocoa accord of 1986, causing a very large deficit and billions of dollars in lost revenue. The situation was a first in our history. Under the very difficult

Bonding with President Houphouët

circumstances, I repeatedly stated to the president that we had to stop paying our debt and reorganize our finances. Although he took what I said to heart, he always seemed distracted and speechless. I continued to hammer home my opinion at every opportunity, until the president of the World Bank, Barber Conable, came to Abidjan. He was accompanied by his advisor, Ismail Serageldin, an Egyptian architect. Serageldin was also Benbrahim's boss and played a very influential role at the World Bank.

President Houphouët-Boigny hosted them for two days. During their meetings, he took the decision to pay the country's debt. Still, he was uncomfortable with the consent he had given on the debt settlement deal, because there were strings attached. When we sat down at the table for the family dinner later that evening, he expressed his sentiments to me. I reemphasized my initial position and recommended a temporary freeze in the payment of the debt until he sorted things out. Before parting ways, he pulled me aside and asked if I was really resolute in my position. "Mr. President, in my opinion, it is the right thing to do." I gave him a hug and left.

The phone rang at 4:00 a.m. "Berrah, are you sleeping?" It was the president. He sounded a bit apprehensive for the abrupt wake-up call. "No, I am wide awake," I said. "About our conversation last night, are you still convinced that yours is the right path?" "Papa, my opinion has not changed, and as you know, I would not compromise with matters concerning the country," I addressed him astutely. "Our guest, the president of the World Bank, is staying at the presidential palace in Plateau," he said. "Could you please go and pay him a visit and bring him the news that Côte d'Ivoire will not be able to honor our commitment to pay our debt at this moment?" He sounded very firm. "We will freeze all payments temporarily." I assured him that I would carry forth the news. "You will start by waking his advisor up." He was always keen on the minor details.

As soon as I hung up, I contacted Serageldin and asked to see him within the hour. They were scheduled to depart the country in the morning. I did not hesitate to inform him that the president had placed me in charge of the mission and I had some business to discuss with his boss. He reacted swiftly, stating that his boss had already spoken to the president and had officially concluded the meeting. As far as he was concerned, their mission had been accomplished. Again, I emphasized the importance of communicating some pertinent facts to the president of the World Bank. We decided to meet at the palace. I arrived in Plateau, the business center of Abidjan, at about five in the morning, merely minutes after we'd hung up the phone.

Serageldin was waiting for me in an office on the first floor. We immediately sat down and began our discussions. I informed him of the president's decision and highlighted the dire nature of our financial state of affairs to illustrate why Côte d'Ivoire could not honor its commitments. As we spoke, Mr. Conable walked into the office. When Serageldin informed him of my mission, they could not disguise their surprise.

Mr. Conable as an honorary Akan chief.

Bonding with President Houphouët

He brandished a copy of the day's newspaper, *Fraternité Matin*, featuring a picture of him posing in an Akan costume after a local village had coronated him as a tribal chief the day before. He posed on the cover with the caption, "The President of the World Bank has come to help us solve our economical problems." I ignored the headline and focused on our discussions. "The president has reconsidered his position because he cannot impose undue burdens on his citizens," I said. "He will soon be here to reaffirm his position." I walked into an isolated office to call and update the president on the mission. Within minutes, he walked in, confirmed his decision, and left.

During a visit to France not long after the episode, the president stood on the steps of the Élysée Palace and declared, "We want to pay our debt, but we are not able to do so." Coincidentally, I learned from my cousin Ghazi Hidouci, the Algerian Minister of Finance, that the director of the World Bank had visited some other African countries after leaving Côte d'Ivoire. His last stop was Algiers, where he discovered to his amazement that Algeria had unknowingly adopted the same position as Côte d'Ivoire and decided to freeze payments on their national debt. Without revealing the name of the country, Barber Conable mentioned that in the course of his African trip, one other country had also adopted a similar position.

Entrusting me with the responsibility of the missions to his brothers and colleagues—Presidents Boumédiène, Sadat, Bourguiba, and Siad Barre; Morocco's King Hassan II; Chairman Arafat; and last but not least, the mission with President Jimmy Carter—was the greatest mark of confidence bestowed upon me by President Houphouët-Boigny.

I only recently realized the significance of the president's trust when I stumbled on a black suitcase the size of a hand luggage at home. It had been secured and so well hidden that I had all but forgotten about it. It was an archive of all my notes and documentations from my confidential missions. I canvassed the introductory statements written about me by the president in highly confidential documents depicting my various missions and was exposed to the measure of his confidence and affection for me. As I reviewed the contents, a few words of wisdom from his favorite statements echoed through my mind:

"I have no ambition to view myself as a prophet, but I expect my disciples to spread my thoughts and actions."

I thought about our many sessions on the terrace of the presidential residence, where I frequently encountered his pet peacocks. The sheer elegance of the amazing colorful birds added to the tranquil ambience on the compound. We brainstormed through political affairs of the day and beyond, graced by those wonders of creation. The peacocks' strong colors make their importance more visual than literal. I marveled at the beautiful flocks that patronized the terrace, sometimes wandering toward the glass door to glance curiously at the guests in the living room. They showed off their vivid blue bodies, radiant with emerald iridescence, accented by the slender neck and head, some crowned with a graceful crest, and a moderately bulging physique. Oddly enough, they never spread their tail feathers for anyone other than President Houphouët-Boigny. At first, I did not know the extent to which the birds would go to uphold their allegiance to him, but I soon came to admire their devotion to their father. Whenever he came on the terrace, they trailed along in a drooping train to greet him by spreading their green, turquoise-spotted tails into stiff, colorful filigreed fans. This was just their way of saying, "Hello, Papa." It was always a delightful sight to behold.

The terrace was his private retreat where we discussed strategies to bring peace to conflicts in many parts of the world. He dictated messages meant to be delivered to world leaders during my classified missions, and I wrote them all down in several notebooks. I rewrote the notes again at home to create duplicate copies for my missions. The originals were kept in a secure place, but I had no need to review them at the end of my assignments. In May 2010, the long-lost documents resurfaced in a storage space. When I began browsing through some of the notebooks, I was captivated by the content. I measured their value to history. The discovery coincided with my decision to write my memoirs, and the choice was made to publish the original documents alongside my story.

My friend Nana Yalley managed to convince me to give an account of my life in an autobiography. I had pondered the idea many times, only to end up placing it on the "Greek Calendar"—in other words, it was an idea that was endlessly "worth exploring at a later time." I had not followed the pressing advice of many of my friends, most notably my brother and friend President Bouteflika, who had encouraged me repeatedly to portray my bonds with President Houphouët-Boigny—a relationship that had intrigued many.

Mr. Nana Yalley and wife, Namuli.

A Dream for Peace

For her part, Mrs. Houphouët-Boigny expressed her wish to have me reveal the heretofore unknown aspects of her husband's innermost thoughts and body of work. I was not ready at the time, but my young Ghanaian friend was the catalyst. Hence, I began to rethread the patterns—to weave and retrace the paths of my life.

A Dream for Peace

Throughout the many excruciating challenges we faced trying to get to the altar, our love for each other was only strengthened by our faith in the Almighty. Ultimately, we knew that if it were meant to be, our union would culminate in a happy marriage.

Chapter Eight

Murky Waters of Love

President Houphouët-Boigny did not hesitate to stand with me against all odds when I found myself beset by extraordinary difficulties.
On May 30, 1970, I met the one being that God had predestined for me: My First and Last Love.

I was part of the delegation that accompanied the president and his wife on a trip to the Netherlands for an official visit as guests of Queen Juliana, scheduled from June 2 to June 5. We planned for a two-day stopover in Switzerland before the actual visit. When we arrived in Geneva the afternoon of Saturday, May 30, I knew that most businesses would be closed at five o'clock. This was not unusual across Switzerland. Mindful of the fact that my long-tail tuxedo needed ironing, I headed to the residence of Ambassador Bénié Nioupin, the Permanent Representative of Côte d'Ivoire to the United Nations in Geneva. We had gotten to know each other over the years, and I was a regular visitor to his home.

As soon as the butler ushered me into the residence, I saw a young lady making her way down the stairs toward the garden level. Our eyes met for a brief second. I was instantly bedazzled, but I composed myself and summoned the butler to give him instructions on what to do with my tuxedo. I left and returned the next day. When I spoke with Ambassador Nioupin, I asked about the young lady and expressed my desire to get to know her. "She is my niece," he told me. "Her dad is an Ivorian businessman. She is a student at the University of Lausanne, here in Switzerland, studying to become a pharmacist." "It's just incredible," I said. "The few seconds I caught a glimpse of her were more than enough to induce my fascination. She left an indelible impression on me." He wasn't at all surprised by my candor. To my absolute delight, he promised to make an introduction in the near future.

I was invited to a dinner event at his residence after we came back from the Netherlands. I arrived excited and in great spirits. He made certain that I sat beside the young lady. When I took my seat, I was a bit shy at first, but she and I found a topic of mutual interest—biology. Our small talk about her biology program at school slowly progressed into a more in-depth discussion about James Watson and Francis Crick's double helix structure of DNA. Interestingly enough, we both seemed comfortable having a conversation about science at the dinner table. Not so typical conversation of the romantic kind, but still, I was fascinated by how much we had in common. "James Watson preceded me in the department where I conducted my research in Bloomington," I told her proudly. Nibbling at our delicious meal, we shared our thoughts on other matters of historical significance.

When dinner was over, I asked if she would join me for an afternoon tea as soon as her uncle gave his permission. She said she would be happy to. I quickly obtained his consent and came back to pick her up at the residence a few days later for our very first date.

I sat in the tearoom at La Perle Du Lac, a restaurant on the shores of Lac Léman in Geneva, with the love of my life. The chic tearoom restaurant was my choice for our rendezvous. We immersed ourselves in the beautiful setting, and I felt an overwhelming sense of joy. As we warmed up in the conversation, we decided to refrain from calling each other by our formal last names, which was always preceded by Mister and Miss. "*Just call me Ghoulem,*" I told her. "It is pronounced with an airy sounding 'H' at the beginning." I explained it was customary in Arabic enunciation, and she simply said her name was Titi. She was the *one*. I was completely overcome by her striking presence. It was the first time I had ever experienced the magnificent allure of love, and I wanted to submerge myself in the feeling for the rest of my life. As our *tête-à-tête* progressed, I could no longer hold back; I just had to tell her how I felt. "I want to marry you. I would like you to be my wife." As expected, she was totally taken by surprise. Amazingly, she neither consented nor rejected. "It seems a bit premature," she said very nicely as she mustered up a beautiful smile. I just smiled back, and we continued talking. After a while, I asked her permission to receive her phone number. "Would you mind if I called you?" I asked. "No, I won't mind," she said. "When can I call you, I wouldn't want to bother you," I told her. "You can call me whenever you wish." That was good enough for me.

After a delightful afternoon, we headed back to the residence. When we parted ways, I continued to feel completely dumbfounded by the overwhelmingly powerful feeling of being in love. I thanked the ambassador for making our encounter possible. I also spoke to him about our conversation and mentioned the part when I expressed my desire to marry his niece, followed by her modest response. "Just allow time to follow its course," he said. I nodded in agreement and said goodbye. That same evening, I sent a pretty postcard of Lac Léman to Titi. Evoking memories of our romantic moment together, I added, *"With the hope that one day we could talk about the radiance of Geneva to remind us that she hosted the birth of our burgeoning love."*

I stayed in touch with her as often as time would permit. Titi had become the object of my love, and with each phone call to her, my love grew stronger. I wrote to her almost every day to tell her what I was up to, at times even describing my daily activities while I was on various missions. But my letters were always meant to express my love for her. More than once, I flew from Abidjan to Geneva and drove to Lausanne just to invite her to have dinner with me. I made my way back to Geneva the same evening and flew back to Paris early the next morning to catch a flight to Abidjan. I was determined to prove my love for her.

After courting her for about a year, I finally passed the test. She agreed to become my wife, once her studies were completed. I was the happiest man in the world. I told her that I would inform President Houphouët-Boigny and request that he formally ask her parents for her hand on my behalf, since he was like a father to me. She promised to inform her parents when she returned to Abidjan for the summer.

We were both very happy. But unfortunately, we were not adequately prepared for the sequence of events that would soon follow. To our utter surprise, the situation took an unexpected dramatic turn. As soon as she arrived in Abidjan, her father, Mr. Gabriel Ollo, welcomed her with a very icy reception. He'd learned of our relationship from someone who was probably looking to earn his favors. Titi, whom I'd chosen to be my wife, was the oldest of Mr. and Mrs. Ollo's six children. She had five siblings—a brother and four sisters. Mr. Ollo was a very powerful and highly influential personality in Côte d'Ivoire, who would have absolutely nothing to do with our plans. He expressed his displeasure to his daughter and called Usher to ask that he advise me to break up with her immediately. Oddly enough, despite having been very supportive months earlier when I first expressed my feelings to him, Usher, my friend and brother, suggested that I let her go. His instant shift was very painful to me. I felt like I had been stabbed in the back.

The father of the woman I loved more than anything in the world called and invited me to his pharmacy one early morning. Mr. Ollo and I had met several times in the past, because I was a regular customer at his pharmacy, long before I even met his daughter. If he happened to be at the counter when I patronized the pharmacy late in the day, he would personally attend to me and offer to accompany me to my car. At times, I apologized for the inconvenience, but he would assure me, "It is always a pleasure. I enjoy accompanying you to your car. It allows me to talk some more." Occasionally, he would also praise President Houphouët-Boigny *"for surrounding himself with bright young people like you."*

But he was a totally different man when I went to see him. The warmth was all but a thing of the past. He immediately ordered me to break off the relationship with his daughter. I remained calm and respectful as he vented, stern and boisterous. When I interjected, I did so politely and tried very hard to make him understand that I was sincere in my feelings for his daughter. I assured him that I took nothing for granted and explained wholeheartedly that I intended to take appropriate steps to formally ask for her hand. However, circumstances had not yet provided a suitable opportunity for me to approach the family. I hoped he would reconsider and give us a chance, but he was steadfast and my appeals fell on deaf ears. It was painfully clear to me the more we spoke that he had a set criteria and profile for her ideal husband. In his heart, I wasn't quite good enough for his oldest daughter. Titi had cautioned months after we first met that being a divorced man might complicate matters. But a past marriage in Islam has no bearing on a future marriage and therefore couldn't be an obstacle that forbade one from getting remarried.

I felt emotionally drained, extremely distressed, and utterly disenchanted. When my Love and I met at a discreet location later that afternoon, we spoke candidly. She knew I was troubled, but she was more disappointed at her father's stubborn indignation. "My father is very protective of me," she said soberly. "He means no offense by this, so please don't take it the wrong way." I understood her. "Perhaps, time will reveal a better outcome," I said. "I believe so. He loves his children passionately, and he is convinced nobody is worthy of marrying any of his daughters. As far as I am concerned, nothing has changed. My sentiments for you are still intact." I was warmed by her affectionate words and moved by the way she tried to soothe my pain, even though her own heart needed some comforting. As we gazed into each other's eyes, she searched for answers to her father's uncaring intransigence. "I must say that there was no need for him to overdramatize our situation. Either way, I have given you my word," she reassured. "Nobody can make me change my mind. You know, I love my parents dearly. They have been exceptional; they have always pampered us, catered to all our needs, and placed us in the best conditions possible. I am very grateful for what they have done and continue to do for my siblings and I. In recognition of their sacrifices, I have done my best to make them happy in every single way. I even decided to become a pharmacist, not of my own volition, but to honor the wishes of my parents. As a matter of fact, I don't even have a background in science. I am more at ease with literature." I listened and was touched by her expressive release of untapped emotions. "I have never asked anything of them. Always done whatever they've asked of me. But now, for the first time in my life, I am asking for their blessing for something so dear to my heart—just a simple acceptance of the one being that I love, and I can't even get through to them!" She cried, and I was moved to tears. I felt her pain so very deeply. "I have the hardest time grasping why they have become so hermetic!" It was tough to bear, but we knew that we had to remain hopeful and pray for some divine intervention. She had only two years left at the university. We thought there was still a possibility that her father would come around and warm up to the situation by her graduation.

Due to the rapid escalation of events and my hectic work schedule, I had not had the opportunity to inform President Houphouët-Boigny about the unfolding situation. When I finally went to see him, I narrated the story in its entirety, beginning with our first meeting in Geneva, where she aroused immense passions in me, and ending with my desire to marry her. "I did not want to tell you about the encounter prior to obtaining Titi's consent," I told him. "But at the moment, we are faced with the outright opposition of her father," I lamented. Upon hearing what I had to say about the matter, the president calmly reassured me and said Mr. Ollo was a friend of his, therefore I need not worry. He suggested that before asking for her hand on my behalf, it would be wise of him to meet her on our next visit to Geneva.

Mr. and Mrs. Ollo.

I immediately went to meet up with her in Lausanne as soon as she returned to the university and offered a pear-shaped solitaire diamond ring as a token of my love. We were officially engaged. We knew that we had balked at tradition by agreeing to the engagement without the blessing of her parents, but we felt as though we had no choice. I embarked on many international flights to see her as much as I could, while continuing to conduct my duties to the president. I traveled from Abidjan to Geneva to see her every single weekend, carrying with me many of her preferred delicacies. I had a feeling that she craved some local foods from time to time. I usually stopped at the food section in the Treichville market to pick up some freshly pressed palm oil, along with some *appiti*, a delicacy consisting of a mixture of mashed plantains and rice, cooked in a banana tree leaf. This was a favorite of my Love's. The first time I visited the stall of the vendor, she was intrigued by my knowledge of the popular native delicacy. "Sir, your wife is from the Apollo tribe," she stated confidently, referring to a tribe in Côte d'Ivoire. I responded with an amused smile. When my Love gave a thumbs-up to the vendor's recipe, I became a regular customer. I even brought along some sweet Fanti bread, baked by the women of the Ghanaian Fanti tribe. Plantains and mangoes were also part of the package. I put so much care into packing everything to ensure freshness and prevent anything from getting damaged on my flight.

I used to leave Abidjan on Saturday morning and arrive in Geneva that same night. From there, I drove to Lausanne to see her. On Sunday evening, I headed to the airport and caught a flight in order to arrive in Abidjan early Monday morning. When I was on diplomatic missions, my trips were much easier because I would always transit through Geneva.

While visiting Geneva, President Houphouët-Boigny asked his nephew Lambert, who was traveling with him at the time, to call and invite my fiancée to his private residence in the La Capite neighborhood. She accepted the invitation and made the trip from Lausanne to meet with the president for the very first time. Lambert ushered her to a small living room, where she sat calmly, waiting for the Ivorian leader. Within a few minutes, he walked into the room, looking overtly passive, absolutely expressionless, and gave her a handshake. According to her, he came across like a "father figure." Their small talk revolved around relationships between parents and children. True to his personality, the president had a few choice words. "At the end of the day, all parents want the best for their children," he said to her. The topic was switched, and the conversation became fixated on his sentiments about me. "Berrah is very dedicated and committed to his duties. He has helped me a whole lot, and I know I can always rely on him. He is my best adjutant." In a sudden shift, he quickly digressed: *"You know that Berrah loves me more than he loves you, don't you?"* He spoke in a serious tone. She was completely caught off guard by those unexpected words. She'd come to see him hoping to get some comfort, but regardless, she kept her composure in spite of the awkward moment. Through a subtle smile, she mustered up a sincere statement straight from the heart: *"Indeed he loves you very much, but ours is not the same type of love."*

She left the meeting feeling somewhat puzzled and completely mystified. Of all people, she thought, President Houphouët-Boigny, the "Sage of Africa," a political icon of international repute and a world-class diplomat with an innate ability to resolve the most difficult conflicts, had just compared two unique loves with nothing in common! She recalled the words of General De Gaulle, in his book *Mémoires d' Espoir*, describing the president as "a first-class political brain." I consoled her, saying, "I'm sure it is probably his way of breaking the ice." "The girl commands respect," the president confided when I heard from him. It was an extraordinary compliment coming from an experienced man with exceptional stature.

As promised, upon his return to Abidjan, the president invited Mr. and Mrs. Ollo to the presidential residence to ask for the hand of their daughter on my behalf. They received a hearty reception when they arrived for the private luncheon. As the conversation progressed, their interaction quickly became awkward. He felt as though he was talking to a wall. His overtures were brushed off with blatant abandonment and discord. But nevertheless, ever so considerate, President Houphouët-Boigny concluded that I shouldn't allow myself to be discouraged. He advised me to let the unwavering passage of time allow the situation to mature into the new reality, and he promised to try a second time, after my fiancée had completed her studies.

My fiancée, ever so magnanimous, often reminded me that her parents' continuous disapproval should not be an obstacle to our love. She stated that it was simply *"the thorns on the bountiful roses of our love."* Throughout the many excruciating challenges we faced trying to get to the altar, our love for each other was only strengthened by our faith in the Almighty. Ultimately, we knew that if it were meant to be, our union would culminate in a happy marriage.

Luckily for us, the situation was slightly enhanced when President Houphouët-Boigny asked me to help establish a Pasteur Institute in Abidjan. To acquire the necessary accreditation, I had to take up a year's residence at the Pasteur Institute in Paris. At least for the time being, the project, and a World Health Organization scholarship I received for the Pasteur Institute in 1971, would place me a little closer to Lausanne and my fiancée. We were very happy to share a closer distance, enjoying many beautiful moments for several months. I commuted to Lausanne every weekend, and she took the train to Paris to spend some time with me during study intervals from school. We enjoyed many wonderful moments in the City of Lights, visiting art museums, going to the theater to see various plays, and sampling a few cuisines in the many restaurants on the quaint island of Île Saint Louis. We just wanted to be together. I even worked with her on her assignments to ensure that she graduated with flying colors. I attended to my presidential assignments, went on diplomatic missions to the OAU summits, and appeared at UN sessions with Usher while working very hard to obtain a certificate on rabies and a degree in epidemiology at the Pasteur Institute.

I returned to Abidjan in the summer of 1972. Without delay, the president appointed me to the position of deputy director of the Pasteur Institute of Adiopodoumé, near Abidjan. The French director of the institute and I had our occasional disagreements on the most efficient way to run the institute. Despite our differences, I continued to do my best to help organize the institute, but much to the relief of the director, I soon left the post due to the complexities of juggling scientific and diplomatic activities.

Whenever I went to Lausanne to see my fiancée, I marveled at her very presence each and every time. She successfully obtained her degree after a few months and returned to Côte d'Ivoire to assist her father at his pharmacy. At the same time, the Middle East problem became scorching hot and my diplomatic activities intensified. We had hoped that after two years, her parents would have had enough time for some kindhearted reflection on our loving relationship and soften their stance enough to bless our nuptials. President Houphouët-Boigny took the time to invite them to ask for the hand of my Love once again, despite his demanding schedule. For the second time, his overtures were categorically rejected. Things took a turn for the worse from there.

While my fiancée continued to see me on a regular basis, her father began to exert constant pressure on the president. He called him a couple of times to complain that my relationship with his daughter was causing extreme tensions in the family. He even blamed the situation for having an adverse effect on his wife's health. The president assigned his personal cardiologist, Professor Bertrand, to oversee my fiancée's mother's health issues. He received regular updates from the doctor and informed me of her daily progress.

After my fiancée's father contacted the president to complain about his wife's health for the third time, he reached out to me again. I felt downright insulted and embarrassed. The unbearable situation permeated my work environment and left a poisonous essence in the air around me. I had to face the music and make a decision. When the president offered to have me settle down with my fiancée in a country of my choice, assuring me of his help, I knew I did not need his help.

    The internal debate for me was existential in nature. I became introspective and began to question my life's purpose. I had left my country, my family, and my scientific career to come and assist the president, hoping to work with him and make the world a better place. I could not abandon him at a critical time when there was so much work to do. We had established a harmonious operation without any discord between us. Ultimately, I came to the realization that it was time for my fiancée and I to have a heart-to-heart conversation. Ours had become a situation that was tantamount to Greek mythology, even the Cornelian tragedies, with duty and honor on one side and love on the other.

    I was totally flustered when I saw her later that day. I shared President Houphouët-Boigny's proposal with her, but she did not jump for joy. She knew instantly that we could not take the president up on his offer because of her own unwavering sense of commitment. Fully aware of my involvement in secret diplomatic missions on the world stage, she refused to interfere with my diplomatic efforts. The year 1974 was marked by the first oil crisis and my many missions to President Boumédiène and others.

    Titi was committed to a purposeful life. She was a practicing Catholic, molded by her Jesuit education at Sainte Marie de Neuilly near Paris, where she completed high school. Whenever I had to go to the war-torn region of the Middle East to meet with President Sadat and Chairman Arafat, she inspired me with many words of wisdom. She constantly emphasized that God would guide and protect me throughout my mission and reminded me that it was our duty to embrace the Creator's project for each of us. I frequently embarked on my missions, knowing that I was the object of her affection and pride. Her prayers accompanied me wherever I went.

Hence, I was without any fear, because I believed then, as I do now, that each day is a gift from the Almighty.

But on the last day of May 1974, amid a heavy tropical morning rainfall, just two days before departing on a diplomatic mission to Cairo, we made the agonizing decision to sacrifice our love. With a broken heart and my soul in great pain, we parted ways. Our emotions had surpassed a higher than normal peak, and we had arrived at a sad place. I was speechless. Her only comment was that the unfortunate outcome would not benefit her parents. My legs trembled on the way to inform the president of my decision to remain in Côte d'Ivoire. I was visibly shattered.

That was the last time I saw my Love in Abidjan. I thought I will never heard from her again. Some mutual friends told me that she had written a letter thanking her parents for their love and for their efforts toward her education. Referring to the situation, she apologized for not being able to live in a "golden prison." She departed Côte d'Ivoire for an unknown destination without telling them. Deflated with a thorn in my heart, I managed to go to Cairo to meet with President Anwar Sadat. I was President Houphouët-Boigny's personal representative at the historic Palestinian National Council conference and the only non-Palestinian on the list of attendees.

Over the years, I had grown closer to Dr. Isam Sartawi, Chairman Arafat's advisor. We were like brothers. He had known Titi for some time, because we often welcomed him to my house together. She liked him a lot, and the feeling was mutual; he even wrote poetry for her. I met with him prior to the conference and shared my dismay at the unfolding drama. He was repulsed by the events. In his view, her parents' actions amounted to gross disrespect and an assault on my dignity. I explained that the ensuing heartache from the rupture was unbearable. Our conversation was full of passion, and it became highly charged. In the midst of the confusion, there was even talk of quickly moving into another relationship to assure Titi's parents that we had really moved on with our lives. But those were mere words from a distressed, confused, and dispirited soul. Still, Sartawi offered to help me, provided that I was willing to get into a marriage in accordance with Arab tradition. He even mentioned that he could introduce me to one of the prominent Palestinian families in Cairo, who would be honored to give me the hand of a young woman in marriage.

    I was fully aware that it was all foolish talk. I could not just get into another relationship without allowing myself some time to heal. In the meantime, I tried to stop thinking about my Love, who I knew was most certainly suffering as much as I. My attempt to turn the page and find closure for that part of my life was not very easy. Oddly enough, each time I reflected on my conversation with Sartawi, I found myself gradually warming up to the idea of a "marriage of reason." Still, I was torn and haunted by Titi's words: "*I love my parents so much. They are exceptional individuals. I have always done everything to please them.*" In the ideal painting, perhaps, I would be portrayed as a troublemaker. I wondered what could have been or what the future might bring. Her parents would certainly choose for her, a husband from their Abouré tribe, and the family would be reunited again. Memories of us would soon fade, and she would eventually forget about me. Perhaps, if I moved into a new chapter, it would be a worthy sacrifice that would transform the idea of being the troublemaker in a united family and make everyone whole again. I thought that if I got married to someone else, Titi's parents would be assured that our ties had been definitely broken. Everyone would be relieved of my presence we would all be free again, and my honor would be restored. They would no longer disturb the president with incessant complaints, and he and I would calmly resume our work to advance peace in the world. Soon enough, I would reach out to Dr. Sartawi and give my consent.

    In the meantime, I focused on my mission and attended every Palestinian National Council meeting. When I arrived at my

Murky Waters of Love

decision by the end of the ten-day conference, Dr. Sartawi and I went to visit an influential Palestinian family from Gaza. He'd come to know them very well over the years as a respectable and proud family. They greeted us with humility at their house in a Cairo neighborhood where they had relocated. We talked for a while, over coffee and some assorted pastries in a traditional setting. A young woman appeared after several minutes. "Meet my daughter Saousan," said her father. Judging from her looks, she struck me as a warmhearted person. She sat quietly beside her mother and listened to the conversation between us men. Whenever I elaborated on my profession and worldviews, her dad probed for more stories about my past. The mood was quite jovial. As I made light of even the most serious situations, I noticed I had begun to captivate Saousan's attention in a big way. She seemed to take a keen interest in me. Her demeanor was important under the circumstances, because in their tradition, the young lady retains the power to choose her suitor from among those who are introduced to her. Overall, the atmosphere was very cordial and relaxed. At the end of our visit, her father invited us to a family dinner. We were treated to a traditional Palestinian meal at their house the following day. I was ready to move forward with the process. On our way to the hotel, I gave Sartawi permission to proceed with the next steps. Apparently, Chairman Arafat was delighted when he heard the news. Sartawi visited the family a few days later. "I have come here on behalf of my very good friend and brother, the official guest of honorable Chairman Arafat, to ask for the hand of your daughter in marriage," he said to the parents. "I consider your request a great honor," her father responded without any hesitation, giving his consent. When Sartawi shared the family's sentiments with me, we convened a meeting at their house the next day. "I would like to take the opportunity to thank you for your trust. I promise to return for the customary formalities," I told them. Saousan could not hide her joy; she gave me her picture before I left.

A Dream for Peace

For me, the process had no sentimental bearings, but I promised myself that I would make an infinite effort to ensure a successful marriage.

I took an early morning flight back to Abidjan. A few hours after I landed, I reported on my mission to the president. When I told him of my latest matrimonial commitment, he asked to see a picture of Saousan. Looking at the photograph, he mustered a big smile and gave me his blessing. "Invite the family to Abidjan," he said. "Will do, Papa. Thank you." I returned to Cairo after a few days to consummate the traditional formalities and honored the president's request by bringing Saousan, her mother, her uncle, and her brother to Côte d'Ivoire.

The family was treated to presidential-level hospitality throughout their three-day stay in Abidjan. They dined with the president every day. Once, when my mother-in-law opted for a second serving from the dinner menu, the waiter presented me with the same dish. "No thanks," I said. The president inconspicuously nodded his head, signaling to me that I needed to go for seconds to complement the mother of my future wife. At the end of the visit, he advised that I return to Cairo with our guests to expedite the official wedding ceremony. Everything happened very quickly—the trip to Egypt, the marriage ceremony in Cairo, and finally, the return to Abidjan with the new bride.

I settled into a new chapter in my life with my new wife in Abidjan. Not surprisingly, the ensuing rumors among my Ivorian brothers ran rampant. They had no idea about what had transpired, but some of them felt that I had been playing games with my Ivorian fiancée. President Houphouët-Boigny, on the other hand, adapted to my new reality. His special assistant was married to a Palestinian woman, at a time when on the international stage, the volatility of the Israeli-Palestinian conflict was at its peak. We resumed our work immediately. I was sent on numerous missions to see President Boumédiène, Chairman Arafat, as well as other heads of state.

Murky Waters of Love

Time had passed, but my heart had tasted the delights of love with my Ivorian fiancée, yet it persisted in not following my reason. I could not fully adapt to my new situation. Nonetheless, I persevered in the effort. My wife was very beautiful; this was reason enough to flatter my ego. I thought maybe my heart would eventually come to terms with my reasoning, but that was not the case. Soon, I could barely recognize myself in what I considered a cowardly act—a reprehensible and abominable mistake, which should never have happened to begin with. As the months passed, I was ever beset by new torments. I still performed my duties to my wife, but she could not in any way alleviate my torment. I did not want to settle in hypocrisy, being an open and direct person, but after several months, it had finally become abundantly clear that we were not a good match for each other.

I began to nurture the idea of a separation. I even pondered taking her home to Cairo to inform her parents of the gradual deterioration of our marriage. Hence, after the passage of time, I decided to reveal my feelings to her and express my intentions. Clearly, my love life had not proven to be an easy one.

While wrestling with these thoughts in my head, I was also focused on my diplomatic missions. I embarked on a trip that transited through Geneva. During my stopover, divine providence knocked at my door once again.

Powered by a *je ne sais quoi*, I chose to stay at the Hotel Ambassador, an unassuming and well-managed place on the Quai des Bergues, a waterfront location in the beautiful city. I had never stayed there before. In true Maquis fashion, prior to settling down in my room, I decided to go around the block and familiarize myself with the area in case of an emergency. The second rule of the Maquis is to take a position to see an approaching enemy and to always face the door. On my way out, I walked past the hotel reception and headed for the exit. To my utter shock, there she was—Titi, the love of my life. I thought I was dreaming. She was looking radiantly beautiful and dazzling, as she'd ever been. I stared in her direction, and after a few seconds of standing there in a haze of dizzy bewilderment, I approached her. I was shamefaced. She was obviously as astounded as I, but she was composed and very receptive. She agreed to join me for a drink. I wasn't surprised to learn that she'd heard I had gotten married. I began apologizing profusely and explained the circumstances that led to my predicament. It didn't seem to matter to her either way. "Well, it was a decision you made, and I respect that," she told me.

Looking for a place to stay in Geneva, she had also checked into the same hotel a few minutes earlier. In order to avoid detection by her parents, she decided not to visit the residence of her uncle, the Ivorian ambassador. Having paid a hefty price for her freedom, she was not emotionally ready to get back to the family fold. I was curious to know where she'd gone after she left Abidjan. "I went to stay with some close friends—the Sarraf family, in Beirut," she said. The Sarrafs owned the Wella Cosmetics manufacturing plant in Beirut. They also owned a pharmacy in Achrafieh, a residential neighborhood in the city. Their son Ghazi, a charming young man whom I met while he was attending the school of pharmacy in Lausanne, offered her a job in the family pharmacy. "From the moment I landed, I was greeted at their home and treated like a family member. Ghazi's parents, Tante Charlotte and Oncle Jean, showered me with much affection and kept me pampered throughout my stay. They did their absolute best to help me recover from my emotional wounds." She seemed to have recovered and was feeling much better.

After only six months, political turmoil began to take hold in Beirut. Israeli planes flew over the city nonstop. Residents were subjected to frequent roadblocks by the Lebanese army, which lasted for hours. The Phalangists, known by the locals as the Kataeb, demonstrated loudly, and on a daily basis, in Achrafieh, a well-known Christian district. This was the precursor to the painful civil war in Lebanon. During her stay, she even visited a Palestinian refugee camp in Beirut and experienced firsthand the Palestinian issue. What she encountered was deeply disturbing to her. Unable to endure the volatile climate, she thanked the Sarraf family for their generous hospitality and left for Casablanca. Dr. El Khatib's sister, Naïma, and her husband, Abdelkrim Boujibar, invited her to come and stay with them.

My beloved brethren catered to her every need and made her feel at home. Abdelkrim, also a pharmacy owner in the city, offered her a job. She struggled to communicate with customers in a neighborhood where a vast majority only spoke Arabic. As a result, she decided to return to Switzerland after only two months.

"I went to stay with Trang Hoang and her sister, Anh, my Vietnamese friends from college," she said. "Ah, *bon*, how are they doing?" I asked. "Very good. Trang is pursuing her doctorate in biochemistry and molecular biology." Titi and I were frequent dinner guests at their place, back when I was always commuting between Lausanne and Abidjan. They welcomed her to their home with open arms. She lived with them until she found a seasonal position as a replacement pharmacist at a pharmacy in Champéry, a ski resort in the Valais. She worked there for three months and came to Geneva at the end of the season to look for a job and a place to stay. "I plan to find a part-time job and pursue a postgraduate degree in history and political science at the Graduate Institute of International Studies," she told me. The research institute, affiliated with the Carnegie Endowment, was where most Swiss diplomats received their formation. "I was lucky enough to be admitted after a grueling interview with Dr. Jacques Freymond." She had not majored in history, a prerequisite for admission, but she aced the interview. I was beside myself with joy. "Thank God for the unexpected turn of events. Otherwise, I am not sure if we would have crossed paths at this juncture," I said.

"I find myself in a tormented relationship with my wife. I have actually decided to end the marriage," I confessed. She looked unfazed. "I am still in the process of mending my broken heart," she confided. "What you are going through is not a concern of mine. I can't be bothered with your personal troubles." I wasn't really surprised by her remark. Although she was adamant that I assume responsibility for my difficult situation, I believed our chance meeting was a fateful occurrence that only God could have planned. For several minutes, we caught up on other lighthearted matters before going our separate ways. We did not exchange personal information, but still, I felt confident that the Almighty had charted a path for us. At that moment, the future remained uncertain; even if time was not of the essence, sooner or later perhaps, destiny would bring us together for eternity. Until that fateful day, I thought, I would nurture the deepest hope and continue to wisely walk in God's chosen path.

  When I accompanied Saousan to see her parents in Cairo, I was certain that annulling our marriage would be a healthy decision for both of us in the long run. Her parents expressed regret at the unfortunate outcome. Dr. Sartawi as well was disappointed to hear the news.

  The process of ending the marriage lasted much longer than the actual marriage proposal. But despite the delays, everything happened in a peaceful and cordial manner. I returned to my normal routine. Saousan and her family adapted to their new reality.

  After the divorce was finalized, I tried my very best to locate my one true Love. While in Geneva on an assignment, I took a chance and went to the Lac Léman area, specifically to the adjacent Parc Barton, a public park belonging to the Graduate Institute of International Studies. The beautiful pink mansion was just a stone's throw away from the La Perle du Lac restaurant. While strolling through the park and taking in the sun, I observed the mischievous behavior of playful squirrels and watched closely the foot traffic coming in and out of the building. Suddenly, I caught a glimpse of my Love and ran toward her. As soon as she saw me approaching, she gasped and stopped. I was overjoyed. We gave each other a long bear hug. From that moment, we knew that we would be inseparable.

    She had grown accustomed to living a serene life in Geneva. In the Champel neighborhood, a chic part of the city, she had rented a small room in an apartment owned by an iconic Swiss political activist. Her uncle and aunt knew of her whereabouts, and her parents were even planning to visit her on their next trip to Europe. Madame Marie-Louise Dumuid, her eighty-two-year-old roommate, was the former proprietor of a hotel in the city. When I met her, I was impressed to learn of her militant past and passionate involvement in global politics. She recalled an unforgettable moment at the hotel with some media personalities during the signing of the Evian Accords, the document that established a cease-fire between Algeria and France. Everything seemed to be lining up fantastically. I was on cloud nine when I returned to Côte d'Ivoire. Smiling broadly, President Houphouët-Boigny said he wasn't surprised at all that we found each other again. "The love that you share with your fiancée is exemplary. I always knew that your separation would be temporary, and the source of the spring of your love would never run dry." Until today, his words continue to resonate in my heart.

    Our lives returned to normal again. When I resumed my travels between Geneva and Abidjan, it was as if we had never gone our separate ways at all. There was no need for us to rekindle our passions, because our love blossomed from the moment our paths intertwined again, and our bond became much stronger. When she went to meet her parents in Paris, it was a happy, yet sober get-together. Still, they were relieved to see her again.

    After our reunion, the topic of marriage did not cross her mind for a couple of years. I had asked her on several occasions, but she needed some time. Eventually, my Love warmed up to the idea and began to ponder the thought of getting married and returning to Côte d'Ivoire. When her parents offered her a pharmacy

A Dream for Peace

in Abidjan, she had them assure her that before accepting the gift, there would be no hidden caveat with respect to our private life. They gave their word. There were no strings attached.

At the time of our wedding, she did not concern herself about her parents' position. We had both come to accept their recalcitrance. But President Houphouët-Boigny was more than delighted to oversee our marriage vows. He even offered to organize the ceremony—"the ceremony of his son," he called it, would take place either at his palace in Yamoussoukro or in Abidjan. My Love did not share the president's proposition with her parents, because she did not want to subject them to such an affront. Either way, we knew that if we tied the knot in Côte d'Ivoire, the entire event would be televised without her parents in attendance. She suggested a more private wedding in Geneva. The president understood her concerns and welcomed the idea. Out of respect for her, he proposed that we use his private residence in the La Capite neighborhood for the festivities. Yet again, she opened up and shared her unease at the thought of having the ceremony anywhere other than her living father's house. She preferred a neutral location. Therefore, she chose the residence of the Côte d'Ivoire Embassy, a new and sumptuous property, formerly owned by the family of Maria Teresa Mestre, Grand Duchess of Luxembourg. President Houphouët-Boigny, always selfless and considerate, did not take umbrage to her wishes, telling her, *"My daughter, we will do anything for your peace of mind."* He agreed to facilitate her every need and make her happy to the very end.

The rules of the Catholic Church required that we had the proper dispensation of marriage before the commencement of our interfaith wedding. We sought the council of Abbé Jean-Pierre Kutwà on how to go about fulfilling our obligations. He approached Cardinal Yago, the appropriate authority, to get his approval and had him sign off on the dispensation.

My Love met privately with her mother and received a

Murky Waters of Love

memorable blessing before departing for Geneva to oversee preparations for our wedding. Her entire family was invited to the event, but other than her supportive sister Mireille, the only family members who committed to attending were her cousins. Mireille conducted herself magnificently under the difficult circumstances. From my side of the family, my sister Fifi was in delicate health and couldn't attend. Neither could my sisters Missa and Yasmina, who were both stay-at-home mothers. But my brother-in-law, Saïd, and my niece Seïda agreed to make the trip from Algiers. Abdelkrim and Naïma Boujibar confirmed they would be coming from Casablanca. Fortunately for us, the president asked the Ivorian Embassy to help with the event. When Titi arrived, she only had to approve the details of certain essentials with the invaluable help of Ambassador Amadou Traoré, Côte d'Ivoire's Permanent Representative to the UN in Geneva, and his wife, Worknesh.

Imam Sheikh Bouzouzou.

The nuptials began with a Muslim wedding, officiated by Imam Bouzouzou. He delivered an interfaith sermon, the *khutbah*:

A Dream for Peace

"In honor of this interfaith union between a Muslim and a Catholic, I would like the bride to know that I'd be talking about the importance of the Virgin Mary in Islam. The mother of Jesus has one of the longest *surahs* [chapters] in the Holy Qur'an," he declared. Two days later, we visited the official residence of the Ivorian ambassador for the civil ceremony. Ambassador Traoré officiated the event in a room designed to serve as a temporary consular section. Following the ceremony, we drove in a convoy to the Immaculée Conception Church, a stonemason's monastic masterpiece of simplistic architecture in the Geneva countryside enclave of Vésenaz. This was an ideal place for the Catholic wedding, beset in a tranquil and classical Benedictine spirituality. President Houphouët-Boigny, my best man, was accompanied by his daughter, Marie, who had always been like a sister to me. Mrs. Posset-Viaud, a longtime friend of my in-laws, was the bride's maid of honor.

Mrs. Posset-Viaud.

Murky Waters of Love

Two Ivorian priests, Abbé Jean-Pierre Kutwà and Abbé Marcel Eboï, presided over the wedding with the support of the parish's resident priest, Abbé Robert de Mesly. Like a place out of a fairy tale, the church was decorated in accordance with the wishes of my Love. There were white and blue flowers honoring the Virgin Mary adorning the ends of the pews all the way to the bottom of the altar. I stood in silence waiting for my Love to make her entrance. The quiet ambience of the church soon gave way to the rich timbres of a powerful hymn emanating from an organ, and I glanced over my shoulder to catch a glimpse of the bride. Wearing a beautiful white taffeta silk dress, she walked down the aisle, looking dazzling, with four flower girls behind her guiding the long train. Through the netted veil partially hiding her lovely face, our eyes met. We both knew then the moment had finally arrived. She held firmly to a bouquet of white and blue flowers. The serene atmosphere in the church was overwhelming. When she reached the altar, the music faded into the silky soft voice of the priest chanting the verses of a prayer in Latin. We remained focused and serious throughout the entire ceremony. Having said our separate vows, we spoke in unison to thank the Almighty for our love. It all felt like a wonderful dream. It wasn't until we were seated in the back of our limousine that the magnitude of the moment dawned on our conscience. Our love had finally been memorialized forever.

We returned to the ambassador's official residence for a two-day royal celebration with the blessing of the president. Several of our friends and family made their way to our seats to take pictures and wish us well. At the end of the cocktail reception, we went outside for the dinner event. Relaxing inside the blue and white tents on the scenic grounds of the garden, we took in the spectacular views of the Cologny golf club.

A Dream for Peace

My niece Seïda with her dad, Saïd.

Abdelkrim and Naïma Boujibar.

Murky Waters of Love

A sumptuous feast featuring an exotic blend of Ivorian and intercontinental foods was served to the delight of all, in a merry atmosphere with our many guests. My wife and I were thrilled; our dream had finally become reality. After dinner, we took to the dance floor for our first dance, to the amusement of all the guests. The wedding cake was wheeled in on a cart, and we posed for the cutting ceremony. The entire compound echoed with a fusion of hot rhythmic dance tunes from Ivorian and international music, sung by the sultry voice of Ernesto Djedje. We enjoyed ourselves on the dance floor and left the party around midnight, but our guests partied until the wee hours of the morning.

President Houphouët congratulating me.

A Dream for Peace

Mons. Kutwà and Abbé Eboï directing the president.

President Houphouët with daughter Marie.

Murky Waters of Love

Relaxing at the reception with President Houphouët.

My sister-in-law, Mireille, joins us for a picture.

A Dream for Peace

The president joined my wife and I at the Immaculée Conception Church in celebration of thanksgiving the following day. Most of our guests were also in attendance. Everyone returned to the residence for an exquisite Sunday brunch. We planned to depart for our honeymoon after the festivities were over. But when we went to thank the president for his kindness and generosity, he insisted we stay with him for a few more days of spiritual reflection. He never underestimated the importance of God in everything. His words and sentiments echoed wisdom and a simple adage:

Leaving for the residence.

"My children, you must bond together like a snail in its shell." During our time with him, we shared lots of deep and meaningful conversations.

Our honeymoon was in the Brazilian Amazon, where an excursion by canoe on the Negro and Solimões rivers was first on our agenda. From the small motorized canoe, we watched in utter amazement the tributaries of the two rivers intersecting before their confluence. Words cannot express our joy and happiness on our unique adventure. After a couple of days in the region, we traveled to Rio de Janeiro to bask in the sun on the beautiful beaches of Ipanema. Before our departure to Côte d'Ivoire, my Love wanted to see the much-acclaimed newly built city of Brasilia. Ivorian Ambassador Charles Gomis was at the airport to welcome us. We met his wife and daughter at a specially arranged congratulatory lunch later that afternoon before embarking on a tour of the city. I was mostly the one who enjoyed the architectural marvels, even though a majority of the infrastructure was still under construction. Our Brazilian chauffeur, a spirited character, exposed us to the local culture and traditions throughout our stay.

From that moment on, we transformed every day of our new reality into a dream; we continued to live each day together like a dream. Forty years after we first met, our love has remained unchanged, and I love my wife as if it were our first day.

As a newly wed couple, we had just begun to settle into our rotation in Abidjan. Meanwhile, my father-in-law did not miss the opportunity to show his discontent at what had transpired. He had a message delivered to us by some people who were close to the family: *"Let them know that I do not wish to see them, nor do I wish to have any contact with them."* His wrath did not stop with us; he also refused to speak to everyone who attended our wedding celebration, including President Houphouët-Boigny and Mrs. Posset-Viaud. As far as he was concerned, Mrs. Posset-Viaud had committed a sinful act. My sister-in-law, Mireille, persisted in being extraordinarily supportive. She continued to see us every time we visited Paris, where she lived, always eager to welcome us at the Concord terminal of Charles de Gaulle Airport whenever we arrived as part of the presidential delegation. Knowing fully well that word would get out to her father, she socialized with us, fearless of his wrath. Mrs. Posset-Viaud remained unmoved by his judgmental and dogged attitude. We received her fervent love and support throughout the difficult times. In the absence of her parents' love, President Houphouët was a natural father figure and the pillar that provided my wife with warmth and affection.

I found some solace in my wife's courage. She expressed no regrets; neither did she make mention of the intransigent attitude of her parents, nor did she ever display a lack of regard for them. We were resigned to expect no change in their behavior. They watched with suspicion and disappointment as our lives evolved. But we were very happy.

My wife and I with the president on his birthday.

Maintaining an archetypal relationship with us, the president never lost sight of his role as a father. He ensured that Titi accompanied me on every foreign trip. Each time I went on a mission, I'd get my itinerary and a plane ticket from the state. But the president offered her a separate ticket to keep us together. At every destination, she found a way to take care of personal business and went about tackling different activities while I focused on my mission. At home in Abidjan, she always joined the president and I for a family dinner at his residence. The atmosphere around us was peaceful, relaxed, and eternally jovial. It didn't take her long to adapt and grow accustomed to being at the house. Carine, Marie's daughter who lived with the president while she was completing high school at the Lycée Français d'Abidjan, was placed under my wife's care. She became a daughter to us. We surrounded her with lots of warmth and loving tenderness, even though I did not hesitate to strongly admonish her when she deserved it.

My wife experienced an unexpected medical situation and was scheduled to undergo two surgeries. Thankfully, years earlier, I had taken precautions to ensure that she and I were covered under the best medical insurance premium in Switzerland. I went with her to Geneva to help select the best surgeons. Two eminent surgeons were recommended to us: Dr. Trần Ngọc Trần and Dr. Jean-Marc Fiala. I demanded that her surgery be performed at the Clinique de Genolier, located about thirty kilometers outside Geneva. The facility had an excellent reputation at the time, but the logistics of bringing two surgeons with divergent schedules was not so easy: Dr. Fiala, a very kind man, had no problem being there for my wife's surgery at 10:00 a.m. However, Dr. Trần had a previously scheduled surgery at 3:00 p.m. that same day back in Geneva, at a different health-care facility, Clinique de la Tour. He stated apologetically that it was not possible for him to leave Genolier and make it in time to tend to his "other" patient. Hence, he declined to take on the responsibility. He was a surgical prodigy, and I was not about to give him up. "I can rent a helicopter to take you to Genolier. I will have the pilot wait for the duration of the surgery, and then he will take you back to the Clinique de la Tour in Geneva in time for your next surgery," I pleaded. From his reaction, it was obvious that he was heartened, because the proposition simplified matters for him. He immediately made the necessary arrangements to attend to my wife.

The president was extremely concerned. Like a caring father, he called her before the operation to give reassurance that she would be fine. He followed up each hour to stay abreast of her surgery. When she awoke from the procedure, she was wheeled into the recovery room and told she needed an immediate blood transfusion. Fearing that the blood might be contaminated, she refused to give her consent. I was on the phone with the president at the time and handed the phone to her per his request. She was quiet and attentive. Listening to his soothing and nurturing words, she eventually warmed up to the idea and agreed to go ahead with the transfusion. It went well. To my relief, a nurse wheeled her up on a gurney within a couple of hours. I had arranged to have a bed next to hers in her private ward. Soon after the president took it upon himself to inform her parents about the unfortunate medical condition, my mother-in-law flew to Geneva. She stayed for a couple of days and visited the ward on a regular basis, returning to Abidjan only when she was convinced her daughter was on the mend. Despite maintaining a hectic schedule, the president was always the first person to call and check on my wife's progress each morning. He kept up the habit until she left the clinic. I'd hoped that the occasion would usher in a new era of improved relations between my in-laws and us, especially after her mother's visit, but those hopes were dashed. We never heard from them.

    Dr. Trần went beyond the call of duty and conducted himself with excellence. He lived up to his Mandarin heritage with class and asked that I refrain from renting the helicopter. He even refused to be compensated for the surgery and follow-up visits. When my Love began her convalescence, one of my nieces arrived from Algiers to be with her. I returned to work in Abidjan with the intention of coming back as soon as I could. Upon learning about the lengths Dr. Trần had gone to accommodate us, the president invited him and his wife to visit Côte d'Ivoire. The Trầns reshuffled their schedules no more than a few days later and came to see us in Abidjan. They were given a tour of the country, going from south to north, spanning Abidjan to Korhogo. Designated officials at every destination, including Yamoussoukro, the president's hometown, received us. They were even treated to a luncheon at the palace and given a tour of the city by the mayor. The president gave them the red carpet reception in Abidjan, taking the time to spend all of his leisure hours with them in intimate dinner settings. I had many great conversations with the man who had put out his best effort to salvage my wife's condition. I was sure he could tell that my appreciation extended beyond our relationship. The visit culminated in a memorable interaction on the eve of their departure. I knew from then on that we would continue to maintain a valuable friendship for years to come.

My Love and I enjoyed relative peace and quiet for a few years, without much disturbance from my in-laws. Occasionally, my very thoughtful and graceful sister-in-law Geneviève went out of her way to bring along her kids for a discreet visit. Ever fearful of her dad's wrath, her sporadic visits were always cloaked in total secrecy, even going as far as to admonish the kids to keep their lips sealed. Her beautiful daughter, Audrey, was my wife's goddaughter. We had watched her grow up and came to appreciate the rare moments we shared with her, nurturing and showering her with love and affection. She had just turned sixteen, and we were so proud of her vibrant personality. I was particularly impressed by her tender nature and exceptional qualities.

When Geneviève called to tell us that Audrey was in critical condition at a local hospital, we could not believe our ears. She had had a bad reaction to some medication. We stormed out of the house and rushed to the hospital. God had called her by the time we arrived. We stood there in the hallway of the intensive care unit in a state of shock, mystified and speechless. Geneviève was devastated and beyond grief stricken. We wept with her and tried our best to console her at the same time. The drive to her home was particularly difficult and painful. For obvious reasons, we had never been to their home because we did not want my in-laws to find out and give her a

A Dream for Peace

hard time. Titi knew she had to be emotionally strong for her sister. She continued to commute to Geneviève's home and stayed by her side for as long as she was needed.

My wife with niece Audrey.

Audrey's funeral brought the family together for the first time in several years. It was an extremely difficult time for everyone. During the burial ceremony, Geneviève stood between my wife and her mother for support. I decided to stand behind my father-in-law with my friend Essy beside me. Overcome by emotions, he almost fell, but for the quick hands of Essy and I. We held him until he regained his composure. After the ceremony, all of us did our best to contain our grief. We walked quietly to our cars and drove to Geneviève's house. Titi continued to visit her sister until she decided to move to Benin, a neighboring country, to recuperate and center herself again. Relations with my in-laws did not change. My Love became increasingly distraught over the fact that she had been deprived of a normal interaction with her goddaughter over the years.

    The situation finally reached a climax for me. Too much time had passed, and the family feud had to come to an end, no matter what. The president often asked me if there had been any new developments with my wife's parents. I grew tired of answering in the negative. "Because of you guys, my brother refuses to speak to me," the president would say dejectedly on occasion. "I am sure we need to continue to cultivate patience," he'd say in closing. The time had come to find a solution to the situation. It seemed to have been going on for eternity.

    I pondered the irony—I had once seized the moment to mend fences between Presidents Houphouët-Boigny and Boumédiène, who had a strong dislike for each other. I lent a helping hand in organizing the first meeting between Israelis and Palestinians, whose hatred for one another is a mystery to no one. If I was unable to sow peace in my own family, I would have failed in my mission of peace. The Creator had used my in-laws as instruments to give birth to my wife, the love of my life. Without a semblance of doubt in my heart, I knew that I had to give it my all in a limitless and passionate determination to bridge our differences.

    With these thoughts still brewing in my head, I finished my Maghrib[34] prayers one evening and asked my Love to get ready to go on a visit to her parents' house. We had been at loggerheads with them for over nine years. She was reluctant at first, but I engaged her in a conversation and emphasized that I was the one who had been

---

[34] The fourth of the five formal daily prayers performed by practicing Muslims.

the object of their hatred for a long time, yet I was ready to forgive and move on, even if I had to face another humiliation. Either way, I would not be affected by their posture, because it would be me who decided to make peace in order to silence any sense of misguided pride. I advised her to also find it in her heart and take the bold step. She finally came around and saw things my way.

We pulled up at the entrance of her parents' majestic villa in the residential district of Cocody Ambassades. They lived just a few yards away from President Houphouët-Boigny's private residence. I introduced myself to the guards at the gate, and they ushered us through within a few minutes. We strolled down the small walkway across a beautiful pond to the front door of the house. The housekeeper led the way to our seats in the living room. I breathed a deep sigh and took in the fact that it was my first time in the elegant home of the Ollo family. The place was an architectural masterpiece. Looking around, I immediately noticed that we shared the same taste in décor. I also had an affinity for Rose du Portugal marble. My father-in-law walked in, smiling gently, visibly pleased to see us. He embraced each of us with a very warm bear hug and apologized for the absence of his wife, who was somewhere in Europe at the time. Like inseparable friends, the two of us talked as if there had never been a single moment lost in our relationship. My Love listened and did not utter a word for the entire hour-long visit. The more we spoke, the better I felt. It was an overdue feeling of relief. In the end, he promised to invite us for dinner when his wife returned home. We bid him a hearty farewell and took our leave. The heavy weight had been lifted from my shoulders.

Eager to share the news, I suggested we head straight to President Houphouët's residence. Obviously pleased, he congratulated us for taking a step in the right direction. I thanked him for his flawless support and for being there for us over the years.

My father-in-law kept his word and called to invite us to dinner a few days later. We stopped at the president's residence for a few minutes on the way to their house that evening. Our hearts were a little heavy, but for the president, it was a bittersweet moment in a way, because for the first time in many years, we were not about to have a family dinner with him. Overwhelmed by emotions, we came out of the residence and noticed my father-in-law standing on the edge of the street, waiting to greet us. We were greatly touched by the scene. He welcomed us with open arms and undisguised joy. Titi's mother was visibly delighted to see us in their home. They pulled out all the stops and gave us a wonderful reception. There were five of us at the dining table, including a friend of theirs who sat beside us for the veritable feast. We kept a lively conversation, but my Love was a lady of few words that evening. We left their house late and came home shortly before midnight. Like clockwork, my father-in-law called exactly at midnight. "You are not sleeping, I hope," he inquired in a pleasant voice. "No, not at all," I said. "Good enough. I just called to make sure you arrived safely and also to tell you I had put aside some mangoes for you to take home but forgot to give them to you." He knew Titi loved mangoes. "If you don't mind, I'd like to bring them over in a few minutes. I want her to enjoy them for breakfast." "Most certainly, she'd like that," I said happily. "I will meet you at the door." He came shortly after the call. His love and affection for his daughter had remained intact after all those years. It was abundantly clear that he had suffered from the long separation.

From the moment we reconciled, he couldn't get enough of us. Every time we left the country, he reached out to let us know that he wished to see us back much sooner than later. Our interactions were always uplifting, and we never spoke about the past. I found out very quickly that in the Ollo family, genuine warmth and kindheartedness were natural traits. They overwhelmed me with deep love and surrounded me with unabated kindness. "It delights me greatly to see the tender side of the Ollo family," the president joked at our morning breakfast meeting. We became very close, and

A Dream for Peace

I began calling them *"Papa"* and *"Maman."* *"Mon grand fils"* was my mother-in-law's preferred name for me. After spending a two-week vacation with Titi and I in the US, she took time to write me a memorable letter that conveyed her most affectionate tenderness in its introduction:

> À *mon grand fils "Amour".*
> *Mon grand fils, I have learned to know you better: You are all about "love". I want you to know that I love you much as deeply as a child born out of my very womb . . .*

I was truly shaken to the core of my soul. So much time was lost on Love in order to reach Love . . .

Cruising Lake Lucerne, Switzerland.

Murky Waters of Love

A Dream for Peace

Murky Waters of Love

A Dream for Peace

"I am an African and an Arab, but if history was to impose on me a choice between the two, my choice is quickly made: I am an African."

President Houari Boumédiène

Chapter Nine

The Abidjan-Algiers Axis

Harmony with my wife's family was the happy medium that had been difficult to reach, but it was the painful events surrounding young Audrey's calling into God's kingdom that led to an open dialogue and a meeting of the minds with my in-laws. Throughout the period of tumult in my love life, I continued to engage the most ardent militants in dialogue for the sake of finding peaceful solutions to political conflicts. Again and again, I experienced constructive outcomes on many diplomatic fronts, but I never managed to crack the code when it came to solving the dilemma with my father-in-law until the time was right. This was the case too with the complex nature of my diplomatic missions and highly classified presidential assignments. On matters concerning the Arab world, the Palestinian question, and multifaceted political issues of the so-called socialist African countries, I was always fervent in my approach but patient in the face of the many obstacles in my path. "*These problems must remain between you and I,*" the president would say regarding the secretive nature of my missions. "*You have no need for a secretary. We will work together in private, here at my residence.*" He overemphasized the discreet manner in which I was to conduct my unique diplomatic duties and assignments to ensure that state secrets were never compromised. As Minister of Foreign Affairs, Usher was in charge of all official diplomatic matters of the republic, as were all those who succeed him in the position—Ministers Siméon Aké and Essy Amara. But even they were inclined to inform enquiring minds that certain missions in foreign diplomacy were highly classified matters of state, exclusively restricted to "Dr. Berrah's domain."

President Houphouët had been a skeptic of the Non-Aligned Movement since its inception, because he doubted that the actions taken at past summits yielded constructive results. This was because he believed that the member nations were indeed aligned with either of the two blocs. Nevertheless, to honor an invitation by his great friend President Boumédiène, he decided to attend the September 1973 summit in Algiers for the very first time. Every head of state from the Third World countries was expected to attend, including Cuban President Fidel Castro, who made no secret of his disdain for the Ivorian leader, whom he thought of as the archetypal valet of imperialism.

President Boumédiène received a copy of the Cuban leader's speech hours before Castro was to address the summit. When he noticed that the content was full of personal insults directed at President Houphouët, he decided to intervene and prevent a major diplomatic incident. Summoning Abdelaziz Bouteflika, his foreign minister, to his office, he directed him to work with his Cuban counterpart and persuade President Castro to tone down his rhetoric. Not surprisingly, Castro wouldn't cooperate. An irate President Boumédiène made me aware of the hot-button issue at the very last minute. "Mr. President, let Castro go ahead with his speech," I said, after pondering the matter. "We will cut off his microphone feed to everyone's headphone as soon as he gets to the insults and pretend there was a technical problem. He will continue to speak, but no one will hear that part of his speech. The technical glitch will be 'fixed' as soon as he moves on to the next topic." The president liked my idea. Much to everyone's relief, the plan was perfectly executed at the time of Castro's speech, and none of the attendees, including President Houphouët, picked up on the anomaly.

Barely a month after the incident, the October War began

The Abidjan-Algiers Axis

in the Middle East. I was dispatched on many diplomatic missions to Algiers, bearing messages from both presidents. The main topic of contention was regarding President Houphouët's reluctance to join with a majority of African leaders who had ceased diplomatic relations with Israel in solidarity with Egypt. The president thought that a diplomatic rupture with the Jewish state would not provide a solution to the conflict, especially since they were the beneficiary of US aid and military support. He'd rather continue to explore diplomatic channels. Côte d'Ivoire would therefore remain on the sidelines as a neutral observer.

President Boumédiène was eagerly awaiting my arrival when I walked into his office at the presidential palace in Algiers. On this particular mission, I was there to deliver a detailed message about President Houphouët's recent visit to see President Nixon at the White House. But the issue of continued diplomatic relations between Côte d'Ivoire and Israel seemed to weigh heavily on his mind. "All of us must have clear positions, because Israel is occupying a part of Africa's territory," he said. "If unfortunately, and this is not our wish, foreign troops were occupying a part of Côte d'Ivoire and threatening Abidjan, and I was asked 'What can you do?' will the Ivorian people expect any less of me than an expression of solidarity?" I agreed with his premise. He was passionate about pursuing a united and active African solidarity front to teach Israel a lesson for occupying the west bank of the Suez Canal on the African shore of Egypt.

Algeria had already set the tone by sending some of its elite fighters to the Egyptian and Syrian fronts and absorbed enormous financial burdens arming both fronts. Having made such a commendable commitment, he could not comprehend the reluctance of Côte d'Ivoire to join with the rest of the alliance in severing relations. I understood our position because I had debriefed President Houphouët and discussed the issue at length. He never took a decision without pondering the dynamics of a long-term impact that yielded successful outcomes. We believed that the US had to be pushed into the forefront of the issue and be made to play more of an active role in order to force Israel's hand. President Boumédiène was not aware that President Houphouët had discussed the matter with President Nixon and received some positive assurances. "Nixon needs peace in the Middle East. It is in their best interest," I said. "But unfortunately, he finds himself in a position in which he can neither require nor even recommend anything to Israeli Premier Golda Meir due to the developing Watergate scandal." This was a delicate balancing act for me personally, because I did feel his passion and agreed with him on the timing of our decision, yet I wanted him to reflect on the issue from a broader perspective. "Nixon reaffirmed his position in a letter to President Houphouët, promising to do everything in his power to bring about a peaceful resolution." He was quick to respond to that idea: "Under the current circumstances, we cannot simply settle for Nixon's promises. We have to adopt a clear position. That is the least we can do."

Assessing his mood, I knew it was imperative that I use all of my God-given talents to find a solution to the issue. President Houphouët and I had a big-picture view of the entire situation, and it was within those parameters we approached the subject of breaking off diplomatic relations. The Palestinian problem was at the heart of our concerns, coupled with the fact that a cessation in relations with Israel carried with it certain risks of total alienation and, most importantly, a breakdown in dialogue. "We are not asking for economic, financial, or material assistance; just an official position. I do not think that this is asking the impossible," he stated passionately and, without missing a beat, continued to make his point: "Côte d'Ivoire is a great country, and more than anyone, I am convinced about the sincerity of Houphouët. He is not motivated by material motives or anything else. He is an honest politician with a moral and intellectual integrity beyond any doubt. He is honesty personified!" "Mr. President," I said, "President Houphouët shares

The Abidjan-Algiers Axis

your exact sentiments and holds you in high regard. His friendship with you is unencumbered by extraneous pressures." He could sense that I was on the same page. We were, after all, brothers motivated by a common purpose, duty, and honor. "I do not wish to see my friend Houphouët-Boigny isolated, or to find himself outside of our current unanimity. If he stayed out of this consensus, his position would certainly be respected, but nobody would agree with him." I took my notes and listened. "He is a great African leader, and this is why his role with us is vital. If I thought for a moment there was a glimmer of hope that he could do something with Nixon, or if I had a glimmer of hope that Golda Meir would listen to him, I would stand behind him against all odds. If I knew that, although isolated, he could do something, I myself would ask him not to break off diplomatic relations. But the events have taken a turn for the worse, and the situation is quite dramatic." Without adding much to his eloquent rhetoric, I left the meeting, assured that I needed to do my very best to convince President Houphouët that indeed time was of the essence and that his decision was fundamental in impressing upon the world that we were one with our brothers.

On October 31, within twenty-four hours after I left Algiers, I returned to give him a response from President Houphouët—"Your message was faithfully transmitted. I take pride in the friendship and trust that you have bestowed in me. Yours was a moving—very moving—message, especially because you touched the sensitive string of the sacred ideals of solidarity and unity, to which I have consecrated all my often-solitary life, even though I have too often been misunderstood by my own brothers. This is the reason why I returned to Addis earlier this year, a return that offered me the happy occasion to meet you, and weave this fabric of kinship, which Algerians are capable of; a friendship which I hold in great honor. In life, the most reliable friends are not always those who agree with you."

President Houphouët-Boigny was a goldsmith of diplomacy;

A Dream for Peace

his sensitivity and tactfulness were second to none. I engaged him in lengthy discussions, conjuring up every side of the equation, until he finally understood that we had no choice in the matter. "Mr. President," I said. "This is a situation that has been imposed on us, and our country must not fail in its duty of solidarity with Africa." He paused for a moment. "Let me reflect on that. I will get back to you in a couple of days."

On November 8, 1973, Côte d'Ivoire severed diplomatic relations with Israel. Before the news broke, the president dispatched me on a mission to Algiers. He was adamant that I should be by the side of President Boumédiène when the historic announcement was made on television. Through the monitors, we heard President Houphouët-Boigny's forceful narrative about Egypt's territorial rights and the illegal occupation of an African territory by Israeli forces. I had a feeling it was a solemn moment for him, but for a much-delighted President Boumédiène, the announcement could not have come at a more perfect time. President Houphouët's actions deprived Israel of its relations with the bloc of Conseil de l'Entente[35] countries, because the Ivorian ambassador represented the bloc in Israel.

President Boumédiène, the visionary who kept alive the dream of a powerful African continent in a postcolonial era, maintained a puritanical outlook, which was shrouded by his warm, thoughtful demeanor. A distant observer would have assumed that his austere appearance was part of the reason why he was revered by most. But he was more of a pragmatist; a magnanimous person with an incorruptible presence who was passionately dedicated to improving the lives of Africa's people. There was a constant exchange of ideas and views between him, President Houphouët-Boigny, and myself. The two leaders shared a common vision of the world and often consulted each other to define and adopt similar strategies

---

[35] Council of Accord: West African regional cooperation forum.

The Abidjan-Algiers Axis

on global matters. "We are very good friends now, and I do not hide anything from you. You trust me, and I trust you completely," President Houphouët affirmed, and President Boumédiène echoed similar sentiments: "You have my trust and my support." He told me repeatedly that he would continue to cultivate a sincere friendship with Houphouët-Boigny.

My own private meetings with President Boumédiène often lasted several hours, and we tackled many wide-ranging topics. We discussed world affairs and pondered constructive solutions to diplomatic stalemates. We also considered different strategies to help free our brother countries that were still submerged under colonial oppression. Africa's development in the postcolonial era, the Israeli-Palestinian conflict, and the Arab-African dialogue were at the epicenter of our conversations. He and I routinely analyzed the impact of the new world economic order on Africa's relations with other continents and reassessed our role on the global stage. He was always adamant on the need for Africa's continued independence, free from the influence of the two major ideological blocs. We developed such a strong rapport that he even began going against protocol on several occasions and accompanied me to my official vehicle.

Not long after the first oil crisis, the two leaders sought to valorize all raw materials, using oil as a vehicle to bring coffee, cocoa, and iron—the riches of the soil and subsoil of Africa—to the forefront of political discourse. President Georges Pompidou of France was also on board with the idea. President Houphouët wanted Africa to be in some ways "the body of the bird," with Europe taking up one wing while the oil-producing Arab and Gulf countries took up the other, but the plan was torpedoed by the US from the beginning.

"I am an African and an Arab, but if history was to impose on me a choice between the two, my choice is quickly made: I am an African."

A Dream for Peace

Those were the words of President Boumédiène. He inspired an active engagement by some Arab states who deemed the approach as a tool that could be used to help resolve the Palestinian issue. There were meetings between African and Arab leaders that were designed to improve cooperation between developing Arab states and underdeveloped African countries. However, the rich Arab states rarely engaged the poor African countries, and every proposition was calculated to the cent of the dollar. It wasn't always clear to me whether the Arabs were incapable of understanding or simply refused to comprehend that oil-based wealth was only temporary, while Africa's vast resources in raw commodities—agricultural, mining, and minerals—were virtually inexhaustible. Initially, the overall objective of the proposed trade alliance, which was founded on principles of interpenetration for mutual benefit, received enthusiastic support from all the regional powers. But there remained some sporadic intransigence on the way to securing commitments from some Arab states to take part in the summit.

EL MOUDJAHID
la révolution par le peuple et pour le peuple — quotidien national d'information

AUDIENCE PRESIDENTIELLE

* **LE Dr BERAH**
Envoyé spécial du Président ivoirien

Le Président du Conseil de la Révolution et du Conseil des ministres, M. Houari Boumediène, a reçu hier matin au siège de la Présidence, le Docteur Berah, envoyé spécial du Président Houphouët-Boigny.

The Abidjan-Algiers Axis

Eventually, my tireless diplomatic efforts, coupled with relentless pressure from President Boumédiène, paid off. "My opinion is not conjectural. It is my deep conviction. I do not want to win over the heart of Africa to the Arabs or the heart of the Arabs to Africa, but I have the firm conviction that our fate is common, that the two regions are complimentary." The first summit in March 1977 was attended by the OAU countries and their Arab League counterparts (with the exception of Malawi, an avid supporter of Israel). Even though we Africans came to accept the charter of the organization, the Arab countries continued to procrastinate on all pertinent matters. It became an impossible marriage: in championing the cause, Presidents Boumédiène and Houphouët expended their resources to improve relations among the group of countries.

A concerted effort to integrate the African continent economically began in earnest with plans to amalgamate an Afro-Arab league. Our pursuit of the establishment of a common global market for raw materials and petroleum products was relentless, and both Presidents Houphouët-Boigny and Boumédiène remained consistent with the underlying principles in our objectives. In speaking to them before each mission, I always emphasized the importance of accelerating the political and socioeconomic integration of the African continent through the promotion of sustainable development that transcended cultural levels to expedite the integration of African economies. I believed that an equal level of development across our vast continent would ultimately lead to peace. After identifying a number of areas where sound measures could be taken toward the elimination of trade barriers as we focused on the revalorization of raw materials, President Boumédiène suggested that it was imperative he present our case to the UN General Assembly.

He sent a letter to Secretary-General Kurt Waldheim requesting an opportunity to address the body in a special session. President Houphouët-Boigny knew that the creation of a common market was an ambitious goal, especially if it were to favor the so-

A Dream for Peace

called Third World countries. But we were fully aware of the difficult measures to be taken by the individual member states, both within the OAU and the Arab League, and also at the individual levels. Nonetheless, without bold measures at a continental level, the goal of imposing a new and equitable international economic order would not be attainable. In his historic address to the UN General Assembly on April 1974, President Boumédiène made a convincing case for the integration of raw materials and oil, and he underscored to Afro-Arab heads of state not to focus on oil pricing alone but to embrace the merits of the bigger picture. Otherwise, he stressed, developing countries would continue to depend on the pace at which barriers to trade were eliminated. We had performed extensive studies on finding the right approach to establish a new world economic order by focusing heavily on raw material revalorization. Although the conversation had begun in earnest, I was convinced that in order to reach the ultimate goal of making revalorization a standard universal policy for international trade, our league of Afro-Arab nations had to remain united, but that idea would be easier said than done.

The year 1974 brought about many unique challenges for raw material valorization. There was one crisis after another, particularly between the developed and underdeveloped countries. One such crisis hit close to home for both leaders. Algeria was a frequent purchaser of coffee and bananas from Côte d'Ivoire. While they were working on finding a solution to the valorization issue, Algeria purchased nineteen thousand tons of coffee at an agreed-upon price, which had been negotiated by the director of the Caisse de Stabilisation[36] and his Algerian counterpart, the director of ONACO. But the deal was executed without the approval of President Houphouët-Boigny.

A week later, speculators at the world coffee trade exchange doubled the price of coffee. The president conducted a quick

---

[36] State agency in Côte d'Ivoire responsible for managing raw material prices.

investigation and was not happy when he discovered that his director had overstepped his competence and consummated a deal without his knowledge. He called and suggested that I pay a visit to his "brother" President Boumédiène in Algiers. "Tell him that the West will laugh in our faces if they discover that we worked very hard to revalorize the prices of our raw materials when dealing with them but then turned around and negotiated a different price among ourselves." He wanted an immediate readjustment in the price of coffee to ensure that the northern region of Côte d'Ivoire could reap the financial benefits. The news would coincide with his first-ever visit to oversee rural developmental programs and break ground on a massive well-digging project in a region that was poorer than the southern part of the country. He asked that I raise awareness on the plight of the Muslim people of northern Côte d'Ivoire while in Algiers.

Before embarking on the mission, I arranged a meeting with both the director of the Caisse de Stabilisation and the Minister of Agriculture and asked to see the records for the Algerian coffee transaction. The agreement's contents were accurate, with no irregularities, but the president still insisted that I go and see President Boumédiène. "It is a political matter," he assured me, "not a commercial one." I gathered my courage and went to Algiers.

Under the circumstances, I asked Mr. Pierre Angora, the Ivorian chargé d'affaires in Algeria, to accompany me to the Boumédiène meeting. It was his first meeting with the head of state of his accredited country, and he was more than happy to come along. Our discussions with the president began promptly in the early morning. He listened attentively as I explained the problem in detail and asked, "What would you do if you were in my shoes?" I did not hesitate with my response: "I would give satisfaction to the request of your friend and brother." He seemed relieved. On my way out, he placed a quick phone call to Mr. Layachi Yaker, his Minister of Commerce.

A Dream for Peace

I went to see Mr. Yaker in the afternoon, accompanied by the Ivorian chargé d'affaires. Surrounded by staff, he and I reminisced briefly about our college days in France before we got down to business. President Boumédiène had instructed him to readjust the price of the twenty thousand tons of coffee, but he needed some further clarification on the matter. I shared my thoughts and elaborated on President Houphouët's concerns. I also proposed that a readjustment was in order, and it had to be in line with the day's valuation. "The deal cannot be renegotiated in accordance with the quote of the day, because Algeria would have to pay twice the price for the transaction," Mr. Yaker told me. I held back from reminding him that his president and I agreed on the premise. "Berrah, you have no experience in the coffee trade business, unlike your Minister of Agriculture and Abdoulaye Fadiga, your director of the Caisse de Stabilisation." He laughed, but he failed to look at the matter constructively as we had done, taking into consideration the larger repercussions and imminent fallout from the global community. I took a diplomatic code of silence and listened. He said, "Let's reconvene another meeting after the president and I discuss the matter in detail. There will be significant financial consequences to such a decision. I believe he should know about that." "Fair enough," I said.

From there, I went to see my cousin, the Director of Political Affairs, at the Foreign Ministry. "The rumor around Algiers is that you have come to take your country's money to give to Côte d'Ivoire," he said. The news had spread like wildfire. "President Houphouët-Boigny is a noble man," I replied. *"What he receives with his left hand, he gives back with his right hand."* He smiled and quickly switched the conversation to a more casual topic. Yaker called within minutes to summon me to his office. "I do not know what you've done to President Boumédiène, but regardless, he has instructed me to do what you asked of me." He spoke as though his authority had been undermined. I was relieved at the outcome. We executed a new contract with the agreed-upon terms, and Côte d'Ivoire recouped several millions of dollars.

When I reached the president on the phone, he was on an official visit in the Ivorian town of Khorogo in the north. Elated at the news, he promptly asked me to catch a flight to meet him in the region without delay. I flew to Paris to connect back to Abidjan and boarded a single-engine propeller plane at the military airport to Khorogo. Prior to takeoff, I received some impromptu precautionary instructions from the pilot. "Just in case of any emergency," he said. I learned how to keep the control lever between my legs and land the plane if necessary. Thankfully, the flight took me to the destination without any adverse events. But the president had already left the town for another destination, and staff members were there to usher me onto a waiting helicopter on the tarmac. I was quite exhausted when we finally met, but all he really wanted was for me to participate in the donation of the much-awaited wells to the community. It was a joyous occasion.

After returning to Abidjan, the Minister of Agriculture called to thank me for my participation in the coffee transaction and requested a meeting. "Here is a little something for you," he said, handing me a check while we sat in his office. "I am sorry, what is this for?" I asked. "It's your bonus check for being the intermediary in the coffee transaction. This is the usual custom at the Caisse de Stabilisation." I was offended. "I cannot begin to imagine what President Boumédiène and my Algerian brothers would think of me if I accepted this check." I could not hide my outrage. I had to try hard to keep from giving him a real tongue-lashing. Our meeting came to an abrupt end. On my way to see the president, I replayed in my mind, the decision I made in asking the chargé d'affaires to accompany me to the meeting in Algiers for the sake of transparency. I knew the president had no patience for unethical practices in his administration, and the minister would not go unpunished. We discussed the matter, and I contrasted the actions

A Dream for Peace

of the two gentlemen. I praised the conduct of his chargé d'affaires in Algiers and singled out the culture at the Caisse de Stabilisation as an unfortunate sequence of ill-advised practices that needed to come to an immediate halt. "I apologize for the pathetic actions of the Agricultural Minister," the president said. "He was totally out of line. I promise I will look into the matter and remedy the situation." I accepted his apology. The minister in question was reprimanded for his shady management style, and by presidential decree, the chargé d'affaires was awarded the ambassadorship to Spain.

President Boumédiène had long been reluctant to reinstate Algeria's diplomatic relations with the US and establish some form of proactive dialogue. Despite his position, both President Houphouët and I held out hope that over time he would warm up to the idea. I had personally discussed the issue of Algeria's frigid relationship with the United States since the 1967 war and told him it was a defeatist strategy with no particular mechanism for constructive measures to tackle the important issues. I was pleasantly surprised during a visit to the official presidential residence at the Arab summit in Rabat in October 1974. Beaming from ear to ear, he asked me to convey a message to President Houphouët: "*I wish to inform you that during the last visit by US Secretary of State Henry Kissinger, I decided to restore diplomatic relations with the United States. You are definitely correct. They are a major power to reckon with. One cannot turn their backs on both reality and history indefinitely.*" He seemed relieved. I was extremely happy that he had come around to our position. Our relationship strengthened in the coming weeks and months, and he developed a persistent habit of requesting my presence to help resolve every difficult diplomatic conundrum.

While returning from an official visit to Tripoli, President Hamani Diori[37] of Niger was on a phone call with Libyan President Muammar Gaddafi. The conversation was partially intercepted by

---
[37] President of Niger: November 10, 1960–April 15, 1974.

The Abidjan-Algiers Axis

Algerian secret services as he flew over their airspace. The two leaders were involved in discussions regarding the supply of uranium to Libya. Concerned, President Boumédiène contacted us and asked that we look into the matter. We sought the assistance of the French secret services and cross-checked the facts as they came in. His suspicions were confirmed by our findings: President Gaddafi had obtained a commitment from President Diori to deliver uranium from Niger. The deal had just been executed in Tripoli, and a euphoric Gaddafi had offered his personal plane to bring Diori back to Niamey when the interception was made.

We were almost at the end of March 1974, and President Boumédiène was far more puzzled than ever because only a couple of weeks earlier, Diori had signed a defense agreement with Libya without informing Algeria, Niger's neighbor to the north. "I cannot comprehend why Diori has forged ahead and executed a defense agreement with Libya," an exasperated Boumédiène confided. "Naturally, he knows that we have problems with Gaddafi, but regardless, let's hope that whatever problems exist between us today are only temporary. What would Libya defend Diori against, and against whom? His students? I do not envision the Libyan Air Force moving in to crush the students in Niamey or Zinder." He was beyond livid. "This treaty goes beyond the borders of Niger. Is it aimed at Nigeria? Is it aimed at Algeria? I would like a clear answer, and I will do anything to get it. I consider this an extremely serious move on his part." "But Mr. President," I said, "if I may interject. It seems to me that the attitude of Gaddafi may deliver a heavy price to all of us. He thinks that he can buy everyone. But in my opinion, I believe he is somewhat intoxicated by his success." He paused on my statement and implored me to inform President Houphouët about the situation. I assured him that we would spare no effort to bring some light to the matter.

Before we had a chance to engage in any diplomacy, Diori was overthrown in a coup d'état that was masterminded by Jacques

A Dream for Peace

Foccart, France's chief advisor on African policies. Knowing fully well that France's defense treaty with its former colonies shielded Diori from such plots, Foccart purposely asked the field commander at the French military base in Niger to go hunting for some game animals. He then signaled Niger's putschist guerrilla fighters to move into the capital in the dark of night, evading the unsuspecting French military forces, and thus ridding the country of its leader. President Houphouët-Boigny learned about the plot as it was unfolding. He spoke with Foccart via radio communication and urged him to stop the coup attempt, but Foccart pretended not to know what was going on. I could overhear them going back and forth until Foccart finally admitted that it was much too late to stop the putschists.

As the First Lady of Niger, Diori's wife had been a spendthrift. She was mainly interested in enriching herself, and her husband had ignored her guilty pleasures. The USAID organization was not aware of the fact that the citizens of Niger were consumers of millet. They sent a large shipment of wheat to the country following a year of severe drought. Mrs. Diori sold the wheat to the general mills of Abidjan and retained all the earnings. Coincidentally, the German government shipped some cows to Niger as well, and Mrs. Diori kept the entire herd to herself. She was assassinated in the coup d'état, and poor President Diori remained a widower, exiled to a prison in the desert until he almost entirely lost his sight. He was abandoned and forgotten by his former friends and allies, proving that their friendship had been limited to their access to uranium.

But President Houphouët-Boigny tried his best to secure Diori's release from prison and took care of him and his children when they landed on Ivorian soil. Throughout his presidency, Diori had kept me at bay. Oddly enough, he mistook me for a spy with covert ties to my native country. Having been abandoned by all of his phony friends, he started making amends upon his release. He asked me for some Arabic books to help him make good use of his time. President Houphouët invited him to dine with us on several occasions. He even adopted Diori's children and treated them like his own, sending them abroad to study in Canada and in the end giving them away in marriage when they were ready to settle down.

Over time, President Diori became increasingly embittered by life. While in power, he stood firm on the side of King Hassan II of Morocco in his Western Sahara dispute with Algeria. He asked for President Houphouët's opinion on his plans to pay a visit to the king. The president said simply, "Kings do not wish to be grateful." I had a feeling he did not get the point. He went to Rabat and discovered to his disappointment that his host was not as gracious. He was offered an entire equipage to play golf, but the king never received him. He passed away shortly after his return. His children remained in the entourage of President Houphouët-Boigny until he also passed away.

President Houphouët accorded the same kind of hospitality to the families of all the former presidents from the Conseil de l'Entente member countries. His kindness was even extended to Andrée Touré, the wife of President Sékou Touré[38] of Guinea. He gave her a house next to his residence. On the occasion of one of my pilgrimages to Mecca, the president asked me to consider taking her along. I was only happy to oblige. She remains a friend of our family till this day. Sadly, after President Houphouët-Boigny passed away, all the former First Ladies and their families were evicted from their homes by his successor.

The issue regarding the Western Sahara had long been a nagging culprit in the relations between Algeria and Morocco. Soon after Algeria gained independence, the country found itself at a tumultuous crossroads, dealing with internal political instability triggered by President Ben Bella's autocratic decisions. In short order, cross-border skirmishes with Morocco sparked a broader war. I was extremely disturbed by the nature and timing of the conflict

---

[38] First president of Guinea, 1958–1984.

between our two sister countries, knowing firsthand how Algerian fighters had benefitted from the invaluable aid of Morocco during the bloody liberation war. Only a few years earlier, I recalled going on reconnaissance missions across the border, almost on a daily basis, supported by fellow Moroccan brothers, united in a common cause. But the so-called Sand War did not foster a spirit of fraternity in the region. Rather, it evolved into a stubborn conflict in the Western Sahara, with Algeria supporting a Sahrawi faction (the Polisario) that sought self-determination, as opposed to Morocco's territorial claims of the former Spanish colony. Boumédiène's decision to further provide a haven for Polisario and receive Sahrawi refugees in Algeria's Tindouf Province cultivated an air of mistrust, which exacerbated the already icy diplomatic relations.

When in 1975, out of growing concern for rising tensions, President Boumédiène decided to reach out to President Houphouët-Boigny and seek his counsel, the matter concerning the Western Sahara was thrust squarely into the forefront of our diplomatic maneuverings. At the time, Ambassador Siméon Aké was Côte d'Ivoire's Permanent Representative to the UN, assigned to the Western Sahara issue. He was dispatched to Algiers to meet with President Boumédiène, who requested at the end of their meeting that Aké ask President Houphouët to send "our trusted man, Dr. Berrah" for further consultations.

When I arrived in Algiers, I found myself in the presence of a very irritated and perplexed president. *"My dear brother, I am sure by now that you may have deduced why I requested your presence regarding the question of Western Sahara. I would like to inform President Houphouët-Boigny in detail without asking for anything else. I have said repeatedly that Algeria has neither ambition nor claims to the territory or the soil of Western Sahara. By contrast, I have kept you informed of the secret agreement between Morocco and Mauritania's plan to divide Western Sahara as soon as the issue is ruled in their favor."*

The Abidjan-Algiers Axis

He maintained his composure even though, inside, he was fuming. *"For almost six months, all the Moroccan media have been mobilized against Algeria, sometimes accusing us of expansionism, claiming that we are an ally of the colonialists and other disreputable falsities. I have given strict orders for us not to respond. Our position is clear. Our attitude is dictated by the consistency of our policy. What we always ask for is the right to real self-determination, without maneuvering in the wording of the referendum, neither from Spain nor from anyone else. There is a lot of demagoguery in this case. King Hassan II is in the process of practicing a head-in-the-sand policy. To understand the problem, we must take a little trip back to the recent history of Hassan II's regime. Morocco has experienced two tragic events: the Skhirat tragedy and the attack on the royal Boeing aircraft, all in the space of a year and a half. Unfortunately, the motives and causes of these events have not changed. Hassan II thinks that he has found a loophole in the Western Saharan issue, which allows him to temporarily neutralize the opposition and create a kind of mass mobilization on this issue for which he has sensitized everyone. They have no other scapegoat than Algeria."*

At the time, it seemed obvious to me that he feared Spain might decide to withdraw hastily, which could potentially create a political vacuum and pave the way for Morocco to enter Western Sahara.

"Mr. President, perhaps a healthy dialogue will help ease the tensions." He paused for a few seconds, shook his head, and took in a deep sigh. After about an hour of discussions, I wandered out of his office, overwhelmed by an intense feeling of distress. President Houphouët-Boigny saw the issue as a painful dispute between two sister countries. He outlined a plan that was best suited to the national interests of both countries and asked Amadou Thiam, the Ivorian ambassador to Morocco, to send a warm message to King Hassan II.

Soon after the International Court of Justice at The Hague

A Dream for Peace

ruled that there existed at the time of Spanish colonization legal ties of allegiance between the Sultan of Morocco and some of the tribes living in the territory of Western Sahara, King Hassan II organized the "Green March," a peaceful march of 350,000 Moroccans into the territory. I was back in Algiers a week before the march, my presence having been requested by President Boumédiène. He expressed his views on the rapidly deteriorating relationship with the king. *"What bothers us is that Spain is begging us to leave the Western Sahara and there are a lot of deals that are made over the heads of the poor Sahrawis. Spain is being offered various provisions, rights, and divestitures. Other than asking women and children to march into the Sahara, the King of Morocco has yet to come up with a better idea. He does not seem to measure the consequences, but rest assured that I will not yield to the provocations. Civilians are escorted by the army, which would perhaps use their weapons. Is Morocco being pushed to create this tension in our region?"*

President Houphouët greets Algerian Ambassador Mohamed Sahnoun.

The march progressed without any anomalies, but unfortunately, the fallout finally reached a climax. Nine days after the march, Spain hosted a conference (Madrid Accords) with Morocco and Mauritania. Most of the details of the accords remained a secret

The Abidjan-Algiers Axis

long after it had been drafted and executed by all three countries. Boumédiène, who had not been consulted regarding the accords, was blindsided by the news. He had in fact launched a campaign in support of an independent Western Sahara prior to the signing of the agreement. Shortly after the deal, the Moroccan army entered the Western Sahara town of Dakhla and was soon joined by Mauritanian troops. In response, Boumédiène dispatched Algerian troops into the region to provide logistic support for Sahrawi refugees and retaliated by ordering the expulsion of Moroccans from Algeria. President Houphouët and I were greatly disappointed by the decision to deport innocent families who had absolutely nothing to do with the political stalemate. I personally voiced my concerns regarding his reasoning and recommended that he reevaluate his decision for the sake of fraternal harmony.

Despite there being a threat of war with Morocco, he chose to invest resources elsewhere. He decided to recruit workers from Algeria's National Services to build the trans-Saharan road, a major thoroughfare connecting Algeria with Mali. The project was part of his vision for the continent to open up the channels of communications between North Africa and sub-Saharan Africa.

A waterhole in the Western Sahara town of Amgala was used as a staging point for refugees being evacuated to Algeria by the army. They were supplying them with food and medical supplies when they were attacked by Moroccan troops. In what would be known as Amgala I, the battle lasted about thirty-six hours, and the ill-equipped Algerian army was severely beaten. Recounting the incident, then Morocco Minister of Defense Aherdan bragged: "With all due respect to Algeria, I could have had tea in Algiers."

Boumédiène avenged the Amgala I incident a couple of weeks later by launching a surprise attack in a second Amgala episode. This caused several dozen deaths and wiped out an entire Moroccan garrison. Months after the battle, the international community raised concerns about the continued presence of Algerian soldiers

A Dream for Peace

in Western Sahara. I was dispatched to Algiers by President Houphouët to get to the bottom of the matter. Boumédiène was very forthcoming: *"Indeed, having lost the battle at Amgala I, I went to the Soviet Union to acquire some very sophisticated weapons and I beat the Moroccans in the Amgala II engagement. I promise you that currently, we do not have a single Algerian soldier in Western Sahara."*

With President Boumédiène.

Emphasizing the importance of dialogue, President Houphouët tried his very best to mediate between the two heads of state. Other leaders certainly did try their best to help ease tensions. We were elated to learn that secret meetings aimed at setting the stage for an encounter between King Hassan II and President Boumédiène were taking place at a high level. Sadly, destiny intervened. President Boumédiène fell sick and was called by the Almighty.

"In diplomatic terms, the fact that an emissary pays frequent visits to a country is a sign that relations are excellent. In that regard, relations between Côte d'Ivoire and Algeria are excellent. You, my brother, are also doing a phenomenal job for both sides."

Houari Boumédiène

A Dream for Peace

We had successfully arranged the first-ever dialogue between the ICIPP and the PLO. There had been no emotional outbursts, only expressions of deep-rooted feelings and raw sentiments, which could barely be contained—something powerful, almost unreal, had illuminated from the participants.

Chapter Ten

Israel and Palestine—Our Plea for Peace

For President Houphouët-Boigny, solidarity was not expressed with mere words. He believed it should be followed by actions that would have an impact on real life. He liked to repeat that it was not enough to sit alongside his brother to mourn with him but rather to take the necessary action to find a solution to his problem so that he never had to cry again. He was a fervent believer in dialogue and discreet mediation, which was for him the only effective means for resolving conflict between human beings and nations—a belief I totally espoused. The Israeli-Palestinian conflict would not be an exception to this rule.

At the service of peace toward the painful Israeli-Palestinian conflict, I used all the talents that the Almighty bestowed upon me, including a dogged determination, without ever holding back any effort. The president devoted all of his strength and energy toward a secret diplomacy—I was his trusted emissary.

> "It must be clear to all that only the love of man and the love of peace guides my actions in the interest of all. I wish that in the passionate pursuit of peace and by resorting to the Creator, all the stakeholders will have confidence in me and give me complete freedom of action. I do not hide the fact that there are difficulties, but it is because there are seemingly insurmountable difficulties that I rest in the belief that God can once again lead men out of the difficulties they have created by turning their backs to the love and justice that emanate from Him."
>
> Félix Houphouët-Boigny

A Dream for Peace

Considering the excruciating pain and suffering inflicted on my people in the aftermath of the Algerian war, a bloody war that had left in its wake countless numbers of martyrs, I made the determination to work for a better world and find an alternative to war. I decided to dedicate my life to public service and work to establish a better understanding among all people through *dialogue*—for the sake of *peace* and *justice*.

In the beginning, Arab countries took a hard-line position on the Palestinian issue, even more so than the Palestinian leaders themselves. We had received word that Palestine Liberation Organization (PLO) Chairman Yasser Arafat wished to have an office in Abidjan. However, on the diplomatic chessboard, their objectives were not aligned with the official position of Côte d'Ivoire. In all international affairs, Côte d'Ivoire always voted in line with the US and France.

I had been approached at a previous OAU summit by Dr. Sartawi, a prominent US-educated heart surgeon from an affluent Palestinian family. He was a well-cultivated man, a poet, and a great diplomat, in possession of a highly classified message from Chairman Arafat to be given to President Houphouët, which he was keen to deliver himself. He complained to me that Côte d'Ivoire's votes at the body were not in compliance with the humanitarian spirit of President Houphouët-Boigny. That particular topic had been paramount in our many meetings at the OAU. I did convey his wishes to the president, along with a docket containing the details of our discussions, and made it known that he was greatly admired by the Palestinians. Not long afterward, the president agreed to receive him in Abidjan.

After meeting with Dr. Sartawi at the end of 1972, the president realized that he personally could contribute to peace in the Middle East in an active and concrete way. He expressed his sensitivities and objectives regarding the Palestinian issue and maintained that he was determined to help by remaining behind the scenes. He made it clear that there was no need for a PLO office in Abidjan, as opening one would undermine his own ability to be more effective in his diplomatic maneuverings. I took the initiative and began to focus on a rapprochement between him and the Palestinians with the sole objective of contributing to peace.

President Houphouët-Boigny always felt that peace depended in large part on the American superpower, an unconditional friend of the Israeli nation, and without their cooperation, there could be no peace. To advance peace and create the conditions for dialogue between the Israelis and Palestinians, it was necessary to seek the involvement of the United States, with whom the president had an excellent relationship. He had met with all the White House residents since President Dwight Eisenhower, who he met while on a mission in 1958 as the Minister of State and Public Health under General De Gaulle. Once he became the president of Côte d'Ivoire, he followed up on his meetings with President Eisenhower's successors—Presidents Kennedy, Johnson, Nixon, Carter, Reagan, and Bush Sr.

He also benefited from the friendship and respect of the Israelis. In 1962, he opened an embassy in Jerusalem. I wondered who had advised him to take a decision that was obviously a mistake, even though the US Embassy was located in Tel Aviv. That same year, he embarked on an official visit to Israel and in a speech, he recommended that the Israelis take up negotiations to solve the Arab-Israeli conflict. Over time, he met with Israeli Prime Ministers Meir, Rabin, Begin, Shamir, and Peres.

He was viscerally attached to the Israeli-Palestinian conflict for spiritual and ethical reasons. Both he and I believed that the territory, a landmass not much bigger than a handkerchief on the global scale and the birthplace of three major religions, should not be at the center of such carnage and unrivaled injustice. Something had to be done to help restore peace.

A Dream for Peace

President Houphouët, Prime Minister Ben-Gurion, and Minister Golda Meir with the First Ladies of Côte d'Ivoire and Israel.

In the aftermath of the Second World War, the Jewish people were clearly traumatized by the malevolent actions of the Nazis. However, after being resettled in a new homeland, they placed the Palestinian people at the receiving end of a brutal Jewish oppression. Therefore, the president and I were faced with the question of reconciling the two traumatized people while dealing with the extremists on both sides. Proponents on the Israeli side advocated for a Greater Israel in which the Palestinians were nonexistent, suggesting that they should be integrated into the neighboring Arab countries. On the Palestinian side, there were those who supported the idea of "Israel to the sea" in order to recover the historical Greater Palestine. We knew that we had set an impossible task for ourselves. By way of objective reasoning, we had to try and convince politicians on both sides to adopt a realistic attitude in order to achieve a meaningful peace.

The Israelis will not realize their vision of a Greater Israel and neither will the Palestinians be able to fulfill their objective of creating a Greater Palestine. Therefore, the only realistic approach would be the establishment of an independent Palestinian state living side by side with the state of Israel.

For President Houphouët and I, our mutual ideal was peace. We dreamed together for the rebirth of a just and lasting peace. With its distant geographical position to the Middle East, there could neither be any allegations of bias on the part of Côte d'Ivoire, nor could there be any reproach of some strategic interest on our part. Finding himself in the unique position of enjoying the trust of both parties, President Houphouët-Boigny was fully aware of the fact that the value of his repeated interventions would eventually allow the truth to pave the way. "Motivated by love," he would often say, "I must press on." We committed ourselves to convince the Palestinians and the Israelis of the need for *dialogue between enemies*, while continuing to work tirelessly and relentlessly toward achieving our main objective.

After the initial meeting between the president and Sartawi at his Cocody residence, I received a call from Raphael Leygues, the ambassador of France. This was a first. The president thought it was odd, and so did I. But nonetheless, he advised me to take the lunch meeting with the ambassador. When I arrived at the compound of the French Embassy, he and I sat at the terrace of his residence, just the two of us, and enjoyed an intimate lunch. He was aware that the president had received a Palestinian delegation and that the officials carried a message from Chairman Arafat. The French were so well informed about what was happening in Côte d'Ivoire that I wasn't really surprised to learn that they had their facts straight. But the more he spoke, it became quite clear to me that he wasn't well versed on the Palestinian question. When he probed for more information, I did not disclose much, for obvious reasons. The president and I discussed the matter and concluded that my visit might eventually prompt a commitment on the Palestinian issue and perhaps keep the

A Dream for Peace

French engaged. Somewhat exasperated by the nature of the French intrusion into our internal affairs, I commented to the president about the manner in which all of our communiqués with the outside world were easily accessible to the French government. They had access to everything, including our original transcripts. The palace was overrun with French loyalists, from the president's own chief of staff to most of his advisors. When the secretary-general of the government, a French prefect of Algerian origin, asked about the visit of "Chairman Arafat's advisor," I responded by handing him a copy of the meeting summary between myself and the ambassador. He returned my report with a thank-you note a couple of days later.

The historic encounter with the president prompted Sartawi to send a memorable letter to me personally on February 26, 1973, in which he expressed his feelings and the sentiments of the Palestinian leadership:

> Berrah, my dear brother.
>
> It is difficult to express in words the deep impression aroused in me by Côte d'Ivoire, especially because of the high ideals it embodies in this world of conflict, disturbances, selfish materialism, and hatred. The philosophy of love and brotherhood so convincingly exposed by the great Houphouët-Boigny imbues Côte d'Ivoire with a halo of spiritual humanism that transcends regional boundaries and reaches the dimensions of a universal appeal of redemption and atonement. The great privilege of mine is to have been a happy recipient of the message that beset my immense spiritual obligation to spread what I have been fortunate to receive. Whether I have succeeded or not is a question of which I cannot be the judge.
>
> I have tried, however, to transmit to the Palestinian leadership, and in particular to His Excellency Chairman Arafat, some of these impressions. The results were very encouraging, and our people and their leadership are now convinced that we have in Côte d'Ivoire a great ally. In the person of His Excellency, President

Israel and Palestine—Our Plea for Peace

Houphouët-Boigny, we have a great friend and supporter. It was impossible, of course, to speak of the president without mentioning his spiritual son and disciple, my brother, Dr. Berrah. Chairman Arafat instructed me to convey to you his personal invitation, asking that you pay him a visit in Beirut, at your convenience, to continue the previous discussions that began in Yamoussoukro and in Abidjan. It goes without saying that I anticipate your arrival with the greatest pleasure.

Isam Sartawi

President Houphouët-Boigny managed to earn the friendship and trust of the Palestinians. He met with Arafat in September of 1973 during the Non-Aligned Movement summit in Algiers. Theirs was a warm meeting that strengthened the bonds of friendship in the coming years. He maintained the momentum and never missed a day without tackling the Israeli-Palestinian issue head-on. Even prior to meeting Arafat, he had met with Israeli Prime Minister Golda Meir as early as January 1973, when she was on a trip to Europe. They met at his private villa in Geneva when she transited through the city from Rome. The press was not invited to the three-and-a-half-hour meeting in which he presented a road map for peace in the Middle East and expressed the need for an immediate Israeli withdrawal from the occupied territories. In an urgent call for an end to the refugee crisis, the president underscored the rights of the Palestinians, insisting that they were entitled to a part of Palestine. Expounding upon the future, he alluded to the continued threats of an all-out war, consequences of which could have far-reaching implications on Africa, claiming that such a bloody war would delay the development of the continent. Mrs. Golda Meir shared his concerns and agreed with his premise, primarily because her country had already suffered diplomatic setbacks in Africa in the preceding year. She returned to Israel later that evening and revealed the details of their discussions to President Nixon. Eight

A Dream for Peace

months later, President Houphouët-Boigny arrived at the White House for a high-profile meeting.

Inspecting the honor guard with President Nixon.

    I was visiting with Chairman Arafat in Beirut when the president summoned me to join him in DC. The initial discussions were centered on issues regarding Côte d'Ivoire's economical development and its bilateral trade with the United States. The complicated Israeli-Palestinian problem was tabled until the next morning. At that meeting, we disagreed on the principle of a measured approach to the very idea of assimilating the Palestinians into Jordan. Even though the US had initiated a process to protect its own strategic interests in the region, President Houphouët managed to convince Mr. Nixon to commit to bringing the issue of

Israel and Palestine—Our Plea for Peace

resettlement to the UN Security Council for discussions. The dialogue between the two leaders was extremely friendly and constructive. In the end, we were shown a great deal of consideration and given the necessary platform to make the case for establishing the road map to peace:

> "As we begin a visit which will be important and fruitful for our common future, I should like to re-create our faithful friendship and our very deep esteem. But it would be a betrayal of this friendship, esteem, and confidence, Mr. President, if before I conclude I did not share with you the very deep preoccupation I feel, as a man, as a leader, as an African in one word, about the very serious problem in the Mideast. Your action on behalf of peace, which is already so remarkable, and history, will note that your capital role would remain incomplete if you did not succeed in acting with the leaders of the Soviet Union, not to impose, but to create and foster conditions for a just and durable peace in that part of the world where one should speak only of peace, love, and brotherhood."
>
> Félix Houphouët-Boigny.

The visit was very productive. It compelled the Nixon administration to realize that Arab mistrust over Israel's commitment to withdraw from the territories it had occupied in 1967 could alter the balance between the superpowers in the region and impose strategic difficulties on the United States. In an effort to try to convince the Arabs that the United States was fully committed to the peace process, Secretary of State Henry Kissinger forged ahead with the so-called "shuttle diplomacy." President Houphouët-Boigny confided that he felt President Nixon seemed sincere in his desire to create conditions for peace. He was confident that he had found a reliable partner in him. I was cautiously optimistic. Nixon had just authorized a major airlift of weapons and sophisticated military equipment to aid the Israelis in the war, at the same time as the

A Dream for Peace

Soviet Union was striking a deal to deliver defensive weapons at an inflated price to the Arabs for the Syrian-Egyptian front. The situation became extremely volatile even before we left the US, and I suspected the brewing proxy war might bring the Soviets and the Americans to the brink of a nuclear confrontation. But by the same token, I knew that it wouldn't be in the best interest of the superpowers to take things that far. Ever since President Houphouët severed diplomatic relations with the Soviet Union following their subversive activities at the port of Abidjan, both he and I had grown weary of their motives. He strongly believed that the Russians planned to sustain the state of war in order to bolster their presence in the Mediterranean Sea.

The October War confirmed Israel's military superiority. As the reality of the outcome became vividly transparent, the president and I were more convinced than ever that it was incumbent on the parties to find a way to resolve the problem by peaceful means. I made several trips to see Chairman Arafat for discussions on taking the necessary steps to achieve peace and to focus on drafting a measure that defined the scope of an Israeli-Palestinian road map. Although it was not easy to develop the idea in an environment where the extremist wing of the PLO supported the Greater Palestine view (as outlined in their charter), the leadership began to consider the adoption of such a policy.

Not long after the war, Arab members of the Organization of Petroleum Exporting Countries (OPEC) imposed an embargo against the United States in retaliation for their decision to reinforce the Israelis with military supplies and for attempting to gain influence in the postwar peace negotiations. Countries that supported Israel were also included in the embargo. Petroleum exports to the targeted nations were banned, and the production of oil was greatly reduced. President Houphouët-Boigny foresaw the events long before the embargo took effect. He cautioned Golda Meir about maintaining a stranglehold on the rights of the Palestinians with

Israel and Palestine—Our Plea for Peace

the help of the United States. In his opinion, the policy was a gross miscalculation. These concerns were addressed to Nixon while we were in DC, but I did not expect him to make any moves to adjust the policies of the US. As I told the president, "the Americans would stick with the Israelis through thick and thin, even if it were to their own detriment." The start of the embargo led to an upward spiral in oil prices with global implications. Most economies took a major hit when oil prices skyrocketed, pushing local consumers to pay dearly at the pump. In Côte d'Ivoire, however, the president was not fazed. He saw the situation as a "minor bump" on the road and attempted to tie the high price of oil to the revalorization of raw materials. With mounting pressure on the dollar, its eventual devaluation imposed significant challenges on the global financial markets, which ultimately forced the United States to negotiate an end to the embargo under severe domestic economic conditions.

During one of Dr. Sartawi's trips to Abidjan, I obtained an audience with the president after Sunday mass and prepared to personally escort him to the residence. Since the Security Services were very familiar with me, I usually went in and out of the residence without ever being stopped. When I pulled up to the security gate on this particular day, Dr. Sartawi was behind me in a separate vehicle. For some odd reason, the Security Services refused to allow the guest to go through the gates. I was surprised and dumbstruck. Despite clarifying that our visit had been prescheduled, they stuck to their guns and remained stubbornly mum. From the look of things, I sensed some racial profiling of our guest. I felt extremely embarrassed and powerless. Although I knew that I could just call the president and remedy the situation immediately, I chose not to. I just shook my head in total dismay and motioned to Sartawi to back up. We reversed our cars and left. My first instinct was to save him from further humiliation by making him wait while I took the appropriate initiatives. I offered my sincere apologies to him and asked that he return to the Hotel Ivoire to check himself out.

A Dream for Peace

My job was to defend the interests of Côte d'Ivoire and the dignity of the president. Hence, the dignity of official representatives from the many organizations and countries with whom we dealt had to be held in high regard. I went to pick him up in my car, and we drove to the airport to catch his return flight to Beirut.

As expected, I received a phone call from the president as soon as I got home. "Where is our guest?" he asked. "We only got as far as the main gates before the Security Services complicated matters for us," I replied. "Realizing we weren't getting anywhere, I took him to the airport, and he is now on his way to Beirut by way of Geneva." Surprised and utterly repulsed by the incident, he summoned me to the residence without delay. He quickly convened a meeting with the Chief of Security and the commanding general of the palace. They were still engaged in discussions when I arrived. I sat quietly and listened as they attempted to justify their actions and chimed in when I'd heard enough. "I am deeply disturbed by the entire episode. There were subtleties of racial motives behind your deliberate attempt to impede our progress. This is totally unacceptable." They had been sworn in their capacity to provide the maximum level of security for the president, but the timing of the incident seemed orchestrated to offset our strategic objectives. After getting an earful from the president, they were dismissed with orders to refine their due diligence process.

The president and I reassessed the Sartawi situation and came up with a face-saving plan. He called our UN ambassador in Geneva and asked him to intercept Sartawi at the airport and render apologies on his behalf. Per the president's request, Sartawi returned to Côte d'Ivoire at his earliest convenience. The Palestinian delegation stayed with us for two days of a working vacation in Yamoussoukro. We learned that the PLO leadership was in a state of distress, and Sartawi had initially come to seek the president's help to revisit the two-state solution in accordance with the 1947 resolution. He was personally frustrated by the fact that voices of reason at the PLO camp were being drowned out by extremists, and he'd begun to notice a worrisome escalation of communist rhetoric among some key figures in their ranks. All of this was happening because he believed the US was increasingly looked upon as an adversary with a biased policy that typically appeased the Israelis. The delegation hoped President Houphouët would use his influence to convey the PLO's message of peace to the US and other moderate leaders of the world. Sartawi was mostly in a philosophical mood during the two-day roundtable. In an unusual spiritual gesture on the second day, he offered a Bible to the president as a gift from the Palestinian people. I was just as surprised as the president. The fact that a devout Muslim had gone through such lengths meant the world to me, a believer in interfaith dialogue, but most notably, the president welcomed the thoughtful gesture with these heartfelt words for Chairman Arafat:

"By sending me a Bible through Dr. Sartawi, you have indeed brought tremendous joy to my heart. What comforts me the most is the thoughtfulness that inspired your choice for this priceless gift. Our thoughts are indeed joined together because of the relief we expect from God."

On occasion, we broke away from the lengthy talks and went for walks around the president's compound. The place was like a tropical paradise with meticulously arranged exotic palms, well-manicured gardens, and a beautiful lake with a few primordial African crocodiles. Fenced off from the rest of the property for good reason, due to the well-reputed nature of the beasts who are known to be vicious predators, I was quick to assure the delegates that the caretakers on the grounds usually fed them a diet of chickens. As it was customary for visiting guests to tour the site, I arranged to take them to watch the feeding frenzy. The large amphibians amused us with their aggressive movements through the shadowy water, hurdling their large bodies like a missile to snatch the meat with their riveting jaws.

A Dream for Peace

In the midst of the conflict, the Arab states lodged a complaint at the Security Council which prompted the UN secretary-general to organize the Geneva Conference for Mideast Peace in December 1973, cochaired by the United States and the Soviet Union. When President Houphouët-Boigny found out that the PLO was not represented, he sent a message to President Nixon stating that the warring factions must be at the table to ensure a balanced approach to peace.

There was much talk by many world leaders about Palestinian rights, but nothing was done. As early as January 1974, President Sadat was involved in the disengagement talks with the United States and Israel, but he did not make any mention of the Palestinian issue. I was sent by President Houphouët-Boigny to meet with him on several occasions and draw his attention to the absolute necessity of including the rights of the Palestinians in all negotiations.

When I met with him in Cairo on June 8, 1974, I was the bearer of a powerful message from President Houphouët-Boigny.

My dear President,

>*I hereby send my most trusted confidant, Dr. Berrah, to hand deliver this congratulatory letter to you, for the courage you have shown in facing the challenges created by the unfortunate situation in the Middle East. I renew my congratulations for the determinant role you played in favor of the disengagement, not only on the Egyptian front, but on the Syrian front as well. You deserve the title, "Man of Peace." For peace to be sustainable, it must be fair, and it can only be fair if there is a restitution of all occupied territories and the return of Palestinians to their homeland. Why were there all those successive wars in the Middle East? I believe the answer is—because the wars were fought to establish the Palestinians their legitimate rights.*
>
>*Today, we stand at a difficult crossroad in history; I do not know if the Americans are aware that the solution to the Palestinian*

Israel and Palestine—Our Plea for Peace

problem is almost as important as the evacuation of the occupied territories and can only be disassociated for tactical reasons. The question must be presented as a prerequisite. All the problems should find a beginning of a solution before the end of President Nixon's term in two years.

The longer the Palestinians are ignored, the longer chances for a lasting peace become difficult, because the Russians are not stupid. They will use all available means to avoid losing the Middle East. They will surely take advantage of the extremist wing—and then the moderates who now seem to have the situation under control will be vanquished. The acts of desperation will not only multiply against the Israelis, but it will do the same to the Arabs as well, and there will be no peace.

If we are not careful, a land that has seen God reveal Himself to man on three occasions, this very land of love, might become the tomb of humanity.

Félix Houphouët-Boigny

In our discussions, I developed abundantly all aspects of President Houphouët's message, but still, my efforts were fruitless. In his initial meetings with Dr. Sartawi, President Houphouët expressed the need for all Palestinians to return to their own state and allow refugees to resettle in their regained homeland. Emphasizing the urgency of the situation, especially due to the mistreatment of Palestinians in the Arab countries that hosted them, he stated that in order for the dream to be realized, the PLO would have to recognize Israel.

The Palestinians felt betrayed by President Sadat. Their issue had become a part of a chronic problem on a slippery slope with many unexpected twists and turns, serving as a daily reminder that an adaptation of different strategies was always at hand. The PLO continued to debate the merits of reaching its goal by peaceful means, focusing mostly on scaling back its armed struggle for the occupied territories and opting for direct negotiations—the dialogue between enemies, Palestinians and Israelis. In 1974, there were a lot of back-and-forth discussions between President Houphouët-Boigny and Chairman Arafat. Dr. Sartawi came to Abidjan on many occasions, with messages from Arafat and the Palestinian leadership. I followed suit with a few trips to see Arafat somewhere in Beirut or in Cairo for high-level discussions.

With Egyptian President Anwar Sadat.

Abandoning their pursuit of the Palestinian issue, Syria, which had also signed the Disengagement Agreement in May of 1974, ended its participation in the Geneva Conference. Although the Arab countries claimed to fight for the restoration of Palestinian rights, the PLO believed that by not taking up the issue of their rights, the Egyptians and the Syrians had, by implication, denied

Israel and Palestine—Our Plea for Peace

their very existence. Dr. Sartawi was Chairman Arafat's emissary to President Houphouët-Boigny, and among the Palestinian leaders, he was without a doubt the most intelligent. Both he and Arafat, as well as other leaders of the Palestinian directorate, were aware of the difficulties they faced within the PLO in adopting the policies that were dictated to them by reality.

After one of Sartawi's visits to Côte d'Ivoire, the president sent me to Beirut to see Arafat and hand him a letter detailing some specific points we had debated previously with Sartawi:

My dear Chairman,

> *I hold dear your discreet wish, which was forwarded to me by your envoy, Dr. Sartawi, and I understand your discretion, since you are in the midst of a frightening tragedy. I took note of the fact that after the acknowledgement of your rights, your desire is to one day come to a sincere understanding with Israel, and God willing, to the realization of a federal union, where all Christians, Muslims, and Jews would live in concord and harmony.*
>
> *My envoy, Dr. Berrah, in whom I have placed my trust, is delivering this letter to you, and he will brief you at length on this matter. I will be happy to know upon his return that you have confirmed your expressed intention, which I repeat, was an inspiration to you from God, the Master of all of us, the Supreme Judge.*
>
> *Félix Houphouët-Boigny*

Chairman Arafat pondered and reflected for several minutes after reading President Houphouët's letter. He admitted that the narrative exposed his utopic view, however given the denial of the Palestinians' true existence, we were far away from there. I agreed with his premise, but I was hopeful that things would eventually begin to move in the right direction.

In the life of each Palestinian is a hidden trauma and a tragedy;

A Dream for Peace

Isam Sartawi was no exception to the rule. He was born in Acre, near Haifa, in Galilee, bordering the Mediterranean Sea. He described his birthplace to me as a beautiful ancient city, fortified with ramparts and the remains of all the civilizations that had succeeded each other—Greek, Roman, Arab, and the Ottoman Empire, which paved the way for the British Mandate. During the Crusades, Acre was the most important port and back then, the Christians referred to the city as Saint John of Acre. There are many beautiful mosques and churches in the city where he spent his childhood, surrounded by Arabs of both Muslim and Christian faiths, constituting the majority population, living side by side with only a handful of Jews. Dr. Sartawi's knowledge of religion was quite vast; he had read the Bible from which he could quote a few passages in their entirety.

When the United Nations enacted a resolution in 1947 for the partition of Palestine, Acre was part of the area allocated to the Arabs. Isam Sartawi was only fourteen when the war broke out in 1948. The city was besieged by the Haganah army, later known as the Israeli army. They expelled the majority Arab population from the area. His distressed family was forced into exile and had to immigrate to Iraq. Since then, he counted each year that separated him from his homeland. During a meeting with President Houphouët-Boigny, he recalled that twenty-nine years had passed and he had yet to return home.

As a teenage boy in Iraq, Isam excelled in high school and went on to study medicine. Prior to leaving for the US to complete his education, he tied the knot with Widdad, an Iraqi woman of high prestige and wonderful personality. He could have maintained a comfortable lifestyle in the United States as a cardiac surgeon. However, at the onset of the Six-Day War in 1967, he could not bring himself to sit on the sidelines and watch as his people were systematically stripped of their remaining land. Motivated by an irresistible desire to join the fight, he returned to the Middle East and formed his own organization. Sometime later, he enlisted with Yasser

Israel and Palestine—Our Plea for Peace

Arafat's Fatah movement, which had taken up the fight against the Israeli army after the Egyptian and Syrian armies brokered a cessation to the war. He also helped establish the Palestine Red Crescent Society and quite often, he spoke of having taken part in the Battle of Karameh in 1968—a dreadful battle in a small village in Jordan in which the Palestinian forces had emerged victorious against the Israelis. His organization played a role in an attack on a bus loaded with El Al passengers at the Munich airport, in which an Israeli actress (Hanna Maron) was seriously injured. Shortly after the Black September war, he relinquished armed struggle for peace advocacy.

Dr. Isam Sartawi.

Sartawi was realistic about events and understood the complexity of the situation. I used to host him at my house while he was waiting to meet with the president. He was quite a talkative, cheerful, and witty person who loved English and Arabic poetry. Sometimes, he would compose Arabic or English poems in minutes, but almost suddenly, his mood would get darker and he would grow

A Dream for Peace

serious, unable to hide the pain that consumed him. He would then sit back and finger his prayer beads nervously. Whenever I saw him like that, I rushed to play Frank Sinatra's "Strangers in the Night" (his favorite song) on my turntable. As soon as the power of the music filled the room, his demeanor became more relaxed and the meditation beads found a lenient touch along his fingertips. The sultry and magical voice of the crooner never failed to bring out the joyous side in him, and his energy unwound with the crescendo of the chorus. It was not unusual for him to rise up from his chair and recite a newly composed poem.

Once again, President Houphouët renewed his call for Chairman Arafat to take the initiative and demonstrate his desire for a peaceful resolution to the problem. After the PLO received recognition from the United Nations, the president determined it was imperative that Arafat set the right tone with his overtures of peace. I went to Beirut to meet him in April of 1974 for some lengthy discussions, during which he expressed his desire to move forward in the direction of achieving peace. He also expressed his readiness to establish a Palestinian state alongside Israel within the borders of the returned territories. Additionally, he informed me that he would invite President Houphouët-Boigny to attend the next Palestinian National Council (PNC) session to be held in June that same year in order to witness a historic milestone in the making.

During the June 1974 PNC session in Cairo where I personally represented President Houphouët-Boigny, I was also the sole non-Palestinian attendee. I was seated at the right-hand side of Chairman Arafat, Dr. George Habash[39] was seated to my right, and Nayef Hawatmeh[40] was seated immediately to his right. They were the heads of the major Palestinian factions. The PNC was a large national legislative body for the Palestinian people. I listened intently to the

---

[39] and [40] Palestinian Christians and cofounders of the Popular Front for the Liberation of Palestine (PFLP).

presentations by the various heads and representatives of the PLO, who were based in different Arab countries. I observed that they seemed to endorse the position of the countries in which they lived rather than support the Palestinian cause itself. It became clear to me that Arab solidarity had its limitations and that there was a point at which the interests of the Arab countries would no longer converge with those of most Palestinians. I analyzed the attitudes of the representatives and concluded that their peculiar behavior stemmed from the unfortunate predicament of living in the host countries that continued to impose political pressures on them. At any time, they and their families were subjected to retaliatory actions. Grasping in vivo the complexities of administering and legislating within the PLO body, I realized how the role of dissensions within the organization would eventually prevent them from adapting a unified structural road map. President Houphouët-Boigny, who never had to resort to taking up arms for the liberation of his country, was nonetheless a great strategist. Whenever I was dispatched on a mission to meet with Chairman Arafat, the president would ask me to implore Arafat to stick to a clear and permanent position. Yasser Arafat's Fatah movement, whose members included Isam Sartawi, Abu Jihad, Mahmoud Abbas, and other leaders, represented 95 percent of the various factions that operated under the banner of the PLO. Fatah represented the moderate wing, though there were more extreme groups that made up the remaining 5 percent.

Those hard-line groups operated under the influence of the Assad regime in Syria, which took its orders from Moscow. The moderates, who were ignored by the United States, continued to encounter intransigence from within by the extremists, who viewed their expectations as unrealistic. The success of the PLO was growing thanks to the help of President Boumédiène at the Non-Aligned Movement summit, and the opening of several offices in Europe had also strengthened Fatah within the movement.

I was struck by the democratic structure of the Palestinian

A Dream for Peace

National Council. The historic Ten Point Program marking a major step forward for the PLO was unanimously adopted at the end of the debates. The new resolution was coated with revolutionary slogans to accommodate the extremists, but it stipulated the establishment of a "Palestinian National Authority" in each part of the liberated Palestinian land, which equally implied a clear recognition of Israel. This happened to be the key decision that Chairman Arafat wanted to bring to the attention of President Houphouët-Boigny by inviting him to the Palestinian National Council summit. Additionally, Chairman Arafat wanted to shed some light on the complex nature of the internal operations within the PLO, coupled with the pressure from extremist groups, which added to the difficulties. When I finally submitted my formal report to President Houphouët-Boigny, he clarified that I had explicitly expressed what he feared and already knew. He also stated that the Palestinian issue was at the core of the actions of the various movements that had attached themselves to it, only to reproduce their objectives within the Middle East and beyond. I continued to attend and monitor other Palestinian National Council summits in the coming months.

President Houphouët was not satisfied with the lack of results from the United States. The sudden departure of President Nixon from the White House ushered in a level of uncertainty to the situation and made matters worse. Even though the State Department maintained its focus, the Kissinger peace initiative was a nonstarter because it did not adequately address the Palestinian question. In the days after the first oil crisis in 1974, I escalated my trips to the Middle East. During the same period, Secretary Kissinger embarked on many diplomatic missions to the region to propose his Mideast peace initiative, which was deemed acceptable by most Arab leaders even before they had thoroughly vetted the scheme. There were occasions when he and I arrived either in Egypt or in Saudi Arabia at exactly the same time. The Egyptian press corps mistook me for him a couple of times. But I was once forced to

Israel and Palestine—Our Plea for Peace

call a television station to straighten out the mix-up after I saw myself on TV with the caption, "Henry Kissinger arrives for talks..." Most of my trips to the Middle East were focused on the Palestinian problem. A letter written by the president to Chairman Arafat placed me squarely at the forefront of his foreign policy agenda—"In the presence of my Minister of Foreign Affairs, Mr. Usher, I have asked Dr. Berrah to serve as an intermediary, because no one can doubt his sincerity, and because, more than anyone, he embodies the impact of this drama. He will be departing next week to establish communication links to enable you reach us at any time. Our country is open to you at any time."

I was inclined to seek a peaceful resolution to the problem, and I hoped to convey a powerful message to all who were involved in the process, but Secretary of State Kissinger did not strike me as an honest broker. He was skillful at manipulating everyone to suit a biased objective that in my opinion was highly tilted toward facilitating the state of Israel. Benefitting greatly from the confidence bestowed upon him by President Nixon, he modeled the policies for the Department of State in his own unique way, albeit in accordance with the Israeli vision of the Middle East. It seemed that most Arab leaders in the region were being purposely complacent. They were quick to react and embrace the road map without performing their due diligence responsibilities. I was appalled by their credulous acceptance of Secretary Kissinger's positions and their readiness to embark on his pathway to peace doctrine.

Since he had severed diplomatic relations with the Israelis, President Houphouët-Boigny did not have any formal means of contact with the Rabin administration. However, he continued to deliver messages through some influential friends within the Jewish diaspora. His main leitmotif was an emphasis on both the evacuation of the occupied territories and the recognition of the legitimate rights of all Palestinians.

The concept of dialogue between enemies was a belief that

set the president apart from most leaders. Although the state of war had certainly become a concern for the entire world, the direct repercussions on the life of the general populations was a matter of concern for the warring factions. The future of the children, families, Israel, and a new Palestinian state were all at risk of being impacted by continued atrocities. We pushed for a face-to-face encounter, hoping that the enemies would learn to know each other, assess each other's motives, and hamper the efforts of outside agents who only cared for their own interests, which did not necessarily embrace a peaceful resolution to the conflict. The president and I spent many hours discussing the advantages of a conclusive peace emanating from dialogue between enemies. "A more constructive peace can be achieved without the intervention of superpowers. Henceforth, neither the Israelis nor the Palestinians would be beholden to anyone," he expressed philosophically.

When talks came to a grinding halt, Chairman Arafat and Dr. Sartawi reached out to us to express their dismay about the stalemate. The president sought to encourage them, even though they could not bring themselves to imagine that there were some Israelis who supported peace. But the president was speaking from experience.

"*Since 1956, without any particular intervals, I was kept as a hostage by every successive government in France, until General De Gaulle made me his trusted right-hand man. That gave me an opportunity to learn, not only about problems concerning the French, but also about European and African issues. I was privy to the intricate details of problems in the Middle East, and especially the Algerian decolonization war. I studied the Algerian issue in the span of eight years and regardless of the intensity of the fight, the French government maintained contacts with the fighters. I understood then that diplomacy is key in every struggle.*"

I was impressed by his recollection of events. The narrative was an effective one to the ears of Arafat, because he, like other

Israel and Palestine—Our Plea for Peace

Palestinians, had been an admirer of the Algerian liberation struggle. He appreciated the president's chronicle of events.

In the aftermath of Arafat's historic reception at the United Nations General Assembly in November 1974, the president asked him to prove to the world that he was indeed ready to abandon armed struggle in pursuit of peace. Speaking to Sartawi, the president stated his position: *"Chairman Arafat is now a 'responsible man.' From the moment he was recognized by the UN, he became a leader with whom one must deal, even though he has no territory. Now, he and his comrades must define the goal and determine the means to get there. He is no longer a 'troublemaker' or an 'outlaw' but a head of state. His responsibility is to consider all avenues, including the slower ones, which lean toward his goal."*

Emphasizing that a policy shift would yield a twofold effect in the eyes of the world, the president was quick to point out that primarily, such a shift would influence international public opinion and persuade the Israelis to come to the negotiating table. Secondly, the shift would trigger a ripple effect within Israel itself and harvest the birth of a peace initiative to acquiesce a desire for peace with the Palestinian people.

His face expressed sadness, pessimism, and the immense burden of responsibility for his people whenever he was not smiling. Chairman Arafat, discreet, friendly, with a heightened sensitivity, could immediately detect all the nuances in the attitude of those speaking to him. While expressing his will to persevere in the direction of peace, his concern, his constant concern, was the reaction of the Palestinian extremists. "What would be the response of the Israeli government following the demonstrations of goodwill on the part of the Palestinians?" he asked. "None." He answered his own question before I had a chance to chime in.

For the extremists, this realization was akin to showing all their cards and having nothing in return. Thus, they responded by carrying out violent guerrilla actions in Israel, denying the existence of the Israeli nation in the process. The victims of those skirmishes were innocent men, women, and children going about their daily activities. Consequentially, the reckless actions of the extremists would result in the demonization of all the Palestinians in the eyes of the Israeli population and the world at large. In retaliation, the Israeli army would target Palestinian refugee camps in Beirut in a relentless bombing campaign and kill many innocent people. Both sides were teaching hatred to their children. The Palestinians began setting up training camps to train their children (boys and girls) in the art of war, escalating the vicious cycle with no apparent end in sight. Sartawi came to convey the following message to the president:

"These modern times impose two types of behaviors on us: success, or suicide. Each has its own deep motivations, but life and death have the same meaning, and death can sometimes be a form of relief. Nonetheless, we are fully aware of the dangers in place. Especially Chairman Arafat, whom you regard as a responsible man; however, we are not capable of controlling everybody, or every Palestinian in despair. We cannot, nor can any other leader."

For some time, Pierre Gemayel, founder of the Kataeb Party, was publicly sympathetic to the Palestinian cause. But he changed his position and called for an end to armed Palestinian presence in the country after the Israelis began to bombard Lebanon in retaliation for attacks by Palestinian guerrillas. An attempt was made on his life by Palestinian gunmen as he was leaving church on a Sunday morning. In retaliation, Kataeb gunmen ambushed a busload of Palestinians, mostly civilians, and killed twenty-seven passengers. Immediate clashes between Palestinian Muslim forces and Kataeb forces followed, marking the beginning of Lebanon's bloody fifteen-year civil war in the spring of 1975.

Arafat and I were at his office discussing the merits of some proposals from the president when Kataeb forces besieged the compound. We were suddenly thrust in the middle of a fierce gun battle between Palestinian militias and the attackers and were quickly escorted to a secure area by his bodyguards. After several hours of intense fighting, the confrontation came to an end. I was truly distressed by the level of carnage all around me. The body count was over a hundred—casualties of a senseless war. The Kataeb forces received their arms from the Israel Defense Forces, who had become their allies. Even though Arafat knew that peace with Israel was imperative, he never underestimated the difficulty of the mission in pursuit of an independent Palestinian state. Regardless, the president and I believed that our proposals could serve as the basis for constructive discussions within the Palestinian leadership. Back in Abidjan, President Houphouët was more relieved than ever to see me. "All praises go to the Almighty for protecting you through the volatile situation in Lebanon," he prayed. We discussed the state of affairs in detail and concluded that the right course of action was for us to maintain our communication channels with the Israelis through our friends in the Jewish diaspora.

The prolonged conflict and its immediate impact on the people of Lebanon was not something the world was expecting. But needless to say, President Houphouët and I were prepared to do our part to help stave off the mounting refugee crisis that brought many Lebanese citizens to Côte d'Ivoire. Initially, the Interior Ministry had issued orders to immigration officials directing them to refuse entry to the refugees, most of whom were arriving without identification. The president rescinded the rules after the Minister of Interior went to complain to him about the crisis. "When one's life is in danger," the president said, "one has neither the time to search for their ID nor the forethought to find their shoes. They find the most expedient way to escape. God has sent them to our country. Let us welcome the poor Lebanese people with open arms." With that, he issued an executive order allowing all Lebanese citizens arriving on Ivorian soil to find sanctuary in the country.

President Houphouët's idea of dialogue helped create a profound revolution within the Fatah movement. The group

A Dream for Peace

underwent a major political transformation when they relinquished their armed struggle, just as the seeds of dialogue had begun to quietly take root within the Palestinian leadership. Henry Kissinger attached a private addendum to the 1975 agreement between Israel and Egypt, which called for a withdrawal of Israelis from territories that were seized in the Sinai during the 1973 war. The document stipulated that if the PLO wanted to establish political dialogue with the United States, the leadership would have to accept Resolutions 242 and 338 and publicly acknowledge Israel's right to exist as a nation. Until such time as the PLO acted in accordance with the restrictions, the US would ban all high-level contacts with the Palestinian National Authority. The president and I had made some inroads with Chairman Arafat long before Kissinger set forth the US conditions in his addendum. We had advised Arafat to alleviate his hard-line stance against Israel by embracing moderation and acknowledging the need for a two-state solution.

    I left Abidjan for Geneva to meet with Sartawi, who had initially been scheduled to meet with the president and I in Côte d'Ivoire, but circumstances had led to a change in venues. It was obvious from the moment I landed that there had been some major developments within the PLO leadership. Our meeting venue was at the Ambassador Hotel, where he expressed in clear, succinct detail that the PLO had decided on talks with Israel, as long as such a meeting could be held in absolute secrecy. He indicated that President Houphouët was the ideal voice of moderation, and in accordance with his wishes, the PLO had decided to establish contacts with the Israelis.

    "Chairman Arafat has decided, and we are happy to confirm, that Abidjan is our city of choice for an eventual meeting with the Israelis. Perhaps, not tomorrow, but certainly within six months to a year—no one really knows. However, we have determined that it is vital to proceed in absolute secrecy."

    It was clear that neither he nor I could predict where

things might end up. He was understandably frustrated because the PLO had made several attempts to gain recognition from the United States, but their overtures were always received with some suspicion. They started to believe that President Gerald Ford was purposely doing whatever he could to push them into an alliance with the USSR.

When Sartawi asked that I deliver a message from the PLO expressing their gratitude and affectionate regard for the president's continued support, I sensed a major diplomatic push in the making. He reiterated that it was Chairman Arafat's wish to embark on a secret mission to Abidjan, sponsored by the president. As a caveat, the proposition was subject to our helping secure a meeting with the United States, and they truly hoped the move would be proof of their goodwill. He went as far as to state that Chairman Arafat had committed in writing to giving the president carte blanche to defend the interests of the Palestinian people. But President Houphouët and I were astute in our diplomatic overtures. We understood the gamesmanships within the PLO camp and were at times weary of Arafat's political maneuverings. Nonetheless, we gave him the benefit of the doubt and did our best to accommodate the PLO whenever feasible. We were always aware that the Israelis, the Americans, and others who had a stake in the peace process had to be assured that indeed there was a trustworthy partner on the other side of the negotiating table, and Arafat, despite his own shortcomings, was in fact the face of the PLO. We had seen too much suffering in the Palestinian territories. For us, taking a back seat and doing nothing was out of the question. A higher level of diplomatic pressure had to be sustained on the parties to ensure an outcome that would ultimately be embraced by them.

Sartawi continued to be an honest broker, despite finding himself in a sea of jealousy among his peers. As an emissary to the chairman, he was limited in how much he could do or say, because he was at times circumvented by official PLO spokesperson Farouk

A Dream for Peace

Kaddoumi (Minister of Foreign Affairs), who made statements to the press contradicting Sartawi's views. This was, of course, Arafat's doing, as he had a habit of using both resources to fulfill his promises to certain allies and gain some political advantage. The president and I saw through all of that but refused to buckle to the innuendos of the doubters and naysayers, because we viewed the peace process with a different set of lenses. Those who wished to use and manipulate were usually not on the side of peace but could be made to see things our way. We rose above the shenanigans and maintained our resolve with the strictest discipline to not fall short of our ultimate objective.

In the summer of 1975, when Sartawi returned to Abidjan, he informed us that they were beginning to see some encouraging signs from a small but growing number of Israelis who were supporters of the idea of "peace with the Palestinians." "But nevertheless," he added, "in the midst of this gloomy picture, Chairman Arafat has asked that I deliver some good news: there is an increasing number of Israelis who are becoming aware that a solution is only possible through Arab-Jewish solidarity, and they are fighting for the establishment and creation of a democratic Palestinian state. The evolution of this feeling among Israelis, granted among the minority of course, is the result of your predictions and prophecies about dialogue as the only true path to a solution."

Even the PLO's representative in London, Said Hammami, he told us, had been in secret contacts on a regular basis with Uri Avnery, a former member of the Knesset who had deployed considerable efforts to effectuate and advance the idea of peace within the Israeli domestic policy.

The president and I were quite pleased. He voiced his sentiments to Sartawi: "I would like to take the opportunity to express my gratitude to Chairman Arafat for the confidence he has always bestowed in me. I have a weakness that is articulated by my loyalty to principles, and to my friends, as well as my unwavering commitment to peace and justice. This will tell you that I have not changed, and will never change my position on the negotiated settlement of the Palestinian problem. It is through these complexities that we must arm ourselves with the necessary serenity to search for the diminutive thread in the midst of this labyrinth, which will lead us to the desired peace; peace and justice, peace for the reconstruction of the Palestinian nation."

Sartawi signed off with his own uplifting message: "The entire leadership of the PLO and the Palestinian people believe in your faith in dialogue, love, and peace—as opposed to the futility of terminating dialogue and contact even between enemies."

With that, the president and I assumed we could move forward and begin making some progress, not realizing that there was still a great deal of hesitation inside the Palestinian leadership. Sartawi returned to Abidjan in less than two weeks to deliver some new suggestions from Arafat. For the president and I, it seemed they were procrastinating.

"Dialogue presumably involves two parties who commit to engage in discussions," he proceeded to say. "Before engaging in discussions, the law of engagement requires the recognition of each party by the other. These are the basic fundamentals of dialogue; hence, the basic criteria for dialogue between parties. We chose to recognize the Israelis in our statement—to consider them as full citizens. However, they have chosen to refuse to recognize us."

President Houphouët's answer was compassionate, steadfast, and encouraging:

"*I have listened with the utmost sensitivity to the statements you just made, and I cannot ignore the normal reactions of the Palestinians in a situation that seems to be deteriorating by the day. Gambling is worthy of blame. Even so, if one has to gamble, the cards must be played on the table, not beneath the table. All modesty aside, I will keep moving on, because I still believe there is room for hope.*" Sartawi welcomed the president's words as food for thought for the Palestinian leadership.

Benefitting from robust American economic aid, Egypt had gone ahead and executed a second disengagement agreement with Israel under the aegis of the US. Negotiations had been concluded without ever revisiting the Palestinian issue. Thus, having been rejected in Lebanon and ignored by President Sadat, the Palestinians could no longer contain their anguish. They were willing to advance their objectives and engage in a substantive dialogue but insisted their counterparts at the table must be influential personalities in Israeli society, whose positions could influence public opinion and have an impact on the decisions of the Knesset. It was under such ideal conditions that the leadership of the PLO could be encouraged to take the risk and face the violent reactions of the extremists. In those days, the majority of Arabs and Jews viewed all forms of contacts between the Palestinians and the Israelis as high treason. This was also the case for any Israeli who dared reach out to a member of the PLO.

The Israeli Council for Israeli-Palestinian Peace (ICIPP) was founded in Israel in December 1975 by an eminent Israeli group. They released a manifesto in February of 1976, which among other things advocated for a return to the 1967 borders as well as the establishment of a Palestinian state alongside the state of Israel. They also recognized the PLO as the sole representatives of the Palestinians and the negotiating body with whom the government of Israel would engage on the basis of mutual recognition. Ironically, the Lebanese Civil War was still raging and the Israelis were getting increasingly involved, hoping to weaken or eliminate the Palestinians altogether. The president and I continued to pursue all the avenues of dialogue at our disposal, reaching out to our various friends in the Jewish diaspora, mostly well-established businessmen in France who had business ties to Côte d'Ivoire. Members of their families with whom they were in constant contact lived in Israel and by extension, they also had relationships with influential people in the

Israel and Palestine—Our Plea for Peace

country who were willing to help.

In the midst of all of these efforts, an Egyptian Jew by the name of Henri Curiel appeared on our radar. He had been a supporter of the partition of Palestine while living in Egypt in 1948. He participated in demonstrations with his friends, hoping to motivate the Farouk monarchy to pursue the establishment of a Palestinian state alongside Israel. King Farouk, fighting a war against Israel for the restoration of a Greater Palestine, expelled Curiel from Egypt. He later settled down in Paris as a political refugee. Other Egyptian Jews arrived in France not long afterward, and they formed a support group around him. He was an energetic activist, instrumental in helping the FLN organization with its underground network operations. When the Algerian war came to an end, he worked with his support group to assist other liberation movements in the Third World. They were mostly wealthy businessmen, very generous and well organized, and above all, they were absolutely discreet. Peace between the Israelis and the Palestinians was a subject that was very dear to their hearts.

It seemed that everyone who was interested in maintaining any form of dialogue was reaching out to help, and one such individual was an Israeli physicist by the name of Daniel Amit. In 1975, during a brief sabbatical in Paris, he was introduced to the Curiel circle, and eventually he became their liaison to the ICIPP. Curiel was also a close friend of Pierre Mendès-France, former President du Conseil of France, an advocate of peace, and a supporter of the peace process. Hence, with absolute discretion, Curiel initiated contacts with the ICIPP. Ultimately, our collective efforts paid off, and the Curiel group agreed to host the first dialogue between the Israelis and the Palestinians in Paris in absolute secrecy. The setting was perfect.

As soon as I received the confirmation from the Curiel group, I reached out to the Palestinian leadership and they assured me that they were ready to engage in the secret dialogue with the

A Dream for Peace

leading members of the ICIPP. We determined that I was to meet the Palestinian delegation in Paris, and Henri Curiel would be responsible for initiating contacts with the ICIPP through his liaison, Daniel Amit. I flew in from Abidjan and arrived just in time to meet with Dr. Sartawi, who was heading the Palestinian delegation. He seemed a bit nervous, but he exuded some confidence because he knew that this was a historic moment and that the time had come to perform his distinguished duty with courage and determination. It was also an act of survival to restore the identity of his people, whom he loved passionately. *This was the only way to take up the fight for a Palestinian passport to be granted to his people.*

Dialogue was a strategy—not a form of capitulation. Dialogue was a means of reaching out to influence the public opinion in Israel (through the ICIPP) in order to have the people move from hatred to the recognition of Palestinian rights. Since public opinion is the engine of democracy, in the long term, our efforts could influence the Israeli government. Nonetheless, we were still aware of the fact that the government for its part retained the ability to influence public opinion with a more powerful bully pulpit by way of the media. The summer of 1976 offered a sliver of hope and led us down a historic pathway for some very constructive discussions at a Paris home provided by a member of the Curiel group. I arrived at the venue as scheduled and warmed up to the cordial atmosphere, joining both the Israeli and Palestinian delegations in interacting with the host, Henri Curiel. Mattityahu Peled, a reserve general in the Israeli army at the time, acquainted himself and introduced me to former secretary of the Labor Party Aryeh "Lova" Eliav and two other members of the ICIPP.

As a neutral observer, I felt a great sense of relief that we were able to hold the talks, even if it was not in Abidjan, as anticipated by the Palestinians and the president. Although he had quietly hoped to provide a safe venue for the historic meeting, President Houphouët shared my sentiments. At no time was I left with the impression of being in the presence of two enemy factions. Besides English, I also heard Arabic and Hebrew being spoken among the members of both delegations. The chairman of the ICIPP and head of the Israeli delegation, General Peled, was an architect of the Six-Day War in 1967. He retired from the Israel Defense Forces about two years after the war and went to study Arabic literature at UCLA, earning a PhD and electing to teach the subject at the University of Tel Aviv.

We were still engaged in small talk when the members of the Curiel group excused themselves and left the room. Going around the table, the individuals in each delegation introduced themselves formally and gave a detailed description of their backgrounds. Collectively, they were all men of bravery and veterans of war who had committed themselves to a new struggle with the same measure of courage and determination toward the fight for peace. As a veteran of the Algerian liberation war, I felt very close to them, and I was especially astounded by their differing pathways that had motivated them to reach the decision for the need to make peace.

The approach of Dr. Sartawi, which had been explored in very minute detail over the course of many years by the Palestinian leadership as well as the president and I, was finally presented to the panel. He spoke passionately and eloquently about the need for a road map to peace. The Israeli delegation reacted warmly, and they concurred with the Palestinian objective. The discussions were very cordial and constructive on both sides.

During the Six-Day War, the participating Arab nations and the Palestinian population suffered a great deal of devastation in the aftermath of the unprecedented Israeli victory. Yitzhak Rabin, the commander of the Israeli armed forces during the war, was later hailed with prestigious honors in Israel, alongside Matti Peled and other companions. However, for General Peled, the evocations of these victorious feelings quickly dissipated. He reminisced on his experience in the immediate aftermath of the war. "The Israeli army," he said, "had set up a delegation of prominent members charged with the responsibility of visiting each family to notify them of the death of a next of kin." I noted the inclusion of a medical doctor among the delegation. He explained that on many occasions, when the delegation arrived at their designated location to break the devastating news to the soldier's family, someone would succumb to the shocking news and faint. The accompanying doctor was always ready to resuscitate the victim. Clearly, the entire experience had affected his view of the situation. He had witnessed too many disturbing scenes and had begun to question the senseless war—a war with no end in sight. "Ultimately, I continue to believe that it is time to offer the Arabs their land in order to make peace. I retired from the IDF and decided to change careers because the upper hierarchy did not embrace my ideas." His candid reflection was met with a big sigh of resignation by the rest of the panelists.

The two opposing factions had not come all the way to participate in a historic meeting in order to criticize the past. Indeed they were determined to focus on building the future. There was one substantive point of mutual agreement for the parties: the terrorist sees himself as a freedom fighter, but the irony is that a freedom fighter is seen as a terrorist in the eyes of the enemy. Uri Avnery, a founding member of the ICIPP, who was noticeably absent at this particular meeting, once told me that the British saw him as a terrorist in the past. This was during his stint as a fighter in a nationalist underground Jewish group. The veteran fighters became soldiers of peace, determined to succeed.

After the parties created an outline for more future dialogue, they emphasized the absolute necessity of maintaining the discreet nature of their meetings until the circumstances had improved. The Israelis would have preferred to publicize the meeting, but the Palestinians insisted on preserving the secrecy, suggesting that it was much more important to advance the process in stages. They were mindful of the extreme political wing within the PLO whose intransigence could lead to violent confrontations.

Israel and Palestine—Our Plea for Peace

At the end of the day, the parties were definitely in agreement that the meeting had been mostly substantive and they seemed propitiously impressed with not only the tone of what had transpired but also with each other. I felt as if we had just completed a long journey, which had seemed unimaginable only a few days earlier.

We had successfully arranged the first-ever dialogue between the ICIPP and the PLO. There had been no emotional outbursts, only expressions of deep-rooted feelings and raw sentiments, which could barely be contained—something powerful, almost unreal, had illuminated from the participants.

For my part, I felt a sense of liberation and pride. With the grace of the Almighty, I had been able to perform a duty and offer my humble contribution to the peace process. Henri Curiel and his friends had put forth an exemplary organization, and our collective efforts had yielded something substantive. Although, he knew that the road ahead would be long, the president was pleased with the historic milestone.

Sartawi with Matti Peled.

The president and I continued with our efforts. He worked tirelessly in his attempt to influence the decision of political leaders

A Dream for Peace

in Israel. As early as February 4, 1977, he met privately for three hours with Israeli Prime Minister Yitzhak Rabin in Geneva. During their meeting, he informed Rabin of his contacts with the PLO through their representative, Dr. Sartawi, whom he deemed to be trustworthy, and he elaborated on the ICIPP's positive impact. Prime Minister Rabin commented that the ICIPP represented a tiny fraction of the population, and he even referred to General Peled as his comrade-in-arms. President Houphouët pleaded for peace through dialogue and called for the evacuation of the occupied territories on the basis of UN Resolutions 242 and 338 and for the birth of a Palestinian state. However, Rabin was not ready for a Palestinian state. Rather, he sought a solution within the framework of a peace agreement with Jordan. The president later described their meeting to me as "direct and frank."

President Houphouët and Premier Yitzhak Rabin.

I went on a mission to debrief President Anwar Sadat in Cairo about the Rabin meeting on February 8. In reaffirming that Côte d'Ivoire had not wavered from its position regarding Palestinian rights, I assured him that the president and I would continue to push

Israel and Palestine—Our Plea for Peace

for Israeli evacuation from all the occupied territories. President Houphouët wanted me to let him know that he had suggested Yitzhak Rabin accept his proposal and establish dialogue with the upper hierarchy of the PLO. I was in a very good mood at the meeting. Earlier, he had been exceptionally courteous in welcoming me to Cairo. Though a bit peculiar, the level of hospitality was accorded me from the moment I heard a gentle knock on my hotel suite in the early hours of the morning, right before our scheduled meeting. The butler apologized and begged to bring in a large cart with a plethora of dishes, including the traditional Egyptian meal *fūl*,[41] accentuated with platters full of pastries. "Excuse me, you have the wrong suite. I have not requested room service." He was insistent. "No, sir, not at all. This is a special order from President Sadat for his esteemed guest," he said, overzealously delighted to be of service. He finished setting the table and exited my room gracefully. I worked up a quick appetite and indulged myself in the Egyptian national dish. I had no idea that the meal was a renowned breakfast delight.

Meeting President Sadat.

---

[41] Egyptian dish: cooked and mashed fava beans, vegetable oil, and cumin.

A Dream for Peace

Sadat was a secretive and truly pious man who often sought solitude in different palaces on the outskirts of Cairo. I had met with him several times in the past in one of his palaces. When I arrived on a previous mission, I was escorted into a waiting room. My focus was soon diverted from reviewing President Houphouët's introductory letter to the sound of footsteps echoing through the hallways, growing louder as they came closer, and then suddenly he appeared in the doorway with a smile on his face. I stood up and gave him a firm handshake. It was like seeing a long-lost friend. On a return visit, I stumbled upon him praying in a meeting room. Utterly surprised at myself for the accidental intrusion, I stood still and meditated until he was done.

With President Sadat.

The annual Palestinian National Council meeting was held from March 12 to March 22 in 1977. President Houphouët-Boigny was widely criticized by every speaker on the podium for having

Israel and Palestine—Our Plea for Peace

met with Rabin. I listened to all the dissenting voices for the entire first week of the summit, feeling perturbed, knowing how much effort the president and I had put forth in our attempts to foster communication links between the Israelis and the Palestinians. In the president's defense, Arafat took to the stage on the seventh day and explained that President Houphouët had no ulterior motives other than the fact that he sought to protect and defend the rights of a people who had been rendered voiceless. Finally, a resolution was adopted at the end of the conference. It stipulated the initiation of dialogue with non-Zionist forces in Israel and elsewhere and embraced the idea of the establishment of a Palestinian national state.

Heated rhetoric and repeated threats by some members of the Palestinian hard-line groups were a frequent occurrence. Dr. Sartawi and Arafat knew fully well that the extremists were passionately against the peace efforts and that their lives were in permanent danger. For his part, Arafat took extreme precautionary measures to avert any assassination attempts on his life. He remained elusive and spent the night in different homes to avoid being tracked down. Even Sartawi had a very hard time reaching him while in Paris. He often sought the help of Abu Mazen (Mahmoud Abbas), the only person who knew of Arafat's movements, to relay messages regarding progress at the ICIPP meetings.

The risks were not restricted to the Palestinian camp. There were many death threats against their Israeli counterparts too. But regardless, everyone maintained their resolve. When I accompanied Sartawi to a subsequent ICIPP meeting, I marveled at the similarity between the delegations representing the two enemy nations. I found their behavior and their attitude so identical that at some point, I expressed it to him: "You look so much alike that I find myself at a loss for words. What are the differences between the two of your peoples?" "There is none," he remarked, "except when we eat, the Palestinians combine cheese and milk with meat. The Jews never mix their meat with milk or cheese." I found that to be true during our meal break. The harmonious interaction was heartwarming. Most of the conversation between General Peled and Sartawi was in Arabic, and the two shared a common interest in Arabic poetry. For a moment, I briefly recalled a passage from a Madame de Staël essay, later published in a book (*De l'influence des passions sur le bonheur des individus et des nations*), about the impact of geography and the environment on people.

Elections had recently ended in the United States, and newly elected President Jimmy Carter was proving to be a more willing listener. President Houphouët was encouraged by a letter he received from him, asking that he take a more hands-on role in the peace process. I grew increasingly hopeful that we were beginning to take a step in the right direction. Regarding the Middle East, Carter's first foreign policy decision was to put forward a plan that separated the Sinai issue from the complex Palestinian question. In so doing, he intended to push for a peace treaty between Egypt and Israel and force the Israelis to return the Sinai territory in exchange for diplomatic recognition and access to the Suez Canal, among other things. As for the conflict between Israel and Palestine, he envisioned an outline of principles for future negotiations in the region, suggesting that Israel grant autonomy to the Palestinians in exchange for peace with its Arab neighbors.

Not bothered by the criticisms at the Palestine National Council conference, President Houphouët forged ahead and met with Israeli Foreign Minister Yigal Allon for two hours at the president's Paris apartment. He summoned Allon to discuss the merits of the Carter approach and to get a feel for the official Israeli position prior to Allon's meeting with US Secretary of State Cyrus Vance. Despite projecting his thoughts into the process, the president spoke with much humility to the press when asked about his own efforts on the peace process. "I put up no ideas of my own for a Middle East peace," he said. "I just pick up suggestions and pass them along. As for peace making, you are asking too much of me. Our discussions were conducted in a frank and trusting atmosphere, and we covered a broad array of topics affecting the world, but with special emphasis on the Middle East." Months of secret diplomacy continued to bear fruit behind the scenes. Six months after he spoke publicly about his discussions with Allon, Secretary of State Cyrus Vance and Soviet Minister of Foreign Affairs Andrei Gromyko issued a joint statement, calling for a negotiated solution to the Israel-Palestine problem. In pushing for a negotiations framework, the superpowers had set the right tone by including the Palestinians in a new Geneva conference involving all parties. But the upbeat atmosphere quickly dissipated when, to our surprise, the Israeli government began to move forward with a planned settlement policy. Suddenly, talks came to a grinding halt.

The president and I regrouped and refocused our Mideast plans, especially in anticipation of what was to come after Sadat's historic visit to the Knesset. He had opened the door to Camp David after becoming the first Arab leader to set foot on Israeli soil. When he stood in front of the Knesset to state that the genesis of the conflict was the Palestinian issue and that there could be no peace without a just solution for the Palestinians, we hoped he would lay out the principles for future negotiations in the area, based on the idea that Israel should grant autonomy to the Palestinians in exchange for peace with its Arab neighbors. But he did not go that far. Instead he revisited certain aspects of discussions that President Houphouët and I had taken up with him, shortly after the Rabin meeting, and he did so effectively, by insisting on Israel's withdrawal from the occupied territories and the restoration of the Palestinians' legitimate rights. Even the United States, Israel's main ally, concurred with him as to the reinstatement of those rights. The irony was that he made his statements without any mention of the PLO, a move that was seen by Arafat as a breach of their authority and, predictably, a move that may have weakened their position in

A Dream for Peace

the peace negotiations. The decision angered the Palestinian people, triggering riots and insurrections in the refugee camps.

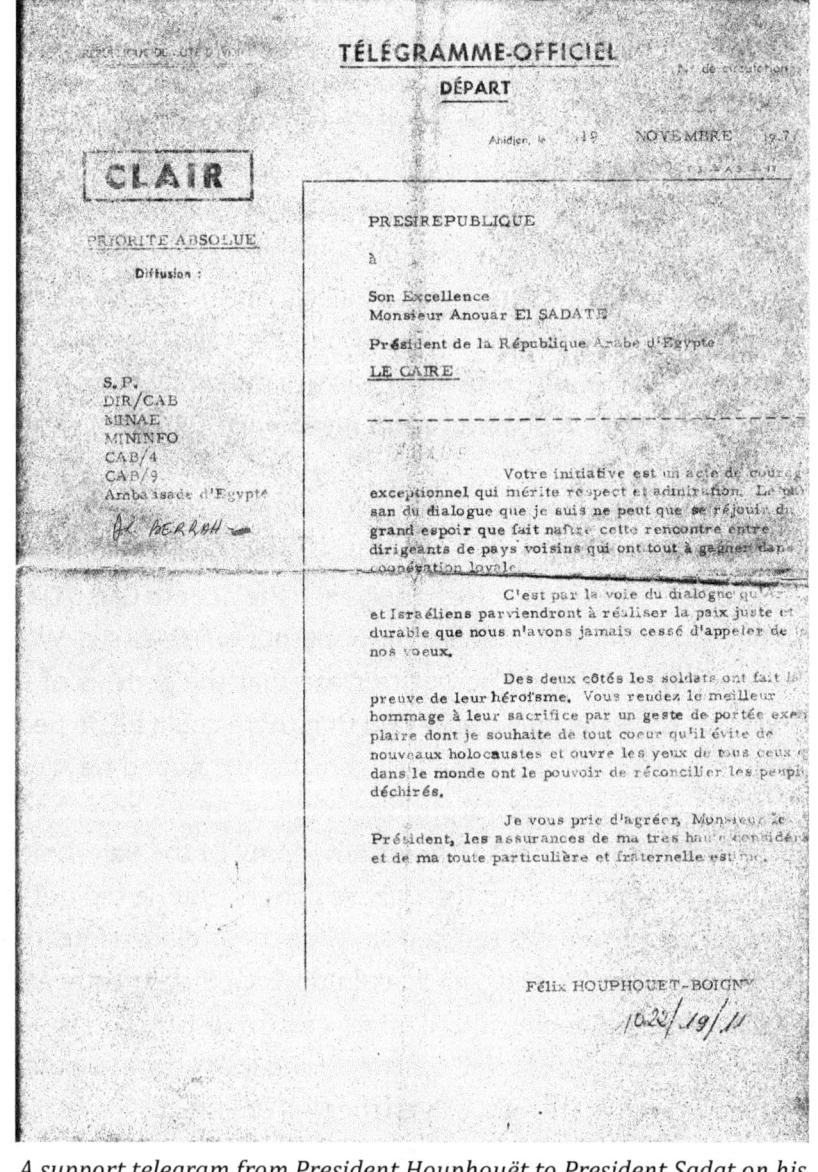

A support telegram from President Houphouët to President Sadat on his trip to Israel, November 19, 1977.

Israel and Palestine—Our Plea for Peace

I was dispatched to Cairo by President Houphouët-Boigny on November 30 with a letter for Sadat, explaining in detail the reason behind our severance of diplomatic relations with Israel in 1973 (the Israeli army occupied a part of sovereign African territory in the Arab state of Egypt). We sought to reemphasize the importance of maintaining a strong solidarity, speaking in unison to ensure continued unity in our pursuit of a just peace. Although he applauded Egypt's pursuit of dialogue with the Israelis, the president declared that Sadat had placed us in an untenable position by remaining silent after his visit to Israel. We had been hoping to receive some diplomatic overtures from him, acknowledging our support and declaring publicly that members of the alliance that had supported Egypt may also at some point establish diplomatic relations with Israel. But needless to say, our relationship with Sadat had always been somewhat complicated. Since the very beginning, he came across as not being forthright in any of our discussions. It seemed he always had something up his sleeve. He was hard to read. Either way, I waited in Cairo for four days. Before we finally sat down for our meeting, his security team expressed regret for the delay due to the president dealing with a major blowback from other Arab leaders, especially those who had gathered in Tripoli for the major anti-Egypt summit on December 2. All the PLO factions had been in attendance with Libya, Syria, Algeria, Iraq, and South Yemen. After condemning Sadat for three days, he responded by severing relations with the attending countries (who had formed an alliance known as the Steadfastness and Confrontation Front).

We had our face-to-face meeting a day before the end of the Tripoli summit. During our discussions, I impressed upon him the fact that we had nothing against his choosing to restore relations with Israel, but the timing of events was paramount. Rather than imposing radio silence, a nonproductive silence in the aftermath of such a historic move, he needed to give some serious consideration to our suggestions and make some public statements. Referring to the following statement by President Houphouët, I reemphasized our commitment to do our very best to help him: "I am geographically very far from the region, but I am also independent, and everyone knows me as a man of truth—one who respects the given word. By having a free hand, I can talk about what it takes and deliver the befitting words to Chairman Arafat, the United States, Israel, and even the Arab states. I am only motivated by the desire for peace. President Carter wrote to me and stated, 'Help us.' So did President Giscard d'Estaing. I will be able to effectively help you calm the upheaval that lurks against Egypt and her courageous president."

He was in a somber mood, and I predicted he would give me the cold shoulder. I was right. He dismissed my suggestions and refused to lend any credence to the Arab states that had reacted negatively to his trip.

I left Cairo and went to see President Bourguiba in Tunis to explain our position on the situation. He had previously proposed an Arab-Israeli dialogue with himself serving as the initiator and go-between. Although he was very pleased that President Houphouët initiated consultations with him prior to restoring diplomatic relations with Israel, he declared that long before any such moves by Anwar Sadat, he had advocated opening a direct dialogue with Israel (prior to the October War of 1973)—a suggestion for which he was roundly censured by the Arab camp. We outlined a series of strategic measures for follow-up discussions with President Houphouët before I left for Algiers that same day. My meeting with President Boumédiène was constructive. He accepted our position that the severance of diplomatic relations with Israel no longer had a purpose. I emphasized the fact that President Houphouët, a man not motivated by any desire for material gains or other assistance, was ready to reinstate diplomatic relations with the Jewish state in pursuit of peace. He knew of the sincerity and commitment of the president on the Israeli-Palestinian issue and made no objections.

At the end of the Tripoli summit, Sartawi was dispatched to

Israel and Palestine—Our Plea for Peace

Abidjan to inform President Houphouët that Chairman Arafat was "forced" to adopt a position that imposed sanctions on Egypt. He reiterated that it was the PLO chairman's wish to assure President Houphouët before all things of the "love" and "respect" that he had for Sadat. In addition, he emphasized his belief that the alliance with Sadat was crucial in the Palestinian objective for peace in the Middle East. Arafat wanted us to convey to Sadat that he had acted under pressure, particularly from the Syrian leadership, and that he had no choice but to align himself with the Steadfastness and Confrontation Front in Tripoli. As a result, he had placed himself in quite a predicament; therefore, he sought the help of President Houphouët to clarify his position, albeit discreetly, to Sadat.

Sartawi took up the compelling statement with the president: "I appeal to you to play the role of an intermediary between President Sadat and Chairman Arafat and help them navigate through their positions. In order to accomplish this, I would like to ask, if I may, that you dispatch Dr. Berrah on a mission to Cairo to meet with President Sadat and present the situation as I have described, and proceed to talk to Chairman Arafat. I also propose that Dr. Berrah meet with King Fahd to discuss some options regarding how to rein in the Arabs to take on a clear position toward achieving peace."

I moved quickly to dispel any perception of dissent by embarking on a trip to Cairo for an emergency meeting with President Sadat, but he couldn't see me due to logistical reasons. Instead, I took up the issue with Vice President Mubarak. Both President Houphouët and I knew better than to give carte blanche credence to such message shifts from Arafat, especially due to his vacillating tendencies. I knew why he sought to appease extremists in the Palestinian camp or kowtow to external pressures from Arab leaders who supported the Palestinian cause. The lack of an organized administration in an independent state with a functioning government had rendered the Palestinians a hopelessly dependent and voiceless people with very few friends.

A Dream for Peace

١٩٧٨/١/١٠

رسالة للسادات من رئيس ساحل العاج

تسلم حسني مبارك نائب رئيس الجمهورية امس رسالة الى الرئيس انور السادات من الرئيس فيليكس هوافيه بوانيه رئيس ساحل العاج خلال مقابلة تمت بينهما امس .. واوضح نائب رئيس الجمهورية لمبعوث ـ ساحل العاج آخر تطورات مشــــكلة الشرق الاوسط .. وكان الدكتور غلام براخ وصل القاهرة يوم الخميس الماضي.

With Egyptian Vice President Hosni Mubarak.

But their predicament highlighted certain character flaws in Arafat that did not entirely encapsulate his persona. We understood why the Israelis and the Americans, who had some difficulty trusting his word, were at times hesitant to take up discussions with him at the negotiating table, but the fact is, we were also realistic in knowing that he indeed was one of the true voices of reasoning in the Palestinian camp. As such, we tried our very best to maintain a balancing act in diplomatic circles—to keep the ball rolling for the sake of peace.

The coming to power of Israeli Prime Minister Menachem

Israel and Palestine—Our Plea for Peace

Begin,[42] a member of the Likud Party, brought about a higher level of intransigence toward the Palestinian issue. He announced plans for the expansion of West Bank settlements and spoke openly about moving his offices to East Jerusalem. Such rhetoric made a comprehensive agreement ever more difficult to achieve. However, the shift in policy neither stopped nor discouraged President Houphouët-Boigny in his pursuit of peace. Labels did not matter to the president. His objective was to reach out and touch the hearts of his fellow man to draw their attention to the truth, regardless of how rigid their positions may be. He never despaired in the face of a setback. As far as he was concerned, there could always be a sudden or gradual conversion of thought. One of the greatest apostles of Christ, Saul, was once a persecutor of Christians and went on to become Saint Paul after his conversion. It was with these convictions that he would meet with Prime Minister Begin. He expressed the same truths to Begin and emphasized the need to make peace with the Palestinians through dialogue, emphasizing Israel's withdrawal from the occupied territories and the establishment of a Palestinian state as the only way to guarantee secure borders. Prime Minister Begin remained unfazed. He stuck to his doctrine of a Greater Israel and moved to increase settlements in the occupied territories. Though the Begin administration initiated policies that were counterproductive, amid their hard-line stances, the ICIPP and their Palestinian counterparts began soliciting support from some well-known personalities in the international community. Pierre Mendes-France, who they visited at the end of their very first meeting, was already on board, but Austrian Chancellor Bruno Kreisky[43] threw the full weight of his office behind them. Other prominent personalities followed suit. At the same time, the extremists and other enemies of dialogue within the Israeli and Palestinian camps made their voices

---

[42] Israeli Prime Minister, 1977–1983.
[43] Austrian Chancellor, 1970–1983.

A Dream for Peace

heard through the use of violence. The year 1978 was marked by assassinations in a disturbing frequency. First was the assassination of Said Hammami in London, Henri Curiel a few months later in Paris, and then there was the brutal murder of PLO representative Azzedine Kalak, also in Paris. The price for peace had become quite hefty.

In the midst of these setbacks, a determined President Carter forged ahead with his main objective: the pursuit of a peace agreement between Egypt and Israel—his framework that was to be negotiated at Camp David, which he believed was the only viable and most palatable solution for the Palestinian problem. Ultimately, we expected his proposals to include some form of compromise that balanced Israeli security with a recognition of the rights of a Palestinian state.

Soon after his trip to Jerusalem, President Sadat broke ranks with most of his Arab brothers. He continued to negotiate with the Israeli and US governments. The Egyptian economy was on the brink of collapse, and understandably, he set his sights on repairing the damages from the previous war and focusing on building a consensus around his domestic agenda. I appreciated the complexity of his position but empathized with those in the Palestinian camp who had hoped that he would continue to maintain the Israeli-Palestinian issue on his list of priorities. But as far as the PLO was concerned, Sadat had minimized their influence in the region. The president and I understood their frustration. Still, we encouraged Arafat to remain vigilant in his push for peace and asked the parties to rise above the fray and not lose sight of the bigger picture.

Though he lacked the support of a majority of senators on the Israeli-Palestinian issue, President Carter was the first US president to declare the illegality of settlements in the occupied territories. He was rendered powerless by the intransigence in Congress, and his influence on Begin, an unwilling ally, began to wane. I was hopeful that the thirteen-day Camp David summit in the Maryland hills would establish a milestone in the peace process. But unfortunately, the final agreement from Camp David provided less clarity than we had anticipated. Beyond that, the West Bank negotiations could have been premised on UN Resolution 242 for a clear path toward Palestinian self-determination. Sadly, we encountered some vague provisions that provided no specificity on the final outcome of the negotiations. Hence, the ensuing peace treaty between Egypt and Israel was catastrophic for the Palestinians. The Begin administration had been great at maneuvering through the process and succeeded in isolating President Sadat in order to secure Israel's border with Egypt.

The repercussions of the Kissinger addendum were felt by several high-level diplomats, notably, the US ambassador to the United Nations under President Carter, Andrew Young, a great friend and an advocate of peace who had to resign from his position unceremoniously in August 1979. A month earlier, Young had attempted to delay a report by the United Nations Division for Palestinian Rights that had called for the creation of a Palestinian state because he felt that the administration was dealing with too many other issues at the time. He proceeded to meet with UN representatives of several Arab countries, who agreed in principle to delay the report as long as the Palestine Liberation Organization also agreed. As a result, Young met with Zehdi Terzi (the PLO's UN representative) at a reception in the apartment of Kuwait's UN ambassador. News of their highly controversial meeting became public within days, and after denying any complicity in what the press had dubbed the "Andy Young affair," President Carter asked Young to resign four days later. President Houphouët and I were very disappointed when we heard the news. After his tenure in office, he visited Côte d'Ivoire on several occasions and we became very close.

We maintained contacts with the ICIPP and other participants in the Israeli-Palestinian dialogue. At times I stopped at Sartawi's office or at some other location in Paris for a few hours to get a refresher on new developments. Occasionally, Aryeh Eliav, General

A Dream for Peace

Peled, or Uri Avnery would show up for the discussions. Sartawi dealt with the mounting pressure from Palestinian extremists by voicing his ideas on the ongoing dialogue with the Israeli peace activists at lectures and conferences. He received the Austrian Bruno Kreisky Prize in 1979, jointly with Aryeh Eliav, for seeking an end to the Arab-Israeli conflict. Within the PLO, he faced direct attacks by opponents of the talks. Eventually, he reached a point where he could no longer sit by idly and watch as Chairman Arafat danced the tango with the hard-liners in his attempts to rally support from them. The opponents of dialogue refused to let Sartawi take the podium and speak at the Palestinian National Council meeting. Soon thereafter, he tendered his resignation to Chairman Arafat, who refused to accept it.

Meanwhile, he was placed on the hit list of the Abu Nidal terrorist organization, which had been threatening him for some time, and he became a hunted man. Over the years, we developed a habit of meeting each other whenever he passed through Geneva. I encountered him once while he was on a brief transit en route to a European destination, and I expressed my concern for his health. He had become a chain smoker. "Don't worry, my dear friend," he said, seemingly nervous and resigned. *"What matters to me is my dedication to serving the people for whom my love is without limits."* On April 10, 1983, I received a heartbreaking call regarding his assassination in Albufeira, Portugal, by a member of the Abu Nidal group. President Houphouët and I felt as though we had been hit on the head with a sledgehammer. "Please go and represent me at the funeral," he begged, with a heavy heart. Titi was totally devastated by the news. With her by my side, we embarked on the long journey to Amman to pay our last respects. I meditated during the trip and reflected on the times I asked Sartawi to tread lightly and cautiously around the extremists. His haunting words echoed loudly in my thoughts again and again. "If it is the will of Allah, then I have nothing to fear," he would say. "I know that they

Israel and Palestine—Our Plea for Peace

might succeed in taking my life someday, but the sacrifice would have been worth it." We went to see his family and expressed our heartfelt condolences to his wife, Widad. She was very dignified under the difficult circumstances. "How are the children holding up?" Titi asked. "They are in Paris," she said, holding back the tears. The burial ceremony took place a day before our arrival, with Arafat and other members of the various factions of the PLO in attendance. But we went to the cemetery to pay our respects at his graveside and stayed in Amman for two days to be with his family. Each day was filled with conversations about the heroism of the great son of Palestine.

President Houphouët at Rose Garden with President Reagan.

President Houphouët arrived for talks with President Ronald Reagan at the White House on June 7, 1983, and he asked that the US remain committed to resolving the Israeli-Palestinian conflict. At the time, the only communications between the US and the PLO amounted to what former Secretary of State Kissinger described as "low-level technical contacts." When President Houphouët pressed for a lifting of the ban on dialogue to bring the parties to the table,

A Dream for Peace

Reagan emphasized the need for Chairman Arafat to renounce terrorism, adding that if an official declaration recognizing Israel's right to exist was made by the PLO leader, he would immediately have the ban lifted with the stroke of a pen. Days after the meeting, the president and I discussed the issue at length, and he expressed to me with much certainty that President Reagan would not budge until Arafat had taken the next step. Despite several difficulties in the midst of more Israeli settlement expansions into Palestinian territories, we ramped up our diplomatic efforts in an attempt to push the PLO leadership to officially recognize Israel's right to exist.

A few months later, in the summer of that same year, I received a phone call from General Peled and Uri Avnery, who were both in Geneva for the Conference on Palestine. My wife and I happened to be in the city at the time, and we arranged to meet for lunch at the Au Vieux Bois, an upscale restaurant adjacent to the UN compound in Geneva. From the moment we sat down, it was clear that they were still in a state of shock. We had lost a mutual friend, someone very dear to our hearts, and the unfortunate murder served a somber reminder of the dangerous nature of our efforts to achieve a peaceful resolution in the Israeli-Palestinian conflict. Their commitment remained intact, and the struggle continued. The encounter had a profound effect on Titi. "I really admire the courage of both men, but especially their devotion to peace," she said. She was particularly impressed by the compassion that emanated from the face of General Peled.

We maintained an intense diplomatic posture with our Israeli counterparts. Likud Party member Premier Yitzhak Shamir[44] flew to Geneva for a private meeting with President Houphouët to clarify his position on impending negotiations with Lebanon. Discussions were frank and straightforward, with the president insisting on finding a solution for the massive refugee crisis, which had imposed

---

[44] Israeli Prime Minister, 1983–1984 and 1986–1992.

unwarranted suffering on ordinary Palestinian families. He let Shamir know that the war in Lebanon remained at the epicenter of our foreign policy. There was lots of blame to go around, and the conversation only scratched the surface of the bigger issue. The fact that Israel had thrown their military might behind the Phalangists had exacerbated the problem, despite the PLO's own culpability in the bloody insurrection.

When the organization was expelled from Lebanon in 1982, remnants of hard-line fighters continued to battle the Phalangists for several months. In the midst of the sporadic fighting, Lebanon's newly elected president, Bashir Gemayel, was assassinated. Although there was no evidence of the perpetrator's origins, the PLO was blamed for the murder. The Phalangists, with the help of the Israeli military, entered the Shatila refugee camp in the Sabra neighborhood. Over three thousand Palestinians and Lebanese Shiites were massacred. We were appalled by what was deemed a genocidal act by the UN. All parties, we insisted, had to cease atrocities and bring the civil war to an end, and most importantly, Israel had to get out of Lebanon before we could restore official diplomatic relations.

The situation improved two years later, and President Houphouët convened a meeting in Geneva with Israeli Premier Shimon Peres. A joint declaration was issued on this occasion, *"We have decided to recommend to our governments to reestablish diplomatic relations. I imagine that our governments will follow our recommendations."* Following the announcement, diplomatic relations were restored. When Premier Yitzhak Shamir paid a visit to Côte d'Ivoire months after, President Houphouët, the consummate diplomat, ensured that the theme of his foreign policy strategy revolved around arguments of a two-state solution and a cessation of Israeli settlements. Unfortunately, Shamir remained rigid, ever true to his vision of a Greater Israel, and more determined than his predecessor to expand the Israeli settlements.

A Dream for Peace

President Houphouët-Boigny and Premier Shimon Peres.

The resettlement of Jews in the occupied territories and the seizure of more Arab lands did not go unnoticed. This policy had endured for several decades, stemming from when Israel permanently annexed East Jerusalem soon after the Six-Day War and began setting up military administrations in the occupied territories. Frustration among the Palestinian people had been mounting ever since. I sensed the beginnings of an uprising during a pilgrimage to Jerusalem with my wife and took note of that. When I went to visit Arafat in Tunis shortly after the pilgrimage, I elaborated on my suspicions, telling him about the imminent rise of a populist movement intent on establishing a Palestinian state, no matter the cost. I implored him to take the bull by the horns before the situation got out of control.

By the beginning of December 1987, the year that marked the twentieth anniversary of Israel's conquest of the Gaza Strip and West Bank, over two thousand armed Jewish settlers were occupying about 40 percent of the Gaza Strip, while close to seven hundred thousand destitute Palestinians were contained within the other 60 percent, making the Palestinian portion of the tiny Gaza Strip one of the most densely populated areas in the world. Palestinian despair had given birth to a grassroots movement (the Unified National Command of the Uprising) with ties to the PLO, and there were signs to indicate that people were fed up with the unbearable conditions. The situation was gravitating to a boiling point. December 9 was the spark that ignited the flame. This was the day when an Israeli truck crashed into a station wagon carrying Palestinian workers in the Jabalya refugee district of Gaza, killing four and wounding ten. Palestinians in Gaza determined that the incident was a deliberate act of retaliation against the killing of a Jewish man in the area several days earlier, and they took to the streets in protest, burning tires and hurling rocks and Molotov cocktails at the Israeli police, who responded with live ammunition. The riots exploded into a revolution (the intifada) and spread from Gaza into the West Bank. I was not surprised by what I saw on the news, and neither was the president. Due to the volatile situation, our efforts to get the parties to begin talking with each other entered a highly critical phase. Flabbergasted, I watched helplessly as Chairman Arafat moved to control the situation from his base in Tunisia. Our calls to Prime Minister Shamir and PLO leadership did not yield anything constructive.

Arafat had been banned from entering the United States due to the Kissinger addendum, which had imposed restrictions on contacts with the PLO. But after the Arafat condemned terrorism and recognized the state of Israel during a December 1988 speech in front of the UN General Assembly in Geneva, President Ronald Reagan moved to end the thirteen-year ban, effectively authorizing the US to begin "substantive dialogue" with the organization. His successor, George H. W. Bush, shortly after winning the Gulf War, went in front of Congress to declare the following statement: "The time has come to put an end to the Arab-Israeli conflict." Within months, he organized the Madrid Peace Conference and brought together for the first time all of the parties to the conflict for talks

A Dream for Peace

on holding direct negotiations.

We had followed closely the electoral process in the US and knew that the incoming Clinton administration would approach the Israel-Palestine issue with much vigor and diplomatic fortitude. Hence, there was valid reason for optimism in the Clinton administration's tenacious posture. When our sources informed us about a draft resolution in the works that established interim governance arrangements as well as a framework to facilitate negotiations for a final treaty between Israelis and Palestinians, we wondered if President Houphouët's constructive approach to dialogue was going to become a reality. Personally, I knew that although the 1987 intifada had failed to end Israel's occupation of the West Bank and Gaza Strip, it had in essence influenced the dialogue and at the very least prompted Chairman Arafat to shift gears and push for Palestinian statehood in the West Bank and Gaza Strip. Within months after Clinton was sworn in, Israeli and Palestinian negotiators had agreed on a "Declaration of Principles," and just as we had implored him to do years earlier, Yasser Arafat renounced armed resistance and vowed to remove the destruction of Israel from the Palestinian National Charter. The president and I were elated.

In message after message, the president told Arafat that all he really needed to do was create a framework allowing for Palestinian statehood in exchange for Israeli security. Accordingly, when President Houphouët nudged Prime Minister Rabin in their last meeting in Geneva, Rabin had in fact promised to respond to such a move by recognizing the PLO as the legitimate representative of the Palestinian people if Arafat took the necessary steps. We were indeed impressed that Rabin kept his word and began to negotiate peace with Arafat. These were the makings of the Oslo Accords. When I watched the ceremony at the White House lawn on the news, my heart was warmed by thoughts of endless journeys frustrated by countless setbacks, baby steps, and hampered accomplishments

Israel and Palestine—Our Plea for Peace

that had finally been crystallized into the annals of history. Perhaps this had been a worthwhile undertaking that could lead to a just and lasting peace. I rushed over to see the president, who was recovering from surgery at the time, to inform him of the remarkable execution of the accord between PLO and Israeli representatives. He held my hand, smiling broadly, and prayed that Arabs and Jews would one day live peacefully with dignity in the land where "God revealed Himself to Man on three occasions."

Barely three months after the historic handshake between Rabin and Arafat, President Houphouët-Boigny, a tireless advocate for peace, was called to the kingdom of God on December 7, knowing in his heart at least that his efforts had not been entirely in vain, that he had transferred his torch, even if in part, to others who were destined to come along and leave their mark in the name of peace.

My heart was broken and my spirit was weakened by the loss of my dearest friend and adopted father—my partner in the quest for peace. For several months, I mourned privately and reminisced over our diplomatic efforts. Our deep commitment to Mideast peace and our highly sensitive yet secretive overtures behind the scenes were part and parcel of what ultimately helped push everyone to take the historic step on the sun-splashed South Lawn of the White House, where a deal was consummated and executed by Shimon Peres and Mahmoud Abbas to seal the "Declaration of Principles on Self-government Arrangements" in Israeli-occupied Gaza and the West Bank. This was essentially everything President Houphouët and I had envisioned and worked on since 1972. At least, I thought, he had witnessed the occasion, and I knew that somewhere in heaven, Dr. Sartawi smiled down upon the ceremony. Though that particular chapter came and faded into the annals of history, the words of Mr. Yitzhak Rabin stuck with me:

"We the soldiers who have returned from the battle, stained with blood . . . We who have fought against you, the Palestinians, we say to you today in a loud and clear voice: 'Enough of blood and tears!

A Dream for Peace

Enough!'"

The response from Chairman Arafat had been etched on my conscience too: "*Our two peoples are awaiting today this historic hope, and they want to give peace a real chance.*"

As I readied myself for permanent retirement from politics and diplomacy-related assignments, I was at peace with the fact that our secret diplomatic efforts and undaunted commitment to Israeli-Palestinian peace efforts and sacrifices that lasted for over two decades would neither be at the forefront of Mideast political discourse nor on the front pages of international print media. Our historic actions and determined campaign for dialogue were simply aimed at ensuring peace for our brethren in the land where "God revealed himself on three occasions." But much to my surprise, the international jury chaired by Dr. Henry Kissinger et al. to oversee UNESCO's Félix Houphouët-Boigny Peace Prize decided to award the prize to Chairman Arafat, Yitzhak Rabin, and Shimon Peres at an event in Paris.

And so, on July 6, 1994, an emotional Mr. Shimon Peres stood at the podium and stated, "*It is truly an honor to have been awarded this Peace Prize named after the great leader and unforgettable friend, Félix Houphouët-Boigny.*" He then shared a personal story about the president: "Upon concluding his visit to Israel, President Houphouët-Boigny talked about a young Israeli of whom he had asked, 'How come the Sea of Galilee and the Dead Sea are located on the same longitude and draw their water from the same river, yet one of them, the Sea of Galilee, is vibrant with life, while the other, the Dead Sea, contains death?' The young Israeli thought for a while and responded: 'The Sea of Galilee draws its water from the Jordan River and passes it on. In other words, this is a sea that gives and takes. On the other hand, the Dead Sea draws its water and keeps it for itself. It is a sea that just takes.' President Houphouët-Boigny then concluded by saying that, '*The difference between giving and taking or just taking may become the difference between life and* death—*the distinction between a peace that guarantees life, and a war that carries death.'"*

Quite profound. Everyone was very emotional, and the memories of the great "Sage of Africa" ruled writ large in the hall. When Yitzhak Rabin spoke, he channeled a classic President Houphouët saying: *"Let us proceed slowly, for we are in a hurry."* He continued: *"Ladies and Gentlemen, it is summer here in Paris, and we have come from a small patch of land in the Middle East. We have arrived at the most decisive stage on the way to reconciliation between Israelis and Palestinians. This is the stage where we bring an end to the dreaming phase. The time has now come to roll up our sleeves. Again, 'let us proceed slowly' as our friend, Houphouët-Boigny, who is sorely missed here, once said. Today, we miss his statesmanship and wisdom."*

Chairman Arafat was the last to speak:

"I wish first and foremost, to express my sincere gratitude and pride to be honored by the Félix Houphouët-Boigny Peace Prize, together with Mr. Yitzhak Rabin and Mr. Shimon Peres. We have been partners in seeking to achieve the peace of the brave in our region, and we still continue our pursuit in order to consolidate that peace and attain its objectives. It is only natural that this prize should acquire such a remarkable status, since it carries the name of one of the outstanding and faithful sons of Africa—a judicious leader, who has worked his entire life for peace, mutual understanding, and dialogue. We are really saddened that he is not in our midst today to witness one of his foremost objectives come to fruition, being that he was once the chairman of the committee of 'the Wise Men of Africa' that was set up years ago to find common ground for Arab and Israeli viewpoints. He also blessed and supported the efforts made by the late Dr. Isam Sartawi, a Palestinian martyr and hero, who was assassinated while fighting to achieve peace."

A Dream for Peace

The Félix Houphouët-Boigny Peace Prize Award ceremony: Mr. Peres, Traoré, Arafat, Mayor, Rabin, Kissinger.

I was humbled by the memorable optics and optimism shared by the recipients on the podium. I felt assured that the torch had been passed successfully on our long and arduous journey in search of a fleeting peace. It brought hope to my heart once again, as I reflected on the everlasting words of President Félix Houphouët-Boigny:

"Tell Arafat that I will remain until my death, the servant of peace—a just and lasting peace."
Félix Houphouët-Boigny, August 25, 1975.

A Dream for Peace

During the Muslim call to prayer, we could also hear the Christian procession praying loudly as they made their way past the mosque en route to the Holy Sepulchre—while at the same time, the Jews prayed at the Wailing Wall. Together, all the prayers of the various faiths, emanating in unison, rose toward the sky. A sign of our common faith in one unique God.

Chapter Eleven

Our Common Faith

President Houphouët-Boigny and I revered each other's devotion to the Almighty. Our convictions were intertwined in an unabated set of religious principles and deep spirituality, born out of a common faith in one unique God.

R eligion has always been my ultimate sanctuary. I practiced my faith with an innate and inescapable awareness that I also needed to take a stand on some things, albeit in a discreet way. My convictions and beliefs are essential to my sense of purpose and loyalty to the Almighty. Endowed with these principles, my commitment extended beyond the personal to the needs of the faithful who sought to pray in a safe haven.

I finally decided to embark on a long-awaited trip to the village of Satama-Sokoura—the hometown of my faithful chauffeur, Touré Mama, to meet his family for the first time. We drove for hours to the central part of the country. On the outskirts of town, he turned on a small street and passed by a nineteenth-century mosque, distinctively situated a few yards from the main road. Out of sheer curiosity, I asked him to pull over. I inched closer to the property and touched the retaining wall. The cascading sun-dried bricks were molded from mud and clay, and hand-plastered by workers typical of an epoch of bygone times. Massive blocks of sandstone had been used to reinforce the main entrance, and support beams had been nailed together to hold up the outer and inner perimeter walls. In keeping with tradition from the period, red clay was used for surfacing on the outside, around the windows, and inside the arches of the doorway. I was fascinated by the historical significance of the monumental structure, which was seemingly in danger of falling apart. "I have to do something about this," I said. The mosque must be saved from further structural damage," Touré agreed.

Within weeks, my architectural team provided details on the scope of conservation work needed to preserve the structure's relics. After lengthy discussions, I put forth a plan to restore and expand the space. I wanted to modernize without compromising its original features, but most importantly, I wanted to ensure that it would be developed to accommodate the growing community. I counted on the local workforce of mostly self-taught masons and apprentices to take up the task, and I wasn't disappointed. Everyone was disciplined and reliable. We completed the project on time, to the delight of the community's faithful Muslims.

The Adjamé mosque located in a very popular and crowded neighborhood can be seen towering over the open marketplace, especially in the evening, when the waning sun begins to set, casting a blissful ray of light across Abidjan. It stands tall in the northern part of the city's impoverished neighborhood. In the past, the massive building presented a fading, corroding structure that seemed more like a concrete façade, bridging an outward appearance to conceal a less-pleasant reality. The wear and tear had been due to neglect and insufficient maintenance over the years, worsened by adverse effects of seasonal rains and other climatically hazardous factors. Having successfully completed the Satama-Sokoura project, I was motivated to take on another reconstruction project to improve the neighborhood.

When I first set foot on the property, the pillars and columns reminded me of the mosque in the holy Islamic city of Medina. Although the frames of the building were well preserved, the structure required substantial conservation work in addition to a paint job, flooring, and installation of new facilities. A team of experts assured me that they could restore the fading ceiling to its original appearance. This was a key factor in my decision to award the contract. To get the project underway, I raised the much-needed funds and provided additional financial infusion of my own. I hired the most skillful construction workers in the city and set out to micromanage the process like a seasoned project manager, without fully appreciating the daunting demands it was about to place on my schedule. New flooring was the first to be installed by my team, but the rebuilding of amenities was outsourced and the final painting touch-ups were completed at the end of the project. President Houphouët-Boigny was one of the financial backers. His generosity and support was unmatched. He was eternally committed to the success of such projects, regardless of their religious orientation, but especially, in the case of Islam—the religion of the poor. I knew I could always count on him.

As a passionate devotee, the president took his faith very seriously. He had the great misfortune of watching his mother die in his arms. "In her final moments, I conjured up enough courage to baptize and give her the name Marie," he confided. "That was quite an extraordinary act of faith, Mr. President," I said. "I can't even begin to imagine how difficult the experience must have been." After years of attending mass with his wife in the neighborhood parish, he decided to transform an office in his private residence into a chapel. From then on, he celebrated mass at home with the local Apostolic nuncio.

At the time, Archbishop Justo Mullor Garcia, the papal nuncio and advisor to His Holiness Pope John Paul II, had been in Côte d'Ivoire for several years and developed a very deep friendship with the president. He had become his personal confidant and was more than happy to officiate mass at the chapel. The standing invitation to join in prayer sessions was a privilege for my wife and I, and we looked forward to hearing Monsignor Mullor's powerful sermons, imbued with deep interpretations of biblical passages.

A Dream for Peace

On a few occasions, the mild-mannered and polite Secretary of the Nunciature, Monsignor Timothy Broglio, was the substitute celebrant, ever so graceful and spiritually adept. As a practitioner of Islam, and one who is well versed in the teachings of the Holy Qur'an, I recognized the similarities between both religions.

The relationship between President Houphouët and Monsignor Mullor evolved into the space of confessor and spiritual counsel. However, Monsignor Timothy Broglio moved away after years of service in Côte d'Ivoire and took on another assignment at the Vatican, where he quickly rose through the ranks until Pope Benedict appointed him archbishop for the US military.

With Monsignor Mullor and the president.

My wife and I arrived at the official residence on a beautiful Saturday afternoon to join the president for mass. When he walked into the living room, he seemed a bit bothered. He had been speaking privately with an individual who pressed him for a favor and rubbed him the wrong way. "I am very disappointed at the irrational context of the conversation," he expressed quietly to me as we walked into the chapel. Once seated, we were directed to the Gospel according to Luke, chapter 6, verses 29b, 30, and 31, the liturgy of the day. The topic was about responding to solicitations:

"And from him who takes away your cloak, do not withhold your tunic either. Give to everyone who asks of you. And from him who takes away your goods do not ask them back. And just as you want men to do to you, you also do to them likewise."

These words took on a deeper meaning for the president. As far as he was concerned, what he heard in the Gospel amounted to a divine call for immediate action. He came up to me after mass and asked that I summon the individual to his residence. It was then that I realized the profound impact of the Gospel's effect on his judgment. I was deeply touched. The gentleman was beyond grateful to be at the receiving end of the president's generosity.

The clergy had set aside a large plot of land for a future cathedral building in Plateau's business district right in the heart of Abidjan. The spectacular city views provided a backdrop for what was expected to become a masterful architectural work of art. Planning for the project had gone on for months with the involvement of many faithful Catholics in the community, but we encountered difficulties in our attempts to secure adequate financing. When the president stepped in and made a large contribution to break ground on the construction, Aldo Spirito, a highly respected Italian architect, was hand-picked to design the cathedral. His final model was a mockup of the towering figure of Saint Paul.

Monsignor Mullor rolled up his sleeves and got down to work like a master foreman. He was very engaged in the many phases of construction, maintaining a shrewd vigilance and exceptional tenacity to ensure a perfect outcome. As the designated interior designer for the cathedral, he oversaw décor, selecting a number of beautiful stained-glass tableaux that pulled in a cast of colorful rays from the sun. The Archbishop of Notre Dame d'Afrique Basilica in Algiers donated the church bells. Monsignor Mullor was hands-on until the very end.

A Dream for Peace

He arranged the second visit to Côte d'Ivoire by His Holiness Pope John Paul II for the consecration on August 8, 1985. The neighborhood echoed with sounds of heavenly bells that announced the commencement of the magnificent ceremony. I was in attendance with my wife, who had been selected by Monsignor Mullor to join the lucky few to receive the Holy Communion from the pope. Within minutes after the ceremony's conclusion, Monsignor Mullor and the pontiff boarded a helicopter to the airport for a chartered flight to Cameroon.

Saint Paul's Cathedral.

Circling over the city of Abidjan, His Holiness praised the grandeur of President Houphouët-Boigny during an especially candid moment: *"It would suffice one more head of state such as the one I met in Côte d'Ivoire to change Africa and perhaps the world."* Monsignor Mullor, who had become a dear friend of ours, shared the extraordinary moment with my wife and I.

President Houphouët with Pope John Paul II.

Murmurs from the country's majority Muslim population grew louder by the day, mostly due to the much-acclaimed publicity regarding the scope of the president's involvement in a "Christian project." Some complaints of a lack of fairness in needed investment distribution across the two major religions were duly noted, but such sentiments were not expressed openly. It had long been clear to me that the city of Abidjan, with its modern infrastructure, was in dire need of a new mosque. There was an open tent with aluminum roofing in the exclusive Cocody neighborhood of Riviera Golf, where my fellow Muslims and I congregated for Friday prayers. We had been subjected to many a difficult situation, particularly during the monsoon season rains. The stacks of aluminum sheeting on the roof of our prayer shelter were not exactly soundproof, and the clatter of the heavy tropical rains rattling off to deafening levels made it impossible to hear the Imam's sermon (*khutbah*). As I prayed, I imagined being in a tranquil space, insulated from all distractions, and I continued to reflect on a viable solution to end the torment. I prayed to Allah to show me the way. At the completion of prayers on a stormy Friday afternoon, I took to the floor and announced to everyone, "The president will build a mosque for us." The statement came out of my mouth, and I meant every word with all my heart. The only problem was, I had not discussed the matter with the president. The congregation responded with much elation and a collective sigh of relief. Some applauded and chanted "*Allahu Akbar*"—praise the Lord.

    I went from there to have lunch with the president at the residence. His close confidant, Abdoulaye Diallo, who had been at the mosque that afternoon, had arrived earlier to thank the president for his "selfless commitment." President Houphouët was surprised, but he played along until I got there. During lunch with two of his ministers and I, he suddenly looked at me and smiled. "So, I heard that Dr. Berrah has taken it upon himself to enlist my commitment for a new mosque in the Riviera?" I laughed and nodded approvingly. However, the Minister of State, a Protestant, did not attempt to hide his displeasure. The president deflected his concerns and continued the conversation.

    It wasn't very long before he quietly threw his support behind the project. I secured a large plot of land only a few yards away from the old mosque. The final blueprints included an adjacent complex to house a conference room with two or three lecture halls and a large parking lot. The local mayor, who was not very pleased with the idea of a mosque in the neighborhood, carved out a piece of the plot and set it aside for a "future project." His underhanded actions, which were revealed long after construction had begun, angered many of the youth in the Muslim community.

We halted the bidding when renowned architect Pierre Fakhoury, a Lebanese Christian and a Prix de Rome recipient, donated the blueprints of a model inspired by the beautiful Obhur Mosque in a suburb of Jeddah, Saudi Arabia. I wasn't familiar with that particular mosque, even though I had visited the city several times before. The task ahead was more difficult than I anticipated. After weeks of pursuing leads, I learned of a major breakthrough from the president when I paid him a visit following the completion of Friday prayers. "The family of Bintou wishes to donate proceeds from the sale of her estate to help finance the project," he told me. I was pleasantly surprised and elated to hear the great news. He was referring to a very dear friend, Mrs. Bintou Camara from among the Muslim community, who had been called by the Almighty not so long ago. It was the will of Allah that had worked such a miracle, and I was certain that she was smiling upon us. The president himself made a large contribution and decided to convene a meeting with leaders of the Muslim community, Pierre Fakhoury, and the director of the Grands Travaux,[45] Mr. Antoine Cesareo.

Attendees to the town hall included the head of the Economic and Social Council (the third most influential person in the country), young Muslim organizers, and prominent officials from affluent Muslim circles. President Houphouët presented the project to the audience and introduced Pierre Fakhoury, who unveiled the model and described the structure in detail. "Can you come up to the stage, Dr. Berrah, and say a few words?" the president beckoned. I took to the podium. "Actually, Mr. President, I believe that everything

---

[45] A state agency that oversees major construction projects.

has been said." A security guard walked up with a large suitcase and placed it beside me. "The suitcase contains all the money for construction-related expenses," the president revealed confidently through the loudspeakers. For the most part, illiterate workers did not have bank accounts; hence, they had to be paid in cash. A few attendees protested loudly: "Why is Berrah favored at the expense of his elders?" I leaned into the microphone and said, "Mr. President, I wish to thank you for your confidence. I am sure you understand that this is a major undertaking. In my own humble way, I ask that you insulate me from any financial involvement by depositing the funds into a local bank account, and coincidentally, there is a bank president among us. He is a trusted Muslim intellectual who attends Friday prayers at the mosque. I am confident that he wouldn't mind overseeing all financial processes for the entire project. I also recommend that we employ the services of a technical director, someone I believe would be the best man for the job. May I introduce to you Mr. Antoine Cesareo, the director of Grands Travaux and one of the seventeen greatest engineers in France." The audience applauded loudly. Fired up and animated by the atmosphere, the president took to the podium and spoke energetically: "This does not preclude your responsibility in the adventure, Dr. Berrah." I applauded him and gave a thumbs-up.

I assembled a team of workers from across sub-Saharan Africa, headed by a highly competent foreman from France. We broke ground on the project about a couple of weeks after the town hall meeting and proceeded quickly to beat the deadline. Because of our limited budget, we sought the help of construction companies and received *ex gratia* contributions of equipment, including a tower crane, for the project's duration. The local business community came together to donate all the needed gravel, woodwork, and glass frames. Their commitment and support exceeded my wildest expectations.

I kept a keen eye on daily progress and oversaw the

recruitment of various specialty handymen like a seasoned construction foreman. The workers' morale was key to ensuring their efficiency on the job. I urged them to put their heart and soul in the project and led by example by designing the intricate details of the geometrical interior mosaic on the floor and walls. My strict adherence to perfection rubbed off on the crew. For fear of having to redo substandard work, they did their best to ensure that every step of the design phase was up to par with my standards. Our collective sacrifice was a modest gift to Allah. I treated all the workers to a drink and weekly meals on Fridays and brought my wife along every so often to explain the building process. She was always astonished and impressed by the speed of progress, but I said very little to the president because I wanted to keep him guessing until the grand finale.

    Plans to install the dome on the minaret had been in the works for sometime. The delicate process had to be mapped out strategically with a team of experts to guarantee a foolproof installation. When the long-anticipated time finally came, I was excited and nervous, because I knew that we were inching closer to a successful completion. The tall and slender spire is a typical addition to a mosque. For this project, the structure was designed to be a working minaret. It had a balcony for the *muezzin* whose chant would call the faithful to prayer. The erected minaret stood at over a hundred feet tall on the corner of the platform of the mosque, and it was symmetrically designed to complete the architectural composition.

    My Love and I joined the few spectators who were already on the scene to watch the dome installation from under a spotlight in the heat of the night. Skilled workers secured a magnificent crescent moon to the large dome and lifted it off the platform with the tower crane. Mr. Cesareo and his team of experts monitored every inch of the nail-biting process, while we prayed for divine intervention to prevent any accidental mishaps. We watched anxiously as it made its

A Dream for Peace

way across the moonlit sky, drifting back and forth on the harness, until it was finally placed onto the apex of the minaret with decisive precision.

The beautiful minaret.

    Everyone breathed a collective sigh of relief and applauded the men. Cheers echoed into the neighborhood, and we rejoiced alongside local residents who had flocked to the site and stood for over three hours to witness the historic occasion. I was so happy that I was moved to tears. I expressed my deepest gratitude to Mr. Cesareo, each member of his team, and all the workers. With the last piece of the puzzle finally fitted in place, the project had come to a successful conclusion in all its glory, bringing everyone a little bit of respite and a semblance of pride.

Riviera Mosque.

I owed a debt of gratitude to the many corporate donors whose generous contributions helped us build the mosque without exceeding our budget. But for Mr. Cesareo, the Riviera Golf Mosque, as exquisite as it now stands, would never have been completed. It remains a gem and a true jewel for the faithful, and the best part is the fact that we managed to complete the project at a modest price. After interacting with everyone on site and expressing our sincere appreciation for a job well done, my Love and I left for the night. On the drive home, I sat silently in the car and reflected on the magnitude of the historic endeavor. Titi beamed with pride and showered me with praises for the successful outcome. "All this would not have been possible without the guidance and intervention of Allah, to whom belongs the glory," we both agreed.

President Houphouët was pleasantly surprised and reacted with utter amazement at the record-breaking construction phase.

A Dream for Peace

"Congratulations," he said. "It has barely been two years!" "*Merci,*" I replied, "but most of the credit goes to Mr. Cesareo. A committee is already hard at work, planning the inaugural ceremony." I knew how important it was for him to preside over the grand opening. When the day finally arrived, most of the leading imams showed up in force with hundreds of the faithful. The extraordinary moment was chronicled in an unforgettable ceremony. The president was the main guest of honor. He delivered the introductory welcome through a wireless PA system, a cutting-edge technological innovation at the time, and served up an eloquent speech about our common faith: "*I cannot emphasize enough, the importance of our service to the Almighty for the general good of all mankind.*"

President Houphouët-Boigny did not just intend to facilitate the economic success of Côte d'Ivoire; he also wanted to nurture the spiritual development of the population, particularly among the youth. Our goal did not begin or end with the erection of a mosque. The objective was to lay a sound foundation for the young intellectuals who populated the Riviera area. We both believed that the mosque had to be led by an imam who was well versed in Islamic theology. Several qualified candidates appeared on the radar, but I ended up selecting Sheik Tidjane Bâ. He spoke Dioula[46] and French and could also express himself in perfect Arabic. But most importantly, his deep understanding of Islamic theology was unmatched. In my opinion, he was the ideal imam with supreme spiritual intellect to nurture the faith. Due to his proficiency and religious qualities, His Holiness Pope John Paul II invited him to join the Assisi ecumenical prayer[47] in Italy. For years, I looked forward to hearing the theme of his *khutba* at Friday prayers, because his profound wisdom helped foster my thoughts. My Love was tangentially affected by those moments when I came home from

---

[46] A Mande language spoken in Burkina Faso, Ivory Coast, and Mali.
[47] The first World Day of Prayer for Peace, held in Assisi, Italy, organized by His Holiness Pope John Paul II.

the mosque and discussed the context of the sermon with her. She appreciated the fact that the spiritual wisdom of the message brought some nourishment to our spirits.

Imam Tidjane Bâ.

The Riviera Golf Mosque reached its maximum capacity for Friday worshippers in only a few months. I began to witness an increase in the number of young intellectuals among the congregation. Religious pride brought them a sense of belonging and an extra spring in their step. The humble, gracious, and extremely considerate Tidjane Bâ was truly an amazing imam and quickly became everyone's favorite celebrant.

He once went on a pilgrimage to Jerusalem and brought back a rosary for my wife, a practicing Roman Catholic. She was pleasantly surprised. A rosary from an imam was a gift so precious and profoundly thoughtful that she continues to cherish it to this

A Dream for Peace

day.

"*Bonsoir, Docteur,*" Abdoulaye, a day laborer from the Riviera Golf Mosque project with a reputation for persistence and professional conduct, greeted me as soon as I arrived at my wife's pharmacy on a late afternoon. He stood back nervously and forced a sparkling smile, hoping I would know who he was. I gazed back at his thin, tall frame. "*Ah, bonsoir, Abdoulaye. Comment vas tu?*" I was curious to know how he'd been since the last time we saw each other at the construction site. He was seeking a recommendation letter for a new job. I had grown accustomed to such encounters. In the days after the end of the project, many of the workers in and around the city approached me whenever they recognized my car, and the theme was always about jobs or personal struggles. Several months of long and laborious toiling on the grounds had brought us closer. We felt like a big extended family. I did not hesitate to ask Abdoulaye to come to my apartment at exactly 5:00 a.m., and he wasted no time bringing a couple of his trusted friends along, right on schedule. Rumors began to spread like wildfire around the day labor community, and before long, many of them came to see me. They queued up at my doorstep, in the stairway, and around the terrace every morning at five, shortly after I was done with my dawn (Fajr) prayers.

My Love and I were living a quiet life in a modest first-floor apartment with lovely views of the Ébrié Lagoon in Cité Esculape, in the Plateau commune. For years, the serenity was fiercely guarded and our peaceful retreat remained undisturbed until everyone suddenly knew where we lived. She had converted the entryway into a flowered terrace and decorated our open patio with colorful hibiscus flowers. The terrace had become a favorite spot of mine to relax and have my morning cup of tea. I quickly turned it into a temporary field office—a meeting spot for the relief seekers and I to engage each other. After my morning prayers, I appeared with a pencil and paper, pulled up a patio chair, and greeted everyone, "*Bonjour, mes amis.*" They came at me, one by one, or sometimes as a couple. The issues were not limited to job search and recommendations, but also were about economic hardship and personal endorsements. I grappled with the nagging question of how best to help everyone on a daily basis. It was quite a challenge and a constant struggle for me, but I never lost sight of the fact that they were very hard workers. From the moment I hired them for the Riviera Mosque project and got to experience their sense of gratitude for the opportunity to be a part of something special, I knew that they were proud people, but most importantly, they were not looking for handouts. They had come from local and far-away places inside Côte d'Ivoire and from countries in the sub-Saharan delta to seek employment. I was just as committed to their struggle as they were, and they saw that in me.

And so, the routine continued. Like clockwork, they would come to queue up in the wee hours of the morning and wait for me to finish praying. At times, the line extended from my first-floor apartment all the way to the ground floor. They were courteous to each other and kept a respectful distance in the queue to allow some privacy for their peers. I interacted with them for exactly two hours every weekday. On the weekends, no one came to disturb us. As time went by, more and more people who had nothing to do with the construction project came to present me with a variety of issues. I was okay with extending a helping hand to everyone as long as they remained disciplined and took my recommendations to heart. Their gratitude was delivered with deep sincerity and an extension of heartfelt thoughts and prayers, especially among those who received introductory letters from me. The expression of appreciation left me speechless every time. I wished each individual a great deal of luck and watched him or her disappear into the tropical morning dew, hoping they would nail the job interview, maybe secure a permanent one, or at least find temporary placement.

There were certain unique circumstances when I felt the

need to help resolve some disputes for the sake of fairness. Even though I hoped to end my early morning commitments at my terrace, there were times when I became a resolute advocate for those who were victims of unjust treatment in labor disputes. I took on the responsibility and made time in my day to visit former employers to address the matter and bring some relief to the workers. My wife was an avid volunteer of her services as well. She was an accredited pharmacist running her own business and told me many times to never hesitate to call upon her if I needed her help. I tried hard to not involve her in what had become an unprecedented labor of love, but at times I had no other choice, and she was more than happy to keep her word. When I sent those who lacked funds to pay for their prescription, they went to see her with a special note from me. Without hesitation, she processed the order and went over the instructions with them.

At times, I did my best to insulate her from the pressures by validating the prescriptions on my own and giving some money to those dealing with urgent medical situations. All in all, my favorite interactions were with the fathers who came to me seeking letters of recommendation to enroll their children in schools of higher learning. I rarely encountered a high school graduate with a low grade-point average seeking entrance into a vocational institution, but it did happen once or twice, and I made sure they got an earful from me before handing them a note.

Out of the many individuals who came to see me on the terrace, the overall majority were genuinely honest and hardworking people. But there were those who came on occasion hoping to take advantage of the situation. I admonished a young man who asked that I contribute to the repair of an air-conditioning unit in his car, "Nonsense. What do you think this is? Don't come here again." I reprimanded him for wasting my time and asked him to be more considerate of others.

I never felt apprehensive, nor did I harbor second thoughts

about interacting with the group of mostly strangers who came to see me for help. There was just a warm and compelling kinship with everyone. I wouldn't say so for the president's palace commander, General Kouassi, who came to see me one morning out of concern for my safety because he'd heard that I was always "intermingling with all sorts of people at dawn." I thanked him for caring and assured him that all was well; however, I wasn't about to change my routine anytime soon. I couldn't quite understand why he worried about my well-being because I never envisioned a violent attack or robbery. The people needed me to be there for them. When I fell ill at some point and didn't show up on the terrace, the first person in line anxiously rang our doorbell shortly after five in the morning. He knocked softly a few more times until my Love opened the door and apologized for my unfortunate absence. "Please come back in a few days, my friends," she told them. I could hear the instant chorus of well wishes from the bedroom as they dispersed into the morning fog.

    I had pondered on a few occasions how I could personally put some of them to work again and convert my benevolent outreach into a real sustainable project for the most competent among them. The only item on my list was a plan to build a house for my wife and I. I owned a piece of land in the Riviera golf area, and I had been saving up to build my dream house, my own Taj Mahal, which I would offer to my Love as a surprise gift. I would call the residence "A Hymn to Love" and have it designed like a classic Italian Palladian villa formed in a U-shaped structure and fashioned after a pink Greek temple, with accents of multiple white Ionic columns. I first saw a villa like that in southern Louisiana during a student excursion, but I was sold by its grandeur when I saw a rendered depiction in the movie *Gone with the Wind*. Pierre Fakhoury would be the architect of choice when the time was right. Little by little, I inched closer and closer to the design phase after months of visualizing the finished product. When I called on him, I was 100 percent sure of exactly

A Dream for Peace

how the design of my dream house would look like. He loved the concept and seemed excited to take on the project. His final design was a well-crafted blueprint projecting my vision in concise detail. I was ready to pay for his hard work, but he handed it to me as a gift from the heart.

It had been months since that day, and the time to break ground arrived while I was still living at the apartment. I hired each and every one of the workers who were involved in the Riviera Mosque project. They were among the lucky few. By then, the lines had softened a bit. The stream of disenfranchised folks had lessened, but they still showed up nonetheless, prompting me to wonder what would become of them once I vacated the premises and settled in on the other side of town, far away from the area. I thought long and hard about a way to help them and decided to direct everyone to meet me in the conference room of the Riviera Mosque, a more convenient location.

Knowing fully well that my imminent transition would have an impact on how I balanced my daily schedule, I began to focus on activating a systemic approach to what had clearly become more of a social welfare program on my terrace. The consistent flow of aid seekers to my doorstep for several months wasn't something I anticipated, nor was it a situation I could sustain as an individual. I moved beyond extending a helping hand to proposing a bill to the president. At the time, both he and I were fully cognizant of the promise of our nation's success and its influence on neighboring countries whose economies were teetering on the brink of collapse. Many day laborers who immigrated to Côte d'Ivoire came searching for a prosperous life, and those who employed the workers benefited greatly from their hard work. I thought it was only fair that the state impose a minor tax levy on employers to help fund a new social welfare system, the Fonds de Solidarité. The objective was to use collected taxes to build vocational institutions and retrain able-bodied workers for the emerging economy. My bill was voted on and adopted as the law of the land to be implemented for the benefit of society.

The hardworking men completed the magnificent villa in record time, and miraculously, the project was delivered under budget. They enjoyed a brief but stable period of sustained employment, which gave them some breathing room and accorded them ample time for reflection. With the new law in place, most of them made appropriate career moves, and the illiterates pursued further education.

To celebrate my wife and show my appreciation for her unyielding support and understanding, I offered a custom-designed solid-gold key as a symbol of my everlasting love. I handpicked some of the workers to stay on as house help and security personnel, and I referred others to a variety of jobs.

I soon embarked on another development project with my dear friend and brother Essy Amara in his hometown. The tiny, sleepy village of Kouassi Datekro in Côte d'Ivoire's Bini region of about two thousand inhabitants was a mishmash of religions, comprising mostly of Animists, Muslims, and Catholics. He had returned from a pilgrimage to Mecca, where he miraculously found himself praying inside the Ka'aba, a most revered shrine, after losing his footing while embedded among thousands of circling pilgrims. A divine premonition inspired him to build a mosque in his hometown, but the council of elders, including his beloved father, advised him to include a rundown Catholic Church in his plans to ensure continuing religious harmony in the community. His wife, a devout Catholic, was pleased to hear the news. He came to see me at home in Abidjan after the decision was made. "My brother," he said, "I need your help to make this happen." I embraced the idea right away. Within days, we went to the town and held court with the elders. We surveyed the site for the two projects—a mosque beside a church—and reviewed our options. He had already donated some building materials for the construction, but we joined forces with the village elders to set up a fund, and we both initiated the seed investment.

When I informed the president about our plans, he championed the vision and pledged his support through a significant contribution to the fund. I was overjoyed by the idea of erecting two buildings for two unique devotions, side by side, to illuminate the beauty of our common faith.

The local village priest, a young Frenchman by the name of Père Alain Derbier, impressed us with his extensive background in construction when he came forward to volunteer for the project. We welcomed the idea and gave him full responsibility to oversee the entire construction. As the country's Permanent Representative to the UN, Essy spent most of his time in New York, and I traveled on occasion for work, but I took on the responsibility of managing both projects. The commitment entailed a whole lot of road trips between Abidjan and the village. I spent several hours of my leisure time at the construction site, working from sun up to sun down, and then I drove back home late at night. The priest tried his very best to keep me in the loop even though it was almost impossible at times due to infrequent phone problems. We used a courier to deliver messages during lengthy periods of communications blackout.

The exceptional opportunity to interact with neighbors from both faiths brought out the best in everyone. All the day laborers worked hard on both projects interchangeably, regardless of their religious affiliations. Everyone seemed eager to bring the project to a successful close. At its completion, we inaugurated the mosque and the church on the same day and organized a major celebration for the entire village. I joined Essy and his family to take in the joyous occasion with everyone. Though he could not attend, President Houphouët-Boigny was very pleased to hear the news. He was extremely proud of the hard workers. I could not stop praising the Almighty for allowing me to witness the exemplary flow of harmony and display of selflessness among the people.

It wasn't very long before an unusually long dry season

ushered forth a discordant atmosphere that prompted a surprise visit from the young French priest. He drove all the way to see me in Abidjan to report on rising tensions between Catholics and Muslims in the village. "This was all brought on by the lack of rains," he said regretfully. The residents were in the midst of the worst drought in memory, and members of the Muslim community gathered to lead a special prayer session for the rains to come. Amazingly, during their prayer session rain clouds began to gather, followed by the sound of thunderstorms, and heavy rains began to pour. Convinced that Allah had heard and answered their prayers, the grateful Muslims planned a thanksgiving ceremony: they would sacrifice four sheep for the village, and they thought it was only fair that the Catholics purchase two of the four. When they approached the Catholic leaders, they refused, arguing that it was a novel ritual that was foreign to their beliefs. I sensed his frustration, but I also understood the mindset of those who were antagonizing his congregants. He stated his dismay over the entire incident in a very composed and reflective manner. "It is my opinion that the Catholics are being forced to participate in an Islamic sacrament," he said dejectedly. I expressed my sincere gratitude to him for taking the time to come to see me and let him know that I sympathized with his point of view. We spoke about the importance of continuous unanimity among the people in the village, which was so prevalent among the faithful during the inaugural ceremonies.

The conversation had a calming effect on him. "Mon Père," I sighed. "This is all a simple misunderstanding. I would like to make a contribution on behalf of my Catholic brethren and pay for the two sheep, if that is okay with you." He listened. "As you know, the principle of giving thanks to the Almighty was endowed to us through the teachings of all religions. Sometimes, we differ in the way we give thanks, but we all share one common faith." "Well said," he agreed. I assured him that I was at his disposal to talk about anything, especially matters that caused friction in the village.

A Dream for Peace

"It means the world to me to know that everyone in the village continues to live in peace." He left my house with a little less weight on his shoulders. A few days later, he called to confirm that the village had regained concord and harmony.

President Houphouët-Boigny's dream was to build a basilica in Yamoussoukro with the help of his family and name it "Our Lady of Peace" in honor of the Virgin Mary. Ever since His Holiness Pope John Paul II blessed the cornerstone for the building, shortly before the consecration of the Saint Paul Cathedral in Abidjan, he continued to pray and meditate over the project. I knew how much it meant to him, and I felt his life force whenever he spoke to me about his vision.

Our Lady of Peace Basilica.

From around the world, we faced criticism the moment we broke ground. Throughout the entire construction phase, there were a few ambiguities in articles published somewhere around the globe. For some reason, Western journalists in particular focused only on the monumental size of the proposed building and nothing else. However, critics at the newspapers who authored the numerous articles about the basilica did not sway the president in any particular direction. He looked forward to the completion of the process, and he nourished the deepest wish for a new trip from the Holy Father for the consecration. Mr. Antoine Cesareo, the project's manager who oversaw every aspect of the Pierre Fakhoury masterpiece, immersed himself and committed to safeguarding the architectural integrity of the construction from beginning to end. After five years of meticulous labor, with the utmost attention to every minute detail, the basilica was finally completed and heralded as a pioneer in its capacity, among the best architectural feats ever accomplished on Ivorian soil. Today, the magnificent structure stands as a historical jewel.

Nothing could guarantee the coming of His Holiness. Dissenting voices and critics speculated that there could possibly be some obstacles that might prevent the pope from making the trip. President Houphouët-Boigny was shocked when he learned of the perversion of facts by critics who spread falsehoods, claiming that the construction of the basilica was designed to stop the advancement of Islam in Côte d'Ivoire, but such rumors had not caused discontent among the much larger population of Muslims. The reaction from the Vatican became increasingly reserved, and the coming of the Holy Father seemed to be in jeopardy. The president and I were aware that bad press had placed His Holiness in an untenable position and that the public discourse could prompt him to stay away for fear of inciting the Muslim population and causing friction in the country.

President Houphouët was caught off guard by the intensity and magnitude of the harsh rhetoric that was being espoused by the skeptics. As a concerned Muslim, I finally decided to embark on a mission to the Vatican to wipe away all the disparaging criticisms once and for all. When I arrived, I was received by Cardinal Angelo Sodano, the Secretary of the Council for the Public Affairs of the Church, in the presence of the Ivorian ambassador to the Vatican,

A Dream for Peace

Mr. Joseph Amichia. *"For the Muslims in Côte d'Ivoire, there is nothing too large or too beautiful for God."* Those were the first words I uttered, in all sincerity, to Cardinal Sodano. We spoke for several minutes and connected spiritually, but the full force of my earnest approach and purity of my genuine disposition resonated beyond any heartfelt words between us. At the end of the visit, he promised to deliver my message to the Holy Father. We were both in awe of the moment. Ambassador Amichia told me after Cardinal Sodano escorted us through the hallways of the magnificent premises that it was highly unusual for him to walk any guest beyond the doors of the meeting room. We took in the jaw-dropping sights of the frescoed Renaissance-age paintings and decorations in the resplendent architectural building one last time.

With Aillot-About, Pope Paul VI, and Minister Usher.

Despite having been to the Vatican a couple of years earlier, I still could not get enough of its majesty. At the time, I joined Minister Usher and Charles Aillot-About, Ivorian ambassador to Italy, for formal talks with Pope Paul VI on opening the Holy See's first Ivorian Embassy. I made sure to visit the Vatican Museum just to admire the impressive array of renaissance paintings. I ventured inside the Sistine Chapel to view Michelangelo's nine paintings on the magnificent ceiling and trace his depiction of God's creation of the world, God's relationship with mankind, and mankind's own fall from God's grace. I stopped at every painting along the hallways and corridors to peruse priceless gems by Sandro Botticelli, Pietro Perugino, Pinturicchio, Michelangelo, and others. It was an art lover's delight within the walls of a spiritual haven that pays homage to the Almighty.

Cardinal Sodano delivered my message to Pope John Paul II, and it was well received by His Holiness because shortly after my return to Côte d'Ivoire, we heard that the pope would commit to the trip. Within a few weeks, his plane touched down in Yamoussoukro for the historic occasion. I went to greet him at the presidential palace on the eve of the consecration and held his hand in my palms. *"Your Holiness, I am Ambassador Ghoulem Berrah. I was the one who came to the Vatican to affirm that the Muslim community would be more than happy to see you at the basilica. I'd like to welcome you to Côte d'Ivoire, and I wish to extend to you my sincerest gratitude for making the long journey on this historic occasion."*

Greeting Pope John Paul II.

I mingled with the select few who had arrived for the

reception. The pope's exceptional tenderness could be felt in an atmosphere of intense spiritual energy. After endless months of construction amid all the media frenzy, the day had finally arrived, and we all took in the memorable minutes of mystical indulgence in the presence of His Holiness, who sat humbly in our midst, smiling modestly, and receiving everyone in his good graces. He showed subtle signs of fatigue from a whirlwind trip that had taken him across the Mediterranean to three East African countries prior to arriving in our beloved Côte d'Ivoire. The president engaged him in a quiet conversation for about half an hour before he was escorted to the waiting papal limousine for the drive to his private residence on the basilica compound.

As soon as he left the reception, my wife and I went to see a group of imams around town to solidify their commitment to attend the consecration. Every Muslim leader in Côte d'Ivoire had been invited to the ceremony, which was planned for September 10 in the year 1990, and most of them had arrived in the day. Monsignor Mullor flew into Abidjan from his station in Geneva a few days earlier and stayed at our house. We drove to Yamoussoukro together to ensure that the on-the-ground logistics were in order. He was always tremendously helpful and ever ready to lend a helping hand. We went to tackle our duties separately and planned to meet up for dinner later that evening. I owed him a debt of gratitude for his moral commitment, something akin to a natural trait in an unrelenting and vibrant personality that reigned supreme from the moment we broke ground on the project until the very end.

After a hectic series of meetings with the imams, Titi and I were assured that they would all attend the consecration. We breathed a sigh of relief only when we were convinced that our outreach and overtures to the Muslim community had paid off in the name of peace and continued harmony between the two major religions. Monsignor Mullor met us for dinner at the Hotel Président. The restaurant was packed mostly with dignitaries and others from the pope's entourage. I told him, "*My dear brother. I would like to convey a message to the Holy Father. Please get the word to him that I am assured of the attendance of Côte d'Ivoire's imams for tomorrow's event. I have the full commitment of each and every one.*" The words flowed from my lips to the happy ears of Monsignor Mullor, who had barely sat down. "Ah, Ghoulem. This is very, very important." He excused himself and scurried off to invite Joaquín Navarro-Valls, the pope's personal spokesperson, to our table. With a high level of astuteness and disciplined restraint typical of the Opus Dei, Mr. Navarro-Valls looked into my eyes with curious expectation. I delivered the same message to him. He thanked me, shook our hands, and promised to notify the Holy Father.

Pope John Paul II began a powerful homily with one memorable sentence: "*I would like to thank the imams of Côte d'Ivoire for their presence in this basilica and for attending the ceremony. I welcome each one of you.*" When the cameras of the world were finally focused on them in the basilica, viewers around the world were almost blinded by the sea of white *boubous* gracing the pews. The historic scene transformed our critics into instant admirers. Lest we forget, peace and harmony had won over the naysayers, and the whole world had become a platform for unity among humans in celebration of our common faith.

My Love has always respected the precepts of Islam, and I have also respected those of the Catholic religion. Hence, I have never experienced the feeling of having a faith that differs from hers. We will forever continue to share our common faith in one God.

The month of Ramadan was always as meaningful and exciting to my wife as it was to me. "*Chéri*, please remember to bring home a calendar from the mosque today." Those words had been repeated by her, each year, at almost the same time, over decades. She remembered to remind me at least a week or two before the beginning of the season. For years, Titi maintained the same practice of ensuring that she stayed abreast of my routines

A Dream for Peace

to help me break fast. Even when I lagged behind the start time for prayers, she was always quick to give a tender reminder to let me know that it was time for my Dhuhr[48] or Asr[49] prayers. During the holy month of Ramadan, Muslims usually begin to fast from predawn and break the fast at sunset. Right on time, my table was always perfectly laid out with a selection of mouthwatering dishes like Ivorian cream of rice, coffee, milk, dates, *burek*,[50] and my all-time favorite Aïn Beïda dish, *chorba frik*.[51] She prepared the meals and waited patiently to eat with me after I broke the fast. She even kept me company when I woke up to have a late-night snack. With a little help from my sisters, she managed to stock up on most of the base ingredients: fresh green *frik* and other essential produce varieties that were native to Algeria. *Zrir*,[52] a key ingredient for breakfast concoctions at the end of Ramadan, was a key addition to her inventory. At times, she served a delicious couscous or *tajine*[53] with prunes. I looked forward to the last course of desserts after a hearty meal. My Love knew that the most difficult aspect of Ramadan had very little to do with abstaining from eating or drinking. It was a deeper commitment that enforced to the faithful the importance of self-discipline. Speaking ill of others, uttering offensive words, commenting negatively, or acting in a way that could be perceived even in the slightest terms as causing harm to one's neighbor are actions that must be resisted. The main objective of every believer is to undertake a spiritual awakening through prayers and good deeds in order to strengthen the soul and be closer to the Almighty.

Titi also maintained some cohesion with me during Ramadan. We fasted together for the first three days, and then she joined me to fast once a week, including the twenty-seventh day—the Day of

---

[48] Noon prayer. One of the daily prayers performed by practicing Muslims.
[49] Afternoon prayer. One of the daily prayers performed by practicing Muslims.
[50] Family of baked or fried and filled pastries made of a thin, flaky dough.
[51] Gravy soup (*chorba*) with green wheat (*frik*).
[52] Mixture of sesame seed, dried fruits, honey, and butter.
[53] Meat or poultry stew combined with vegetables, flavored with spices.

Our Common Faith

Destiny. I spent the holy month in the small French-Swiss border town of Annemasse and worshipped at a local mosque from time to time. Always mindful of the importance of dialogue between the faiths, I insisted that my wife invite the priest from her parish to break the fast with us. Though soft-spoken, the young priest, Père Alain Viret, had an upbeat personality and was very curious about world affairs.

As a matter of fact, he was seduced by the idea of celebrating the spiritual feast at our house. I welcomed him at the front door on a mild spring evening and led him into the living room. "Thank you for having me, Dr. Berrah. I am delighted to make your acquaintance. I can hardly wait to learn about Islamic customs." "You are welcome, mon Père. It is a pleasure." Titi walked in with some dates and milk. "It is time to break the fast," she said. Seeing the puzzled look on his face, I felt the need to explain the tradition. "We usually break the fast with something sweet to compensate for the low blood sugar levels after a full day of going without eating. Please enjoy, and excuse me while I go and say my sunset prayers. We will have dinner as soon as I am done." He nodded. "But of course. Please take your time."

He was in deep conversation with Titi when I returned. I overheard him highlight the similarities between Ramadan and the Lent observance by people of the Catholic faith. "Essentially, the objective is to get closer to God. However, for us Catholics, we indulge mostly in prayers and penance, whereas Muslims tend to submit physically in many ways. The intensity of fasting is a telltale sign of their very own unique approach." Over dinner, he spoke about the need for all humans to take heed and fulfill in their hearts the teachings of their religion. He hoped to develop a forum for Christians and Muslims to meet and interact for better understanding of the commonalities of faith. He was an interesting character who soon found out that the subject matter was very dear to my heart. My entire life had pivoted naturally at the intersection of religious harmony among all faiths. "Well, it has been a lovely conversation in great company," I said. "But unfortunately, tradition is beckoning yet again. I have to take my leave and go to the mosque." Titi chimed in, "*Ah oui*. It is time for him to go." The priest was gracious. "I understand. *Merci beaucoup*, Dr. Berrah. It has been an honor. Hope to see you again very soon to continue our insightful conversation." It was part of my routine in the holy month to go to the mosque and pray the Taraweeh[54] after breaking fast. He remained with Titi and they spoke in depth about faith and servitude to the Almighty.

The Holy Qur'an must be read by the faithful in its entirety during the month of Ramadan. Each year, Titi never missed the opportunity to ensure that I completed the process. She always stayed up late at night until I returned from my Taraweeh prayers, and she would muster up enough energy to ask for an update, sometimes prompting me to recite parts of the holy verses to her. Eid al-Fitr, the festival of breaking of the fast, is one of Islam's two most important celebrations, and it begins at the end of Ramadan. Prayers and festivities at mosques around the world mark the culmination, but the faithful are especially prayerful and charitable at the end of the fasting season. Although Muslims from around the world are expected to visit their local mosques to affirm their undying dedication to their faith, the Annemasse Mosque was never large enough to accommodate everyone. Frequently, organizers would bus people to a larger venue elsewhere. I had come to expect this to be a normal annual routine for several years, but I had no idea that my Love had quietly been contributing money to fund the transportation until a member of the organizing committee said something to me about how much she was appreciated. I was pleased but not surprised, as it was in her nature to give of herself without drawing attention to her deeds. For years, I thought that I was the sole beneficiary of her undivided attention. Never could I

---

[54] Special evening prayers performed during Ramadan.

Our Common Faith

have imagined that she had been going out of her way to shower my Muslim brethren with so much selfless kindness. My Love has always been more than a devout Catholic who has dedicated herself to the faith with the utmost devotion. She is a magnanimous individual plain and simple. She worries about the comforts of others and acts in accordance with the altruistic principles of our common faith.

My wife receives the Holy Communion from Pope John Paul II.

Titi's undying wish was to receive the papal benediction from Pope John Paul II himself. Though His Holiness had previously sent the apostolic blessing to be delivered at our wedding by Monsignor

A Dream for Peace

Kutwâ, I promised to do whatever I could to make her wish come true someday. Not very long after we tied the knot, I asked the Ivorian ambassador to the Vatican, Mr. Amichia, to help us gain audience with the pope. The tireless and dedicated civil servant was more than happy to deliver. Weeks later, Titi and I arrived at the Vatican as scheduled to meet with Pope John Paul II for the very first time.

With my wife, Ambassador Amichia, and Pope John Paul II.

The momentous occasion left me with an indelible and profound impression of the pious yet meek pope. I was captivated by his innate ability to interweave strength and tenderness with unbridled warmth and humility. Embodied within his saintly persona was a man with a great sense of humor. It was an easy interaction for several minutes, with my wife and I listening intently to his every word and immersing ourselves in his divine, wisdom-filled oratory.

Our Common Faith

When we were done praying, he handed a rosary to my wife, and then he gave one to me. Our hearts were forever stirred with unmatched emotions after the encounter.

My wife receiving a rosary from Pope John Paul II.

My Love and I have forever cherished our yearly anniversary. We always look forward to the day like no other, and she asks her priest for a thanksgiving mass, no matter where we happen to be. In Geneva, we pray at l'Eglise de l'Immaculée Conception, the enchanted church in nearby Vésenaz, where we tied the knot. In any other part of the world, she locates a Virgin Mary–affiliated church and asks for a special mass. I have never had second thoughts accompanying her to church, or to the ICAO[55] chapel, and never once have I hesitated to celebrate Sunday mass with the president at his chapel, because I believe that no matter how or where we pray, we all reach the same God.

---

[55] French acronym for Catholic Institute of West Africa.

A Dream for Peace

Leaving San Marco Basilica, Venice, on our twenty-fifth anniversary.

Some twenty-five years ago, we were exiting the ICAO chapel after our mass when we met a Saint François Xavier Holy Sister from the Sainte Marie High School in Abidjan. She recognized Titi from her high school days at the affiliate school in Neuilly, near Paris. When Titi introduced us, she asked if I wouldn't mind visiting the local school someday to give a presentation on interfaith marriage. I was honored but hesitant, because I did not think I was qualified to speak about the subject. I thanked her graciously and told her that I would ponder the proposal. *In my heart, I never saw any difference between my wife and I. We were two connected souls just living our faith.*

I learned to appreciate the spiritual depth of the sisters at the Saint François Xavier Community, and I valued the importance of their apostolate because of my wife, who maintained strong ties with her former school. She subscribed to and read the alumni quarterly newsletter religiously. It wasn't until we settled into our retirement in the United States that she suggested I read an article in one of her newsletters. I was struck by the content. My mind traced the road map of what seemed to be a common goal in the pursuit of peace. It then occurred to me that the students who had come from all over the world were taught to live together in a climate of mutual respect, with a deeper understanding of the Christian, Muslim, Jewish, Buddhist, and Hindu religions. A light bulb illuminated my thought process, and it dawned on me, the reason why the sister had extended the invitation to me in Abidjan some twenty-five years earlier. I placed the newsletter down and asked Titi to set up a meeting with her former tutors on our next trip to Paris. They told her that they would be more than delighted to receive us for a casual meeting of the minds.

We called from Geneva in the summer and went to meet them for a hearty breakfast at their Rue de Poitiers home in a quiet residential part of the Parisian congregational quarters. It was an honor and a pleasure to finally meet the two Holy Sisters. Sister Jacqueline d' Ussel was a former director of the collective Sainte Marie institutions around the globe and one of the great influences in my wife's early educational experience. She embodied exceptional personal traits: a very open-minded, strong, and forthcoming individual with much profundity. She was with Sister Odile de Vasselot, also quite a remarkable and dynamic woman—a past member of the French Resistance during World War II. She was the founder and former director of Sainte Marie High School in Abidjan.

Despite juggling many responsibilities in their daily routines at the apostolate, they were full of life. Nature had been kind to them over the years; hence, it was impossible to detect any signs of aging in either of them. There was a light behind the flame that kept them animated, and it illuminated the room during our time with them. I congratulated them for their innovative approach to youth education and for encouraging religious tolerance. They were humble and soft-spoken, but with an astuteness that carried over

A Dream for Peace

and filled the atmosphere with the spirit of service to others. We shared many philosophical and religious ideas and engaged their sensibilities in a vibrant and jovial conversation that at times veered into deeper discussions about Côte d'Ivoire, mostly touching on the heydays of President Houphouët, and the future of the country. They were aware of the ongoing political turmoil in the country and affirmed to us that they prayed each day for the people to pull through. Titi and I expressed our concerns about the uncertainties. But for me, the situation had become an especially painful reflection because I was witnessing the daily deterioration of our hard work in three dimension. We all stressed the need for peace to prevail in the world and bonded on sentiments of harmony with unfettered justice for our beloved Ivorian brethren in the days ahead as they prepared for highly contentious elections. We thanked them for their service and dedication and promised to stay in touch often.

Vacationing in Hawaii.

On Christmas, Easter, and other major Christian holidays, I accompanied my Love to church. Some years, we flew directly out of New York at the conclusion of the annual UN session in mid-December to take in the warm and sunny tropics of the Pacific Islands and celebrate Christmas at a midnight mass in Honolulu. If we happened to be in a Muslim country, I found a church for her to celebrate Sunday mass. In Annaba,[56] our nephew Salim always volunteered to escort her to the Basilica of Saint Augustine in Hippone.[57] I looked forward to visiting my old friend Cardinal Léon-Étienne Duval at the Notre Dame d'Afrique Basilica whenever we celebrated mass in Algiers. He lived on an adjacent compound a short walk from the basilica. The cardinal, a Frenchman, had been a friend of Algeria during the lengthy war, having protected several freedom fighters from the colonial forces. He remained an influential and revered personality known for his bravado. The locals gave him the moniker Mohammed Duval.

My friend Essy Amara, my wife, and Imam Tidjane Bâ.

He continued to live in the country even after independence

---

[56] Annaba: city in the northeastern corner of Algeria.
[57] Hippone: the imposing hill over the city of Annaba.

and throughout successive administrations, but he expressed grave concern for the direction of the country during the early 1990s. Those were tumultuous times in Algeria, and I prayed for the Almighty to allow peace to endure over all our troubles. Our house in Abidjan was open to all imams and priests. Monsignor Mullor entrusted Opus Dei, the pope's prelature of the Catholic Church, to me in spite of my faith, shortly before he left Côte d'Ivoire. As a consequence, I met Monsignor Alvaro Del Portillo, a holy man and companion of Saint Josemaría Escrivá, the founder of Opus Dei, as well as his successor, Don Javier Echevarría Rodríguez. Each encounter left me more impressed. The depth of their spirituality was interlocked with all that I knew about my faith, life's principles, and man's ultimate quest to sanctify the ordinary life for the glory of God.

Imam Tidjane Bâ and Monsignor Mullor.

After Monsignor Mullor's departure, his successors in the Apostolic nunciature continued to nurture our friendship. As far as the charming Polish priest Monsignor Janusz Bolonek was concerned, our house was a peaceful haven, second only to the nunciature. He called my wife on many occasions to ask permission to visit us whenever he hosted guests from the Vatican. Titi was always more than delighted and honored to receive everyone for lunch. I also looked forward to those times as an opportunity to mingle and never hesitated to take my leave from the president to help accommodate the guests. A sampling of hors d'oeuvres and appetizers usually followed a tour of the villa, while my Love treated everyone to cultural classics and traditional Ivorian dishes.

Carving some fish for Monsignor Bolonek.

Their favorite main dish was peanut stew with rice, slices of boiled ripe plantain, and yam. Lamb *méchoui* stuffed with couscous, a popular North African delicacy, was always par for the course. As usual, prune *tajine* and a large selection of seasonal tropical fruit with French pastries capped off the lunch. Those were fun times. We

A Dream for Peace

ate and relaxed to meaningful discussions about everything, even sharing a few laughs when we caught ourselves getting too serious.

Monsignor Bolonek and I bonded over time. From the very beginning, he was captivated by our interfaith marriage. He pushed our conversations about Islam and Christianity to deeper levels and highlighted the similarities among all religions. Theology, Muslim dogmas, and so forth had embedded truths that revealed such parallels to the believer. Monsignor Piero Marini, the Master of Ceremonies for Pope John Paul II, was one of the many notable Vatican visitors to our home when he came to Abidjan to prepare for the consecration of the basilica. After Titi and I thanked him for overseeing the massive consecration preparations, he expressed himself with remarkable humility and indulged us in a witty display of pure modesty. "I feel culturally enriched, even though I have only been here a few short days," he said. "You seem to have adapted very well," I replied. "*Merci*, Dr. Berrah . . . *et merci à vous*, Madame Berrah, for the warm hospitality. Indeed, I feel truly pampered."

With Father Touzet, Monsignor Alvaro del Portillo, and my wife.

I grew accustomed to being in the company of the Holy

Our Common Faith

See diplomats. At times, I longed for our interactions because they always demonstrated to me the highest of standards and were extremely effective at every facet of diplomacy. Monsignor Giuseppe Bertello, an overtly friendly and humble man with a selfless personality, succeeded my dear brother Monsignor Mullor as the Holy See's representative to the UN in Geneva. Having been charged with overseeing human rights abuses around the world, he and I were constantly discussing ways to tackle the most disturbing issues in specific countries. His practical approach and remedies were personal attributes that drew me to him, and I reciprocated by introducing constructive measures to solve some of the problems. I emphasized the need for more diplomats from developing countries and decided to reach out to Monsignor Mullor to discuss the possibility of an agreement with the Holy See to open the doors to an internship program at the Vatican for young Ivorian diplomats. Much to my surprise, I found out that as a prerequisite, each aspiring candidate had to be a priest, and they had to go through a selection process in order to be admitted to the Pontifical Academy, of which Monsignor Mullor later served as president. Upon completing the course at the academy, graduates were then required to follow the normal process that took them through the various ranks as a diplomat of the Holy See. It was interesting, but either way, I was disappointed to discover that the opportunity to participate in the program was not available to our Ivorian diplomats.

On occasion, I felt the need to get away from diplomacy and my hectic schedule—to have a more in-depth reflection about the meaning of my actions. These feelings took on a sense of urgency around the holy month of Ramadan, and I usually felt a strong desire to go on a pilgrimage to Mecca. By the grace of the Almighty, I was fortunate enough to record nine such pilgrimages to the Hajj, one of the five pillars of Islam. This is a required commitment for every Muslim to undertake at least once in their lifetime. It is also recommended that all who make the pilgrimage should in turn help others who lack the means to do the same.

At the heart of the pilgrimage is the Ka'aba, known to the faithful as the House of Allah. This most venerated Muslim shrine sits at the center of the Holy Mosque in Mecca. The Prophet Ibrahim built the shrine and many centuries later, it was rebuilt with the help of the Prophet Muhammad (S) to encapsulate the Black Stone. It serves as a focal and unifying point among the faithful, which is why Muslims around the globe turn their compasses toward Mecca during daily prayers to ensure that they are facing the Ka'aba from wherever they may be.

As destiny would have it, I had the immense grace and distinguished honor to be among a select few to participate in the cleaning of the Ka'aba on two memorable occasions. The monument is covered by a kiswah, a gold embroidered black silk cloth with adorned verses from the Qur'an. Traditionally, a piece of the Kiswah is given to each individual who participates in the cleaning ritual. The two kiswah pieces that were given to me at the end of my sacrifice are my most cherished prized possessions.

The pilgrimage to Mecca is from the eighth to the twelfth day of Dhu al-Hijjah, the twelfth and last month of the Islamic calendar. Because we use a lunar calendar, our dates are eleven days shorter than the standard Gregorian calendar, and accordingly, the Gregorian date of the Hajj changes from year to year.

The Hajj is associated with the life of Prophet Muhammad (S) from the seventh century, but the ritual of pilgrimage to Mecca dates back thousands of years to the time of Prophet Abraham, known by Muslims as Ibrahim. At the same time each year, pilgrims by the hundreds of thousands from all over the world converge upon Mecca during the week of the Hajj.

Like my fellow pilgrims, I embark on my spiritual journey in a special seamless white garment, an *ihram*—required clothing to enter Mecca. The custom signifies a renunciation of the outside world for a more humble and pious life. I am always filled with strong spiritual emotions whenever I make my final entrance to the Haram, a designated area encircling the city perimeters measuring about three miles wide and eighty miles long. Each year, pilgrims follow in the footsteps of the Prophet to formally declare their devotion to Allah the Almighty.

The Hajj begins with the welcome Tawaf[58] and the Sa'I[59] ritual once we enter the Holy Sanctuary (al Masjid al Haram), right foot first, through the Bab Al-Salam gate. At the Holy Mosque, we are led in prayer by an imam who chants verses from the Holy Qur'an in a voice so unique and powerful, it sends chills down my spine and literally moves everyone to tears. We then proceed to the small village of Mina to spend the entire day in meditation and prayers in solidarity with the Prophet's ritual. Before sunrise the following day, we head to the Plain of Arafat to meditate and pray on our feet atop Mount Arafat, another solemn and poignant experience for those of us who are moved to tears during the prayer ritual of Prophet Muhammad (S).

We spend the night in reflection under the open skies of the Muzdalifah valley just like the Prophet. Upon awakening in the wee hours of the morning, we collect pebbles for the stoning of the devil ritual and return to the town of Mina to cast the stones at the three walls of Jamarāt. The faithful believe that Jamarāt is where the devil failed in his attempt to persuade Ibrahim to sacrifice his son.

It is at Mina that we commemorate the sacrificing of lamb in a synchronized ritual with Muslims around the world. The feast of Eid-al-Adha represents the sacrifice of Ibrahim. To show gratitude to Allah for his generosity and blessings, most of the meat is given to the poor. Those who are unable to participate in the sacrificial ritual make monetary donations to the needy. The second Tawaf takes us to the small hills of Safa and Marwah for a walkabout

---

[58] Ritual walk counterclockwise seven times around the Ka'aba in meditation.
[59] Moving back and forth seven times between the hills of Safa and Marwah.

ritual that begins and concludes with the drinking of water from the Well of Zamzam. By then, the state of *ihram* is presumed to be fulfilled, except for two more days of ceremonial stoning. We head to the Holy Mosque in Mecca to complete the farewell Tawaf. I felt lighter and spiritually cleansed, but I always had a tough time with my emotions on the day of departure. For pilgrims, the Hajj is not complete until we go to pray at Prophet Muhammad's (S) tomb inside the Al-Masjid al-Nabawī Mosque in Medina, the second holiest city in Islam. The mosque was built by Prophet Muhammad (S) and refurbished centuries later to include the renowned Green Dome, a unique fixture over the Prophet's tomb. I usually began my pilgrimage in Medina and found the memorable experience to be one of reinvigoration and purification, hence year after year, I could not wait to do it all again.

On a couple of occasions, I went to Mecca at the invitation of the Saudi royal palace. But for the most part, I embarked on each of my nine pilgrimages on my own accord and did so without complications. I remain eternally grateful for being so fortunate, because many of the faithful do not always complete the process. Ever mindful of the Muslim calendar, President Houphouët-Boigny always offered pilgrimages to a select group of Muslims each year.

Though my Love and I were inseparable, the Hajj kept us apart, but by the grace of the Almighty, we managed to embark on our very own unique pilgrimage to Jerusalem—the cradle of Christianity, Judaism's most divine sanctuary, and one of Islam's holiest cities. We planned to meet in Tel Aviv after one of my pilgrimages to Mecca. She traveled from Geneva to Zurich, then endured a thorough security check before boarding her flight. We both arrived a few minutes apart and greeted each other at the airport on a beautiful Friday afternoon. For me, the restful weekend was all I needed after my physically demanding pilgrimage, in spite of the unique spiritual fulfillment. On Sunday morning, we were picked up by our chauffeur and shuttled to church. We both grew very fond of Elie, the friendly Sephardic Jew from Morocco, and decided to make him our designated driver for the duration of our stay.

    The beauty of Jerusalem is revealed in the early morning sunshine, a city draped in white cliff-side homes. Varieties of pale dolomitic limestone, common in and around the city, had been used in the construction of buildings since ancient times. When we came back to the Mount of Olives Hotel, where we stayed, we inquired about finding a tour guide and by sheer coincidence were introduced to an Algerian. Ibrahim was a very animated and dynamic person, fluent in Hebrew, Arabic, and English. Years before he was born, his grandfather had come to the British colony of Palestine after a pilgrimage to Mecca and decided to settle down in Jerusalem. We felt right at home with him from the moment we began sharing our trip objectives. For five days he would be at our disposal, and he would be responsible for a memorable interfaith pilgrimage. "Firstly," I told him. "My most distinguished wish is to pray at the Al-Aqsa Mosque. And for my wife, a pilgrimage to the Basilica of the Holy Sepulchre would be in the highest order." We discussed other key must-see destinations in the Holy Land and narrowed them down to a solid itinerary. He knew of all the religious sites.

    On the first day of our pilgrimage, I rose from bed in the early dawn, full of anticipation and looking forward to my maiden pilgrimage to the Al-Aqsa Mosque. Ibrahim was already waiting in the lobby to greet me. Not long after I left, my Love began her morning in the exquisite gardens of the hotel, meditating and reflecting on the experiences of Christ and his Apostles by the Mount of Olives. We took a short trip to participate in the Fajr prayer at the magnificent Dome of the Rock. From there, we headed to the Al-Aqsa Mosque in Old Jerusalem. According to Muslim doctrine, the mosque completes the fifth pillar of Islam. We went inside to meditate for a while before attending the Dhuhr prayer. My heart was overjoyed. I was completely overwhelmed by the weight of the moment, even as I focused deeply on a passage in the Qur'an about the mysterious journey of the Prophet Muhammad (S) from the place I stood in prayer. It was a blessing to have been among the few Arabs to achieve that particular milestone.

When we returned to the hotel at the end of prayers, my Love was ready to get going. We asked Ibrahim to join us for a light lunch before embarking yet again for a trip to Old Jerusalem. The driver pulled up to the pretty square at the entrance of the old town, known as the Damascus Gate, and we walked past the Al-Aqsa Mosque again to show the site to my wife. We stopped at the ancient ruins of the Second Temple, the revered Wailing Wall—Judaism's holiest shrine. It lays at the foot of the western side of the Temple Mount, beside the mosque. The area was bustling with activities, and we saw many Jewish faithful bowing their heads rhythmically in prayer at the wall. Flocks of people stood in line and moved a step at a time to take turns to meditate. We moved across an old narrow road to get to the house of Pontius Pilate, where Jesus Christ was put on trial. There was so much energy around us from the moment we set foot in the area. It felt like a spiritual awakening.

Undoubtedly, the time has come for us to reflect on our common faith in one God, the one who revealed Himself to mankind in three different ways right where we stood.

When we left the house of Pilate, we paced through the pavements of the old picturesque town and made our way toward the Basilica of the Holy Sepulchre. I went into the Mosque of Omar, across from the basilica, to meditate for a few minutes. Walking in the footsteps of the caliph in a mosque that was built within range of the basilica was an experience to behold. The mere historic significance made me shudder as I replayed the story in its context: Omar, the caliph, was at the basilica when he realized that it was time for the Islamic prayers; the site's administrator invited him to pray inside the basilica, but he wisely refused because he did not want his Muslim brothers to take over the holy place in the future. He stood and cast a stone and went to pray where it landed. Hence, a small mosque bearing his name was erected on the very site where he prayed.

As we were entering the basilica, I worried about how my wife would react. She seemed at peace. According to Christian teachings, we were treading lightly on the grounds venerated as Golgotha, the Hill of Calvary, where Jesus was crucified—also known to contain the tomb where Jesus was buried. The sepulchre remains a paramount destination for many Christians and a most important pilgrimage site. When we finally made our entrance, my Love was suddenly overcome by emotions. She couldn't hold back her tears, and I was profoundly affected by her. I grabbed and held her hand tightly to soothe her. We stood side by side in the heartland of Christianity, and with each breath, her soul lent credence to the deepest bonds of her faith. After a couple of hours, we returned to the hotel to unwind the emotions of our first day.

Our second day was marked by a visit to Bethany—the home of Martha, Mary, and their brother, Lazarus. "It is said that Jesus arrived in Bethany six days before the Jewish celebration of Passover," Ibrahim told us. "Martha served dinner in Jesus's honor, and Mary poured perfume on his feet." We reflected on those words and walked across the compound to the tomb of Lazarus.

The Basilica of the Nativity in Bethlehem was next on our list. I was astonished to see for the first time the segmentation of the various Christian faiths—branches of the Orthodoxy, Catholic, Protestant, Methodist, etc. Making our way down two flights of steps to the Grotto, we passed the Altar of the Nativity and arrived at a holy recess with a fourteen-point silver star, surrounded by Latin inscription, proclaiming the site as the birthplace of Jesus. It was a stirring encounter for my wife, who was once again moved to tears as she stood transfixed at the exact spot where Jesus was born. *Where else does one get the power to experience all of this over and over again without going numb?* I wondered quietly. We maintained a silent vigil and exited after a couple of hours. The vendors outside the compound showered us with bargains on religious souvenirs, a welcome sight of ease and comfort. We indulged them for a while until it was time for my Dhuhr prayers at a nearby mosque.

The dry midafternoon heat was enveloped by soft breezes and fragrances of summer. Dominating the distant city skyline of Hebron, Al-Haram Al-Ibrahimi Mosque, Islam's fourth holiest site, seemed closer than we thought. We cruised for several minutes down historical roads before we finally pulled up to what is believed to be Abraham's sanctuary and the Tomb of the Patriarchs. For a thousand years, the mosque has been a consummate interfaith pilgrimage site as the resting place for the Prophets Abraham, Isaac, and Jacob and their wives, revered equally by Christians, Jews, and Muslims. We experienced firsthand the tension between Jews and Muslims in the once peaceful region. The Israeli army was at the mosque's entrance in full force to ensure that the flow of pilgrims moved along peacefully. We came face-to-face with the charged atmosphere for the very first time, providing a reality check, but we chose to meditate on the tomb of the father of all believers rather than allow ourselves to be absorbed by the melee. I followed our guide, Ibrahim, to an area in the southeastern section for the Asr prayers. My Love went on a sightseeing tour that took her to an octagonal room with the cenotaphs of Jacob and Leah passing a synagogue beside the southwestern wall where the faithful stood in silent meditation. *Into all its tenderness, our once-in-a-lifetime journey carried us into the cradle of our common faith, uniting us as one people.*

We took in the scenic sites en route to Jerusalem, basking in the multiplex of beautiful sunset radiance that soon revealed another mosque in a heavenly setting by a desolate roadside. The ancient structure was born out of the remains of an older mosque that had undergone rehabilitation. The driver pulled over for Ibrahim and I to go inside and pray the Maghreb. For five days, he found a mosque for me every time I needed to pray. Back on the road again, we had a lively conversation. Ibrahim, a real angel and a great find, talked to us about the hidden gems in the Holy Land, and Elie, the soft-spoken driver, shared his sentiments on religious diversity. My Love had an insightful take on the matter, wondering how such an awesome opportunity to harness the power and culture of rich religious diversity could go untapped.

At the hotel, we felt the heaviness of tension that had gradually permeated the blissful night and made its way into the restaurant to disturb the serene atmosphere. Unbeknownst to us, there was a brewing Palestinian revolt in the not-so-distant future. We overheard a couple of Arab waiters at the restaurant speaking openly about the intolerable situation. This was my first contact with Palestinians on their native soil. The writing was on the wall.

On day three of our stay, we drove from Jerusalem to Ramallah, the place where Joseph and Mary discovered the absence of the child Jesus when their caravan came to a rest stop. They went to look for him and found him teaching in the temple among the doctors of the law. Ibrahim explained to us that at the time, Ramallah was a hub and a mandatory stop for caravans. We then moved on to Emmaus, where Christ met some of his own disciples who walked with him without knowing who he was.

At the site of Jacob's Well in the province of Samaria, I was astonished to see that the four-thousand-year-old well remained intact and fully functional. The history of Samaria harkens back to a time when Samaritans could not interact with Jews, yet Jesus surprised a Samaritan woman when he asked for a drink of water from the well. "You know," Ibrahim said, "there are still Samaritans living in the area." "Oh, really?" we chimed in unison, totally amazed. "Yes, of course," he replied. "Would you like a visit?" "We would be more than delighted to meet a Samaritan in the flesh," I said. We crossed the street to a small apartment building. When he tapped on the door, a middle-aged man greeted us with a smile and became pleasantly chatty. We could tell that he and Ibrahim knew each other.

A Dream for Peace

We entered the home and relaxed on a sofa in the living room. In line with tradition, our host served some local home-brewed coffee and welcomed us. The male companion who joined us was animated and friendly. Titi and I enjoyed their insightful stories about Samarian culture, which interestingly enough had transcended the fade of time to entrench itself in modern-day practices. Samaritans continue to live reclusive lives in their very own unique community. We thanked our hosts for their graciousness and memorable hospitality.

We left and drove to the Sea of Galilee, parked a few yards from the beach, and walked toward the shore. While Ibrahim narrated a passage from the Gospel, describing Jesus walking across the body of water, we paused for a moment of reflection and cast our eyes across the sea. As we cast our gaze at the distant horizon, we felt the occasional gusts of the moisture-laden breeze caressing our faces. My Love was overcome with emotions. I held her hand firmly, and we walked back to the car.

A few miles down the road, we stopped at the Mount of Beatitudes, where Jesus delivered the Sermon on the Mount. We got out of the car to admire the lush greenery for a brief moment and drove a little farther down to view Mount Tabor from a distance. For Catholics, the textual passages in the liturgy that day were about Mount Tabor and coincidentally, we happened to be at the site on that particular day. My Love seized the moment to reflect on some passages of her faith before we sped up the road and headed to Nazareth, our final stopover for the day. Just about a few minutes into our drive, we decided to stop briefly at the site of the Wedding at Cana while we were still in the province of Galilee.

In Nazareth, the town where Jesus spent most of his childhood, we were surprised to see a very modern and robust city. My Love later expressed to me her disappointment after our visit to the Basilica of the Annunciation. Neither she nor I had been aware of the fact that the church, which was built over the Crusader and Byzantine foundations, had been demolished in 1955 for the construction of the present-day church. She was particularly dumbfounded because she expected to see a site that was reminiscent of the historical venues on our list. For my part, I realized that our guide might have spared us the unfortunate stroke of serendipity had we bothered to ask a few questions beforehand. Nonetheless, we scouted the premises, tracing a path into the vast upper church, which had been decorated with mosaics of the Virgin Mary. My Love excused herself to pray at a nearby altar. As soon as she was done, we walked down to the lower church in the Grotto of the Annunciation, where the angelic announcement to Mary is believed to have occurred. She paused once again for a few minutes of meditation. Our trip back to Jerusalem was a long one, but we had many interesting conversations to keep us occupied.

As usual, our guide awaited us in the lobby on the morning of our fourth day. We invited him to sit with us for some coffee and went over events from the previous day. High on our list for that day was a visit to the Old City of Jerusalem for souvenir hunting. From the Damascus Gate, we mingled with many shoppers and walked into some of the small shops along the cobblestone streets. Though I could express myself in Arabic, the few Palestinian shopkeepers who detected my accent were curious to know my country of origin. When I explained to a vendor that I was Algerian and a former FLN combatant who also happens to be an Ivorian diplomat, he showed us a lot of hospitality and invited us to sit for some coffee. Some family members from the back room soon joined our conversation and expressed their joy at seeing us.

We moved along to an adjacent shop and were again invited to sit for more coffee. But soon enough, we were joined by a small group of shopkeepers who converged around us. Most of them spoke openly and poured out their hearts to us, complaining about their brothers in the Arab countries who had abandoned their cause. "As far as we are concerned, Israel is here to stay," a vendor who had just joined the group spoke louder than the rest. He was echoed by a barrage of vociferous sentiments and statements coming at us one after the other: "We are asking our Arab brethren to recognize Israel, because this is the only way for them to gain the entry permits, which will enable them to come and see us and help us free ourselves." "We feel as though we have been forgotten and they don't even recognize our very existence." "You, my friend, are the only one who has paid us a visit in a long time." "We don't even have a passport, hence we are stuck here, deprived of our freedom to move around freely." The encounter amounted to an educational moment for me. I saw it as an affirmation of the importance of dialogue as the best and only way on the path to achieving peace.

At each stopover, vendors spoke openly about their plight, and we perused souvenirs, gladly picking up some rare items along the way. When we returned to the waiting car, Ibrahim and I strolled off to catch the Dhuhr prayers at the Al-Aqsa Mosque. We joined my wife later to embark on our planned visit to Jericho. Parked beneath a tree alongside a busy street in the small town, we went to see a sycamore fig tree, where our guide recounted a verse from the Gospel. He told us about a tax collector named Zacchaeus, a short man in stature who was hated by the Jews because he worked for the Romans. He had climbed up the sycamore fig tree so that he might be able to see Jesus as he approached the town. When Jesus reached the spot, he looked up through the branches, addressed Zacchaeus by name, and asked him to come down, for he intended to visit his house. Onlookers were amazed by the fact that Jesus, a Jew, would dishonor his reputation by being a guest of a tax collector.

From where we stood, we could see the Jordanian border. I wondered how the West Bank, a tiny slit of landmass, was at the center of so much turmoil in the region. We could also see the River Jordan, where Jesus was baptized by John the Baptist, whose father Zakariya is a known prophet in the Qur'an alongside John. Zakariya's role as one of the men of God is frequently referenced in many verses of the Qur'an. We followed along the river's western border and stopped to watch it converge with the Dead Sea.

From the shoreline of the Dead Sea, we watched the sun emerge from the shadows of Mount Nebo. Jews and Christians believe that the Prophet Moses, to whom the Almighty had given the Torah, was buried on the mountain but that his final resting place is unknown. My wife and I went to dip our hands in the sea to experience its density and high salinity. It seemed at first glance that there was an oily tinge on the surface. We both felt a strange sensation, somewhat oily to the touch, but oddly enough, there was no such residue on our hands. "This is an awesome work of nature," Titi said, and I agreed. "As part of their tradition, some rabbis purify themselves in the Dead Sea before the Sabbath," Ibrahim revealed. We left the area and headed toward Jerusalem. Back at the Mount of Olives, he led us to the Pater Noster Church, where Jesus taught his disciples the Lord's Prayer. We were taken in by the multitudes of gorgeous roses in the beautiful courtyard, the pillars and arches, and the imposing neo-Gothic style of architecture. Our focal point was the cloister, decorated with tiled panels of the Lord's Prayer in several languages. Everything was definitely unique in the Holy Land.

At the end of our day, we sat in the hotel lobby with Ibrahim and discussed our calendar for the conclusion of the pilgrimage. My Love wanted to join her fellow Christians and walk the path of Christ on the "Way of the Cross," starting from the house of Pontius Pilate to the Holy Sepulchre. I wanted to attend the great Friday prayers at the Dome of the Rock and take part in the Asr prayer for the last time at the Al-Aqsa Mosque. After organizing our morning program, Ibrahim graciously left us.

We woke up early in the morning, clearly energized and extremely excited to see the holy sites around the Mount of Olives. After breakfast, we could hardly wait to get started. We went to a small church behind a huge wall, commemorating the place where the disciples brought the donkey on which Jesus rode triumphantly into Jerusalem. Christians honor the event by celebrating Palm

Sunday every year. We passed by the Zion Gate and went to the crest of Mount Zion, sauntering past the partial remains of an ancient building known as the Cenacle, the site of the Last Supper, where Jesus first introduced the Eucharist, commonly known as the Holy Communion. I watched my wife affirm her dedication at the site for a moment. She paused to offer an earnest prayer in silence. Jews know the site as the final resting place of King David.

Our next stop was the Mosque of the Ascension, which is sacred to Christians and Muslims, known as the place of Jesus's ascension into heaven. The site contains what is traditionally believed to be the last footprint of Jesus on earth. Beside the mosque is a small chapel that was taken over after the fall of the Crusader kingdom by Salah al-Din in the twelfth century and transformed from a Christian church into a mosque. There is an underground tomb near the entrance that is venerated by those of the Jewish faith. We stood still and meditated at the junction where the three major religions converged upon one another and debated among ourselves about why mankind continues to be preoccupied with religious differences rather than finding the common ground where we can all relate.

For my Love and I, this has always been commonsensical and never a mystery to us. We have continuously lived our lives as devotees to our personal faiths, always knowing that the love of the Almighty is limitless and without boundaries. I have by no means attempted to convert her to Islam, and neither has she tried to convert me to Christianity. The world as we have come to know it has become a place that yearns for a true understanding of the faiths.

We went to see the Tomb of the Prophets Haggai, Zechariah, and Malachi (a popular pilgrimage site for Jews), located on the upper slope of the Mount of Olives. A beam of sunlight permeated from above and traced its way into the dark catacomb of arguably one of the holiest mountains in the world. It was as if the Almighty was shining his divine light and beckoning to the faithful. In the midst of the surreal scenery, a Hasidic family smiled at us and wandered into the tunnel. We moved past ancient olive trees with two-thousand-year-old roots and crossed into the Garden of Gethsemane, right next to the Basilica of Agony. Christians believe that the roots are symbolic witnesses to the emotional suffering and betrayal of Jesus.

The Church of the Assumption, believed by most to contain the Tomb of the Virgin Mary, was next on our list. We strolled along the foot of the Mount of Olives and made our way down several steps in the dimly lit church to get to the tomb. My Love has a very special place in her heart for the Virgin Mary, to whom she looks for spiritual guidance. She stood silently in the dark and shadowy crypt, and we breathed a heavy fragrance of incense. I meditated as she slowly caressed her rosary. Though we were captivated and in awe of the ambiance, she was on a unique spiritual level, lost in powerful prayers and deep reflection. I glanced over at her and felt every ounce of her energy. After many minutes of extraordinary silence, I held her hand and we made our way out of the crypt.

Ibrahim wasted no time letting us know that the Virgin Mary, mother of Jesus, was taken by Saint John the Apostle to Turkey, where she lived in a stone house on Mount Koressos until her Assumption. The site is both a Catholic and Muslim shrine. We went a little farther down the road to the edge of the Jewish cemetery and were soon rewarded with the best views of the old part of Jerusalem. I became increasingly emotional as the hour of my last great prayer in Jerusalem drew near.

Our final pilgrimage day was slowly coming to a very insightful and enlightening end. I really looked forward to my last day of prayers at the Dome of the Rock with so much zeal and spiritual focus. I was already in a state of meditation when we arrived, and my prayers were very intense. Following the conclusion of the imam's oration, we returned to pick Titi up for the three o'clock commencement of the Via Dolorosa (Way of the Cross) at the house of Pilate. Ibrahim and I escorted her to the meeting place and left

A Dream for Peace

her with the Christian faithful. We hastened back to the Al-Aqsa Mosque just in time for the Asr prayers.

During the Muslim call to prayer, we could also hear the Christian procession praying loudly as they made their way past the mosque en route to the Holy Sepulchre, while at the same time the Jews prayed at the Wailing Wall. Together, all the prayers of the various faiths, emanating in unison, rose toward the sky. A sign of our common faith in one unique God.

I couldn't help but think of a verse from the *surah* AL-MA'IDAH 5:48 in the Holy Qur'an: "*Unto everyone of you have we appointed a different law and way of life. And if God so willed, HE could surely have made you one single community; but in order to test you by means of what HE has vouchsafed unto you. Vie then, with one another in doing good works. Unto God you all must return, and then HE will make you truly understand all that on which you were wont to differ.*"

As soon as we completed our prayers, we walked back to the Basilica of the Holy Sepulchre to meet my Love at the exit. It was shortly before the Sabbath was to begin, and it was also time to part ways with our guide. We thanked him for his masterful teachings and expressed our regrets for the quick passage of time. He shared our feelings for an enlightening experience. I exchanged information with him and promised to get in touch in the very near future. Because of the Sabbath constraints, our Jewish driver did not have enough time to take us to our hotel and make it back home in time. We asked him to drop us off at the Damascus Gate.

Within a few minutes, an unmarked car pulled up to us. "*Habibi*, you want a taxi?" the driver asked, using the Arabic term for "friend." "Oh, yes, yes," I responded. "You are not a Palestinian, *habibi*. What are you doing in Jerusalem?" We had barely sat down in the car. "On a pilgrimage with my wife, *habibi*," I told him. He began to talk about the Israeli-Palestinian conflict. We spoke for about twenty minutes. "I am very well acquainted with Arafat. He is like a brother to me," I said. He acknowledged with a nod. Seemingly at ease with me, he felt more comfortable expressing his political views. We arrived at the base of the Mount and drove slowly up the winding road to the hotel entrance. "With your permission, I would like to pick you up tomorrow and take you to a secret location. I am certain you will appreciate what you see." I did not give it a second thought. "Sure, why not?" I agreed. "It will give you an opportunity to see firsthand and allow you to assess our situation in these occupied West Bank territories," he said. When we came to a stop, he refused to take any payment.

    He picked us up in the morning. After about an hour's drive through isolated mountainous terrains and desert roads, he rolled downhill and dodged some massive potholes before coming to a stop on a desolate road. "We have to walk the rest of the way," he explained, obviously concerned about my wife's ability to hike with us. I asked Titi if she was okay with a trek down the slopes. "*Je préfère rester ici.*" She was such a trooper. She agreed to sacrifice her safety and wait in the car, alone in the desert, in the middle of nowhere. I saw her take out her rosary to assure me that she was in good company. I planted a kiss on her forehead and disappeared with him through the canyons. "It is a difficult slog for a woman," he said. It seemed that way. The ground was filled with stones and gravel spanning a curvy downward incline. "We did not come prepared for a hike," I told him. We passed through some very narrow valleys and navigated carefully across a few steep gorges to get to a well-hidden training camp.

    There were over a hundred young and seasoned fighters on site. They demonstrated an impressive determination to sacrifice their lives for their freedom—a willingness to be among their brethren, united and dedicated to the cause. Each and every one of the young men I spoke to assured me that they stood committed and poised to fight for their liberation, saying, "We stand ready to rid ourselves of this unbearable occupation and form an independent Palestinian state." I listened to their heartfelt remarks and promised

A Dream for Peace

to relay the message to Chairman Arafat.

We left the camp and returned to reunite with my Love about two hours later. She was a bit nervous and agitated when I saw her. She had been wondering what to do in the event I didn't come back. "I thought you would only be gone for no more than thirty minutes," she said. "Very sorry, *mon chéri*," I apologized, acknowledging my recklessness. "I was really taken in by an evolving situation and lost track of time." Nonetheless, I was very relieved to see her too. The encounter occurred in August of 1987, just months before the first intifada. It was then I realized that the volatile situation in the occupied territories was on the brink of a massive flare-up. We said very little during the hour-long drive back to Jerusalem. I mostly reflected on the surprising experience and the long road ahead to achieving a sustainable peace. At the hotel's entrance, we bid farewell to the young Palestinian and wished him well.

"All thanks be to God for guiding us through this momentous and spiritually rewarding pilgrimage," Titi breathed a fitting sigh of gratitude as soon as we closed the door behind us. "Indeed, my Love, *Alhamdulillah*." We paused and began to pack our belongings. I woke up within a few hours to pray at dawn and joined my wife for Sunday mass at the beautiful Basilica of Agony, within walking distance of our hotel. We returned to find our driver waiting to take us to the Tel Aviv airport. The days had gone by very fast, it seemed. When he dropped us off at the curb, we expressed our sentiments and parted ways, hoping to soon return to the Holy Land. For five days, we immersed ourselves in a spiritual excursion that reawakened our core fundamental beliefs. We felt rejuvenated and more grounded in our common faith.

The city of Geneva seemed so far away from the Holy Land, but in reality, it made for a perfect transition due to its serene atmosphere. We rested at home for a few days and returned to Abidjan. In the coming days, we shared the highlights of the trip with President Houphouët. He was particularly taken in by my unexpected adventure to the training camp and suggested I go to Tunisia to share the experience with Chairman Arafat.

I still yearned to complete my knowledge of all revealed religions. After honoring an invitation to a Shabbat dinner by my Jewish friend Melvin Cohen and his family in Tucson, I purchased a book on the symbols of Judaism. Melvin, a religious man, was also involved in teaching the scriptures at the University of Arizona. When we arrived at his charming home on campus, we met his wife and father-in-law, who greeted us in French. Much to our surprise, he was very fluent in the language. His wife was high-spirited and sociable and got along very well with Titi. We were soon joined by their little boy, who was quite polite. The couple did their very best to make us feel at home. When the time was right, they led us to the powder room, where we took turns to wash our hands. The table in the living room was set beautifully with two candles. Mrs. Cohen gave a quick orientation about the significance of the candles: they each represented one of two commandments—the first, in remembrance, and the second, in observance of the Shabbat. The ritual was performed as a way to profess one's faith and follow the example of the Lord, who interrupted the process of creation on the seventh day, the day of the Sabbath.

Mrs. Cohen lit the candles before sundown and waved her hands over the flames after ceremonial rites, and she welcomed the Shabbat with a blessing recitation. Melvin took over and recited some more prayers. They sang some verses from the Psalms, and we joined them in spirit amid the pious atmosphere.

The meal was served with slices of *challah*, a specially blessed Shabbat bread, representing the symbol of *manna*. "It is believed that the *manna* fell from the sky onto the desert," explained the father-in-law, a former Auschwitz inmate. Mrs. Cohen served up an exquisite dinner. We relaxed and engaged in small talk with her father, who shared some harrowing details from his time at the infamous Nazi concentration camp. He revealed a tattooed serial number on his right arm, and I told him I was sorry he had to endure so much pain and suffering. Both Titi and I remained transfixed for several minutes. We all shared his gratitude to the Almighty for surviving the camp. His poignant stories stayed on my mind for a while. It was a deep and meaningful learning experience.

I had read a couple of books on Judaism, but I had yet to come across certain aspects of religious traditions, but through my many friendships, I was given an opportunity to learn something new on occasion. When Irving and Audrey Greene invited us to celebrate two bar mitzvahs simultaneously in Florida, we did not know what to expect. The grandfather, a World War II veteran who served in the US Air Force, was celebrating a renewal of his bar mitzvah and at the same time, his grandson was about to celebrate his first. In Jewish tradition, once a boy reaches the age of thirteen, he becomes a bar mitzvah and goes through a rite of passage in which he transitions from not understanding the Torah to ultimately being considered old enough to begin to understand. Among some Jews, a man who has reached the age of eighty-three will customarily celebrate a second bar mitzvah. The logic being that, in the Torah, a "normal" lifespan is seventy years old, therefore an eighty-three-year-old becomes thirteen again in a second lifetime.

My wife and I accompanied the Greene family to the synagogue to witness the beautiful ceremony for the first time in our lives. One after the other, we watched and listened attentively as the rabbis took to the bimah[60] and delivered some powerful passages from the Torah. I was struck by the depth of the readings of goodness, love, and all the precious values that are prevalent in all religions. "If the Jews applied the precepts of the Torah, the whole world would be changed for the better," I commented passionately to my wife at the ceremony's end. The teachings I derived from my experience were also applicable to Christians and Muslims in the

---

[60] Platform in a synagogue from which the Torah is read.

principles of their faith. I have since concluded that I prefer the company of a good Christian or a good Jew to that of a bad Muslim.

Many a time, the topic of religious diversity would become the centerpiece of my conversation with my dear Vietnamese friend Dr. Tran. He was raised a Buddhist. I had gained some insights on Buddhism in China during my FLN student years. That was long before our paths crossed. I knew that Vietnamese Buddhism was similar to Chinese Buddhism, but through our conversations, I learned that their practice has elements that can be traced to Japanese Zen, Tibetan Buddhism, and another form known as Amitabha, or "Pure Land," Buddhism. Just as Muslim children in my native Algeria are often raised in Qur'anic schools, most Buddhists in Vietnam belong to the Mahayana schools. I came to admire how much Dr. Tran's culture and thinking was influenced and shaped by his Buddhist faith. As far as he was concerned, his faith was a way of life that emphasized disconnection to the present. The main holy book, the Tripitaka, was translated from an ancient Indian language which was very close to Buddha's native dialect. In the book, it is written that people reap today what they have sown in the past.

What really impressed me about Dr. Tran was his enduring patience. This was a key component of his personality. It was at the core of his disposition, having been instilled in him from a very tender age. His wife was much the same way too. Tucked in the corner of their yard was a small greenhouse with a nursery of orchids. She tendered to the plants with the utmost care and forbearance. Some orchids flourished well, others stayed bloomless for years, and although she thought she might never see the rewards of her hard work, she was satisfied with the belief that someone else would enjoy the fruits of her labor someday, long after she leaves this earth. Titi and I often marveled at her selfless inclination to be a steward of good so that others may reap the benefits and perhaps continue the good work. We could relate because it was in perfect synchronicity with the spirit of service to the Almighty. Our own faith teaches us that sacrifice is indeed a moral obligation that is looked upon favorably by Allah.

The foundation of all religions rests upon the concept of morality. The sincerity in leading a religious life, the quest to follow the righteous path, and a desire to practice honesty in judgment, sincerity in speech and in all of one's actions, including aspirations, are intrinsic values that correlate to our faith. The precepts of nurturing a healthy spiritual state of mind are necessary to foster genuine sincerity in prayer and meditation. Our fellow Hindu brethren share similar patterns in worship. What I have seen among adherents of every religion are the commonalities of our specific beliefs and ultimate objective. But there is also a spiritual reality that transcends our finite human experience. The role of religion, therefore, is to serve as a road map to guide us by emphasizing the moral commandments and encouraging humans to follow a better path, to work for peace in the world, and to be tolerant of others.

My wife and I share a common faith in God's plan for us. Like the vast majority of people, we were hoping to be blessed with children. When we realized that God's plans for us would be different, we did not fall into despair. Instead, we reflected on the wisdom of the words of Monsignor Mullor: *"Having children is a blessing; not having any is also a blessing."*

We became very close with the monsignor a few decades ago. Throughout the years, we took turns visiting each other regardless of where we happened to be. When he was at the papal station in Geneva, he was kind and generous enough, going beyond the call of duty, to drive several miles to bring the Holy Communion to my wife at the Clinique de Genolier every single day for a month. We visited him in the Baltics and journeyed to Mexico to see him once. He was the first nuncio to be assigned by the Holy See to the three Baltic states after the fall of the Soviet Union. When I accompanied him to the Lithuanian capital of Vilnius to help with his move into a new sanctuary, I warmed up to the local Secretary of the

Nunciature, Monsignor Mario Cassari. During the few days I spent at the complex, I quickly gravitated to him because his technique reminded me of the level of artistry I aspired to achieve at Indiana University.

Monsignor Justo Mullor Garcia.

I never associated priesthood with artistic talents, but he was a master of surreal abstract paintings, and I took a liking to his creative touch. Moreover, his abilities went beyond the depth of most abstract painters, and when he dedicated two of his prized paintings to me as a gift, I was honored. The portraits transformed his communist experience into a unique artistic interpretation, influenced by colorful details that chronicled an inimitable political journey. He took me on a tour of the underground painting scene in a different part of the city, where I came across multiple spectacular masterpieces by great painters who used their art to depict life in a state of captivity behind the Iron Curtain. Later that day, when we had dinner as usual with Monsignor Mullor, I was tempted to ask my hosts about the permanent diet of baked or fried cabbage with cabbage soup, which had been par for the course ever since I arrived. They both nodded to acknowledge me and began to eat. I shrugged off my own question and joined them. Months afterward, my wife and I managed to get together with Monsignor Mullor in Estonia for the Christmas holidays. Our friendship blossomed deeply over the years, and he joined us on memorable vacations at multiple destinations. To this day, he remains our spiritual brother.

Having the capacity to acknowledge God's presence in our lives has enabled my wife and I to accept the premise that to not have children is to also respond to another one of God's plans. Hence, our fate will serve its purpose by giving us the opportunity to overcome the role of our core biological family and cast a keen eye on the children of others in order to nurture their needs. We have many godsons and daughters around the world, to whom we continue to give our undivided attention. Every single one of them is our source of joy, and this also is a blessing.

Although, not having children has placed us at the disposal of those who providence has positioned in our path, I have always known that not having children has also allowed me to continue my commitment toward achieving peace in search of a better world. I could not begin to imagine facing the torment of being a parent who must abandon their children to fulfill another duty.

For my wife and I, God's purpose is also reflected in the variety of his creation. The beauty of his creation resides in the diversity of

Our Common Faith

human beings whose skin colors are akin to a palette, ranging from milky white to ebony black. It would have been easy for the Almighty to create us all in uniform colors and sizes, but instead, he chose to ensure that each person is a reflection of the unique power of his creativity. Unfortunately, there are still many people who waste a lot of time failing to appreciate the uniqueness of each other. For his part, the Almighty uses each of us in the same way a man and a woman would contribute the XX and XY chromosomes to give birth to life.

Despite our many imperfections and failures, my wife and I will always invoke the power of our unique God in all aspects of our lives. We have embraced the force behind all creation as a source of inspiration on a daily basis as we continue to appreciate every waking moment. All my life, I have tried my very best to serve the Almighty, and in so doing, I have been blessed and he has illuminated the road on which I continue to travel with but one desire: to communicate these sentiments to others who seek happiness in God's guiding light and reaffirm the belief that our religion shall not divide us. For it is God we seek, and in that quest, spirituality must unite us in *one common faith*—and *HIS* world shall be a better place for all humankind.

A Dream for Peace

"He is taking back the port of Berbera from the Russians and charging you with the responsibility of delivering it to the Americans," I said to the president enthusiastically. He paused and smiled back at me. "Hmmm, you don't seem to know the Westerners very well," he remarked. "Between us Africans, we never fail to honor our verbal commitments. But for Westerners, words are without merit. Everything must be in writing."

Chapter Twelve

Memos from the Cold War

My commitment to continue nurturing and fostering a deeper insight on the commonality of our different faiths frequently intersected at a crossroads with the politics of diplomacy. Many heads of state were familiar with the skillful diplomatic abilities of President Houphouët-Boigny and had come to see him as an expert in discreet diplomacy. When they sought his help and counsel to resolve political disputes, I often found myself at the helm of communications between him and an array of world leaders. During the Cold War, many unique circumstances placed us in the midst of the power struggle between the East and the West. The small country of Somalia, located on Africa's easternmost coast, an area known as "the Horn of Africa," was of strategic geographic importance to the superpowers because of its easy access to the Arabian Peninsula and its vast oil reserves. Flowing gingerly between Yemen and Somalia, the Gulf of Aden had quietly become an epicenter for political posturing between the East and the West since the 1950s, even well into the height of the Cold War in the 1960s.

At the start of the Cold War, the US was a reliable ally of Emperor Haile Selassie I of Ethiopia, Somalia's archrival. Upon gaining independence in 1960, Somalia was seen as a beacon of hope for democracy in the Horn of Africa. In November 1962, the country's first president, Aden Abdulle Osman, sent his prime minister, Abdirashid Ali Sharmarke, to the United States for a meeting with President John F. Kennedy to cultivate a political relationship with the aim of positioning them as a more reliable US partner in the region. The delegation arrived in Washington and received a very warm welcome by President Kennedy. But nonetheless, the ensuing discussions did not completely go as expected. The Kennedy administration leaned more toward establishing socioeconomic cooperation with Somalia, falling short of a deal that included military hardware—a key component to the Somalis' objectives. At the time, the US was not prepared to jeopardize an entrenched relationship with neighboring country Ethiopia. But regardless of US sensitivities, a determined President Osman was keen on boosting his nation's resources after having only recently seen their borders redrawn by Great Britain and Italy. Not long after their meeting with President Kennedy, the government of Somalia formed a military and diplomatic alliance with the Soviet Union.

The second president, Abdirashid Ali Sharmarke, was assassinated by a bodyguard in 1969, and the military staged a coup a day after his funeral. Major General Siad Barre of the Supreme Revolutionary Council took over the country, disbanded the country's parliament, suspended the constitution, and began experimenting with a unique form of socialism (scientific socialism) that was reinforced with traditional Islamic principles. The country's bond with the USSR remained strong. Within months, the alliance paved the way for the Soviets to take control of the deepwater port of Berbera, on the northwestern Somali seaboard.

During Barre's tenure as the chairman of the OAU (1974 to 1975), he visited a majority of Arab and African countries. His visit to Côte d'Ivoire in 1974 had the most impact on his political ambitions. It became abundantly clear to us that he had done his homework and knew of President Houphouët-Boigny's many accomplishments. I was particularly taken in by the level of respect and reverence he had for the president. He shared his enthusiasm about Côte d'Ivoire's future and praised our achievements in the agricultural and industrial sectors. In our private conversations, he let President Houphouët know how much he had come to admire him, and he expressed his desire to emulate Côte d'Ivoire's progress in Somalia. I was impressed by how much he opened up to the president—like an old friend. He spelled out his intentions in succinct detail, emphasizing again and again that he saw no obstacles on the way to progress. The vision he spoke of was a bold one that could potentially foster a robust development agenda for his nation. We knew that such sacrifices would be immense, and his political platform would have to be reengineered if his plans to pull his country out of political and economic difficulties were to succeed.

On a factory tour with President Siad Barre.

Barely a couple of months prior to his Côte d'Ivoire trip, Haile Selassie I was overthrown. A communist-inspired military junta took over the reins of power, and as expected, the roles of the superpowers shifted. The USSR was now Ethiopia's new ally and hoped to bring the former enemies under the same umbrella. But for Siad Barre, Russia's alliance with a long-term enemy nation was a deal breaker. He began to focus heavily on developing a stronger bond with President Houphouët-Boigny and solicited his counsel on many matters, especially on the issue of warming up to the West.

A Dream for Peace

Sabti, 5ta Luulyo, 1975

Jaalle Siyaad iyo La-taliyaha Madaxweynaha dalka Ifori Kost, oo wada hadal yeeshay.

With President Siad Barre.

I was thrust squarely in the middle of their diplomatic foray. The topic surrounding the strategic port of Berbera was broached a few times during our interactions, leading me to believe that he was seriously reevaluating his treaty with the USSR. I thought perhaps his new posture could lead to a cooperative agreement with the Americans. When he first came to Côte d'Ivoire, he was in the company of young Somali professionals of great value—graduates of American and British universities. Also present during the visit were his ambassador to France, Mohamed Said Samatar, a bright and active fellow, and his Finance Minister. Ambassador Samatar, who hailed from a prominent Somali family, became our communications liaison in lieu of an embassy in either of our countries.

Memos from the Cold War

A fraternal friendship with President Houphouët began and continued to blossom after Siad Barre's maiden visit. I was dispatched to Mogadishu on many diplomatic errands to follow up on talks with him and provide direction to facilitate his amended political stance. Once our communication routine had been established, he was assured I was always a phone call away, but if he needed some counseling on highly classified and complex matters, he asked Ambassador Samatar to send an invitation requesting my presence in Mogadishu.

He did not hide the fact that he intended to capitalize on President Houphouët's ties with France. To him, the relationship with France was a critical part of his political objectives regarding resolving an issue with neighboring Djibouti. The origin of the Djibouti dispute found its roots years earlier, when Somalia achieved its independence and merged with the former colonies of Italian and British Somalia. The newly independent country's leaders had but one wish: to take back the ancestral land known then as French Somaliland (present-day Djibouti), which was at the time, a French colony. France later changed the colony's name to the Afars and the Issas. But after a referendum, which was contested by the new Republic of Somalia, the colony remained under the administration of the French government. Ten years after Somalia's independence, a revolt started brewing in the Afars and the Issas. Somalia's relationship with France became increasingly strained as the French government's suspicions and accusations of Somali interference in its affairs grew louder. Siad Barre was even accused of masterminding the revolt. He asked for our help to tone down the heated rhetoric and find some common ground.

When I arrived in Mogadishu, he expressed his intentions with a spirit of compassion toward his fellow men. He wanted to end the suffering of his brethren of the Afars and Issas region. "They are being subjected to oppression, injustice, and inequality by France," he told me. "And they have in large part escaped to

A Dream for Peace

Somalia to seek refuge." I felt the intensity of his pain and the level of his distress. The state of affairs was acutely urgent. Somalia was providing asylum to a massive number of refugees, and the situation had placed an enormous burden on the country, which was already one of the world's poorest.

In a letter to President Houphouët, he decried the injustice: *"Our relationship with the French government has been deteriorating day by day, despite our expressed desire to hold discussions in a spirit of harmony with France—with the hope of arriving at a peaceful solution—one that is acceptable to the various stakeholders in the fate of French Somaliland. But the response by the French government has taken the form of an unacceptable provocation. They have sent many troops, most of whom are equipped with ultramodern war equipment, reinforced by a French fleet with missile-launcher units and marines with mobile missiles. All their actions constitute a continuing threat to our sovereignty and threaten the peace and stability of our entire region."*

He instructed me to ask President Houphouët to mediate and speak to French President Valéry Giscard d'Estaing about the principle of independence for the people of the Afars and Issas territory. "Mr. President," I interjected, "indeed, I realize the drama that has been imposed upon you, and I am very saddened by the suffering of our brothers. I will spare no effort to try to ease their pain. Knowing President Houphouët's sensitivity to such humanitarian matters, be reassured that he will dedicate his energy and resources to help you resolve this inextricable issue." We shook hands warmly and I left.

I was deeply perturbed by all that was said. The situation was reminiscent of Algeria's independence struggle with France. I thought about ways and means to prevent further bloodshed—to end the unbearable suffering of my brothers and push for their liberation. President Houphouët could sense my exasperation. I stressed the urgency of the matter, especially, with regards to the refugees, and let him know that I had made promises to the Somali leader on his behalf, saying, "I told him that there was no doubt that my president would commit to reaching out to the French government." "You did well," he commented, with the utmost humility. "We are here to help solve problems. It is a difficult task, but I will try my best, and the Almighty will help us."

President Valéry Giscard d'Estaing attended the annual French-African summit in Bangui (Central Africa) in 1975. Just shy of a few weeks from the commencement date, President Houphouët kept his word and engaged the leader of France in discussions. Even though various leaders from the OAU nations, heads of state from the Arab League nations, and other diplomats had tried their hardest to resolve the volatile situation, either through institutional channels or other reputable sources, no one would be more successful at making inroads with the French government than President Houphouët.

He worked discreetly and pursued his diplomatic objectives without ever publicizing his motives or seeking acknowledgement from anyone. By the summer of 1975, when he felt content enough that he had a solid commitment from France, he dispatched me to Mogadishu to update President Siad Barre on developments. "France has committed, and is ready to grant independence to Djibouti," I informed him. But he was guarded and somewhat skeptical because of the continuing atrocities on the ground. "The Foreign Legion continues to kill men, women, children, and the elderly indiscriminately. The situation in Djibouti is still explosive and despite this, I have never encouraged a revolt. I have always advised everyone to cultivate patience—to negotiate and partake in dialogue," he expressed. "Please implore President Houphouët to be steadfast and persistent in pursuing his mediation. Take with you the following message to him." He shook his head before articulating his thought:

"I have spoken with many brothers regarding the problem of the relationship between France and Somalia, but I could not, through the Arabs who are friends of France, establish any dialogue.

A Dream for Peace

I am counting on you, and you only, to continue to work to help us thaw the situation. And I do so in the best interest of France, as well as that of Somalia. I am quite certain that you will succeed. Know that from our side, you have carte blanche to act and negotiate on our behalf. Regardless of the course of history and events, I promise to stay calm. I will remain calm, even in the face of provocation. We are ready to turn the page, and we are sincere when we say that we want friendship with France."

Before my departure, I handed him a generous donation on behalf of the people of Côte d'Ivoire to emphasize our solidarity with the refugees.

We continued to give him updates on our progress, and he kept us in the loop regarding developments in Djibouti. Eventually, the tension between France and Somalia eased up, but President Houphouët remained resolved and committed to the complete liberation of Djibouti until the country finally gained independence in 1977. Thereafter, Siad Barre adopted a very conciliatory position and requested the reestablishment of cooperative relations with France. But to this day, Djibouti remains a strategically important nation for the French government, and they continue to maintain a military base in the country.

President Houphouët believed that nothing less than prudent cooperation with the USSR was best for the development of Africa. Quite discreetly, he tried very hard to encourage other African countries to resist the communist influence. He used to say that African countries had neither factories to nationalize nor commerce to put under state control, but he insisted we needed to create factories and organize our trade policies. I agreed with his premise and worked with him to achieve that purpose for the sake of peace and freedom.

We sought to protect the Horn of Africa and the entire African continent from communist penetration and tried to prevent the migration of communism into Africa by way of Somalia's shores.

Memos from the Cold War

To achieve our purpose during each of my meetings with President Siad Barre, I would emphasize the advantage for his country to free itself from the grip of the Soviet Union and turn toward the West. While we were trying to make some progress, the antagonism between the East and the West surfaced in Somalia because of the port of Berbera.

In the agreement between the USSR and Somalia, the Russians committed to improve the infrastructure of the port of Berbera in return for full access to the seaport. However, barely a couple of years after the agreement was executed, the word was out about Russia's missiles facility in the harbor. It was widely reported in US print media when journalists were prevented from entering the port to verify the accuracy of the facts, and concerns grew across the great political divide, with the Western nations becoming more anxious.

President Houphouët was contacted by a few key allies in the West to help validate the report. At the time, I was about to leave on a diplomatic trip to Somalia for discussions regarding Djibouti. I met with a baffled yet defiant President Siad Barre in Mogadishu. He appeared a bit embarrassed to be on the radar of the US, because his change of political orientation was still in play. To be seen as an anti-Westerner hiding Russian missiles was the antithesis of a reformed politician.

But nevertheless, he assured me that there was no such base in Berbera. "Tell him [President Houphouët] to reassure his allies in the West that I am a victim of false accusations..." I brought back the following message to Abidjan:

"We are in principle, and by choice, leaning against building any foreign bases on our soil. Allowing the establishment of a base on our territory is to abandon a part of our national sovereignty ... It will be tantamount to mortgaging our tranquility, because such a base can be used against us. A base in the midst of this frantic arms race will lead to the creation of another base. The Russians have never dared to

A Dream for Peace

ask me to build a base on our soil. Some Americans have said that we have a base in Berbera. Berbera is a Somali port, which is open to all our friends. The French and the Italians have already used our facilities in Berbera, and all of our friends are welcome to use our facilities."

I delivered the message to President Houphouët, who embarked on a fruitless attempt to convince the West of the veracity of Siad Barre's assertions.

The global military competition between the US and USSR, which had led to a period of escalating tensions between the superpowers, found a flashpoint in the Somali invasion of eastern Ethiopia in 1977. Siad Barre had attempted to gain control of the Somali-speaking Ogaden region. The region was granted to Haile Selassie in the aftermath of World War II by the British, with the consent of the United States. After the fall of the Ethiopian Empire, months of uncertainty followed before Mengistu Haile Mariam emerged as the chief of the junta. He became the country's head of state in 1977. In the eyes of the Soviets, he was a genuine Marxist-Leninist, and he quickly gained their favor. When the war broke out, Siad Barre managed to take back some of the ancestral lands. The Russians escalated their military aid to Ethiopia with more arms, while Fidel Castro dispatched some Cuban troops to support the effort. In October 1977, in the midst of the war, I was dispatched to Mogadishu with a series of recommendations for President Siad Barre:

> *"I think that if you were entertaining some illusions about maintaining the same old relationship with the Soviet Union, you have to realize that life has never been neutral. If friends of our friends are supposed to be our friends, it has always been difficult for a man as it is for a state to either maintain a good relationship with two men or two countries that are enemies. The Soviet Union has a duty to choose openly between Somalia and Ethiopia, and they revel such a favorable situation. They enjoy the simultaneous*

confidence of two enemy countries. Thus, it is clearly up to you, my dear brother, to make that choice."

Félix Houphouët-Boigny.

Handing over documents to President Siad Barre.

He seemed exasperated, not by the content of the letter but, as he expressed to me, by the very notion of being taken for granted. "President Houphouët is right," he said. "The Russians, for better or for worse, are quite the pragmatists. They are taking advantage of the situation to satisfy their own objectives." I told him that it was in fact President Houphouët's hope that he sever ties with the Russians without delay. He knew that his next move was vital. "*The two superpowers are extremely powerful, and yet they do nothing for Africa other than things they can use directly or indirectly for their own prestige,*" he lamented. "*Our cooperation with them is only a side affair which they can easily dispose of. They only view us as satellites of power.*" "I share your opinion, Mr. President," I said, "but the Western bloc does not constitute an obstacle to our development. We are always free to choose our options, knowing all along that the ideology of communism is fatal to Africa. It embraces a path which kills our fundamental aspirations—to make our continent a developed continent." He breathed deeply and let out a sigh of relief, nodding in agreement. "My dear Dr. Berrah, I will reflect on President Houphouët-Boigny's proposal and adopt at my earliest convenience a decision in the best interest of Somalia."

I went back to Abidjan. Less than two weeks after I last saw him, he abrogated the treaty of friendship and cooperation with the USSR and expelled his Soviet advisors from the country. By mid-December of that year, the Russians escalated their support and asked Castro to dispatch twenty thousand Cuban troops to Ethiopia.

In the midst of the skirmishes, I received an urgent call from Ambassador Samatar, sometime in December 1977, summoning me to see President Siad Barre. I was unable to find a direct flight to Mogadishu that very night but figured I could catch a flight from Sanaa, Yemen. Under normal circumstances, a Russian propeller aircraft would not have been my first choice, but that was my only option. It was a low-wing cantilever monoplane with tricycle landing gear. I was offered a boarding pass as long as I agreed to carry my suitcase aboard. Stepping off the narrow stairs onto the aircraft, I lost my footing and grazed my head on the edge of the doorway. My scalp started to bleed profusely. The crew attended to me with a first aid kit, but the blood had dripped enough to stain my shirt. Amenities on the plane were practically nonexistent, but thankfully the duration of the flight was just under two hours. I waited patiently until we landed in Mogadishu and hopped into a waiting car. My sense of duty and the urgency of the situation overwhelmed every aspect of my concerns regarding my tawdry appearance. I was not remotely tempted to ask the driver to drive to my hotel for a chance to tidy up and change clothes. By the time I arrived at the presidential palace, I had stopped bleeding, but there were a few traces of dried blood on my forehead. President Siad Barre was astounded to see me in my bloodstained condition. He ordered a palace attendant to escort me to the nearest bathroom, and I soon appeared refreshed after a few minutes to begin my assignment. "Mr. President, thank you for the courtesy," I said. "It's my pleasure. I hope you are okay to proceed," he replied. "But yes, of course." When I said I was, he continued: "*I would like to convey to President Houphouët-Boigny all rights to the port of Berbera, which as you know, has been in the hands of the Russians for some time. I would like him to oversee the transfer of unencumbered rights of use to the Americans. I believe he is correct. We have nothing to do with the Russians, and with his help, I can align myself with the Americans.*" I suspected there was a major diplomatic maneuver on the horizon, based on our most recent communiqués, but this was a significant turn of events, and I was ecstatic. It was well worth my dramatic entrance.

    The magnitude of his decision placed me in a very celebratory mood, and the resulting euphoria flooded me with more than enough excitement to trigger a sudden lapse in my otherwise very professional composure, despite many years of diplomatic experience. After having made such a bold statement, it never crossed my mind to ask President Siad Barre for a written confirmation of his historic decision. President Houphouët-Boigny was the one who pulled me back on track when I reported to him.

    "He is taking back the port of Berbera from the Russians and charging you with the responsibility of delivering it to the Americans," I said to the president enthusiastically. He paused and smiled back at me. "Hmmm, you don't seem to know the Westerners very well," he remarked. "Between us Africans, we never fail to honor our verbal commitments. But for Westerners, words are without merit. Everything must be in writing," he cautioned. "I will

A Dream for Peace

be taking the next flight to Mogadishu," I promised.

I went to meet Ambassador Samatar in Paris, and we flew together to Mogadishu. It took about four days for the letter to be composed and executed by President Siad Barre, but I enjoyed the company of his ministers and other dignitaries. When we met at the presidential palace, I received a thirty-six-page confirmation letter for President Houphouët-Boigny. Ambassador Samatar accompanied me to Abidjan and presented the letter to the president. I later translated it into French for him. In official context, the letter bequeathed the strategic port in the Gulf of Aden to the US. Without hesitation, he contacted the US ambassador in Abidjan to inform him that he was in possession of an urgent message for President Carter. It was Christmas season.

I was immediately dispatched to Egypt, where I hoped to catch up to President Carter, who was on an important official trip to India and the Middle East (Iran, Saudi Arabia, and Egypt). I camped out in Cairo until the US ambassador to Egypt asked me to fly to Saudi Arabia to connect with President Carter, who was scheduled to arrive in the country on January 3, 1978.

The flight to Riyadh was about two hours. I was greeted by members of the Saudi royal protocol and taken to see US Secretary of State Cyrus Vance. We traveled together to meet with President Carter at the royal palace in Riyadh. We met at approximately 2:00 a.m. local time. "This is wonderful," he said, after reading the letter. "Please give my warmest gratitude to President Houphouët-Boigny." We shook hands. "I will, Mr. President. Indeed I will." Then he asked: "By the way, is King Khalid aware of this?" "I don't think so, Mr. President," I told him. "The Saudis are stakeholders in this matter," he responded. "You need to inform them, because the port is as important to the US as it is for them." "Certainly, Mr. President, it will be my utmost priority this morning," I promised. "Good night, Mr. President. It was a privilege to make your acquaintance." I returned to my hotel.

Memos from the Cold War

I met with the Special Advisor to the King, a very influential Syrian, to inform him of what President Houphouët-Boigny was able to obtain from President Siad Barre. In the midst of our discussion, he received a call alerting him that President Boumediène would soon arrive at the airport, on transit to Algiers after a trip to Iran. Boumediène was at that time negotiating a solution to the conflict between Iran and Iraq. The advisor asked me to join him and King Khalid to welcome Boumédiène with the royal entourage. However, it was against my diplomatic protocol. I went to meet with Boumediène at his hotel that evening, and as expected, he was pleased to hear the news. I returned to Abidjan within hours.

Indeed, the document could have been delivered to President Carter by Somalia's US ambassador in Washington. But Siad Barre had chosen President Houphouët-Boigny for his sincerity. He had hoped that with this extraordinary gesture, the US would begin to fully throw its weight in the fray and give credence to his government's objectives. Months following his expulsion of the Russians from his country, the US remained on the sidelines, hesitant to give him their full backing because they deemed him the aggressor in the Ogaden War. Moreover, they sought to avoid a proxy war with the USSR. Nonetheless, Somalia had finally become their ally on the Horn of Africa, and their alliance would eventually be effectuated, sometime after the end of the war, when Somali troops had retreated behind their country's borders.

A Dream for Peace

RÉPUBLIQUE DE CÔTE D'IVOIRE

SERVICE DU CHIFFRE

CLAIR

Diffusion :

A.E
DIR/CAB
S.P
CAB/4

TÉLÉGRAMME

ARRIVÉE

Origine : MOGADISCIO
Adresse : ABIDJAN

N° de circulation : 215
Date d'émission : 1500/26/0
Date de réception : 0907/27/1
1976

H.E. FELIX HOUPHOUET-BOIGNY PRESIDENT
OF THE REPUBLIC OF IVORY COAST ABIDJAN

N° 62/ EXCELLENCY CMA EYE AM CONFIDENT THAT YOUR
EXCELLENCY IS WELL AWARE OF THE CRITICAL SITUATION
PREVAILING IN FRENCH SOMALILAND AND THE LATEST DANGEROUS
POLITICAL DEVELOPMENTS IN THE TERRITORY WHICH IF UNCHE-
CKED COULD HAVE UNFORTUNATE CONSEQUENCES FOR THE WHOLE
REGION. FOLLOWING THE OVERWHELMING AND UNSWERVING SUPPORT
GIVEN BY THE OAU AND INTERNATIONAL COMMUNITY THROUGH
INTERLIA THE UN GENERAL ASSEMBLY RESOLUTION APPROVED
BY 109 MEMBER STATES DECEMBER LAST TO THE PEOPLE OF
FRENCH SOMALILAND FOR THE ATTAINMENT OF IMMEDIATE CMA
UNCONDITIONAL INDEPENDENCE AND THE WITHDRAWAL OF FRENCH
MILITARY FORCES AND BASES CMA THE FRENCH COLINIAL POWER
IS NOWW RESORTING TO DESPICABLE STRATEGEMS AND MANOEUVRE
AIMED AT GRANTING A FORMAL AND HOLLOW INDEPENDENCE TO
FRENCH SOMALILAND IN ORDER TO APPEASE INTERNATIONAL
OPINION WHILE AT THE SAME TIME CREATING A PUPPET REGIME
HEADED BY ITS FAITHFUL STOOGE ALI AREF CMA AN INDIVIDUAL
WHO DOES NOT ENJOY ANY SUPPORT WHATSOEVER FROM THE
PEOPLE OF THE TERRITORY. IN ORDER TO PRESERVE ITS STRATE
GIC INTERESTES IN THE TERRITORY CMA THROUG THE IMPOSITIO
OF THE ALI AREF PUPPET REGIME CMA THE FRENCH COLINIAL
POWER IS FULLY DEPLOYING ITS HUGE MILITARY FORCES STATIO
NED IN THE TERRITORY AND IS CURRENTLY ENGAGED IN THE
PROCESS OF INCREASING TIS FORCES AND ENLARGIN ITS
DEFENCE INSTALLATIONS OF THE TEERITORY. THUS THE OPPOSIT
PARTIES AND LIBERATION MOVEMENTS CMA WHO ARE THE
LEGITIMATE REPRESENTATIVES OF THE PEOPLE CMA ARE BEING
SUBJECTED TO CONSTANT HARASSMENT CMA ARRESTS AND TORTURE

.../...

CMA ARE BEING SUBJECTED TO CONSTANT HARASSMENT CMA ARRESTS AND TORTURE CMA WHILLE MANY OF THEIR LEADERS ARE SUMARILY BEING DEPORTED FROM THE TERRITORY . ALL POLITICAL ATIVITY AND OPPOSITION TO THE LOCAL REGIME IS THEREFORE PROHIBITED AND THE VOICE OF THE MASSES IS SILENCED THROUGH INDISCRIMANATE KILLINGS CMA CONSTANT SEARCHING IN THE HOMES OF THOSE SUSPECTED OF SYMPATHISING WITH THE PROGRESSIVE FORCES AND A STATE OF INCREASING TENSION IS DAILY DEVELOPING AND AN EXPLOSIVE EMERGENCY SITUATION IS PREVAILING THREE. IT IS MY CONVICTION EXCELLENCY THAT IN VIEW OF THE ABOVE CRITICAL SITUATION AND ITS IMPLICATIONS FOR THE STABILITY AND PEACE IN THE REGION EYE DEEMED IT NECESSARY TO INFORM YOU AND APPEAL TO YOUR EXCELLENCY SO THAT YOU MAY INTERVENE IN THE MATTER AND RENDER JUSTICE AND ALL POSSIBLE ASSISTANCE TO THE PEOPLE OF FRENCH SOMALILAND IN ORDER TO ENABLE THE TO ATTAIN THEIR SACRED RIGHT TO GENUINE AND UNCONDITIONAL INDEPENDENCE. FINALLY EYE CONSIDER IT PERTINENT TO INFORM YOU ON THE CONSISTENT VIOLATIONS OF THE INTERNATIONAL NORMS AND PRACTICE RELATING TO THE DIPLOMATIC IMMUNITY. AS A MATTER OF FACT THE SOMALI CONSULATE GENERAL IN DJIBOUTI HAS BEEN SUBJECTE FOR MORE THANT TWO WEEKS TO A STATE OF SEIGEBY THE COLONIAL GENDERMARINE AND THE STAFF AND THEIR CARS ARE BEING DAILY PERQUISITIONED AND HARISSED DESPITE STRONG PROTESTS TO THE FRENCH GOVERNMENT BY THE SOMALI DEMOCRATIC REPUBLIC. IT IS UNFORTUNATE TO NOTE THAT THE FRENCH GOVERNMENT HAS NOT SO FAR GIVEN ANY JUSTIFICATION TO THE VIOULATIONS.

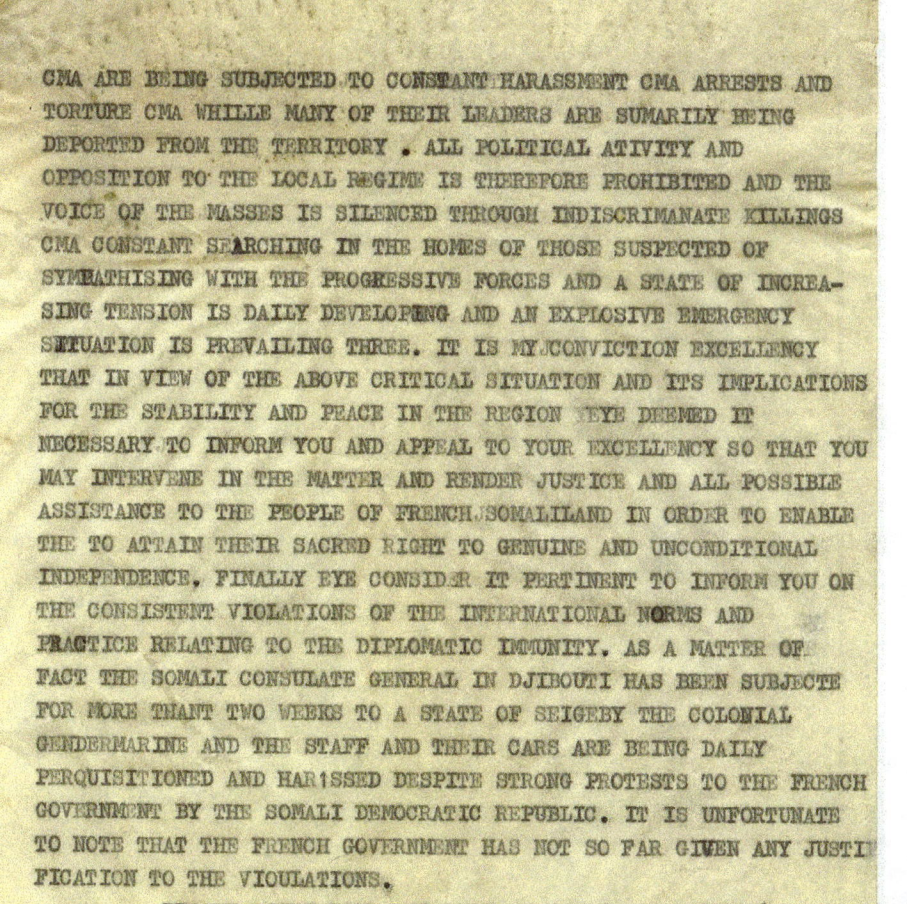

PLEASE ACCET YOUR EXCELLENCY MY HIGHEST ESTEEM/-

MAJOR GENERAL MOHAMED SIAD BARRE
PRESIDENT OF THE SUPREME REVOLUTIONARYCOUNCIL./-

A Dream for Peace

JAMHUURIYADDA DIMUQ. SOOMAALIYA Madaxtooyada Golaha Sare ee Kacaanka MADAXWEYNAHA	**SOMALI DEMOCRATIC REPUBLIC** Presidency of the Supreme Revolutionary Council THE PRESIDENT

My Dear Brother,

Allow me first and foremost to extend, on behalf of the Supreme Revolutionary Council, the Government and the people of the Somali Democratic Republic and in my own, to Your Excellency and through you to the Government and fraternal people of Ivory Coast my brotherly greetings and sincere best wishes for Your Excellency's good health and for the progress and prosperity of your people.

Indeed, I recall with great pleasure the memorable visit which I have had the honour to pay to your great and beautiful country in late 1974 and the warm reception and hospitality extended to me and my delegation which no doubt was a clear manifestation of the close and deep fraternal sentiments of friendship and brotherhood happily existing between our two peoples.

I also recall with a sense of inspiration our very fruitful discussions touching upon our bilateral relations as well as

H.E. FELIX HOUPHOUET-BOIGNY,
PRESIDENT OF THE REPUBLIC OF IVORY COAST,
ABIDJAN.

JAMHUURIYADDA DIMUQ. SOOMAALIYA Madaxtooyada Golaha Sare ee Kacaanka	**SOMALI DEMOCRATIC REPUBLIC** Presidency of the Supreme Revolutionary Council
MADAXWEYNAHA	THE PRESIDENT

- 2 -

African and international issues, which afforded me the opportunity not only for a brotherly exchange of views but also the occasion to benefit from your wisdom, sagacity and able-statesmanship; particularly on matters pertaining to African unity and co-operation as well as the total liberation of our continent from colonial bondage and racial domination. This has left a positive and lasting imprint on my mind since your constructive ideas have and would, I am confident, continue to contribute to the furtherance of the noble ideals and fundamental principles for which we all yearn and resolutely stand for and in particular our long cherished cardinal goal of eradication of all forms of colonialism and racial domination from Africa.

Excellency, I wish at this juncture to address myself to the issue of the decolonization of the Somali Coast (French Somaliland) which, as you no doubt are aware, has now reached a crucial stage which will be decisive in the determination of the future destiny of the people of the territory.

In this regard Your Excellency is no doubt as much aware that the Government of the Republic of France has been in contact with the Somali Democratic Republic recently. During the course of official discussions, we called upon the French

A Dream for Peace

JAMHUURIYADDA DIMUQ. SOOMAALIYA	SOMALI DEMOCRATIC REPUBLIC
Madaxtooyada Golaha Sare ee Kacaanka	Presidency of the Supreme Revolutionary Council
MADAXWEYNAHA	**THE PRESIDENT**

– 3 –

Government to take the necessary measures in order to create an atmosphere that will enable the people of the territory to fully exercise their rights under the fullest democratic conditions for the attainment of their noble aspirations to genuine immediate and unconditional independence in accordance with the relevant Resolutions of the Organization of African Unity, the Arab League, the Non-Aligned nations Conferences and the United Nations.

I sincerely trust, confident as I am in Your Excellency's firm commitment and dedication to the cause of total liberation of our continent, that you will spare no effort in rendering your valuable contribution to the immediate realization of genuine and unconditional independence to the people of the territory.

With these considerations I have pleasure to send you this message with Jaalle Dr. Hussein Abdulkadir Kassim, our Secretary of State for Mineral and Water Resources, who will brief Your Excellency on the latest major development in our country as well as on the issue of decolonization of the Somali Coast and discuss with you our bilateral relations in particular and the situation in Africa in general. I have given him full

./

JAMHUURIYADDA DIMUQ. SOOMAALIYA	SOMALI DEMOCRATIC REPUBLIC
Madaxtooyada Golaha Sare ee Kacaanka	Presidency of the Supreme Revolutionary Council
MADAXWEYNAHA	THE PRESIDENT

- 4 -

credence in discussing these vital matters with you on my behalf and you may also wish to convey to me through him any advice or idea designed to further the African cause and to further enhance our bilateral co-operation.

Once again, please accept Excellency and Brother the expressions and assurances of my highest fraternal consideration and esteem together with my sincere wishes for your continued health and happiness and for the progress and prosperity of your country.

Mogadishu, 13th April, 1976.

MAJOR-GENERAL MOHAMED SIAD BARRE,
PRESIDENT OF THE SUPREME REVOLUTIONARY COUNCIL.

A Dream for Peace

Sheryl P. Walter   Declassified/Released   US Department of State   EO Systematic Review   20 Mar 2014

Message Text

SECRET

PAGE 01   ABIDJA 00003   011601Z
ACTION SS-25
INFO OCT-01 ISO-00 SSO-00 /026 W
------------------053755 011602Z /44

O 011425Z JAN 78
FM AMEMBASSY ABIDJAN
TO SECSTATE WASHDC NIACT IMMEDIATE 6767

S E C R E T
ABIDJAN 0003

EXDIS

FOR EXECUTIVE SECRETARY - PLEASE PASS TO SECRETARY VANCE AND REPEAT REF (C) AND (D)

E.O. 11652: XGDS-2
TAGS: PGOV, IV, US
SUBJECT: HOUPHOUET'S MESSAGE TO PRESIDENT CARTER AND SECRETARY'S MEETING WITH GHOULEM BERRAH

REF: (A) SECTO 13024; (B) TOSEC 130029 (STATE 309968); (C) ABIDJAN 11931; ((D) ABIDJAN 11909

1. AT PRESIDENT HOUPHOUET-BOIGNY'S NEW YEAR'S DAY RECEPTION FOR DIPLOMATIC CORPS THIS MORNING HOUPHOUET TOOK ME ASIDE TO DISCUSS BRIEFLY HIS MESSAGE TO PRESIDENT CARTER. CONTRARY TO MY ASSUMPTION (REFTEL B), MESSAGE DOES NOT RPT NOT DEAL WITH ARAB-ISRAEL QUESTION BUT WITH HOUPHOUET'S RECENT INITIATIVE TO PERSUADE SOMALI PRESIDENT SIAD BARRE TO IMPROVE RELATIONS WITH KENYA (REFTELS C AND D). HOUPHOUET SAID HE WAS EXTREMELY GRATIFIED WITH SIAD BARRE'S RESPONSE AND BELIEVED THAT SOMALI PRESIDENT'S WILLINGNESS TO SIGN NON-AGGRESSION PACT WITH KENYA SHOULD OPEN THE WAY TO COMPLETE NORMALIZATION OF SOMALI-KENYA RELATIONS. HOUPHOUET WISHED PRESIDENT CARTER TO HAVE A DIRECT ACCOUNT OF THESE DEVELOPMENTS, SINCE US AS WELL AS UK INFLUENCE WOULD BE ESSENTIAL TO KEEP MATTERS ON COURSE, AND HAD WRITTEN THE MESSAGE TO BE DELIVERED BY GHOULEM BERRAH FOR THIS PURPOSE.
SECRET

Memos from the Cold War

Sheryl P. Walter Declassified/Released US Department of State EO Systematic Review 20 Mar 2014

SECRET

PAGE 02   ABIDJA 00003 011601Z

2. I TOLD HOUPHOUET THAT SECRETARY VANCE WOULD BE GLAD TO RECEIV

BERRAH IN RIYADH (REFTEL A) AND THAT AS SOON AS I RECEIVED FURTHER INFORMATION ON THE TIME AND PLACE I WOULD PASS IT ALONG TO HOUPHOUET'S AIDE, GEORGES OUEGNIN, SO THAT BERRAH COULD BE ALERTED.
I ASKED HOUPHOUET WHETHER HIS MESSAGE TO THE PRESIDENT ADDRESSED

OTHER SUBJECTS THAN SOMALI-KENYAN RELATIONS. HOUPHOUET SAID THAT IT DID NOT, BUT THAT BERRAH FOLLOWED MID-EAST DEVELOPMENTS CLOSELY ON HOUPHOUET'S BEHALF AND ANY THOUGHTS THAT SECRETARY VANCE COULD IMPART TO BERRAH ON THE STATUS OF EGYPTIAN-ISRAELI NEGOTIA- TIONS, AND RELATED DEVELOPMENTS, WOULD BE OF GREAT VALUE TO HOUPHOUET.

3. I SAID THAT I WOULD CONVEY THIS TO THE SECRETARY AND HOUPHOUET ASKED THAT I ALSO EXPRESS HIS NEW YEAR'S GREETINGS. AND PERSONAL REGARDS TO PRESIDENT CARTER AND TO THE SECRETARY HOUPHOUET GREATLY APPRECIATED THE SECRETARY'S WILLINGNESS TO SEE BERRAH IN RIYADH AND HOPED HE WOULD FIND HIS MESSAGE TO PRESIDENT CARTER ENCOURAGING AND USEFUL.
STEARNS

SECRET

NNN

A Dream for Peace

After hosting Prime Minister Vorster in Yamoussoukro on September 21, 1974, he informed me that the meeting had been very constructive. He went on to say that he first observed a mulatto among the South African delegation and made light of the situation. "What is the origin of the many mulattos in your country?" he nudged the unsuspecting prime minister.

Chapter Thirteen

Concord in Africa

The president and I shared a profound love for our African continent. Liberty, freedom, and peace were intrinsic to our philosophies, and our values were deeply rooted in the principle of total independence from colonial rule for every nation.

He had begun promoting his ideas long before I entered the fray. In the aftermath of the Second World War, colonial powers became increasingly aware that colonial rule could not be maintained forever. People in Africa had the right to be free and independent, and colonial governments were placed in the untenable position of having to justify why they were keeping African societies under their rule, despite a United Nations declaration that all people had the right to self-determination. But indeed, some were not ready to hand over self-governance to the African people, claiming that the Africans would have to be "prepared" to run their countries.

Colonial governments forged ahead and began investing in education in their colonies, resulting in a growing number of young educated African elite who were hungry for an end to colonial rule. President Houphouët-Boigny, as well as a handful of activists from sub-Saharan colonies, including Kwame Nkrumah of Ghana (the Gold Coast under British rule), organized their political platforms while living in Europe. "Kwame Nkrumah traveled from London to meet with us in Paris sometime in 1946," he confided, recalling their fateful encounter. "At the time, my francophone colleagues and I were the African representatives at the French National Assembly. Nkrumah came to invite us to participate in the West African Conference in

A Dream for Peace

London. We spoke of the upcoming French Union and I told him about our plans to form the RDA [Rassemblement Démocratique Africain] in Bamako, October of that year." Although the push for unity and solidarity on the continent began intensifying in the French and British colonies, only two African members of the French parliament, Léopold Senghor of Senegal and Sourou-Migan Apithy of Dahomey, managed to attend the conference in London.

Responding to demands for independence, the British colonial government introduced the Burns Constitution, giving the people of the Gold Coast more self-autonomy but initially allowing for only those with money and property the right to vote. Thus, the majority of the people, many of whom were blue-collar workers, were excluded from government. Hoping to gain more political influence within the colonial government's power structure, a group of affluent Ghanaians, including chiefs, lawyers, and merchants, seized the opportunity and financed the formation of the United Gold Coast Convention (UGCC). Nkrumah accepted an invitation by the political movement's founder (J. B. Danquah) to join the party. But after only two years, he left to form the Convention Peoples' Party (CPP). Aiming to counter the disenfranchisement of the ordinary citizen by organizing peaceful demonstrations in the country's capital, the grassroots movement grew in popularity very quickly. His core supporters were a more nationalistic wing that sprouted out of the UGCC. They helped him rally and mobilize the masses to oppose further repression. Emboldened by the fervent support of those constituents, he proposed to the colonial government a model that was similar to the Statute of Westminster, drafted by the British Parliament in 1931. The framework of the statute imposed universal franchise without property qualifications, while establishing a separate house of chiefs and self-governance of the people by the people. Although the proposals were roundly rejected by the British administration, the Burns Constitution ultimately proved an important step toward Ghana's independence.

Concord in Africa

Once Ghana achieved independence, Nkrumah set out to offer assistance to other colonies that were engaged in the battle for self-rule. After the francophone countries reached their final political milestone toward achieving independence, the unity of Africa and its total liberation became a priority for President Houphouët. As opposed to Nkrumah, who had embarked on a "Marxist-Socialist" path, the president was more pragmatic in his approach to governing. In the advent of Côte d'Ivoire's independence, Houphouët-Boigny, then president of the Territorial Assembly, was faced with a broken economy and almost no infrastructure. Having neither industrial plants nor properties to nationalize, he opted for a more capital-infused policy in a free market economy, relying heavily on French technical expertise as well as private investment. Nkrumah, on the other hand, moved further to the political left of President Houphouët.

A dictum of Nkrumah's—"*Seek ye first the political kingdom and all else shall be added unto you*"—followed a commitment to fellow Ghanaian citizens of an economic utopia, a promise of unencumbered wealth for the people of the newly independent country. Barely a month after achieving his groundbreaking accomplishment, he accepted President Houphouët-Boigny's challenge, in a bet that became known as the "West African wager." "When I last spoke with Nkrumah," the president told me, smiling as he reminisced, "I made a bet with my fellow Akan neighbor that we would meet in ten years to assess and compare developments in our respective countries. Based on the outcome, the less efficient of the two will change their orientation and adopt the path that led to success."

Nkrumah was overthrown about nine years after the wager. Having fallen short of achieving his promise of an economic utopia for Ghanaians in his quest to transform his country into a socioeconomic powerhouse, he would have been on track to losing his wager with President Houphouët. But his ideological vision of a socialist socioeconomic transformation for both Ghana and Africa was not borne out of a simple, evanescent bluster. His move to the political left was part of a much broader doctrine within the circles of a new breed of African nationalists who were keen on creating a more egalitarian society along socialist ideological pathways to achieve a lasting, robust developmental success.

President Houphouët and Dr. Kwame Nkrumah.

Nkrumah had declared on Ghana's independence day that his country's independence would be meaningless unless it was linked to the total liberation of Africa. From the onset, he made no secret of the fact that the total unification of African countries was an urgent matter, high on his list of priorities. The ultimate Pan-Africanist, he pursued a bold idea of a federation of African states, modeled after the US, which he envisaged would serve all two hundred million citizens of a united African continent and would be designed in scope to hold its own against the likes of Europe, an emerging India, China, and the US, in an incipient socioeconomic global environment. He reinforced his rhetoric with the slogan, "*We must unite, or we will perish.*"

Concord in Africa

Ghana had trail-blazed the path to independence for all sub-Saharan countries at a time when Côte d'Ivoire was still under French domination. As early as 1958, Kwame Nkrumah organized a conference in Ghana's capital, Accra, for some independent nations, including Ethiopia, Egypt, Sudan, Morocco, Libya, Tunisia, and Liberia. "Here is a challenge which destiny has thrown out to the leaders of Africa," Nkrumah later wrote in his book, *Africa Must Unite*. "It is for us to grasp what is a golden opportunity to prove that the genius of the African people can surmount the separatist tendencies in sovereign nationhood by coming together speedily, for the sake of Africa's greater glory and infinite well-being, into a Union of African states."

President Houphouët-Boigny focused on creating regional structures of unity within a continental organization supported by all nations. He spearheaded the creation of the Conseil de l'Entente, an organization comprising of francophone satellite nations Côte d'Ivoire, Dahomey (Bènin), Upper Volta (Burkina Faso), Niger, and Togo. The cooperative structure between the nations included aid and a solidarity fund. Additionally, he launched the Organisation Commune Africaine et Malgache (OCAM), an organization comprising twelve countries across the continent, whose purpose was to foster economic, cultural, and social cooperation among the francophone states.

The differing approaches of Presidents Houphouët-Boigny and Kwame Nkrumah for the unity of Africa shed light on differences in opinion regarding the best way to navigate the path of concord. Two groups were formed: Casablanca Group, supporters of a federation of African states sharing President Nkrumah's ideas, and the Monrovia Group, favoring a more flexible organization. Always driven by the need for concord in Africa, the president requested the mediation of President Tubman of Liberia and Nigerian Prime Minister Tafawa Balewa, both of whom enjoyed the respect and confidence of Nkrumah. After several attempts at reaching a

A Dream for Peace

consensus among the countries, an agreement was arrived at with the help of Emperor Haile Selassie I of Ethiopia, an avid Pan-Africanist who worked diligently behind the scenes to organize a conference of foreign ministers of the two groups in his country.

They met in Addis Ababa in May 1963. The objective was to launch a program for a summit conference at the same venue immediately following the meeting. Participants managed to set aside their differences and agree on a charter that defined the articles of the Organization of African Unity (OAU). Although the charter did not meet everyone's expectations, it was formally adopted on May 25, 1963, a day that became known as "African Day." The president expressed how relieved and happy he was at the advent of what was a great victory for concord in Africa. I was overjoyed at the announcement, which I read in a local newspaper while completing my doctorate in Indiana. Total liberation of the African continent, a common objective among the nations, remained at the helm of discussions at every summit for some time, as successive leaders continued to push for continental cooperation, peace, and unity among the nations. After a series of amendments to the charter over several consecutive years, the OAU became known as the African Union (AU).

Among his peers, President Houphouët continued to play a major role in the Conseil de l'Entente. He was consulted frequently and traveled with them to various events. I joined them on occasion. The government of Côte d'Ivoire helped in the development of the member countries, most notably in the building of the Bobo Dioulasso Airport in the second largest city of Burkina Faso. The French government considered him their key partner in OCAM and in the subregion. He maintained privileged relations with France through his friendship with General De Gaulle. When US President Eisenhower passed away, Foreign Minister Usher and I represented President Houphouët-Boigny at the funeral. After the memorial, General De Gaulle invited us to join him aboard his plane to Paris in

Concord in Africa

honor of his friendship with the president. I met him for the very first time when he came and greeted us at our seats. He stood out for his towering height, but more so, he was an intelligent and savvy political leader whom I personally respected for his significant role in laying the foundation for Algeria's independence. When he spoke, he struck me as a man of modest mind and great self-confidence. He wished President Houphouët were aboard the flight because he missed seeing his old friend, whom he hadn't seen in person for several months. I assured him the president was well, and we thanked him for his kind gesture. Côte d'Ivoire's relations with France have fluctuated over the years, especially when France was ruled by the Left. According to President Houphouët, French President Francois Mitterrand, a former colleague from the mid-1940s, was an unpredictable personality.

President Houphouët and General De Gaulle.

The president believed that any notion of development should be preceded by peace. *"There can be no progress without stability. Stability can only be based on peace and justice for the full development of the citizens,"* he declared repeatedly. He lived by those words and worked tirelessly for peace in Africa. Whenever he was confronted with issues pertaining to a sovereign country anywhere on the continent, he rose to the occasion and lent a helping hand, often using the few but limited resources of Côte d'Ivoire in that regard. Though I knew the president was a highly compassionate man who dealt straight from the heart, I was clearly conflicted about his decisions on occasion. For instance, when President Mobutu of Zaire[61] informed him that he lacked enough funds to pay his army and President Houphouët-Boigny took the necessary steps to provide the needed financial resources, I cried foul. I was outraged and expressed my reservations about his decision. "My son, we need peace in Africa," he said. "Can you imagine the consequences and impact on our fragile continent if the Zairian soldiers were to take matters into their own hands?" I agreed with his principles, but in the absence of a stringent due diligence to ascertain enough credible data to assure us that Mobutu's difficulties amounted to a well-managed economy that continued to fall short of projections due to past colonial misappropriations, the president had to take him at his word.

I had observed the developmental progress and cooperation among the nations on the African continent and understood the difficulties that had plagued most countries after gaining independence from their former colonial governments. But notwithstanding, there were remnants of mismanagement of postcolonial budgets by many administrations across the continent, which led us down a path of self-destruction. During Mobutu Sese Seko's regime (1965 to 1997), Congo, which he renamed Zaire in 1971, was riddled with foreign debt to the tune of some $14 billion, and the standard of living of the Congolese people declined further from pre-independence levels. But Mobutu and his closest allies grew their personal fortunes to extraordinary heights. We were not completely aware of the severity of corruption at the time,

---

[61] Central African state, currently the Democratic Republic of the Congo.

yet I hoped the president would curtail his actions and embrace a tough-love stance, because more than once he responded positively to similar solicitations from leaders across the continent. He had excellent relations with all the African countries and never hesitated to give credence to their needs.

Not long after my arrival in Côte d'Ivoire, we learned of the assassination of President Houphouët's dear friend, Nigerian Prime Minister Sir Abubakar Tafawa Balewa, in a coup plotted by mainly junior military officers of the Igbo tribe from the southeast. Balewa's body was discovered by the side of a road days after his murder, triggering a passionate cry for justice by his tribesmen of the north, who sought vengeance at all cost. A countercoup about six months later brought to power Colonel Yakubu Gowon from the country's Plateau State, who instituted a series of preventive measures to ensure stability in the country. However, northerners continued the massacre of Igbo tribesmen in their region, leading to further tribal mistrust and urgent calls for secession of the southeastern region. The leader of the secession movement was a junior army officer, C. Odumegwu Ojukwu.

The atrocities continued to escalate along tribal lines. Northerners were mobilized in the belief that the Igbos wanted to enslave everyone else in the country. Predictably, the push for secession led to a civil war (in July 1967) that came to be known as the Biafra War, named after the Bight of Biafra in Nigeria's southernmost Atlantic coast. At the height of the military hostilities between southeastern Nigeria and the federal government, Gowon's regime warned that any country that recognized Biafra as an independent sovereign state would be viewed by his government as interfering in the country's internal affairs. The OAU member states were inclined to make condemnation statements and speeches appealing for a peaceful resolution.

When Usher and I attended the OAU meeting in Kinshasa in September 1967, it was abundantly clear that member states wished to resolve the crisis. None of the nations wanted a partitioning of the country. During the session, African heads of states succeeded in persuading Nigeria to bring the issue to the floor of the General Assembly on the condition that no member nation would interfere with its internal affairs. A committee was dispatched to Lagos to emphasize the OAU's position and assure Gowon that the Nigerian government would determine the nature of the organization's involvement in its internal affairs.

About a year into the brutal war, Emperor Haile Selassie I of Ethiopia and other East African leaders held a joint news conference and appealed for a cessation in atrocities. I was appalled by the OAU's lack of urgency on behalf of the browbeaten Igbo civilians. They even failed to take up a resolution when Lesotho's head of state introduced a proposal asking member states to consider a variety of ways to end the conflict. There was a lot of rhetoric floating around and very little action on the part of the member states. President Houphouët was so perturbed by the horrific images on the media, depicting the massacre of tens of thousands of people for the sake of keeping a unified Nigeria, that he moved to recognize Biafra as a sovereign nation. Although he was supported by the leaders of Tanzania, Zambia, and Gabon, this was a highly unusual and controversial move on his part, and many leaders were quick to condemn his decision. He expressed privately to me that he wished to bring the opposing factions to the negotiating table and that he thought the OAU needed to pursue a more proactive engagement to achieve peace and justice.

I wondered if his decision amounted to a unique approach, or perhaps a savvy political maneuver, but I knew that he believed in doing something to dislodge the self-inflicted bureaucratic mess within the organization. The body was at a gridlock, with member states suddenly finding themselves inadvertently dragged down the path of neocolonial upheaval. Most of the leaders were indecisive on the Biafra issue. While his decision was seen as a breach of the

OAU charter, he also risked promoting an atmosphere of dissent that could potentially inspire other secessionist groups in newly independent and fragile nations on the continent. A majority of nations had inherited arbitrary and precarious borders from reckless colonial governments. In the aftermath of many such blunders by other well-meaning leaders, I was convinced that their indecisions might have diminished the organization's moral authority to act. Nonetheless, it was a tough situation that had reared its ugly head on a continent that was in the process of picking up the pieces from colonial transgressions. Sadly, the organization was ill prepared to deal effectively with the issue at the time.

Côte d'Ivoire admitted over nine hundred malnourished and disenfranchised Igbo children into the country's welfare system. The government hosted them in an Abidjan neighborhood, which became known as Biafra. The president personally attended many local events, organized by selected committees for the children's benefit. He interacted with them during many of his visits to the compound and inquired about their well-being.

When I asked the question during the OAU conference, Nigerian Minister of Foreign Affairs Dr. Arikpo had a hard time explaining the federal government's road map to peace. Even after recognizing Biafra's right to secede, the president remained impartial and continued to work feverishly behind the scenes with both parties. He believed that Gowon had a responsibility, whether it was humanitarian, political, or for the sake of peace. Either way it was a critical choice, and it was imperative that a diplomatic solution was arrived at. Therefore, he put forth several proposals and kept the pressure on both parties to meet at the negotiating table. In the meantime, the war continued to take its toll. Although the Igbo forces found a formidable and resolute military opponent on the opposite end of the spectrum, their leader, Ojukwu, seemed more determined to strong-arm himself into power.

The war raged on for months with no end in sight, but

A Dream for Peace

ultimately the federal government's military pressure was insurmountable. In January 1970, we learned Ojukwu had relinquished the dream and was en route to Côte d'Ivoire. We were relieved that the Nigerian people would be reunited at last, and the sufferings of the Igbos had come to an end. Gowon diplomatically proclaimed that the war had yielded "no victor, no vanquished." The president maintained his friendship with the opposing parties, especially, with General Obasanjo, commander of the federal forces. Ojukwu enjoyed his exile in the country, while Biafran children in Côte d'Ivoire were identified by the UN High Commissioner and returned to Nigeria to be reunited with their families in the summer of 1970. The president, who had grown fond of the children, thought about them quite often. He had hoped to hear from them after they were resettled in their homeland, but sadly no one reached out to him.

President Houphouët-Boigny's unique approach on South Africa had been subject of much controversy. Although his position remained true to his philosophy of dialogue, his actions caused a myriad of misinterpretations among many leaders on the African continent. Some dissenting voices went to great lengths to discredit him, claiming he was cruelly indifferent to the suffering of our black brothers in South Africa, and by contrast, he cozied up with the white tyrants in an unnatural Manichean alliance. But such critics were unaware of the fact that in private, he mourned the suffering of his brethren under apartheid, feeling deeply in his own flesh the very pain of the burning flames that they continued to endure. In the midst of receiving some severe blowback for taking the lead and initiating talks with South African Premier B. J. Vorster and suggesting that the leadership of the OAU member countries follow suit, I had an in-depth conversation with him, privately at his residence. I sought to dig deeper into his mindset and extract the essence of diplomatic ingenuity that propelled him to go against the status quo. Admittedly, he was not attempting to pioneer an engineered solution to a delicate and highly charged problem; he was merely seeking dialogue with the enemy. I never forgot what he told me: *"When a black man is a victim of racism in Japan, a country so far away from the shores of Côte d'Ivoire, I still feel the chills resonate deeply in my very soul."*

By June 1948, as a majority of countries on the African continent were preoccupied with the struggle for freedom from colonial rule, newly elected Prime Minister Dr. D. F. Malan of South Africa had already declared in a campaign speech for the first time that apartheid must be projected as a policy of race relations in his country. South Africa was already immersed in an atmosphere of fascist oppression. Upon winning the elections, his National Party (NP) introduced a registration system for whites and non-whites, thereby institutionalizing a policy that required non-whites to carry with them a permit at all times. His government spearheaded the development of reservations for the Bantu (African) population. Declaring that only Africans who were guaranteed work would be allowed to live in urban areas, they forged ahead with the principle of residential and public segregation ensuring that the Africans who lived in close proximity to the white areas could not have any political rights but could be represented in the Senate by Europeans. Non-whites were not admitted to white universities, and interracial marriage between whites and blacks was criminalized.

In May 1950, at a Johannesburg congress of the African National Congress (ANC), African People's Organization, South African Indian Congress, and Communist Party of South Africa, Walter Sisulu was chosen to act as secretary and organizer of the National Protest Committee together with Y. A. Cachalia. The congress adopted a resolution that directed all non-whites to stay away from work. Police action to protect non-strikers resulted in a fierce clash in which eighteen blacks lost their lives, and a day of mourning was declared on June 26 by the ANC to honor those who were killed. Almost two years later, the ANC launched its Campaign for the Defiance of Unjust Laws. At the time, Nelson Mandela was the president of the organization's Youth League. The Defiance Campaign was expected to be a mass civil disobedience campaign that would snowball from a few selected volunteers in the hopes of attracting more ordinary people to culminate in mass defiance. Mandela was arrested, but the court found that the ANC advised their followers to adopt a peaceful course of action and refrain from violence. He was convicted of contravening the Suppression of Communism Act and given a suspended prison sentence.

President Houphouët-Boigny had been following the developments in South Africa throughout his political career; as an assemblyman in France and as Côte d'Ivoire's president of the Territorial Assembly. He observed helplessly on the sidelines as the government of Prime Minister Hendrik Verwoerd declared a state of emergency in South Africa and banned both the ANC and the Pan Africanist Congress. On the eve of achieving independence for his own country, he read about the massacre of blacks outside a police station in the township of Sharpeville with a heavy heart. It came as no surprise to him that the ANC would respond to the oppression by creating a military unit led by Nelson Mandela and adopting guerrilla tactics across the country. While the South African government presented itself as a buffer of the West against communist penetration in southern Africa and possibly across the continent, Mandela was deemed a communist and a terrorist by the CIA. Successive regimes under apartheid became the West's sentry during the Cold War.

Côte d'Ivoire was elected as a member of the UN Security Council in June 1964. Usher was the first African to preside over the council. The president asked him to initiate and introduce a draft resolution to the Security Council demanding the release of all political prisoners in South Africa. Usher worked on the resolution with his colleague, Morocco's Permanent Representative to the UN, and presented the draft to the Security Council on June 8. It was adopted by a vote of seven in favor and four abstentions. Two days before a verdict was pronounced in South Africa, convicting Mandela, Walter Sisulu, and other valuable activists of crimes against the state, the Security Council called for the South African government to postpone the trial and release the prisoners. However, Mandela and his companions were sentenced to life in prison and transferred to Robben Island. The struggle nonetheless had to continue for the release of Mandela and the abolition of apartheid.

Beginning in 1966, I attended every OAU summit as well as the annual General Assembly meetings at the United Nations. Faced with the sad reality that the South African government remained deaf to every condemnation by the OAU and having exhausted several attempts to stop the infernal machine of violent repression, President Houphouët-Boigny took it upon himself to try a unique approach in 1971. He embarked on an extremely difficult path of diplomacy and outreach, decried by the vast majority of sovereign African nations—the path of dialogue with South Africa. President Hastings Banda of Malawi had already lent his voice to the call for dialogue. But President Houphouët's announcement that he was in favor of dialogue to cure the "political leprosy" of apartheid was more pronounced. "We wish to open talks with this country, South Africa," he proclaimed. "But that does not mean we intend to recognize it." He went on to say that force was no use against the South African regime and emphasized that the only invasion he wished to see would be that of African diplomats. Although he faced a heavy backlash, he was not entirely isolated in his position. Eventually, he was supported by the likes of Prime Minister Kofi Busia of Ghana as well as the leaders of Gabon, Malagasy, and Dahomey. For him, the decision was not one of complimentary dialogue akin to that of leaders in the West who were entrenched in their own interests in South Africa. He held a strong belief that pleading the cause of his brothers in a face-to-face dialogue was the right thing to do.

It is worthwhile knowing that at the very heart of the

complexity of understanding and embracing the notion of an enemy and enmity lies the recognition that it is a most potent and grave emanation at the crossroad of opposing views. I understood that as difficult as his decision was, one must attempt to transcend the norms of basic principle and resist the temptation of archaic belief structures spanning generations of warfare to opt for sincere dialogue and solve even the most vituperative problem. Talking with South Africa at a time when the rest of Africa was mired in a geopolitical flirtation with capitalism, communism, business globalization, and cultural identity was, in essence, a significant step and a symbolic level of discourse.

At the OAU, Côte d'Ivoire was constantly the target of harsh criticism, but Usher and I were relentless in explaining the position of President Houphouët-Boigny. I was attacked by the representatives of socialist countries, particularly my Algerian brothers, for aligning myself with the traitor to Africa's cause. After organizing the meeting between President Houphouët-Boigny and President Boumédiène at the 1973 OAU summit in Addis, I seized the opportunity to explain the president's position as best as I could. On one of my missions to Algiers, Boumédiène informed me that he was mystified by the president—*"I must admit that before our historic meeting in Addis, I was puzzled by him. I disagreed with him on his Biafra position. We have no reason to hold talks with the whites in South Africa. If ever the situation called for it, dialogue would have to be between South Africa's whites and blacks."* I understood his point. *"But Mr. President,"* I added, *"as far as the dialogue is concerned, I believe that President Houphouët-Boigny's idea has been gravely distorted. His position is in the spirit by which you explained your point of view, and he is committed to those same principles."*

The UN finally adopted a resolution equating the practice of apartheid to a crime against humanity on November 30, 1973. The president and I applauded the decision; though we felt that the move was not enough, we believed it was a step in the right direction.

President Houphouët's discussions with South Africa were always direct and frank, never failing to highlight contradictions in rhetoric and unbecoming practices. After hosting Prime Minister Vorster in Yamoussoukro on September 21, 1974, he informed me that the meeting had been very constructive. He went on to say that he first observed a mulatto among the South African delegation and made light of the situation. "What is the origin of the many mulattos in your country?" he nudged the unsuspecting prime minister. "Is apartheid restricted to the daytime and not at night?" Vorster seemed surprised but knew the joke was on him. "Do you mean to tell me that no one has taken measures to thwart the behavior that produces interracial offspring?" The red-faced premier managed to sneak a smile but remained speechless. In typical fashion, the president used the opportunity to offer some advice to Vorster: "Your country would do better to integrate all its citizens into a genuine society, and then perhaps, Mr. Prime Minister, you can begin taking steps to join the rest of the continent." His clever wit was astonishing, but the simplistic wisdom he used to tackle the subject of apartheid was enough to cause some in the seated delegation to bow their heads disquietly.

Six days later, I was dispatched to see President Boumédiène to deliver a message that read: "I have no economic relations with South Africa, unlike those who yell while maintaining with that country all types of interactions, directly or indirectly. The planes leaving or returning from South Africa land elsewhere in Africa—not in Abidjan. My dialogue with South Africa has but one aim, which is to work for racial equality, not through the use of violence but through dialogue, and to forestall what we were unable to avoid with Israel in the beginning. As you now know, we have agreed to talk with Israel; at least those of us who are doing so are doing this under very difficult conditions. Those who support Israel will support South Africa in order to stall developmental progress on the African continent, but without ever impacting progress in South Africa itself. And by the way, the South Africans will soon build their own nuclear bomb. They are, after all, the world's number one producer of uranium, which brings them more money than gold. We need to be realistic and acknowledge these facts, not because we fear that we might develop a complex of inferiority or wallow in despair."

Boumédiène was swayed by the message, and he set aside his reservations on the matter. I delivered a letter to President Houphouët-Boigny affirming Boumédiène's support. "When it comes to dialogue with South Africa," it read, "I personally trust you."

President Houphouët-Boigny did his part in an attempt to shed light on some of the inconsistencies in South Africa's domestic policies and international posture. In one notable move, he dispatched the Ivorian Minister of Information, Laurent Dona Fologo, a black African, on a mission to South Africa. Fologo arrived in Pretoria with his wife, a white woman from France. By using the image of a powerful interracial couple, the president intended to send a strong and captivating message directed at the apartheid laws that forbade mixed marriages. The Fologos were welcomed officially by South African Information Minister Dr. Connie Mulder. After touring the townships and meeting with various segments of the general population, Fologo returned home to deliver an incisive report to the president.

Three months after Mulder visited Côte d'Ivoire with a South African delegation, riots broke out in Soweto. President Houphouët-Boigny put on hold all plans for cultural exchange celebrations with the apartheid nation. I attended the OAU conference in Port Louis, Mauritius, around the same time of the Soweto uprising. At the weeklong twenty-seventh session of the Council of Ministers that preceded the summit, there were heated debates regarding the efficacious impact of imposing sanctions on South Africa. The Soweto massacre not only resonated loudly on the international scene, it triggered the most vociferous debates in the organization's history. During our breaks, I was cornered by different delegates in the conference corridors and questioned about the logic behind Fologo and Mulder's visits to each other's country. Explaining the advantages of dialogue to our detractors was a burdensome task. Yet, I hoped to restore some sanity to the discourse by illustrating to everyone that the mechanism of peace was hard at work and the goal was attainable, however patience remained a virtue.

A boycott of the Montreal Olympics to express the OAU's opposition to New Zealand's participation in a rugby tournament in South Africa was a major topic for debate. The body condemned the governments of France, West Germany, and the United Kingdom for cooperating with South Africa on the building of nuclear centrifuges and denounced the collusion between Israel and the apartheid regime. We moved to adopt resolutions condemning a policy that created a separate territory for the Bantus and voted to not recognize the secession of Transvaal, a breakaway republic that was planning to proclaim its independence in October of that year. One of the items on the agenda—the need to ensure compliance with the charter and effectuate the OAU resolutions—was introduced by the government of Benin with the aim of punishing the member countries that did not enforce implementation of the resolutions. Stating his case, the delegate from Benin alluded to the fact that certain countries had ongoing relations with South Africa and delivered a fiery tongue-lashing directed at Côte d'Ivoire, obviously due to the visits of Fologo and Mulder. He went on to admonish the countries that allowed the landing of South African commercial flights on their soil. Sensing his hypocrisy, I obtained the list of those African countries with the most frequent stops from the Committee of Anti-Apartheid Workers and shared the information with Oliver Tambo and the ANC. We were in a very strong position to expose the culprits but decided not to embarrass some of our friends.

Notwithstanding, Usher interjected to bring up some relevant articles in the OAU's charter just to point out that certain member countries were in violation of Chapter III and Article 13 of the organization's budgetary rules. Accordingly, he suggested that sanctions be imposed on those nations that were delinquent with their dues. It just so happened that the most vociferous of the critics were the ones who had not paid their dues. Following the intervention of Usher, the item was removed from the agenda, and we avoided a mass condemnation by our peers on the panel.

In the end, the OAU did its very best to send a strong message. Member states were directed to adopt sanctions against the brutal apartheid regime, and a bill was introduced to ensure that countries that violated such sanctions were put on notice that they could face potential penalties themselves. But in a bid to shield and protect Côte d'Ivoire from further political fallout, Usher emphasized that not every member state at the OAU would be bound by the resolutions adopted by the Council of Ministers. After reviewing my report, the president advised that we cultivate patience, and he admitted he had reached a point where he had to embrace the issue as a school of thought.

The president's purpose was not limited to dialogue with the South African government; he lent his support to many apartheid-era exiles who followed the rise and fall of domestic South African resistance from foreign lands and lived with the dream of a peaceful resolution. There were those for whom being in exile felt like a huge burden had been lifted off their shoulders, liberating them from the trauma and confines of apartheid, and there were others for whom the distance from their ancestral land made them feel as if they had been thrown in a prison of their making. With each encounter we had with South Africans in diaspora, I was always reminded of how homesick they were. It brought me great sadness, knowing the impact their predicament was having on their families. When the president met with activists during private dinners at his home in Geneva, it accorded them the opportunity to interact and speak in Afrikaans, Zulu, or Xhosa, perhaps even laugh at their plight. Even their arcane mother tongues and unspoken sadness of being exiled never broke their spirits.

President Houphouët continued to hold talks quietly behind the scenes with South African Prime Minister Pieter Botha,[62] who began to scale back some of the highly restrictive laws. Yet the martyrdom of our brothers continued with countless numbers of people dying at the hands of the brutal security apparatus. I nurtured a great friendship with Oliver Tambo and stayed in touch with him as often as I could, offering him my full support and assurance in times of despair. But when we ran into each other unexpectedly at the airport in Geneva, I could hardly recognize him. He seemed a broken man, and I was greatly disturbed by his despondent resignation. Years in exile and a longing for normalcy had taken a toll on his spirits, but he was not down for the count.

With his wife beside him, we spoke about the struggle and progress since the Soweto massacre. I shared a bond with the ANC and appreciated their push for liberation. Although I had been on the frontlines of battle to free Algeria from the jaws of colonial oppression, in the case of South Africa, I was particularly impressed by the fact that women had risen up en masse and joined the fight, becoming more militant by the day. I was very familiar with the heroics of women such as Djamila Bouhired, an Algerian activist and former freedom fighter during our liberation war. At a time in my country's history when even the most basic political and civil rights were being denied to my people, our only solution was to fight for our liberation. Algerian women helped to provide provisions for those of us on the front lines, and some engaged with us in armed operations in the city. Djamila Bouhired was a major factor in the historic Battle of Algiers, which took place in 1957. When she was shot in the leg, arrested, and subjected to torture by French security forces, she stood up boldly and told them, "*I know you will sentence*

---

[62] South Africa Premier, 1978–1984; first Executive President, 1984–1989.

A Dream for Peace

me to death, but do not forget that by killing me, you will not only assassinate freedom in your country, but you will not prevent Algeria from becoming free and independent." She walked into the prison limping on one leg and chanting, *"Jazayerna"* ("our Algeria").

Our compatriot Djamila Boupacha was also captured and tortured by the French. My dear friend Zohra Drif was subjected to torture and imprisonment after several attempts to extract valuable information about the FLN. They were never broken. I felt a common kinship with the ANC and understood the tactics in their strategic efforts to secure liberation at all cost. I applauded black South African women for refusing to sit idly by and allow the apartheid minority government to destroy their family structure and take down the basic fabric of their respective societies. They were left with no other alternative but to form women's federations and become very active in trade unions.

Mrs. Tambo herself was a prominent anti-apartheid activist in political exile and was regarded as a hero of the liberation struggle against apartheid in her country. It was the women of her generation who rose up and fought to change the laws, hoping to bring an end to the so-called "Bantu Education Act" after their children had been massacred by the police force in Soweto. They made an effective contribution to the struggle for liberation and increasingly attracted the attention and solidarity of women and men around the globe. I was particularly encouraged by Winnie Mandela's famous dictum, *"It is only when all black groups join hands and speak with one voice that we shall be a bargaining force which will decide its own destiny . . . We know what we want . . . We are not asking for majority rule; it is our right, we shall have it at any cost. We are aware that the road before us is uphill, but we shall fight to the bitter end for justice."*

We met for some coffee at an airport cafeteria, and I couldn't help but notice my good friend Oliver Tambo's failing health. I prayed silently that the world was on course to witnessing the eve of apartheid's demise. They were on their way to a clinic in London for a treatment. I sensed that the great activist was nearing the end of his final days and began to extract from him every detail about his health and medical history, while extending my well wishes to soothe their concerns. "Don't give up the struggle, my brother and sister; you are in my prayers," I said with hugs before we went our separate ways. Back at the president's villa, I informed him of Oliver Tambo's perilous condition. The president was so moved by his story that he immediately dispatched his ambassador, Essy Amara, to London with instructions to deposit the necessary funds to pay for all the medical expenses of the South African liberation leader.

Prior to his ascension to the head of South Africa's National Party and his election as president, Frederik Willem de Klerk had spent five and a half years in the nation's parliament and eleven years in the cabinet. At first, he was seen as a political conservative, having gone on record for supporting segregated universities while he was Minister of National Education. But in September 1989, he was sworn in as president of South Africa in Pretoria as successor to P. W. Botha. I breathed a sigh of relief when I heard him utter the following words while recalling his swearing-in ceremony: "*It was as though I stood before God, promising that I would execute the task he had given me on the basis of the biblical principles of justice, peace, and neighborly love.*"

When President Houphouët-Boigny met him, he recommended that he pursue a policy of reconciliation in order to circumvent the dogmatic "suitcase or coffin" scenario that occurred in Algeria. He encouraged him to move away from segregationist policies. De Klerk himself seemed to embrace the simplest of basic human principles—a belief that belonging and identity are essential to everyone, no matter what creed or color. He was in total synchronicity with our political outlook, tapping into the need to respect all the different religions, cultures, and ethical practices in his country and stressing the importance of bringing everyone together in a rainbow society, regardless of who they were, what

A Dream for Peace

they believed, and how they practiced their beliefs. I replayed in my mind, what Mandela had said at the Rivonia Trial: *"I have cherished the ideal of a democratic and free society in which all persons will live together in harmony and with equal opportunities. It is an ideal which I hope to live for. But, my lord, if need be, it is an ideal for which I am prepared to die."* I watched Mr. De Klerk's actions closely and shared my opinions with the president. Though he was still tarnished by allegations of complicity in the violence that seeped across South Africa in the late 1980s, I knew with all his imperfections, his heart was in the right place, and I sensed his good intentions from afar.

One of his first actions in office was to appoint the first woman ever to serve in a South African cabinet. He moved swiftly to lift restrictions on protest marches, enabling Archbishop Desmond Tutu, a social rights activist and Anglican bishop, to organize the largest anti-apartheid march in the country's history. He ended many of the petty restrictions of apartheid, including segregated beaches, parks, lavatories, and restaurants.

Only four months into his presidency, the world's press descended on Cape Town, South Africa's coastal capital, for what seemed a momentous occasion, perhaps the biggest news story in our continent's fragile history. I witnessed on television young whites mixing happily with black demonstrators carrying the black, green, and gold flags of the banned African National Congress (ANC) party in the heart of the city. Archbishop Desmond Tutu was at Saint George's Cathedral with his flock, which included more whites than blacks, ready to celebrate the announcement of the official end of the apartheid system by Mr. De Klerk, whose Afrikaner forbearers had embraced the brutal policy over four decades prior to his presidency.

Yet on that fateful day of February 2, 1990, Mandela told De Klerk that he didn't want to be released from detention. He said he wasn't ready. Besides, he told government ministers that he needed more time to prepare, reminding them that he had been in prison

Concord in Africa

for twenty-seven years, and an additional week or two would make no difference to him. But he had no idea of what President De Klerk had in store for the ANC and the people of South Africa that day.

With my wife and invited guests At UNESCO ceremony.

Nine days after the speech, the release of Mandela was made official. As a man of faith, Frederik Willem de Klerk attained peace for the good of mankind. The opposition of many white conservatives did not stop him in his perilous march, and it was well worth the risk. Mandela and De Klerk stood shoulder to shoulder as one—the ideal partners in the search for a true sustainable peace in South Africa.

They were both recipients of the first-ever 1991 UNESCO Félix Houphouët-Boigny "Prize for Peace Research." Titi and I had the privilege to attend the award ceremony on February 3, 1992. Seeing the two men standing side by side had a profound impact on me. In his speech, De Klerk remarked that he was determined to embark on his quest and complete his resolute path toward achieving peace, despite the stubborn resistance of the supporters of apartheid. After the ceremony, a gala dinner was hosted by President Houphouët-Boigny to honor the recipients. My wife and I shared our table with

A Dream for Peace

the Director of Protocol for the South African government and his spouse. They were quite the charming couple and an integral party to De Klerk's immediate entourage. The event offered us an opportunity to learn a little more about the faith and humility of the South African head of state.

President Houphouët, De Klerk, and Nelson Mandela.

By the early 1970s, most of Africa's countries had gained independence, though Portugal continued to maintain a stranglehold on its colonies. Having the political foresight and wisdom, President Houphouët-Boigny asked General De Gaulle over a decade earlier to convince Portugal's President António de Oliveira Salazar to ensure a peaceful transition toward independence for its colonies. But his attempt to prevent further misery and suffering for those under Portugal's oppressive rule fell on deaf ears. Salazar stated emphatically that he believed a move to relinquish power could potentially lead to the spread of communism, a risk he was unwilling to take. Therefore he disregarded the sound recommendations. His stubborn indignation led to the formation and propagation of various liberation movements in those countries.

Independence movements were oppressed and activists were persecuted, jailed, or exiled for merely speaking out about a need for change. Many freedom fighters found refuge in Algeria with the blessing of President Boumédiène. They received tactical training in guerrilla warfare from Algerian special forces. President Houphouët extended considerable assistance to such movements when they appeared on his radar. The National Union for the Total Independence of Angola (UNITA), Popular Movement for the Liberation of Angola (MPLA), and the National Liberation Front of Angola (FNLA) were all supported equally by the president. I personally got to know some of the guerrilla fighters in Angola's liberation struggle. Most of the leadership gravitated to me during OAU conferences, mainly because they felt that I shared their convictions. Some prominent activists began to ask for my advice and counsel after learning of my involvement in the Algerian revolution. I bonded with the likes of independence leader Antonio Agostinho Neto and some dedicated revolutionaries on matters of strategic importance to their cause. Over time, they grew accustomed to my patronage and felt very comfortable confiding in me regarding more personal matters.

Some of their problems amounted to the most basic of needs, and it was for me a very discomforting feeling of helplessness. On several occasions, I was a constant reminder to President Houphouët of their untenable plight and depravity, and he took steps to provide as much aid as possible. However, his generous contributions never got to the intended recipients. When I discovered what was happening, I began to offer some financial help to a select few freedom fighters of my choosing. It gave them quite a morale boost to know that both President Houphouët-Boigny and I were sympathetic to their situation.

Agostinho Neto was a physician, poet, and a very mild-mannered guerrilla fighter. He and I became quite close, having consistently kept in contact ever since we met. When I first learned about his background as a young man in his homeland under an oppressive Portuguese colonial government, I connected deeply with his heart. He spoke about the high levels of illiteracy in his country and the struggle to make secondary education available to all. His father was a Protestant pastor and his mother a teacher. Other than the fact that he and I found commonality in the fight for national liberation, we also shared a passion for medicine. Growing up during a very difficult time in his country's history, he dreamed of becoming a doctor someday. The ruling Portuguese government's policy was designed to ensure that the darker-skinned Africans were kept at the bottommost levels with little or no education, while the light-skinned Angolans, descendants of mixed Portuguese-African heritage, were mostly ushered up the ladder in society. In those years, he became a prominent figure in a cultural movement that began to sprout from the grassroots under the slogan, *"Let's learn about Angola."*

He was arrested and jailed three months for collecting signatures supporting the Stockholm Appeal for World Peace. The World Peace Council, an international organization that advocated for independence and peaceful coexistence, had made the appeal about two years earlier. But apparently, to advocate for world peace was a crime under the Portuguese fascist colonial regime that controlled Angola because at the time, the government was on a major crusade against the USSR, hoping to deter individuals and groups from aligning themselves with communism. Notwithstanding, however, most guerrilla fighters were nonideologues, leaning toward neither side of the political spectrum. The USSR, with its anticolonial policy, attracted liberation movement leaders who sought their assistance, only after being shunned by the West. Years earlier, I explained this dichotomy of strange bedfellows to the Senate Committee on Foreign Relations in Washington, DC, when I was asked about the FLN.

      Neto managed to save up some money to pursue his medical studies in Portugal. In his second year of studies, he received a scholarship from an American Methodist church to help him get by. But he was picked up by the brutal Portuguese secret police in Lisbon for his activism, just weeks after publishing his first collection of poetry. In jail for more than two years, he gained prominence on the international scene when Amnesty International declared him "political prisoner of the year" in 1957. Months afterward, he was released and went on to finish his medical studies. His work as a gynecologist in a Lisbon hospital lasted for a very short time. In 1959, he returned to Angola to provide medical services to poor women. He took on the leadership mantel of the MPLA, an organization that had sprouted out of a convergence of smaller political movements in 1956. But life in the motherland wouldn't proceed unperturbed. Barely a few months after he settled into a normal routine, the chief of Portuguese security forces personally went to arrest him in his Luanda medical office for no particular reason. He was sent off to prison in Lisbon, later confined to the island of Santo Antão, and then shipped to Santiago Island in the Cape Verde archipelago. Undeterred, he continued servicing the medical needs of the people of Cape Verde and, in particular, his exiled comrades in arms. When he was freed some two years later, he was ordered by the Portuguese government to live in Portugal. But he devised an escape plan with the help of some freedom fighters and left Portugal with his wife and small children. After a perilous journey, he arrived in the capital of Congo, where the MPLA had its headquarters.

A Dream for Peace

The OAU had welcomed Angola's liberation movements for many years without knowing that they were in fact opposed to one another. It had been presumed that they shared the same objectives to rid their nation of Portuguese domination, but unfortunately, they were undermining their own brothers. Such was the case in the bitter struggle between the MPLA, the FNLA, and UNITA. For the sake of peace, President Houphouët-Boigny continued to give counsel to each of the movements, but he remained neutral and restrained from meddling in their internal strife.

The son of the first black stationmaster during the colonial Portuguese period, Jonas Savimbi took pride in the fact that his father was one of the early converts by American Protestant missionaries in Angola, which paved the way for him to attend a missionary school as a boy. He was very studious and showed a great deal of determination to get into secondary school at all cost, knowing at the time that the privilege was accorded strictly to the mulattos in his country. He was even a part of the youth wing of the MPLA. But nonetheless, as a black child with absolutely no traces of Portuguese blood in his lineage, he overcame the odds and managed to get a scholarship to study medicine in Lisbon. While he was being persecuted by Portuguese police for associating with the Communist Party, he rejected offers of scholarships to study in Moscow, opting for social science studies in Switzerland after escaping from Portugal. Jonas Savimbi founded his own movement, UNITA, with fellow Angolan Antonio da Costa Fernandes and went to China for combat guerrilla tactical training.

Angola's three liberation movements continued to fight against each other and against Portugal. The overthrow of Portugal's dictatorship by low-ranking left-wing military officers increased the momentum for the decolonization of its colonies. General António Spínola, a moderate and former governor of Guinea Bissau, became the leader of the new provisional government in Portugal. Although he supported autonomy and self-determination for the colonies, he projected a more gradual transition from colonial rule supervised by a federation led by Portugal. A majority of the junta disagreed with his ideas and proposed an expedient disengagement from all of Portugal's colonies. The internal disagreements slowed down the transition process for several months.

Meanwhile, in a desperate bid to stop the fratricidal feuds among the nationalist movements in Angola, a committee of OAU heads of state invited the FNLA and the MPLA to a summit in Bukavu, Congo, and talked them into agreeing on the formation of a common front to negotiate the independence of their country. But the matter was complicated in part thanks to Angola's nonsensical trivial tribal woes. Each of the freedom movements had a popular ethno-regional power base: the Mbundu tribe supported the MPLA, while UNITA was the pride of the Ovimbundu tribe, and the FNLA was a favorite of the Bakongo. Additionally, beliefs and values were contradicted by the leaders of the movements, making it very difficult for them to see eye to eye on plans for independence negotiations.

Having been a longtime admirer of President Jomo Kenyatta of Kenya, Savimbi reached out and asked for his mediation. Mombassa, Kenya, was welcomed as a neutral venue for all the freedom fighters. They convened there and engaged in dialogue that became a precursor to a formal agreement with Portugal's government for Angola's independence. They pledged to share a common platform and build a just and democratic society. Even so, they were neither prepared to assume nor share power. Hence, when Portugal handed over the reins of governance and self-autonomy, the suspicion and infighting resumed.

Ultimately, the MPLA managed to position itself to rule Angola with the help of the Soviet Union and support from Cuba. Soon after becoming president, Agostinho Neto declared his regime Marxist-Leninist. By contrast, Savimbi and his UNITA movement positioned themselves as moderate stewards of the free world and sought assistance from the continent's moderate countries as well as the West. Not surprisingly, he received the support of President Houphouët-Boigny.

Neto was faced with Soviet interference into his administration's domestic affairs. In order to continue receiving aid from the Kremlin, he was given a list of milestones that suited Russia's objective to create a Bolshevik state in Africa. The new leadership under Leonid Brezhnev wanted to see significant progress in the nationalization of Angola's industries and institutionalization of land ownership reforms to ensure that its people supported a cultural revolution in alliance with communist ideology. With the backdrop of a brewing political instability, Neto had come to rely heavily on military assistance from the USSR. His period in office had been marked by armed conflict with the FNLA, which was supported by Zaïre's President Mobuto, as well as with Savimbi's UNITA, a beneficiary of military support from South Africa and the US. Thus, Neto had no other recourse but to rely on Cuba and the Soviet Union while doing his best to cozy up to the West for investment in his country's oil production.

While attempting to distance himself from the Russians, the hard-line communist wing of his party made it abundantly clear that they opposed any overtures to the West. He responded by cracking down against them. With the help of Cuban forces, he survived a Kremlin-backed coup attempt by the leftists. President Houphouët and I attended an OAU summit in Libreville a few months after the failed coup of May 1977, and met with his prime minister, Lopo do Nascimento, to discuss strategies for a cooperative relationship with the West. He wished to convey to the president that the vast majority of his country's citizens would rather not have the Russians and Cubans on their soil. "I meet people all the time, and they ask why we rid our country of the Portuguese, only to replace them with Russian and Cuban masters," he told the president. We supported Neto's objectives, but by the same token, the president thought it would be best for him to reconcile his differences with Mobutu, because the two countries shared a common border and Mobutu was a darling of the West. The suggestion was easier said than done, however, since the two leaders had developed a great deal of mistrust and were not quite ready to make peace. Mobutu rejected our efforts. On the other hand, I had been adamant in suggesting to the president that we bypass Mobutu all together. But he stuck to his guns, knowing fully well that without a cooperative strategic agreement in place, the continuation of cross-border incursions would undermine the fragile peace. He remained hopeful that our efforts would eventually pay off in the months to come. Sadly, Neto lost his battle with cancer and died in Moscow. The unfortunate turn of events was extremely painful to us and became one of the most regretful episodes in our peace-making endeavors. The president dispatched Justice Minister Camille Alliali and I to the funeral on his private jet.

I was taken in by the somber atmosphere and an overwhelming ambience of an entire country in mourning. The body of Neto, a national hero, was borne through the streets of Luanda, the country's capital, for the solemn funeral ceremonies at the Palace of the People. The crowd was immense. Women with black scarfs wailed as the glass-topped coffin draped with flags was accompanied by Dr. Neto's widow, Maria Eugenia Neto, party and state leaders, African leaders, and the president of Portugal. I paid my last tributes to my dear friend and brother with a heavy heart and remained in Angola until the succession was decided. Because of my relationship with the likes of Lúcio Lara (president of the MPLA), a potential successor, and other leaders of the MPLA, President Houphouët wanted to have me on the ground to monitor the situation closely and deliver a detailed analysis on the outlook of a fragile peace. I knew at the time that Angola was an important axis around which the Cold War revolved, and therefore I was acutely aware of the fact that the balance of power could switch in a moment's notice in that part of Africa if the successor favored the policy of opening up

A Dream for Peace

to the West, in accordance with Neto's objectives. He had already endorsed some contracts with Texaco, an oil conglomerate, and sought the establishment of diplomatic relations with Washington. But the power shift could potentially be derailed by the Soviets, whose motives were quite clear—to usher forth a successor who would be willing to put in place a communist administration.

They got their wish when Eduardo Dos Santos, then Minister of Planning and interim president at the time of Neto's hospitalization, became the successor. He earned his graduate degree in petroleum engineering from a university in the Soviet Union. I returned to Abidjan after he was sworn in, feeling somewhat pessimistic about the chances for a sustained peace. It was clear that the country was on track to becoming a hotbed for Cold War tensions.

The United States channeled its support for Savimbi through Côte d'Ivoire. As a dear friend of Savimbi's, the president tried to talk him out of continuing the atrocious civil war that had gotten out of hand, causing the deaths of thousands of Angolans. Despite the propositions, he continued to report about advancements from the front lines of battle whenever he phoned the president. He came to Abidjan on occasion to update us on his successes. During our talks at lunches and around the dinner table, I became quite familiar with Savimbi and came to regard him as a courteous and well-spoken personality, but I couldn't grasp with much certainty what drove his political objectives. He was a complex man. However, the president, a firm anti-communist, believed Savimbi could potentially help stave off the emerging threat of communism on the continent. He became his protégé and showered him with lots of affection, even helping him gain the support of other leaders in the West. His wife soon warmed up to Titi, and they became good friends.

After years of discussions and consultations with his troops, he finally gave in to the president's urgings. He agreed to recognize Dos Santos as the president of Angola, paving the way for the withdrawal of all foreign troops from his country. He even agreed to participate in free and open elections after peace had been restored. Cautious yet very confident, President Houphouët-Boigny prayed to give peace a chance. He met with President Dos Santos in Paris in February 1986. The encounter was a debacle. It was also a missed opportunity for peace because Dos Santos was unbending to Savimbi's proposals. He did not wish to see Savimbi on Angolan soil but in exile in the United States. When I saw the president at the end of their discussions, he couldn't hide his disappointment. "It is no longer an ideological fight, my son," he told me. "It has become personal. All of this fighting at the expense of the Angolan people makes absolutely no sense to me." We marveled at the audacity of forcing the son of a sovereign nation—a military leader representing the ideology and interests of a large portion of the population—to go into exile after fourteen years of fighting. The motive was sinister at the very least, designed to deprive him of an electoral platform. Such spiteful posturing amounted to a major act of disrespect to those who had sacrificed their lives and a slap in the face of those who accepted reconciliation. Once again, the fleeting nature of peace slipped through our fingers and came to a grinding halt.

Since the president could neither reach out with a coherent response nor give him a feedback on his proposals, Savimbi concluded that Dos Santos was not ready for peace. The fighting intensified. In mid-1987, he made some inroads and took over some key districts in the Battle of Mavinga with the help of the South African military. This was a morale-boosting victory and a major advancement for his UNITA movement. President Houphouët thought that a proposal by South Africa's government that linked the departure of Cuban troops from Angola to recognizing Namibia as a sovereign independent nation could potentially end the South African aid to UNITA. They entered into an agreement (the Brazzaville Protocol) with Cuba and Angola while involved in talks regarding Namibia's independence (the New York Accords). The president and I finally breathed a sigh of relief but remained cautiously optimistic. We foresaw some

A Dream for Peace

difficulties on the road ahead for Dos Santos with the departure of the Cubans and the arrival of Mikhail Gorbachev as the head of the USSR. Aid to Angola from Russia was rolled back significantly, and soon he lacked other means of vital support, giving him no other alternative but to contemplate negotiating a peaceful settlement to bring about political stability in his country.

The president encouraged Savimbi to refrain from actions that could hamper the peace efforts. He stopped his offensive in February 1989; then in September of that same year, despite more urging from the president, Savimbi refused to attend a crucial meeting in Kinshasa that had been orchestrated by the US and chaired by President Mobutu. Savimbi and his team suspected an imminent plot by Mobuto to have him killed. The president and I were surprised by the news. Faced with the prospects of making peace with the enemy, the seasoned fighter feared for his life. His decision was contradictory to my personal conviction; as a former freedom fighter I always believed that in taking up arms, the most important pledge is the sacrifice of one's own life. Well aware of the friendship between President Houphouët and Jonas Savimbi, President George Bush Sr. sent a letter of inquiry regarding the decision to stay away from the Kinshasa summit. In his response, the president assured Bush that he was at a loss for words, because he had exhausted every possible avenue to ensure Savimbi's participation. Not to be outdone, Mobutu directed some unwarranted criticism at President Houphouët, blaming him for the debacle. In a rare rebuke, President Houphouët voiced his disenchantment to me: "Mobutu must not forget all the moral support I offered to him throughout the difficult phases of his not-so-rosy political career. I do not understand his criticism toward me, but I'm used to this nonsensical behavior, and his words do not affect me. Although I pity the man, I will continue to support him in his efforts."

The president declared further, "What matters to me is neither a victory by Dos Santos nor Jonas Savimbi, but a victory by Angola in peace and reconciliation of all her children." Finally in 1991, the Bicesse Accords, outlining the framework of a transition to multiparty democracy in Angola under the supervision of the United Nations, were drafted in Portugal and executed by Dos Santos and Savimbi. The accords detailed a specific road map that led to the disarmament and demobilization of both political parties in the conflict prior to free and open multiparty elections in 1992. When the final votes were tallied, Savimbi accounted for 40 percent to Dos Santos's 49 percent, with the remaining 11 percent going to other candidates. Following the finalization of the preliminary voting, it was required by Angola's constitution that either a second round of voting must take place to elect a candidate with an absolute majority, or an arrangement between the candidates was required to solidify majority rule. Instead of proceeding in accordance with the constitution, the fighting resumed.

As for President Houphouët, he was never the one to lose faith in the process. He remained hopeful and patient and pushed for further peace talks through the United Nations. But in the aftermath of Savimbi's loss at the ballot box, the UN Summit for Peace in Abidjan broke down. His decision to not return the president's phone calls while his representatives were at the summit was a major disappointment to us. The president had not only been a broker of the resolution for peace but also a staunch, relentless supporter and a friend in time of need. The two men never had another moment to speak and reconnect again, because the president passed away just a few months after the botched summit.

Faced with constant conflicts and failed peace attempts, finding concord in Africa became a thorny dream for those of us who were indefatigably committed to bringing harmony among the nations of our beautiful continent. Although peace in Angola was elusive for several decades, leaving perplexed politicians and policy makers in its wake, the transcendent conflict, like all other conflicts on the continent, managed to transform itself from a struggle for independence to a multinational proxy war that brought in the Cold War actors with deadly consequences. But the dumbfounding nature of a conflict that ushered forth a highly charged struggle for personal power resulted in an overwhelming tragedy, having claimed the lives of more than half a million citizens and displaced over half of the country's population after the dust had settled. Despite our very thoughtful, perhaps sometimes passionate pledge to achieve peace in a forum designed to accommodate constructive international mediation, the president and I learned the hard way that the negotiation process was always littered with complex scenarios that could never be predicted. As well, Africa's future may at times be in the hands of impulsive play makers and personalities who are bent on determining the final outcomes to appease their self-serving interests, which isn't always aligned with a genuine search for peace and reconciliation.

A Dream for Peace

"Young man with piercing blue eyes!" she exclaimed in a high-pitched voice. "You are so young, and yet you are decorated with medallions from almost every country in the world. My goodness, what did you do to deserve so many acknowledgments?" I smiled broadly and said, "Madame, I really don't think I deserve these medals, but I wear them because others think I am worthy."

Chapter Fourteen

Diplomacy of Smiles

The intricacies of diplomacy lend themselves to the complexities of negotiating many a difficult issue or even an obscure political event on the world stage. At times, my mind navigates a glimpse into the past and lands squarely in the thick of stubborn episodes of lighthearted bloopers that trigger a momentous smile or unbridled laughter. In all seriousness, both President Houphouët and I loved to laugh.

Barely two years after joining his administration, I was part of a large delegation that accompanied him to Tunisia in March 1968. By then, I had become accustomed to working with everyone in the president's cabinet, including his French advisors. Oddly enough, weeks before the trip, presidential protocol received word that Tunisian President Habib Bourguiba had specifically asked that our entourage must only consist of African nationals. President Houphouët agreed, and the French stayed home.

During the welcome ceremonies in Tunis, I noticed that I was the object of undue attention from President Bourguiba. In his interactions with our delegation, he frequently gazed over at me with uninhibited curiosity. I caught his gazes from the corner of my eye, but I continued to enjoy the impressive spectacle on display. The reception was magnificent.

Over the years, both leaders had nurtured a very deep friendship and affection toward each other, and they seemed very much immersed in each other's company. At the end of the day, I returned to the hotel with other members of our delegation. In honor of his treasured friendship and esteemed regard for President Houphouët, the Tunisian president arranged for him to stay at the villa of his son, Habib Bourguiba Jr.

Shortly after my Fajr prayer in the early morning, I received a phone call from the hotel's front desk, "Good morning, sir. The president is waiting for you and the driver is here to pick you up." "Thank you," I replied. "I will be down shortly."

Somewhat surprising, I thought to myself, because it was unusual for the president to not call me directly if he wished to meet at an early hour. This was certainly an unexpected situation. I did, however, recognize the driver as soon as I got to the lobby. I hopped in the back seat of the car without asking any questions. It wasn't until I noticed we had driven past President Houphouët's residence that I wondered out loud, "*Je m'excuse, mon ami,* we just passed the villa where the president is staying." "You are absolutely correct, sir, but President Bourguiba is the one who wishes to see you." I was puzzled.

As soon as we arrived at the presidential palace, I was escorted to a grand living room where a smiling President Bourguiba was waiting. "Good morning, young man," he greeted vibrantly and motioned for me to sit. "Good morning, Mr. President, pleased to see you."

"You know, young man, because I was looking forward to meeting with my African brothers, I was mystified when I saw you yesterday in the midst of the Ivorian delegation. I asked Houphouët, '*We were supposed to be interacting among us Africans. Who is this white man?*'" He paused to look at me point blank, and he flashed a smile. I acknowledged. "Do you know, young man, what he said to me?" I bobbed my head, encouraging him to continue. "*He is your son.*" He became animated, moving to the edge of his seat. "What do you mean by 'he is my son?'" "Yes, of course he is your son; he is a young man from your neighboring country, Algeria." He mimicked the president with such accuracy it made me laugh. "Is that right,

Diplomacy of Smiles

Houphouët? An Algerian by your side? No wonder you've been such a calm personality of late!" He chuckled at himself, and I laughed at his wittiness. He impressed me as a very down-to-earth man, direct and carefree. "Those Algerians," he alleged with some sarcasm. "They are usually a bunch of bustling characters. But I trust that this young man is very special. This is why I can't wait to meet him." We both burst into a hearty laughter. "I am honored to make your acquaintance, Mr. President," I said.

Meeting with President Bourguiba.

Interestingly enough, he wanted to know more about the story of my life. I shared my global political vision and told him about how I met President Houphouët. The conversation was punctuated by "Oh, really?" and "Very good, young man, very good. I like that." He was so moved by my story that at the end of our official visit, he awarded me the country's highest distinction, Commandeur de l'Ordre de la République de Tunisie (Commander of the Order of the Republic of Tunisia).

A Dream for Peace

With President Nyerere in Bouaké.

  I enjoyed going on extracurricular tours around the country with visiting heads of state. When we arrived in Bouaké with Tanzanian President Julius Nyerere, we were received by the hyperenergetic mayor, Djibo Sounkalo, in a traditional welcome ceremony fit for visiting royalty. In fact, unbeknownst to him, the stage had been set to anoint President Nyerere as honorary Baoulé chief. He seemed somewhat overwhelmed and bashful. After a spirited speech with many funny punch lines, the mayor draped him in a colorful Baoulé *pagne* fabric and placed a large crown on his head. Not quite familiar with the customs of traditional dress code, he felt a bit awkward and looked out of place. It was funny watching the mayor's futile attempt to help him own the costume. We later paid a visit to a frog farm on the outskirts of town. The country was well known for exporting frog legs overseas, especially to many French restaurants of high repute, yet President Nyerere was a bit reluctant to embark on that particular tour. He held my hand in a firm grip as soon as he stepped out of the car. "Please don't leave me alone. I can't stand frogs, let alone the thought of eating them. I have a very strange feeling that this will be a tough visit. Just the thought of eating a frog leg is making me sick already." "But of course, Mr. President. No problem at all," I assured him. When I alerted official protocol that the visit would be shorter than expected, we were quickly escorted to the cafeteria where the anxious maître d' presented the president with a platter of freshly cooked frog legs. He inhaled deeply and held his breath. "Thank you," I said, "but the president will not be tasting any frog legs at the moment." I dismissed the maître d' and we had a memorable chuckle. "I owe you a debt of gratitude, Dr. Berrah."

Because of his fear of flying, President Houphouët avoided the use of airplanes as a means of transportation. Although he compelled himself to overcome his fear on occasion, this was a well-known fact among those in his inner circle. I was aboard an official Ivorian flight with him and other leaders of the Conseil de l'Entente, including President Maurice Yaméogo of Upper Volta (renamed Burkina Faso), President Hubert Maga of Dahomey (renamed Bénin), and Hamani Diori of Niger. Suddenly, the plane encountered severe turbulence and dropped several feet in altitude. We heard a hair-raising scream. One could have guessed that it was President Houphouët, but I did not recognize his voice. After several minutes of bumps and shakes, the plane stabilized and the rattled nerves were soon forgotten. "It was without a doubt Houphouët who screamed. The poor man was frightened!" exclaimed one of his peers. "Not at all, it was definitely Diori," President Houphouët responded. "He was more courageous than I. He could at least express himself, but I was too petrified. I had turned into a rock, unable to move, let alone open my mouth to scream." Everyone burst into a contagious laughter.

On June 2, 1970, while on a three-day official visit to see Queen Juliana of the Netherlands, we cruised the canals of Amsterdam on the royal yacht with Her Highness. I was among a few key members of the delegation who joined President Houphouët and the First Lady for a sumptuous lunch with Her Royal Highness aboard the vessel.

A Dream for Peace

Shortly after sampling some desserts, the queen disappeared to the lower cabins. After several minutes of waiting, President Houphouët wondered about her whereabouts and asked me to check on her. I found her sprawled across a chaise lounge on a lower deck balcony, sleeping soundly. She had succumbed to the serenity of the summer breeze. I reckoned the heavy meal might have had a role to play in her unintended snooze. We chuckled at the thought of being abandoned in such an informal manner by our royal host.

On deck of the Netherlands royal yacht with the president.

Our entire delegation stayed at the royal palace in Amsterdam. During a brief interval in our official schedule, the president's nephew, Lambert Aka, asked if I could accompany him to the city in search of a special Dutch cheese. "This wouldn't be necessary. No need worrying about such errands when you are a guest of the royal palace," I reminded him. "I am sure that a palace employee would gladly facilitate your wish." He ignored my advice and pressed me to go with him into the city. The friendly palace guards greeted us warmly on our way out and called for a driver to take us to a bustling commercial area. We searched and found the cheese at a popular family-run business with a long tradition of artisan cheese making in the city center. When we returned to the palace, we were stopped at the gate by the same guards and asked to use the back door. I glanced over at Lambert and saw the puzzled look on his face. "You see," they told us, "it is improper to return to the royal palace hauling grocery bags. This is a job for palace employees." I couldn't stop myself from laughing as we sauntered off into the alley.

President Houphouët and Queen Juliana.

The trip was definitely special, albeit with a very strict protocol. Each of us was assigned a Dutchman as our minder. While I was getting dressed for the gala dinner, I heard a knock on the door. A high-ranking air force lieutenant in an immaculate uniform had come to see if I needed his help getting into my shawl collar shirt and peaked lapel tailcoat. "Oh, no thank you," I said confidently. "You are so kind, but that won't be necessary," I dismissed him.

An elderly lady sitting next to me at the dinner table couldn't keep her eyes off the many medallions on my jacket. "Young man with piercing blue eyes!" she exclaimed in a high-pitched voice.

A Dream for Peace

"You are so young, and yet you are decorated with medallions from almost every country in the world. My goodness, what did you do to deserve so many acknowledgments?" I smiled broadly and said, "Madame, I really don't think I deserve these medals, but I wear them because others think I am worthy." Her face lit up with subtle admiration, and it made everyone laugh.

In formal attire with medallions.

After the gala dinner I returned to my room, and within minutes my minder from the air force came back to inquire if I needed his help getting out of my attire. Again, I declined. "No, no, no thank you. Have a good night." I tried to remove my white bow tie as soon as the door closed behind me and realized I could not even unbutton my collar. Out of self-respect, I decided not to call him back. I exhausted every feasible attempt to free myself from the menacing outfit and began to appreciate the fact that I was trapped. Hopelessly tired, I collapsed onto the bed, tilted my head backward on the soft pillow, and passed out. My minder was amazed to see me in the same garb when I answered the door in the morning. Sparing him the details of the night's experience, I apologized profusely for not taking him up on his offer and expressed my warmest gratitude after he relieved me of my agony.

President Houphouët shared a memorable tale with me, after he returned from a visit to the United Kingdom. I had fallen ill prior to his departure and was unable to accompany him on the trip. Upon arrival, the president and First Lady were welcomed by Her Majesty, Queen Elizabeth II, and invited to stay at Buckingham Palace. As a courtesy, aides at the palace came to pick up the dinner attire of the delegation, as well as of the president himself, for dry cleaning. Delivery of the outfits was rushed to the delegates shortly before the dinner deadline. Unfortunately for Ambassador Georges Ouégnin, the president's Director of Protocol, a thin, long-limbed man, his vest was about three times his size. The president's personal physician, Dr. Salmon, a tall, heavyset man, did not fare any better; he received a *petite*-sized vest, more than likely belonging to Ouégnin, but neither man had any idea, and there was hardly time to sort things out. All of this happened just shy of a few minutes before dinner. Without hesitating, Dr. Salmon's wife came up with the only remedy available to her. Grabbing a pair of scissors, she slit the back of the vest from top to bottom and handed the two half vests to her husband. He smiled approvingly, threw on his tailcoat, and *voila!* Problem solved. The situation in Ambassador Ouégnin's room was frantic but not as stressful. With some safety pins, he folded the back of the vest and lined up an oversized inward crease. He wore it gently and moved gingerly, ever mindful of the threatening needles beneath his tailcoat. Everyone made it just in the nick of time for the gala dinner.

On the way to the Belgian suites of the palace after the reception, Georges Ouégnin was sharing his story with the president when Dr. Salmon overheard them and began to laugh uncontrollably: "So, it is you who is wearing my vest." "*Oh, mon Dieu!*" exclaimed Georges Ouégnin. "Does that mean you are wearing mine? That's impossible!"

The laughter was contagious. "You couldn't even begin to imagine the clownish spectacle before my eyes when I asked them to take off their jackets, Berrah," the president recalled. Fortunately for them, Her Majesty was nowhere in sight.

Colonel Gaddafi was less than chivalrous during his usual mood swings. He used to refer to President Houphouët as a "valet of imperialism." On a particular occasion, he went as far as to ask a Libyan newspaper to publish a highly discourteous and offensive article lambasting the president in a myriad of distorted facts. I was immediately dispatched to Libya to meet with Gaddafi and shed some light on the matter to prevent further dissemination of falsities.

The Minister of Foreign Affairs, Ali Triki, whom I had known for years, dating back to his days in New York when he was Libya's UN representative, was on hand to welcome me at the airport in Tripoli. On our way to the hotel, he informed me that state protocol would be in touch regarding my meeting with Colonel Gaddafi. I called Triki at the end of the day to remind him that I still hadn't heard from state protocol. "I will be taking the next flight back to Abidjan if I don't meet with the *raïs* [president] within twenty-four hours." "My apologies," he said. "Let me check on it and call you back." He reached out about a couple of hours later to confirm the meeting for the following day.

Diplomacy of Smiles

With Colonel Gaddafi.

I was greeted at the presidential palace by Gaddafi and invited to take a seat. He sat across from me, but rather than face me, he turned sideways and only showed me his profile. I waited patiently, thinking he was gathering his thoughts or focusing on some artifact on that part of the room. After a few minutes had gone by, I couldn't imagine what else he was doing.

A Dream for Peace

Clearly he was alert, because I could see him blinking. I cleared my throat in a fruitless attempt to get a reaction. Realizing this was a game of some sort, I proceeded to address him. "I am a native of Algeria. Perhaps, you don't know me, but President Boumédiène will be able to provide you with more information about me." That did it. He immediately turned to face me, giving me his undivided attention.

I explained the purpose for my mission and highlighted the misinformation in the article. He listened intently and apologized when I was done speaking. "My brother," he said. "Extend my sincere apologies to President Houphouët. I will see to it that the editors of the newspaper retract and correct the story in their next issue." I thanked him and took my leave.

When Foreign Minister Triki came to take me to the airport, he handed a parcel to me. "It is a gift from our guide, Colonel Gaddafi." I gathered my thoughts for a few seconds. "Thank you very much, my brother, but I cannot accept any gifts," I said regretfully. "I couldn't begin to envision the idea of President Houphouët under the assumption that I have been corrupted by Gaddafi." "I implore you to accept the gift my brother," he begged, "because I run the risk of being incarcerated if I return the parcel to the boss."

I suddenly had a moral dilemma, and it had to be resolved on the spot. For security reasons, I asked him to open the box to ensure that it wasn't booby-trapped. He obliged and opened the package, his fingers shaking as he fidgeted his way into the box. To our relief, it was a very costly Rolex watch. "Ali, I definitely couldn't live with myself if you were sent to prison because of me. I will take your boss's gift with me to Abidjan." He breathed a huge sigh of relief. "My sincere gratitude, my brother. Thank you very much for accepting the gift." We left for the airport.

As soon as my flight landed in Abidjan, I went to see the president and gave him the watch. "It is Colonel Gaddafi's gift to you." He smiled reassuringly. "You should give the watch to one of the faithful at a Friday prayer," he suggested. "Thank you, Mr. President, but I believe that you do have ample opportunity to meet people. You might run into someone who will be interested in the gift." He stared at me and said nothing. I proceeded to debrief him and went home shortly afterward without the watch.

    I wore a suit and tie on a daily basis, except for when I went to pray at the mosque on Friday afternoon. The traditional *boubou* was my preferred outfit of choice and a personal favorite. When I went to see the president on a beautiful morning shortly before Friday prayers, I ran into Madame Plazanet, his French secretary. "*Bonjour*, Dr. Berrah," she chimed. "*Mes hommages, madame*," I replied. Her eyes zigzagged across my outfit from head to toe. "Is there a particular reason for playing dress-up today," she asked curiously. "Absolutely not, madame. Indeed, I am dressed in the outfit of my ancestors. I only play dress-up when I wear a suit." She stood speechless and forced a quick smile. "Enjoy the rest of your day, madame." I left her hanging in the hallway.

    My wife and I went on a private visit to Paris with President Houphouët. French President François Mitterrand invited him to lunch at Le Palais de l'Élysée shortly upon arrival. In stereotypical fashion, he started his early morning routine with the usual power walk around the compound, followed by a thorough review of his meeting agenda. We decided to go and call on him at his Parisian residence about an hour before he was scheduled to leave.

    His official car, adorned with the Ivorian orange, white, and green flag, was parked behind the gate, gleaming in the sun, ready to go. I went looking for him and was told to my utter surprise that he was having lunch in the dining area. Titi and I found him, looking absolutely relaxed and comfortable, enjoying his favorite Baoulé dishes: *yam foutou*[63] dressed with *gnangnan*[64] and *kopé*[65] sauce,

---

[63] Pounded African yams.
[64] Bitter eggplant stew.
[65] Okra sauce.

infused with chicken. He smiled at us when we walked in.

"Good morning, Papa," we chimed. "Good morning, daughter; good morning, my son. How are you doing?" "We are well, Papa," I said and inquired, "Have you altered your schedule?" "Not at all," he laughed. "*C'est pour pouvoir faire la fine bouche à l'Élysée,*" he declared ("*I will play the role of the picky eater when I arrive at l'Élysée Palace*").

Distinctions and Medallions granted to Dr. Ghoulem Berrah during his diplomatic carrier

Order of Merit of the Federal Republic of Germany

Officier de L'Ordre de la Valeur de La République Fédérale du Cameroun (Cameroon)

Grand Commander of the Star of Africa, Republic of Liberia

Commandeur de L'Ordre de la République de Tunisie (Tunisia)

Commandeur du Wissam Alaouite, Maroc (Morocco)

Commandeur de L'Ordre de Belgique (Belgium)

Commander de Orde Van Oranje Nassau (Netherlands)

A Dream for Peace

*W*ithout any hesitation, I proceeded to advise him: "Papa, I think it is time for you to create a position in the administration. We need a person in charge of managing domestic dissension and tackling the nation's financial affairs." He was one step ahead of me. "I am looking for someone who doesn't have any skeletons in their closet."

Chapter Fifteen

Côte d'Ivoire's Political Radar

The pursuit of happiness for the average Ivorian in a society where concord and fraternal harmony reigned writ large denoted to me that I commit to a tenacious and feverish effort to reach certain milestones within the standards of modern-day politics. The quest for a sustained dynamic economy in Côte d'Ivoire was an essential piece of the puzzle, and likewise, enshrined in our ideal criteria were the basic tenets of freedom of religion, freedom of speech, decent living standards for the citizens, and the goal to achieve multipartyism. I believed in a vibrant society where each individual could aspire to reach their potential and where our thoughts intersected at the center of the ideals of liberty, peace, and justice. Envisioning a twenty-first-century mindset, I knew that the task ahead would be hard for the president, but nevertheless, as a public servant, I was entrusted to serve for the good of all citizens and was prepared to dedicate my tireless efforts to an endeavor that solicited the best in us—everyone in the administration. I believed with all my heart that we were stewards on a mission to leave a better society for future generations.

Within the president's inner circle, I was on the forefront of the nation's politics, and I observed firsthand the intricacies of policy implementation. I first brought up the subject of a multiparty system with him in 1966. "You know, my son," he told me. "I am not against the idea. I must emphasize that I proposed the article be inserted into the constitution of the new republic." He had inherited from France a nation that was severely underdeveloped economically and socially. "There were only two factories in the entire country, and a mere total of 8 percent of the people were enrolled in school, hardly enough of a base to field political parties and exploratory committees," he explained. "An immediate institution of a multiparty system would have ushered in an era of tribal division fueled by heated deliberations and discordant debates that could have derailed our constructive agenda." He was convinced that a vibrant political institution should be planned in incremental steps, albeit in tandem with future socioeconomic progress. Hence, he opted for a pragmatic path toward an open market system of development and began to focus on building a solid national foundation on which the country could flourish.

Observing the ministers of the administration over several months, I detected that they had a tendency to congregate around their fellow tribesmen. From the office director to the errand boy, tribal instincts overrode qualifications. I understood the president's point regarding a fragmented society. Such a problem is still prevalent in Africa. Tribalism continues to be rampant across the continent, and consequently, establishing a neutral source for a basic think tank or other committee to operate fluidly remains a formidable challenge. The president was an alchemist of interior politics who ensured that the many tribal factions in Côte d'Ivoire were each represented by one of their own in his administration. He believed that educated executives and professionals from diverse backgrounds constituted a healthy economic and political fiber for the nation. In essence, he envisaged a society where a vibrant multiparty system would automatically blossom out of a well-cultivated political structure. He inserted the basic idea and guaranteed its implantation in the constitution.

Plans had been in place since its inception for the Parti Démocratique de Côte d'Ivoire (PDCI) to not only organize party meetings and conventions but to also serve as a body that nurtured and trained individuals who could then provide advice and ideas on specific political or economic problems. In 1967, almost a year after I joined his administration, the president formed the Conseil National, a forum that brought together leaders from across the land, charged with meeting biennially to participate in three days of dialogue aimed at gauging the pulse of the country and finding solutions for matters of national development. Traditional chiefs, union representatives, heads of corporations, social groups, peasants, and workers from all professions were invited to participate. The interactive event took place in a forum designed to engage the president in a robust exchange of ideas and constructive feedback.

In October 1970, I was given a major domestic assignment to survey and report on a violent uprising in the western region of Guébié where a tribal insurrection against the local administration had gotten out of hand. The backdrop was a grassroots movement spurred by a political activist, Kragbé Gnagbé, who returned to Côte d'Ivoire following years of studies in France. Shortly after he arrived, he recorded his intent to form an opposition party in accordance with Article 7 of the constitution. At the time, however, a lack of national preparedness for accommodating multiparty platforms and mass political rallies was a matter of concern for the administration. Arrangements for a planned framework and further deliberations were suggested by the PDCI to help them assess how to properly handle the matter. Meanwhile, Gnagbé envisioned the secession of his tribal region from the country altogether and initiated the formation of an embryonic opposition party, Parti Nationaliste Africain (PANA), in 1967.

He and his supporters continued to stir passions on the streets of Gagnoa township, the main city in the region and beyond. In Abidjan, he was picked up by the authorities after distributing leaflets with antigovernment propaganda and inciting tribal rebellion, accusing the central government of illegal annexation of his ancestral lands. His claims were totally baseless, because the administration was inclusive of public servants from the different tribes in the country. When he received a presidential pardon, he escaped into the forest as soon as he was released. From his hiding place, he urged his supporters to participate in civil disobedience. The situation quickly got out of hand. Armed with rudimentary weapons, his supporters, largely made up of dissidents along tribal lines—Guébié, Zabia, Paccolo, and others from surrounding villages—took to the streets in violent demonstrations. They attacked fellow citizens from other regions of Côte d'Ivoire who had relocated to the area. A group of them used overwhelming violence against local state representatives when they seized the city hall in Gagnoa and hoisted a flag to declare the official secession of an independent state known as "Eburnie." Having been pushed to their limit due to the scale of unprecedented rioting and widespread looting, police precincts were rendered powerless. The full force of the army was called in to restore order, but they were not adequately trained to deal with civil unrest of that magnitude. No martial law was imposed on the communities. Making matters worse, the unruly soldiers resorted to levels of unrivaled violence in an attempt to keep the peace.

    I toured the area by helicopter before going to meet with the regional minister and other local officials on the outskirts of town. Having witnessed firsthand the impoverished living conditions on the ground, I returned to Abidjan profoundly perturbed by the state of affairs. "Mr. President, the people are living under such dire circumstances that I am not too surprised they are being influenced by someone who promises them a better way of life." He was astonished. "Granted, violence is not the solution to resolve their problem, but they are being led along a path which, in my opinion, Mr. President, is highly coercive and self-destructive." I also emphasized the use of brute force in the army's undisciplined crackdown, calling it a disproportionate response, and he agreed. "I made it categorically clear that the army must not resort to extremes to bring an end to the violence and restore the peace, my son. The leadership was explicitly ordered to remain calm and resolved."

Immediately after receiving the details of my report, he summoned the key leaders of the military and subjected them to a scathing rebuke. We then took up a discussion regarding how to quell the situation and move forward. It was determined that a face-to-face dialogue with Kragbé Gnagbé was in order. The president sent out an urgent invitation to meet, but it was much too late. We received word that Gnagbé had died alongside many other victims in the midst of the military mayhem. We were absolutely shocked by the unfortunate news. To my utter disgust and dismay, false rumors spread like wildfire within certain political factions in the opposition about the president's role in the killing. He directed the heads of the military to launch a thorough investigation into the reckless actions that took the lives of so many of the country's citizens, but he faced substantial cover-up within their ranks. Ultimately, it was concluded that a surreptitious confrontation caused the wrongful death of the PANA leader. It was mind-boggling. I remained rattled and incensed for several weeks.

In the years following the Guébié episode, the country's economy continued to show signs of improvement. We noticed the gradual rise of a vibrant middle class in Abidjan and an influx of young graduates returning home, mostly from universities in France, but also a handful came back from US institutions. There was much patriotic fervor in the air, and it seemed everyone was eager to participate in the country's development. Many unique enterprises blossomed around the country, resulting in a robust expansion in our economy and a GDP rate somewhere north of 7 percent. Global financial experts characterized such promising economic indicators as the "Ivorian miracle." The president recalled in a conversation with a visiting journalist:

"Members of the PDCI agree with me on the fact that any evaluation of our progress must be done, not by us, but by foreign visitors to our country. In general, progress is not easy, especially for a young country. I haven't managed to take some time off since 1957. My people expect a lot from me and have placed an overwhelming amount of trust in my leadership. I believe that only God's guidance and protection endows me with the strength needed to tackle my duties as the head of this nation. Besides my obligations and commitments to the people, I also deal with a number of countries that have established contacts through a variety of means."

Due to Côte d'Ivoire's very robust economical success, the country began to attract many immigrants from around the continent, thereby prompting the president to introduce a bill to the Conseil National in 1972 proposing dual citizenship for West African immigrants. He admitted that the proposition was modeled on the merits of the so-called "melting pot" idea in the United States, a country he greatly admired. The scheme was a part of a preemptive measure to strengthen immigration through a legal institutional framework. He was ahead of his countrymen. But in the face of a massive outcry, the Conseil National expressed disenchantment, and the president retracted the proposal. Had the bill become law, Côte d'Ivoire would not have undergone an identity crisis in the years to come, and the concept of "Ivoirité"[66] (introduced by his successor) would have been averted.

He was a seasoned farmer who knew how to cultivate and grow crops. His vast experience transcended agriculture and loomed large on his policies. I observed when I first arrived in the country that there wasn't a threat of an imminent food shortage. The fertile soil and the president's own emphasis on a robust agricultural program ensured the abundance of food. When rapid population growth at a yearly rate of about 4 percent posed unexpected challenges to the nation, he pivoted toward a mass reorganization of the food culture, utilizing the power of state-owned companies to expand

---

[66] Initially, the word was used as a common cultural identity for everyone living in Côte d'Ivoire. However, it shifted in meaning, due to nationalist and xenophobic politics, to distinguish populations from the south and east.

production of vital subsidies.

For several years, Côte d'Ivoire was the world's largest producer of cocoa and the third largest producer of coffee. The country's economy was dependent on those two main exports and until 1979, the favorable terms of international trade had a positive effect on its balance sheets. After that year, however, the nation underwent a series of intermittent economic growth with periodic highs and lows, triggered by instability in global markets. Prices of cocoa and coffee stagnated while the value of imported goods skyrocketed, resulting in a steep decline in GDP.

Toward the end of the 1970s, we red-flagged a series of questionable government contracts and presented our findings to the president, who took the necessary steps to remedy the situation. He hired Antoine Cesareo, the French civil engineer, acclaimed for some of the world's most important structural engineering, and had him oversee the development of the country's vital infrastructure expansion. Cesareo's work will go down in the country's history as the most constructive. Shortly after he came aboard, he established the DCGTX (Grands Travaux), an independent public works division charged with auditing the books and every single contractual bid, tightening contractual oversight, and eliminating corruption. He was a very hands-on man, literally getting down and dirty in the trenches with manual laborers at every opportunity.

Some ministers in the administration viewed him as a troublemaker who stood in their way, since they no longer could engage in the same old tribalism and cronyism practices. But the president saw him as a godsend—a strict, incorruptible, no-nonsense disciplinarian who saved the country loads of money and kept projects on track. I often visited him at the Grands Travaux to discuss state affairs and came to appreciate his sense of hard work and commitment.

After going through a long period of severe drought (1983 and 1984), there was considerable decrease in crop harvests in the country. The economy took a hit. Even the 176-megawatt hydroelectric facility on the Bandama River at Kossou suffered as a consequence of the drought. All the lakes behind the five dams were almost dried up. We had to reactivate two smaller thermal units in the northern and western regions in order to redirect our load-balancing needs to the Vridi facility on the outskirts of Abidjan. Electricity production fell significantly, causing power outages in the city, which resulted in considerable losses to productivity in the industrial sector. Across the country, everyone endured intermittent blackouts. From his terrace, the president used to sit and gaze in silence at the city below. "This is real sad. I just can't bear to see my beautiful city in the dark," he whispered quietly. I felt his pain, and the sense of helplessness had a reflective effect on me.

    A minor surge in commodity prices and exports led to a brief economic recovery. Record cocoa harvests in 1985, combined with improved prices for coffee and cotton, boosted exports, increased earnings, and restored confidence in the economy. Côte d'Ivoire's national currency, the CFA, was pegged to the French franc and the dollar. When the value of the dollar fell in conjunction with a major decline in raw cocoa and coffee exports, the unexpected situation forced a precipitous drop in state revenues, prompting the country to suspend payments of its foreign debt in 1987. The budget surplus of 1986 was soon transformed into a budget deficit in less than a year.

    We were pressured by the World Bank to introduce austerity measures without further delay. The president issued orders directing the Finance Ministry to implement procedures aimed at raising revenues, leading to an extension of the value-added tax on wholesale and retail trading. There was a gradual increase in import tariffs, customs duties, and tobacco taxes. We secured a substantial loan from the Paris Club and the commercial lending institution the London Club in December 1987 and March 1988. Faced with more challenges, the administration decided to privatize most state enterprises and enter into joint ventures with companies to help revitalize the industrial sector.

The recession impacted every sector of the economy, but low-income workers felt more of the pinch because of rapidly rising inflation. With a steep decline in household consumption rate per capita and a rollback in consumer spending, most average citizens began to feel demoralized. I sensed the shift in enthusiasm during my leisurely walks around town, which revealed to me in vivid detail the pain and suffering that was suddenly a daily reality for the common man. Perhaps such an unexpected turn of events could have been averted with enough foresight and thorough vetting of the administration's policies, but it was much too late to reverse the tide. Although trust and fraternal harmony received a subtle blow, fizzling along with the boisterous chaos at the marketplace, most people remained resilient and friendly despite their difficulties.

Upon completing our due diligence on the government's international trade policies, we began to understand that the deck had been stacked against us from the very beginning. We had underestimated the extent to which international banking syndicates could impose on us financial challenges designed perfectly to appease their interests, yet to the detriment of ours. Their intent was never to operate on a leveled playing field. They controlled the commodity markets as well as the currency exchange boards and profited when the global price of goods fell. They also hedged their bets against our fragile currency, which was weakened when our exports declined in value, but they were always the winners. *"I have but one regret,"* the president told me repeatedly. *"My only regret is the fact that I did not create my own currency at the time of our independence."* Unfortunately, we had already signed off on their loans and placed ourselves in an untenable predicament, which allowed them to play us like a fiddle. The president expressed his frustrations in a letter to President Bush Senior:

A Dream for Peace

> *"Is it fair and honest to play with the work of the poor peasants by manipulating the prices for the products in a single day with price fluctuations that do not reflect reality? In other words, does the price of a cup of coffee or a chocolate bar change every two hours or every day? They play with the work of men as if they were playing in the casinos. Everyone has the right to indulge themselves and risk their money at a casino, but no one has the right to gamble with the money of others, let alone with our products. These are the processes that must disappear from the relationship between humans when we know that our world is moving towards total peace—the peace of hearts and minds. It is up to men like you to attach their name to the current transformation of mentalities that we denounce and that do not honor mankind. Whether we like it or not, the Africa that I know best will have sufficient professionals capable of transforming its raw materials, because it is the continent that is currently the poorest, but potentially, the richest. Its professional workforce I say, one day, sooner than we think, will rise to the challenge of underdevelopment.*
>
> *But I wish, as a sincere friend of the West, that it will be done in friendship, in love and why not, in the love of our grandchildren and great-grandchildren."*
>
> Félix Houphouët-Boigny

The dire circumstances prompted a major overhaul in the political and social landscape of Côte d'Ivoire. Oddly enough, we found out the hard way that we were dealing with a "hidden hand" in the banking institutions' rigid decisions. This was evidenced by their blatantly dismissive approach, thumbing their nose at us, regardless of our constructive propositions, all the while mindful of the fact that such shenanigans could potentially lead to a destabilization of the government. When the people began taking to the streets of Abidjan in mass protests, PDCI leaders retreated to their homes. None of them bothered to go to their districts to explain the situation to misinformed constituents. In a desperate move to evade protesters, mostly all the leadership abandoned their very recognizable government-issued vehicles, opting to move about discreetly in their private cars. The opposition seized the moment and recruited more people to boost their ranks.

Civil unrest became a daily occurrence for several weeks on end, raising security concerns around the country. At an early morning meeting, some within the president's inner circle began to suggest that he ask the French military to intervene. He enjoyed his breakfast and listened to the chatter but said absolutely nothing to any of us. When he was done eating, he laid down his napkin and walked calmly to his living quarters. I was perturbed by the strident and desperate spirit that had permeated the air, but I remained silent. There would surely be a price to pay, I thought, and major repercussions were we to decide to involve the French army in our sovereign nation's affairs. I went straight home to tell my wife that I was prepared to break ranks with the president if he resorted to such extremes. "*I did not fight to liberate Algeria from France,*" I told her, "*only to join forces with the French against my Ivorian brethren some years later. When I decided to accept my Ivorian citizenship, I made a conscious decision from the heart. In this regard, I will be on the side of the ordinary Ivorian through the hard times and the good times, whatever the circumstance. It is my preference that we solve our problems as Ivorians.*" She agreed with me.

Fortunately, civility prevailed throughout the period of unrest. I relayed my thoughts to the president weeks after the situation had stabilized. "*Berrah, you know I will never involve the French army in our domestic affairs.*" He seemed utterly astonished that I even entertained the thought. "*I will never fire on my own brothers to maintain a hold on power.*" There was an innate feeling of selflessness in his emphasis on the word "power," characteristic of his compassionate and peace-loving nature. "*Papa,*" I said, "*you just gave me one more reason to admire you.*"

During a midafternoon drive in April 1990, I passed by the

A Dream for Peace

landmark CCIA[67] building in the heart of the business district of Plateau. An unusual thing caught my eye: written in bold graffiti at a bus station was the inscription, "Houphouët is a thief!" This was a first, and also a most unusual eyesore. The city had absolutely no graffiti anywhere at the time. I was taken aback. I returned to the presidential residence and shared my observation. Without any hesitation, I proceeded to advise him: "Papa, I think it is time for you to create a position in the administration. We need a person in charge of managing domestic dissension and tackling the nation's financial affairs." He was one step ahead of me. "I am looking for someone who doesn't have any skeletons in their closet," he said. "I assume you are referring to our representative at the International Monetary Fund? The gentleman who serves as the governor of the BCEAO[68] in Dakar who pays you frequent visits?" I searched for clues in my thoughts, but he kept mum on the topic.

A few days later, he created a new position and appointed Alassane Ouattara as "Chairman of the Inter-ministerial Committee," responsible for coordinating and stabilizing the nation's economic recovery program. With the exception of myself and a handful of others, almost every politician in the president's inner circle seemed troubled by his selection. After the announcement, I asked why he hadn't just gone ahead and made Ouattara his prime minister. "I am moving in incremental steps," he told me, "I took the decision to ensure that everyone adapt to the idea and grow accustomed to my new appointee before promoting him further to the position of prime minister."

As a former director of the African Department for the IMF, Ouattara was more than qualified to serve in his new position, but there were some who begged to differ with the choice, only because they did not understand that under the circumstances, the nation

---

[67] International Commerce Center of Abidjan.
[68] Central Bank of West African States.

needed to employ the services of a candidate from outside of Côte d'Ivoire's political radar. Encouraged by the president's support and the confidence of the banking institutions, Ouattara collaborated with the IMF and the World Bank to propose economic reforms. In the interim, prospects for the country improved and more Ivorians managed to put on their work boots after the long, dismal stretch that had seen gross domestic product shift abruptly into reverse. Data from the Finance Ministry showed the economy had gradually began to show some signs of recovery. We hoped the momentum shift would continue.

Around the same period, the country recorded an average literacy rate of 70 percent, and we were on track to achieving our most robust infrastructure expansion since independence. I was very happy to point out to the president that we had reached a milestone worth celebrating. Moreover, he agreed that it was time to revisit the framework for implementation of multipartyism in accordance with Article 7 of the constitution. Within weeks after the official announcement, the Interior Ministry registered a number of political parties, the most influential being the Front Populaire Ivoirien (FPI)[69] led by Laurent Gbagbo, a well-known dissident who had served a couple of years in prison for subversive acts against the regime. Following his release, he joined the faculty at the University of Abidjan and pursued a doctorate degree from a university in Paris. He formed the FPI in 1982 and left on a self-imposed exile to France. When he returned in 1988, he was elected to lead his party. Barely two years after his return, the country entered a new era in its politics.

On an unusually rainy morning, we were about to wrap up the day's briefing when the president gave his closing remarks and informed me that our prized infrastructure engineer, Cesareo, had turned in his resignation after claiming mental and physical

---

[69] The Popular Ivorian Front.

A Dream for Peace

exhaustion stemming from thirteen years on the job. Knowing how close I was to Cesareo, President Houphouët asked me to try and talk him out of his decision. I agreed with the president that losing the engineer would be tantamount to eliminating an unbreachable financial fire wall that had proven worthy since the scheme was adopted. I went to meet with Cesareo and his wife at their lovely home to discuss the issue over some tea. When I broached the topic, she stared directly into my eyes, moved to the edge of her seat, tensed up, and expressed her sentiments: "Dr. Berrah, I must tell you that lately, my husband has been on the receiving end of vicious insults and verbal attacks from certain ministers and government officials who refuse to play by the book. There are times they even go as far as to reject requests for files and other documents. I pray that my husband does not get depressed or, even worse, suffer a heart attack. I would rather leave Côte d'Ivoire holding his hands than leave with his body in a coffin." She grabbed his hand and held on firmly. Her words went straight to my heart, and I sensed a deeper level of sadness in the air. It was true that he had complained to me in the past about encounters with some menacing characters who had grown weary of his straight and narrow approach. I soothed his concerns on a few occasions, but this time was quite different. I couldn't bear the thought of having an adverse outcome on my conscience. "I'd like you to know that I respect your decision and to also assure you that you will truly be missed. Thank you for all you have done for our country." The president organized a farewell show of gratitude for his services to the nation. He also gave him a medal of honor in a highly emotional ceremony. We were very sad to see him go.

Out of the doldrums of the international scene, Henri Konan Bédié suddenly reappeared on the domestic political radar. The first Ivorian ambassador to the United States and Canada after independence, he took up the post of Minister of Economy between 1966 until 1977, and then in 1978, he moved on to serve as a special

Côte d'Ivoire's Political Radar

advisor to the World Bank Group's International Finance Corporation, in Washington, DC. I saw him in Geneva in the summer of 1980 at the presidential residence while waiting for the president to wrap up a meeting. I wasn't aware of who exactly he was meeting with until Bédié walked up to me, looking quite pleased. "I am returning to Côte d'Ivoire," he perked up and told me through a gleaming smile. "Good for you," I responded, a bit surprised. "I am happy to hear that." We chatted briefly on our way to the exit. During his two-year tenure in Washington, Bédié had increasingly felt exiled for some reason, hence the opportunity to return home could not have come at a more appropriate time. Speaking after reviewing the day's calendar, the president reaffirmed to me that he had accepted Bédié's request to return home to run for office.

By the autumn, Bédié won the PDCI district elections and joined the National Assembly of Côte d'Ivoire as a member of congress. A couple of months later, he replaced Philipe Yacé as the President of the Assembly. This was a vital step that positioned him in line to become the constitutional successor of President Félix Houphouët-Boigny.

In the beginning, he seemed content in his new post. He ran in two subsequent elections and won. But he had long nurtured an impatient desire to become the country's next president. He once invited Apostolic nuncio Monsignor Mullor to his home for lunch and handed him an envelope containing 500,000 CFA (approximately $1,000) "for the Church." My dear friend Monsignor Mullor thanked him for the charitable "donation," but he was shocked to learn that there was more to the gesture. "You are the president's friend," Bédié whispered. "He listens to you. Can you ask him to resign and hand over the reins of power to me?" The Monsignor later confided in me that he was rendered speechless, dumbfounded, and insulted by the blatant display of audacious impudence. "I cannot convey such an impossible request," he told him in a composed tone, though his disenchantment was vividly clear. Soon after the bizarre episode, he gave the envelope to the Sanctuaire Mariale and tried his best to dismiss the "unfortunate blunder" from his thoughts.

I received a phone call from General Kouassi, a former Commander of the Palace, on June 5, 1990, shortly after lunch with the president. There was an unusual sense of urgency in his voice. He was also a Baoulé tribesman, a protégé of the president's, and a trusted deputy chief of the Ivorian armed forces. He stated dramatically that it was imperative that I went to meet with him. "The matter cannot wait," he said. "I am requesting your immediate presence at my house. He did not live very far from the president's residence. I went to see him.

He welcomed me at the entrance of his home, dismissed his bodyguard, and led me down the hallway. I had no clue what was about to transpire. We ended up holding court in his bedroom. When the door slammed shut behind us, he began talking: "The president is getting old. I plan on picking him up tonight and replacing him with Bédié." I was stunned by his frank delivery and didn't know what to make of it. His lips quivered through a calmly articulated speech pattern that was laced with impromptu stutters. But when his words began to set in and envelope my sense of reason, I felt like I'd been hit with a sledgehammer. I sat down on a couch, speechless and shell-shocked. It seemed the man had been transformed into a different person. Yet I could tell by the latent look in his eyes that he was torn at his very core. I struggled to contain my emotions and did my best to maintain an apparent calm.

He cast his gaze across the room and then back at me as he breathed a deep sigh, then he interrupted the deathly silence with his raspy voice. "Yesterday, the ambassador of France, Michel Dupuch, invited my boss to lunch. The ambassador introduced my boss to a French general who had been dispatched from Paris by President François Mitterrand to discuss strategies for replacing President Houphouët-Boigny." His boss, General Ory, was the chief of the Ivorian armed forces. Listening to him, I wondered why he had chosen to confide in me. I wasn't quite sure if he really hoped to achieve his objective. He knew that I was the president's closest aide and the last person to whom he should divulge such a treasonous plot. I managed to conjure up the words "*Merci, mon frère*" and made my way to the exit.

The rest of my day was turned upside down, but I remained composed until I walked through my front door; then I began to feel extremely distressed. Like a caged lion, I paced back and forth in deep thought, not knowing what to do. In my mind, I imagined the aftermath of a coup, and I analyzed the conversation, replaying again and again the shocking encounter. When I finally told my wife about the plot, she reacted with jaw-dropping shock. She couldn't believe that the "mild-mannered Kouassi" would mastermind such a Machiavellian scheme. "*Mon Dieu*. That's just impossible! This makes absolutely no sense. Why did he choose to divulge the information to you?" She was appalled. We both agreed that the future of the entire nation depended on my next move.

I wondered if there was perhaps a remote possibility that General Kouassi might have been coerced by the plotters, and with little or no choice, he'd agreed to go along with the plan. Maybe he reached out to me because he was searching for a way out, hoping I'd inform the president about the conspiracy instead of having to do it himself. I concluded that I was the missing conduit in his face-saving plan. We took turns praying. For a couple of hours, we meditated and reflected deeply, seeking divine intervention. When I was done with the Maghreb prayer, I asked my wife to accompany me to the president's residence.

He was holding a meeting on the terrace when we arrived. My wife stayed behind in the living room as I approached the president and asked him to dismiss everyone, including his bodyguards. I then broke the news of the impending coup. Though surprised, he remained calm and composed. He gently reached for the phone and summoned Ambassador Dupuch, whom he had always held in very high regard.

The ambassador arrived within minutes. I ushered him in and remained standing at the entrance of the terrace when he sat down with the president. "Berrah has informed me of the plot. I do not need verification of the facts, because he has my full confidence." The president was stern. He handed the phone to Dupuch. "Call your president and ask him to put a stop to his adventure." With fingers trembling, the ambassador dialed the Élysée, but President Mitterrand was unreachable. He dialed a different number and got a hold of Roland Dumas, the Minister of Foreign Affairs. "President Houphouët is onto us." He paused for a moment and hung up. The president stood up and asked me to escort the ambassador to the exit. I promptly led the way. Simplice Zinsou, the president's son-in-law, walked into the residence at that very moment. He greeted us and offered to walk Dupuch to his car.

General Ory and his deputy, General Kouassi, were both dismissed that same evening. President Houphouët put all the military's trustworthy colonels through a thorough vetting process and reorganized the hierarchical structure. Colonel Robert Gueï was promoted to chief of the Ivorian armed forces on June 6, 1990; however, most Ivorians woke up to the news twenty-four hours later, after his confirmation by the Council of Ministers. The plot that would have forever altered the political landscape of Côte d'Ivoire had been averted. Internal investigations pointed to Bédié's collusion with the French, but for the sake of peace and harmony in the country, the president never took any disciplinary measures.

He called up for duty General Ory and appointed him ambassador to Egypt about a month later. General Kouassi was appointed ambassador to Algeria and Tunisia. From that moment forward, Ambassador Dupuch tried his hardest to avoid bumping into me at the presidential residence. If he saw me coming his way, he wouldn't wait for the chauffeur to pull up to the main entrance. Rather, he would move briskly to the waiting vehicle in the parking lot. I mostly ignored him.

The president was lonely at the top, but he always endured and remained a strong leader, forever patient and indifferent in the face of many social upheavals and a fragile peace. He held true to his preferred method of dialogue and continued to speak with representatives from the different social and professional groups, as well as from around the political spectrum. He engaged in prolonged meetings until the middle of the night, often up to three, four, or five in the morning. He hardly ate, and he barely slept a few hours each day. Nevertheless, I did my very best to perform my duties in lockstep with his tasking routine. On many occasions, my wife and I waited patiently in his living room for several hours along with family members. We were there to assure him of our unwavering support and affection. When he surfaced for dinner, sometimes as early as 4:00 am, he would flash a broad smile—"Well, let's go get the dinner-breakfast started." Naturally, the warmth of his jubilant voice brought smiles to our heavy-eyed faces. *"This is not easy, but I always wish to listen to everyone and then I go to get on my knees to summarize everything in the presence of God,"* he used to say. We all felt his company in a deeply spiritual way. He was energetic, and his penchant for humor was never lost in those moments.

In the midst of all the hectic back and forth, the president maintained frequent contacts with old friends, using the cherished moments to reflect and reminisce on many a fond memory. This perhaps was not just a way for him to defuse and escape the demanding political pressures; it was his way of remaining faithful to his friendships and staying rooted. He once invited a fellow physician, a very dear friend from his medical school days, to an intimate family dinner at the residence. From the moment the very vibrant and jovial Mr. Johnson arrived, he took center stage at the table and shared some funny tales with all of us. They compared versions of similar stories and were soon mired in a debate on who was the more agile of the two. "*D'accord*, Johnson? Let's put our agility to the test." "Oh really?" Mr. Johnson responded. "Okay let's see." My wife and I watched in awe as the more than eighty-year-old president sat upright, lifted his leg, and stooped low to touch his chin to his knee. He kept his balance without flinching. For Mr. Johnson, however, the nuisance of old age stood painfully in the way. "*Félix tu es fort!* [You are really good!] There is no way I could do that!" The president initiated a different posture. "How about this move, Johnson, huh?" He stretched out in a leg split like a yoga guru. "Oh, no, Félix, I really can't do that one." They amused themselves until we could not stop laughing at them.

He maintained the same untiring pace throughout the social crisis and steered the country clear of imminent financial calamity. Just as the situation was beginning to improve, there was an unexpected mutiny by a division of the air force, commonly known as the GATL—the Air Transport and Liaison Group. The move followed the abrupt closure of the Abidjan airport and was the last straw. The nation woke up to an early morning surprise: planes could neither take off nor land. General Tanny, a trusted military leader, was dispatched by the president to order the rebel GATL troops to stand down. He phoned the president after their meeting. "Monsieur le President, it is my conclusion that the troops have been victims of negligence and dereliction of duty by the air force leadership." The president asked to speak with their spokesperson. "Sir, are you really President Houphouët?" a wound-up voice inquired in disbelief on the other end of the phone. "Yes indeed, I am the president," he responded calmly and listened to the young man's grievances. Then he said, "I'd like to meet all the leaders. Let's continue the conversation at the presidential residence. Come immediately." They soon arrived and were directed to meet with the president at a formal reception. He got to the bottom of the matter within the hour and ordered a speedy investigation. Before long, the problem was resolved and the relieved soldiers called off the boycott. They begged the president's pardon and left.

Only divine intervention could have prevailed over our many challenges in the year 1990. Fortunately, the nation managed to avert some potentially hostile consequences. I took some much-needed time away from my administrative duties and went to offer prayers of gratitude in Mecca. As a sacrificial gesture for peace and harmony, I shaved off my hair during the Hajj. When I returned to Côte d'Ivoire after the pilgrimage, I had a renewed sense of commitment. I was ready to redirect my energy to fight for our party's success in upcoming elections.

I went to meet with President Houphouët to assess his personal political outlook and measure his level of commitment to our party's future. We relaxed at the terrace, shortly after breakfast. "Papa, when are we going to retire from politics?" The question had been nagging me for quite a while. "A captain does not abandon ship under difficult circumstances," he said thoughtfully. "I wish to reorganize the house before I step aside, my son." It was clear to me he had pondered the answer long before I posed the question. His decision to move the nation toward multipartyism had been pragmatic and well timed. "You deserve to win by a landslide, Papa." I was highly motivated to campaign vigorously for him.

Due to leadership complacency, the PDCI had lost its luster. Hence, when the time came for the nation to hold its first multiparty elections, the usual exhilaration from the base was hard to detect. The Bureau Politique decided to hastily convene the PDCI congress and prepare for the party's internal nominations as we neared the end of the five-year term, but I disagreed with their decision and recommended to the president that we wait until the general elections were over. "It will be counterproductive to convene a congress for the purpose of nominating party leaders who could potentially be defeated in the general elections," I clarified at lunch. "The outcome could be disastrous, but also embarrassing, and it could undermine the structural integrity of the party." He kept nodding. I paused for a few seconds, hoping to get his feedback, but he said nothing. "Papa, if that were to happen, we could find ourselves in the unenviable position of having to decide whether to replace our nominees with newly elected members." I couldn't gauge whether we were on the same page, because he maintained silence even after I was done talking.

Days after I shared my opinion, Alassane Ouattara approached me following a morning meeting with the president in Yamoussoukro. "Ghoulem, you won," he said. "Excuse me? I don't quite follow you." I really didn't know what he was talking about. "The congress will convene after the general elections," he explained with a delicate smile. "*Au contraire, mon ami*," I replied. "The party and Côte d'Ivoire have won. But I am happy to hear the news."

When the pre-congress convention was hosted by the PDCI in October 1990, key assemblies within the various party structures were set up; however, many seats were left empty in anticipation of the general elections. The period between the pre-congress convention and the general elections was plagued by fierce infighting among potential candidates competing for positions in the Bureau Politique and the Comité Directeur. But dedication among the candidates willing to campaign for the president's reelection was sparse to none. I joined forces with the "*J'aime le PDCI*[70]" movement—the party's youth wing—and we forged ahead with preparations for a vigorous campaign. We launched a passionate drive in the ten communes[71] of Abidjan, tirelessly dedicated to ensuring a landslide victory for the president, whose primary opponent for the first time in the nation's history was Laurent Gbagbo.

All across the country, political activities were at a fever pitch. It seemed everyone was enthusiastic about charting a new course in our politics. For the first time in thirty years, congressional seats were up for grabs in the general elections, and candidates of the PDCI

---

[70] French for "I love the PDCI."
[71] Third-tier units of administration. All departments are split into communes.

were poised to face off with the opposition. Notwithstanding, some members in our party assumed that my administrative obligations would keep me from campaigning for the president, but I knew I was unstoppable even if I faced some blowback within my own party. A handful of old-guard party faithful made it clear that my presence on the campaign trail was unwelcome. They went to complain to the president in person. Others reached out to him by phone to voice their disapproval of my constant public presence. One such call came through while I was at the residence. "Listen to what they are saying about you." He handed the phone to me. I wasn't discouraged by the voice of the lethargic party elder on the other end of the line. I thanked the president for his continued support and went on to campaign with reenergized passion.

On the trail, we frequently came across the loud and boisterous Laurent Gbagbo supporters, but our strategy was to engage and educate the voting public. Focusing primarily on the younger generation, we highlighted the greater opportunities awaiting the nation and the need for continuation. The party's youth expressed their love for the country and explained the president's accomplishments to potential voters on the streets. Their impact on political discourse was not lost on the old guard. Some were concerned that they might be forced to a runoff against more vibrant candidates and potentially lose their seats. Fully aware of the stakes, they began to reshape their messages and focus on their vast political experience.

Our daily rallies usually commenced with a group prayer that begged the Almighty to remove any lies from our lips and fill our hearts with abundant love for others. In the spirit of tradition, I often wore a *boubou* on the trail. My choice of attire became a punch line among some members of the opposition party. They dubbed me the "ayatollah." It all seemed silly to me. They even posted unsavory articles in newspapers criticizing me, but I refused to waste my valuable energy reacting to their trivial antics. I remained

A Dream for Peace

determined to work harder and push the limits of our formidable campaign. Disseminating information and ensuring that the message got to the masses was a bit tricky in those days, for lack of social media. Either way, we persevered, using some good old-fashioned political mobilization strategies within the ranks of the PDCI.

A gentleman from the north was attacked in his home in Marcory commune just ten days before the presidential elections. He was a party member who owned a fleet of campaign vehicles. I visited him at home with a few members of the party's youth wing and saw the mess that was once a very tidy and beautiful house. The entire place had been vandalized by hooligans from the opposition. I consoled the man and assured him of the Party's continued support. He seemed more determined than ever to work even harder for the campaign. We were soon back on the trail, walking a few blocks past the local police precinct. I wondered why the station was closed and unmanned at a time when the police were required to be on high alert. To mark our presence, we stayed for a while in front of the precinct and then we moved the growing procession to the working-class suburb of Koumassi for our campaign rally. A large group of the opposition FPI were on site, itching for trouble, when we arrived at the Grande Place. I commended our party's youth for resisting the urge to engage them. We commenced with our program without any complications.

From where I stood on the podium, I saw the crowd growing even larger when I began to speak. I addressed the need for improved communication within our party and criticized the old guard for failing to engage the people, especially for being absent during the crisis in the country. I emphasized our renewed commitment to a constructive path forward and outlined the party's strategy to connect with the people in the future. Admitting our past mistakes as a party, I implored the supporters to renew their confidence in the PDCI and promised to earn back the trust of those who had moved to join the opposition. My speech ruffled the feathers of some key veterans who believed that our party was beyond reproach. But I knew that the election was ours to lose.

We concluded the rally and began our march to Port-Bouët for a larger gathering. As the sunset hastily faded, soaking up the dry season's tropical night air, cheers from waiting supporters echoed in the distance. I stepped up to the microphone, pumped my fist at the sky, and chanted party slogans. The crowd accompanied with a thunderous roar. I led into my fiery speech and endorsed some of the young candidates on the podium. Rhythmic chants of *"J'aime le PDCI"* grew louder as my speech came to a climactic end.

When I returned home by midnight, my wife informed me that she had just gotten off the phone with the mayor of Port-Bouët, who had called to complain about the rally. She had done her best to soothe the mayor's concerns, going as far as to apologize on my behalf for any logistical headaches caused by our presence. "I even told the mayor that you were not running for any office, that you were mainly campaigning to assure victory for the president, the PDCI, and Côte d'Ivoire."

Given that this was my first public exposure in the heat of national politics, my brothers were suspicious about my motives. But I had no plans to position myself in the future of Côte d'Ivoire; I aimed to position Côte d'Ivoire in the future. My plans for the future had long been established; I harbored a strong desire to return to the United States, the world's epicenter for global decisions. This was the only place I knew I could go to continue to serve all of humanity.

I was fighting for the country to maintain its course and to prevent us from spiraling into a path of self-destruction. Regardless of the competence of the opposition party's candidate, I was always mindful of the delicate nature of governing a nation through crisis, which requires more than proficiency in civics and social policy advocacy. The FPI was a novice on the scene, without a solid plan to create jobs for the middle class or build upon the president's major accomplishments and ensure sustainability. The president had learned from experience before taking on the responsibility, having served for fourteen years as a representative in the French National Assembly and as a minister under five consecutive governments. The distinction between him and Laurent Gbagbo was clear.

Touré Mama, my trusted chauffeur, was so troubled by the constant hostile comments being directed my way that he went behind my back to have a private chat with my wife. "*Madame*, I have a feeling *monsieur* is in danger," he warned. "I'm afraid someone might try to kill him." In her typical style, she let her deep spiritual faith drive her response to him. "Touré, please do not worry about anything. God is the master of our lives," she assured him. He went to see her a few times to caution that the situation was worsening, and each time she put him at ease. Even the president began to grow a bit apprehensive. "It is rather he who protects us, Mr. President," a young member of "*J'aime le PDCI*" who accompanied me on the trail with a few of his peers told him when instructed to do his best to ensure my well-being. During the last weeks of campaigning, I slept very little and rarely had time to go to the presidential residence for lunch. I lived mostly on Touré's supply of street-side charcoal grilled plantains and Fanta.

For a brief period, a majority of citizens remained under the impression that the FPI had become the predominant party in the country. I was acutely aware of our odds. The country had sustained a one-party system for three decades, and most of the electorate had grown accustomed to the guaranteed reelection of the president. However, there was suddenly a formidable opposition candidate on the scene who could possibly defeat the president. We did our best to spread the word to eligible voters, informing them of what was at stake. After weeks of campaigning, educated minds seemed ready to make their voices heard. We saw a spike in the polls during the final stretch and were assured that the youth had gotten the message.

The issue of personal identification was a major hurdle to

overcome. Most eligible voters lacked essential documents and couldn't register to vote. I discovered the magnitude of the problem with very little time left before the voting deadline. I tapped into our campaign reserves and ordered a bunch of typewriters. People with secretarial skills were recruited to deal with identifying and filling out applications for thousands of voters who could potentially be disenfranchised. Other volunteer teams were put in place to direct voters to locations where they could go to apply for an ID with their birth certificates. Illiterate villagers and the elderly were accompanied by witnesses to attest to their identity at every location.

Although frustrated by the timing of the last-minute push in our democracy, I wasn't very surprised by the reckless abandonment of responsibility by those in the Interior Ministry who had sat on their hands for months. Here I was, trying my hardest to conduct their duties in order to ensure free and fair elections. The president, for his part, was always made aware of certain lapses either toward the end of a deadline, or in some instances he found out much too late. Such was the state of affairs—a bit nonchalant perhaps, but surely a destructive pattern that caused incessant stagnation in the system. I had grown wearily accustomed to it. To his credit, the president tried his best to remind all public servants about their sworn obligations to the country.

I followed up daily with the national printing press to ensure that they had everything they needed to deliver a sufficient number of identity cards to every precinct and encouraged more volunteers to go out and assist the voters. Out of nowhere and without any proof whatsoever, some fictitious informants went to inform the president that I was issuing fake ID cards. I received a call from the president asking that I cease and desist and report to the residence immediately. The egregious allegations did not sit well with me at all. "How could I even entertain such a thought?" I searched for an answer. "I have only been trying to do what's best for the electoral system." There is a very transparent process in place at local precincts at the moment, and everyone without identification, regardless of party affiliation, is welcome to go and register. These assertions are totally ridiculous." He seemed to agree. "Moreover, Papa, I am quite certain that you know fully well that I would not commit such political deception. All our efforts are crystal clear." "Berrah," he answered, "all eyes are on you because you are a respected public servant, loyal to our party's pledge and to our nation. I know you wouldn't stoop to such lows."

I remained undaunted, forging ahead with my efforts and doing my very best to safeguard the transparent process. I instructed the printing presses to make duplicate copies of the electoral lists to back up the originals. The administration took measures to guarantee the safety of the general public during the elections. Security was present at almost every location, although there were a few sporadic outbreaks of violence in certain areas. When thugs from the opposition ransacked a polling station at Abobo, destroying some ballot boxes, we sent copies of electoral lists from all ten communes to the precinct to ensure that every vote was accounted for. The Interior Ministry brought in some additional ballot boxes to replace the damaged ones. Braving the humid climate, resilient voters waited patiently in long lines until order was restored.

Observers at the polling station in Plateau informed voters to remain in place after closing hours to cast their vote. Throngs of people joined long lines to cast their vote, and the polling stations stayed open until midnight to accommodate everyone. Despite being new to the democratic process, the electorate gave political leaders a real lesson in civics. The elections concluded without further complications or complaints of irregularities. Opposition candidate Laurent Gbagbo received 18 percent of the final vote count. I believed that the opposition would have had fewer votes if the PDCI leadership had committed more of their energy to fulfilling their electoral duties. But in the end, it was a great victory for the president, the party, and for Côte d'Ivoire. Alassane Ouattara became the prime minister after the elections.

I suffered from extreme exhaustion when it was all over. The president was in a playful mood when we sat for lunch a few days later, and I told him of my intent to go on a brief medical sabbatical to Switzerland. He encouraged the idea, but he also wanted to share some news. "You know, Berrah, Gbagbo wanted to submit his wife's name in Gagnoa's mayoral race, but the Bété people did not look favorably at electing a woman, especially someone from the south. She switched her candidacy to the Abobo district." I had a feeling he was asking me to stay and campaign for the PDCI candidate. "Oh well. I guess I will postpone my trip and lend a helping hand to the party."

The mayoral campaign was almost as intense as the presidential elections. Mrs. Gbagbo ran her campaign in strict accordance with electoral rules, and she maintained a civil discourse. However, she went on to lose by a large margin to our candidate, Adama Sanogo. I finally took a much-needed break and went for a medical checkup.

When I returned to the country, I met with the *"J'aime le PDCI"* members to thank them for their commitment and promised to propose their integration into the PDCI's upper echelon. I thought the party needed a reboot. The president and I discussed the matter prior to our special congress in April 1991. He agreed that something needed to be done. We began to unveil our road map of gradual systemic changes but discovered very quickly that the old guard would have nothing of the sort. The president stepped back and reappointed them yet again to their posts. Like the youth, I was also disappointed, but for the sake of peace, I believed it was best for the nation.

We met for our morning briefing the day after he had proposed the final decree. I was eager to request some time off after noticing a brief lull in my hectic schedule. With his blessing, my

A Dream for Peace

Love and I departed a couple of days later on a trip to Annemasse at the Swiss/France border. The time we had to ourselves was precious. We caught up on much deserved rest and recreation. I checked in with the president on a regular basis to keep apprised on progress back in Côte d'Ivoire. About two weeks into our vacation, I received a call from him—"My son, I need you to come back. It is an urgent matter." His voice resonated with a sense of urgency. But whatever the issue, he decided not to go into further details. I expressed regret to my Love, who as always gave her support and understanding. We caught the next flight and arrived in Abidjan the following day. Our chauffeur took us straight to the presidential residence.

From the way he greeted us, it was as if we had been away for several years. It was a magnanimous and joyful welcome. We left my wife in the living room and strolled off to the terrace to indulge in small talk for a few minutes. "I can't wait to hear about the urgent matter. Tell me, Papa, what's going on?" "Berrah," he interrupted. "You must be exhausted after your very long trip. Why don't you go home and get some rest. We can talk about everything tomorrow." I gave in hesitantly. I was tired, and I knew my Love was also exhausted. We went home. "His behavior seemed a bit strange," I mustered the energy to tell my wife. "Based on the call, I assumed something important had come up. Perhaps an emergency of some sort, but he didn't want to talk about it. I don't have time to rest if there is indeed an emergency situation." She agreed.

I returned to the residence first thing in the morning. The president kept going in and out of meetings throughout the day until much later. I finally got a chance to ask about the urgent call. "My son, I am a bit tired today. Let's talk tomorrow." I tried to digest his peculiar behavior, but I couldn't put two and two together. I turned to his daughter, Marie. She was always witty and straightforward. Fortunately, she was visiting him that day. I caught up to her in the living room. "Papa asked me to come back from Switzerland to attend to something urgent, but he doesn't seem interested in discussing anything. What's going on with him?" She laughed and teased: "Ghoulem, someone must have put some sand in your *attiéké*." She was referring to the traditional dish, made with a dried pulverized cassava root. I chuckled at her sense of humor. "There's no more *attiéké* left on my plate. I am down to my last grains of sand." She giggled and changed the topic. We talked about my vacation, and I left without pressing her on the matter.

When I arrived at the residence the next day, the president and I walked hand in hand to the smoking room that was primarily reserved for confidential one-on-one conversations with him. He was a nonsmoker, and no one ever smoked on the premises.

"My son, are you maintaining contacts with the '*J'aime le PDCI*' youth?" He had something on his mind. "But yes, of course." He breathed a sigh of relief and leaned back in his seat. "I am disenchanted with the new secretary-general of our party. I want to find a way to bring the youth into the upper nucleus. Will you be able to help me do something about that?" I knew that preserving a robust party was important to him, but if he needed to speak with the youth, I thought perhaps he could have done so while I was in Europe. He had obviously been in a reflective mood and wanted to get my opinion on the matter. "With all due respect, Papa, I believe it's a bit late for me to get involved at this point. If there's one lesson you have taught me, it is that a person has to know their limitations. Every available position is already filled. All powers and authority have been assigned to our party's veterans. I don't think that I can do anything for the youth." For the first time in decades, I had said no to him without offering advice or presenting viable alternatives. Short of firing people or creating new offices, there were no other solutions. At that juncture, I knew the time had come for me to roll back my involvement in the party's internal affairs, and deep inside, I also felt the time had come to turn the page. Although at the very least, I was willing to stay and serve him until he was ready to retire from office.

A Dream for Peace

Both Ouattara and Gbagbo had gained much prominence on the Ivorian political landscape. Due to popular demand, the two gentlemen were invited to face off in a debate on a highly rated television program, *Le Fauteuil Blanc*. When the show aired, all the political aficionados in the country, including the president, joined many viewers that evening to hear the candidates square off on the nation's political orientation. He had fully embraced the multiparty system when it was adopted in Côte d'Ivoire, and he continued to envision the country's future in light of that context. The day after the televised event, my wife and I, along with other members of the family, were at the residence waiting to have dinner with him. He showed up a bit later than usual in a jovial mood. "Do you know who I have been speaking with for the last two hours?" "No," we answered in chorus. "Laurent Gbagbo." He paused for a reaction. "During yesterday's televised debate against the prime minister, I couldn't help but notice several shortcomings. He is a son of this country, and he may one day become the president. I asked him to come over to have a conversation on overcoming his deficiencies." This was on the eve of Gbagbo's trip to the United States. The president liked to say that he had no room for hatred or resentment in his heart. Côte d'Ivoire was all that mattered to him. He had such a passionate love for his country.

The oft-repeated rumor that President Houphouët-Boigny did not prepare his succession is unbecoming. When I discussed the issue with him, he clarified that he had begun preparing the next generation long before his ascension into office by facilitating the formation of many high-level executive positions. He emphasized that Côte d'Ivoire was not under a monarchial constitution and that Ivorians were fully capable of electing future leaders and political representatives. He also saw to it that his immediate family stayed out of politics, claiming that his stint in office had been enough to outlast two family generations. Nonetheless, in case of an unexpected power vacuum, the nation could always count on the enforcement of the constitution. His successor would complete the remainder of his five-year term, followed by presidential elections open to all, in a multiparty system.

For the party's secretary-general, the bitter struggle for succession was blatantly obvious behind the scenes. Although the door was open to competition, the struggle for power was prominent among the Baoulé trio consisting of Camille Alliali, Jean Banny, and Henri Konan Bédié. As a student in Paris, Alliali vacationed on occasion at the residence of Congressman Houphouët-Boigny, sometimes in the company of local Ivorian students. He practiced as a lawyer, defending the natives against the laws of the ruling colonial government in Côte d'Ivoire. His mentor, Houphouët, had been very supportive and influential, going as far as to advise him to run for office in 1957 while the country was still under colonial rule. He was successful in that bid and became the vice president of the Territorial Assembly, which was later transformed into a legislative assembly in the autonomous territory in 1958. After the proclamation of independence in 1960, the president appointed him as the nation's first ambassador to France. Between 1963 and 1989, he held three separate ministerial positions in the administration. Alliali was a high-ranking PDCI member in the Bureau Politique, responsible for organizing the party's congress. By 1980, the president, along with congress, created the Comité Exécutif for the upper echelon of the party membership, headed by Alliali.

Jean Banny, also a lawyer, knew the president from childhood. He belonged to the party's upper hierarchy many years before the country's independence. The president appointed him Minister of Defense in 1960. While in office, he was arrested along with others, tried, and given a heavy sentence in 1963 on charges of plotting to overthrow the government. Notwithstanding, after a lengthy and thorough investigation that lasted over three years, the facts came to light, and it was discovered that he had been falsely accused. He received a presidential pardon in 1967. Years later, as token gesture of goodwill and apology for the injustice, he earned back his ministerial position at the Defense Ministry in 1981.

The unfortunate drama unfolded among the three men, who continually attempted to outmaneuver each other before the disappointed eyes of the president. He confided in me that their actions saddened him greatly. Establishing a historical parallel with the olden days, he recalled that competition used to be fair, open, and honest; all the best talents, whether they were jewelers, weavers, or singers, gained their claim to fame by winning over their peers, who pushed them to the forefront. There was never any room for mediocrity. He pointed out that selection processes were always based on Darwinian principles, not the present-day method of doing things with an all-out political expediency mindset, prevalent in today's environment, where most people's objective was to ensure that everyone stays out of their way.

President Houphouët presided over the Conseil des Ministres, and the prime minister was in charge of overseeing all other ministries and reporting to him. Alassane Ouattara gradually took control of the country and administered his duties with the mindset of an IMF executive. This was where he had built his career. He committed to honoring the country's debt payments in a timely fashion, and his discipline earned him the president's unequivocal trust. He went beyond the strict protocol of our payment obligations and imposed even harsher measures on a country that was in dire financial straits; he collected the coins from the State Public Transport Company (SOTRA) in order to secure the required minimum monthly payments. He had lunch with the president at the residence every Wednesday after the Conseil des Ministres meeting. I always had lunch with them and listened attentively to his words, which in my opinion went too far at times, especially with regards to the management of state affairs. Notwithstanding, however, I believed that he was committed to doing a fine job. I had a very cordial relationship with him.

In the interest of increasing state revenues to meet the

Côte d'Ivoire's Political Radar

country's debt requirements, Ouattara established a resident permit for foreigners. The decision in the context was premature; it begged to be studied in detail because it caused a lot of frustration in the West African population, particularly among nationals of the former Upper Côte d'Ivoire, in addition to stripping them of 5,000 CFA each year. I once brought up the issue at lunch in his presence and clarified the immeasurable political consequences that we foresaw by singling out a part of the population in that way, especially since they could legally lay claim to the Ivorian nationality without ever having to consider that they needed to go through the process.

After France created the Upper Volta colony in 1919, they began transplanting a part of the population of the new colony into Côte d'Ivoire to work on the plantations. The great famine in 1932 prompted the French to divide the Upper Volta into three colonies: Niger, Sudan, and Côte d'Ivoire. As a result, more than half of the territory was attached to Côte d'Ivoire, and then by 1938, the merger was completed with the creation of Upper and Lower Côte d'Ivoire, going beyond the borders of Ouagadougou (Burkina Faso). Representatives for both Upper and Lower Côte d'Ivoire were given a seat in the French National Assembly. President Houphouët-Boigny recounted his election campaign in Upper Côte d'Ivoire: "Myself, Ouezzin Coulibaly, and Zinda Kaboré were all elected as representatives for Côte d'Ivoire at the French National Assembly in 1946."

In 1947, the impulsive French colonial government suddenly decided that the Upper Volta needed to be reconstituted into a colony. After independence, all those who remained in southern Côte d'Ivoire became de facto Ivorians. Hence, it was easy to imagine the frustration of a seventy-year-old man, an immigrant to southern Côte d'Ivoire in 1920, decades before the reconstitution of the Upper Volta colony, who had become a victim of police harassment in 1990. After being profiled and stopped by the police, they demanded that he show his resident permit because his surname sounded "foreign."

A Dream for Peace

The president was moved by the man's story, and he promised to address the problem at a later time. It was important to address the immigration issue, but the matter had to be studied in order for us to find the right solution. However, Alassane was on the eve of a trip to Senegal on behalf of the president for the inauguration of reelected President Abdou Diouf. We decided to pursue the discussion upon his return. The resident permit problem unfortunately opened the door to what was to become the Ivoirité concept. Unfortunately, the president fell sick and had to undergo a medical procedure in France, which he never recovered from.

He later went through a long, agonizing battle in Yamoussoukro. His anguish was one of the most painful moments of my life. I was incapable of bringing myself to appreciate the will of the Almighty. My adoptive father, friend, confidant, and exceptional boss was inevitably on his way to meet his Creator. Day in and day out, I observed the last days of this great man, whom I considered a historic monument. I could not even turn to my wife to ease my pain, because she was also grief stricken and inconsolable. I focused on my prayers, aided by multiple readings of the Holy Qur'an. Despite the pain and emotion that gripped me, I tried to pull myself together by imploring the Almighty to give me strength and courage to fulfill my last duties toward the president and Côte d'Ivoire. To maintain the integrity of his work, I had to ensure that the constitution would be respected and that the transition, although painful, would be conducted smoothly and, for the sake of all Ivorians, in a peaceful and orderly manner.

During this period, Prime Minister Alassane Ouattara, whose own Ivorian nationality would soon be subjected to questionable challenges, enjoyed absolute powers. The Ministries of Interior and Homeland Security, the Joint Chiefs of the Armed Forces headed by General Guéi, and the police were all within the auspices of his control. I went to Ouattara's residence after my prayers at the mosque wearing a *boubou* and was received by his wife. When I asked to see him, she said he was still at work, but she graciously accepted my request and went to give him a call. She came back to the living room to inform me that he would be arriving shortly. I was eager to talk with him. As soon as he arrived, we retreated to his home office. Once seated, I placed my Qur'an on the center table and addressed him. "This Holy Book unites us. You have all the power in your hands. What do you wish to do?" "Thank you," he replied. "I will defer to the constitution." He had given me his word, and I left his house with a reassured feeling.

Accompanied by a young man from *"J'aime le PDCI,"* I called on Henri Konan Bédié, the constitutional successor, at his villa in Yamoussoukro the very next day. In light of the events that our unforgiving destiny had imposed on us, the critical nature of what was about to transpire was beyond anything our young nation had ever experienced. When I met with him, my questions revolved around his readiness to accede to power at the appropriate time. I urged him to undertake the full and effective implementation of the constitution for the unhampered continuity of the affairs of state. Admittedly, he had not fully come to grips with the fluid situation. He had instead moved to surround himself with a handful of ministers who had pledged their allegiance to him. In any event, my intent was to emphasize the importance of setting up a crisis committee to deal with matters that could destabilize the nation. "Have the ministers been briefed on what to do in case things do not go as planned?" I asked. He stared at me, somewhat bewildered. I realized I had to rephrase the question. "Have you organized the ministers into a crisis committee, and are they ready to implement critical measures to avert a national crisis?" I nitpicked my choice of words to suggest indirectly that he might want to have a discussion with the ministers. His answer was exactly what I suspected: "Not quite." He paused briefly. "But I have a planned dinner engagement with the ministers tomorrow evening. We will go over everything at that time." "Fair enough," I replied. "If you wish, I can come back to meet with everyone." I wanted to be there to ensure that the proper framework would be drafted for everyone to know that they had been commissioned, and moreover, that they belonged to the same committee. He seemed relieved. "Better yet, why don't you join us for dinner and we can have the meeting after that?" We shook hands. I sunk into my seat and the driver took to the highway for the 250-kilometer drive back to Abidjan. I was in a reflective mood, and the surreal moment weighed heavily on my heart. Along the way, I opened the window to breathe in the crisp subtropical breeze and caress the night sky with my thoughts as I meditated to clear my mind.

Driving back to Yamoussoukro the following afternoon, we hit a traffic jam. A logging truck had overturned and spilled its load, obstructing the highway for several minutes. There were large timber logs in both lanes. We waited patiently until a road crew arrived to clear the way. When we got to the villa, the ministers were enjoying the last course on the menu, some fruit salad. The atmosphere was subdued. I joined them at the table and had a glass of water. As I was talking to one minister, I noticed that a couple of them were preparing to leave. "*Mes amis*, I would like to have a word with all of you." "Berrah would like to say a few words," Bédié chimed in. They returned to their seats and gave me their undivided attention. I presented a framework and elaborated on the need for the committee, how to maintain communication in critical moments, and the importance of knowing each other's role. Someone wondered about the whereabouts of my close friend, Foreign Minister Essy Amara, who was noticeably absent. "I attest on his behalf," I reassured them. They pledged their commitment to unite and remain vigilant when faced with any attempt to destabilize the nation. The meeting progressed late into the night until Bédié finally proposed that I reconvene with the ministers the next day in Abidjan.

Though I knew that I was doing exactly what the president

would have asked of me at a time when the country had reached a major crossroad, I missed him deeply and longed to be in his presence. The long drive back to Abidjan felt very short. When I arrived home, I held a vigil with my wife until the wee hours of the morning.

We met as planned at the home of Interior Minister Emile Constant Bombet. The only person missing at the meeting was the secretary-general of the PDCI, Laurent Dona Fologo, who I was told had a prior commitment. I asked Bombet to call him and hand me the phone. As soon as I heard his voice on the line, I expressed the imperative nature of his presence. In accordance with the PDCI charter, Fologo was responsible for overseeing the transition of the presidency. He arrived a few minutes after I hung up with him. Everyone at the meeting assured me of their commitment to the implementation of the constitution, pledging to expedite the succession of Bédié and to hold fast in case there was a crisis. After our discussions, I knew in my heart that the president's wish was being fulfilled and as far as I was concerned, I could go on into the twilight, knowing in my heart that I had accomplished my duties and managed to facilitate a peaceful transition of government. Feeling a dismal sense of melancholy, I went home to pray and fast with my wife. We sought strength in our time of turbulence and prayed for the Almighty to bless and protect the president.

During the wee hours of a Tuesday morning on December 7, 1993, only a few days after we had begun our fast, President Félix Houphouët-Boigny was called by his Creator. Upon hearing the news, an entire nation was stricken with immense sadness. It did not matter on what side of the spectrum you were—an era had come to a sudden end. His powerful presence would forever remain enshrined in the annals of our history. Tears poured out from my broken heart. Time stood still in the midst of a fleeting array of memories suddenly engulfed in flames of immeasurable pain.

Alassane Ouattara broke the official news of the president's passing, around 1:00 p.m. That same evening, Bédié took to the airwaves to announce that the implementation of Article 11 was in full effect and that a smooth succession had taken place. At the time of his statement, there was still some confusion whether Ouattara had in fact given up the reins of power. Nevertheless, the transition proceeded as planned. As soon as Bédié ascended to the presidency, the Mitterrand administration in France proposed that Alassane Ouattara remain prime minister. He passed on their suggestion and resigned. A few days later, he assumed his new post as the Deputy Managing Director of the International Monetary Fund.

Shortly after the funeral ceremonies for the president, I left the country to begin my retirement in the United States. Not long afterward, I was greatly saddened to see Côte d'Ivoire descend into gradual disarray and spiral into the abyss of Ivoirité-ism—a form of xenophobia that was stirred up by the Bédié administration. Barely six years after he became the country's president, a group of young soldiers toppled him in a coup and replaced him with former armed forces chief of staff, Robert Guéi. It was as if our beloved nation had suddenly embarked on its own "Way of Grief." I felt totally helpless and perplexed, observing the planting of the unfortunate seeds of hatred among what was once a harmonious populace.

I was mystified when Guéi adopted the same xenophobic pattern and banned Ouattara from politics after accusing him of foreign parentage. In 2000, a year after being in office, Guéi faced off in an election with Laurent Gbagbo. Not surprisingly, he refused to accept the results and he was deposed in a popular uprising. I could not believe what was happening to our country. Each time I received a phone call or read the newspapers, the headlines were filled with depressing news. Muslims from the north, who felt alienated, joined a troop mutiny in 2002, triggering a fierce civil war that ended in 2004. The country remained divided. France and the UN had to bring in some peacekeepers to patrol a buffer zone, separating the north from the rest of the country.

Côte d'Ivoire's Political Radar

Occasionally, my wife and I went to spend a few days in Côte d'Ivoire. The "Pearl of the Lagoon," as the city of Abidjan was called in its heyday, stood in gradual dilapidation with a crumbling infrastructure. The archetypal Ivorian smile was missing from the faces of people, and public services seemed to have all but dissipated with the passage of time. We returned on a couple of occasions, hoping to see the implementation of some constructive reforms and a revitalized economy, but to our disappointment, our expectations were a bit far-fetched. The fragile peace lasted until new elections aimed at bringing the conflict to an end were held in 2010. I wondered what President Félix Houphouët-Boigny would have thought of all the killings, all the displaced refugees, and those who had been exiled in neighboring countries as a result of the cycle of violence in a never-ending power struggle.

But in light of the painful setbacks, I held out hope that sanity would prevail and that people would begin to nurture love for each other. I prayed for the day when the leaders would be motivated to restore concord and fraternal harmony.

A Dream for Peace

I was immersed in deep affliction and became immeasurably flabbergasted, for it was not a war against French colonialism that we were fighting. This was about Algerians killing their own brethren after having sacrificed more than seven years in the war for independence. When I heard the news in 1999 that my brother and friend, Abdelaziz Bouteflika, was running for president, I was elated and overjoyed.

Chapter Sixteen

Algeria—Cry of the Crestfallen Heart

During my time as a freedom fighter in Morocco, I dreamed of returning home to serve an independent Algeria someday. Unfortunately, when the time was right, I happened to find myself at the heart of a major crossroad between fate and destiny. The circumstances were contrary to all that I had envisioned for my beloved country. Ahmed Ben Bella's administration was in charge of the country's policies, and the Trotskyist experiment was front and center of everyday politics. I frankly could not imagine playing a role in any particular field in the country.

Algeria from its inception has always been a difficult country to rule. The Tell and Saharan Atlas mountain chains pose a disruptive ease in communications between the northern part of the country and the south, thereby confining merchant marine commerce to a few natural harbors and making trade with the hinterlands an almost impossible task. The native tribes, mostly Berbers with their own language and dialects, managed to form a monolithic trading bloc with their neighbors in a mostly peaceful region until the first Arab military incursions into the Maghreb in the seventh century resulted in the spread of Islam. In stark contrast to our regional neighbors, my ancestors, the Berbers, showed a greater resistance to Arabization in Algeria. But for centuries, the period was marked by constant conflict, political instability, and economic decline. After a massive incursion by Bedouin Arabs from Egypt in the first half of the eleventh century, the Arabic language became widely used in the countryside by the native Berbers, who became gradually Arabized.

A Dream for Peace

However, Muslim dynasties that originated in Algeria were few and far between, and none had a lasting power or dominance. Internal conflicts dominated the region for centuries. Algeria became a part of the Ottoman Empire until the French came to colonize my ancestral land in the summer of 1830. Initially, the French government organized northern Algeria into three distinct regions, each with its own representative in the National Assembly of France. But the traditional Muslim population within the confines of the rural areas remained separated from the modern economic infrastructure of the European community. Their attempt to control the entire country was met by fierce rebellion, led by El Emir Abdelkader. However, after a decade-long battle, he was exiled to France and later permitted to resettle with his family in Damascus, Syria. Until today, the much-revered Emir remains the quintessential symbol of Algerian national resistance.

Algeria endured 132 years of colonial subjugation under a foreign non-Muslim power that had forced its way into our way of life. The French annexed our ancestral lands and distributed plots to colonial settlers after redrawing the country's borders. All our traditional leaders were purged, replaced, or sidelined. Our traditional educational system was largely dismantled, and social structures were pushed to their limits. The oppressive rule of the French, who viewed my people with condescension and disdain, left an indelible mark on the psyche of my generation. In order to be fully appreciated, today's Algeria must be viewed through a prism of colonial rule spanning a century and a half, starkly juxtaposed with fearless resistance to Western domination.

Messali Hadj was a mythical figure when I was growing up. He founded the Algerian People's Party (PPA) and voiced the first nationalistic demands seeking independence from France. His platform attracted the youth of the day. Other national heroes came along during World War II. Ferhat Abbas, a former assimilationist who drafted a manifesto for presentation to the French authorities

Algeria—Cry of the Crestfallen Heart

seeking recognition for an independent country, stood out the most. General Charles de Gaulle declared to the French National Assembly that "the loyalty of the Algerian people" to his country had indebted France to the Muslims of North Africa. In March 1944, French citizenship was extended to "certain classes of Muslims." Three years after that, the French National Assembly voted into law a unique statute defining Algeria as "a group of regions endowed with civic responsibilities, financial autonomy, and a special organization."

I was only a child when Nazi Germany surrendered in May 1945. That same day in the town of Sétif, thousands of Algerians took to the streets to demonstrate for their liberation. Most banners were indicative of the people's desire to see a free country. Some Messali Hadj supporters carried signs asking for his freedom. The peaceful march quickly turned violent when a French policeman attempted to confiscate an Algerian flag from a young man who refused to give it up. The young man was shot and killed before the police force began firing into the crowd and triggering mass pandemonium, which filtered into the streets and resulted in the killing of over a hundred French settlers. The governor called in the army, whose heavy-handed crackdown led to the killing of over 45,000 Algerians in the area and other rural communities close to my hometown. Everyone was understandably traumatized by the horrific episode, which has been forever memorialized in the nation's consciousness. Resentment against the French rocketed to levels never before seen in the country. Throughout our fearless struggle for independence, more and more disillusioned youth became politically active and ardently militant, and once-moderate members in the Mouvement Pour le Triomphe des Libertés Démocratiques (MTLD), the Messali Hadj organization, began to grow increasingly frustrated with his tempered approach.

On November 1, 1954, nine disenchanted young freedom fighters from the movement determined that justice for Algeria could only be realized through open rebellion. They formed a new movement, Front de Libération National (FLN), and issued a decree stating that the aim of their organization was to restore Algeria to a sovereign state. The group advocated social democracy within an Islamic framework that accorded citizenship and equal rights to all residents in Algeria. Their vision was prefaced by the recognition that Algeria had fallen behind other Arab states in emancipating itself socially and nationally, therefore the only remedy was a difficult and prolonged struggle. They came up with plans and drafted a method of war against the French, primarily focusing on guerrilla warfare at home, backed by diplomatic activity overseas, in particular at the United Nations.

They formed a guerrilla wing, Armée de Libération Nationale (ALN), and trained tactical units to attack the French within Algeria's Wilayas as well as on French soil. Across France, they recruited Messali's followers from the large expat community and launched the so-called "Café Wars." The Fédération de France du FLN, a stealthy group of combatants popularly known as Wilaya 7, spearheaded covert actions in France. Other divisions of fighter units were dispatched to the Morocco and Tunisia borders. The combatants were placed under the command of army Colonel Houari Boumédiène when he became chief of staff in the ALN. After clashing with the FLN's Algerian provisional government-in-exile (the GPRA), a group that attempted to dismiss him toward the end of the war, he moved to support an alliance of FLN politicians led by Ahmed Ben Bella. In a daring display of self-determination, he went against their post-independence government plans and marched the ALN toward Algiers to occupy the city. Ahmed Ben Bella became president and Boumédiène was named Minister of Defense. In his new position, Boumédiène used his military muscle to wield powerful influence over the Ben Bella regime. He secured his grip over the army by promoting and supporting old friends and colleagues from his service in Oujda. They formed their own alliance, the Oujda group, becoming a very powerful pro-Boumédiène faction within the political and military ranks of the newly independent country.

Due to rising tensions between pro-Boumédiène supporters and the Ben Bella base, Ben Bella informed Boumédiène that he planned on reassigning responsibilities within the army. In the three years since he ascended to power, Ben Bella had managed to relegate the country's religious leaders to the sidelines and jail Ferhat Abbas and other outspoken intellectuals. But Boumédiène wouldn't go quietly. He staged an army-led coup d'état, overthrew Ben Bella, and placed him under house arrest for several years.

Despite being a hard-liner, he earned the people's respect because he ran a disciplined and noncorrupt administration that saw to the exponential growth and expansion of a robust economy. In the country's secondary sector, he put in motion an ironclad state-driven industrialization strategy that relied heavily on oil and natural gas resources to boost production. His sole objective was to turn Algeria into an industrial powerhouse for the Maghreb, Africa, and the rest of the Third World.

His years in office were marked by consistent economic growth engineered by a vigorous industrial diversification and an astute global political acumen. The country's industrial development was strengthened by a metallurgy of iron complexes such as the impressive El Hadjar, which attracted a large workforce to the town of Annaba. He built refineries, developed a petrochemical production facility, and urbanized the electrical industry, mobilizing the Algerian people and empowering them to aim for higher productivity and enable the country to compete among developed nations. The results were impressive.

I took the opportunity to congratulate him on his record-breaking accomplishments during a diplomatic meeting in Algiers. "We are still very far away from reaching our objective, my dear brother," he assured me. "Our objective is to make Algeria a developed country. If the Europeans succeeded in doing the same with their countries, why not us? Unlike them, we don't need to take as much time. These days, technology is prevalent. I am sure we can catch up quickly. The only thing I ask from the Algerian people is to work hard."

He remained anxious about the transfer of technological knowledge from the West to aid Algerians in the management and utilization of heavy industrial equipment. Because of these concerns, the government set up strategies for an innovative business model with industrialized nations; rather than operate in line with the classic "key in the hands" concept, they moved to institute a "product in the hands" concept which ensured that foreign corporations would work side by side with Algerian personnel from the construction phase through to the final system testing phase. This guaranteed that Algerians would absorb the knowledge and be well versed in maintenance services, ultimately building similar factories with the acquired expertise.

On Boumédiène's watch, the country's steel manufacturing plants produced many different grades of steel. His government negotiated a product-in-hand cooperative agreement with Berliet, a French automobile manufacturer, paving the way for a large engine assembly plant to be built in the country. This was mostly a strategic move, aimed at improving the aptitude of Algeria's workforce. Due to critical shortages in our developing nation's engineers, he encouraged graduate students to take up engineering and focus on science and technology. Boumédiène believed that development could not be bought. It had to be produced. Although he imposed timely austerity measures, he ruled by example and advanced his agenda by leading a passionate call for sacrifice and discipline. All of this endeared him to the vast majority of Algerians. I was ever hopeful for the country's future.

Throughout the many years of our friendship, I was ever ready to be of service whenever he sought my advice on a myriad of issues or other complex matters of state. His outlook on the future of the country had a profound impact on his plans for drafting the republic's constitution. The security and political stability of the nation's future administrations were embodied within a framework that served as the principal foundation on which a new constitution was to be adopted. He took steps to systematically set in motion a procedure by which the country's future constitution would be amended for the sake of opening up a process for gradual democratization.

As chairman of the Council of the Revolution, Boumédiène ruled by decree. But he slowly began to reinstate constitutional rule and encouraged the restoration of civilian political institutions. Occasionally, we discussed and exchanged ideas on the reorganization of state institutions. My official duties in Côte d'Ivoire did not prevent me from lending a helping hand when he reached out to me. The health and stability of Algeria was always prominent on my mind, and I never hesitated to contribute to the future of my beloved country. I was extremely happy when he mentioned to me that as soon as a new parliament was elected, he would commit to reviving political activism within the FLN and begin reestablishing state institutions to enable the hierarchical movement of local and regional assemblies through to the national level. The news was music to my ears, because I was quite familiar with the experiment, having seen such practice within the PDCI in Côte d'Ivoire. I appreciated his openness and commitment to the process and remained hopeful about his ever-evolving well-meaning intentions and vision for Algeria's future. After a period of open debates on the merits of several government-backed proposals, the initial constitutional draft was adopted by referendum in 1976. Shortly after that, he was elected as the president of the republic in accordance with the guidelines set forth in the constitution, reintroducing the office of presidency.

While he was in power, the highest military rank was that of colonel. Following his call by the Almighty, the hierarchy promoted themselves to superior ranks without any particular rationalization.

A Dream for Peace

Present-day Algerians find themselves in the midst of generals, superior generals, and notable high rankings that make up the hierarchy in the country's power structure.

I experienced the dawn of the situation firsthand when Boumédiène returned from Moscow, where he was undergoing treatment for an unidentified health problem. I was dispatched to Algiers by President Houphouët to stay and monitor his progress. This was a token gesture of our friendship, love, and compassion.

Upon arrival, I realized that he was in dire straits. His health was deteriorating quite rapidly. Surrounded by doctors who could not figure out what was wrong with him, chaos and confusion had poisoned the power base. The tragic experience was distressful and severely painful to cope with. Whenever I returned to my hotel, I sunk into the couch in my suite and phoned my wife to share the emotionally draining ordeal. She remained a pillar of support in those crucial moments when the life of a dear friend was hanging by a thread. Her soothing assurances always culminated in prayers for Boumédiène and the people of Algeria. President Houphouët, whom I kept up to date with the fleeting developments, prayed long and hard every single day, hoping for divine intervention.

I went on routine visits to see my friend every morning at the hospital's intensive care unit. On a particular morning, I was walking briskly to his ward, hoping to see him with eyes wide open, or at the very least get an opportunity to speak with one of his physicians. I imagined a miraculous recovery and signs of improvement. His nurse approached in the hallway and broke the sad news to me. My brother and very dear friend Boumédiène had passed away. I was immediately frozen, flustered, and deeply shocked at the news. It took me some time to regain my composure. When I returned to my hotel and informed President Houphouët of our mutual loss, he remained speechless, and we both kept a moment of silence before we hung up. Algeria had just lost a great leader. When the media broke the news, the nation came to a standstill. People reflected

Algeria—Cry of the Crestfallen Heart

and shared their memories and all around the country, patriots expressed their sadness and indescribable angst at the life that was cut short by a mysterious illness.

The day of the funeral was extremely challenging, both emotionally and mentally. I sat in the front row, flanked by Commandant Abdelmadjid Allahoum and soon-to-be successor, Chadli Bendjedid. We were surrounded by other high-ranking military officers. As Minister of Foreign Affairs Abdelaziz Bouteflika was concluding the eulogy, Chadli fainted and fell into the arms of Allahoum.

The military's high command had decided on his successor while he lay sick at the hospital. Chadli, the highest-ranking colonel at the time, was their choice. However, Algeria's constitution clearly spelled out that the interim presidency belonged to the head of the People's National Assembly (APN). He had the power in accordance with constitutional rule of law to enact measures to elect Boumédiène's successor. I prayed that the successor would continue to work hard and sustain the process of growth. But the question remained whether the next leader would be equipped with the proper acumen, passion, patriotic dedication, and vision to continue on the path of progress. I knew that only time would tell.

The day after the funeral, I attended the official bestowment of commiserations at the Palais du Peuple and was received by Chadli as the first representative of a foreign country. In my statement to him, I conveyed our heartfelt condolences on behalf of President Houphouët, a friend and brother, and the Ivorian people. "We hope to maintain our bilateral relations and uphold the unique bond that our countries hold so dear," I said. This type of communication was not unusual among diplomats and leaders even in times of bereavement. Affairs of state must go on regardless. "Presidents Houphouët and Boumédiène shared the same worldviews, with particular emphasis on how to deal with the Western Sahara, cooperation with Europe, and Africa's role in the world. It is our hope

A Dream for Peace

that we stay on the path in the spirit of solidarity between our two nations." I paused for some feedback. His response was brief: "We will see." He seemed removed from the moment. "Very well, Mr. President. Let's continue to act cautiously, but expediently. History will not wait on us," I pressed, assuming he was a bit overwhelmed by events and wasn't particularly focused. On the way to my hotel, I pondered the departure of President Boumédiène, and suddenly I was flooded by the immense nature of the loss. Reality began to set in gradually, and I knew that we were going to miss him.

Following the effective takeover of the Algerian army whose generals seemed more inclined to enrich themselves and secure the future of their own families rather than govern to create prosperity for the people, I grew increasingly concerned and flabbergasted. The once booming economy began to slide toward a downward spiral, and soon the country found itself in a state of stagnation. It was as if things had taken a 360-degree turn for the worse. The leadership organized for their own benefit a questionable import policy scheme and secured vital import licenses for themselves and those in their inner circles, at times camouflaging their deeds behind corporate entities. Public enterprises were abandoned and as a consequence, national production began to decline, followed by high unemployment. A small group of individuals took control of oil revenues and misappropriated state funds into private holdings.

The generals behaved like despots and continued to maintain an unfair and illegal authority over an unhappy Algerian populace, defending their legitimate hold on power by arguing that they were veterans of the liberation army. Every aspect of life for the average Algerian, including every avenue of prosperity, was controlled by the powerful generals. The road to success in Algeria was suddenly vested in their hands, and one had no choice but to endure an unavoidable allegiance to them. After all, it was the army that confirmed, appointed, and removed everyone it saw as "undesirable."

Algeria—Cry of the Crestfallen Heart

A wide net was cast over the category of those classified as undesirables. My nephew, who had earned his PhD in seismology at MIT when he was only twenty-four years old, was sacked for no apparent reason whatsoever. He is the son of an eminent professor, Abdelhak Berrah, who was well known within the corridors of medicine and even had a facility named after him at Mustapha Hospital in Algiers. Upon his return to Algeria, my nephew was appointed director of the École Polytechnique. A few years later, he was suddenly dismissed from his post and replaced with the daughter of a general who lacked the required academic background and experience.

When I heard the news, my heart broke for the young man. I recalled introducing myself during a phone conversation with the Dean of International Students at MIT. Upon hearing my surname, he immediately asked, "Professor Berrah, do you have any family ties with a young man by the name of Berrah?" Without giving me a chance to answer, he continued. "The lad has set an outstanding example in our records here at the university." "Oh yes of course," I told him. "He is my nephew." I felt such a sense of great pride.

The brain drain among young people was easily understood. Both President Houphouët and I had discussed the matter at length on many occasions and concluded that the trend had posed unique challenges to some newly independent African countries. But unlike other countries, Côte d'Ivoire had been immune from the mass exodus. A journalist brought up the subject and President Houphouët responded, "Most developing countries are losing their competent young professionals to developed nations. I remain convinced that Africa's future lies squarely in science and technology, and I also understand that the foundation of a prosperous nation is strong when the youth are well educated." At the time, I thought his statement was insightful, but the repercussions of brain drain had not hit close to the home front for us, because Côte d'Ivoire had no such issues.

A Dream for Peace

Either way, his words were not mere rhetoric. They echoed far into the future and encompassed the challenges facing Algeria's youth in a country that had deprived them of a chance at decent living due to its high unemployment rate. As I observed across the country, the vast majority of highly qualified individuals remained unemployed for lack of connections to an influential network or affiliations among the upper echelons of the military. It was not surprising that groups of talented youth, the "cream of the crop," continued to leave for greener pastures in Europe and Canada. But in spite of the migration, many able-bodied and bright young patriots had chosen to remain in the country because of family ties or emotional reasons. It is still worth noting that those who have stayed represent an untapped resource of bright minds. A nation cannot trend positively on the GDP scale and blossom if it is faced with a major migration of skilled workers.

By late 1988 into 1990, Algeria had reached a crossroads of sorts, with record high unemployment and inflation threatening to derail the government's socioeconomic policies. During one of many trips to the country, I sensed an increase in popular dissatisfaction among the youth and hardworking families and became concerned. The issues of brain drain, high unemployment, and slow technological development were at the root of the nation's instability.

Driving down a long and serene country road on the way to Aïn Beïda in the spring of 1989 after visiting Missa, my beloved sister in Annaba, Titi marveled at the rows of beautiful perennial flowers growing wildly on the sun-drenched landscape. The array of stunning colorful blossoms dotted the hillside as if to greet us. Suddenly, we observed a cloud of black smoke in the distance and cruised slowly toward the animated shadows pacing the middle of the road. "What in the world is going on?" I wondered. We pulled up to a roadblock of burning tires and suffocating smoke in the air and came face-to-face with about ten menacing teenage boys. When they encircled the car, I stepped out to confront them, obviously agitated by the commotion. They chanted angrily, "We are fed up! We don't have jobs, we don't have any freedom of speech in this country. We are the forgotten ones. We have nothing! Absolutely nothing!" "Okay, okay, calm down," I said, but my initial attempts to tame their raucous behavior fell on deaf ears. They yelled louder and talked over each other, feeding off the adrenal rush. It all seemed staged for the unsuspecting audience. The ringleader stepped forward. "Each time we try to voice our discontent, the military folks subject us to severe beatings!" he cried out, "Many of our brothers have been killed. It is in their memory we stand here to call the world's attention to our plight." I put up my hand and asked them to be quiet. "Listen up, young men. I am from Aïn Beïda, but I serve the Ivorian government as a diplomat. I came home to spend the holidays with my family. This is not the way to go about things. You are disturbing the peace of those who are not responsible for your situation." "Sidi, if you are indeed a diplomat, please get our story out to the United Nations," the ringleader chimed. "I will. Now please let us get back on the road. Thank you." They moved some tires out of the way and waved us on. Back in Algiers, I called first thing in the morning and spoke to the Interior Minister and a few friends in government. I warned that matters could worsen unless adequate measures were taken to tackle public dissension. Everyone assured me that they were seriously focused on making improvements in the domestic agenda, hoping to promote sustainable growth in rural areas and provide employment opportunities for the youth.

The incident occurred at a time when the Chadli administration had instituted a multiparty system. But regardless, the discontent of the masses continued to spread around the country, leading to the formation of a few hard-line political factions, the so-called "Islamists," known for their clear opposition to the government. They were the voice of millions. Among them, the most important party was the Front Islamique du Salut (FIS, the Islamic Salvation Front), which gained recognition after the adoption of multipartyism

A Dream for Peace

in the new constitution.

The military leadership annulled the first round of an election for the National Assembly that had been won by the FIS and forced Chadli to step down because he disagreed with the decision to annul the election. The FIS organization was immediately banned and a large number of the party's members were arrested, but many went underground and some escaped to the mountains. The advent of ten dark years in the nation's history began in earnest, with a malicious, bloody, and vicious civil war resulting in the deaths of thousands of Algerians.

I was immersed in deep affliction and became immeasurably flabbergasted, for it was not a war against French colonialism that we were fighting. This was about Algerians killing their own brethren after having sacrificed more than seven years in the war for independence. The abominable war started while I was in Abidjan. It was a traumatic psychological roller coaster of shocking proportions watching the country descend into the deep abyss on the daily news. I held my breath and pulled my hair, struggling with an array of diplomatic solutions that could pave a path toward achieving peace, but all of my overtures and viable proposals were deemed as nonstarters. I felt powerless.

My wife and I passed the serene waters of la Lagune Ébrié on a sunny tropical afternoon, admiring the display of cheerful flowers with abounding colors adorning the roadside on the way to our villa. It was two minutes to 4:00 p.m. when I checked the time. I asked Touré, my trusted driver, to dial up Radio France International (RFI) for the news. At the top of the hour, the reporter started with the breaking news: "Terrorism continues to strike Algeria. Today, the victim is a well-known personality in Algiers, Mr. Khoudir Berrah, a civic servant who served as the head of several Daïras around the country." "What? Allahu Akbar! [Oh God Almighty!]" I exclaimed to my wife. "That is my cousin Khoudir!" I could not believe my ears. Titi gently took my hand in hers and held on firmly. I was paralyzed, stunned, and dizzy. "Mr. Khoudir Berrah was gunned down in a blaze of machine gun fire right in front of his son's school," the reporter continued. "Terror-stricken schoolchildren and parents ran for their dear lives as the perpetrators escaped from the scene of the crime." I thought about his son, my nephew Chakib, and the trauma he had experienced, having witnessed his beloved dad gunned down in such a horrific manner.

After speaking with Khoudir's grief-stricken wife, Mounira, who maintained exceptional courage and remained dignified under the dire circumstances, I felt feverishly sick. Needless to say, I was powerless. I was unable to sleep for several days. I mourned my cousin deeply and couldn't stop thinking about him. He had been by my side every single minute during our three-day stay in Algiers. That was just two years before his untimely passing. I remembered him for his active lifestyle and how he was always ready to cater to my various needs. He was a witty man who found a way to make me laugh about many nonsensical things. During our stay in Algiers, he accompanied us everywhere from the wee hours of the morning until the late evening. The last time we saw him, I apologized for taking too much time away from his hectic schedule. He assured me not to worry about anything. "When I'm with you, I do not lose a second of my service to the nation," he said. "I am in constant contact with the office. But it is an immense pleasure and a privilege to spend these precious moments with you. It is a rare opportunity that happens once in a lifetime." Perhaps, I thought, it was his farewell to us.

Despite being in a state of shock, my wife did not relent in trying to alleviate my pain. She was the pillar of support that I needed, and she became a sanctuary for my emotional distress. She knew that beyond crying for Khoudir, I was also crying for Algeria. As the years wore on, the situation in Algeria took a turn for the worse. I made the decision to organize family reunions in Tunisia, a neighboring country. At the time, I grew ever more doubtful that there was even the slightest chance that things would ever get back to a semblance of normalcy.

I prayed very hard and continued to hope for an end to the unsettling situation. When I heard the news in 1999 that my brother and friend Abdelaziz Bouteflika was running for president, I was elated and overjoyed. He appeared on the scene like a savior, ready to rid the country of the military scourge. I have never had anything against the military as such. I have always believed that the noble nature of the army is to constitute forces for the defense and security of the nation. But the military must neither interfere with politics of state nor hamper progress in the daily life of the citizen. The country's political radar must always be in the capable hands of the head of state, who serves as the commander in chief of the armed forces.

The notion of what constituted the role of the military was so mired in confusion that younger Algerians had a hard time discerning between reality and what was supposed to be the norm. I once asked a high school senior in Algiers about his aspirations during a family visit. "Sidi, after completing high school, I plan to attend military school," he told me. "Congratulations, Mohammed, so you want to defend your country!" "Not at all," he answered in all candor. "I want to be a military man so that I can help my parents out." "How can you help your parents by being a soldier?" I asked. "If I join the military," he responded, "I will be welcome in any office and I will manage to obtain whatever I need. In this country, anyone in the military forces can do whatever they want." I then asked, "So, Mohammed, as a soldier, if faced with a dangerous situation, what would you do?" "Simple," he said. "I will run away!" Though preposterous, this seemed to be a prevailing mindset among the innocent youth. I spoke to him about aiming for a higher purpose in light of his muddled views. Thankfully, he was quite receptive, and I embraced the belief that all hope was not lost.

It seemed to me that placing an emphasis on more civics

programs in primary schools would be essential to the country's future. The benefits of innovative curriculums endure in a person's life, especially when the notion of patriotism and love for country is grasped at an early age. In order to preserve our national identity, my generation was ready to die for Algeria. We were groomed that way, and we took pride in fighting for our sovereignty. Today's youth must build a pathway to success and help foster a deeper understanding of what it is to be Algerian. Were it not for the resolute struggle and sacrifice of more than a million and a half martyrs, our nation would not have gained its autonomy. The colonialists were more than happy to dissect our beloved nation into three French "departments." Today's generations and those far into the future must be proud of our painful yet glorious past. Harnessing the power of their inheritance will propel them into the future and exhort them to excel with a fierce determination to do better than the older generation. The young soldiers who face security challenges every day are at the forefront of a noble commitment. By honoring their sacred obligation to defend the land and its people, they are memorializing those who stood in the line of fire to liberate our country. Their pledge should constitute a pact with the state, more or less, a vow that instills in the minds of every child our traditional and national values.

Abdelaziz Bouteflika and I shared a fifty-year friendship. Our relationship outlasted his political isolation and endured even at a time when his friends had grown scarce. We used to meet in Paris and in Geneva at my house in Annemasse. Sitting on the terrace, sharing a glass of mint tea or a soft drink, we looked out at the majestic Mont Blanc and talked about Algeria and other worldly affairs for many long hours. At times, we went for a long drive to Lausanne or somewhere else in the region. We really enjoyed being in each other's company. Titi took a liking to him, and he in turn showed her a great deal of affection. When she was recovering from surgery in Switzerland at the Clinique de Genolier, he flew in

A Dream for Peace

from Paris to spend an entire day with her, knowing that I was in Abidjan at the time. And like a true brother, he gave her his undivided attention until it was time for him to catch the last flight to Paris.

I grew accustomed to his astute nature and bright personality. When he won the election, I was convinced that he would use all of his talents and diplomatic abilities to bring about peace and usher in a new era for Algeria. The country's citizens had opted for positive change. One of his first acts in office was to enact La Concorde Civile, a bill that granted total amnesty to those who had been implicated in acts of terror against the state, as long as they were willing to cease all criminal activities and relinquish their arms. The bill was implemented after a referendum vote by close to 90 percent of the Algerian people, just five months after he came into office.

A few days later, he flew to New York to attend the annual UN General Assembly session. Once on the ground, he met with a select group of Algerians at the Intercontinental Hotel. My wife and I flew in for the special occasion from Denver, where we lived at the time. It was our first meeting since he became president. He appeared relaxed and resolute and appealed to every Algerian in diaspora to return home and help him reconstruct the country. When I went to see him just days after the gathering, I emphasized that most able-bodied Algerians would heed his calls only after peace and security had been restored in the country. Although he had taking steps toward achieving such objectives, he had yet to convince the various groups to lay down their arms.

My wife and I continued to observe gradual but exponential changes in the country whenever we visited the city of Algiers. Most of the citizens we spoke to were enthusiastic about the direction of a new Algeria under President Bouteflika. New restaurants flourished in the city, and commerce was fluid for families from all walks of life. Unlike the past, women were no longer afraid to drive or walk unaccompanied in the streets, and his administration pushed for infrastructure investments to improve housing and expand access

Algeria—Cry of the Crestfallen Heart

to clean water.

The president pampered and spoiled us plenty during our visits. We were always given the red carpet treatment. But what mattered the most were the leadership qualities of the head of state the Algerian people had chosen to run the country's affairs.

President Abdelaziz Bouteflika.

We were his guests at a time when la Charte Pour la Paix et la Réconciliation Nationale (the Charter for Peace and National Reconciliation, an amnesty bill for thousands of fighters who had surrendered their arms) was drafted in 2005. My wife and I followed the campaign for the referendum closely. President Bouteflika embarked on an energized crusade. He traversed the deepest regions with his walking stick, relentlessly preaching about peace, love, and reconciliation with so much zeal and devotion. All of that was profoundly moving to me, having dedicated my entire diplomatic career to similar values and virtues. Images from north to south, west to east, depicted him as a trailblazer leading his people.

A Dream for Peace

I dispatched my nephews and nieces to the far provinces of the country to help spread the word, and I called on my brother-in-law, Djilali Mehri, an eminent businessman in Paris, to put out a full-page ad in a major newspaper in support of the referendum. This particular decision was an important step, because he was known by most as an avid supporter of Ali Benflis, a former prime minister turned opposition presidential contender. My wife and I attended two of the president's rallies in Algiers. One of the events was held at a venue called La Rotonde, where he electrified the capacity audience with an impressive speech that brought joy to my heart.

While doing my part to help the referendum campaign, I encountered several people on occasion who speculated about the president preaching pardon and peace among the Algerian people, and meanwhile they wondered why he hadn't addressed issues among the leaders at the top of the political spectrum. Though it seemed most of those inquiries, stemmed from rumors and innuendos, I knew the facts, but I declined to share details with anyone regarding my discreet efforts behind the scenes. Indeed, there was some dissention and antagonism between the president and others of a different political persuasion who didn't see eye to eye with his vision for the country. I had thought long and hard about a comprehensive and cogent approach on how best to get everyone working together to maintain cohesion. We were at a major crossroads in the nation's history, and I believed strongly that joining forces was central to the president's agenda.

I had frequent discussions with some of my former student-activist friends from the UGEMA years who had gone on to become highly influential political personalities in Algeria. My plan was to reach out and do whatever I could to help them find common ground between their needs and the hardships facing the country. I knew Ahmed Taleb Ibrahimi as the son of our traditional religious leader, Sheikh Bashir El Ibrahimi, who was persecuted by the French. I was always supportive of him with regards to UGEMA affairs and even throughout his sentencing on trumped-up charges during the war, when he was sent off to the Prison de la Santé in Paris. Even though I had enlisted with the Maquis, I remained a fervent advocate for his release. After Boumédiène came to power, he called him up and offered him a position in his administration. They got along very well, and he held a couple of ministerial positions until Boumédiène was called by the Almighty. At the time, he was the president's closest advisor. He made the transition into Chadli's government and served as Minister of Foreign Affairs.

Like Bouteflika, Ahmed Taleb threw his hat in the ring for the presidential elections in 1999 but withdrew his candidacy just before the vote began, claiming undue and fraudulent interference by the military. He formed a new Party (WAFA) soon after Bouteflika had been sworn in, but the organization was banned from participating in national politics because of alleged links to the FIS. For the same reasons, he was prohibited from running in the 2004 presidential elections. When I went to see him, we chatted about the past for the most part, but when our conversation turned to politics, he was straightforward and unabashedly blunt about his views. He asserted repeatedly that he had nothing against the president and confirmed that he supported what he considered was a "very good initiative" on the ballot. I sensed his sincerity because he was always a straight shooter with me. We both elaborated on the need for unfettered fraternity and concord among all Algerians. He was a very positive and committed patriot who was willing to put aside his personal reservations in the name of peace. We met on two occasions, and he reassured me that he wouldn't stand in the way of progress. I was pleased with the outcome.

By contrast, our mutual friend and UGEMA comrade, Redha Malek, who played an essential role during the war as the editor of the clandestine FLN newspaper El Moudjahid, had earned himself the moniker "the Eradicator" for his hard-line stance on the issue of terrorism. Having served briefly as prime minister after Chadli's resignation, he was absolutely not ready to forgive those who had committed crimes against the state. Initially I was somewhat surprised, recalling a time when he was the spokesperson for the Algerian delegation at the Evian meetings for peace. In the Boumédiène administration, he held consecutive ambassadorships to France, the United States, the USSR, and Great Britain, transitioning to a ministerial stint that progressed into the Chadli changeover.

In conversations with him, it was hard to miss the traces of deep philosophical studies that had shaped the verbosely articulate personality behind the man. Such fundamentals drove his proclivity for highlighting distinctive patterns in the gray areas of individual, collective, or national consciousness. I enjoyed our talks because we touched upon many thought-provoking variants that seemed to endlessly stimulate the brain's creative visualization and placed things into perspective. In the end, I managed to convince him that individual consciousness is a by-product of a person's innate tendency to embrace their own moral dispositions—"Indeed, when we deal with social and political issues, we find ourselves in a cultural sphere, which in essence alters the equilibrium, and then the narrative of national consciousness is revealed." He sat quietly and absorbed the words, a wry smile on his face. When I left his place, he came to my hotel the next day to invite me to eat some couscous in accordance with old Aïn Beïda traditions. His father was the town's beloved qadi when we were growing up.

A day before the referendum vote, my wife and I attended a ceremony that awarded Bouteflika the Louise Michel peace prize, reaffirming the support of the international community. The bill was adopted in spite of an ardent pushback by opponents. In the end, even those who had been hurt or affected in some way by the war agreed to vote for it because he earned their trust. He shot to the peak of every poll and rose in popularity, hailed by the people as the first true leader for the country in quite a while.

I sent a message to him when I returned to the United States

Algeria—Cry of the Crestfallen Heart

expressing my pride and confidence in a bright future for Algeria. I believed that the country had set a great example for other nations that were mired in long-lasting conflicts. His actions harkened back to his days as the country's Minister of Foreign Affairs, when he promoted messages of peace in diplomatic circles.

But my joyful enthusiasm did not last long. He was rushed in an emergency to a hospital in Paris after falling mysteriously ill. I was extremely alarmed and gravely concerned not only for his well-being; I also prayed that his health issues and prolonged absence would not drive the country down the abyss of war and destruction. His presence at the helm of the nation was imperative, as it amounted to a guarantee of sustainable peace in the region as well.

I hoped that the generals would not take advantage of the temporary vacuum and rush to reclaim control of the reins of power. My wife was relentless, moving heaven and earth to get in touch with him and obtain some information about his condition, but her efforts did not bear fruit. Meanwhile, we continued to pray for him. We asked some imams to keep him in their prayers and celebrated masses on his behalf with priests and bishops.

To our relief, he returned to Algeria about two months after taking ill. The media broadcasted pictures of his triumphant welcome in the midst of patriotic fervor, flanked by hundreds of people expressing their love and well-wishes for his sustained health.

My brother and friend did not miss the opportunity to call and comfort our hearts. I received an early morning call to our Florida home: "Sabah al kheir a khoya [good morning, my brother], Abdelaziz speaking." I was overjoyed to hear his voice again. He had called to reassure me of his good health and vitality. He exchanged a few soothing words with Titi before hanging up. He really made our day. It was then that I was convinced he had returned to duty and was in full control.

In the aftermath of the successful referendum, I was motivated to send a message to my dear friend and praise him for his

A Dream for Peace

sacrifices to the nation. "The brutality of war does not solve anything. It only stirs the pot of hatred and disgust," I wrote. "I commend you, for the bloody massacres in Algeria could never have been brought to an end without pardon, mercy, and love for the people." His approach to peace had been a welcome breath of fresh air in Algeria and in the region. He had set out to move the country forward with the help of its citizens, a vast majority of whom were poised to safeguard his development agenda. Tens of thousands of booklets, aptly titled The Charter for Peace and National Reconciliation, had been distributed to members of the public. When he and I spoke, I suggested that he take the message of peace to a level that would ensure profound consequences. "The people will surely embrace the message, especially after familiarizing themselves with the contents of the booklet. Open debates and robust discussions in community think tanks will help enrich them and produce enough leaders who can educate others in parts of society." He was quite receptive. "You are right. The message of peace can make its way into our secondary schools and universities, even workplaces, zaouias,[72] and mosques." "But of course," I said. "Peace and reconciliation must be the focus of every single Algerian, man and woman alike. All the various political parties must be charged with the responsibility of ensuring the program's success. It is the only way to sow the seeds of peace." I envisioned a well-tailored message of peace and love reverberating around the globe and taking root in conflict-riddled regions. Algeria could be the beacon of light in a world that prayed for victory against terrorism.

I was certain that given the opportunity, our Palestinian and Iraqi brothers who were killing each other at the time would rethink and embark on a different approach, because there was no love, no pardon, and no reconciliation in their objectives. Everyone seemed driven by their desire and love for power.

---

[72] Islamic religious schools. (The term is Maghrebi and West African.)

Algeria—Cry of the Crestfallen Heart

Education has been an essential component that underlies the development of every vibrant society. But most people in developed nations I observed had gradually lost touch with their spirituality. I contemplated the unfortunate consequences of advanced nations in the Western Hemisphere whose citizens found themselves trapped in a life that had spiraled out of control, leaving their souls trembling at their core. There was an absence of life's purpose. It seemed as if everyone was entombed in a moment of unbridled ambition, floating somewhere between a feeling of dissatisfaction and a distorted view of true happiness. Consequentially, people were not only lost, but they also found themselves stuck in an infinite loop of soul searching. Such were the thoughts that kept me awake in the very late hours of the night, prompting me to reach out yet again to President Bouteflika. I came up with a plan that set forth a framework to help the Algerian people achieve education without losing their spiritual foundations. Even though I wasn't completely sure if we had arrived at a point of no return, I sensed a dire need to frame the message for future generations. It was time to deliver the memo and help educate every developing nation that sought to achieve such vital objectives.

"In Algeria's case, our people are in dire need of basic education," I wrote. "Obviously, everyone must work and love to work, because wealth is generated by hard work. But wealth is not what makes us who we are."

In 2006, I heaped praises on him for building new schools, ultramodern universities, and advanced institutions, and I commended him for urging his countrymen to get to work. But by 2010, when I realized that Algerian universities were ranked almost at the bottom of the world's list of accomplished universities, I grew increasingly frustrated. I wondered if it mattered that we had brand-new buildings without a capable, innovative staff to deliver professional services that benefitted our youth. Another issue that I found disturbing was the fact that employment in the country's emergency services was sparse, almost nonexistent, because there were no wage and collective bargaining incentives in place to attract enough workers. Hence, after a flood in the town of Skikkda, the municipality was forced to rely on a team of experts from China to clean up the town. Such a decision would have triggered a massive outcry and no less than political repercussions in any European country. I wondered if he had taken note of the fact that in France, Algerians were at the helm of municipal services, tasked with performing the hardest and least rewarding duties. By contrast, those workers in France were rewarded with good pay and benefits, and they never had to fret about putting their children through good schools.

I commented on the need to institute measures to help young entrepreneurs and make available small business loans to keep the wheels oiled for the country's industrial development. The times were favorable because of the rise in oil prices, and I was happy to see the president using oil revenue to launch major infrastructure projects, such as the East-West Highway, for the benefit of average Algerians. The agricultural sector began to show signs of recovery when both the young and able-bodied middle-aged citizens were given the necessary assistance to acquire arable farmlands.

I liked the way my dear friend was inspired to serve the Algerian people, but I wasn't sure that those around him were as committed and dedicated to the same sense of service. For infrastructure development projects, I recommended that he contract a professional with a similar profile and integrity as Antoine Cesareo to help him negotiate the terms of any major project. Unfortunately, he did not heed my advice and ended up ensnared in problems of delays, greed, and shady intermediaries. Most of his projects were hard to keep in check.

The country's brain drain continues to dog its very foundation. I addressed the issue of enticing Algerians, especially those in medical practice, back to the homeland. We had lost very capable brainiacs to Europe and Canada over the years. The president and I agreed that it was important to accommodate our educated elite in diaspora whose talents Algeria needed desperately to ensure the nation's upward mobility. At the Saint Julien en Genevois hospital by the Franco-Swiss border, the cardiology and radiology departments were headed by Algerians, who were among thousands that ply their trade in France. In the backdrop is the homeland, whose citizens receive free health-care benefits, yet its substandard medical infrastructures need a facelift. Under most circumstances, a patient is required to bring along their own catgut and gauze to a hospital that lacks adequate drugs or medical equipment; otherwise they risk not receiving the care they need. Some hospitals have even experienced severe shortage of beds, a rather disenchanting fact, when Algeria, with the world's tenth largest natural gas reserves and sixteenth largest oil reserves, has actually benefitted from a surplus of nearly $200 billion in the recent past. The burdens on the country's general hospitals were expected to be alleviated by the emergence of private clinics that have sprouted in the country like wild mushrooms. But those clinics continue to operate beyond the financial reach of the average Algerian. The question remains how the vast majority of medical practitioners I met, who were all willing to relocate, could be guaranteed decent wages and affordable housing.

In light of the difficulties, most affluent citizens or those related to a member of the military who required medical care were evacuated to France, all expenses paid, by the government. The irony is that during the colonial era, the Faculty of Medicine in Algiers was second only to its sister facility in Paris. The caliber of talent that emerged from the institution was second to none on the continent, a fact that was affirmed by the Élysée's choice of Professor José Aboulker, the surgeon who operated on General De Gaulle.

The challenges that Algeria continues to face are mostly unique to developing countries. It is true that economic growth and

A Dream for Peace

prosperity can be achieved through an implied partnership between state and local governments, but also, state and local governments must assume primary responsibility for the education system in order to produce a more skilled and dynamic workforce. As such, it is essential to introduce research programs that are vital to stimulating private-sector growth and guarantee that the noninflationary macroeconomic policies would generate improvements in the standard of living.

When a woman was promoted to the rank of general, I applauded the move as a historic step because Algeria's women played a key role in the fight for liberation. Even though they had no political rights during the colonial days, they joined in the struggle when the war broke out; some even took part in active combat. I encountered a few of the fighters who joined the National Liberation Army, knowing fully well that their numbers matched the percentage of European women who took part in the Second World War. This was quite impressive, but nevertheless, while residual terrorism remains on the fringes in today's Algeria, security and public safety will continue to be a problem for everyone.

Either way, long after the referendum of amnesty, it was business as usual for the generals, who had signed off on refraining from their past deeds yet continued to practice "appropriation." I was particularly disappointed in the generals for their apparent display of impervious arrogance. These were public servants who had sworn to serve the people of Algeria. Notwithstanding, my dear friend and brother remained hermetically silent. I wondered what was going on and prayed that the Almighty would continue to guide and protect him. After ten years of civil war and mass confusion, governing can be immensely challenging. I trusted, however, that he had a vision and a plan. Someday, historians will recognize him as a man of peace and the architect of peace in Algeria, but he must acknowledge that his accomplishments must stand on two pillars to be perennial or they run the risk of becoming an incomplete symphony. He needs to commit to engaging political structural changes to include participatory democracy and equality among all citizens. The rule of law must be strictly enforced, and the independence of the judiciary must be enshrined in the constitution. I am accustomed to his sincerity and the logical march of his rigorous and subtle thought process as he threads his cautious and patient temperament. He always waits for what seems to him the right and most appropriate time to undertake any action, never missing an opportunity to lay down the foundation for the second pillar of his exalting work.

As a person, Bouteflika is to me a selfless individual with a nationalistic zeal that transcends parochial motivations. At the dinner table in my home in Annemasse, Rabeha, a fervent supporter, stated candidly, "If someday Mr. Bouteflika became president, he will make Algeria like the United States." His modest but somehow approving smile meant a lot to me, and our continuing discussions corroborated the ambitious dream of the future president who hoped to endow Algeria with all the attributes of a developed nation.

He encountered a high unemployment rate when he was sworn into office in 1999 and managed to lower it drastically, though incomes stagnated for nearly four years. He tackled the minimum wage with periodic increases from 2004 until 2009. But by then, he still had fallen short of his goal to improve the quality of life of Algerians. Rising prices for basic goods and utility services had an adverse impact on the purchasing power of everyone in the country, even high-ranking workers like university professors and doctors. There were massive strikes by workers from many sectors. He still enjoyed high approval ratings and a high level of support from the people. The vast majority knew that he was a dedicated workaholic, but his efforts would be lackluster without the full commitment of his cabinet members. The challenge, therefore, was finding a way to communicate his nationalistic zeal to those in the administration who were charged with managing the nation's affairs. When I started writing this book in 2010, the country was quasi immune from debt, with a budgetary surplus to boot. But a nation that is blessed with vast petroleum reserves could utilize many tools in its arsenal to develop other sectors. The time has come to expedite and embrace a diversified economy. As petroleum prices continue to fluctuate, and as the developed nations embark on a clean energy agenda, more and more hybrid and electric cars are being produced. When I was a young boy in Aïn Beïda, the entire region was a mass producer of wheat, generating enough quantities to cater to domestic consumption and exports. By investing in the agro-industrial sector, the region would become productive once more and contribute immensely to the national economy.

More investments must be made in Algeria's tourism sector. All the way from the northeast, where visitors can immerse themselves in the beauty of Constantine, the city of suspended bridges on the mouth of the Rhummel River (a sight that fascinated my young eyes when I was at the Lycée d'Aumale), to the picturesque Mzab Valley, the face of Ghardaïa and the door of the desert, where local donkeys maintain a good mood despite the heavy coloful rugs sitting on their backs, our country offers an awesome opportunity to learn about the unique Mozabite culture and more. The spectacular landscape of the breathtaking dunes at Timimoun in the Sahara is also unforgettable. Promoting and marketing the country's vast nature reserves to attract domestic tourism would help its citizens appreciate their country and embrace their cultural identity. Children born in the north will have so many things to learn by visiting the south and vice versa, instituting a formal complete regional integration. Such strategy would foster a boon in the hotel industry and boost the private sector by spurring young talent to secure degrees from schools of tourism. Even local governments could take part in the process by helping alleviate the administrative constraints to ensure a mass revival of small businesses. This could be a factor in the quantitative approach to reducing unemployment among the youth. If those in charge of the economy were to roll up their sleeves and work hard to promote a diversified economy, Algeria would sustain a robust economy and the future should be bright.

Bouteflika is known for his acute and exceptional diplomatic skills. He is a diplomatic maestro whose reputation dates back to the 1960s. His talent and his artistry has aided him immensely in the resolution of different conflicts. Soon after his election, he ended the country's diplomatic isolation by working hard to restore Algeria's standing on the international stage. His diplomatic resurgence began at the OAU and reached its peak when he succeeded in restoring peace in Algeria. I praised his fruitful experience in the fight against Algeria's terrorism and mentioned in my letter that he would become a role model in the fight against terrorism. Algeria is now regarded as a key antiterrorism partner by major powers like the United States and the European Union. As such, Algeria's ongoing stalemate with Morocco regarding the border closure, which at first glance seemed like a silly squabble between two brother countries, is now a matter of grave concern to me.

Although, the government's position differs from Rabat's stance on the Western Sahara issue, this could lead to a manifestation of profound consequences unless both leaders engage in a deeper dialogue for the sake of peace. Algeria and Morocco were allies throughout the struggle for our liberation, but our historical ties predate colonial intrusion. In August 1959, King Mohammed V refused to cooperate with General De Gaulle when asked to help redraw new borders between Algeria and Morocco, preferring only to do so with his Algerian brethren once they gained their freedom. He urged De Gaulle to end the war and hasten the process toward Algerian independence. He solicited the help of President Eisenhower in the hopes that he would exert pressure on De Gaulle to expedite the course of action.

When five FLN leaders were arrested aboard a flight that belonged to King Mohammed V while en route from Tangier to

A Dream for Peace

Tunis, it was Dr. El Khatib, a Moroccan, who discovered to his dismay while the men were at the Prison de la Santé in France that they were embroiled in a bitter dispute over who was best qualified to lead the FLN. Beyond cautioning them and asking that they cultivate patience, Dr. El Khatib summoned Bouteflika and sent him off to France with a Moroccan diplomatic passport to mediate and counsel the five leaders on maintaining peace until the end of the Algerian liberation war.

During the days of our liberation struggle, I helped to reinforce loads of trucks carrying Moroccan fighters bound for the border. Weapons and logistics were exported from Morocco to Algeria with invaluable assistance and oversight from local authorities. At a time when our nation couldn't issue travel documents to its citizens, Algerian students who supported the revolution received Moroccan passports to travel abroad for studies. When we gained our independence, those were the graduates who formed a crucial part of the intellectual fabric of the country.

The five leaders—namely Ahmed Ben Bella, Mohamed Boudiaf, Hocine Aït Ahmed, Mohamed Khider, and Mostefa Lacheraf—were eventually released from prison in the spring of 1962, just in time to manifest their presence at the National Congress of the Algerian Revolution in Tripoli. After the proclamation of independence on July 3, GPRA President Benyoucef Benkhedda, along with members of the provisional government, were welcomed to Algiers by a large cheering crowd. About a week later, Ahmed Ben Bella made his triumphant entrance into Tlemcen from the Moroccan town of Oujda. He established himself in the western part of the country and formed the Tlemcen group, which attracted the likes of Ahmed Francis, Ahmed Boumendjel, and Ferhat Abbas. Not to be outdone, Benkhedda and a group of GPRA ministers formed an opposition group in Tizi Ouzou, the Kabylia capital and Berber stronghold, setting the stage for a complex political showdown among various factions that lasted for several weeks. Ultimately,

Algeria—Cry of the Crestfallen Heart

Ben Bella became the nation's first president.

In August 2008, my wife and I visited Dr. El Khatib and his family at their seaside residence of Sidi Bouzid. It was clear he was agonizing over the painful stalemate in Morocco-Algeria relations. After all, he and I had campaigned feverishly for the unity of the Maghreb. "My father was Algerian," he told me. "I studied for four years at the Faculty of Medicine in Algiers and fought for the independence of Algeria. It is very difficult to imagine that today, I don't even have the basic right to cross the border on foot like I used to." "Si Abdelkrim," I said with a heavy heart. "You and I can hold hands and go across the border. No one will stop us." "Ghoulem, it is not about me," he replied. "It is for the sake of our peoples."

After a three-day stay, we left to celebrate Ramadan in Annemasse. On the twenty-seventh day of fasting, exactly a month to the day after our visit to Morocco, we received the heartbreaking news that Dr. El Khatib had been called by the Almighty. My friend, big brother, comrade—a great man who I deeply admired—had left us. I mourned him, reminiscing about the intense journey we shared when our paths crossed in this life, and felt consoled that I had at least spent some valuable time with him prior to his ascension to the kingdom of Allah. Sadly, he left without witnessing the restoration of fraternal unity between our two nations.

We packed our bags and flew to Casablanca to pay our last respects. Grief stricken and inconsolable, we were escorted to Rabat by my beloved relatives, Naïma El Khatib and Abdelkrim Boujibar. We arrived in time for the Eid al-Fitr ceremonies. I had a difficult time holding myself together when I encountered his wife, Meftaha, sister Lalla Hiba, Fatima Hassar, and the rest of my Moroccan family, but I did the very best I could to maintain my composure during the ceremonies.

President Bouteflika's chargé d'affaires in Rabat delivered a message of condolences to the family. "It is Ghoulem, Dr. El Khatib's great friend, who must respond to the Algerian president's

A Dream for Peace

message." Much to my surprise, the calls came from some notable voices in the political elite of Dr. El Khatib's family—Lalla Hiba, Hosni Benslimane, Commandant of the Palace, his nephew, Secretary of State for the Interior, and his son-in-law, leader of a major political party. Indeed, I was touched by their confidence and consideration. I took heed of their wishes and sent a warm response to President Bouteflika.

My last encounter with Dr. El Khatib.

I pressed Bouteflika to use the unique opportunity to reopen the borders and allow the free movement of people. He remained deaf to my calls, but on the anniversary of Dr. El Khatib's passing, he asked Youcef Khatib, a former member of the Liberation Army and one-time contender for Algeria's presidency, to deliver his condolences to the family. I felt strongly that he had missed out on a great opportunity, one that could have led to a peaceful beginning in the dialogue between Morocco and Algeria.

I also felt that his refusal to make a genuine gesture of goodwill toward Morocco, a gesture that would have resonated positively for Algeria, would ultimately unleash adverse ripple effects and cause delays in plans for implementing the Arab Maghreb Union. Such regional cooperation is paramount for economic and security reasons. The pursuit of a mutually beneficial strategy to confront the many border challenges, such as drug trafficking and terrorism, is something that we all agree on. It is therefore imperative to accelerate and intensify efforts on both sides in order to overcome our differences. The people of the Maghreb recognize that peace is essential and absolutely necessary for the unity of North Africa. A united Arab-Maghreb zone extinguishes the need to curry favors with the European Union, improves fraternal relations with sub-Saharan Africa, and fosters the development of a stronger continent. As an artisan of peace, Algeria's president knows how to take the bull by the horns and work for the construction of the Maghreb. The people of North Africa deserve better, and they are waiting patiently for the dream to become reality.

A Dream for Peace

From the Presidential Papers of Dwight David Eisenhower:

Document #1525; May 5, 1960 To King Mohamed V
Series: EM, AWF, International Series: Morocco ; Category: Secret
The Papers of Dwight David Eisenhower, Volume XX - The Presidency: Keeping the Peace Part IX: Shattered Dreams; March 1960 to July 1960
Chapter 22: Disaster in Paris

Your Majesty: I have reflected most carefully upon Your Majesty's letter of April twenty-second expressing eloquent concern over continuation of the Algerian conflict. In doing so I also recalled the thoughts Your Majesty conveyed to me on this subject at our meeting in Casablanca.

The United States Government fervently hopes for an early end to this war, and to all the suffering and danger which it entails. Moreover, it continues to be alert to take any feasible step which could be a positive contribution to a just peace in Algeria.

I discussed this subject with President de Gaulle during his recent visit to Washington, and in particular I asked him whether his offer of self-determination to the Algerian people remains valid. The President assured me that he stands by this offer, and it remains the official policy of France.

Since there had been some reports that French policy might have changed, I was relieved to have the President's assurance, both because I believe that the principle of self-determination is the key to peace in Algeria, and because I repose such confidence in the sincerity and determination of President de Gaulle.

In addition, I am most grateful for Your Majesty's letter of April sixteenth. I have instructed Ambassador Yost to cooperate fully in the discussions which are envisaged.

Algeria—Cry of the Crestfallen Heart

Allow me to express once again my personal esteem for Your Majesty and to restate the friendship which all Americans feel for the Moroccan people.

Bibliographic reference to this document:
Eisenhower, Dwight D. Secret To King Mohamed V, 5 May 1960. In The Papers of Dwight David Eisenhower, ed. L. Galambos and D. van Ee, doc. 1525. World Wide Web facsimile by The Dwight D. Eisenhower Memorial Commission of the print edition; Baltimore, MD: The Johns Hopkins University Press, 1996, http://www.eisenhowermemorial.org/presidential-papers/second-term/documents/1525.cfm

A Dream for Peace

Dialogue has replaced warfare in today's Africa after decades of wars and coup d'états, and the bloodletting has given way to a more conscious Africa. Though the continent's woes may not be over, the world is witnessing the birth of a new generation, the grandsons and daughters of those who wove the fabric of innovation and forward-thinking into the veins of this new breed of vibrant and confident pioneers.

Chapter Seventeen

Dialogue for Humanity's Sake

A country was once measured by the physical courage of its infantrymen and the temerity of its forces. That era is long gone. In today's world, the value of a country's standing is measured by its nuclear deterrent and, most importantly, its robust economic strength. The energy crisis of the 1970s imposed structural challenges to the stability of Western economies and induced the dollar's devaluation, thereby prompting a global recession. Fearing that the long-term possibility of high oil prices and recession would trigger a rift within the Atlantic Alliance, the US, which had thus far sought to impose itself as the world's police, threatened to use force to occupy the oil fields of the Persian Gulf in order to safeguard its economy.

President Houphouët-Boigny, who remained an avid advocate of dialogue, emphasized repeatedly to anyone who would listen that dialogue was the weapon of strong men. After all these years, that dogma holds true, and I dare anyone to prove otherwise. The willingness to use dialogue requires some self-control and mastery of instincts, as well as the inclination to compromise without sacrificing integrity.

Is it not more difficult to convince ourselves that dialogue is an absolute necessity, rather than defer to war for the sake of vanquishing the enemy? Our primal instincts do not differentiate us from animals, but those of us who continue to struggle daily against our innermost instincts by mastering the ability to rid ourselves of selfishness, misappropriation, self-centeredness, and other shortcomings would have successfully become better human beings.

President Houphouët-Boigny once reminded a foreign journalist that human instincts were more or less under control in ancient African society before the arrival of Europeans. The village delegated its best artisans, its best artists, and best jewelers for regional competitions. The African society did not practice secret ballot elections. This spirit of negative competition and jealousy as we have come to know today did not exist. It was imported from abroad.

Is there anything more uplifting than to see your brother admired by foreigners? Looking back, one of my proudest moments was when a delegation from a powerful country paid a visit to Côte d'Ivoire. After listening to a presentation that was typical of President Houphouët-Boigny, the head of the delegation asked to speak. "Mr. President," he began, "you have said everything, and after listening to you, we understand how you have managed to achieve such a spectacular economic milestone—the Ivorian miracle. I only have but one regret . . . the fact that you are not the one who rules my country."

There is a popular saying that goes, *"No man is a prophet in his own country."* The Ivorian people refused to support the vision of President Houphouët-Boigny on the matter of dual citizenship, and most African heads of state criticized him for promoting the need for dialogue with South Africa. He was only guilty of seeing the issues clearly and being a decade ahead of everyone. When he gave a press conference in Paris, advocating for the first time the importance of dialogue, he went through great lengths to set the right tone for the speech. Yet every single African leader subjected him to fierce criticisms, and furthermore, there were murmurs on the floor of the OAU summit when his foreign minister stood at the dais to address his peers.

The concept of dialogue has since found some traction, and today we applaud wholeheartedly, in a unified chorus, the artful dialogues that continue to take place among African countries and, at times, in concert with nations from other parts of the world, resolved to finding solutions to many issues. Those who were familiar with President Houphouët-Boigny cheered even louder, because they knew that he refused to accept the honor of taking credit for the authorship of any idea or policy. He was always steadfast on his primary motivation. He pushed forth the core objective and urged on its arrival at the final destination. It made no difference to him who was in the final stretch of the race or who bore the torch in the process.

The African continent managed to celebrate the liberation of territories formerly held by Portugal—the last bastion of colonial European holdouts. Nevertheless, very hard lessons were learned in the aftermath of the bloody wars that were imposed for lack of dialogue, but the naysayers pivoted and threw their weight behind efforts to bring Ian Smith, prime minister of Rhodesia (Zimbabwe), to talk at the round table with the so-called rebels. We reached a major milestone in the region when South African Premier Vorster stated, "*Things will change.*" Passionate and euphoric was his rhetoric, after venturing into an African capital once opposed to any form of dialogue with his apartheid regime. Though everyone believed that things were bound to change, albeit gradually, we celebrated the fact that a process had begun. Little by little, he baby-stepped measures to dismantle the oppressive pieces, one sliver at a time, and we nudged him to keep going. We saw him open the doors of Pretoria's largest theater to our black brothers and expounded upon our sentiments, because if that wasn't a virtue of dialogue, then by no means did humanity have a leg to stand on.

Decades after some of the continent's greatest events, the power of dialogue continues to resonate in a resolute march into the future, leaving behind giant footprints in its wake. An indelible impression was recorded in history after the first OPEC summit of heads of state and government in Algiers in 1975 that drove the organization's unyielding efforts to broaden its mandate in order to address the plight of poorer nations, while calling for a new era of cooperation in international relations to bring about world economic development and stability. Those talks led to the establishment of the OPEC Fund for International Development in 1976 and propelled member countries to embark on ambitious socioeconomic development schemes. Other noteworthy events, such as the Franco-African summit in Bangui, the historic meeting between heads of Arab and African states, and the tripartite conference between energy producers and consumers, came to pass with remarkable recorded outcomes, and for now, Third World nations, longing for peace and stability, have begun to unearth the strategy of those who aspire to divide us—our detractors.

When African and Arab leaders marched to the tripartite conference as a united front against the conspirators who sought to divide us, our reasoning was both simple and logical: There was on one side the oil-producing countries, and on the other, consumers from major oil-consuming nations that also imported billions of tons of other commodities. Then there were the other smaller consumer nations from the Third World. It was our belief that the non-oil-producing countries of the Third World would be committing political, if not economic suicide by asking to sit at the negotiating table on the consumer side. It was our sacred duty to tighten our ranks more than ever, expecting that the oil-producing nations would act in solidarity with us, the nonproducing countries that were at the time underdeveloped just like they were. Collectively, we constituted a powerful unit, bolstered by vast energy resources and raw materials—both agriculture and those of the subsoil.

The layman would be surprised to learn that oil is a by-product of most manufactured goods, and a vast majority of raw materials are imported from developing countries. Hence, it is worthwhile exploring technological development as a way forward in the dialogue between developed and developing countries, between consumer and poor nations. The consumer nations managed to reach a robust level of development because of their exploitation of the Third World. The developing countries were always exploited and, through no fault of our own, have become the eternal victims of the instincts of those we first referred to as slave traders, who morphed into colonialists and finally became the neocolonialists.

One cannot have his cake and eat it too. The developed countries ate their cake and proceeded to take huge chunks of our cake too.

The Europeans arrived in North America and discovered a vast land that was fabulously wealthy, but they lacked the manpower to develop a vibrant society. As is their tendency to always search for easy and gratuitous solutions to enrich themselves, they went to import blacks from Africa. Alas, the country was built on the backs of the slaves, the economy grew exponentially, and their children were educated. After vital natural resources were exploited and pushed to their limits, they embarked again on another search for easier and virtually free solutions. Raw materials were plundered from their source countries, mostly in the Third World, where they had found their labor force in the seventeenth and eighteenth centuries. The point is, if in the past one has shamelessly exploited their fellow humans and deprived them of their potential while depleting their lands of natural resources, it is only fair that we speak of the sad reality of today and say no to further exploitation, no to plunder, no to injustice. However, we must be consistent with ourselves and not repay evil deeds with evil acts, but be mindful about keeping our instincts in check while learning to forgive and forget.

We can forget the past and continue to be proponents of dialogue in order to cultivate peace and understanding among all nations of the world. Only dialogue can save humanity from the perils of war. In the dialogue between developed countries and the Third World, the topic must be about a fair compensation for our raw materials and our backbreaking labor. Developed nations must honestly acknowledge that every ounce of energy that is expended by workers at Ford, Renault, Mercedes, Fiat, and Toyota to accomplish their duties is just as equal to the energy expended by the laborer, the farmer, or mine worker in any country of the world to accomplish their task.

As for mine workers in modern-day developing countries, it is not unusual for them to experience preventable accidents and various diseases in the workplace. Their socioeconomic predicament and lack of adequate health programs exposes them to toxic environmental pollutants such as mercury, while subjecting them to lung-related infections. Worst yet, in countries like the Democratic Republic of the Congo, children as young as seven years old are hoisted down narrow mines shafts and sent into hazardous underground excavations to extract precious cobalt used to manufacture lithium batteries for electronic devices. How can we lend credence to those who fight for the rights of mine workers in the West, only to behave ruthlessly and refuse to act for the betterment of their fellow humans, whether it is the plight of innocent children, workers, or peasants in the developing world?

Karl Marx, Lenin, Malthus, or modern economists and other theorists from the past did not invent anything new. The world does not need a Marxist theory to promote a just and fair labor manifesto for every workingman or woman. When we question a sclerotic economic system and replace it with a fair and more equitable economic order, society will be better off. In their quest for a frank and open dialogue, most Third World nations have denounced past practices that have remained in place for decades. They are determined to prompt a sea change by imposing a platform for restructuring the broken system, which has proven to be a major culprit in the deterioration of global trade accords.

People share a common physiological function. Yet the powers that be continue to guide us on a path of injustice that could potentially lead humanity to a collective suicide. The old adage proclaims, *"Render unto Caesar what belongs to Caesar."* The West may have burned its candle, perhaps, on both ends, but one must not lose sight of the fact that we in the developing world do have on our side the intellectual, moral, and economic honesty to recognize that developed countries have accumulated undeniable and invaluable wealth, as well as indisputable technological advancements, by mastering the art of invention. If our two worlds collaborated in a forum for positive dialogue, fashioned in an honest and serene atmosphere, the end result would be a just and humane order.

Prosperous nations need raw materials from developing nations, and developing nations need technological innovations in return. Logic should prompt the wealthier nations to embrace the type of robust cooperation that is essential for all. Times have changed. What was once affordable by many just over a decade ago is but a far-fetched dream for most in today's world.

We the people of the Third World neither feel the need, nor harbor a desire in all honesty, to switch places with the wealthy nations. We do not wish to see them become impoverished while we become rich. But the wealthy nations must understand that we refuse to let ourselves bleed to death while they sit back nonchalantly and enrich themselves on our backs.

Dialogue should also be open at the Third World level and, on a smaller scale, between Africans and Arabs. Though the Arabs have a trump card in this game that is played between developed and developing countries, it is their duty to support their fellow African brethren. History, geography, and economics compel the two to cooperate to build such an alliance into a comprehensive political partnership, aimed at maintaining a solid front. It is crucial, however, that the Arabs commit to becoming partners in Africa's development. The relationship between Arabs and Africans must move from the asymmetrical level to a reciprocal cooperation between both sides. In Afro-Arab history, Arabs have been at times conquerors and sources of new ideas. We shared a common trade bloc, and frequently, parts of sub-Sahara Africa were exposed to the crescent moon of Islam as it shadowed the commercial caravan into the marketplace.

Africa's leaders have always responded courageously in support of most issues that are dear to the Arab cause. The continent has been unanimously present during the call for solidarity. Hence, the Arab world must not continue to disappoint their African brethren; otherwise, both parties risk falling back into medieval decadence. African solidarity toward Arabs has never been, and should never be, circumstantial or financially motivated. In unified chorus, every African responded "present" and continued to stand united against the injustice and contempt surrounding the restoration of Palestinian rights and the evacuation of the occupied territories. Africans are a principled people. Arabs are no less. It is therefore my hope that our two complementary communities continue to find creative ways through the use of dialogue to harness our strengths.

Despite ongoing instances of political stability and turmoil, some Arab nations benefit from vast energy and financial reserves, more so than the vast majority of Africa's developing countries. Having access to a continent that is very rich in human resources and vital raw materials is beneficial, as both communities can work together to foster trade and economic development across regions. Why then do our Arab brothers search so far, sometimes too far, to invest in horses that have run out of breath? Why not invest in new and resourceful countries? Is it because the United States continues to float the "sword of Damocles" over the heads of Arab leaders, as if to say, "If you refuse to cooperate with us, we will cut off the vital supply lines."

In the past, Arab leaders, in their zeal to conduct business with the West, have inadvertently exposed their nations to much blackmail. Their priorities have been ill-placed. Still today, in the new century, only a handful of countries are looking to the African land with its more-than-sufficient resources, enough to feed all of humanity and then some. The Chinese understand this and have taken the bull by the horns by investing heavily in Africa. Back in the 1970s I advised some Arab leaders about Africa's industrial and agricultural potential and suggested that they consider investing in the continent's wheat, rice, corn, and soy cultivation. President Houphouët built an agronomic laboratory in Yamoussoukro to demonstrate the many possibilities.

The continent's opportunities have always been vast and ripe for constructive development. However, absent a borderless cooperative agreement between Arab and African countries, economies remain unstable and the paradigm shift continues to force Africa's developing nations to adopt policies that safeguard socioeconomic stability. Some are left with no other alternative but to persist on their engagement with the West. China knows this more than any other nation and has sought to capitalize on the situation. Driven by a desperate need for raw materials and a zeal to gain a stronger foothold on the continent, the Chinese are rising above political correctness to fill a void that has exposed the EU's many mistakes in its historical dealings with the continent.

Dialogue has replaced warfare in today's Africa after decades of wars and coup d'états, and the bloodletting has given way to a conscious Africa. Though the continent's woes may not be over, the world is witnessing the birth of a new generation, the grandsons and daughters of those who wove the fabric of innovation and forward-thinking into the veins of this new breed of vibrant and confident pioneers.

By the end of President Houphouët's administration, Côte d'Ivoire was full of promise. The sub-Sahara delta's socioeconomic regions had begun to establish institutions designed to foster political stability and economic growth. When war and disunity engulfed a nation once harmonized across tribal and religious lines, the doctrine of dialogue had failed once again. But lo and behold, the African community stood up and refused to embrace

A Dream for Peace

the ultranationalist propaganda that placed northerners against the southerners. The people's undaunted faith in the Almighty, irrespective of one's religion, became the *force majeure* that pulled the country together to defend the principle of democratic elections. There is no better example to illustrate the importance of dialogue between all faiths to enhance communication and foment understanding among all humans. There are some who pretend to be true to Islam and relapse into acts of terror in the name of their faith, blatantly disregarding the fact that such acts are the antithesis of Islam. But those extremists generate global mistrust and hatred toward all Muslims by nurturing an unfortunate fear of Islam.

Extremism should not divide us. We are all victims of the plague, Muslims included. Through the use of dialogue, the greater world can stand as a common and unified front in the fight against extremism. When extremists see us united as one, empowered by the knowledge of each other's faith and standing in solidarity for a shared cause, their source of recruitment will ultimately dry up.

While the world stood in shock after witnessing the apocalyptic scenes of September 11, 2001, I received an invitation to speak at the Saint Gabriel Episcopal Church in Cherry Hills Village, Colorado. Only a couple of days after the horrific incident, the pastor reached out to ask that I come and address the congregation about the recent event and explain the linkage, if any, between such ungodly acts of terror and the Islamic faith. Leaders of the church knew me only as their neighbor, a retired ambassador, a Muslim married to a Christian. We maintained a very cordial relationship. Although I was still dumbfounded at what most perceived was an act by Muslims, I saw the invitation as a call of duty and accepted.

I began my brief but detailed presentation by praying for the families who had lost their loved ones, and I expressed my sincere sentiments to the congregation. Humanity as a whole had been assaulted by the evil actions of a few criminals who had hijacked Islam with a false ideological sense of conviction. *Those who pretend* to be Muslims and act to bring harm to their fellow humans must understand that nothing in their actions emanate from the tenets of Islamic faith or its principles. I assured the congregation that such vile behavior could only be attributed to those who believe in an unfortunate misinterpretation of the Holy Qur'an and a twisted misconception of the Muslim faith.

The Holy Qur'an clearly states that Muslims must respect the People of the Book, the Torah and the Holy Bible, because they predate ours, and further, they must embrace all of God's creatures. During the Q&A session after my speech, I was struck by the candor of the congregants. Mostly everyone probed for a deeper understanding of Islam. In the final analysis, I circled back to the catastrophic occurrence and reminded everyone that every single Muslim had been victimized twice: first, by the scourge of a terrorist act, and secondly, by the twisted perception that all Muslims are terrorists. For the attendees, the episode was their first interactive discussion with a devout Muslim, and for me, I concluded that the forum was essential for sewing the seeds of peace and harmony among all humanity.

The day all humans embrace wisdom and learn to love our neighbors as we love ourselves, and do unto others as one would do unto oneself; the day we master and control our sordid instincts and restrain ourselves from selfishness and self-centeredness—that will be the day we would have come full circle. On that fateful day, the generosity, the nobility of the soul, and the meaning of humanity would have reached a pinnacle of excellence and ushered forth the golden rule for a purposeful existence.

Epilogue

After circling the world forty times, I took the decision to retire and settle down in the United States, having resigned from my tenured professorial commitment at Yale University a little over three decades earlier to answer the call of Africa. My purpose was to go back and serve the continent. I was obligated to work hard for a better world. My most esteemed wish was to support Africa's development and create conditions to allow every newly independent country to excel among the concert of nations. Reaching that milestone would not only enhance relations among all nations, but more importantly, it would motivate the youth of the world to interact in harmony. The rapprochement, I believed, would serve as an augmentation of consciousness and mobilize future generations to embrace the spirit of oneness on planet Earth. We sail on the same boat, though each of us disembarks on a different day and hour to join our maker.

Memories of my African experience emanate from a mixture of complex outcomes and constant frustration in the struggle for economic development. In the immediate aftermath of colonial withdrawal, the continent was caught flat-footed in the middle of the Cold War, with many nations becoming a pawn in the political ideologies and mounting tensions between the Eastern and Western blocs. Worst of all, our economic oppression was fair game, and our raw materials were in play. Price fluctuations and currency devaluations were a standard daily occurrence and a major concern for leaders all over the Third World. Plans were hampered by uncertainties of the times, and developmental projects were derailed.

I often thought about one of the great American presidents,

my personal favorite, Abraham Lincoln, who, upon winning reelection, stated in his inaugural address on March 4, 1865, "*It may seem strange that any man should dare to ask a just God's assistance in wringing their bread from the sweat of other men's faces.*"

More than five decades after independence, many African countries are lagging behind a majority of nations in Asia. While most in Asia are seeing exponential and rapid development, the overall majority of Africa's sovereign countries are struggling to gain traction. Failed policies by corrupt governments have led to a vicious cycle that has forever anchored down the mobility of progress. We see the economies of nations with the world's largest natural resources dipping into the red and staying there for decades on end. Rather than place their faith in commodity exports alone, it would be wise for today's governments to learn from the mistakes of the past and diversify their economies, empower their citizens with knowledge of science and technology, and design an environment for innovative minds to excel. The young generation needs solutions at home. They are hungry and determined to succeed, but opportunities must be made freely available, and access to quality education and global interactivity in the cyberspace must become a standard norm. We live in a world that is getting smaller by the day, and a paradigm shift is forcing change at a pace never before seen in human history. If Africa seizes on its potential, it would go a long way to solving its own problems.

My diplomatic experience in global politics has helped shape my worldview. The role of the US in finding solutions for the world's problems cannot be denied. One of the reasons why I decided to retire and settle down in the US was because she wields such sphere of influence around the globe. All eyes are on this nation. After getting my education in America and becoming a lecturer, the transformational experience became a part of my very being. No society embodies so much unity in such a diverse way. I have always treasured the fact that the entire world seems to exist in the

Epilogue

United States, and as a workaholic, I came to appreciate the values of hardworking Americans, most of whom are to be commended for taking absolutely nothing for granted and for believing that success is borne out of hard work. Not long after President Houphouët passed away, my wife and I left the shores of Côte d'Ivoire for a tranquil neighborhood in a Denver suburb. We became American citizens, quickly immersing ourselves in society and engaging in our civic duties like most decent Americans.

Although imperfect in its democratic experimentations, it is still the people who give mandate to their representatives to act on their behalf. Even if some in Congress may be animated by noble ideals, they are sworn to work to fulfill the agenda of their constituents. In many instances, however, they yield to the influence of campaign financiers and lobbyists in their decision-making, and as a result, commonsensical measures are not implemented. President Barack Obama had to deal with a partisan Congress that placed ideology of party over the interests of the nation and obstructed his entire agenda in an abhorrently divisive way.

As a country of immigrants, where many come to ply their trade, perfect their craft, and deliver unmatched transformative innovations to the world, the US is the place where each person's ingenuity is embraced with an open mind. The world remembers a country that dispatched its military to fight two wars on two occasions to liberate Europe and defend the free world. But the quagmire in the Middle East has long been the most challenging foreign affairs conundrum the country has ever faced. Due to America's ever-evolving political balancing act and perceived bias toward Israel in the quest for a sovereign Palestinian state, the world has resigned itself to deal with a status quo that is begging for a revolutionary change. At every turn, the US continues to squander an opportunity to be a genuine broker—a neutral force for good, a nation that must lead the Palestinians and Israelis to peace. The world's leaders could use a moment of reflection to channel the

A Dream for Peace

wisdom uttered in the words of President Lincoln at his second inaugural address: *"With malice toward none, with charity for all, with firmness in the right as God gives us to see the right, let us strive on to finish the work we are in, to bind up the nation's wounds, to care for him who shall have borne the battle, and for his widow and his orphan, to do all which may achieve and cherish a just and lasting peace among ourselves and with all nations."*

As a diplomat, I risked my life in the pursuit for peace, working with organizations like the ICIPP and the PLO. I sat in think tanks with the likes of General Peled and Dr. Isam Sartawi and searched for ways to bring Israeli and Palestinian representatives to the table. Dr. Sartawi was assassinated by his Palestinian brothers because of his pursuit for peace with Israel. Prime Minister Rabin, who once told President Houphouët that he would embark on the road to peace as long as Chairman Arafat agreed to take similar steps, was also assassinated by an Israeli extremist. Though the road to peace has been painfully littered with dangerous outcomes, achieving the ultimate goal in the very near future would go a long way to honor the heroic efforts of those who have been martyred.

When I watched Senator Obama speak on television at the Democratic National Convention in 2004, I called out to my wife and asked her to take note. "This young man has the attributes of a head of state," I told her. "I believe he will become the president of the United States someday." She agreed. I followed his political activities closely until he threw his hat into the 2008 presidential race. As soon as he entered the primaries, I began to campaign for him. He was to me the only candidate among the aspirants who stood for dialogue and peace. His worldview was up to par with superior leadership qualities, and his mere presence seemed to profess a reset in how America would conduct its business on the international stage. I campaigned on the streets of Miami throughout the primaries and into the general elections. After his historic win, Mr. and Mrs. Obama sent a thank-you letter to me, and I also received an invitation from

Epilogue

the inaugural committee to attend the historic event, but I couldn't make it to DC because of a severe bout with the flu.

In March 2009, I wrote him a letter to express my gratitude for his thoughtful gesture and to wish him well. He had a large mandate at the time, and his popularity was at record highs. I shared some insights on the Middle East problem and expressed my grave concerns for the political posture of the US under the watchful eyes of previous presidents. I felt it was my duty as an American and a human being to speak up.

It is my view that Israel has the right to exist in peace and security, but illegal settlements have encroached on almost 89 percent of Palestinian lands, going far beyond the allotted 51 percent that was bequeathed to Israel through a United Nations resolution in 1947. Given the structure of the UN, only five permanent members of the Security Council have a veto power in all decision-making processes. Each of those nations is in a position to block any resolution. As such, we are seeing more deadlocked outcomes. Historically, the United States has used its veto power to support Israel, thereby allowing the Hebrew nation to behave with impunity, without any recourse, despite recommendations by the very body that created Israel. We have acknowledged for decades that the illegal expansion of settlements amounts to a major obstacle to peace. Yet, whenever the General Assembly votes to force the Israeli government to refrain from further land annexation, the US has vetoed the bill and prevented the body from condemning Israeli actions. Where do we stand?

One has to be realistic. Hamas is condemned because they refuse to abide by the status quo. But if Hamas were to disappear, another group will reappear from the grassroots. This was the spirit of the intifada: just say no to the status quo. That doesn't mean they are ideologues like the leaders who refuse to accept the right of Israel to exist; all they ask is to control their future in their own homeland. I would recommend dealing with the Palestinian

A Dream for Peace

people without any labels. The solution of the problem lies in the hands of the Palestinian people. While the PLO's leaders live in a cozy environment, they will continue to accept the situation to the detriment of their people. Meetings with heads of state have led nowhere, and we continue to witness on a regular basis more construction of illegal settlements on occupied lands, authorized by the Israeli government, under the false pretext of "protection against terrorism." The United States has no choice but to force a two-state solution. By sitting on the sidelines, we have become accomplices to a dire situation, witnessing an unprecedented annexation of Palestine by Israel today, and tomorrow perhaps, the whole of Palestine, all because we have failed to speak the truth to our friends by turning a blind eye to injustice.

Our tango dance with the Israeli-Palestinian problem is not constructive and will not lead to peace. As the greatest power in the world, we should fear no one but respect everyone and maintain a position of strength. To reestablish the US as an honest broker in the peace process, we have to lead the process of change. There is no substitute for American leadership. If we want to be true to ourselves, we know that in the long run, nothing will do more to ensure Israel's security than a two-state solution. Such an outcome would be better than any wall. It would be their best shield.

Currently, Iran finds itself playing an active role in the Middle East because of the Palestinian question. They finance Hezbollah and Hamas, both Shiite organizations, and they forge a divide between the Shiites and the Sunnis, who are backed by the Saudis. Hezbollah controls all of Southern Lebanon, and they create nothing but instability in that country. Iran remains popular even among the handful of Sunni Muslim countries despite the fact that they are Shiites. If the Palestinian issue were solved, Iran's role would be diminished. Meanwhile, let's not pretend that if Israel were to bomb Iran as they have threatened to do on many occasions, the repercussions would not be catastrophic.

Epilogue

Once the problem is solved, the US will regain the trust of all the people of the region and control the geopolitical cards. Instead of being a permanent sentry in the region, we will have trusted allies, and all the members of the Arab League will normalize their political and diplomatic relations with Israel. They stand ready to resume economic and security cooperation when this happens. The invasion of Iraq was a grave misstep, and we will continue to see and feel the residual impact of our failed foreign policy in the aftermath of that war. The country continues to be a cradle of insecurity, and it will be a recruiting center for global jihadists for the foreseeable future. Shortly after the war in Iraq ended, US administrators under Paul Bremer's leadership decided to get rid of the mostly Sunni members of Saddam Hussein's Baathist Party in the country's civil and military services. Al-Qaeda, the terrorist group known for its strike against America on September 11, 2001, was more than happy to recruit disgruntled Iraqi Baathists into their fold. They formed Al-Qaeda in Iraq (AQI) to fight against the US occupation. The fighters frequently went across to Syria to get weapons from unknown sources. When Syria's leader, Bashar al-Assad, began to shoot at his own citizens and the situation turned into a bloody insurrection, AQI moved into the country and established itself as ISIS, the Islamic Caliphate.

This is an illustration of just how dangerous the Israeli-Palestinian conflict is. The issue has served as a call to arms by those who see the injustices of oppression and rampant destruction as a means to an end with evil intent. Now more than ever, jihadist groups like Al-Qaeda, ISIS, and other little-known agents are committed to the destruction of Western civilization because of the West's historic destabilizing impact and cultural influence in the developing world. They plan to use any means necessary, and they will continue to morph into different movements, depending on their objectives, until they are hard to control. These groups are capable of unspeakable terror in every global corridor because their members are everywhere, and with social media, they are finding new ways to influence and recruit the youth at record levels.

Since the war against terrorists cannot be fought like a conventional war, we need the active cooperation of the leaders in Muslim countries and a more pragmatic approach to stemming the tide of recruits who are more than willing to sacrifice their lives for the cause. But Islamophobia is not the answer. Not all Muslims are extremists. As a matter of fact, the vast majority of Muslims who wish to live in peace are the ones who suffer the brunt of terrorist acts. I have envisioned a forum where most people of all faiths come together in an interfaith setting to find common harmony. Now more than ever, we must understand that democracy cannot be exported from the United States to the Middle East. The West, but especially the US, must allow each country to grow at its own pace, and we must not undertake covert actions to undermine them, as we have done in the past. In Iraq's case, the country needs another strongman to create stability. These were some of the thoughts and ideas I expressed so passionately in my letter to President Obama.

America has its share of domestic problems, some of which can be attributed to the anachronistic policies that at times inhibit the flow of progress and upward mobility. Perhaps unbridled capitalism might be to blame, due to a perceived lack of fairness to everyone, no matter what their background, race, or creed. The downside of capitalism can be equated to the belief that money buys happiness. While it is indeed a very good thing to be a great businessman and make lots of money, a misguided desire to achieve riches at all cost can lead to conceited patterns of thought and in many ways induce people to turn their backs on those who may be less fortunate. It seems as if the entire world has descended into the depths of materialism, and henceforth, it has become increasingly difficult to operate in harmony with transcendental truths. We are succumbing slowly but surely to that which is materialistic and becoming worshippers of matter. We are at risk of losing our spirituality and turning our backs on the true meaning of happiness.

Epilogue

The soul of the modern man yearns to indulge in all his desires, and it tempts him to embrace materialism, which has now replaced religion to rule over his mind and spirit. The belief that there is no other goal in life than to accomplish material success is something without truth or merit, and like a prisoner, such belief entraps one to become oblivious to their true sense of self and makes them lose their spirituality. A man therefore runs the risk of losing any sense of warmth from his human nature, thus making him seem indifferent to others.

This happens at the top of the ladder, from the boardroom to the executive branch, from upper management to the corridors of politics. For instance, whenever the issue of minimum wage comes up for discussions in Congress, the topic produces divergent views along party lines. Certainly, jobs must be created, but workers must be paid a decent salary for a hard day's work. Those at the top tend to forget that this is a necessary component to alleviating poverty and hardship.

Racism is still rampant in our country, despite the denial by some. When Obama was elected, there were many who claimed that the historic moment was proof of the end of racism. I cried on the night he won the election. Like others from my generation who have suffered in their hearts after witnessing firsthand the tyranny of segregation, I am not nostalgic, nor do I yearn for a return to the tenebrous past. Though significant progress has been made since my days at Yale in the 1960s, we still have a long way to go. Recurrent incidents taking away lives of innocent individuals are painful and troublesome.

Race and culture are real forces in American life because they are entrenched in politics. Take, for instance, the process of filling out an administrative questionnaire at your local government office, where one is almost always asked to specify their ethnicity. It is a requirement that at first seems to be rooted in archaic processes from bygone days, hardly a twenty-first century custom. As a matter of fact, identifying one by their race is a procedure that was invented for statistical data-mining purposes. Though this simplistic strategy has served society by ensuring that today's legislatures can mine data to support their ability to conduct a more reliable census count, even identify and log migration patterns of the various ethnic groups, still, records from their findings are being used to determine how to regulate and control the allocation of federal funds to the states. As with any well-intended practice, politicians tend to find a loophole in the system to exploit. The policy of gerrymandering has become standard practice in a sinister strategy to prevent minorities from voting, or worse yet, districts in minority communities are redrawn in such a way that their votes will not make a difference.

A society's racist shortcomings are not by default. The tendency to segregate by race and count individuals by their ethnic and cultural heritage is, by definition, prejudicial and divisive. It promotes a spirit of "us and them" and carries forth a conception of "rich neighborhood versus poor neighborhood," and alas, the public systems in those poor communities are deprived of vital resources for lack of representation. It's no mystery why so many feel left out of the system or do not feel like they stand a chance in achieving the American dream. My hope is to one day see the tail end of the plague of racism as it is extracted from its very roots, leaving in its wake the birth of a new society—the ultimate utopia.

No one would argue against the fact that not everything should be decreed by law. Most decisions can be motivated by our very own genuine aspiration to do what is right for each other—to speak out and to stand up for others, without being indifferent to anything. I place my faith and trust in the youth to meet the challenges by saying no to hatred and doing their very best to make the world a better place. While getting rid of clichés and by thinking with their own heads, they might reveal the best part of themselves. Only then, will their vital impulses and their creative genius take over. Peace starts with each of us; it should not be a dream. We

Epilogue

must make the pursuit of peace our constant reality. Young people have their own way of seeing things. They are all connected through social media and want more interaction to understand the rest of the world. They seem poised and ready to undertake actions and get to the root of problems. It is imperative that America remains fully conscious of her responsibilities, be full of wisdom, and lead by example instead of continuing to impose our rules on the rest of the world. When we attempt to force change by manipulating one group over the other just to protect our interests, we are failing as a nation. Today's youth are a different breed. They are intent on changing the world by being fair and transparent.

In light of my faith, and knowing fully well that each one of us has a specific mission to fulfill during his or her lifetime, I ventured to put all my heart in whatever I tried to accomplish at every single moment, and I embraced all humans as unique in the eyes of the Almighty. The attributes that define me are faith, honor, duty, love, justice, peace, and dialogue. These are characteristics that can move mountains. While we are still sailing in a common vessel known as planet Earth, I believe in my heart that I have accomplished my life's mission. I can now sense that the time has come for me to get ready to disembark and go to meet my Creator.

Twenty years of divine grace.

Forty years of divine grace.

By the grace of the Almighty, our love has lasted through the test of time.

Acknowledgments

As the widow of my beloved husband, Dr. Ghoulem Berrah, I am honored and duty-bound to write these few words of appreciation on his behalf:

First and foremost, my most sincere and heartfelt thanks go to Mr. Nana Yalley for managing to convince my late husband that his memoir was worth writing, and assuring him that at least, more than one individual would be interested in reading about his life. It took some nudging and some divine intervention, but Nana's persistence paid off. In reminding my husband that the odyssey of a purposeful life was a story worth sharing, his words would not be lost on my husband's conscience, as he conveyed to him that he would otherwise have to explain his failure to complete this fated duty when he meets his maker. My husband, who was always consumed by the need for world peace, long envisioned setting up a non-profit interfaith foundation. He began to ponder the merits of producing such a book for a humanitarian cause, and became deeply animated by the thought of making a modest contribution toward promoting peace.

On a momentous day, he awoke in the wee hours of the morning and prayed the Fajr prayers. As he gazed across the ebbing ocean, charmed by the rising sun on the brilliant horizon, he reflected on his life's mission and began to record his thoughts on the mini tape recorder that he received from Nana. With his fountain pen, he wrote the first few words of a memoir that had been etched in his psyche his entire life. This became his routine in the months ahead.

When my Love asked me to proofread his material, I gladly accepted, without knowing that I would discover some very interesting aspects of his life that had been buried deeply in his memory, some of which were new revelations to me. I became an avid reader of every chapter, with the exception of the one titled "Murky Waters of Love," which he secretly kept at bay, knowing fully well that I would have vetoed the story of our very private life. I was so captivated by his storytelling capabilities that I wondered at times if I had lost all sense of objectivity, an attribute that has served as the golden rule of my life.

This became his very last project. It was an assignment that he took just as seriously as anything else he had been involved in. He entrusted Nana to direct and oversee the project and to review the minutest details of his manuscript until the book was published. I did not know that in his heart, he was quietly preparing for his departure. He invited Nana for some midafternoon tea at our home and organized a long working session immediately after. Several memorable pictures and documents were laid out in rows across the large conference table, deliberately sectioned to synchronize the various chapters of his planned book. Missing were the decades-old pictures of Chairman Mao Zedong, Vice Chairman Li Shaoqi, and Premier Zhou Enlai, which he'd searched feverishly for, to no avail. The pictures had circulated among friends during interactions over the years and had been lost along the way. In an effort to reassure himself that we were on the same page, he revealed his choice for the book's cover picture. He wanted to ensure that we knew exactly what to do just in case. The Lord called him not long after he had completed his manuscript, and Nana did not fail to keep his word.

Meticulously attentive to detail, and fully committed to the project, he demonstrated a desire to achieve absolute perfection, and he put his heart into the autobiography from the moment the French script was translated into English. Displaying an immense talent, he dove right in and crisscrossed every detail in the editorial process as he worked with me to tackle each missing puzzle in the enduring process. He even helped design the book's layout in

Acknowledgments

accordance with my husband's wishes. Thank you, Nana, from the bottom of my heart.

I would also like to extend my heartfelt gratitude to Mr. Regis Zoula, who helped translate the French version of the manuscript into English. This was a process I supervised and monitored to ensure accuracy in the transmission of nuanced expressions in their purest form to the English language prior to being edited by Mr. Yalley. Regis is a very nice and courteous gentleman who handled himself well throughout the process, always ready to undertake any task assigned to him. He was more than happy to become a proofreader, eagerly reading loudly during our sessions and assisting in pertinent research on many occasions.

A very warm thank-you to Mr. Brove Soto, who enjoys all things related to photography. He was more than delighted to scan and adjust all the pictures for the book.

Thank you to Mrs. Caroline Adjoussou, who after reading some of my husband's writing, shared the words that resonated with him: "Uncle, this is really fascinating!" A huge thanks to Mrs. Karine Diby, who worked on the original translation from French to English, and Dr. Alley Djouka, for his contributions throughout the project.

Last but not least, my infinite gratitude goes to the Almighty for blessing me with a unique and wonderful human being and gracing my life with a dream husband.

Photo Credits

Chapter 5
"Presidents Kennedy and Houphouët-Boigny with First Ladies" – Collection: White House Photographs. Photo credit: Robert Knudsen, John F. Kennedy Presidential Library and Museum, Boston
"Algerian flag" – Photo credit: Keystone France.

Chapter 6
"With cabinet members in 1956, Houphouët-Boigny, seated" – Photo credit: L'Ours.
"With President Houphouët and Dr. Julius Nyerere" – Photo credit: ITN Great Britain.
"With President Houphouët and President Tubman" – Photo credit: Indiana University Collection.
"With President Kaunda and President Houphouët" – Photo credit: https://untilourindependence.files.wordpress.com.
"With Ghana Premier Dr. K. A. Busia" – Photo credit: ITN Great Britain.
"With President Houphouët and Robert McNamara" – Photo credit: ITN Great Britain.
"With Minister Usher and US Secretary of State Dean Rusk" – Photo courtesy of US State Department.

Chapter 9
"President Houphouët greets Ambassador Sahnoun" – Photo credit: ITN Great Britain.

Chapter 10
"President Houphouët, Prime Minister Ben-Gurion, First Ladies, and Minister Golda Meir" – Photo credit: Israel National Photo Collection.
"Inspecting the Honor Guard with President Nixon" – Collection: White House Photographs. Photo credit: Karl H. Schumacher, Richard Nixon Foundation Library.
"Dr. Isam Sartawi" – Photo credit: Palestinian Academic Society for the Studies of International Affairs.

A Dream for Peace

"Sartawi and Matti Peled" – Photo credit: Just World Books.
"President Houphouët and Premier Yitzhak Rabin" – Israel National Photo Collection. – Photo credit: Saar Yaacov.
"President Houphouët at Rose Garden with president" – Photo credit: Collection: White House Photographs. Ronald Reagan Presidential Library.
"President Houphouët and Premier Shimon Peres" – Photo credit: Israel National Photo Collection.
"The Félix Houphouët-Boigny Peace Prize award ceremony – Photo credit: Copyright © UNESCO.

Chapter 11
"The beautiful minaret" – Photo credit: Cecil Images, Charles O. Cecil.

Chapter 13
"President Houphouët and Dr. Kwame Nkrumah" – Photo credit: Fondation Houphouët-Boigny.
"President Houphouët and General De Gaulle" – Photo credit: Keystone France.
"With my wife and invited guests at UNESCO ceremony" – Photo credit: Copyright © UNESCO.
"Presidents Houphouët, De Klerk, and Nelson Mandela" – Photo credit: Copyright © UNESCO.

Chapter 14
"Meeting with President Bourguiba" – Photo credit: ITN Great Britain.
"With President Nyerere in Bouaké" – Photo credit: ITN Great Britain.
"On the Deck of royal yacht with the president" – Photo credit: ITN Great Britain.
"President Houphouët and Queen Juliana" – Photo credit: ITN Great Britain.

Chapter 16
"President Abdelaziz Bouteflika" – Photo credit: Ricardo Stuckert, Agencia Brasil.

CPSIA information can be obtained
at www.ICGtesting.com
Printed in the USA
FSHW010408271019
63371FS